Windows XP:
The Complete Reference

About the Authors

John R. Levine is the author of two dozen books, ranging from *Linkers and Loaders* to *The Internet For Dummies*. He also runs online newsgroups and mailing lists, hosts a hundred Web sites, and consults on programming language and Internet topics. He lives in the tiny village of Trumansburg, New York, where in his spare time he's the water and sewer commissioner. John is also active in the anti-spam movement, is a board member of CAUCE (Coalition Against Unsolicited Commercial E-mail), and runs the **abuse.net** Web site.

Margaret Levine Young is the coauthor of over two dozen books with various coauthors, including *The Internet For Dummies, Internet: The Complete Reference*, and *Poor Richard's Building Online Communities*. She holds a B.A. in computer science from Yale University, helps run the Unitarian Universalist Association's online communities at **uua.org**, lives in Vermont, and experiments in e-commerce at her family's Great Tapes for Kids Web site at **http://www.greattapes.com**.

Doug Muder is a semiretired mathematician who has contributed to a number of books about computers and the Internet, including *Internet: The Complete Reference* and *Dragon Naturally Speaking For Dummies*. He is the author of numerous research papers in geometry and information theory, and dabbles in various forms of nontechnical writing. (Check out his fiction and essays at **http://www.gurus.com/dougdeb**.) Doug lives in Nashua, New Hampshire with his wife, Deborah Bodeau, whom he met while getting his Ph.D. in mathematics from the University of Chicago.

Alison Barrows has authored or coauthored books on Windows, the Internet, Microsoft Access, and other topics. In addition to writing books, Alison writes and edits technical documentation and training materials. She holds a B.A. in international relations from Wellesley College and an M.P.P. from Harvard University. In real life, she hangs out with her toddler, Parker; aspires to compete in Agility with her Portuguese Water Dog; and tries to carve out some time to practice yoga. Alison lives with her family in central Massachusetts.

Rima Regas is a freelance writer, technical editor, and a specialist in the networking and hardware fields. She has contributed to many Internet, networking, and hardware books. Rima is also a multiplatform networking consultant.

About the Technical Editor

Diane Poremsky is a consultant who specializes in Microsoft Windows, Outlook, and Office training and development. She is a Microsoft Outlook MVP (Most Valuable Professional) in recognition for her technical support of Microsoft Outlook. She is a technical editor for a number of computer books and is a columnist, author, and technical reviewer for *Exchange and Outlook* magazine. Diane currently resides in East Tennessee with her family.

Windows XP:
The Complete Reference

John R. Levine, Margaret Levine Young,
Doug Muder, Alison Barrows, and Rima Regas

Osborne/**McGraw-Hill**

New York   Chicago   San Francisco
Lisbon   London   Madrid   Mexico City
Milan   New Delhi   San Juan
Seoul   Singapore   Sydney   Toronto

Osborne/**McGraw-Hill**
2600 Tenth Street
Berkeley, California 94710
U.S.A.

To arrange bulk purchase discounts for sales promotions, premiums, or fund-raisers, please contact Osborne/**McGraw-Hill** at the above address. For information on translations or book distributors outside the U.S.A., please see the International Contact Information page immediately following the index of this book.

Windows XP: The Complete Reference

34567890 CUS CUS 01987654321

Book p/n 0-07-219299-2 and CD p/n 0-07-219298-4
parts of
ISBN 0-07-219297-6

Publisher	**Acquisitions Coordinator**
Brandon A. Nordin	Alex Corona
Vice President & Associate Publisher	**Technical Editor**
Scott Rogers	Diane Poremsky
Acquisitions Editor	**Compositor**
Megg Bonar	Interactive Composition Corporation
Project Manager	**Series Design**
Betsy Manini	Peter F. Hancik

This book was composed with Corel VENTURA™ Publisher.

This book is dedicated to
Robert J. Levine's
first 80 years.

Contents at a Glance

Part V

Windows XP on the Internet

Part VI

Networking with Windows XP

Part VII

Windows Housekeeping

Part VIII

Behind the Scenes: Windows XP Internals

Contents

Part I

Working in Windows XP

Part II

Managing Your Disk

Part III

Configuring Windows for Your Computer

Part V

Windows XP on the Internet

Part VI

Networking with Windows XP

Part VII

Windows Housekeeping

Part VIII

Behind the Scenes: Windows XP Internals

Acknowledgments

The authors would like to thank the following people for valuable assistance in writing this book: Megg Bonar, Betsy Manini, Alex Corona, and Alissa Larsen at Osborne/McGraw-Hill; and Brittney Corrigan-McElroy at ICC, for making the book happen; Erika Kauppi, Paul Medoff, and Marilyn Smith, copy editors; Linda Medoff and Nelda Street, proofreaders; Diane Poremsky, technical editor and general catcher of errors; Lisa Robbins and Marti Lucich at Waggener Edstrom; Jesse Derick, for checking chapters as Windows XP changed out from under us; and Kathy Ivens, Matt Ronn, Robert Schlabbach, Tyler Regas, Jordan Young, and everyone on the Microsoft Beta Support Team, for answering lots of questions. We also thank our friends and (most of all) our families for putting up with us during the seemingly endless process of updating such a long book.

Introduction

For years, Microsoft has had two series of Windows versions: the Windows Me/9x series (which includes 95, 98, 98 Second Edition, and Millennium Edition, or Me) for individual users, and the NT series (Windows NT and 2000) for corporate users and network servers. And for years, Microsoft has been trying to merge the two (slightly incompatible) series, so that everyone could run more or less the same version of Windows. With each new Windows release, Microsoft promised that the *next* release would be the one that combines these two strains of Windows.

Microsoft has finally done it. Windows XP is the upgrade to both series of Windows, Me/9x and 2000/NT. Windows XP (also known by its prerelease code name, *Whistler*) does away with the legacy architecture of the Windows 9x series. Windows 95 and its successors were based on DOS, the pre-Windows, non-graphical operating system that PCs started with. Windows XP removes the underlying DOS environment for increased reliability, and it uses the Windows NT/2000 file system for better security.

Windows XP is based on Windows 2000 and combines the technical core of NT/2000 with the ease of use of Windows 98 and Me. Because of its business-oriented lineage, Windows XP has some great new capabilities for Windows Me/9x users, including password-protected user accounts and system management programs. But Windows XP also adds people-friendly features that were lacking in Windows NT and 2000, along with a completely redesigned (and spiffy-looking) screen design called

Luna. This book helps you to make sense of the world of Windows XP, find your way through all the new and sometimes confusing options, learn the new interface, and make it work for you.

Initially, Windows XP comes in two versions: Home Edition (for home use) and Professional (for small-office and workstation use). These two versions are intended for workstations—that is, computers that people sit in front of and use directly. Two additional versions, Windows .NET Server and .NET Advanced Server, will be available in 2002. (Despite the ".NET" in their names, these are high-end versions of Windows XP.) These versions run on servers—computers that provide services to other computers over a network. This book describes Windows XP Home Edition and Professional as they are used on desktop and laptop workstations at home and at work. We hope that this book—both on paper and on the CD-ROM in the back—will help you make the most of Windows XP.

Later in this Introduction are sections titled "New Features in Windows XP," an overview of Windows XP's features, and "Differences Between Windows XP Editions," descriptions of the various versions of Windows XP.

Who Is This Book For?

This book is for everyone who uses Windows XP Home Edition and Windows XP Professional. You might already have Windows XP installed on your computer, or you might be considering upgrading a Windows Me, Windows 98, or Windows 2000 system to Windows XP. You might have a lot of experience with other computer systems, or Windows XP may be your first exposure to computing.

Your computer might be the only one in your home or office, or it may be one of many on a local area network. You probably have a modem or network card, although Windows works perfectly well without either. Chances are, your computer is connected to the Internet, or will be soon.

If your computer is connected to a large network, we don't expect you to be the network administrator, but if you're in a small office with two or three computers, we tell you how to set up a small, usable Windows network. If you have a modem, we discuss in detail what's involved in getting connected to the Internet, because Windows XP includes all the software you need to use the Internet.

Note *If you are the network administrator of a domain-based local area network, or if you need to know about the security and networking options for large networks, consider getting* Windows .NET Server: The Complete Reference *(by Kathy Ivens, published by Osborne/McGraw-Hill). It's the companion volume to this book for information technology staff members who support Windows XP servers and networked workstations.*

What's in This Book?

This book is organized around the kinds of things that you want to do with Windows, rather than around a listing of its features. Each part of the book concentrates on a type of work you might want to do with Windows.

Part I: Working in Windows XP

Part I covers the basics of using Windows. Even if you have used Windows forever, at least skim through this section to learn about XP's entirely new interface environment. If you are new to Windows, you'll want to read it carefully.

Chapter 1 starts with the basics of working in Windows: using the mouse and managing your windows. Chapters 2 and 3 explain how to run and install programs beyond those included with Windows—including using the new Compatibility Mode options that can run even the oldest DOS and Windows Me/9x programs. Chapter 4 covers the newly revamped Help And Support Center, including how to get assistance from friends, coworkers, and Microsoft over the Internet. Chapter 5 looks at the many ways to move and share information between and among programs. User accounts, which have been vastly improved in Windows XP, are described in Chapter 6.

Part II: Managing Your Disk

All the information in your computer is stored in disk files and folders, and Part II helps you keep them organized and safe. Chapters 7 and 8 cover day-to-day file and folder operations, including how to use Windows Explorer (also known as My Computer) to manage your files. Chapter 9 describes the backup program that comes with Windows, and how to set up a regular backup regime.

Part III: Configuring Windows for Your Computer

Windows is extremely (some would say excessively) configurable. Part III tells you what items you can configure and makes suggestions for the most effective way to set up your computer.

Chapter 10 covers the all-new Start menu, the gateway to the features of Windows. Chapter 11 details the desktop, the icons, and other items that reside on your screen. Chapter 12 explains your keyboard and mouse (yes, lots of options exist just for the mouse), and Chapter 13 tells you how to add and set up additional hardware on your computer. Chapter 14 covers printing, including setting up printers and installing fonts, and using the built-in fax features. Chapter 15 highlights the special features that are useful to laptop computer users. Chapter 16 covers the accessibility features that make Windows more usable for people who may have difficulty using conventional keyboards and mice, seeing the screen, or hearing sounds.

Part IV: Working with Text, Numbers, Pictures, Sounds, and Video

Chapter 17 discusses Windows' simple but useful text and word processing programs and calculator feature. In Chapter 18, you read about new features for viewing, printing, e-mailing, and making Web pages with your pictures, including ordering prints over the Internet. Chapters 19 and 20 examine Windows' extensive sound and video multimedia facilities, including the powerful new Windows Media Player 8.

Part V: Windows XP on the Internet

Windows offers a complete set of Internet access features, from making telephone or network connections to e-mail and the World Wide Web.

Chapter 21 explains the intricacies of setting up a modem to work with Windows, whether you use a dial-up account or a high-speed cable, ISDN, or DSL connection. Chapter 22 tells you how to use that modem to create and set up an account with an Internet service provider or online service. Chapter 23 describes Outlook Express 6.0, the Windows accessory program that handles your e-mail. Chapter 24 covers Internet Explorer 6.0, Microsoft's updated Web browser. Chapter 25 examines online chatting and conferencing with Windows Messenger and NetMeeting, and Chapter 26 discusses the other Internet applications that come with Windows.

Part VI: Networking with Windows XP

Because it is based on Windows 2000, which itself was derived from a network server operating system, Windows XP has extensive built-in networking features. You can set up your Windows machine as a workstation in a large network, as a server in a small network, or as both.

Chapter 27 introduces local area networks, including key concepts such as client-server and peer-to-peer networking. Chapter 28 walks you through the process of creating a small network of Windows systems. Chapter 29 tells you how to share printers and disk drives among your networked computers. Chapter 30 explains how to use Internet Connection Sharing to share one Internet account and modem among all the computers on a LAN. Chapter 31 covers the improved network security features that Windows XP provides, including the Internet Connection Firewall.

Part VII: Windows Housekeeping

Windows is sufficiently complex that it needs some regular maintenance and adjustment, and Part VII tells you how. Chapter 32 discusses disk setup, including removable disks and new hard disks that you may add to your computer, as well as NTFS and FAT32 partitions. Chapter 33 tells you how to keep your disk working well and how to use the facilities that Windows provides to check and repair disk problems, including defragmenting and taking out the garbage. Chapter 34 explains how to tune your computer for maximum performance, and Chapter 35 reviews the process of troubleshooting hardware and software problems. Chapter 36 describes the other Windows resources available on the Internet and elsewhere, including Automatic Updates, which can automatically identify and install updated or corrected Windows components.

Part VIII: Behind the Scenes: Windows XP Internals

Part VIII covers a variety of advanced Windows topics. Chapter 37 describes the configuration files that Windows uses, and Chapter 38 describes the Registry, the central database of program information that is key to Windows' operation. Chapter 39 covers the Command Prompt window that enables you to run DOS programs. Chapter 40, the final chapter, concludes with the Windows Script Host, a sophisticated system to automate frequently performed tasks.

Appendix, Glossary, and Instructions for Installing the Book's CD-ROM

The Appendix describes how to install Windows XP as an upgrade to a Windows system, from scratch on a blank hard disk, or as part of a dual-boot configuration. The Glossary describes all the terminology you need to know to understand Windows. At the very back of this book, you'll find a page of instructions for how to use *Windows XP: The Complete Reference E-book*, which is stored on the accompanying CD-ROM. (For more information, see "About the E-book" later in this Introduction.)

Conventions Used in This Book

This book uses several icons to highlight special advice:

 A handy way to make Windows work better for you.

 An observation that gives insight into the way that Windows and other programs work.

 Something to watch out for, so you don't have to learn the hard way.

When we refer you to related material, we tell you the name of the section that contains the information we think you'll want to read. If the section is in the same chapter you are reading, we don't mention a chapter number. If you find yourself skipping around the book, consider reading the text on the screen using the CD-ROM (see the next section).

When you see instructions to choose commands from a menu, we separate the part of the command by vertical bars (|). For example, "choose File | Open" means to choose File from the Menu bar and then choose Open from the File menu that appears. If the command begins with "Start |," then click the Start button on the taskbar as the first step. See "Giving Commands" in Chapter 2 for the details of how to give commands.

About the E-book

The CD-ROM in the back of this book contains the entire text of the book as a set of several hundred interlinked Web pages that you can display with Internet Explorer or any other Web browser. Our goal is for the e-book edition on the CD-ROM to be your reference and tutorial companion as you use your Windows system.

For instance, as you read in Chapter 33 about disk management and you want to know more about how to recover from faults and crashes, you can click a link on the e-book Chapter 33 to jump to that material. The e-book makes it easy to follow links from topic to topic until you get the information you need—without flipping to the back of the book to consult the index.

Wherever the book says "See Chapter so-and-so," the e-book has a link that you can follow with a single click. In the printed book, we refer you to related information by saying "see Chapter 18" or referring to other sections in the current chapter. The e-book has been coded—using Web-style hyperlinks—to provide references to related topics. When you read the e-book, you can click links to jump directly to the section of the book that contains the related information.

We've also added other useful links both within the book and to external resources on the World Wide Web. For example, if Microsoft's Web site has more information about a topic, we provide you with a clickable link to the page you want. We also provide Internet addresses for companies that provide Windows-compatible products and information. The book also has its own Web site (at **http://net.gurus.com/winxptcr**) where you'll find the latest Windows XP information we think you'll find useful.

The key to the e-book is the electronic Glossary page that you'll find one click away from the CD's opening screen. This Glossary provides an alphabetical list of Windows-related and Internet-related terms, each linking to the section of the book that introduces that concept. To learn about a topic, find the term in the glossary and follow the link into the text.

A page of instructions at the very back of this book describes how to install and use the e-book on the CD-ROM.

New Features in Windows XP

At first blush, Windows XP looks very different from its predecessors—the new Luna interface can be a startling change, with its simplified desktop and Start menu. Windows is still under there, though—and, as we'll show in Chapter 11, you can

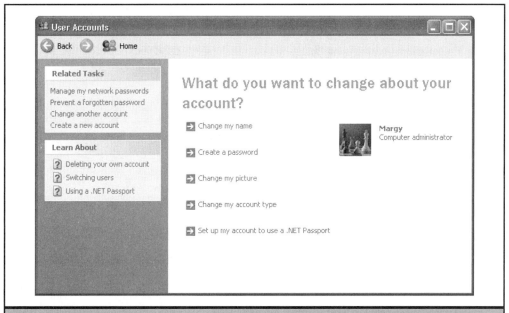

Figure I-1. *User accounts are easy to set up, and provide password-protect folders for each user's files.*

switch the Windows desktop back to a more familiar style. But the Luna interface isn't the most important new feature. Here is a list of other new features:

- The **CD Copy Wizard** built into Windows Explorer makes it easy to copy your files (including music and graphics files) onto CDs (see Chapter 7, section "Making Your Own CDs").

- **Backup** is back! Microsoft used to provide a backup program with earlier versions of Windows, but recent versions have left it out (see Chapter 9). We're glad to see that it's back, as running backups regularly is vital to keeping your files safe. If you use Windows XP Home Edition, you'll need to install it from the Windows XP CD-ROM.

- **Internet Explorer (IE)** version 6.0 is an upgrade to Microsoft's powerful Web browser, and **Outlook Express** 6.0 is the newest version of Microsoft's e-mail and newsgroup program (see Chapter 24, section "What Is Internet Explorer?").

- **Fast User Switching and password-protected user accounts** make it convenient to create and use a separate user account for each person who uses a single computer (see Figure I-1). If you assign passwords to the accounts, users can have a private, password-protected folder for their files. Fast User Switching lets several people stay logged on at the same time, with a new keystroke—WINDOWS-L—to switch from one user to another. If you use the NTFS disk format, you can password-protect files and folders, too (see Chapter 6).

- **Windows Messenger** challenges AOL Instant Messenger and other instant-messaging programs (see Chapter 25).

- **Windows Media Player 8** is a step up from the previous version, with DVD support, audio CD creation, and even automatic downloading of audio CD cover art from the Internet (see Chapter 19).

- **Photo printing** and **Web publishing** are built in: when Windows encounters a folder that contains graphics files, it offers wizards that can upload your pictures to a Web site or send them off to a photo-printing service (see Chapter 18, section "Printing Your Pictures at Home"). You can see your photos as a filmstrip or slideshow, too.

- The **Files And Settings Transfer Wizard** helps you move your stuff from one computer to another, including your documents and settings (see Chapter A, section "Transferring Your Data Files and Windows Configuration Settings").

- The **Internet Connection Firewall** protects your computer (or your whole LAN) from intruders on the Internet (see Chapter 31, section "Enabling the Internet Connection Firewall Between Your PC and the Internet").

- **Web Folders** enable you to work with files and folders on FTP and Web servers using Windows Explorer (see Chapter 26, section "Working with FTP and Web Servers Using Web Folders").

- The **Last Known Good Configuration** option lets you recover from Windows crashes by returning to a Windows configuration that worked (see Chapter 35, section "Startup Modes").

- **Remote Assistance** enables you to ask a friend, coworker, or a support professional to take over your computer via the Internet and fix a software problem (see Chapter 4, section "Allowing a Friend to Control Your Computer").

- **Product activation** requires you to "activate" Windows over the Internet or phone within a grace period, or the program stops functioning (see Appendix, section "How Does Product Activation Work?"). Activation doesn't require personal information from you (it's not the same as registration) and is designed to stop software piracy.

Windows XP also removed a few programs that came with some earlier Windows versions. Windows XP doesn't come with FrontPage Express (an HTML editor for creating Web pages), Microsoft Chat (an Internet Relay Chat program for chatting over the Internet), or Active Movie (which has been replaced by Movie Maker and Windows Media Player 8).

Differences Between Windows XP Editions

Windows XP comes in various versions: Windows XP Home Edition (for home and small-office users), Windows XP Professional (for corporate workstations), Windows XP 64-Bit Edition (for Itanium-based workstations), Windows .NET Server (for network servers), and Windows .NET Advanced Server (for network servers that need advanced features).

Windows XP Home Edition and Professional

These two versions of Windows XP are very similar: Microsoft has disabled a few features in Home Edition and made a few cosmetic changes. Here are the major differences:

- **Backup**   The Microsoft Backup program comes with both editions, but must be installed separately in Windows XP Home Edition (see Chapter 9, section "Installing the Backup Utility").

- **Multiprocessor support**   Home Edition supports only a single processor (CPU). Luckily, the vast majority of computers have only one processor. However, users of high-end scientific and analytical workstations need to install Professional.

- **Domain-based network support**   Home Edition cannot log onto a domain-based network. The networks within most large organizations use domains, so Home Edition won't suffice for corporate workstations. However, small-office and home users can use Home Edition on smaller workgroup-based peer-to-peer networks (see Chapter 27).

- **User administration**   Professional has a more flexible system of user accounts. Home Edition enables you to set up accounts for each user of the computer and choose whether they are administrative (with the ability to give any command) or limited (within all administrative privileges). See Chapter 6.

- **File Encryption**   Home Edition doesn't support file or folder encryption on NTFS-formatted disks (see Chapter 6, section "Can Windows XP Keep Files Private?").

- **Remote Desktop**   Home Edition doesn't include this Web-based application (also called Terminal Server client), which enables you to see the desktop of another computer on your own.

- **Offline Files And Folders**   Home Edition doesn't support this feature, which allows you to copy files from a server to a laptop before going on the road, and then synchronize the files when you reconnect to the network.

- **Upgrades**   You can't upgrade from Windows NT or 2000 to Windows XP Home Edition, only to Professional. You can upgrade from Windows 98 or Me to either version of Windows XP.

Microsoft has a comparison of Home Edition and Professional at **http://www.microsoft.com/windowsxp/home/guide/featurecomp.asp**.

Windows XP 64-Bit Edition

This edition of Windows XP adds support for the Intel Itanium processor family. These processors are used on high-end engineering, scientific, and graphics workstations.

Windows .NET Server and Advanced Server

These versions of Windows are, as the names imply, designed to run on servers rather than on workstations. That is, they are designed to provide services to other computers on a network rather than being used for day-to-day work by someone sitting at the keyboard. They are based on Windows XP, but include these additional features:

- **Slower performance as workstations**   These editions are optimized for network services, not for workstation performance.

- **Support for server software**   Many server programs, such as Microsoft Exchange, Advanced Server Pages, and SQL Server, require Windows .NET Server or Advanced Server, and don't run on Windows XP Home Edition or Professional.

- **Clustering**   Servers can be linked together into clusters to handle large network demands.

Talk to Us

We love to hear from our readers. Drop us an e-mail note at **winxptcr@gurus.com** to tell us how you liked the book or just to test your e-mail skills. Our mail robot will answer right away, and the authors will read your message when time permits (usually within a week or two.)

Also visit our Web site at **http://net.gurus.com/winxptcr** for updates and corrections to this book.

The
Complete
Reference

Part I

Working in Windows XP

The
Complete
Reference

Chapter 1

The Basics of
Windows XP

Windows is the most widely run computer program in the world, and *Windows XP* (short for "experience") is the latest version of Windows. Most of the software written for personal computers—indeed, most of the software written for any computer—is written for computers running Windows.

This chapter explains what Windows XP is and explains the objects you see on the Windows screen—the desktop, icons, the taskbar, the Start menu, and windows. It also explains the Control Panel, a collection of programs that enable you to control how Windows and your computer work. Many Control Panel programs run *wizards*, special programs that step you through the process of creating or configuring an object on your computer. Properties are another way of choosing settings for the objects in your computer. This chapter also describes how to start Windows, shut it down, and suspend Windows operation when you're not using your computer.

If you've used Windows 95, 98, Me, or 2000, you can probably skip this chapter since you already understand windows, icons, and the desktop. Just skim through to see what's changed!

What Is Windows XP?

Windows XP is the latest desktop version of Microsoft's Windows series of programs. It's the upgrade to the consumer versions of Windows (95, 98, and Me) as well as to the business, server, and power-user versions (Windows NT and 2000). Windows is an

Versions of Windows XP and Windows 2002

For years, Microsoft has produced two editions of Windows, one for desktops (that is, for individual users, including for use on laptops) and one for servers (computers that provide services over networks). The desktop versions were Windows 3.1, 95, 98, and Me, and were intended for workstation use—that is, on computers that people used directly. The server versions were Windows NT 4, NT 5, and 2000, and were intended for use on servers (computers that provide services to other computers on a network) as well as by high-end users.

Windows XP is designed to work for individuals and power users, and comes initially in three versions: Home Edition (for home and small offices), Professional (for offices), and 64-Bit Edition (for technical workstations that use the Intel Itanium CPU). At the end of 2001, Microsoft plans to release two more editions of Windows XP, renamed Windows .NET: Windows .NET Server and Advanced Server (for server machines on small and large networks). This book describes Windows XP Home Edition and Professional, with notes where features are available in one edition and not the other. If you plan to use the Windows .NET Server or Advanced Server versions, refer to *Windows .NET Server and Advanced Server: The Complete Reference* by Kathy Ivens (Osborne/McGraw-Hill, 2001). The Microsoft web site contains details about Windows XP at **http://www.microsoft.com/windowsxp**.

operating system, a program that manages your entire computer system, including its screen, keyboard, disk drives, memory, and central processor. Windows also provides a *graphical user interface*, or *GUI*, which enables you to control your computer by using a mouse, windows, and icons. You can also use the keyboard to give commands; this book describes both methods.

You can upgrade to Windows XP from Windows 98 or Me, or you can do a "clean install" to replace any previous version of Windows on your computer. You can also buy a computer with Windows XP preinstalled. Once Windows XP is installed, you can run Windows-compatible *application programs* (programs for getting real-world work done).

Windows XP comes bundled with many programs, most of which aren't actually part of the operating system, including Internet connection software (dial-up connections), an e-mail program (Outlook Express), a Web browser (Internet Explorer), a simple word processing program (WordPad), an instant messaging program (Windows Messenger), local area network support, utilities that help with hard-disk housekeeping, and dozens of other programs.

What Hardware Do You Need?

Windows XP requires the following computer hardware:

- A Pentium II, Pentium III, Celeron, compatible, or better CPU running at a speed of at least 300 MHz.

- At least 64MB of RAM memory (although Microsoft recommends at least 128MB—it's not reliable with only 64MB).

- A hard disk with at least 2GB total space with at least 650MB free, depending on which options you choose to install. (You may need more for temporary files.)

- A CD-ROM or DVD drive from which to install Windows and other software.

- A monitor, keyboard, and mouse or other pointing device.

- If you plan to listen to sounds played by Windows and other programs, you need a sound board and speakers attached to your computer (see Chapter 19, section "Configuring Windows to Work with Sound"). To participate in voice or video chats, you need a microphone or digital video camera, too.

- If you plan to use your computer to connect to the Internet, you need a dial-up modem and a regular phone line, an ISDN modem and an ISDN line, a DSL modem and a DSL line, a cable modem and cable connection, or a local area network connection (see Chapter 27).

What Appears on the Screen?

Like previous versions of Windows, Windows XP uses windows to display information on your screen, icons to provide pictorial buttons for you to click, and a taskbar, a "mission control" center for your computer. All of these objects appear on your Windows desktop—your screen. Microsoft made a major effort to clean up the screen in Windows XP: you'll see many fewer icons and menu commands. Of course, you can always create icons and add commands for the programs and files you use frequently—in fact, Windows does this for you.

What Is the Desktop?

Windows uses your screen as a *desktop*, a work area on which you see your programs. The desktop, shown in Figure 1-1, can contain windows, icons, and the taskbar. You can think of the icons, windows, and Web pages that appear on your screen as "sitting" on your metaphorical desktop, like the papers and folders on your real desktop. (Your PC's desktop may display a picture or background color: we show a white desktop, because it is clearer when printed on paper.)

The Windows XP desktop starts uncluttered, with few icons. As you install and use programs, you (and the programs) will create icons on the desktop for programs and files you use frequently. You can add or delete icons from the desktop (see Chapter 11, section "Changing Icons").

Chapter 2 explains what windows are and how to use them.

What Is an Icon?

An *icon* is a little picture on your screen. When you click or double-click the icon, or select the icon with the keyboard and press ENTER, something happens. Windows uses icons to represent programs, files, and commands.

Throughout this book, the instructions tell you what icons you can expect to see, what happens when you click them, and when to use them.

  Many programs provide labels for their icons. Icon labels may appear just below the icon, or they may appear in a little box when you rest the mouse pointer on the icon for a moment.

Welcome to Windows XP!

To see a tour of Windows XP, choose Start | All Programs | Accessories | Tour Windows XP (that is, click the Start button in the lower-left corner of the screen, click Help And Support, and click Tour Windows XP).

You can choose how the icons on your Windows desktop and those in Explorer windows work when you click them—they run when you double-click them (like Windows 95 and 3.1) or click them once (like a Web page). See the section "Choosing Between Single-Click and Double-Click" later in this chapter for how to control how Windows icons behave.

Icons on your desktop that include a curved arrow in a little white box in the lower-left corner of the icon are *shortcuts* and represent files or programs on your computer (see Chapter 8, section "What Is a Shortcut?"). You can create your own shortcut icons.

What Is the Taskbar?

The *taskbar* is a row of buttons and icons that usually appears along the bottom of the screen, as in Figure 1-2. You can configure Windows to display the taskbar along the top or side of your screen (see Chapter 10, section "Moving the Taskbar"). You can also tell Windows to hide the taskbar when you aren't using it.

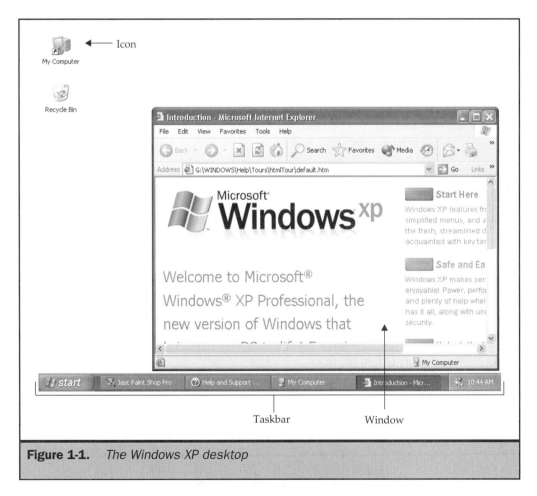

Figure 1-1. *The Windows XP desktop*

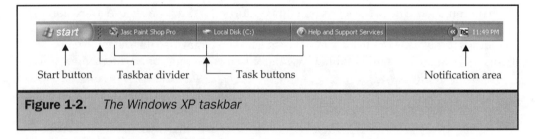

Figure 1-2. *The Windows XP taskbar*

The taskbar has several parts:

- The Start button is usually at the left end of the taskbar.
- The task buttons represent each window that is open on the desktop.
- The taskbar can contain one or more toolbars (sets of buttons). (None appear in Figure 1-2.)
- The notification area contains icons for Windows programs that require your attention, along with a clock. This area used to be called the system tray.

What Is the Start Menu?

When you click the Start button on the taskbar, the Start menu appears. You can also display the Start menu by pressing the WINDOWS key (if your keyboard has one) or by pressing CTRL-ESC.

The Start menu lists commands and additional menus that list most of the programs that you can run on your computer. It looks something like this:

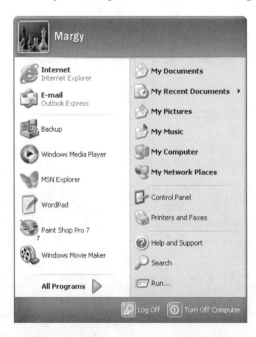

The Start menu has fewer commands than appeared in previous versions of Windows. The Settings and Favorites commands that appeared in Windows 98 and Me are gone. As you use your computer, Windows adds commands for your frequently used programs to the Start menu. Installing some programs adds commands to the Start menu, too. You can customize which programs appear on the Start menu and how they are arranged (see Chapter 10, section "Reorganizing the Start Menu"). Chapter 2 has more information about how to run programs from the Start menu.

In this book, we indicate commands on the Start menu and its submenus like this: "Choose Start | Help And Support" means you should click the Start button and then choose the Help And Support command from the menu that appears.

Most of the programs available on your computer appear on the Start | All Programs menu (click All Programs on the Start menu to see it). This menu was called Programs in previous versions of Windows.

What Are Task Buttons?

Task buttons are the buttons on the taskbar that represent each program that is running (see Figure 1-2). If a program displays more than one window, more than one task button may appear. Each task button displays the icon for the program and as much of the program name as can fit. Some programs display other information on the task button; for example, Notepad displays the name of the text file that is open. The task buttons used to be called the Task Manager in previous versions of Windows, but Microsoft has reassigned that name to a system management program (see Chapter 35).

Click a window's task button to select that window, that is, make that window active (see Chapter 2, section "Switching Programs"). You can also right-click a button to see the system menu, a menu of commands you can give regarding that window, including opening and closing the window (see Chapter 2, section "What Is the System Menu?").

If the taskbar gets too full to fit task buttons for all the open windows, Windows groups the buttons together, with one button for each application. For example, if you have two Internet Explorer browser windows open, you see one button for the program, with a 2 in the label, like this:

Click the task button to see a menu of the windows displayed by that program.

What Is the Notification Area?

The *notification area* appears at the right end of the taskbar and contains the system clock along with a group of tiny icons:

When you move the mouse pointer to the clock, after a moment the current date also appears. The icons in the notification area represent programs that need your attention. Windows XP displays fewer icons here than previous versions of Windows did, displaying them only when you need to do something.

Some programs add icons to the notification area. To find out the name of an icon, move the mouse pointer to the icon, without clicking. After a moment, the icon's label appears. Some icons display information rather than a label (for example, the Power Management icon that appears on the system tray of most laptops displays how much charge is left in the laptop's battery). To change the settings for the program that displays the icon, or to exit the program, double-click or right-click the icon and choose a command from the menu that appears.

If there are too many icons to fit in the notification area, you see a left-pointing (<) button that you can click to see the rest of the icons. This button allows Windows to hide the icons that don't fit, so they don't clutter up your taskbar.

What Is the Mouse Pointer?

The *mouse pointer* indicates which part of the screen will be affected when you click your mouse's buttons. As you move the mouse, trackball, or other pointing device, the mouse pointer moves, too (see Chapter 12, section "Configuring Your Mouse"). A separate indicator, the *cursor*, which usually appears as a blinking vertical line, shows where text you type will appear.

How Do You Configure Windows and Other Programs?

To use Windows effectively, you need to configure it to work with your computer's hardware and with your other programs. When configuring Windows, you encounter these concepts:

- Properties, which are settings for many different objects in your computer's hardware and software

- The Control Panel, which enables you to see and change many Windows settings

- Wizards, which are programs that help automate the processes of installing hardware, installing software, and configuring software

What Are Properties?

Every object in Windows—the hardware components of your computer, software programs, files, and icons—has *properties*, the settings that affect how that object works.

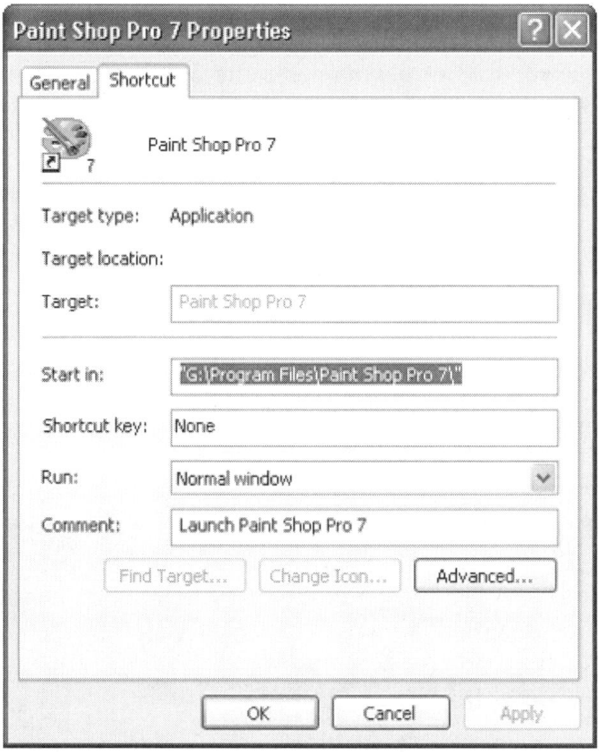

Figure 1-3.   *A Properties dialog box displays the properties of an object and may enable you to edit them.*

For example, a file might have properties such as a filename, size, and the date the file was last modified.

To display the properties of almost anything you see on the screen in Windows, right-click the item and choose Properties from the menu that appears. You see a dialog box with a title that usually includes the word "Properties." Figure 1-3 shows the properties of an icon on the desktop.

If the object has too many properties to fit in a dialog box, tabs may run along the top of the dialog box. Click a tab to see the settings on that tab. Windows may let you change some of the settings, depending on the type of object.

For example, to see the properties of the Windows desktop, right-click the desktop in a place where it is not covered by icons or windows. You see the Display Properties dialog box (see Chapter 11, section "What Are Display Properties?"). When you have finished looking at the properties shown and possibly changing some of the properties that can be changed, click OK to save your changes or Cancel to cancel them, and exit the Properties dialog box.

What Is the Control Panel?

The *Control Panel*, shown in Figure 1-4, is a window that displays icons for a number of programs that enable you to control your computer, Windows, and the software you have installed. These programs help you see and change the properties of many parts of Windows.

To see the Control Panel, choose Start | Control Panel. Windows XP displays a newly redesigned window with categories of tasks—Windows calls this *Category View*. Clicking a category in the Control Panel displays a list of tasks in that category.

If you are used to the "Classic" Windows 95, 98, or Me Control Panel icons, click the Switch to Classic View option. You see most of the same Control Panel icons that appeared in earlier versions of Windows; double-click them to run them. These icons also appear in Category View, below the tasks.

The details of what you can change in each category and what each Control Panel icon does are discussed throughout this book, in the related chapters.

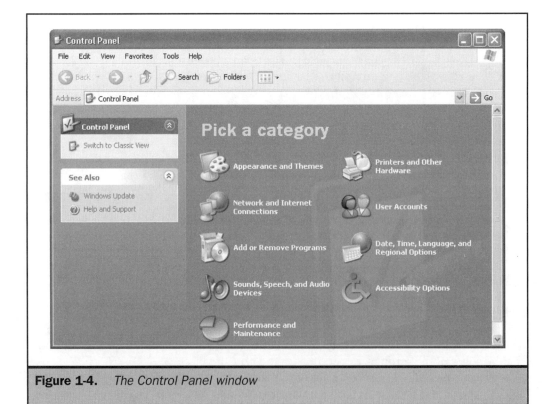

Figure 1-4.   *The Control Panel window*

What Is a Wizard?

Windows, like many other Microsoft programs, includes many *wizards*, programs that step you through the process of creating or configuring something. For example, the New Connection Wizard leads you through the many steps required to set up a dial-up connection to the Internet (see Chapter 22).

Wizards include instructions for each step, telling you what information you must provide and making suggestions regarding your choices. Most wizards display window after window of information and questions, with Back, Next, and Cancel buttons at the bottom of each window. Fill out the information requested by the wizard and click the Next button to continue. If you need to return to a previous wizard window, click the Back button. To exit the wizard, click the Cancel button. The wizard's last screen usually displays a Finish button because there's no next screen to see.

Starting Up Windows

On most systems, Windows starts automatically when you turn on the computer. You see whatever messages your computer displays on startup, followed by the Windows *splash screen* (logo). If your computer is on a LAN or is set up for multiple users, you also see a welcome screen, showing the user accounts defined on the system (see Chapter 27). Click your user account name: if the account requires a password, type your password and press ENTER.

If your computer system has been suspended, Windows hasn't been shut down; instead, it is "sleeping." To start up where you left off, just resume operation of your computer, which usually is accomplished by moving the mouse, pressing a key (such as the SHIFT key), or (if you use a laptop) opening the cover.

Another possibility is that someone locked the computer screen by pressing WINDOWS-L (that is, holding down the WINDOWS key, which not all keyboards have, and typing L). If so, you see the same welcome screen you saw when Windows started: click your user account name to continue.

Tip   *If your computer's hard disk contains more than one bootable partition (that is, another section of your hard disk that contains an operating system), you may see the message "Please select the operating system to start," with a list of bootable partitions. Use the arrow keys to select the operating system you want and press ENTER. For information about partitions, see Chapter 32.*

Shutting Down and Restarting Windows

When you need to turn off the computer, you must shut down Windows first to allow Windows to close all its files and do other housekeeping tasks before terminating. To shut down Windows, choose Start | Turn Off Computer, click anywhere on the desktop and press ALT-F4, or press CTRL-ESC and choose Shut Down. You see the Turn Off Computer dialog box:

Your options are

- **Stand By**   Stores the programs and data that are currently open, and then shuts down Windows so you can turn the computer off. The next time you turn your computer on, you can pick up just where you left off.

- **Turn Off**   Shuts down Windows. Windows displays a message when you can safely turn off the computer. Don't turn off the computer until you see this message. Computers with advanced power management shut off automatically.

- **Restart**   Shuts down Windows, and then reloads it (useful if your computer starts acting funny).

When Can You Turn Off the Computer?

We recommend you *do not* turn off the computer when you have finished using it. Windows likes to perform housekeeping tasks when you aren't using the computer, so leaving it on, even when you're not working, is a good idea. You can schedule programs to run at specified times (see Chapter 2, section "Running Programs on a Schedule Using Task Scheduler")—for example, you can schedule Windows to collect your e-mail at 7:00 every morning.

Many computers power down the screen, hard disk, and fan after a set time of inactivity. The computer itself, however, is still running. If your screen doesn't power off automatically, you should turn off your screen when you aren't using the computer. Computer screens use the lion's share of the electricity consumed by the computer (see Chapter 15, section "Managing Your Computer's Power").

If programs are running, Windows closes them before shutting down, switching to standby, or restarting. If a program has unsaved files open, the program should ask you whether you want to save your work before the program exits.

 With previous versions of Windows, restarting Windows every day or so was important. Windows' housekeeping wasn't perfect, and previous versions lost track of system resources over time (see Chapter 34, section "Monitoring System Use with the Task Manager"). Windows XP is much better at remaining stable over long periods of time. However, to ensure that the maximum system resources are available for your use, restart Windows.

Setting Windows to Shut Down by Itself

Windows includes *OnNow*, technology that powers down the computer when nothing is happening and powers back up when the computer is needed again, if the computer's hardware permits. To use OnNow, choose Start | Control Panel, click Performance And Maintenance, and then run the Power Options program (see Chapter 15, section "Managing Your Computer's Power").

Suspending Windows XP

Some computers have a *Suspend Mode, Hibernate Mode,* or *Standby Mode* in which the computer remains on, but the disk drives, fan, and screen turn off. If your computer has such a mode, a Stand By option appears on the Turn Off Computer dialog box. To switch your computer to Suspend Mode, choose Start | Turn Off Computer and click Stand By.

Tip *To wake up a computer that has partially powered itself down, press the SHIFT key a few times.*

Choosing Between Single-Click and Double-Click

You can choose how icons on the Windows desktop and in Explorer windows behave (as you could in Windows Me and 98 Second Edition). Your choices are

- **Single-click** (Web style) To select the icon without running or opening it, move your mouse pointer to the icon without clicking, and wait a second. To run or open the icon, click it once. Icon labels appear underlined (like Web page links).
- **Double-click** (Classic Windows style) To select the icon, click it once. To run or open the icon, click it twice. Icon labels are not underlined.

Figure 1-5. *The General tab of the Folder Options dialog box, where you can specify how Windows icons work*

Follow these steps to choose between single- and double-click:

1. Choose Start | Control Panel. Click the Appearance And Themes category.

2. Click the Folder Options icon near the bottom of the Appearance And Themes window. You see the Folder Options dialog box, as shown in Figure 1-5. If the General tab isn't selected, click it. (Windows XP Home Edition doesn't include the Offline Files tab.)

Whether you use single-click or double-click, you can right-click icons to see a shortcut menu of commands you can perform on the icon (see Chapter 2, section "Choosing Commands from Shortcut Menus").

3. In the Click Items As Follows box, click Single-click or Double-click. If you choose Single-click, choose whether you want icon titles to be underlined all the time (Consistent With My Browser) or only when your mouse pointer is on the icon (Only When I Point At Them).

4. Click OK.

The
Complete
Reference

Chapter 2

Running Programs

Running Windows XP itself doesn't get you very far. The point of Windows is to let you run programs that help you get work done. To take advantage of Windows' capability to multitask (do several things at the same time), this chapter explains how to run several programs at the same time and how to switch among them. Because programs display information in windows, you also learn how the windows you see on your screen work.

You can control the size and location of the windows in which programs display information. Once a program is running, you can give it commands using the mouse and keyboard. This chapter also explains how to configure Windows to launch the programs you always use automatically so you're ready to work as soon as you start Windows, how to schedule programs to run at preset times, and how to define shortcut keys for quick-starting programs you use frequently. Windows XP's new compatibility mode enables many older programs to run without problems.

 If you've used previous versions of Windows, you probably know everything in this chapter—just flip through to familiarize yourself with the terms you'll see throughout the rest of the book.

What Are Programs and Windows?

A *program* is a sequence of computer instructions that perform a task. Programs are stored in *program files*, which have the filename extension .exe or .com. When you run a program, your computer executes the instructions in the program file.

Programs can do several things at once; for example, a word processing program may be able to print one document while you edit another. One program can run several *tasks* or *processes* at the same time. Windows itself runs many tasks at the same time, including tasks that monitor the hard disk, screen, and keyboard; update the onscreen clock; and run programs on a schedule, for example. The heart of Windows is its capability to *multitask*, that is, to run many processes at the same time.

An *application* is a program that does real-world–oriented work. Word processors, spreadsheets, and databases are widely used types of applications. A *systems program* does computer-oriented work—an operating system like Windows itself is the most important systems program you use. Printer drivers (which control the actions of a printer) or disk scanners (which check disks for errors) are other examples of system programs. A *utility* is a small, simple, useful program (either a small application or a small systems program). Windows comes with many utilities, like Calculator and Notepad.

 If you have user accounts on your system, you can run a program as if you logged in as another user, assuming that you know the user account's password (see Chapter 6, section "Running a Program as Another User").

Each program displays information in one or more *windows* (see "What Do the Parts of Windows Do?")—rectangular areas on the screen that display information from a running program. Some windows are divided into sections called *panes*. To run more than one program at the same time, go ahead and run one program, then another, then another. The first program you run continues to run when the second program starts. Each program's window(s) can be minimized, maximized, or restored (see "Controlling the Size and Shape of Your Windows"). A button appears on the taskbar for each program.

One window is always *on top*, which means it is the *active window*. The title bar of the active window is a different color than the title bars of all the other windows on your screen; in the default Windows desktop color scheme, the title bar of the active window is blue, while the other title bars are gray (see Chapter 11, section "Choosing a New Color Scheme"). Where the active window overlaps with another window, the active window obscures the other window.

Whatever you type on the keyboard is directed to the program in the active window. The programs in the other windows continue to run, but they don't receive input from your keyboard. To type information into a program, you switch the active window to a window displayed by that program.

What Do the Parts of Windows Do?

Figure 2-1 shows a program (this example shows WordPad, a simple word processor that comes with Windows) running in a window. Although what's inside the window

16-Bit Versus 32-Bit Applications

Older personal computers process data 16 bits at a time. These 16-bit computers are based on older CPUs (central processing units), like the Intel 8088 and 80286.

Newer personal computers process data 32 bits at a time. These 32-bit computers are based on newer CPU chips, like the Intel 80386, 80486, Pentium, and Pentium Pro.

DOS and Windows 3.1 run on both 16-bit and 32-bit computers. Windows 9x, Me, NT, 2000, and XP, as well as Linux and OS/2, all require 32-bit computers.

Some programs are designed to run with DOS and Windows 3.1; these programs are called *16-bit applications*. Other programs are designed to work with later versions of Windows and are called *32-bit applications*.

As a Windows XP user, you can run both 16-bit and 32-bit applications. (If you have Windows XP 64-Bit Edition running on a computer with an Intel Itanium processor, you can even run 64-bit programs!) When you have a choice, run the 32-bit version of a program, though; it takes better advantage of your 32-bit computer, and it usually runs faster and has more capabilities than the 16-bit version. If you have to run an older program, you can use compatibility mode to simulate an older version of Windows (see "Running Programs in Compatibility Mode").

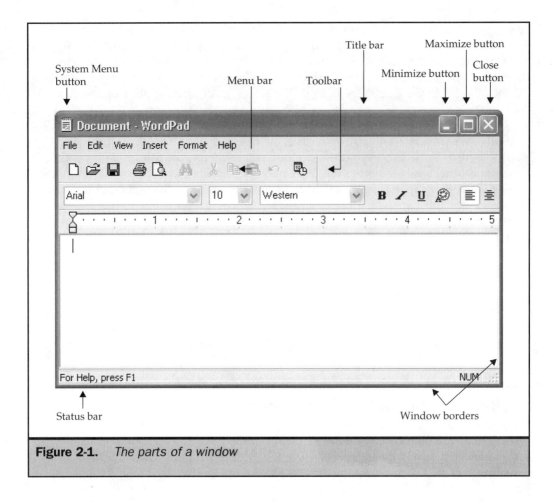

Figure 2-1. *The parts of a window*

frame changes from program to program, most windows you see in Windows include the following components:

- **System Menu button** Displays a menu of commands you can use to move and resize your window (see "Controlling the Size and Shape of Your Windows").

- **Title bar** Displays the title of the window and provides a way to move the window around within the screen (see "Moving a Window").

- **Minimize button** Shrinks the window to an icon on the taskbar (see "Minimizing a Window").

- **Maximize or Restore button** When you click the Maximize button, the window expands to cover the whole screen (see "Maximizing a Window").

Once a window has been maximized, the Maximize button disappears and is replaced by the Restore button. When you click the Restore button (with two overlapping rectangles), the window shrinks to its previous size and the Maximize button reappears.

- **Close button**   Closes the window and exits the program (see "Closing Windows").

- **Menu bar**   Provides a row of menus you can use to choose commands (see "Giving Commands").

- **Toolbar**   Provides a row of buttons you can click to give commands (see "Giving Commands").

- **Status bar**   Displays information about the program. Some programs enable you to give commands by clicking parts of the status bar.

- **Scroll bar**   Provides a way to "pan" your window up and down, or left and right to show information that doesn't fit in the window. Scroll bars may be horizontal (running along the bottom edge of a window) or vertical (running down the right edge of a window). All scroll bars have arrow buttons at each end and a sliding gray box somewhere in the scroll bar; some programs display scroll bars with additional buttons (for example, to scroll one page of a document at a time). The length or width of a scroll bar represents the entire length or width of the document you are viewing, and the sliding box represents the part of the document you can currently see. To change which part of the document you can see, click the arrow button at one end of the scroll bar, or click-and-drag the sliding gray box along the scroll bar.

- **Window borders**   Provide a way to drag around the edges of the window to change the size and shape of the window (see "Changing the Size and Shape of a Window").

What Is the System Menu?

The *System Menu* button is a tiny icon in the upper-left corner of each window. The icon shows which program you are running (if you happen to recognize the icon). When you click the icon, you see the *System* menu, as shown here:

You can also display the System menu by pressing ALT-SPACEBAR or by right-clicking the title bar of the window.

The commands on the System menu do the following:

- **Restore**   Resizes the window to its previous size, the same as the Restore button.

- **Move**   Enables you to move the window around on your screen by using the cursor (arrow) keys. This command does the same thing as dragging the window's title bar with the mouse (see "Moving a Window"). Press ENTER to finish moving the window.

- **Size**   Enables you to change the size of the window by using the cursor keys. This command does the same thing as dragging the window borders with the mouse (see "Changing the Size and Shape of a Window").

- **Minimize**   Minimizes the window, shrinking it to a small icon, the same as the Minimize button.

- **Maximize**   Maximizes the window to cover the whole screen, the same as the Maximize button.

- **Close**   Closes the window, the same as the Close button.

Some applications also add their own commands to the System menu.

Starting Programs

Windows gives you many ways to start a program, including clicking its icon on your Windows desktop, choosing it from a menu, clicking a document you want to edit or view by using the program, clicking the program filename, and typing the program name into a Run or DOS window. The following sections describe these methods.

Starting Programs from the Desktop

If an icon for the program appears on your Windows desktop, click the icon either once or twice to run the program. If the labels under the icons on your desktop are underlined, click once. If the labels are not underlined, double-click. You can control whether you need to single-click or double-click icons to run programs by setting your folder options (see Chapter 1, section "Choosing Between Single-Click and Double-Click").

Starting Programs from the Start Menu

Chapter 1 describes the Start menu, including the all-important Start button. To launch a program from the Start menu, click the Start button. You see the Start menu, as shown here:

Unlike the Start menu of previous versions of Windows, the Windows XP Start menu has two sides. At the top of the left side are Internet and E-mail, which run your default Web browser and e-mail program. You can add other programs, too (see Chapter 10, section "Reorganizing the Start Menu"). Below that are icons for programs you've run frequently and recently: Windows chooses these programs according to your usage. At the bottom of the left side is the All Programs button, which displays menus that usually include the rest of the programs that are installed on your computer.

The right side of the Start menu lists the folders that Microsoft suggests you use for your files (My Documents, My Pictures, and My Music) and My Computer (to run Windows Explorer). If your computer is on a network, My Network Places appears. The other choices are usually Control Panel (for computer administration), Connect To (if your computer is on a LAN or the Internet), Help And Support, Search (for finding files and other information), and Run (for running a program whose filename you know).

If you can't find the program you want, and you think it's been installed on your computer, click the All Programs button on the Start menu (that is, choose Start | All

Programs). You see the Programs menu, which looks like the Programs menu in previous versions of Windows:

When your mouse pointer is on a menu name, a submenu appears (usually to its right). Point to menus until you see the name of the program you want to run, then click the program name. Most programs appear on the Programs menu or on its submenus (because most installation programs add commands for the programs that they install). You might need to try several menus to find the one that contains the program you want. You can always press ESC to cancel the menu you are looking at (moving your mouse pointer off the menu usually cancels the menu, too). For example, WordPad appears on the Accessories submenu of the Programs menu. To run WordPad, choose Start | All Programs | Accessories | WordPad.

Note   *In this book, we tell you to run programs from the Start or Start | All Programs menus where the programs appear in a standard Windows XP installation. If you've customized your Start menu, commands may not be where we say they are. Also, if you've run a program recently, it may appear on the left side of the Start menu—if so, ignore our instructions for finding the program and click the command you see.*

You can rearrange the programs on your Start and Programs menus so the programs you most frequently run appear on the Programs menu or the Start menu rather than on a submenu. You can also create desktop icons for any programs on these menus (see Chapter 10, section "Reorganizing the Start Menu").

You can change the order of the items on the Start and Programs menus by dragging them up and down on the menus. You can also drag an item from one menu to another, or "pin" a program to the top-left side of the Start menu by right-clicking it and choosing Pin To Start Menu. If you don't intend to reorganize your menus, don't click-and-drag the commands on them.

Starting Programs Using the WINDOWS Key

You can run a program without using your mouse. If your keyboard has a WINDOWS key, press it to display the Start menu; if not, pressing CTRL-ESC does the same thing. Press the LEFT-ARROW, RIGHT-ARROW, UP-ARROW, and DOWN-ARROW keys to highlight a command from the Start menu and press ENTER to choose the command. The same method works for choosing commands from submenus. The RIGHT-ARROW key moves from a command to its submenu (which is usually to the right on the screen). The LEFT-ARROW and ESC keys cancel a submenu and return to the previous menu.

Starting Programs by Clicking Program Filenames

Programs are stored in files, usually with the filename extension .exe (short for "executable") or .com (for "command"). Windows displays the names of program files in Explorer windows. To run the program, single-click or double-click the filename of the program you want to run.

For example, if you double-click the filename Mspaint.exe, Windows runs the Microsoft Paint program. You can usually guess the program name from the filename, though some filenames can be cryptic.

Starting Programs by Clicking Document Filenames or File Icons

Windows knows which programs you use to open which types of files. For example, it knows that files with the .doc extension are opened using Microsoft Word. When you install a program, the installation program adds a file association to Windows, so Windows knows what kinds of files it can open.

To run the program that can open a particular file, you can click or double-click the filename in an Explorer window. If the filenames are underlined, you single-click the filename to open it. If the filenames are not underlined, you double-click the filename. Windows runs the appropriate program to handle that file (if the program isn't already running) and opens the file in that program. If an icon for a file appears on your desktop, clicking or double-clicking the icon tells Windows to do the same thing.

For example, if your desktop icon labels aren't underlined and you double-click a file with the extension .mdb (a Microsoft Access database file), Windows runs

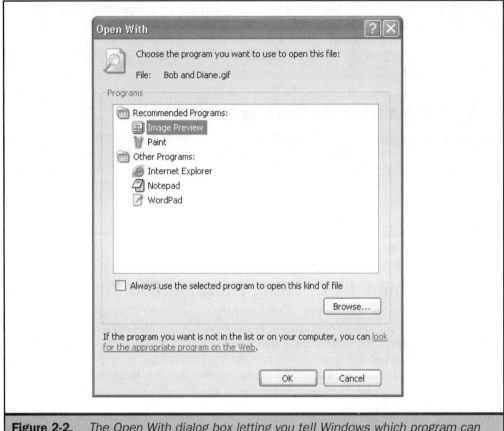

Figure 2-2. *The Open With dialog box letting you tell Windows which program can open the file you clicked*

Microsoft Access and opens the database file. Windows may be configured not to display extensions (the default setting is for extensions to be hidden); you can identify many types of files by their icons. To tell Windows to display full filenames, including the extensions, see the section "What Are Extensions and File Types" in Chapter 7.

If you try to open a file for which Windows doesn't know which program to run, you see a window asking what you want to do. Your options are

- **Use The Web Service To Find The Appropriate Program** Windows runs your Web browser to display information about the type of file that you want to open, and helps you find a program that can open it.

- **Select The Program From A List** Windows displays the Open With dialog box, shown in Figure 2-2. Choose the program that can open the type of file you clicked; if the program doesn't appear on the list, click the Browse button to find the filename of the program. If you always want to run this program when you click this type of file, leave the check mark in the Always Use The Selected Program To Open This Type Of File check box. Optionally, you can type a description of the type of file: This description appears when you select a filename and choose View | Details. Then click OK.

You can control which program runs for each type of file (see Chapter 3, section "Associating a Program with a File Extension").

 If you want to open a file using a different program from the one Windows automatically runs, right-click the filename and choose Open With from the menu that appears. Windows displays the Open With dialog box shown in Figure 2-2, and you can choose the program you want to run.

Starting Programs Using Shortcut Keys

If a shortcut (see Chapter 8, section "What Is a Shortcut?")—an icon with a tiny arrow in its lower-left corner—exists for a program, you can define shortcut keys to run the program. *Shortcut keys* for programs are always a combination of the CTRL key; the ALT key; and one other key, which must be a letter, number, or symbol key.

To define shortcut keys for a program:

1. Right-click the shortcut icon that launches the program and choose Properties from the menu that appears. You see the Properties dialog box for the shortcut.

2. Click the Shortcut tab.

3. Click in the Shortcut Key box (which usually says "None") and press the key you want to use in combination with the CTRL and ALT keys. For example, press M to specify CTRL-ALT-M as the shortcut key combination. To specify no shortcut keys, press SPACEBAR.

4. Click OK.

Once you define shortcut keys for a program, you can press the keys to run the program.

 If another program uses the same combination of keys, that combination of keys no longer performs its function in the program; instead, the key combination runs the program to which you assigned the shortcut keys. However, few programs use CTRL-ALT key combinations.

Starting Programs from the Run Dialog Box

Before Windows, there was DOS, which required you to type the filename of a program and press ENTER to run the program. If you prefer this method, it still works in Windows—sometimes it's easier than finding the program in the maze of Start menu options. Choose Start | Run, and you see the Run dialog box:

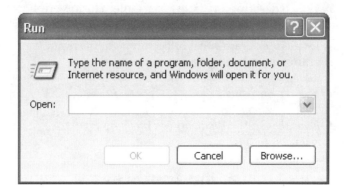

To run a program, type its full path and filename into the Open box (that is, the exact filename, including the folder that contains the file), or click Browse to locate the filename. Then press ENTER or click OK. Windows runs the program.

Depending on the program, you may need to type additional information after the filename. For example, to run the Ftp program (an Internet file transfer program that comes with Windows), type **ftp**, followed by a space and the name of a computer on the Internet (like **ftp.microsoft.com**). When you press ENTER, Windows runs the Ftp program by using the additional information you typed.

 If you've typed the filename in the Open box recently, click the downward-pointing button at the right end of the Open box and choose the filename from the list that appears.

A more arcane way to run a program from a dialog box similar to the Run dialog box is by using the New Task button on the Windows Task Manager. Press CTRL-ALT-DEL to display the Windows Task Manager and click New Task.

Starting Programs from the Command Prompt Window

Serious DOS enthusiasts like to see the old-fashioned DOS prompt (usually C:\>) before typing the filename of the program they want to run. To run programs from the DOS prompt, choose Start | All Programs | Accessories | Command Prompt, or you can choose Start | Run and type cmd and press ENTER. You see the Command Prompt window, a window that looks like the screen of a computer running DOS. Type the filename of the program you want to run and press ENTER.

When you have finished using the Command Prompt window, type **exit** and press ENTER, or close the window by clicking the Close button in the upper-right corner of the window. You can also run DOS commands in the Command Prompt window (see Chapter 39, section "Running Programs on Startup").

Starting Programs when Windows Starts

When Windows starts up, it looks in the Startup folder of your Start Menu for shortcuts to programs (see Chapter 8, section "What Is a Shortcut?") This folder is usually stored in C:\Documents And Settings*username*\Start Menu\Programs (assuming that C: is the partition where Windows is installed). If any programs or shortcuts to programs are stored in this folder, Windows runs them automatically when it has finished starting up. To see the programs in the Startup folder, choose Start | All Programs | Startup and see what programs are listed.

For example, you can use this Startup folder to run your word processor and e-mail programs automatically each time you start Windows. Just create shortcuts in your Startup folder (see Chapter 8, section "Making Shortcuts").

 The Windows Registry, which stores information about Windows and your applications, can also tell Windows to run programs automatically on startup (see Chapter 38, section "Running Programs on Startup").

Controlling the Size and Shape of Your Windows

Windows enables you to control the size and position of most windows, so you can arrange your open windows to see the information you want to view. A window can be in one of three states:

- *Maximized*, taking up the entire screen, with no window borders.
- *Minimized*, so all that appears is the window's button on the taskbar.
- *Restored*, or *in a window*; that is, displayed with window borders (see Figure 2-1). You can change the height and width of restored windows. Most windows on your screen are restored windows.

Moving a Window

The *title bar* is the colored bar that runs along the top of the window. To move a window, click anywhere in the title bar of the window, except for the System Menu button or the buttons at the right end of the title bar. Next, drag the window to the place you want it to appear. Release the mouse button when the window is located where you want it.

You can also use the keyboard to move a window. Press ALT-SPACEBAR to display the System menu, press M to choose the Move command, press the cursor keys to move the window, and then press ENTER when the window is located where you want it. You can also right-click the program button on the taskbar and choose Move from the menu that appears.

Minimizing a Window

A button appears on the taskbar for each program that is running. To minimize a window—make a window disappear, leaving nothing but its taskbar button—click the window's Minimize button, the leftmost of the three buttons on the right end of the title bar, or click the window's System Menu button and choose Minimize from the menu that appears.

You can also minimize a window by using the keyboard. Press ALT-SPACEBAR to display the System menu and press N to choose the Minimize command. You can also minimize a window by right-clicking the window's button on the taskbar and choosing Minimize from the menu that appears. To switch between minimized, and either restored or maximized, click the taskbar button for the program.

 Minimize windows when you want to unclutter your desktop without exiting programs.

Minimizing All Windows

You can minimize all the open windows on your screen by right-clicking a blank area on the taskbar and choosing Bring Desktop To Front from the shortcut menu that appears. Using only the keyboard, you can press WINDOWS-M (using the WINDOWS key, which is next to the CTRL key on many keyboards). If the Show Desktop icon appears on your taskbar (it's on the Quick Launch toolbar, usually right next to the Start button), you can also click this icon to minimize all your windows. (See "What Can Appear On the Taskbar?" in Chapter 10 for a description of the Quick Launch toolbar.)

To reverse this command, right-click a blank area on the taskbar and choose Send Desktop To Back from the menu that appears. Or, press SHIFT-WINDOWS-M.

Maximizing a Window

To maximize a window—expand it to cover the whole screen—click the window's Maximize button, the middle button on the right end of the title bar, or click the window's System Menu button and choose Maximize from the menu that appears. When a window is maximized, its Maximize button is replaced by the Restore button, which returns the window to the size it was before you maximized it. Double-clicking a window's title bar switches between maximized restored.

If the window is currently minimized and you want to maximize it, right-click the button on the taskbar for the window and choose Maximize from the menu that appears.

You can maximize a window by using the keyboard, too; press ALT-SPACEBAR to display the System menu and press X to choose the Maximize command. You can also maximize a window by right-clicking the window's button on the taskbar and choosing Maximize from the menu that appears.

Restoring the Window to Its Previous Size

After you maximize a window, you can restore it—return it to its previous size. Click the window's Restore button to restore the window, or click the window's System Menu button and choose Restore from the menu that appears. The Restore button appears (as the middle button on the right end of the title bar) only when the window is maximized.

If the window is currently minimized and you want to restore it, click the taskbar button for the window.

You can restore a window by using the keyboard, too; press ALT-SPACEBAR to display the System menu and press R to choose the Restore command. You can also restore a window by right-clicking the window's button on the taskbar and choosing Restore from the menu that appears.

The choice between maximizing programs and running them in windows (restored) is a matter of taste. If your screen is small or low resolution, maximize your windows, so you can see their contents as clearly as possible. If you have a large, high-resolution screen, you can run your programs in windows so you can see several programs at the same time.

Arranging All Windows

If you want to see all the windows on your desktop at the same time, you can ask Windows to arrange them tastefully for you. Right-click a blank area of the taskbar and choose one of the following commands from the menu that appears:

- **Cascade Windows**   Opens all the windows so they overlap, with their upper-left corners cascading from the upper-left corner of the screen, down and to the right.

- **Tile Windows Horizontally**   Opens all the windows with no overlap, with each window extending the full width of the screen and one window below another.

- **Tile Windows Vertically**   Opens all the windows with no overlap, with each window extending the full height of the screen and one window next to another.

If you choose one of these commands by mistake, you can undo the command by right-clicking a blank area of the taskbar and choosing Undo Tile or Undo Cascade from the menu that appears.

 If four or more windows are open, Tile Windows Horizontally and Tile Windows Vertically arrange the windows the same way—in a grid.

Changing the Size and Shape of a Window

If a window is minimized or maximized, you can't change its size or shape. Maximized windows always take up the entire screen, and minimized windows always appear only on the taskbar. When a program is restored (running in a window), you can change both the size and the shape (height and width) of the window by using the *window borders*.

To change a window's height or width, click the border around the window and drag it to the place where you want it. If you click along a top, side, or bottom border, you move one window border. If you click the corner of the window border, you move the borders that intersect at that corner. When your mouse pointer is over a border, it changes to a double-pointed arrow, making it easy to tell when you can start dragging.

You can move and resize windows by using only the keyboard, if that's your preference. To move a window, press ALT-SPACEBAR to display the System menu and press M to choose the Move command Press the cursor keys to move the window where you want it; then press ENTER to choose that position. To resize a window, press ALT-SPACEBAR to display the System menu, and press S to choose the Size command. Next, press cursor keys to adjust the window size and press ENTER to select that size.

Closing Windows

In the upper-right corner of almost every window, you see a red button with an X—the Close button. Clicking the Close button performs the same action as choosing File | Close from the window's menu. If the program appears in only one window (the usual situation), closing the window exits the program, the equivalent of choosing the File | Exit command.

If you'd rather use the keyboard, you can close many windows by pressing CTRL-F4. To close a window and exit the program, press ALT-F4.

If the window is minimized, you can close the window without restoring it first. Right-click the window's button on the taskbar and choose Close from the menu that appears.

Giving Commands

Almost every Windows program enables you to issue commands to control what the program does. For example, the WordPad program includes commands to create a new document, save the document you are working on, print the document, and exit the program (among its many other commands). Most programs provide several ways to issue commands, including choosing commands from menus and clicking icons on the toolbar.

Choosing Commands from the Menu Bar

The *menu bar* is a row of one-word commands that appears along the top of a window, just below the title bar. To choose a command from the menu bar or to choose a command from any drop-down menu, click it. For example, to choose the File | Open command, click the word "File" on the menu bar and click the word "Open" on the File drop-down menu.

When you choose a command on the menu bar, a *drop-down menu* usually appears. Each drop-down menu is named after the command that displays it. For example, most programs include a File command as the first command on the toolbar. Choosing the File command displays the File drop-down menu, a list of commands that have something to do with files, such as opening, closing, or saving files:

File	Edit	View	Insert
New...		Ctrl+N	
Open...		Ctrl+O	
Save		Ctrl+S	
Save As...			
Print...		Ctrl+P	
Print Preview			
Page Setup...			
Recent File			
Send...			
Exit			

When a drop-down menu is displayed, you can see a different drop-down menu by clicking a different command on the menu bar. To cancel a drop-down menu (that is, to remove it from the screen), click somewhere outside the menu.

If you are used to using a Macintosh, you can choose commands from menus the same way as you do on a Mac. Click and hold down the mouse button on the menu bar command, move the mouse down the drop-down menu to the command you want, and then release the mouse button.

If your screen doesn't have room for the entire drop-down menu to appear, you see a downward-pointing triangle at the bottom of the submenu; click the arrow to see the rest of the menu. Many programs use a Windows feature that displays only the most frequently used commands or the commands you've chosen recently. At the bottom of the menu is a double-*V* character (a double downward-pointing arrow) that you can click to see the rest of the available commands.

When displaying a menu, many programs display more information about each command as you point to the commands with your mouse. The additional information usually appears in the status bar, the gray bar along the bottom edge of the window.

Symbols on Menus

Other information may appear next to commands on menus:

- Commands that have a rightward-pointing triangle to their right, display another menu.

- Commands that have an ellipsis (three dots) after them display a dialog box.

- Some commands represent an option that can be turned on or off. A command of this type has a check mark to its left when the option is on (selected) and no check mark when the option is off (not selected). For example, a View menu might have a Status Bar command that is checked or unchecked, controlling whether the status bar is displayed. To turn an option on or off, choose the command; the check mark appears or disappears.

- Some menus contain several options, only one of which may be selected. A large dot appears to the left of the selected option. To select an option, choose the command; the dot appears to its left.

- For some commands, a button on the toolbar performs the command. On the drop-down menu that contains the command, the toolbar button appears to its left, just as a reminder.

- Some commands have a keyboard shortcut. For example, many programs provide the key combination CTRL-S as a shortcut for choosing the File menu, and then the Save command. Keyboard shortcuts appear to the right of commands on drop-down menus.

Commands on a menu may appear in gray, indicating that the command is not currently available.

Choosing Menu Commands with the Keyboard

In most programs, one letter of each command in each menu is underlined. Previous versions of Windows displayed these underlines all the time, but with some programs, Windows XP displays them only if you press the ALT key. For example, most programs underline the *F* in File on the menu bar. To choose a command from the menu bar by using the keyboard, hold down the ALT key while you type the underlined letter of the command you want. Or, press and release the ALT key. The first command on the menu bar is selected and appears enclosed in a box. Press the underlined letter of the command you want. To choose a command from a drop-down menu, press the underlined letter for that command. For example, to choose the File | Open command, press ALT-F, and then O.

You can mix using the mouse and the keyboard to choose commands. For example, you can use the mouse to click a command on the menu bar, and then press a letter to choose a command from the drop-down menu that appears.

To cancel all the drop-down menus that appear on the screen, press the ALT key again. To back up one step, press the ESC or LEFT-ARROW key.

Clicking Buttons on the Toolbar

Most (but not all) Windows programs display a *toolbar*, a row of small buttons with icons on them, just below the menu bar, for example:

Clicking a toolbar button issues a command, usually a command that you also could have issued from the menu bar.

To find out what a toolbar button does, rest the mouse pointer on the button, but don't click. After a second, a small label appears near the button, naming or explaining the button (this label is sometimes called a *tool tip*). Some programs display toolbar buttons that contain text along with icons, for people who like words with their pictures.

Some programs let you move the toolbar to other locations, including into a separate floating window. Try clicking a blank part of the toolbar and dragging it to another location in the program window. And some programs that come with Windows XP enable you to lock the toolbar, to prevent anyone from changing or moving it. Right-click a blank place in the toolbar to see if a command like Lock The Toolbars appears.

Choosing Commands from Shortcut Menus

Windows and most Windows-compatible programs display special menus, called *shortcut menus* (or *context menus*), when you click with the right mouse button. The shortcut menu displays commands appropriate to the object you clicked. For example, if you right-click a blank space on the Windows taskbar, the shortcut menu that appears contains commands you can perform on the taskbar or desktop:

Commands on shortcut menus contain the same symbols (ellipses, triangles, and toolbar buttons) that appear on drop-down menus (see "Choosing Commands from the Menu Bar"). Commands that appear in gray are currently unavailable.

After you have displayed a shortcut menu, you can choose a command from the menu by clicking the command (with the left mouse button) or pressing the underlined letter in the command. If no letters are underlined in the commands on the menu, pressing a letter usually selects the first command that starts with that letter. To cancel a shortcut menu, click outside the menu or press the ESC key.

 You can't always guess where shortcut menus will appear or what will be on them. To use shortcut menus, right-click the item you want to work with and see what appears!

You can display a shortcut menu by using only the keyboard; select the item you want to right-click and press SHIFT-F10 to display the shortcut menu. Newer keyboards include an "application key" that looks like this:

The application key has the same effect as right-clicking at the mouse pointer location. Use the UP-ARROW and DOWN-ARROW keys to select the command you want, and then press ENTER to select it, or press ESC to dismiss the menu.

Choosing Settings on Dialog Boxes

A *dialog box* is a special kind of window that enables you to change settings or give commands in a program. For example, in most programs, when you give a command to open a file, you see an Open File dialog box that enables you to specify which file you want to open. You must exit the dialog box before continuing to use the program. Most dialog boxes include buttons to exit, with names like OK, Close, and Cancel.

As programs have gotten more complicated, with more and more settings, dialog boxes (like the one shown in Figure 2-3) have also gotten fancier. They may also include a menu bar, a toolbar, tabs (like the ones on manila folders), graphics, and buttons that display other dialog boxes.

When a dialog box is displayed, choose the settings you want. When you have finished, click the OK or Close button to dismiss the dialog box. You can also click the Close button in the upper-right corner of the window. If you don't want to keep the changes you have made, click the Cancel button or press the ESC key. While a program is displaying a dialog box, the program usually won't accept any other input until you've closed the dialog box.

WORKING
IN WINDOWS XP

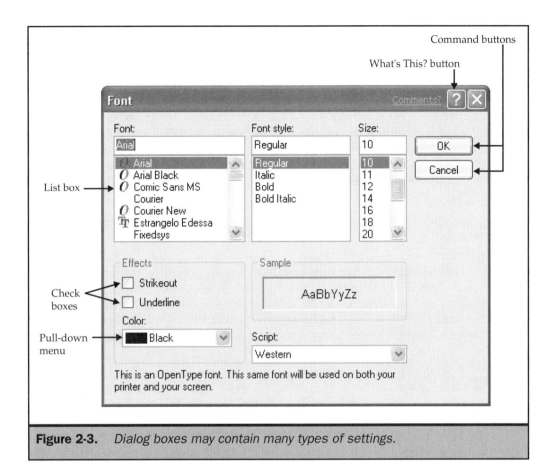

Figure 2-3.   *Dialog boxes may contain many types of settings.*

 If a window has a question mark button in its upper-right corner, click it and then click the setting about which you want help. If the window doesn't have a question-mark button, click the Help button, if there is one, or press F1. Another way to obtain help is to right-click the setting you need information about and choose the What's This? command from the shortcut menu, if it appears.

Settings in Dialog Boxes

Dialog boxes contain various types of settings, and different software companies use different types of settings. The following are the most common types of settings in dialog boxes:

■ **Text box**   A box you can type in. To change the text in a text box, click in the box and edit the text. To replace the text with new text, select the entire contents of the box and type the new text. Some text boxes accept only numbers and have tiny up- and down-arrow buttons that you can click to increase or decrease the number in the box.

■ **List box** A box that contains a list of options, one of which is selected. If the list is too long to fit in the box, a scroll bar appears along the right side of the box. To select an option from the list, click it. When a list box is selected, you can use the UP-ARROW or DOWN-ARROW keys to select an option. In many list boxes, typing a letter jumps down to the first item on the list that begins with that letter—a useful maneuver for long lists. Some list boxes include a text box just above them so you can type an entry in the text box or click an entry from the list box—your choice.

■ **Check box** A box that can either be blank or contain a check mark (or X). If the check box is blank, the setting is not selected. To select or deselect a check box, click it. When a check box is selected, you can press SPACEBAR to select or deselect it.

■ **Radio button** A group of round buttons that can either be blank or contain a dot. If the button contains a dot, it is selected. Only one of the buttons can be selected at a time. To select one button in a group of radio buttons, click it. When a button in a group of radio buttons is selected, you can press cursor-motion (arrow) keys on the keyboard to select the button you want.

■ **Pull-down menu** A box with a downward-pointing triangle button at its right end (also called a drop-down menu). The box displays the currently selected setting. To choose a setting, click in the box or on the triangle button to display a menu and click an option from the menu. When you select a pull-down menu, pressing the DOWN-ARROW key usually displays the menu of options; if it does display the menu, press DOWN-ARROW repeatedly until the option you want is highlighted and press ENTER.

■ **Menu bar** A row of commands, such as the menu bar at the top of a program window.

■ **Toolbar** A row of buttons that give commands, similar to the toolbar at the top of a program window.

■ **Command button** A box you can click to perform a command. Most dialog boxes include an OK or Close button and a Cancel button. If the label on the command button ends with an ellipsis (three dots), the button displays another dialog box. One command button on each dialog box is the default command button and has a darker border. Pressing ENTER has the same effect as clicking this button. When a command button is selected, you can press SPACEBAR to perform its command.

Except for command buttons, most settings have labels (explanatory text) to the left or right (or occasionally above) the setting.

WORKING
IN WINDOWS XP

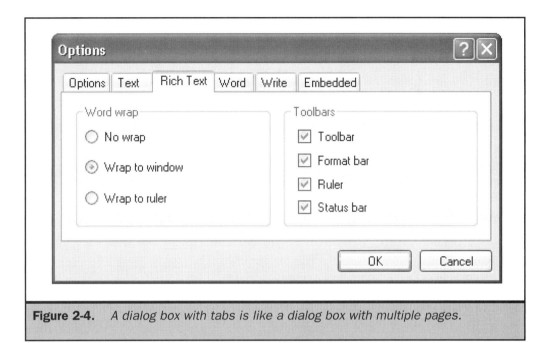

Figure 2-4. *A dialog box with tabs is like a dialog box with multiple pages.*

Some dialog boxes have too many settings to fit in the window, so they contain several pages, or *tabs*, of settings. Figure 2-4 shows a dialog box with tabs running along the top of the dialog box. When you click a tab, the rest of the dialog box changes to show the settings associated with that tab.

Moving Around a Dialog Box

One setting in the dialog box is selected, which means it's currently active. The selected setting is affected if you press a key on the keyboard. The selected setting is highlighted or outlined, depending on the type of setting.

Here are ways to select a setting in a dialog box:

■ Click the setting you want to select.

■ Press the TAB key to select another setting, usually below or to the right of the current setting. Press SHIFT-TAB to select the previous setting.

■ If the setting you want to select has an underlined letter in its label, hold down the ALT key while you type that letter. For example, to select a setting labeled Save In, press ALT-I.

■ If the dialog box has tabs along the top, you can see the settings associated with another tab by clicking that tab or pressing CTRL-TAB or CTRL-SHIFT-TAB. To select a tab along the top of the dialog box, click the tab or press the ALT key and type the underlined letter in the label on the tab. Once you select a tab, you can use the LEFT-ARROW and RIGHT-ARROW keys to display the settings for each tab. The UP-ARROW and DOWN-ARROW keys move from setting to setting, too—though their action varies from dialog box to dialog box.

Open, Save As, and Browse Dialog Boxes

The Open, Save As, and Browse dialog boxes in most programs have some special settings. All three dialog boxes provide you with a way of specifying a disk drive, a folder, and a file to work with. The standard versions of these dialog boxes have a column of icons down the left side and a special toolbar, as shown in Figure 2-5.

Most Open, Save As, and Browse dialog boxes have the following items:

- **Places bar**   Vertical bar down the left side of the dialog box with icons that usually include My Recent Documents (for files you've used recently, regardless of their location), Desktop (for the top-level view of the items in your computer), My Documents (for your My Documents folder), My Computer (for a list of the available disk drives and partitions), and (if your computer is on a network) My Network Places (for a list of network drives). Click one of these buttons to change the view in the folder tree to the right.

- **Look In or Save In pull-down menu**   The Open and Browse dialog boxes contain a Look In pull-down menu that enables you to specify the folder that contains the file you want to open. The Save As dialog box contains a similar Save In pull-down menu that enables you to specify the folder into which you want to save a file.

- **Folder tree**   This large list box displays the current contents of the folder you have selected (see Chapter 7, section "What Is the Folder Tree?") Press F5 to update the display if you think that the folder contents have changed.

- **Go To Last Folder Visited button**   Clicking this button goes back to the last folder you viewed.

- **Up One Level button**   Clicking this button changes which folder is named in the Look In or Save In box by moving up one level in the folder tree (to the folder's parent folder). The folder tree listing is updated, too. You can also press BACKSPACE to move up the folder tree one level.

- **Create New Folder button**   Clicking this button creates a new folder within the current folder (see Chapter 7, section "Creating Files and Folders").

- **View Menu button**   Clicking this button displays a list of the views you can choose: Large Icons, Small Icons, List, Details, and Thumbnails.

- **Files Of Type box**   Clicking in this box displays the types of files currently displayed in the folder tree. For example, in Microsoft Word, the Files Of Type box is usually set to display only Word documents, but you can choose to see all filenames.

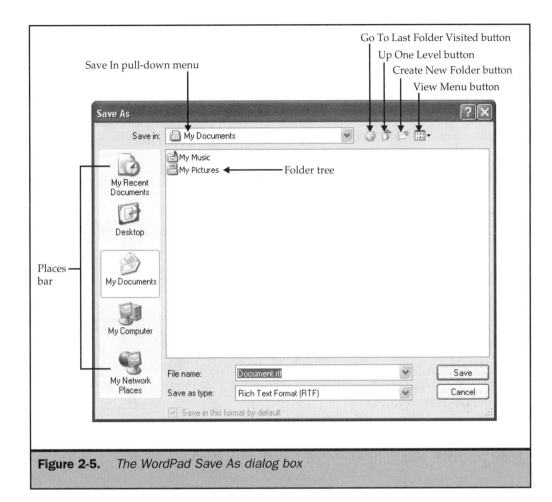

Figure 2-5. *The WordPad Save As dialog box*

Switching, Exiting, and Canceling Programs

Windows enables you to run many programs at the same time, each in its own window. You can exit from one program while leaving other programs running, and you can choose which program window is the active window—the window you are currently using.

Switching Programs

To *switch programs*—choose another window as the active window—you can

- Click in the window for the program.
- Click the button for the window on the taskbar. If the window was minimized, clicking its button returns the window to its size before it was minimized.

■ Press ALT-TAB until the window you want is active, or press ALT-SHIFT-TAB to cycle through the open windows in the reverse order.

■ Press ALT-TAB and don't release the ALT key. A window appears with an icon for each program that is running, with the program in the active windows highlighted, as shown here:

The name of the highlighted window appears at the bottom of the window. To switch to a different program, keep holding down the ALT key, press TAB to move the highlight to the icon for the window you want, and then release the ALT key.

 Perhaps the least convenient way to switch to a program is by using the Switch To button on the Windows Task Manager. Press CTRL-ALT-DEL *to display the Windows Task Manager, select the program you want, and click Switch To.*

Exiting Programs

Most programs provide several ways to exit, including some or all of these:

■ Choose the File | Exit command from the menu bar.

■ Click the Close button in the upper-right corner of the program window. If a program displays multiple windows, close them all.

■ Press ALT-F4.

■ Click the System Menu button in the upper-left corner of the program window and choose Close from the menu that appears.

■ Right-click the program button on the taskbar and choose Close from the menu that appears.

If you have trouble exiting a program, you can use the Windows Task Manager, described in the next section.

Canceling Programs

When you are running several programs at the same time, you can exit a program as described in the previous section. For example, click the Close button for all the windows the program displays or choose File | Exit or File | Close.

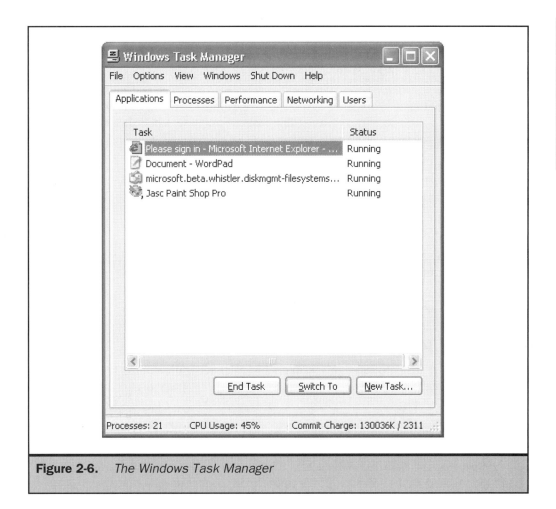

Figure 2-6. *The Windows Task Manager*

Another way to exit a program when multiple programs are running is to press CTRL-ALT-DEL to display the Windows Task Manager (shown in Figure 2-6, and described in more detail in Chapter 35). The Applications tab lists all the programs currently running.

To cancel a program, click the program name in the Windows Task Manager; then click the End Task button. If you were using the program to edit a file, you may lose some work.

Note   *The End Task button is designed for canceling programs that have "hung"—stopped responding to the keyboard or mouse. To avoid losing unsaved work, always try exiting a program by clicking its Close button, pressing ALT-F4, or choosing File | Exit before resorting to the Windows Task Manager.*

Running Programs on a Schedule Using Scheduled Tasks

Scheduled Tasks is the program Windows uses to check the files and folders on your hard disk automatically. You can also use the Scheduled Tasks program to run almost any program at a specified time on a regular basis. When you schedule a task, you must specify the following information:

- What program you want to run.
- How often you want to run it (daily, weekly, monthly, when your computer starts, or when you log on).
- What time you want the program to start running. For weekly and monthly schedules, you also specify what day to start the program.
- What user account you want to use when running the program. You enter the user's name and password (usually your own username and password).

When Scheduled Tasks is running, its icon appears in the system tray at the right end of the taskbar.

Scheduling a Program

To tell Scheduled Tasks to run a program on a regular schedule, follow these steps:

1. Look at the Scheduled Tasks window by choosing Start | All Programs | Accessories | System Tools | Scheduled Tasks; or choose Start | Control Panel, click Performance And Maintenance, and click Scheduled Tasks. You see the Scheduled Tasks window, shown in Figure 2-7.

2. Run the Add Scheduled Task item that appears in the Name column of the Scheduled Tasks window. (If it's underlined, click it once. Otherwise, double-click it.)

3. Windows runs the Scheduled Task Wizard, which takes you through the steps required to schedule tasks to run automatically. Follow the prompts on the screen, clicking Next to move to the next step.

4. When the Scheduled Task Wizard displays all the information you have specified about the program's schedule, including the name of the program and when you want it to run, click the Finish button. The program appears on a new line in the Scheduled Tasks window.

Be sure to leave your computer turned on all the time, so when the scheduled time arrives, Windows runs your program. If your computer is off (or Scheduled Tasks isn't running) when the time comes, the program doesn't run.

 When you schedule a task, Windows creates a file with the extension .job in the C:\Windows\Tasks folder (assuming that Windows XP is installed on your C: drive).

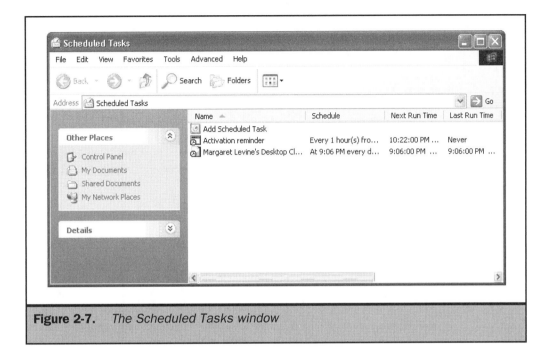

Figure 2-7.   *The Scheduled Tasks window*

Canceling a Scheduled Program

If you decide you no longer want Windows to run the program automatically, open the Scheduled Tasks window, right-click the line for the program, and choose Delete from the menu that appears. When Windows asks you to confirm that you want to delete the file for this job, click Yes.

To cancel running all scheduled programs, choose Advanced | Stop Using Task Scheduler from the menu bar in the Scheduled Tasks window. No scheduled programs will be run until you choose the command Advanced | Start Using Task Scheduler. You can pause the scheduler program by choosing Advanced | Pause Task Scheduler to skip running scheduled programs temporarily and choose Advanced | Continue Task Scheduler to resume. Pausing Scheduled Tasks is a good idea while you are installing new software, for example, so installation isn't interrupted.

Configuring a Scheduled Program

You can configure other settings for a scheduled task. Click or double-click the line for the task in the Scheduled Tasks window (or select the line and click the Properties button on the toolbar, or right-click the program name and choose Properties from the menu that appears). You see a dialog box with all the settings for the scheduled program (see Figure 2-8). Table 2-1 lists all the settings you can specify when you schedule a program to run.

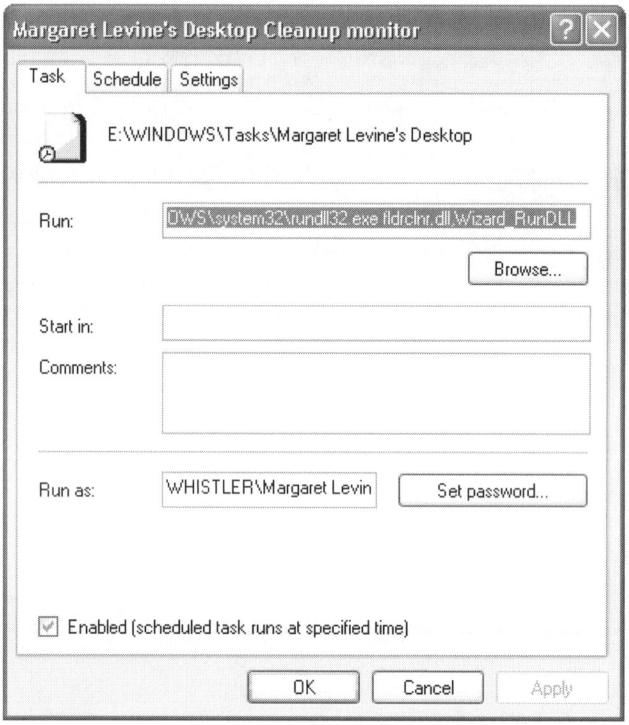

Figure 2-8. *Settings for a scheduled program*

Other Scheduling Options

You can ask Scheduled Tasks to let you know how its scheduled programs are doing. If you want to be notified when Scheduled Tasks is unable to run a scheduled program, choose Advanced from the Scheduled Tasks window's menu bar and make sure a check mark appears to the left of the Notify Me Of Missed Tasks option (if no check mark appears, choose the option from the menu).

You can look at a log file of the results of scheduled programs by choosing Advanced | View Log from the Scheduled Tasks menu bar. Windows displays the log file, which is stored in text format in C:\Windows\SchedLgU.txt, using Notepad. Log entries consist of several lines of text, as shown here:

```
"Activation reminder.job" (oobebaln.exe)
        Finished 7/3/2002 1:39:35 PM
        Result: The task completed with an exit code of (0).
```

The first line describes the program, and the subsequent lines report on the outcome of running the program.

Tab in Dialog Box	Setting	Description
Task	Run	Specifies the pathname (and optional parameters) to run the program. If the pathname includes spaces, enclose the entire pathname in double quotes. Click Browse to find a program.
Task	Start in	Specifies the default folder for the program files (some programs require files other than the program file, and this setting tells the program where to look for them).
Task	Comments	Provides space for you to type comments (ignored by Windows).
Task	Run as	Specifies the user account to use when running the program. Click Set Password to type the password for that user account.
Task	Enabled	Specifies that the task is scheduled. To suspend scheduling the task, clear this check box.
Schedule	Schedule Task	Specifies the frequency the task runs: daily, weekly, monthly, once, at system startup, at logon, or when idle. The rest of the settings on the Schedule tab of the dialog box depend on which frequency you choose.
Schedule	Start time	For daily, weekly, monthly, or one-time tasks, specifies the time Windows starts the program.
Schedule	Advanced	Displays the Advanced Schedule Options dialog box, in which you can specify an end date or number of repetitions.
Schedule	Show multiple schedules	When this check box is selected, a box appears at the top of the Schedule tab from which you can pick from a list of the schedules you have defined.
Settings	Delete the task if it is not scheduled to run again	Specifies that Windows delete the item from the Scheduled Tasks list after running it (useful for programs you have scheduled to run only once).

Table 2-1.   *Settings for a Scheduled Task*

Tab in Dialog Box	Setting	Description
Settings	Stop the task if it runs for *xx* hours *xx* minutes	Specifies the maximum number of hours and minutes the scheduled program can run. If the program is still running after the specified amount of time, Windows stops the program.
Settings	Only start the task if computer has been idle for at least *xx* minutes	Specifies that Windows should start the task only after the specified amount of time with no keyboard or mouse use.
Settings	If the computer has not been idle that long, retry for up to *xx* minutes	If the computer has not been idle for the amount of time specified in the preceding setting when Windows tries to start the program, specifies the number of minutes during which Windows should try to run the program.
Settings	Stop the task if computer ceases to be idle	Specifies that Windows stop the program if you begin to use the computer.
Settings	Don't start the task if computer is running on batteries	Specifies that Windows not start the task if the computer is running on batteries. Some programs, especially disk-housekeeping programs, perform lots of disk access, which can run down your computer's batteries.
Settings	Stop the task if battery mode begins	Specifies that Windows stop the program if your computer switches from external power to batteries.
Settings	Wake the computer to run this task	Wakes the computer when the task is schedule to run, even if it is suspended or in sleep mode.

Table 2-1.   *Settings for a Scheduled Task* (continued)

Running Programs in Compatibility Mode

Some older programs, especially games, don't run correctly under Windows XP or 2000. Windows XP has a new feature called *compatibility mode* that emulates previous versions of Windows—Windows 2000, NT 4.0, Me, 98, and 95. Compatibility mode can also set the display to the lower resolutions that were standard several years ago. If you have a program that used to run well but balks at Windows XP, compatibility mode may fix the problem.

Caution   *Don't use compatibility mode to run programs that are specifically designed for older versions of Windows. For example, a virus checker that is designed for use with Windows 95 should not be run with Windows XP.*

You can set all your compatibility modem options by creating or editing a shortcut for the program, or by working with the .exe (executable) file that you run to start the program (see Chapter 8, section "What Is a Shortcut?"). Right-click the shortcut or .exe file for the program that has compatibility problems, and choose Properties from the menu that appears. Click the Compatibility tab on the Properties dialog box (as shown in Figure 2-9). Click the Run This Program Using Compatibility Mode check box and

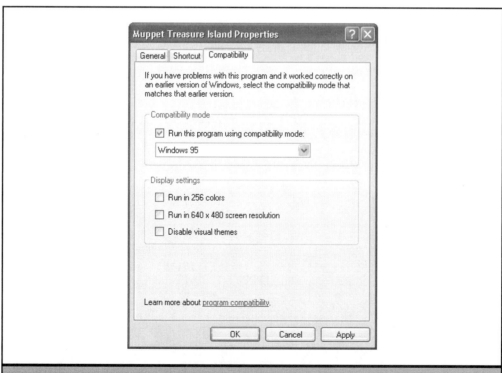

Figure 2-9.   *Setting compatibility options for the shortcut to a program*

Getting Acquainted with Windows by Playing Games

Games have been an important part of the personal computer experience from the beginning. Even people who are intimidated by serious tools, such as word processors and spreadsheets, can be enticed into learning games—and the basic computer skills the games require. Windows XP provides a variety of games:

- **Solitaire**   FreeCell, Classic Solitaire, Spider Solitaire, and Minesweeper.
- **Classic Hearts**   Simulated four-player card game in which the computer plays the other three hands. If your computer is on a local area network (LAN), you can play against others.
- **Pinball**   For one to four players.
- **MSN Gaming Zone**   Internet Backgammon, Internet Checkers, Internet Hearts, Internet Reversi, and Internet Spades. In these games, you play against other people over the Internet. You can also run these games from the Web site at **http://zone.msn.com**.

You can play these games by choosing Start | All Programs | Games. Once a game is running, you can look up rules and strategies on the Help menu.

select a previous version of Windows from the drop-down menu. You can also run the program in 256 colors (also known as *8-bit color*, a much smaller set of colors that are standard for Windows XP), 640 × 480 screen resolution (lower than the usual 800 × 600 minimum for modern PCs), or without visual themes (with desktop themes disabled).

Tip   *You can find out whether a program works with Windows XP by choosing Start | Help And Support and clicking Find Compatible Hardware And Software For Windows XP in the Help And Support Center window. When you see the Product Search window, type the name of the program and click Search. Windows contacts Microsoft's database of compatible products over the Internet and displays a list of products that match the words you typed.*

Note   *If the Games folder doesn't appear on the Start | All Programs menu, or if the Games folder does not contain all the games we mention, you can install them from the Windows XP CD-ROM (see Chapter 3, section "Installing and Uninstalling Programs that Come with Windows").*

The
Complete
Reference

Windows XP

Chapter 3

Installing Programs

W indows XP comes with a number of useful programs, and many new computers come with lots more software preinstalled, but you'll want to install some programs yourself sooner or later. For example, you might want to install some of the programs included on the Windows XP CD-ROM that may not have been installed on your system.

Or, you may want to do just the reverse—uninstall programs that you no longer use or that are outdated. You can free up some disk space by uninstalling Windows components that you never use. Windows comes with a built-in system for installing and uninstalling programs.

When you install a program, Windows keeps track of what types of files the program can create and edit. You can change which program Windows uses to open each file type.

Windows XP omits a few programs that came with Windows 98 and Me, including FrontPage Express (a Web page editor) and Microsoft Chat. If you upgraded your system from an older version of Windows, though, these programs may still be installed.

What Happens During Program Installation and Uninstallation?

Before you can install a program, you have to get it—you have to buy or download the program. You may receive a program on a CD-ROM, as a stack of floppy disks or as a file downloaded from the Internet. Once you have a program, you install it, usually by running an installation program to copy the program to your hard disk and configure it to run on your system.

If you download a program, it usually arrives in the form of an *installation file* (also called a *distribution file*), which is a compressed file containing all the files required for a program to run, along with an installation program. For example, the installation file may contain the installation program, the program itself, the help file for the program, and a few other files that the program needs. You can download (copy) installation files from the Internet or other sources. If your computer is connected to a local area network (LAN), the installation file may be stored on a network disk (see Chapter 29). The files that make up the program are usually compressed to take up less space and so that they can be packaged together as one file.

Note   *When installing programs, you must be logged on with a user account that is a member of the Administrator or Power user group (see Chapter 6). Limited and Guest user accounts can't install programs. If you haven't set up user accounts, you are probably logged on automatically as Administrator (in Windows XP Professional) or Owner (in Windows XP Home Edition), which are both members of the Administrator group.*

What Happens During Program Installation?

Most programs come with an installation program named Setup.exe or Install.exe. When you install a program, the installation program usually does the following:

- Looks for a previous version of the program on your hard disk. If it finds a previous version, the program may ask whether you want to replace the previous version.

- Creates a folder in which to store the program files. Most installation programs ask where you'd like this folder. Some installation programs also create additional folders within this folder. Windows creates a folder named Program Files, usually in C:\ (if Windows is stored in a partition or drive other than C, the Program Files folder is usually in the same partition). We recommend you install all your programs in folders within the Program Files folder.

> **Note** *Some software vendors have the bad habit of installing application programs in locations other than your Program Files folder. You can't do much about this; the additional folders may clutter up your root folder, but they don't do any harm.*

- Copies the files onto your hard disk. If the program files are compressed, the installation program uncompresses them. Usually, the installation program copies most of the files into the program's folder, but it may also put some files into your C:\Windows, C:\Windows\System, or other folders (assuming that Windows is installed in C:\Windows).

- Checks your system for the files and hardware it needs to run. For example, an Internet connection program might check for a modem.

- Adds entries to the Windows Registry to tell Windows which types of files the program works with, which files the program is stored in, and other information about the program (see Chapter 38).

- Adds a command for the program to your Start | All Programs menu (some programs add submenus to the Start | All Programs menu to contain several commands). The installation program may also add a shortcut to your Windows desktop to make running the program easy for you. You can change the position on the Start menu of the command for the program, get rid of the command, or create a command if the installation program doesn't make one. You can also create a shortcut icon on the desktop, if the installation program hasn't done so, or move or delete the program's shortcut (see Chapter 8, section "Making Shortcuts").

- Asks you a series of questions to configure the program for your system. The program may ask you to type additional information, like Internet addresses, passwords, or software license numbers. It may also ask which users should be able to run the program.

Every installation program is different, because it comes with the application program, not with Windows. If your computer is connected to a LAN or to the Internet, the installation program may configure your program to connect to other computers on the network.

What Happens During Program Uninstallation?

The perfect uninstallation program exactly undoes all the actions of the installation program, removing all the files and folders the installation program created, and putting back everything else to where it was originally. Unfortunately, we've never seen a perfect uninstallation program, but most uninstallation programs do an acceptable job of removing most traces of a program from your system.

Installing Programs

Windows includes a program called Add Or Remove Programs that helps you find and start the installation program for a new program. However, you can skip this step and run the installation program yourself, if you know how. Some older programs don't come with installation programs, and you have to perform the actions of an installation program yourself.

For most programs, putting the CD-ROM into the CD drive is all you have to do to start installing the program. An installation program usually runs automatically and steps you through the process.

Installing Programs Using the Add Or Remove Programs Window

Follow these steps to use the Add Or Remove Programs window to help you install a program:

1. Choose Start | Control Panel. You see the Control Panel window.

2. Click the Add Or Remove Programs category. Or, in Classic view of the Control Panel, run the Add Or Remove Programs program—if the icon is underlined, click it once; if not, double-click it. You can control whether you need to single-click or double-click icons to run programs.

3. You see the Add Or Remove Programs window. This window has three buttons down the left side. Click the Add New Programs button so the window looks like Figure 3-1.

4. If you are installing a program from a floppy disk or CD-ROM, insert the disk or CD-ROM into its drive and click the CD Or Floppy button. If you are installing a program from a file on your hard disk or on a network drive,

click the CD Or Floppy button anyway—you'll have a chance to tell it where to look for the program in a minute. Windows looks on any floppy disk or CD-ROM in your drives for an installation program (that is, a program named Setup.exe or Install.exe). If Windows finds an installation program, skip to step 7.

5. If Windows doesn't find an installation program, you see the Run Installation Program dialog box, which asks for the full pathname of the installation program.

6. Click the Browse button and specify the installation program you want to run in the Browse window. You can browse to any disk on your computer, or any disk accessible over your LAN, if you are connected to one. Click Open when you find the installation program.

7. When the pathname of the installation program appears in the Run Installation Program box, click the Finish button. The installation program runs. Follow the instructions on the screen to install the program.

Once you install a program, the program name usually (but not always) appears in the list that the Add Or Remove Programs window displays when you click the Change Or Remove Programs button.

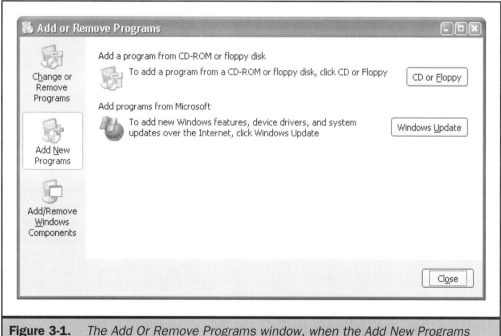

Figure 3-1.   *The Add Or Remove Programs window, when the Add New Programs
button is selected*

Running an Install or Setup Program

If you know the pathname of the installation file for the program you want to install, you can run the installation program directly (see Chapter 2, section "Starting Programs")—double-click its filename in Windows Explorer or use the Start | Run command. Follow the instructions on the screen to install the program.

Installing Programs Without Installation Programs

Older programs, such as those designed to run with Windows 3.1 or DOS, don't have installation programs. Instead, the programs are delivered as a set of files. Some older programs arrive as a *ZIP* file, a file that contains compressed versions of one or more files (see Chapter 8, section "Working with Compressed Folders"). ZIP files have the extension .zip (if you can't see filename extensions in Windows, see Chapter 7, section "What Are Extensions and File Types?" to display them).

To install a program from a ZIP file, you can use the Windows compressed folders feature, which treats ZIP files like folders (see Chapter 8, section "Working with Compressed Folders"). Alternatively, you can install an unzipping program such as ZipMagic (**http://www.ontrack.com**) or WinZip (**http://www.winzip.com**), which come with their own commands for unzipping (uncompressing) and installing programs from ZIP files.

To install a program that you receive as a set of files or as a ZIP file, using the Windows compressed files feature, follow these steps:

1. If you received the program as a ZIP file, open the ZIP file. In an Explorer window, it appears as a folder with a little zipper on it. Otherwise, look at the set of files in an Explorer window.

2. Look at the list of files to find files with the .exe or .com extension; these are executable programs. If one file is named Setup.exe or Install.exe, run it. Then follow the instructions on the screen. The installation program may ask you a series of questions to configure the program for your system. If one file is named Readme.txt (or some other name that suggests it contains instructions), read the contents of the file. If its extension is .txt, click or double-click the filename to see the file in Notepad.

3. Otherwise, look for an executable file with a name like the name of the program; this may be the program itself. For example, if you are installing a program called Spam Be Gone version 2.3, you might find a filename such as Spambg23.exe. To run the program, click or double-click the program name. The first time you run the program, it may ask you for information with which to configure the program for your system.

Finishing Installation of a Program

After you install a program, you may still need to configure it to work with your system. Many programs come with configuration programs that run automatically, either when you install the program or when you run the program for the first time.

To make the program easier to run, you can add it to your Start menu (see Chapter 10, section "Reorganizing the Start Menu"). If the program has an installation program, the installation program may do this for you. The installation program may even put an icon on the Quick Launch toolbar (the small icons on the taskbar you can click to run a program). If not, you can add an icon yourself (see Chapter 10).

You can also add a shortcut for the program to your Windows desktop (see Chapter 8, section "Making Shortcuts"). The installation program may have created a shortcut already. You can create shortcuts right on the desktop or in a folder.

Installing and Uninstalling Programs that Come with Windows

Windows XP comes with fewer optionally installed components than did previous versions of Windows. You get just as many features, utilities, and free applications, but you no longer have a choice about installing them. For example, you no longer have the option of saving disk space by uninstalling Outlook Express, NetMeeting, Windows Messenger, or other programs that you don't want to use.

If you want to install some of the programs that come on the Windows XP CD-ROM, follow these steps:

1. Choose Start | Control Panel. You see the Control Panel window.

2. Run Add Or Remove Programs. You see the Add Or Remove Programs window.

3. Click the Add/Remove Windows Components button. You see the Windows Components Wizard with a list of the types of programs that come with Windows, as shown in Figure 3-2. The check box to the left of each type of program is blank (meaning none of the programs of that type are selected), gray with a check mark (meaning some, but not all, of the programs of that type are selected), or white with a check mark (meaning all the programs of that type are selected). The selections show which Windows programs have already been installed.

4. To select additional programs, click the type of program to install (scroll down the Components list to see the rest of the program types). A description of the programs appears just below the list. A few items have only one program of that type, such as Fax Services. Most of the items on the Components list include a number of programs.

5. To select all the programs of that type, click the check box to the left of the item. To select some of the programs, click the Details button to see the list of programs of that type. Click each of the programs you want to select and click the OK button to return to the Windows Components Wizard window. For Accessories And Utilities, choose either Accessories or Details, and click Details again to choose individual programs.

6. You can uninstall previously installed programs at the same time you install new programs. To uninstall a program, deselect it; that is, clear the check in its

check box by clicking the box. Don't clear a program's check box unless you want to uninstall it.

7. After you select all the programs you want installed and deselect all the programs you don't want installed, click the Next button. Windows determines which programs you are installing and which you are uninstalling, and copies or deletes program files appropriately. The wizard may ask you to insert the Windows XP CD-ROM.

8. Depending on which programs you install, you may need to restart Windows when the installation is complete, and you may be directed to run Wizards or other configuration programs to set up the new programs.

Note   *A few programs on the Windows XP CD-ROM don't appear in the Windows Components Wizard. Look in the /Valueadd folder on the CD-ROM for Microsoft programs (in /Valueadd/Msft) and programs from other companies (in /Valueadd/3rdparty). For example, if you installed Windows XP Home Edition, the Microsoft Backup program doesn't appear as a Windows component: you have to install it yourself (see Chapter 9).*

Figure 3-2.   *You can install additional programs from the Windows XP CD-ROM.*

Associating a Program with a File Extension

Many programs create, edit, or display files of a specific type. For example, the Notepad program (a text editor that comes with Windows) works with text files that usually have the filename extension .txt (the extension is the part of the filename that follows the last dot in the filename). When you open a file with the extension .txt, Windows knows to run Notepad.

The Windows Registry stores *file associations*, information about which program you use to edit each type of file. Installation programs usually store this information in the Registry, but you can, too. Chapter 38 describes how to view and edit the Registry with the Registry Editor program, but you can use other tools to change your file associations.

Windows offers three ways to create or change a file association: the Open With dialog box, the Folder Options dialog box, and the Edit File Types dialog box. The third method is rarely used.

Associating Files with Programs when Opening a File

In an Explorer window, you can tell Windows which program to use when opening files with a particular extension. Follow these steps:

1. In an Explorer window, find a file with the extension that you want to associate with a program.

2. Right-click the filename and choose Open With from the menu that appears. (If Open With doesn't appear on the menu, you have to use another method of associating the file type with the program; see the next section.) You see the Open With dialog box shown in Figure 3-3. (If a small submenu of programs appears, select Choose Program to display the Open With dialog box.)

3. Select the program to run, or click Browse to find the program file.

4. Click the Always Use The Selected Program To Open This Kind Of File check box and click OK.

Windows Explorer permanently saves the association of the filename extension with the program, and it opens the file you selected with the program you specified.

Associating Files with Programs by Using Folder Options

Another way to associate a file type (file extension) with a program (or change the program associated with a file type) is to use the File Types tab on the Folder Options dialog box.

Editing an Existing Association

To edit a file association, follow these steps:

1. Choose Start | Control Panel, click Appearance And Themes, and run Folder Options. You see the Folder Options dialog box. (You can also display this dialog box by choosing Tools | Folder Options from any Explorer window.)

2. Click the File Types tab, shown in Figure 3-4.

3. In the Registered File Types list, click the type of file you want to associate with a program. (Scroll down the list—it's long.) When you select a file type, more information about that file type appears in the Details For File Type box. You also see two buttons: Change (to associate one program with the file type) and Advanced (to associate multiple programs with the file type).

4. To see or change which program Windows runs to open this type of file, click Change. You see the Open With dialog box (see Figure 3-3). Select the program to run or click the Click Here link (in "If the program is not in the list, click here") to find the program file. Then click OK.

5. Close the Open With and Folder Options dialog boxes.

Windows now knows to run the program you specified when you open a file of this type.

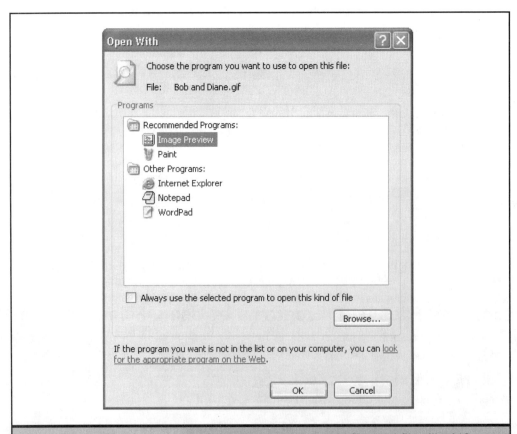

Figure 3-3.   *Which program do you want run to open this file (and files like it)?*

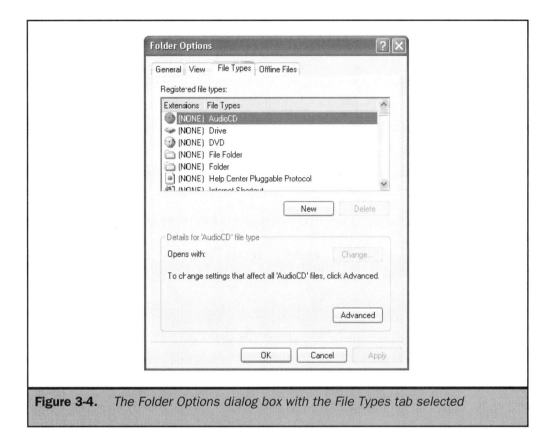

Figure 3-4.   *The Folder Options dialog box with the File Types tab selected*

Creating a New Association

You can create a new file type, with a new extension.

1. Choose Start | Control Panel, click Appearance And Themes, run Folder
   Options, and click the File Types tab (see Figure 3-4).

2. If the file extension doesn't appear in the list of Registered Files Types, click
   New to display the Create New Extension dialog box, shown here:

3. Type the extension in the File Extension box.

4. If you know the Windows file type (that is, the name of the Windows class or
   object that this file extension contains), click Advanced to expand the Create

New Extension dialog box to include the Associated File Type list. Choose the file type from the (very long) list.

5. Click OK. Windows adds the new type at the top of the list (not in alphabetical order, unless you close and reopen the dialog box).

6. Select the program to associate with this new extension by following the steps in the previous section.

Editing a File Association

Rather than telling Windows that one program can handle a file type, you can specify different programs for different actions. You rarely need to do this: installation programs use this facility when registering a new program to handle file types; human beings almost never need to change the details of file type association.

Displaying the Edit File Types Dialog Box

Follow these steps to specify the settings for a file type:

1. Choose Start | Control Panel, click Appearance And Themes, run Folder Options, and click the File Types tab (see Figure 3-4).

2. Choose a file type from the Registered File Types list.

3. Click the Advanced button. You see the Edit File Type dialog box, shown in Figure 3-5. It displays the information that the Registry knows about this file type, including the icon to use for files of this type and a description of the file type. The Actions box lists the tasks that Windows knows how to perform for files of this type: open, print, edit, and other actions. For each action, you can tell Windows which program to use; for example, you can use Internet Explorer to display .gif files, but use Paint Shop Pro to edit and print them.

4. To change which icon appears for this type of file, click the Change Icon button. Windows displays the available icons. Click one and click OK.

5. To see the details of what Windows does when you choose a command like Open or Print from a shortcut menu for a type of file, choose the action from the Actions list and click the Edit button. You see the Editing Action For Type dialog box (Figure 3-6). For information about the entries in this dialog box, see the next section. Click OK when you have finished.

6. Click any of the three settings that appear on the Edit File Type dialog box, if you want to change their settings:

   ■ **Confirm Open After Download**   Specifies to open files of this type after downloading.

   ■ **Always Show Extension**   Specifies the extension always appears after filenames of this type.

■ **Browse In Same Window**   Specifies if the program that opens this program is already running, you want to open the file in the existing program window, rather than opening another window.

7. Click OK to store your changes to the way that Windows handles files of this type.

Actions and DDE Messages Associated with File Types

In addition to telling Windows which program to run for each file type, you can define as many *actions* for a file type as you want. For example, you can define one action that opens files of that type and another action that prints files. There are two types of actions:

■ **Regular actions**   These actions are listed on the shortcut menu that appears when you right-click filenames in Explorer windows. For example, when you right-click a filename with extension .txt, the Open and Print commands appear on the shortcut menu; the Open and Print actions associated with the .txt file type determine what these commands do.

■ **DDE actions**   These actions define how data can be moved from one program to another using DDE (Dynamic Data Exchange, a method for programs to exchange information—see Chapter 5, section "What Is DDE?"). DDE actions do not appear on the shortcut menu when you right-click filenames.

Figure 3-5.   *Specifying which programs open and print one file type*

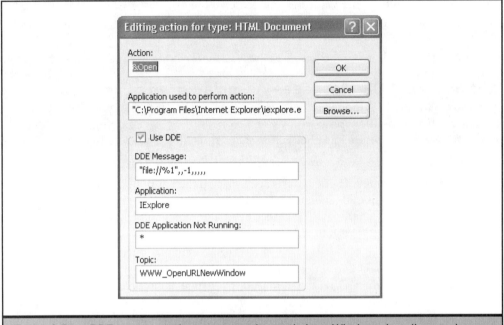

Figure 3-6.   *DDE messages let you control exactly how Windows handles each file type.*

Tip   *Specifying regular actions is useful if you use two programs with files of one file type—for example, you might use your browser to view HTML files, but your Web page editor to create and edit those files. Associate one program with the file type. Add the second program to the actions for that file type. Single- or double-clicking a file of that type runs the first program. To run the second program, right-click the file and choose the program from the shortcut menu.*

In the Edit File Type dialog box, you choose an action and click Edit to see the Editing Action For Type dialog box (Figure 3-6). The Application Used To Perform Action box contains the command line Windows executes when you open files of this type. The command line usually consists of the full pathname of a program, possibly followed by a space and %1. The %1 represents the name of the file you want to open; that is, this command runs the program and tells the program to open the file you double-clicked.

If the Use DDE check box is not selected, it is a *regular* action (that is, a command that appears on the shortcut menu, which appears when you right-click a file of this type). In this case, the dialog box has only two settings:

- **Action**   Specifies the name of the action, which appears in the Edit File Type dialog box and on the shortcut menu you see when you right-click filenames of this type. You don't have to capitalize the first letter of the action: Windows capitalizes the first letter of the action name when it appears on the shortcut menu. You can choose a letter to be underlined on the shortcut menu: precede the letter with an ampersand (&). You can choose a command from the shortcut menu by typing the underlined letter.

- **Application Used To Perform Action**   Specifies the program to run to perform this action on this type of file.

If the Use DDE check box is selected, the action is a DDE action, and you see four additional settings:

- **DDE Message**   Specifies the DDE command for this action.
- **Application**   Specifies the DDE application string to start a DDE link with the program. If this box is blank, Windows runs the program specified in the Application Used To Perform Action box.
- **DDE Application Not Running**   Specifies the DDE command to use if the program (specified in the Application box) is not already running. If this box is blank, Windows sends the same command specified in the DDE Message box.
- **Topic**   Specifies the DDE topic string to start a conversation with the program. The default DDE topic string (used if this box is blank) is "System."

Uninstalling Programs

If you have a program on your computer that you don't use, you can uninstall it to free up space on your hard disk (unless it's one of the many un-uninstallable components of Windows). You can also uninstall older versions of programs before installing new versions. The best way to uninstall a program is by using the Add Or Remove Programs window. If it doesn't appear on the Windows list of installed programs, run the program's uninstall program; if the program doesn't have one, you'll have to delete files manually.

Uninstalling Programs Using the Add Or Remove Programs Window

When you want to uninstall a program, first try using the Add Or Remove Programs window. Follow these steps:

1. Choose Start | Control Panel and click Add Or Remove Programs. You see the Add Or Remove Programs window. If the Change Or Remove Programs button isn't selected, click it, as shown in Figure 3-7. The Add Or Remove Programs window lists many of your installed programs (not including Windows components).

2. In the list of installed programs, click the program you want to uninstall. Windows tells you how much disk space the program occupies, how often you run the program, and when you last ran it.

3. Click the Remove button. Windows uninstalls the program, while messages appear to let you know what's happening.

If the program doesn't appear in the Add Or Remove Programs window, you have to uninstall the program another way (see "Running an Uninstall Program").

Note *Sometimes Windows can't uninstall a program, usually because it can't find the files it needs to perform the uninstallation.*

Running an Uninstall Program

Many programs come with uninstall programs, usually named Uninstall.exe. Look for an uninstall program in the same folder where the program is stored. Run the uninstall program, and then follow the directions on the screen. The uninstall program may also be on the Start | All Programs menu on the same submenu as the program.

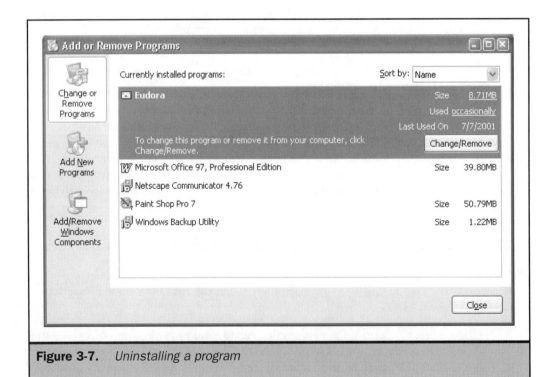

Figure 3-7. *Uninstalling a program*

Uninstalling Programs Manually

What if a program doesn't appear in the Add Or Remove Programs window and doesn't come with an uninstall program? You can delete by hand the program files and the shortcuts to the program. You might not delete every last file connected with the program, but the remaining files usually won't do any harm. Before deleting anything, check the program's documentation for instructions. Be sure to back up your hard disk or create a System Restore checkpoint before uninstalling a program by hand, in case you delete a file your system needs (see Chapter 35, section "Returning Your System to a Predefined State with System Restore").

Tip *Rather than deleting a program, you might first want to rename the folder containing the program files, adding something like "deleted" to the end of the folder name. Wait a few days. If other programs are using those files, you'll see error messages when those programs run. If no programs report errors within a week, then you know it's safe to delete the folder containing the program files.*

To delete the program files, determine which folder contains them. The easiest way to find out where the program is stored is to look at the properties of a shortcut to the program (see Chapter 8, section "What Is a Shortcut?"). Right-click a shortcut to the program on your desktop, on the taskbar, in a folder, or in the folder that contains your Start menu items (usually C:\Documents And Settings\All Users\Start Menu\Programs). Choose Properties from the menu that appears and click the Shortcut tab on the Properties dialog box for the program. The Target box contains the full pathname of the executable file for the program. Click Find Target to open an Explorer window for the folder that contains the program file.

To delete the program, delete the folder that contains the program files and all the files in it (see Chapter 7, section "Deleting Files and Folders"). After uninstalling a program, you might see shortcuts to the program lying around on your desktop, in folders, on the taskbar, or in your Start menu. Delete these shortcuts by right-clicking the shortcut and choosing Delete from the menu that appears, or by dragging the shortcut into the Recycle Bin on the desktop.

Tip *If at all possible, use a program's uninstaller instead of just deleting all the files because the uninstaller is safer and more comprehensive. Uninstallers remove files in C:\Windows, C:\Windows\System, C:\Windows\System32, and other locations in which the program might have installed them. Uninstallers also delete the Registry entries for the program (see Chapter 38).*

The
Complete
Reference

Chapter 4

Getting Help

Windows has always come with *online help*—helpful information stored on your computer that you can look at using a Help command. Windows XP comes with online help, too, but this help is "online" in two senses: the help system includes help files stored on your computer's hard disk, as well as a connection to online help information via the Internet. You look at the online help stored on your own computer by using the Help And Support Center. When you are using a program, you can use its "question mark" Help button to find out what the items on the screen mean.

New in Windows XP is Remote Assistance, which enables you to allow a friend or coworker to take control of your computer over the Internet or a LAN to fix software problems you may have. Microsoft now also offers online newsgroups, discussion groups about all aspects of Windows.

> **Note** *The Help And Support Center contains information about Windows XP and some of the programs and accessories that come with it. Other programs that come with Windows, and most third-party applications, have separate help systems. Most programs have two ways of displaying Help screens: Choose Help, Help | Contents, Help | Help, or Help | Topics from the menu bar, or press the F1 key.*

What Is the Help And Support Center?

The Help And Support Center is a set of Web pages about Windows and the programs and accessories that come with it. The pages are stored on your hard disk and are displayed by a special Internet Explorer window. Other programs you install may also come with their own online help.

Displaying Help Screens

To see the Help And Support Center window (shown in Figure 4-1), choose Start | Help And Support. The toolbar shows many of the same icons you see in any Explorer window, including Back, Forward, Home, Favorites, and History. You also see Index, Support, and Options commands. The Task pane (left side of the window) shows a list of topics from which to choose. The rest of the window displays the help information you request from the Task pane.

When the Help And Support Center window first appears, you see lists of help topics and tasks (click Home on the toolbar to return to it). Click a topic to see a detailed list of subtopics in the left pane. When you see a plus box to the left of a topic, click the plus box to see its subtopics. When you see a topic with a question-mark icon to its left, clicking the topic displays an explanation, and steps to follow, in the right pane. If a word or phrase becomes underlined when you move your mouse pointer over it, click it to see information about that topic.

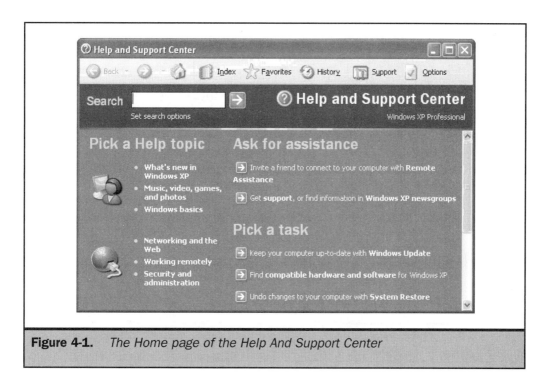

Figure 4-1.   *The Home page of the Help And Support Center*

If your computer is connected to the Internet, Windows automatically updates the home page of the Help And Support Center with news and updates, which appear in the lower-right corner of the window.

Finding Topics

When you click Index on the toolbar in the Help And Support Center, the left pane displays an alphabetical index of help topics, shown in Figure 4-2. The first time you click Index, you may see the Preparing Index For First Use window, which can take a moment to disappear.

To find a topic in the index, you can scroll down the list, but the list is very long. Instead, you can type a word or phrase in the box above the list. As you type the word, Windows finds the first entry in the index that begins with the letters you typed. Scroll down the list to see all the entries that start with that word.

When you find a topic of interest, press ENTER, double-click the index entry, or click the Display button. If there is only one help topic about that index entry, Windows displays it in the right pane. If more than one help topic exists, you see a Topics Found window, with a menu of topics to choose from. Double-click or single-click a topic, and click Display.

You can search for words or phrases wherever they appear in the help text, whether or not an index entry exists for that word or phrase. Click the Search box in the upper-left corner of the Help And Support Center window, type a word or phrase

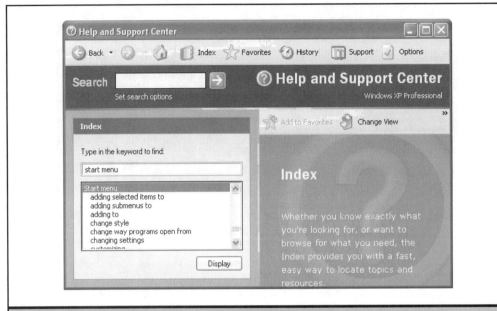

Figure 4-2.   *Alphabetical index of help topics—click one and click Display to see information about that topic.*

in the box, and then press ENTER or click the green arrow button. A list of topics appears in the left pane (as shown in Figure 4-3) in three sections:

- **Suggested Topics**   Pages that Microsoft recommends about this topic.
- **Full-Text Search Matches**   Pages that contain the word(s) in the Search box.
- **Microsoft Knowledge Base**   Pages in the Web-based Microsoft Knowledge Base, which is a huge searchable database of articles about all Microsoft products, at **http://support.microsoft.com**.

Click the heading to see the list of matches in that category, and then click a match to display its information in the right pane.

Copying Help Information to Other Programs

You can use cut-and-paste to copy information from the Help And Support window to other programs (see Chapter 5, section "Cutting, Copying, and Pasting"). Select the part of the text in the right pane of the window that you want to copy. If you want to copy the entire help topic, right-click in the right pane and choose Select All from the menu that appears. Then right-click in the page and choose Copy from the menu that appears (or press CTRL-C). Windows copies the text to the Windows Clipboard. Now you can paste the text into a document by using the Edit | Paste command (or pressing CTRL-V) in the program you use to edit the document.

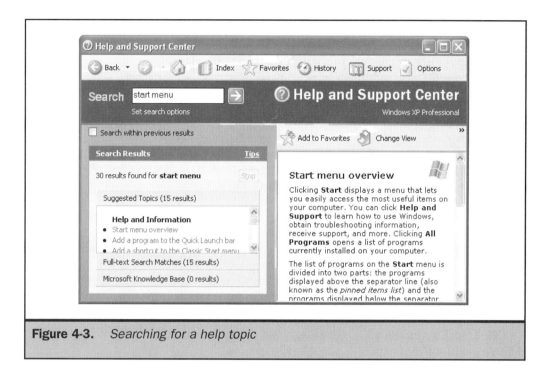

Figure 4-3. *Searching for a help topic*

Taking Tours of Windows Features

The Help And Support Center can also display tours and tutorials about Windows. Click Home on the toolbar, click What's New In Windows XP, and click Taking A Tour Or Tutorial. You see a list of topics about which Windows includes tours and tutorials—click one to start the tour.

Getting Help from Microsoft or from a Friend

You can get helpful information over the Internet about Windows. Click Support on the toolbar to see a list of your options:

- **Ask A Friend To Help** Using Remote Assistance, you can ask a knowledgeable friend to take control of your computer via an Internet connection (see "Allowing a Friend to Control Your Computer").

- **Get Help From Microsoft** If your PC is online, you can sign up for a Microsoft .NET Passport, which identifies you to Microsoft, and get information from the Microsoft Web site. Once you sign in with your .NET Passport name and password, you can contact a Microsoft support technician for help, check on the status of problems you've submitted, or download and install software that enables Microsoft to upload files from your computer to resolve a software issue.

■ **Go To A Windows Web Site Forum**   Participate in online newsgroups
about Windows XP. Your browser runs and displays the
http://www.microsoft.com/windowsxp/expertzone/newsgroups site.
For more information about reading newsgroups, see Chapter 23.

You must be connected to the Internet to use these Internet-based resources.

*If you are asking for help from Microsoft or on a newsgroup, you may be asked for
information about your computer system. In the Help And Support Center window,
click Support and then click My Computer Information in the lower part of the Task
pane to see information about your hardware and software.*

Other Help Options

Here are other things you can do in the Help And Support Center window:

■ Click the Back button on the toolbar to move to the previous topic you
displayed, or click the Forward button to return to the next topic you displayed
before clicking Back.

■ To print a help topic, right-click in the right pane and choose Print from the
menu that appears.

■ To make coming back to the topic easy, add it to your Favorites list by clicking
Add To Favorites. To see your Favorites list, click Favorites on the toolbar. Your
favorite help pages are listed in the left pane: click one to display it in the
right pane.

■ You can choose whether to display Favorites and History buttons on the toolbar
the font size used in help pages, whether labels appear next to toolbar buttons,
and how the Search box works. Click Options on the toolbar, click Change Help
And Support Center Options, and select the appropriate check boxes.

■ If you want to see extra help information about using the keyboard, open the
Accessibility Properties dialog box, click the Keyboard tab, and select the Show
Extra Keyboard Help In Programs check box (see Chapter 16, section "Making
the Keyboard More Accessible"). Then click OK.

Finding Out What an Onscreen Object Is

Many dialog boxes in both Windows and application programs have a small
question-mark button in the upper-right corner, next to the Close button. This
Help button enables you to find out what an object is. Click this question-mark
Help button, and then click an item in the dialog box—an icon, button, label, or box.
A small window appears with a description of the object you clicked. To dismiss the
window, click anywhere in the dialog box.

Another way to display information about an item on the screen is to right-click it. If a menu appears that includes the What's This command, choose it. Or, select the item you want information about and press the F1 key.

Allowing a Friend to Control Your Computer

Programs have been available for years that allow someone to control another computer over the phone or the Internet. Carbon Copy (at **http://www.compaq.com/ services/carboncopy**) and pcAnywhere (at **http://www.symantec.com/pcanywhere**) are popular programs with support technicians because these programs allow them to look at and fix a computer without having to visit the office where the computer sits. In another example of bundling programs with Windows, Windows XP comes with Remote Desktop, which provides this same functionality (see Chapter 15, section "Accessing Other Computers with Remote Desktop"). Remote Assistance is a special version of Remote Desktop that enables you to invite someone to control your PC to help you solve a software problem.

With Remote Assistance, you invite a specific person to take control of your computer. You can contact the person via Windows Messenger or by e-mail. If the person agrees, then the helper can control the mouse pointer and type as if he or she were at your computer. You can also chat by typing or talking (if you have microphones and speakers), and send files.

Inviting a Friend to Help

To invite someone to take control of your PC:

1. Open the Help And Support Center window by choosing Start | Help And Support.

2. Click Support in the toolbar and click Ask A Friend To Help in the Support task list. Click Invite Someone To Help You in the window that appears.

3. Choose whether to contact your helper by using Windows Messenger or e-mail, identify the person, and click Invite. Then type the message you'd like to send with the invitation (something more specific than "Help!" is useful). In the Set The Invitation To Expire box, specify how long to leave the invitation open.

4. Leave the Require The Recipient To Use A Password check box selected: otherwise, anyone who gets ahold of the invitation can take complete control of your computer while the invitation is open. Type a password in the Type Password box that the helper will have to type when taking control.

5. Click Send Invitation.

6. If Outlook Express is configured to let you know whenever another program tries to send e-mail (a useful antivirus feature), you see a warning about it: click Send (see Chapter 23, section "Protecting Yourself from E-Mail Viruses").

7. Communicate the invitation password to your helper by Windows Messenger, e-mail, phone, or other medium.

8. Wait for your helper to get the invitation and to respond. When your helper receives the invitation and types in the password in response to your invitation, you see a dialog box with the helper's name and the message "Do you want to let this person view your screen and chat with you?"

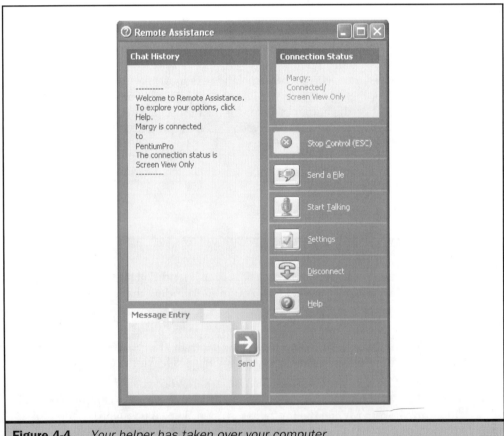

Figure 4-4.   *Your helper has taken over your computer.*

9. Click Yes to proceed. You see the Remote Assistance window shown in Figure 4-4. The left side of the window is where you can chat with your helper.

10. Send a message explaining the problem to your helper by typing in the Message Entry area in the lower-left part of the Remote Assistance window.

Once Windows makes the Remote Assistance connection, you can do the following:

- **Share control of your computer**   When the helper clicks Take Control, you see a dialog box asking whether you want to let the helper share control of your computer. Click Yes to do so. While the helper is using your computer, keep your hands off the mouse and keyboard—it's terribly confusing when two people try to control the mouse pointer or type at the same time! Press ESC (or any key combination with ESC) to end sharing control, or click Stop Control.

- **Send a file**   Click Send A File and specify the file name.

- **Voice chat**   Click Start Talking if you and your helper have speakers and microphones on your computers, to start a voice chat. Click Settings to set the audio quality. If the helper clicks Start Talking first, you see a message asking whether you'd like to start a voice chat.

Click Disconnect when you are done being helped, unless the helper disconnects first.

Responding to an Invitation for Remote Assistance

If you receive an invitation to help someone by using Remote Assistance, you get an e-mail or Windows Messenger message that says something like this:

```
Fred H. would like your assistance. You can easily provide
assistance from your computer by following the instructions at:
http://windows.microsoft.com/RemoteAssistance/en/RA.htm Caution:
* Accept invitations only from people you know and trust. * E-mail
messages can contain viruses or other harmful attachments. * Before
opening the attachment, review the security precautions and
information at the above address.
```

The message includes an attached file named rcBuddy.MsRcIncident. (The first part of the file name may be different.) Click the link in the message to read a Web page about how Remote Assistance works. (This Web page works only in Internet Explorer.)

Follow these steps when you receive an invitation and password from someone you know and want to help:

1. Make sure that you are either connected to the Internet or (if both computers are on the same LAN) to the LAN.

2. Open the attached file. You may see a warning that attached files may contain viruses. Go ahead and open the file. You see the Remote Assistance dialog box:

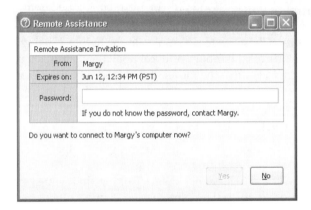

3. Type the password and click Yes to connect. Remote Assistance makes the connection over the LAN or the Internet. You see a Remote Assistance window similar to Figure 4-4, but with an image of the other computer screen in the right side of the window. The left side of the window is where you can chat with the other person.

4. Type messages in the Message Entry area in the lower-left part of the Remote Assistance window, and click Send to send the message to the other computer.

 If someone sends you an invitation to help from a computer that has a higher screen resolution than your computer, you won't be able to see much of the other person's screen in your Remote Assistance window (if you click Scale To Window, it will be unreadable). Set your screen resolution as high as you can.

Once Windows makes the Remote Assistance connection, you can do the following:

■ **Control the other person's computer**   Click Take Control and wait for the other person to give permission for you to proceed. When you see a message indicating that you are sharing control, click in the right side of the Remote Assistance window, where the image of the other person's computer screen appears. While your mouse pointer is in that part of the window, its movements also move the mouse pointer on the other computer. However, the other person can also use the mouse and keyboard, and it gets confusing if you both try to do so at the same time. You can click Scale To Window if the image of the other computer screen doesn't fit in the Remote Assistance window, but it usually becomes unreadable: click Actual Size to display the other computer screen at actual size. Press ESC (or any key combination with ESC) to end sharing control, or click Release Control.

■ **Send a file**   Click Send A File and specify the file name.

■ **Voice chat**   Click Start Talking to start a voice chat. If the other person clicks Start Talking first, you see a message asking whether you'd like to start a voice chat. Both computers need microphones and speakers.

Click Disconnect when you are done helping, unless the other person disconnects first.

| Note | *If you can't make a connection, one of the computers may be behind a firewall, and you may need to ask the network administrator to enable the port used by Remote Assistance (port 3389).* |

The Complete Reference

Chapter 5

Copying, Moving, and Sharing Information Between Programs

Windows XP provides two methods of sharing data between different application programs (although each method has variations): You can cut or copy and then paste using the Windows Clipboard, or you can use OLE, object linking and embedding. In general, cutting-and-pasting (or its variant, drag-and-drop) works well for the simpler tasks—moving text from one application to another, for instance. OLE is useful when you want all the features of one type of program to work with an object in another program. For example, if you want to display an Excel spreadsheet in a Word document, and you want to be able to update a complicated formula and display the correct answer in the Word document, then you need to use OLE.

Sharing Data Through the Windows Clipboard

Copying or moving information from one location to another within a program is easy using the cut-and-paste commands that almost all Windows programs support. Cutting-and-pasting uses the Clipboard to store information temporarily. Moving or copying information between programs is also easy using the Clipboard. You can use the ClipBook Viewer to look at what's on the Clipboard. Some programs also let you use your mouse to drag information from one location to another.

You can use the Clipboard to move or copy text, a range of spreadsheet cells, a picture, a sound, or almost any other piece of information you can create with a Windows application. The Clipboard can hold only one chunk of information at a time, so you either have to paste it somewhere else right away, or not cut or copy anything else until you've pasted the information where you want it. If you cut or copy another chunk of information, it replaces the information already on the Clipboard. To use the Clipboard to move or copy information within or between files, or to share information between programs, you cut or copy the information from one window and paste it in another. You can also use the ClipBook Viewer to see what's on the Clipboard.

Cutting, Copying, and Pasting

Cut-and-paste is a feature of Windows that enables you to select information from one file and move or copy it to another file (or to another location in the same file). Cut-and-paste works by storing information temporarily on the Clipboard. The following cut-and-paste techniques enable you to copy or move information within or between almost any Windows application:

- **Cut**   Removes selected information from its current location and stores it (temporarily) on the Clipboard.

- **Copy**   Copies selected information and makes a (temporary) duplicate of it on the Clipboard.

- **Paste**   Copies information from the Clipboard to the location of the cursor in the active application.

To move information, you select it, cut it to the Clipboard, and then paste it in the new location. To copy information, you select it, copy it to the Clipboard, and then paste it in the new location.

You can cut, copy, and paste information by using the following methods (some methods might not work in some applications):

- **Menu**   Choose the Edit menu's Cut, Copy, and Paste commands.
- **Keystrokes**   Press CTRL-X to cut, CTRL-C to copy, and CTRL-V to paste.
- **Buttons**   Many applications have toolbars with Cut, Copy, and Paste buttons, as shown here:

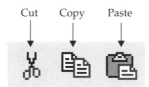

Cut   Copy   Paste

- **Mousing**   Many applications provide shortcut menus that include the Cut, Copy, and Paste commands. Right-click an object to see a shortcut menu.

  The Cut and Copy buttons may be disabled if you haven't selected information in the window, and the Paste button may be disabled if no information is on the Clipboard.

The following steps explain how to copy or move text from one location to another:

1. Select the information you want to copy or move.

   - You can select information by highlighting it with the mouse or by holding down the SHIFT key as you use the arrow buttons. The help system of the application you're using will contain more information regarding how to select in that application.
   - Be careful when you have information selected. Depending on the application, you can inadvertently replace the whole selection by typing a character or space or by pressing the DELETE or BACKSPACE keys. Usually, a simple click deselects the information, ending the danger.

  If you're afraid you deleted something by mistake, press CTRL-Z to undo the change in most programs.

2. If you want to copy the information, press CTRL-C, click the Copy button, or choose Edit | Copy. If you want to move the information, press CTRL-X, click the Cut button, or choose Edit | Cut.

3. If you are copying, you don't see any change on the screen when you give the Copy command. If you are cutting, however (which is useful if you want to move information), the selected information disappears from the screen—it is now stored on the Clipboard.

4. Move the cursor to the place you want the information to appear. This may mean changing applications by clicking a button on the taskbar, or even opening a new application. As long as you don't cut or copy anything else or turn off the computer, the information will be available to be pasted to a new location.

5. Paste the text by pressing CTRL-V, by clicking the Paste button, or by choosing Edit | Paste. The information you cut or copy appears at the location of the cursor.

Once you cut or copy information onto the Clipboard, you can make multiple copies of it by pasting it as many times as you want.

Tip   *Information on the Clipboard takes up RAM, limiting the resources your computer has available to do other things. Therefore, if you cut or copy a lot of information to the Clipboard, paste it quickly. Then, cut or copy something small—one letter or word, for instance—which replaces the large chunk of information on the Clipboard and makes most of the RAM available again. Some programs clear the Clipboard. You can also use the ClipBook Viewer to delete the information on the Clipboard.*

If you use Microsoft Office 2000 or XP you may see the small Office Clipboard window (in Office 2000) or the task pane (in Office XP). The Office Clipboard stores up to 12 (for Office 2000) or 24 (for Office XP) "clips" from Office applications. Rest the pointer on a clip to see its contents. You can paste any clip by clicking its icon on the Office Clipboard. The Office Clipboard opens automatically after you cut more than one selection for Office applications.

Note   *Some programs have problems with cut-and-paste. If you have trouble pasting into a program, first paste the information into Notepad. Then copy it from Notepad and try pasting into the program where you actually want the information to appear.*

What Is Drag-and-Drop?

Drag-and-drop is another method of moving or copying information from one file to another, or to another location in the same file. To move information from one location to another, select it with your mouse and drag it to its new location.

Not all programs support drag-and-drop. Some programs copy the information you drag, rather than move it. Some programs enable you to choose whether to move or copy the information (for example, a program may enable you to copy the information by holding down the CTRL key while dragging).

Using the ClipBook Viewer to Look at What's on the Clipboard

You needn't take for granted that the information you want is on the Clipboard—you can actually look at it by opening the ClipBook Viewer, a program that displays the current contents of the Clipboard. You can't edit what's on the Clipboard, but you can save it as a *Clipboard file*, with extension .clp. (Clipboard files are a form of HTML.)

Note   *ClipBook Viewer seems to conflict with Office XP, so it may not run if you have Office XP installed.*

To open the ClipBook Viewer (shown in Figure 5-1), choose Start | Run, type **clipbrd** and press ENTER, or you can open a clipboard file (with extension .clp) from Windows Explorer. You can see two windows in the ClipBook Viewer, the Clipboard window (with the current contents of the Clipboard) and the Local ClipBook window (with your saved clips).

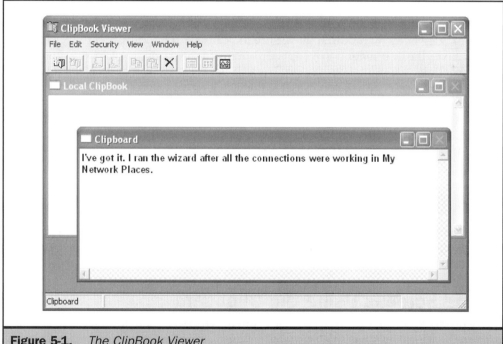

Figure 5-1.   *The ClipBook Viewer*

What Is DDE?

DDE (Dynamic Data Exchange) is another way for programs to exchange information. With DDE, the programs send messages among themselves. For example, say you are running Microsoft Word and you open a .doc file in Windows Explorer. Windows uses DDE to send a message to Microsoft Word, so the .doc file opens in the current Word window, rather than starting up a second copy of Word. You can control what DDE messages your programs send, but programming is required, using macros in programs like Microsoft Word or Excel, or using a programming language like Visual Basic or C++ (see Chapter 3, section "Actions and DDE Messages Associated with File Types").

Note *You might have to install the ClipBook Viewer (see Chapter 3, section "Installing and Uninstalling Programs that Come with Windows")—it isn't always automatically installed. Open the Control Panel, open Add/Remove Programs, click the Windows Setup icon, highlight Accessories And Utilities from the list of components, click Details, highlight Accessories, click Details again and choose Clipboard Viewer.*

You can save the current contents of the Clipboard by using File | Save As on the ClipBook Viewer menu (but first make sure the Clipboard window is active). ClipBook Viewer saves the information in a clipboard file with extension .clp. Open a saved clipboard file by choosing File | Open. The ClipBook Viewer can open files saved in the Clipboard format only—you can give them a different extension, but the file is still in .clp format. When you open a clipboard file and the Clipboard already contains information, ClipBook Viewer asks you to confirm that you want to delete the current contents of the Clipboard.

To delete the contents of the Clipboard, choose Edit | Delete, press the DELETE key, or click the Delete (X) button. Deleting the contents of the Clipboard releases RAM for other uses. You can't cut-and-paste information from the ClipBook Viewer window—the information is already on the Clipboard!

Note *Theoretically, the ClipBook Viewer enables you to save more than one clip at a time, by displaying the Local ClipBook window (with Window | Local ClipBook), pressing CTRL-V, and giving the clip a name. However, we haven't gotten it to work reliably.*

Capturing Screens Using the Clipboard

Many products can take a *screen shot*, a picture of whatever is on the screen. This book is littered with screen shots that are used as figures. If you need to create a screen shot, you can use the Clipboard to create one. Use the PRINT SCREEN key that appears on your keyboard—it often is above the cursor control keys with the SCROLL LOCK and PAUSE keys. You can take two different kinds of screen shots:

- A picture of the whole screen by pressing PRINT SCREEN
- A picture of the active window by pressing ALT-PRINT SCREEN

Once the picture is on the Clipboard, you can paste it somewhere else. You may want to paste the picture into a graphics program, such as Paint; so you can save it in a graphics file format and use it later (see Chapter 18, section "Drawing Pictures with Microsoft Paint"). Or, you might want to paste it into a file, such as a word processing document containing an explanation of that screen or window.

Sharing Information Using OLE

OLE (Object Linking and Embedding) is far more flexible and can be far more complicated than cut-and-paste or drag-and-drop. OLE enables you to use all your software applications to create an integrated document. For instance, you might want to create an annual report that includes these components:

- Text you create and format by using a word processor, such as Microsoft Word or Corel WordPerfect.

- A company logo stored in a graphics file created by Adobe Photoshop, Paint, or some other graphics application.

- Data and calculations on operating costs stored in a Microsoft Excel or Lotus 1-2-3 spreadsheet.

- Graphs and charts, which may come from your spreadsheet package or another graphics package.

These components may not reflect exactly what *you* want to do, but the point is the same—if you want to combine the output of different applications, OLE offers many advantages over the Clipboard. Why? Because, when you use OLE, the original program retains ownership of the object, and you can use the program to edit the object. For instance, if you use OLE to embed a portion of a spreadsheet in a word processing document, you can always use the spreadsheet application to edit the object and the spreadsheet in the word processing document will reflect those changes. If, instead, you use the Clipboard to copy the numbers from the spreadsheet and then you paste the numbers to the word processor, they would just sit in the word processor, oblivious to their origins—you could use only the tools available in the word processor to edit the numbers. This means that if you later change the original spreadsheet, the numbers pasted in the word processing document won't change.

In OLE, an *object* refers to a piece of information from one application that is placed in a *container file* created by another application. For example, a spreadsheet or graphic is an object when it is included in a word processing document. OLE actually is two similar methods of sharing information between applications—embedding and linking. Sticking with the previous example, *embedding* means putting the spreadsheet object in the word processing document (container file) and asking the word processor to take care of storing the object. So, although the word processor enables you to edit the spreadsheet object by using the spreadsheet application, the spreadsheet object is stored with the word processing document. *Linking*, on the other hand, allows the object to retain a close relationship with its origins—so close, in fact, if the numbers in the original spreadsheet file change, the linked spreadsheet object in the word processing document changes to match. This occurs because the word processing document doesn't really contain the object it displays—it only contains a reference to the file where the information is stored.

You may also choose to insert a *package* into another file. A package is a small file that uses OLE, but instead of displaying content owned by another application, it displays an icon, which, when clicked, opens the owner application and displays the object. Packages can be either linked or embedded. Whether you choose to embed or link objects, the process is similar: You create an object in one application, and then link or embed the object into another application.

Although using OLE to link files can be wonderfully convenient and can save you hours of revisions, it should be used judiciously. If you ever plan to move the file containing linked objects or to send it to someone, you must make sure one of the following occurs:

- The linked files also get moved or sent.

- The linked objects don't get updated. This means the host application won't go looking for the information in the linked file. To break the link, delete the object and paste in a nonlinked version instead.

- You edit the links so the host file knows where to find the source files for the linked objects.

Otherwise, your beautifully organized and time-saving document can become a complete mess. If you are going to move a document with linked objects in it, you need to know how to maintain links, a topic covered later in this chapter.

If you don't need the automatic updating you get with linked objects (for instance, if the source file isn't going to change, or if you don't want the object to reflect changes), or if you know you are going to move or send files, then stick with embedded objects—they're easier to maintain. However, embedding a large object may take more disk space than linking.

Note   *Some applications enable you to link one file to another in a different way—by using a hyperlink (see Chapter 24, section "What Is the World Wide Web?"). A hyperlink actually takes you from one file to another, opening the application for the second file, if necessary.*

Creating Linked or Embedded Objects

The way you link or embed an object depends on the application programs you're using—the program into which you want to embed or link the object. Most programs have a menu command to create an object by using OLE, but you may have to use the online help system to find the command. In Microsoft Word, for instance, you can use

Insert | Object to create an object by using OLE. When using Insert | Object in Microsoft Word or its equivalent in another program, you may see the Display As Icon option. This option allows you to create a package, an icon that when clicked, opens the object in its native application. The following two techniques may also work to link or embed an object: dragging-and-dropping and using Edit | Paste Special. Neither technique is supported by all applications.

Embedding an Object by Dragging and Dropping

The easiest way to embed an object is to drag the information from one program and drop it in the other program. For this method to work, both applications must support drag-and-drop embedding. Check the documentation for the program that contains the information you want to embed. When dragging the information you want to embed, use the same technique you use to copy selected information *within* the application: Some applications require you to hold down the CTRL key while dragging the information. For instance, in Excel, you have to click-and-drag the border of the selected area to move or copy it.

Follow these steps to use drag-and-drop embedding:

1. Select the information you want to embed.

2. Use drag-and-drop to drag the selected information to the other application; use the same drag-and-drop technique you use to copy information within an application. If the second application isn't visible on the screen, you can drag the information to the application's Taskbar button—hold the mouse pointer there for a second, and the application window opens.

3. Drop the information where you want it—if the application supports OLE, you automatically create an embedded object.

 You may be able to specify that the information be linked rather than embedded (the usual default when OLE drag-and-drop is supported) by holding down the SHIFT key—try it to see whether the application you are using supports this feature.

Linking or Embedding an Object Using Paste Special

You may want a little more control over the object than you have when you drag-and-drop it—to achieve more control over the object, use the Edit | Paste Special command found in many applications. The procedure is much like using the Clipboard to cut-and-paste, except you paste by using OLE instead, as follows:

1. Select the information you want to link or embed.

2. Press CTRL-C or CTRL-X to copy or cut the information (or use another method to copy or cut).

3. Move the cursor where you want the object to appear.

4. Choose Edit | Paste Special. You see a dialog box similar to the one shown in Figure 5-2. Choose the correct application from the choices displayed. Make sure to choose the application you want to use to edit the object—in the figure, that is Microsoft Word. If you choose another option, you won't be using OLE—instead, you will be using the Clipboard to do a simple paste of information from one application to another.

5. Choose the correct setting either to embed the object in the new file or to link the two files together. To embed the object, choose the Paste option; to link the object, choose the Paste Link option. Figure 5-2 shows the settings to embed a Microsoft Word object into an Excel spreadsheet. Figure 5-3 shows the settings to link an Excel spreadsheet into a Microsoft Word document. Other applications may have Paste Special dialog boxes that look different from these.

6. Change the Display As Icon setting, if necessary. If you choose to display the object as an icon, you don't see the information itself. Instead, you create a *packaged object* that shows the information it contains only when you open its icon.

7. Click OK to link or embed the object. You see the object in the container file, as in Figure 5-4.

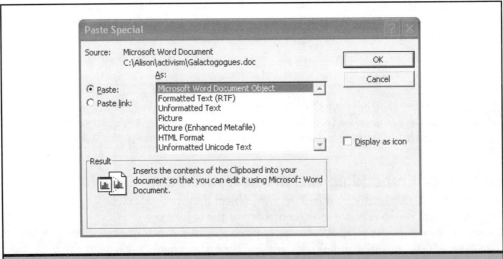

Figure 5-2. *Use this dialog box (or one like it) to embed a Word document into another file.*

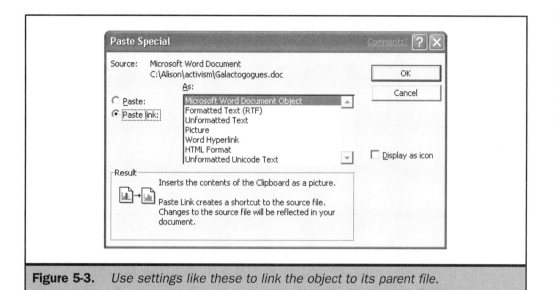

Figure 5-3. *Use settings like these to link the object to its parent file.*

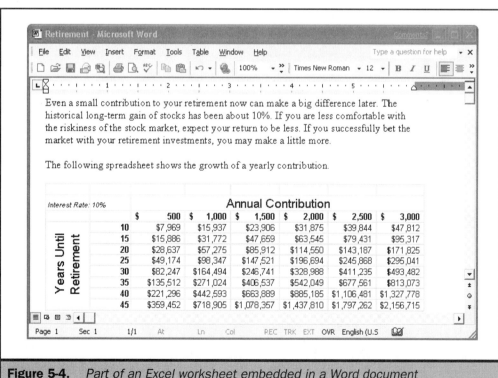

Figure 5-4. *Part of an Excel worksheet embedded in a Word document*

Editing a Linked or Embedded Object

Editing a linked or embedded object is simple—in most applications, you just double-click the object. For other applications, you may need to right-click the object to display a menu with an edit option or change modes so you are in Edit mode (if you're having trouble, check the help system of the application containing the object). Once you figure out how to edit the object, the object's application opens. Next, the menu and toolbars of the window in which the object appears are replaced by the menu and toolbars of the application assigned by the registry to that file type (usually the application used to create the object). In other words, if you're editing an Excel object in a Word document, double-click the object to display Excel's menu and toolbars in Word's window, as in Figure 5-5. You can edit the object by using that application's tools. When you're done, click outside the object to reinstate the regular menu and toolbars, or choose File | Update or Exit. If you're asked whether you want to update the object, answer Yes.

If the object is linked, rather than embedded, you can also edit the object by editing the source file itself. If the file containing the object is also open, you may have to update it manually to see the new information in the object. Closing and opening the file containing the object may be the easiest way to update the object.

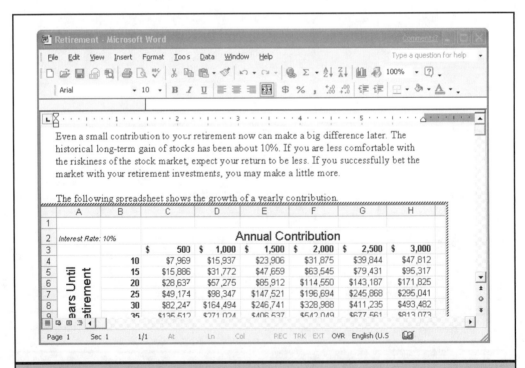

Figure 5-5. *Edit an Excel object in a Word document by using the Excel menu and toolbars that appear when you double-click the object.*

Delete an object by single-clicking it to select it—you'll probably see a box around it—then press the DELETE or BACKSPACE key.

Maintaining OLE Links

If you decide to use a link to put an object in a file, rather than embed the object, you may have to do some maintenance if the linked file or the file containing the link moves to a new location. A link is usually updated each time the file containing the object is opened or printed. *Updating* means that the current information from the linked file is brought into the object.

If the location of a file changes, you may need to "lock" the link so the last available information is retained, break the link so the object becomes an embedded object rather than a linked object, or edit the link so the correct path and filename are referenced. The exact commands may differ by application (check the online help), but usually there's one dialog box where all these tasks can be performed, like this one:

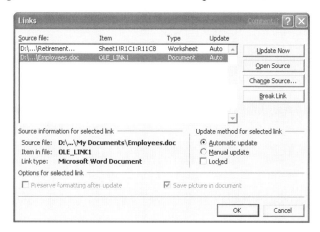

In most Microsoft applications, you can display the dialog box by choosing Edit | Links. The following list explains how to do these three tasks in a Microsoft application. Other applications work in a similar way, but may have different names for the dialog box buttons and options.

- **Lock the link**   Use the Locked option on the Links dialog box to lock the selected link. You can select multiple links to lock by CTRL-clicking or SHIFT-clicking additional links. A locked link isn't updated. To check whether a link is locked, select the link and see whether the Locked option is checked.

- **Break the link**   Use the Break Link (or Cancel Link) button to break a link. When you break a link, the link disappears from the Links list, and you can no longer use the original application to edit the object. A better choice, often, is to lock the link or replace the linked object with an embedded object.

- **Edit the link**   Use the Change Source button to edit the link. This enables you to redirect the link to a different file or to the same file stored in a different location.

Another option is to set up the file to update the links only when you tell it to do so by specifying manual updating. The Links dialog box has an Update Method option that enables you to specify automatic or manual updating. If you set this option to manual, the links are updated only when you display the Links dialog box and click the Update Now button.

Saving Small Bits of Data as Scraps

Not everyone finds scraps useful, but if you need them, they may be a lifesaver. *Scraps* are OLE objects that have been left on the desktop or in a folder. You can keep a scrap on the desktop or in the folder or, at some later point, drag it to another application. A scrap has an icon that looks like this:

Document
Scrap 'Scr...

Scrap icons all look the same, but their names give you a clue as to which application created them. For instance, a scrap from Word or another word processor is called a *Document scrap*, a scrap from Excel is a *Worksheet scrap*, and a scrap from Quattro Pro is a *Notebook scrap* (using the Quattro Pro terminology). Not all applications can be used to create scraps. For instance, Notepad, which doesn't support drag-and-drop, cannot be used to create scraps.

To create a scrap, drag some information to the desktop or copy it to the Clipboard, and then paste it to the desktop (by right-clicking the desktop and choosing Paste). When you open a scrap on the desktop, the application that created the information opens to display it. You can drag a scrap into a different application to create an OLE object out of it.

The Complete Reference

Chapter 6

Sharing Your Computer with Multiple Users

Because Windows XP is based on Windows 2000, it has a bevy of security-oriented features that were never present in Windows Me/9x. Windows Me/9x (like the original DOS operating system on which they were based) had almost no built-in security, with no way to prevent one user from reading another user's files. For example, if you create multiple user profiles on a computer running Windows 98 Second Edition, you see a password dialog box when you start Windows. This suggests that the computer is secure, but you can simply click Cancel and get complete access. Windows XP can require a user name and password, and, if you make too many attempts to gain entry, Windows XP can also deny further attempts for a period of time.

Windows XP also has a new feature, Fast User Switching, so that multiple people can be logged on and running programs at the same time. Once you have created separate user accounts for the people who will use the computer, you can set file and folder permissions to control who can open, run, modify, or delete files and folders. It also provides Simple File Sharing, which makes it easy to share access to files and folders with other people who use your computer. This chapter examines how to set up Windows for multiple users, including creating user accounts, assigning passwords, logging on, and switching users. We also describe how to log on and off, and how to check who's logged on.

Chapter 29 describes how to share files, folders, and printers with other people on a local area network (LAN), rather than users on a single computer. For network security topics, such as how to send secure e-mail, control what information Internet Explorer stores on your disk, or protect your computer from viruses, see Chapter 31.

If your computer is part of a local area network that includes a Windows NT, 2000, or Windows .NET Server, it is probably part of a domain—a workgroup that is controlled by a server computer. If your computer is part of a domain, don't set up or modify user accounts on your computer without consulting your network administrator, because user accounts are probably managed on the server using Windows authentication services. Domain-based networks are covered in *Windows .NET Server: The Complete Reference* (by Kathy Ivens, published by Osborne/McGraw-Hill)—the instructions in this chapter apply primarily to workgroup-based LANs and multiple people using one computer.

| **Caution** | *Windows XP Home Edition doesn't contain all the features described in this chapter. We note which features are missing in Windows XP Home Edition.* |

What Password Protection Does Windows Offer?

Windows has many different resources that can be password protected. The major passwords are the following:

■ **User password**   The password for your user account. You type it when you start up Windows or switch from one user to another, if your computer has user accounts for which passwords have been created. You can change your password at any time. Windows also stores a *password hint*—a word or phrase that would remind you of your password if you forget it, but that wouldn't give the password away to anyone else. If you are truly concerned about forgetting your password (we always are!), you can also create a *password reset disk*, a floppy disk that you can use to log on to your user account even if you forget your password.

Note

You have the option to not have a password. Simply choose not to enter one when prompted by the Windows XP Setup Wizard (as described in the Appendix), or remove the password later. Regardless of your choice, if you plan on being the only user of your computer you can opt to automatically log into your machine. Just make sure you aren't offering free access to sensitive data to unauthorized individuals.

■ **Domain password**   The password used to validate your user name to host computers on a local area network that is controlled by Windows .NET Server, Windows .NET Advanced Server, Windows 2000 Server, Windows NT, or compatible LAN servers. If your domain password is missing or invalid, you can't gain access to disks or printers on the LAN.

■ **Encrypted ZIP compressed folders**   You can assign a password to a ZIP compressed folders (see Chapter 8, section "What Are Compressed Folders?").

■ **NTFS encryption password for a file or folder**   In Windows XP Professional (not the Home Edition), you can assign a password to files and folders stored in NTFS partitions (see Chapter 8, section "What Are Attributes?"). Encryption isn't available on FAT32 partitions.

This chapter describes how to create user passwords to secure your computer and your My Documents folder. See Chapter 31 for additional information if your computer is on a LAN. See *Windows .NET Server: The Complete Reference* for how to create domain accounts and passwords.

What Is a User Account?

When two or more users share a computer, they don't have to argue about what color the background should be, what programs should be on the Start menu, or whether to use single-click or double-click style. Instead, each user can have a *user account* (called a *user profile* in previous versions of Windows). User accounts can be stored in one of two places:

■ **Local user accounts**   Information about a local user account is stored in a folder in the C:\Documents And Settings folder that contains files that describe each user's preferences. Each time a user logs on, Windows finds the appropriate user account and makes the appropriate changes. If you change any of your preferences (for example, choosing a new wallpaper), that information is stored in your user account, so that the change will still be there the next time you log on, but not the next time someone else logs on. Whenever your computer acquires a new user, you should establish a new user account (see "Setting Up a Computer for Multiple Users"). User accounts enable several people to share one computer, or to share folders and other resources on a LAN.

■ **Domain accounts**   Information about domain accounts is stored by the Active Directory (AD) program running on a Windows NT, 2000, or .NET server. When you log in using a domain, your computer gets information from Active Directory about what your settings are and what you have permission to do. Domain accounts are used on larger networks where maintaining accounts stored in each individual computer would be impractical. Domain accounts can use *roaming user profiles*, which allow people to use their own user account from any computer on a LAN, and *mandatory user profiles*, in which only administrators can make changes.

A new feature in Windows XP (new to Windows Me/9x users, anyway) enables you to password-protect the files in your My Documents folder, so that other people using the same computer later won't be able to read them (see "Keeping Your Files Private"). Each user's My Documents folder can be protected from view from the other users.

Another new feature protects your computer if you don't assign passwords to your user accounts. If your user account doesn't have a password, you can log on to your account only at your own computer: you can't use Run As (described in the section "Running a Program as Another User" later in this chapter) or Remote Desktop to use the computer with your user account (see Chapter 15, section "Accessing Other Computers with Remote Desktop").

If your computer is on a small LAN, you can set up local user accounts on all the computers on the LAN so that people can use any computer and see their own files and desktop. See Chapter 29 for details.

 If you are wondering which user account you are logged on as, click the Start button. The user account name appears at the top of the menu.

What Types of Users Can You Create?

Windows XP Home Edition and Professional enable you to set up local user accounts. If you are logged into a Windows .NET, 2000, or NT server with administrative privileges, you can create and maintain domain accounts on a domain-based LAN, but you should talk to your LAN administrator before doing so.

Windows provides at least three types of local user accounts:

■ **Administrator**   Enables access to all accounts. Each computer needs at least one administrator account at all times. You can have more than one, if you

like. When using an administrator account, you can give commands
to create, edit, and delete all user accounts, and you can install software.
Windows XP comes with one administrator account named Owner
(in Windows XP Home Edition) or Administrator (in Windows XP
Professional). Microsoft recommends that you use it only for installing
programs and managing the system.

■ **Limited**   Enables access to your own account. When using a limited
account, you cannot install software, open files in other people's My
Documents folders, change system settings, or change other people's user
accounts. You can run programs that are already installed, and you can
modify your own user account (except that you can't change it into an
administrator account). You should log on with a limited account for
day-to-day work, to avoid viruses and other programs that might try
to install themselves when you aren't looking.

■ **Guest**   Enables access only to programs that are installed on the computer.
Windows has one guest account (named Guest). When using the guest
account, you cannot change the any user accounts, open files in other
people's My Documents folders, or install software.

You can create as many administrator or limited accounts as you want. You can't
create guest accounts. When you install Windows XP, there are at least two accounts:

■ **Owner or Administrator**   An administrator account (in Windows XP Home
Edition, it's called Owner, and in Windows XP Professional, it's called
Administrator). In the rest of this chapter, we'll refer to this account as
Administrator.

■ **Guest**   The guest account.

The installation program asks for the names of the people who will use the computer,
and creates an administrator account for each name. You can create additional
administrative or limited accounts for each person who uses the computer, and you
can rename or delete the Administrator account. Until you create other accounts and
passwords, you automatically log on as Administrator when you start Windows. For
how to create new accounts, see "Creating New User Accounts" later in this chapter.

 *If you are concerned about security (as you should be, if your computer connects to the
Internet), disable the Guest account (see the section "Enabling and Disabling the Guest
Account" later in this chapter). Also be sure to create passwords for each user account,
as described in the section "Adding or Removing Passwords" later in this chapter.
Change all but one or two rarely used accounts from administrator to limited accounts,
to reduce security holes.*

What Are Groups?

Each user account is a member of one or more *groups*, which define what the user can
do. A user account can be a member of many groups. You can create new groups and

you can add user accounts to groups. Groups can be *local groups* (stored on your own computer) or *domain groups* (stored as part of a Microsoft Active Directory system on a Windows .NET or 2000 Server).

(If you need to create and modify groups, you probably have a LAN with a large enough number of computers to warrant at least one computer running Windows .NET Server, with domain-based accounts—see *Windows .NET Server: The Complete Reference* for information.)

Each group comes with *rights* that allow members of that group to perform systemwide tasks, like installing or running programs. A user account has all the rights of all the groups to which it belongs. Groups also have permissions to use certain files and folders (see "What Are Permissions?").

Windows XP Professional comes with nine built-in groups, but for user accounts on a single computer, you usually use only three of them (see the preceding section for descriptions of what each type of user account can do). User accounts belong to these groups:

Group Name	User Accounts
Administrators	Administrator user accounts
Users	Limited user accounts
Guest	The Guest account

 Windows XP Home Edition comes with the same groups as Professional, but with no way to create additional groups or to change settings for a group.

What Is a User Profile?

Table 6-1 lists the some of the files and folders that are stored separately for each local user account. These items are stored in the user account's *user profile*—the folder that contains all the settings for the user. A user profile is usually in the C:\Documents And Settings*username* folder, where *username* is replaced by the name of the user account. (If Windows is installed on a partition other than C:, so is this folder.) You need to configure Windows Explorer to display hidden files and folders to see them (see Chapter 8, section "What Are Hidden Files and Folders?").

Domain-based LANs (that is, networks on which a Windows .NET Server stores all user information) offer roaming profiles that are stored on the server rather than on the user's computer. With roaming profiles, you can log on to any computer on the network and see your desktop and your files in My Documents. (See *Windows .NET Server: The Complete Reference* for more information.)

 If you upgrade to Windows XP from Windows NT and already had user profiles, they may still be where NT stores them, which is usually in C:\WinNT\Profiles.

Item	Contents
Ntuser.dat, Ntuser.dat.log, and Ntuser.tmp files	This user's configuration settings and other information.
Application Data folder	This user's application program configuration settings.
Cookies folder	The cookies stored by Internet Explorer while run by this user (see Chapter 24, section "What Are Cookies?")
Desktop folder	The items that appear on this user's desktop.
Favorites folder	Items this user has added to the Favorites folder.
Local Settings\History folder	Shortcuts to Web sites this user has viewed recently.
Local Settings\Temporary Internet Files folder	Recently-viewed Web pages.
My Documents folder	The files and folders that appear in this user's My Documents folder when the user is logged on. You can tell Windows to look in a different location for your My Documents folder: see "Modifying User Accounts" later in this chapter.
NetHood folder	This user's network shortcuts, which appear in the My Network Places folder when the user is logged on.
PrintHood folder	This user's shared printers.
Recent Documents folder	Shortcuts to files this user has opened recently.
Send To folder	Shortcuts to folders and devices that appear on the Send To menu when the user right-clicks a file or folder.
Start Menu folder	The shortcuts and folders that Windows uses to display the Start and More Programs menus for this user.
Templates folder	Template files for word processors and other programs, used when this user creates a new document.

Table 6-1.   *Information Stored in Local User Account Profiles*

What Configuration Settings Do Local User Accounts Have?

Local user accounts have a number of configuration options, as listed in Table 6-2. See "Modifying User Accounts" later in this chapter for how to change them.

Setting	Description
Name	User name that appears at the top of the Start menu and on the Welcome screen.
Picture	Graphic file that appears on the Start menu and welcome screen next to the user's name.
Account type	Administrator limited, or guest (see "What Types of Users Can You Create?")
Password	The password should be at least seven characters, and ideally longer. You can include lowercase letters, uppercase letters, numbers, and punctuation. Don't use names or words that appear in the dictionary.
Full Name	Full name of the user.
Description	Other text about the user.
User must change password at next logon	When selected, forces the person to change the password when he next logs on. Changing passwords regularly protects the user account from being used by someone who discovered an old password.
User cannot change password	When selected, prevents the person from changing the password. This option is useful for user accounts that are used by more than one person.
Password never expires	When selected, allows the user to continue using the same password indefinitely.
Account is disabled	When selected, no one can log on using this account. When someone won't use the computer for a while, disable the person's account. Don't delete it and make a new one later, because you'll need to redo all the user account's settings.

Table 6-2. *Local User Account Settings*

Setting	Description
Account is locked out	When someone has tried to log on with the wrong password too many times, this check box is selected. Clear the check box to enable the user to use this account again (and assign the person a new password!). See the section "Other Security Options" later in this chapter for how to configure account lockouts.
Member of	Group(s) of which this user account is a member.
Profile path	Pathname of the user account's profile. When blank, the path is C:\Document And Settings*username*\.
Logon script	Script (usually a batch file or Windows Script Hosting script) that Windows runs each time the user logs on. It also runs when Fast User Switching switches back to the user account. See Chapter 39 for how to write batch files and Chapter 40 for how to run other scripts.
Local path	Pathname of the user account's home folder, if it is stored on the local computer (rather than on a network drive) (see "Can Windows XP Keep Files Private?").
Connect *xx* to *xx*	Shared folder name to use as the user account's home folder. In the first box, choose a drive letter, and in the second box, type a UNC network path (such as \\server\users\fred) (see Chapter 29, section "Sharing Your Disk Drives and Folders with Others").

Table 6-2.   *Local User Account Settings (continued)*

Can Windows XP Keep Files Private?

Windows Me/9x had no provision for users keeping files private from each other. Like Windows NT and 2000, Windows XP does, as long as three things are true:

- The disk on which the files are stored is formatted using NTFS (see Chapter 32, section "What Is a File System?"). If your disk is formatted as FAT32 instead of NTFS, you can set up local user accounts and groups, but you can't make files or folders private.

- Simple File Sharing is disabled, as described in the next section.

- You have Windows XP Professional rather than Windows XP Home Edition.

Each user account has its own My Documents folder in which the user can store files. Other users can't open the folder to see the files. Choose Start | My Documents to see the contents of your My Documents folder.

Windows usually stores the My Documents folders for all local user accounts in the C:\Documents And Settings folder. When you create a password for your account, Windows asks if you want a private documents folder (see "Adding or Removing Passwords"). If you click Yes, your My Documents folder can only be opened by you, and by administrative users. If you click No, anyone can open your My Documents folder. (If an administrator creates a new user account, Windows creates the private My Documents folder right away.)

When you are logged on, the C:\Documents And Settings*username*\My Documents folder appears as the My Documents folder. Other user's folders also appear, with names like Zac's Documents and Jordan's Documents. If you try to open a private My Documents folder, Windows displays an error message instead.

You can change the location of your My Document's folder; see the section "Modifying User Accounts" later in this chapter. To control who has permission to use your My Documents folder—or other folders—see the section "Keeping Your Files Private" later in this chapter.

In Windows 2000 and NT, each user had a home folder, which was similar to the My Documents folder. Windows XP provides each user with both a My Documents folder and a home folder, and you can control the location of both. Microsoft recommends using the My Documents folder rather than the home folder.

What Is Simple File Sharing?

Simple File Sharing is a new feature of Windows XP. When Simple File Sharing is enabled (which it is when you first install Windows) and when you share a drive or folder, you share that drive or folder with all user accounts on your computer. If you want to control who has access to drives and folders, you have to disable Simple File Sharing.

You can't disable Simple File Sharing in Windows XP Home Edition, only in Windows XP Professional.

The advantage of leaving Simple File Sharing turned on is that you don't have to make a lot of choices when you decide to share files with other users of your computer or with other people on your network (if your computer is connected to a local area network). However, if you want to be able to give access to some people but not to others, you need to turn Simple File Sharing off.

Follow these steps to change the Simple File Sharing setting on your computer:

1. Run Windows Explorer (choose Start | My Computer, for example).

2. Choose Tools | Folder Options to see the Folder Options dialog box (see Chapter 8, section "Changing the Behavior of Explorer Windows").

3. Click the View tab.

4. Scroll to the bottom of the Advanced Settings box to find the Use Simple File Sharing check box, and select or deselect the check box.

5. Click OK to close the dialog box.

The other requirement for granting permissions for files or folders to individual users is that the files or folders be stored on an NTFS disk or partition. When Simple File Sharing is disabled you see security options when you share a drive or folder, and the Properties dialog box for drives and folders includes a Security tab. However, the options you see depend on whether the drive that you are sharing is formatted with NTFS or FAT32.

What Are Permissions?

Permissions control what a user or group of users can do with a file, folder, printer, shared folder, or registry key. (See Chapter 14 for how to control who can use a printer, see Chapter 29 for how to share folders and printers on a network, and see Chapter 38 for information about the Registry.)

Windows supports permissions only if Simple File Sharing (described in the previous section) is disabled and if your files are stored on an NTFS drive (see Chapter 32, section "What Is a File System?"). Table 6-3 lists the permissions you can

Folder Permission	Allows or Prevents This Operation
Change Permissions	Modifying the permissions of the folder.
Create Files	Creating new files in the folder.
Create Folders	Creating subfolders within the folder.
Delete	Deleting the folder.
Delete Subfolders and Files	Deleting folders and files stored in the folder, even if you don't have permissions for the individual subfolders and files.
List Folder	Viewing the names of the files and folders that the folder contains.
Read Attributes	Viewing the attributes of the folder.
Read Permissions	Reading the permissions of the folder.
Take Ownership	Taking ownership of the folder away from its current owner.
Traverse Folder	Opening the folder to navigate to its subfolders or parent folders.
Write Attributes	Changing the attributes of the folder.

Table 6-3. *Permissions for Folders*

File Permission	Allows or Prevents This Operation
Append Data	Adding information to the end of the file, without changing the existing information.
Change Permissions	Modifying the permissions of the file.
Delete	Deleting the file.
Execute File	Running the program contained in the file.
Read Attributes	Viewing the attributes of the file.
Read Data	Viewing the contents of the file.
Read Permissions	Reading the permissions of the file.
Take Ownership	Taking ownership of the file away from its current owner.
Write Attributes	Changing the attributes of the file.
Write Data	Modifying the contents of the file.

Table 6-4.   *Permissions for Files*

set for folders, and Table 6-4 lists permissions for files. There are other permissions that are not frequently used except in domain-based networks. Each permission either allows or prevents users from performing the operation. To change the permissions for files and folders (assuming that you have permission yourself to do so), see the section "Keeping Your Files Private" later in this chapter.

If a file or folder is stored on an NTFS drive or partition, and if you have Simple File Sharing disabled, then the Properties dialog box for the file or folder includes a Security tab (as described in the section "Setting User Permissions for NTFS Drives" in Chapter 29). When you look at the Security tab of the Properties dialog box for a file or folder, you see the short list of permissions shown in Table 6-5. Each entry on the list represents a group of the permissions listed in Tables 6-3 and 6-4.

What Is Fast User Switching?

Fast User Switching is a new feature of Windows XP that allows you to switch from one user account to another without the first user logging off. For example, a user named Jordan might be running Outlook Express and Microsoft Access. Another user named Meg needs to check her mail and asks to use the computer. Fast User Switching lets Jordan step aside and Meg switch the computer to her user account. Jordan's programs are on hold until Meg is done using the computer. When Jordan switches back to his account, his programs are just where he left them.

Permission	Allows for Folders	Allows for Files
Full Control	All operations	All operations
Modify	Traverse and List Folder Read and Write Attributes Create Files and Folders Read Permissions Delete	Execute File Read, Write, and Append Data Read and Write Attributes Read Permissions Delete
Read & Execute	Traverse and List Folder Read Attributes and Permissions	Execute File Read Data Read Attributes and Permissions
Read	List Folder Read Attributes and Permissions	Read Data Read Attributes and Permissions
Write	Create Files and Folders Write Attributes Read Permissions	Write and Append Data Write Attributes Read Permissions
List Folder Contents	Traverse and List Folder Read Attributes Read Permissions	(Not applicable)

Table 6-5.   *Permissions Shown in Folder and File Properties Dialog Boxes*

Fast User Switching is enabled by default if your Windows system has at least 64MB of RAM. With less RAM, the system doesn't have enough space to store one user's environment, including its running programs and open files, while another user is active.

You can't use Fast User Switching if your computer is part of a domain (that is, connected to a domain-based LAN). You also can't use it if you use the Classic logon screen instead of the Welcome screen for logging on (see "Controlling How Users Log On").

Setting Up a Computer for Multiple Users

When several people share a computer, local user accounts allow each person to personalize the user interface without inconveniencing the other users. The user accounts can have passwords, to prevent people from logging on as each other, or you can dispense with passwords, if security isn't a concern.

We recommend creating a password for each user account, even if it's an obvious one. Passwords prevent toddlers or bored passersby from using your computer, even if the password is simply "xx" or the same as the user name.

When you start using Windows XP, you are automatically logged on with an administrator user account named Administrator (in Windows XP Professional) or Owner (in Windows XP Home Edition), unless you tell the Windows XP Setup Wizard the names of the people who will use the computer (which causes the Setup Wizard to create administrator accounts for each of them). Using this administrator account, you can create user accounts for the people who will use the computer, giving each person the appropriate type of account (administrator or limited) based on the person's level of use.

In Windows XP Professional, user account features can be set in one of two ways: the newly-designed User Accounts window, and the Windows 2000–based Microsoft Management Console. Windows XP Home Edition provides only the User Accounts window: you can't see user account information in the Microsoft Management Console.

The User Accounts Window

To make basic changes to local user accounts or to create new accounts, choose Start | Control Panel and click User Accounts. You see the User Accounts window shown in Figure 6-1. The existing accounts appear in the lower part of the window.

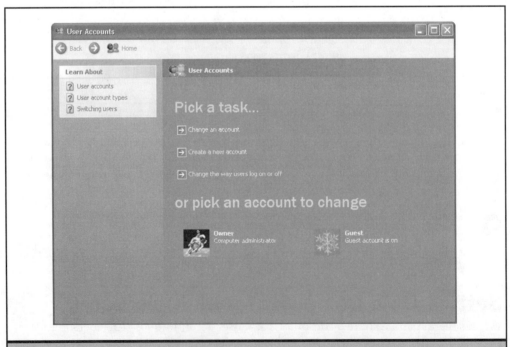

Figure 6-1. *Creating or changing user accounts (when logged on with an administrative account)*

Displaying Local Users and Groups in the Microsoft Management Console

For more advanced settings, you need to use the Local Users And Groups utility in the Microsoft Management Console (MMC), a program that can display various Windows configuration tools (see Chapter 35, section "The Microsoft Management Console"). The Local Users And Groups utility is not available in Windows XP Home Edition, but in Windows XP Professional, choose Start, right-click My Computer, and choose Manage from the menu that appears. You see the Computer Management window. Open the System Tools item in the left (tree) pane, if it's not already open, by clicking its plus box. Click Local Users And Groups to see the Users and Groups folders, and click the Users or Groups folder to see its contents (as shown in Figure 6-2).

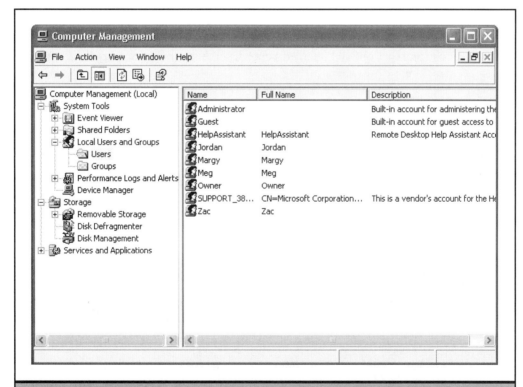

Figure 6-2. *The Computer Management utility displays information about the user accounts and groups defined on the computer.*

Controlling How Users Log On

As the administrator of your PC, you can choose how Windows asks people to log on. You have two choices:

- **Welcome screen** The Windows XP Welcome screen displays a picture and name for each user account, so that users click the one they want. If the user account has a password, a white box appears in which the user types a password.

- **Classic logon screen** Windows Me/9x–style logon screen, in which you type the user account name and password. Fast User Switching isn't available if you use the Classic logon screen (see "What Is Fast User Switching?").

If you use the Welcome screen, you can also choose whether or not to enable Fast User Switching. To choose between the Welcome screen and the Classic login screen, and to enable or disable Fast User Switching, you must be logged in with an administrator account. Follow these steps:

1. Make sure that you are the only user who is logged on (see "Managing Multiple Users").

2. Choose Start | Control Panel, and click User Accounts to display the User Accounts window (see Figure 6-1).

3. Click Change The Way Users Log On Or Off. You see the User Accounts window shown in Figure 6-3.

4. Make your selections using the Use The Welcome Screen check box and the Use Fast User Switching check box, and click the Apply Options button.

If security is a concern, use the Classic logon screen, which doesn't display the names of the user accounts. If a person has to type both a user name and a password, they need to know twice as much to break into your system.

Creating and Deleting Groups

Windows comes with groups for the three types of user accounts: Administrator user accounts are in the Administrators group, limited user accounts are in the Users group, and the Guest account is alone in the Guest group. Windows XP Professional has other groups (Backup Operators, Network Configuration Operators, Power Users, Remote Desktop Users, Replicator, and HelpServicesGroup) which are usually used only on domain-based LANs.

If you have Windows XP Professional, you can create new groups, assign users to groups, and delete groups by using the Local Users And Groups item in the Computer Management window (see "Displaying Local Users and Groups in the Microsoft Management Console"). (Windows XP Home Edition doesn't include the Local Users And Groups program.) You can change a group's name and its members, and you can grant the members of the group permission to use specific files and folders (see "Keeping Your Files Private").

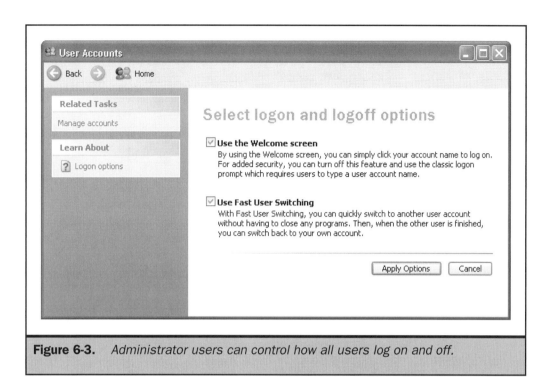

Figure 6-3.   *Administrator users can control how all users log on and off.*

Note   *Domain-based accounts, which are stored in the Active Directory program running on a Windows server, have domain groups. You can't define or change domain groups unless you have access to the Windows authentication services that control the domain's user accounts and groups.*

To create a local group, follow these steps:

1. Log on with an administrator account.

2. Choose Start, right-click My Computer, and choose Manage to display the Computer Management window (see Figure 6-2).

3. Open the Local Users And Groups folder and then the Groups folder.

4. Choose Action | New Group to display the New Group window.

5. Type a name for the group (don't use the name of an existing group) and a description (optional).

6. Click Create. Then click Close. The new group appears on the list of groups.

To add members to a group, select the group from the list in the Groups folder and choose Action | Add To Group. When you see the group Properties dialog box (shown in Figure 6-4), click Add to see the Select User dialog box, type the user account name

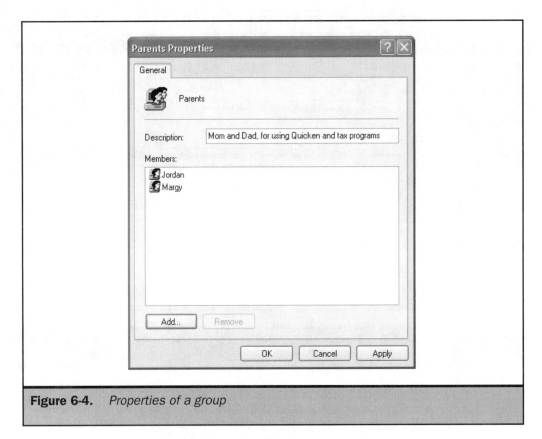

Figure 6-4.   *Properties of a group*

in the Name box, and click OK. (The other settings in the Select User dialog box apply
to domain-based networks.) To remove a user from a group, click the user account
name in the group Properties dialog box and click Remove.

To rename a group, select it and choose Action | Rename. Feel free to rename
groups that you have created, but don't rename any of the groups that come with
Windows, because these names may be referred to in Windows utility programs.

To change the rights that a group gives to its members, the next section describes
how to see and change the User Rights Assignment settings.

Other Security Options

Windows XP Professional (not Home Edition) has many other security options, but
most are of interest only if your computer is on a domain-based LAN. Here's a quick
once-over of *policy settings*—settings that control how accounts, passwords, and
groups work.

If you want to look at policy settings that control users' passwords, how many
times someone can type the wrong password before Windows locks the user account,
and which rights are assigned to which groups, you can open the Local Security
Settings window (see Figure 6-5). Choose Start | Control Panel, click Performance

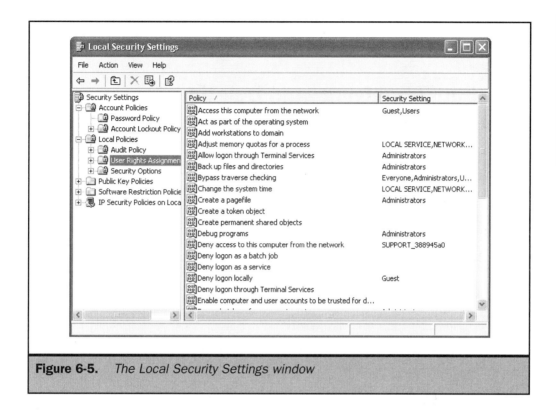

Figure 6-5.   *The Local Security Settings window*

And Maintenance, and click Administrative Tools. From the Administrative Tools window, run the Local Security Policy program. (Or, choose Start | Run and type **secpol.msc** and press ENTER.)

The folders listed on the left side of the window contain groups of policy settings:

- **Password Policy (in the Account Policies folder)**   Control whether user accounts need passwords, how complex they need to be, and how often people have to change them.

- **Account Lockout Policy (in the Account Policies folder)**   Control whether user accounts are *locked out* if someone types the wrong password more than a specified number of times.

- **Audit Policy (in the Local Policies folder)**   Control what security events are included in audit log files.

- **User Rights Assignment (in the Local Policies folder)**   Control which groups of user accounts can perform which types of tasks.

- **Security Options (in the Local Policies folder)**   Include a variety of security settings, including who may install printers, use the CD-ROM and floppy drives, and whether you can shut the system down without logging on.

Click a setting and click the Properties button on the toolbar (or right-click the setting and choose Properties) to see what the options are for that policy setting.

Creating, Modifying, and Deleting User Accounts

If your user account is an administrator account and you run Windows XP Professional, you have full control over local user accounts. If you have an administrator account on Windows XP Home Edition, you can change a limited number of user account settings. (On a domain-based network, you don't have control over domain accounts.) Limited account users can change only their own user account, and the Guest account can't change user accounts at all.

Creating New User Accounts

Follow these steps to create a local user account in the User Accounts window:

1. Choose Start | Control Panel, and click User Accounts to display the User Accounts window (see Figure 6-1).

2. Click Create A New Account. Windows prompts you for the account name and the type of account. You have only two options: computer administrator or limited.

3. Click Create Account. Windows creates the account.

New accounts start with the Windows default settings, as well as settings that have been stored for all users. For example, when programs are installed, they usually create desktop icons and Start menu commands in the C:\Documents And Settings\All Users folder, so that all users, including new user accounts, can run the program.

If you have Windows XP Professional, you can also create new accounts in the Computer Management window, which lets you set many more configuration options for the account. Follow these steps:

1. Choose Start, right-click My Computer, and choose Manage from the menu that appears. You see the Computer Management window shown in Figure 6-2.

2. Open the Local Users And Groups folder and then the Users folder.

3. Chose Action | New User to display the New User dialog box (shown in Figure 6-6).

4. Fill in the information about the user account (see "What Configuration Settings Do Local User Accounts Have?").

5. Click Create. Windows creates the user account and adds it to the Users group. The first time that the user logs on, Windows creates a My Documents folder for the account.

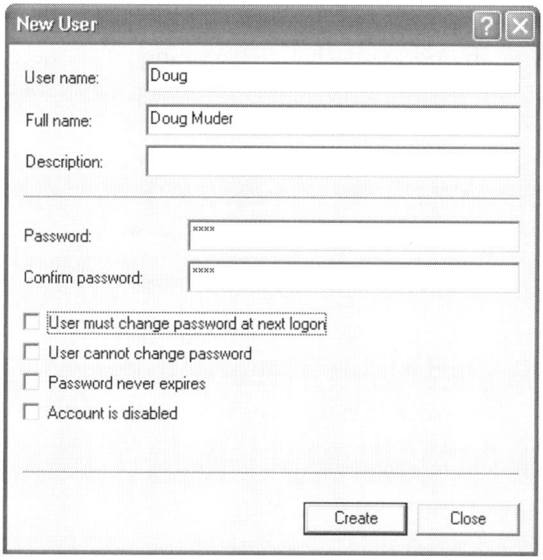

Figure 6-6.   *Adding a new user*

Tip   *Unless you don't care about security, be sure to modify the new account to have a password, as described in the next section.*

Modifying User Accounts

You can change a few user account settings from the User Accounts window, and (if you have Windows XP Professional) most of the rest of the settings from the Computer Management window. A few options, such as the locations of the My Documents and Favorites folders, are set in other ways. The configuration settings you can set for user accounts are listed in Table 6-2 earlier in this chapter.

Modifying Basic User Account Settings

If you want to modify the name, picture, or account type for a user account by using the User Accounts window, follow these steps:

1. Choose Start | Control Panel, and click User Accounts to display the User Accounts window (Figure 6-1).

2. In the lower part of the window, click the name of the account you want to change. You see a list of the settings that you can change. These are

   ■ **Name**   Name that appears on the Welcome screen and at the top of the Start menu. It's also the name of the folder in C:\Documents And Settings that contains the settings for this user account. You can't rename the Guest account. When you rename an account, the renaming doesn't take full effect until you log off and log back on. Renaming a user account doesn't change the name of the user's folder in C:\Documents And Settings—Windows continues to use the folder with the old name.

- **Picture** Picture that appears to the left of the user account name on the login screen and Start menu. Windows XP comes with a small selection of pictures you can use, or you can click Browse For More Pictures to specify a graphics file of your own. Click Change Picture when you have selected the picture you want to use.

- **Account type** Administrator or limited. You can't change the type of the Guest account, and you can't change other accounts to be guest accounts.

- **Password** Password that the user has to type when logging on. The Guest account has no password, and you can't create one. See the next section for how to create a password for an account. Once an account has a password, you can remove the password later.

3. Click a setting and enter the new value.

4. To return to the list of user accounts, click the Back button on the toolbar or click Change Another Account.

If you are modifying your own account, you see another option: Set Up My Account To Use A .NET Passport. Clicking this option runs the .NET Passport Wizard, which asks a series of questions about your e-mail address, a password, a secret question and answer to be used to help you remember the password if you forget it, and your location. This passport enables Windows to identify you when you visit Microsoft-owned Web sites such as **www.microsoft.com**, **www.msn.com**, and **www.hotmail.com**, as well as shopping sites that use the Microsoft Passport service. The Wizard suggests that you use a Microsoft-operated mailbox if you have an address there (addresses at hotmail.com and msn.com—Microsoft still uses Windows to sell its Internet services), but any e-mail address works. Once you've configured your account to use your .NET Passport, you can click Change My .NET Passport to switch to a different .NET Passport or to change information that is part of the Passport. You must be able to connect to the Internet to set up or change your .NET Passport, because Microsoft's servers store that information.

We recommend that you rename the Administrator account to use another name. Breaking into your system is harder if the hacker doesn't know the name of an existing user account, especially an administrator account.

Modifying Advanced User Account Settings

To modify other user account settings you need to use the Local Users And Groups program in the Computer Management window, which is not available in Windows

XP Home Edition (see "Displaying Local Users and Groups in the Microsoft Management Console"). Follow these steps:

1. Choose Start, right-click My Computer, and choose Manage from the menu that appears. You see the Computer Management window, as shown in Figure 6-2.

2. Open the Local Users And Groups folder and the Users folder.

3. Click a user account and click the Properties button on the toolbar. Or, right-click a user account and choose Properties from the menu that appears. You see the Properties dialog box for the user. The General tab contains the same information as the New User dialog box shown in Figure 6-6. The Member Of tab is for adding this user account to groups. The Profile tab is shown in Figure 6-7.

4. Make your changes and click OK.

Tip   *When you specify a pathname that includes the user account name (such as the pathname of the user's My Documents folder), you can type %**user name**% instead of the user account name. This trick enables you to enter the same path for different users' settings.*

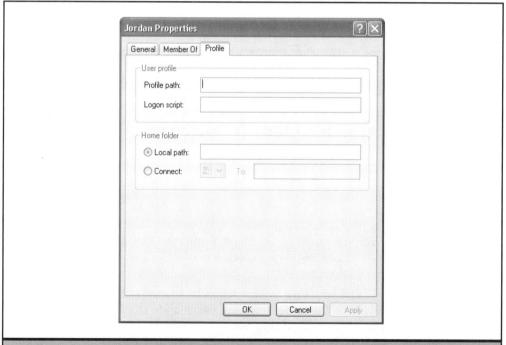

Figure 6-7.   *The Profile tab of the Properties dialog box for a user account*

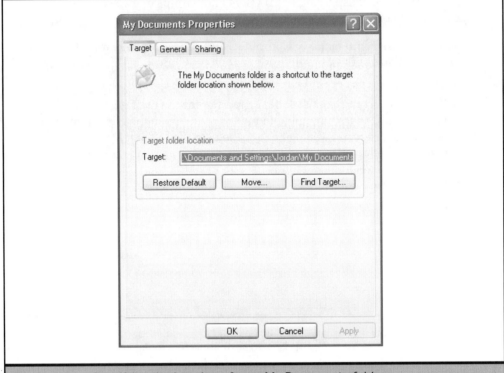

Figure 6-8. *Specifying the location of your My Documents folder*

Changing the Location of the My Documents Folder

The My Documents folder for a user is normally in C:\Documents And Settings\ *username*\My Documents (assuming that Windows is installed on C:). You can tell Windows XP Home Edition or Professional to use a different folder instead, by following these steps:

1. Click Start, right-click My Documents, and choose Properties from the menu that appears. You see the My Documents Properties dialog box, with the Target tab selected (see Figure 6-8). The Target box contains the current location of your My Documents folder.

2. To tell Windows that you want to store your files in another folder, click the Move button and browse to the folder in which you plan to store (or already store) your files. You can click the Make New Folder button if the folder doesn't exist yet. Click the My Network Places link if you want to choose a folder on another computer on your network. Click OK when you have selected the folder.

3. To switch back to the original (default) location of the My Documents folder (in C:\Documents And Settings*username*), click the Restore Default button.

4. Click OK. Windows asks if you want to move the files that are in your old My Documents folder to your new My Documents folder.

5. Click Yes or No.

Keeping your My Documents folder on a separate disk drive or partition makes it easy to back up or move your files separately from your programs. Wherever it is, be sure to back up your My Documents folder regularly.

Changing the Start Menu for All Users

Each user can customize her own Start menu, but an administrator user can customize everyone's Start menus with one command. For example, you might want to add a command to display a program that everyone in your workgroup will use, or a shortcut to a shared folder. Here's how:

1. Right-click the Start button and choose Open All Users from the menu that appears. You see the Start Menu window, which is an Explorer window displaying the files that make up the default Start menu for all user accounts. These files are usually stored in C:\Documents And Settings\All Users\Start Menu (if Windows is installed on C:).

2. If you want the command to appear in everyone's All Programs menu, open the Programs folder. Otherwise, stay in the Start Menu folder to create a command that appears on everyone's Start menu.

3. Choose File | New | Shortcut to run the Create Shortcut Wizard.

4. Following the Wizard's prompts, create a shortcut to the program, folder, or file that you want on everyone's Start menu.

The shortcut you create appears on each user's Start or All Programs menu the next time each person logs on. You can use the Start Menu window to move or delete shortcuts for all users, too.

Adding or Removing Passwords

If you don't want other people to be able to log on as you, assign your account a password. When you create a password for your own account, Windows also offers you the option of a private My Documents folder—one that other people can't open. If an administrator creates a password for you, your My Documents folder is already private.

Follow these steps to add a password to your own user account in the User Accounts window (administrators can use the same steps to add a password to another user's account):

1. Choose Start | Control Panel, and click User Accounts to display the User Accounts window (see Figure 6-1).

2. Click the name of the account to which you want to add a password.

3. Click Create A Password. You see the User Accounts window, as shown in Figure 6-9.

4. Type the password into each of the first two boxes (you see only dots, in case someone evil is looking over your shoulder). You can also type a password hint (that is, a word or phrase that will remind you of your password, without giving it away to anyone else) in the third box.

5. Click Create Password when you have typed the password and password hint.

6. If you are setting a password for your own user account, Windows asks, "Do you want to make your files and folders private?" Click Yes Make Private to create a private folder for your files, or click No not to. If you choose Yes Make Private, your My Documents folder can only be opened by you and by administrators.

7. To create a password reset disk for use in case you forget your password, click Prevent A Forgotten Password on the Related Tasks list in the Task pane. You see the Forgotten Password Wizard.

8. The Wizard steps you through creating a password reset disk. You need a blank, formatted floppy disk, and you need to know your current password.

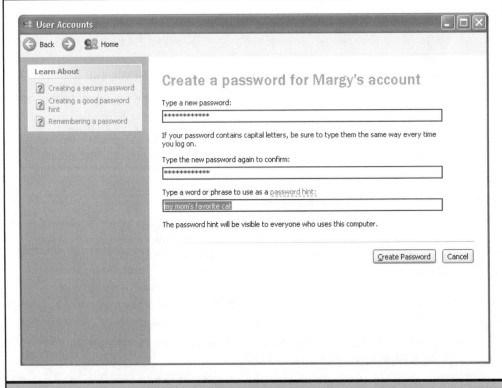

Figure 6-9. *Changing the password for a user account*

If you have an administrator or power user account and you use Windows XP Professional, you can create or remove passwords from a user account by using the Computer Management window. Follow these steps:

1. Choose Start, right-click My Computer, and choose Manage from the menu that appears. Click the Local Users And Groups item. You see the Computer Management window, as shown in Figure 6-2.

2. Right-click the user account and choose Set Password from the menu that appears. You see a dire warning about lost files, but this warning appears to refer to files that the user has encrypted with a password (see Chapter 8, section "What Are Attributes?"). We're not actually sure that *any* information will be lost, but we can't guarantee it. If you choose to go ahead, you see the Set Password dialog box.

3. Type the new password in each of the two boxes and click OK.

4. Let the user know his new password, and suggest that he change it as soon as possible to a password he can remember.

You can remove the password from your own account (or if you have an administrator account, from other user's accounts). If you don't want the user account to have a password any more (so that anyone can log on by clicking the user name on the Welcome screen), open the User Accounts window, click Remove The Password (or Remove My Password, if it's your account), and then click the Remove Password button to confirm.

If you change your password later (and we recommend that you change it from time to time), you don't need to recreate the password reset disk.

We recommend that you create passwords for all your user accounts. If you're not worried about security, make all the passwords the same, but don't omit them altogether, unless your computer isn't connected to the Internet. We don't know of specific holes in Windows XP user account security, but why take a chance?

Enabling and Disabling the Guest Account

If you set up passwords for your accounts, you may also want to make sure that the Guest account is disabled (Windows disables it by default). If the Guest account is enabled, anyone can use your computer without a password.

To disable the Guest account, choose Start | Control Panel, and click User Accounts to display the User Accounts window. Click the Guest account and click Turn Off The Guest Account. You can turn it back on again by clicking the Guest account from the User Accounts window and clicking the Turn On The Guest Account button.

Deleting User Accounts

If someone with a user account on your computer will never, ever use the computer again, you can delete the user account. When you delete the account, Windows deletes the user's internal security ID (SID), and even if you create a new account with the same name, it will have a new SID, and a new profile and settings. So don't delete a user account if the person will be away temporarily—disable it instead.

To delete a user account, an administrative or power user can use either the User Accounts window or the Computer Management's Local Users And Groups utility (for Windows XP Professional users)—we recommend the User Accounts window, because it cleans up the user's account folders when it deletes the account. (You can't delete the account you are currently using.) In the User Accounts window, select the account name and click Delete The Account. Windows asks what you want to do with the files on the user's desktop and in the user's My Documents folder. Click Keep Files to move the files to a folder on the desktop, or click Delete Files to delete them. Either way, the user's folder in C:\Documents And Settings is deleted.

You can also use the Local Users And Groups program in the Computer Management window to delete a user. However, if you use the Action | Delete command in the Computer Management window to delete a user account, the user's folder remains in the C:\Documents And Settings folder, which strikes us as untidy.

To temporarily disable an account in Windows XP Professional, open the Computer Management window (click Start, right-click My Computer, and choose Manage from the menu that appears), click Local Users And Groups, click the Users folder, right-click the user account, choose Properties from the menu that appears, and click the Account Is Disabled check box. While a user account is disabled, it doesn't appear on the Welcome screen, and you can't log onto it from the Classic logon screen, either.

Using a Shared Computer

Unlike Windows Me/9x, with Windows XP you are always logged on with a user account (either a local user account or a domain account). If you haven't yet set up user accounts, you are logged on automatically as Administrator or Owner. Once you set up additional user accounts, you can log on as any user (as long as you know the appropriate password), logging out when you are done. Using the new Fast User Switching feature, you can also switch from one user account to another in the middle of your work.

Don't use Administrator, Owner, or any administrator account for your day-to-day computer work. You can do less accidental damage from a limited account.

Logging On

Once you have created user accounts, whenever your computer powers up or a user logs off, you see a logon screen. If you are not on a LAN, or you are connected to a peer-to-peer workgroup-based LAN, you normally see the Welcome screen, as shown

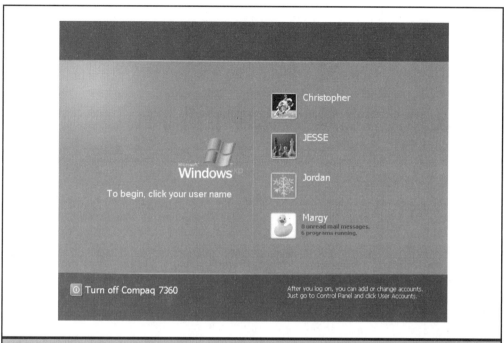

Figure 6-10. *The Welcome screen greets you when you start up Windows, log out, or press WINDOWS-L to switch users.*

in Figure 6-10. If your system is configured to display the Classic logon screen, or your computer is connected to a domain-based network, you see the Log On To Windows dialog box instead (see "Controlling How Users Log On"). Either way, click or type your user name and type your password, if your account has a password (and we recommend that it does). Windows loads your user account and you see your desktop.

When you see the Welcome screen, you can switch to the Classic logon screen by pressing CTRL-ALT-DELETE twice. This trick is useful if you want to log on using the Administrator or Owner account that Windows creates automatically but doesn't usually display on the Welcome screen.

Resuming Work after Locking Windows

If your computer is configured to use the Welcome screen for logging on, pressing WINDOWS-L (that is, holding down the WINDOWS key and pressing *L*) to lock the computer also displays the Welcome screen (see Figure 6-10). Log back in to continue working. If your computer uses the Classic logon screen and you press WINDOWS-L, you see the Unlock Computer window, prompting you to enter your password to continue.

Since Fast User Switching isn't available with the Classic logon screen, if you log on as another user, Windows logs off your original user account.

Logging Off

If you are done working, but you don't want to shut down the computer, you can log off. Choose Start | Log Off, and click the Log Off button to confirm that you mean it. Windows exits all your programs, logs you off, and displays the Welcome screen (or the Classic logon screen).

Switching Users

When Windows starts up, you choose which user to log on as by clicking or typing the user name in the Welcome screen or the Classic logon screen. If Windows is already running, you can switch users by logging off and letting the other user log on.

Fast User Switching provides a faster way to switch users: pressing WINDOWS-L. Alternatively, you can choose Start | Log Off, and click the Switch User button. When you see the Welcome screen, log on as another user. When you switch users with this method, Windows doesn't exit the programs you were running: instead, they continue running in the background until you switch back to the first user account.

Setting the Screen Saver to Require You to Log Back On

If you are worried about someone using your computer when you step away from it, you can set the screen saver to require you to log back in using your user account name and password. Follow these steps:

1. Right-click a blank place on the desktop and choose Properties to display the Display Properties dialog box (see Chapter 11, section "What Are Display Properties?").
2. Click the Screen Saver tab and set the Screen Saver box to an option other than None.
3. Select the On Resume Display Welcome Screen check box.
4. Click OK.

Now when you return to your computer and click a key or move the mouse to wake Windows up, it displays the Welcome screen.

Changing Your Password

You can change your own password any time. Follow these steps:

1. Choose Start | Control Panel, and click User Accounts to display the User Accounts window (see Figure 6-1).
2. If you have an administrator account, you see the list of user accounts. Click yours.

3. Click Change My Password. (If you are an administrator changing someone else's password, the command is Change The Password.)

4. Type the existing password and your new password (twice). Also type a password hint, to remind you of your password if you forget it.

If you created a password reset disk for your user account, you don't have to create or modify the disk when you change your password.

 Be sure to create a password reset disk for yourself: it saves lots of headaches if (when) you forget your password. Choose Start | Control Panel, click User Accounts, and choose Prevent A Forgotten Password from the Task pane.

Keeping Your Files Private

If Simple File Sharing is disabled on your computer (as described in the section "What Is Simple File Sharing?" earlier in this chapter), your folders are stored on a drive or partition formatted with NTFS, and you use Windows XP Professional, you can see and set who has permission to open your folders or files.

To see the permissions for a file or folder, right-click it in an Explorer window and choose Properties from the shortcut menu that appears. You see the Properties dialog box for the file or folder. Click the Security tab, which only appears for files and folders on NTFS drives when Simple File Sharing is disabled (see Figure 6-11).

The Security tab shows who has permission to do what with the file or folder (see "What Are Permissions?"). Table 6-5 (which appears earlier in this chapter) lists what these permissions allow. Select an entry in the Group Or User Names, and the permissions for that group or user account appear in the Permissions list in the lower part of the dialog box. For permissions that are allowed, you can click the Deny check box to revoke this permission for this user or group. For permissions that are denied, you can click the Allow check box. If you don't have permission to change the permission, the check box appears dimmed.

Sharing Files with Other Users

To store your files so that other users of your computer can read, edit, or delete them, store the documents in the Shared Documents folder that appears under My Computer in the folder tree. (This folder is actually called C:\Documents And Settings\All Users\Shared Documents, assuming that Windows is installed on C:.) All users, including the Guest account, can open the files in the Shared Documents folder. To see the Shared Documents folder, choose Start | My Computer and click Shared Documents in the Other Places part of the Task pane.

 If you haven't disabled the Guest account, then files in the Shared Documents folder can be opened by anyone who uses the computer (see "Enabling and Disabling the Guest Account").

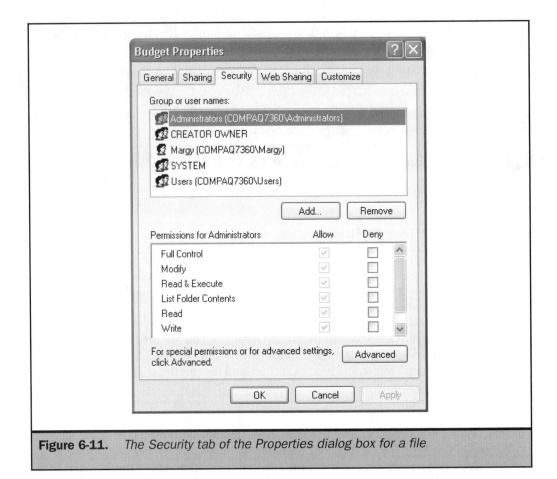

Figure 6-11.   *The Security tab of the Properties dialog box for a file*

If you want only some people to be able to read or modify material you store in Shared Documents, see the preceding section for how to set the permissions for a file or folder.

Running a Program as Another User

If you know the password for another user account, you can run a program as if you were logged on as that user. Some older programs can't run unless the user account has full rights on the system (for example, it insists on making system configuration changes that would ordinarily be forbidden for your user account). The Run As dialog box enables you to run a program and specify what user account to run it as.

To see the Run As dialog box (shown in Figure 6-12), hold down the shift key while you right-click an icon for the program (either on the desktop or in an Explorer

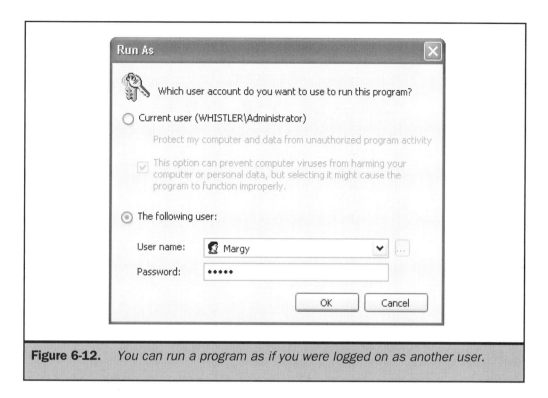

Figure 6-12.   *You can run a program as if you were logged on as another user.*

window). Choose Run As from the menu that appears. In the Run As dialog box, click The Following User, type the user account name, enter the password (or leave the Password box blank if the user account has no password), and click OK.

Note   *Instead of typing the user account name, you can try clicking the down-arrow button at the right end of the User Name box to see a list of user accounts. If no accounts appear, type the computer name, a backslash, and the user account name to specify a user on your computer. For example, if your computer's name is GRACELAND and the user account's name is Elvis, type **GRACELAND\Elvis**.*

You can create a shortcut to a program that is set to run a program as another user. Follow these steps:

1. If the shortcut doesn't already exist, create it: Right-click the program's icon on the desktop or in an Explorer window and choose Create Shortcut from the menu that appears (or use another method to make the shortcut).

2. Right-click the shortcut and choose Properties to see the Properties dialog box for the shortcut.

3. Click the Advanced button on the General tab. You see the Advanced Properties dialog box, which offers the Run With Different Credentials option, as shown here:

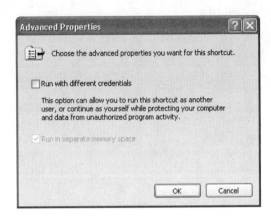

4. Click the Run With Different Credentials check box and click OK.

Each time you run the shortcut, Windows displays the Run As dialog box (shown in Figure 6-12) to ask you for the user name and password. Or, you can right-click the shortcut and choose Run As to see the Run As dialog box (no need to hold down the SHIFT key).

Managing Multiple Users

As an administrator or power user, you can keep track of who is logged on and who has programs running. You can also help users who have forgotten a password.

Managing Logged-In Users

In Windows Me/9x, the term "Task Manager" referred to buttons on the taskbar for the program that were currently running as well as to a program could who you what programs were running. In Windows XP, the Windows Task Manager is a program that can show you the tasks that the computer is currently doing, which users are currently logged on, and more.

The two easiest ways to display the Task Manager are by pressing CTRL-ALT-DELETE and by right-clicking a blank place on the taskbar and choosing Task Manager from the menu that appears. You see the Task Manager, with tabs for Applications, Processes, Performance, Networking, and Users. To see who is using the computer, click the Users tab (see Figure 6-13).

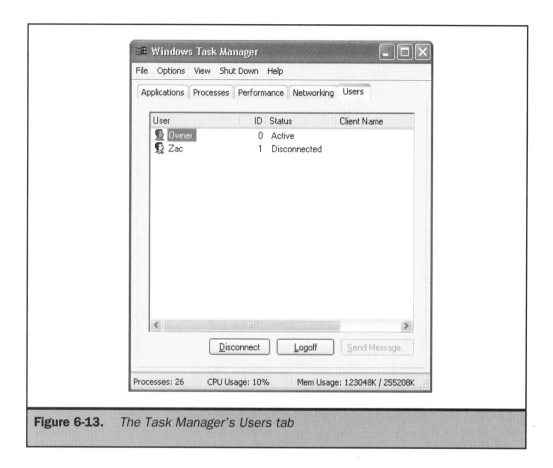

Figure 6-13. *The Task Manager's Users tab*

If you are an administrator, you see a list of the users who are logged on. (Other users just see an entry for themselves.) The user who is currently using the computer (you, presumably) has the status Active, while other logged-on users are Disconnected.

To switch to another user, click the currently active user and click Disconnect. To log a user out, click the user and click Logoff.

You can send a message to another logged-in user by selecting the user and clicking Send Message. When you see the Send Message dialog box, type the text of your message and click OK. The next time you switch to that user, the user sees a message box like this:

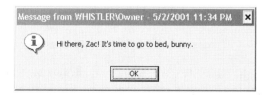

Unlocking a Locked-Out Account

If someone tries to break into your computer, she may try guessing a user's password, entering a series of wrong passwords. You can tell Windows XP Professional to lock an account after someone has tried a specific number of wrong passwords (Windows XP Home Edition doesn't support this). This feature is called *account lockout*.

To tell Windows to lock out accounts if someone enters a series of wrong passwords, you can specify three security policy settings:

- **Account Lockout Threshold**   How many wrong passwords causes Windows to lock out the account. Entering 0 turns off account lockout. To turn on account lockout, enter a number between 1 and 999 (we recommend 3).

- **Account Lockout Duration**   How long the lockout lasts, in minutes. After the duration (usually 30 minutes), Windows automatically unlocks the account. You can enter a number from 1 to 99,999.

- **Reset Account Lockout Counter After**   How long Windows waits after the last wrong password is entered before restarting the account lockout counter, in minutes (usually 30 minutes). After this amount of time, Windows starts counting at 1 again the next time someone starts entering wrong passwords. This must be shorter than, or the same as, the account lockout duration.

To turn account lockout on or off, follow these steps:

1. Choose Start | Control Panel, click Performance And Maintenance, and run Administrative Tools. You see the Administrative Tools window.

2. Run the Local Security Policy program (which doesn't come with Windows XP Home Edition). You see the Local Security Settings window.

3. Open the Accounts Policies folder in the list at the left, and click the Account Lockout Policy folder. At the right, you see the three account lockout settings.

4. To turn on account lockout, click Account Lockout Threshold and click the Properties button on the toolbar. Enter a number 1 or greater (try 3). Click OK.

5. Windows lets you know that by turning on account lockout, you are also setting the other two settings to their default values. Account Lockout Duration and Reset Account Lockout Counter After are now both 30 minutes. Click OK.

6. If you want to change the duration or reset time, click the setting and click Properties on the toolbar.

When someone has tried to log on with the wrong password too many times, Windows locks the account. An administrative or power user on Windows XP Professional can unlock the account before the Account Lockout Duration has passed. Follow these steps:

1. Choose Start, right-click My Computer, and choose Manage from the menu that appears. You see the Computer Management window, as shown in Figure 6-2.

2. Open the Local Users And Groups folder and the Users folder.

3. Click a user account and click the Properties button on the toolbar. Or, right-click a user account and choose Properties from the menu that appears. You see the Properties dialog box for the user.

4. On the General tab, if the user account is locked out, the Account Is Locked Out check box is selected. Clear the check box to enable the user to use this account again (and assign the person a new password!).

Setting Quotas for Disk Usage

For NFTS drives and partitions, you can limit users' files to a specified amount of disk space. Follow these steps:

1. In an Explorer window (choose Start | My Computer), find the drive or partition for which you want to set quotas.

2. Right-click the drive or partition and choose Properties from the shortcut menu. You see the Properties dialog box for the drive or partition.

3. Click the Quota tab, as shown in Figure 6-14. (The Quota tab doesn't appear for FAT32 and FAT drives.)

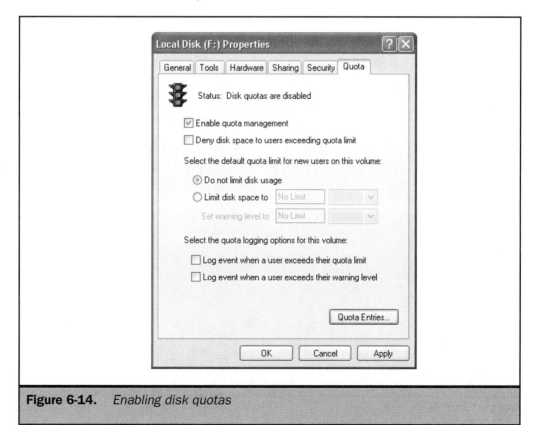

Figure 6-14.   *Enabling disk quotas*

4. Select the Enable Quota Management check box. If you don't want to let people exceed their quotas, select the Deny Disk Space To Users Exceeding Their Quota Limit check box (otherwise, Windows displays a warning, but still allows the file to be stored).

5. Click the Limit Disk Space To *xx* radio button, and set the box to its right to the limit you want to set for new user accounts. Set the amount of space at which you want users to receive a warning, too. Be sure to change the right-hand box from KB to MB unless you are setting a *very* small limit.

6. If you want Windows to create a system log entry each time a user goes over quota, select one or both of the check boxes at the bottom of the dialog box.

7. To set limits for existing user accounts, click the Quota Entries button. You see the Quota Entries dialog box, shown in Figure 6-15. Widen the Name and Logon Name columns by dragging the column header dividers rightward, so you can read the user account names. Listed users who are under their quotas appear with "OK" in the Status column.

8. The Quota Entries dialog box includes an entry for the Administrators group account, with no limit. To set a limit for a user account, choose Quota | New Quota Entry from the menu bar, or click the New Quota Entry button on the toolbar. You see the Select Users dialog box:

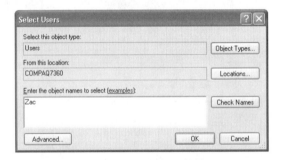

9. Type a user account name into the Enter Object Names To Select box and click OK. You see the Add New Quota Entry dialog box:

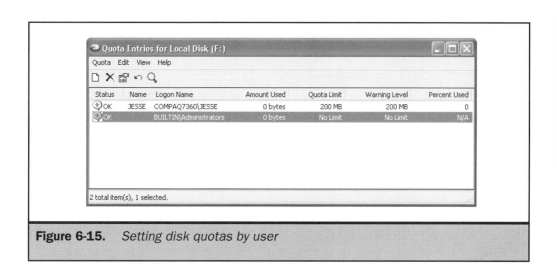

Figure 6-15.   *Setting disk quotas by user*

10. Click the Limit Disk Space To *xx* radio button, and set the limit. Click OK.

11. You can change the limits for existing quotas by selecting the entry in the list in the Quota Entries dialog box and clicking the Properties button on the toolbar (or by right-clicking the entry and choosing Properties from the menu that appears).

12. When you are finished setting quotas, close the Quota Entries dialog box and the Properties dialog box for the drive or partition.

Tip   *If you don't want to limit how much space people use, but you want to track space usage, quotas are still useful. Enable quotas, but don't choose to deny disk space to people who exceed their quotas. Select the check boxes that cause Windows to log whenever people exceed their quotas, and watch your log files. To see when people have exceeded their quotas, click Start, right-click My Computer, and choose Manage to open the Computer Management window. Click the plus box to the left of Event Viewer in the list of items to see the types of logs available, and click the System log.*

The Complete Reference

Part II

Managing Your Disk

Chapter 7

Using Files and Folders

Computers are tools for working with information—creating it, accessing it, and rearranging it. Windows stores information in files and organizes those files into folders. Everything you do with your computer involves files and folders.

This chapter describes the basic file-and-folder skills you need to operate your computer. The next chapter discusses the longer-term issues involved in managing your files efficiently. This chapter explains the anatomy of the Explorer windows in which you manipulate files and folders, and their toolbars. It tells how to use Windows Explorer to create, select, name, open, move, copy, and delete files and folders. You also learn the easiest ways to undo or recover from common mistakes, as well as how to burn your own CDs.

This chapter assumes you are working with the default settings of Windows Explorer—the way Windows Explorer works before you change anything. The next chapter covers how to adjust Windows Explorer to suit your tastes and habits.

What Are Files and Folders?

Files and folders are two of the most fundamental concepts of the Windows operating system. No matter what you use your computer for, you create and organize files and folders as soon as you decide to save your work. If you have worked with any other operating system, you are probably already acquainted with the concept of a file. You probably are familiar with folders as well, though you may know them as *directories*. If you aren't already familiar with files and folders, spending a small amount of time learning their properties will serve you well.

What Is a File?

A *file* is any collection of related information that is given a name and stored so it can be retrieved when needed. A file may contain any kind of information: a program or application (WordPad, for example, is in a file called Wordpad.exe); a document; a part of a document, such as a table or an illustration; a sound or piece of music; a segment of video; or any number of other things.

Many files are part of the Windows system itself. Windows uses files to store the information it needs to function, such as information regarding the appearance of your desktop, the kind of monitor or printer you use, the various dialog boxes and error messages, or how to display different fonts. Similarly, the applications on your computer typically have a number of auxiliary files in addition to the file containing the main program. Some of these files, for example, contain the choices you make about the program's optional settings. When you change these settings, you are not altering the program itself; you are editing some of its auxiliary files.

What Is a Folder?

Because of all the files associated with Windows and the various applications on your computer, your hard drive contains thousands of files before you begin creating files of your own. If your computer is part of a network, you may have access to millions of files. The Internet has billions of files. You would have no hope of keeping track of all those files if they weren't organized in some efficient way. In Windows (as in most other major operating systems), the fundamental device for organizing files is the folder.

Technically, a *folder* is just a special kind of file—one that contains a list of other files. The files on the list are said to be *in* the folder, and each file is allowed to be in only one folder. A folder can be either open or closed. When a folder is closed, all you see is its name and the folder icon, as shown here:

Windows comes with several folders that Microsoft suggests you use for your files—My Documents, My Music, and My Pictures. Another icon, My Computer, looks like a folder, and contains all the disks accessible from your computer. These customized folders have unique icons:

When a folder is open in Windows Explorer, it has its own window, and the files contained in the folder are displayed in the window.

The terms "file" and "folder" were chosen to remind you of a more familiar information retrieval system—the filing cabinet. Like the folders in a filing cabinet, the Windows folders are named objects that contain other objects. For example, a Windows folder named Budget might contain four spreadsheet files for First quarter, Second quarter, Third quarter, and Fourth quarter.

What Is the Folder Tree?

The organizational power of the folder system comes from the fact that it is *hierarchical*, which means folders can contain other folders. This feature enables you to organize and keep track of a great many folders, without straining your memory or attention.

If Folder A is inside Folder B, Folder A is a *subfolder* of B. Any folder can contain as many subfolders as you want to put there, but each folder (like each file) is contained in only one folder. In the same way, a mother may have many daughters, but each daughter has only one mother. And so, a diagram showing which folders are contained in which other folders looks something like a family tree. This diagram is called the *folder tree*, or sometimes the *folder hierarchy*. Windows Help calls it the *folder list*.

Figure 7-1 shows the top levels of the folder tree as they appear in the Folders Explorer bar. At the top of the folder tree (the founder of the Folder family, so to speak) is the desktop. Immediately under the desktop are My Computer, My Documents, My Network Places, and Recycle Bin, plus whatever files and folders you might have copied to the desktop. The manufacturer of your computer may also have put some files or folders on your desktop.

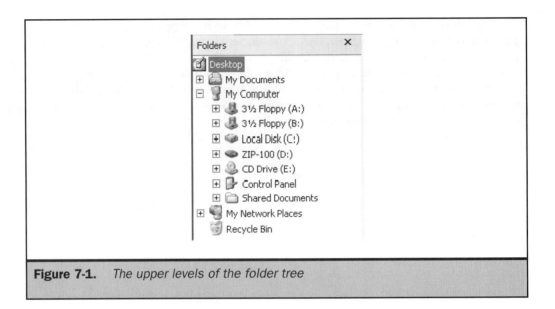

Figure 7-1.   *The upper levels of the folder tree*

   The My Computer icon may not appear on your desktop. But My Computer still shows up directly under the desktop in the folder tree.

Underneath My Computer are icons representing all of your system's storage media: hard drives, floppy drives, CD-ROMs, and so on. (Your system configuration may differ somewhat from that pictured in Figure 7-1.) Also under My Computer is the Control Panel, the window you use for configuring your computer.

What Are Filenames?

To store a file and retrieve it later, Windows has to give it a *filename*. Often you are asked to invent a name for a file. Good filenames are evocative without being too cumbersome. They also have to conform to some rules. Fortunately, the file-naming rules were liberalized when Windows 95 came out, and Windows XP retains these liberalized rules. You can change a filename using Windows Explorer, as well as in the Open and Save As dialog boxes of many applications.

What Filenames Are Legal?

In DOS and Windows systems prior to Windows 95, filenames could be only eight characters long, followed by a three-character extension that told the file's type—Filename.txt, for example. Inventing coherent, easily remembered filenames was an art similar to composing good vanity license plates. Even so, one frequently had to stare at files like jnsdecr.doc for some time before remembering it was John's December report.

Fortunately, Windows 95 changed all that by introducing long filenames, and Windows XP retains that advance. File and folder names can be up to 215 characters long, and can include spaces. So jnsdecr.doc can become John's December Report.doc.

Folders, likewise, can have names up to 215 characters long. These names are automatically of type "folder" and have no extension.

In addition to periods and spaces, some characters that were illegal for file and folder names prior to Windows 95 are now legal, including

+ , ; = [ ]

Still, there are some characters you can't use in filenames, including

\ / : * ? " < > |

and any character you make by using the CTRL key.

What Are Extensions and File Types?

Filenames are still followed by a period and an *extension*, which is usually three letters long. The extension denotes the *file type* and, among other things, tells Windows which program to use to open the file and which icon to use to represent the file. Windows handles most file-type issues invisibly. Files you create with a particular program are typically given a type associated with that program (unless you specify otherwise), and the appropriate extension is added to the name automatically. For example, Web pages usually have the extension .htm or .html, and text files usually have the extension .txt.

You can do many things in Windows without paying any attention to file types; therefore, Windows doesn't even show you the extensions unless you ask to see them. We recommend you configure Windows to display extensions for two reasons: to help you know the complete names of your files and to help you determine the types of files you receive from others. To see the extensions:

1. Choose Start | Control Panel. You see the Control Panel window.

2. Select the Appearance And Themes category, and then click the Folder Options icon. The Folder Options dialog box appears. You can also display this dialogue box by choosing Tools | Options from any Explorer window.

3. Click the View tab. The Advanced Settings box contains a long list of options.

4. Click the check box next to Hide File Extensions For Known File Types. If the box is checked, the extensions are hidden; if it's not checked, the extensions are shown.

5. Click OK to make the Folder Options dialog box go away, and close the Control Panel.

When you install a program, the installation program usually tells Windows the file types the program handles (see Chapter 3, section "What Happens During Program Installation?").

What Are Addresses?

An *address* is information that tells you (and Windows) how to find something. The four kinds of addresses are:

- **File addresses**   Tell you how to find files on your computer. A typical file address looks something like C:\Windows\Explorer.exe.

- **UNC (Universal Naming Convention) addresses**   Used when referring to files on some local area networks (LANs). UNC addresses are in the format *computername**drive**pathname*, where *computername* is the computer's name on the LAN, *drive* is the disk drive on that computer, and *pathname* is the file address on that drive. For example, if you needed to open a file called Budget03.xls in the C:\My Documents folder on a computer named DebB, you'd open \\DebB\C\My Documents\Budget03.xls.

- **Internet addresses**   More properly called *URLs*, specify how to find things on the Web (see Chapter 24, section "What Is a URL?"). The URL of Microsoft's home page, for example, is **http://www.microsoft.com**.

- **E-mail addresses**   Tell you how to find the e-mail boxes of the people to whom you want to write. You can comment on this book, for example, by writing to **winxptcr@gurus.com**.

The Address box in Windows Explorer handles every kind of address except e-mail addresses. Typing a file address into the Address box opens the corresponding file or folder on your computer, typing a UNC address opens the corresponding file or folder on your local area network (if your computer and the computer that has the file or folder are logged into the LAN and you have permission to open it), and typing a URL opens the corresponding Web page on the Internet (if your computer is online).

> **Note**   *E-mail addresses are still handled differently from the other kinds of addresses. You can send e-mail by typing **mailto:** followed (with no space) by an e-mail address into the Address box windows runs your e-mail program and starts a message to that address (see Chapter 23).*

File addresses, also called *paths* or *pathnames*, work in the following way: files and folders are stored on disks. Each disk drive has a drive letter that is its address (see Chapter 32, section "What Are Drive Letters?"). Drives A and B typically are reserved for floppy drives, and C denotes your computer's main hard drive. Subsequent letters are used for other hard drives, CD-ROMs, tape drives, removable drives, drives on other computers on your LAN (if any), and other devices. In file addresses, drive letters are always followed by a colon (:).

Each file or folder address begins with the letter of the drive on which the file or folder is stored. The *root folder*—the main, or top-level, folder on the disk—is designated by a backslash immediately after the drive letter and colon. (So C:\ is the root folder of drive C.) The rest of the address consists of the names of the folders on the folder tree between the given file or folder and the drive that contains it. The folder names are separated by backslashes (\).

For example, the address C:\Windows\Temp refers to a folder named Temp, inside the folder named Windows, which is stored on the C drive. If the file Junk.doc is contained in Temp, Junk.doc's address is C:\Windows\Temp\Junk.doc.

> **Note**   *Both file addresses and UNC addresses use backslashes (\) to separate the pieces of the address. But URLs (for historical reasons) use slashes (/) for the same purpose.*

What Is Windows Explorer?

Windows Explorer is a versatile tool for viewing and manipulating files and folders. It appears whenever you choose Start | My Computer and you can also run it by choosing Start | All Programs | Accessories | Windows Explorer. The program has many features that you can display or hide, and several different views of the features it displays.

Windows Explorer is a twin of Internet Explorer, which is the Windows built-in Web browser (see Chapter 24, section "What Is Internet Explorer?"). Running either program opens an *Explorer window*. The Explorer window is extremely versatile and has many parts, which you may or may not decide to display. When all parts of the Explorer window are made visible, it looks like Figure 7-2.

The major parts of the Explorer window are

- **The title bar**   Displays the name of the open folder and (optionally) the pathname (the list of the folders that contain the open folder).

- **The menu bar and various toolbars**   You issue commands to Windows Explorer by clicking toolbar buttons or making selections off the menus.

- **The working area**   Displays icons corresponding to all the files and folders contained in the open folder. The contents of subfolders don't appear in the working area.

- **The status bar**   Displays information about the objects you select.

- **The Task pane**   Presents easy ways to do tasks that Windows guesses you might want to do with the selected object.

- **The Explorer bar**   In Figure 7-2 this is set to display the folder tree.

You can make the toolbars, Explorer bar, Task pane, or status bar appear or disappear (see Chapter 8, section "Configuring Windows Explorer"). When

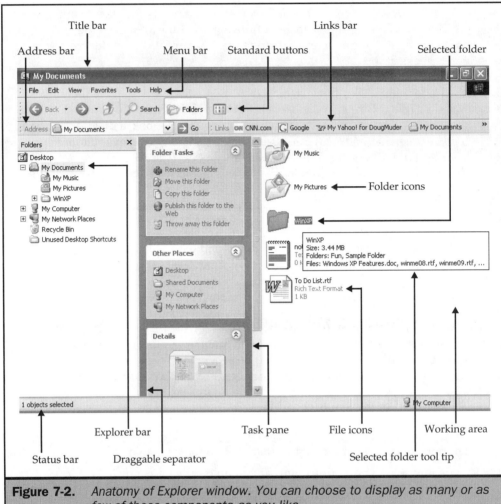

Figure 7-2. Anatomy of Explorer window. You can choose to display as many or as few of these components as you like.

the Explorer window is stripped down to its absolute minimum, the same folder in Figure 7-2 looks like this:

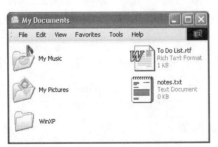

What Is the Address Box?

The *Address box*, which appears on the Address Bar toolbar of Windows Explorer, displays the name of the open folder. The Address box looks like this:

When you click the arrow at the right end of the Address box, a diagram appears. It displays the top levels of the folder tree, and allows "long-range navigation" by clicking any top-level item you want to open.

Another way to choose which folder to view is to type into the Address box the address of the file or folder you want to open. The Address box accepts file addresses, network addresses, and Web addresses (see "What Are Addresses?"). If your computer is online, you can open a Web page by typing its address into the Address box and clicking the Go button to the right of the Address box. Depending on what options you have chosen elsewhere, your computer may automatically dial up your Internet provider to open the Web page (see Chapter 22, section "Setting Additional Dial-Up Options").

What Is the Standard Buttons Toolbar?

The *Standard Buttons toolbar* is an optional feature of Windows Explorer. Like most features of Windows Explorer, you can configure it to look the way you want (see Chapter 8, section "Configuring the Standard Buttons Toolbar"). In the default configuration, it looks like this:

The three leftmost toolbar buttons are navigation buttons: Back, Forward, and Up. They behave like the corresponding Web-browser buttons. The Back button takes the window back to the previous folder it displayed, and the Forward button undoes Back. The Back and Forward buttons have arrows attached to them; clicking the arrow produces a drop-down list of locations to which you can go back or forward. Clicking the Up button causes the window to display the folder that contains the currently displayed folder; that is, it moves the window up the folder tree.

 These buttons behave differently if you have configured Windows Explorer to open each folder in its own window (see Chapter 8, section "Opening a New Window for Each Folder").

The next two buttons—Search and Folders—are Explorer bar options. In Figure 7-2, for example, the Folders button has been clicked, and the Explorer bar displays the folder tree.

The Views button enables you to choose among several options for representing the contents of a folder (see Chapter 8, section "Changing Views"). Right-clicking anywhere in the toolbar enables you to select which toolbars are shown. This menu is the same one you see by choosing View | Toolbars.

What Is the Links Toolbar?

The *Links toolbar* is a toolbar you can fill with links to files, Web sites, or applications. When you first install Windows XP, it contains buttons that connect to various Microsoft Web sites, but you can customize it to contain whatever links you find useful (see Chapter 8, section "Configuring the Links Toolbar"). It can look like this:

In this example, the bar contains links to four Web sites (CNN, Google, My Yahoo, and Amazon), an application (Notepad), and a folder (My Documents). If you have more items on the Links toolbar than can be displayed at one time, a double arrow appears at the right end of the Links toolbar. Clicking this arrow shows you a menu of the remaining links.

What Is the Explorer Bar?

The Explorer window usually contains a separate pane with additional information. Two things can appear there: the Explorer bar and the Task pane (which is described in the following section).

The *Explorer bar* provides a variety of tools to help you find files and get a higher-level view of how your files are organized. To change what you see in the Explorer bar, select an option from the View | Explorer Bar menu or click the corresponding button on the toolbar. The choices are

- **Search** Helps you find files or folders on your computer system, Web pages on the Internet, or people in a directory (see Chapter 8, section "Searching for Files and Folders"). To display it, choose View | Explorer Bar | Search (or press CTRL-E). You can also access the Search Explorer bar by selecting one of the options under Start | Search.

- **Favorites** Shows you a list of favorite files, folders, and Web sites (see Chapter 24, section "Using Favorites, Links, and Internet Shortcuts"). If you are online, clicking an entry for a Web site displays the site. In the default configuration, the Favorites button isn't on the toolbar, but you can always use the menu command View | Explorer Bar | Favorites (or press CTRL-I).

- **Media** Puts a media player into the Explorer bar and displays some links to WindowsMedia.com (see Chapter 19). Choose View | Explorer Bar | Media.

- **History** Displays a daily list to whatever files or Web sites you have opened in either Windows Explorer or Internet Explorer (see Chapter 24, section

"Examining History"). To see it, choose View | Explorer Bar | History (or press CTRL-H).

- **Folders**   Displays the folder tree. When the Explorer bar displays the folder tree, we call it the *Folders Explorer bar*. Choose View | Explorer Bar | Folders.

You can make the Explorer bar disappear by clicking the *X* in the upper-right corner of the Explorer bar or by clicking the selected (pressed in) button on the toolbar. You can resize the Explorer bar by dragging the boundary that separates it from the working area.

In the default configuration, only the Folders and Search Explorer bars have buttons on the toolbar. If you want other Explorer bars to have buttons, you can customize the toolbar (see Chapter 8, section "Configuring the Standard Buttons Toolbar").

What Is the Task Pane?

The *Task pane* (previously called the WebView pane in Windows Me) is a big blue column that sits between the working area and the Explorer bar. (If the Explorer bar isn't displayed, the Task pane occupies the left side of the window.) It has three major sections: Tasks, Other Places, and Details.

- **Tasks**   Suggests some tasks that you may want to perform. Clicking the suggestion starts you on your way to carrying out the task. The Tasks box is context sensitive. For example, if you haven't selected any items in the working area, it offers you the option to create a new folder. But if you have already selected a folder, it suggests copying, moving, or deleting the selected folder. The exact response you get when you click a suggestion varies according to the difficulty of the task. Clicking the Throw Away This Folder suggestion, for example, takes you to a confirmation box; if you click Yes the folder is sent to the Recycle Bin. Publishing something on the Web is a more complicated task, so when you click the Publish This Folder To The Web suggestion, the Web Publishing Wizard opens to guide you through the process. Depending on which folder you are looking at, the Tasks box may be called Folder Tasks, or you may see more than one Tasks box (for example, System Tasks and Folder Tasks).

- **Other Places**   A list of folders that you may want to jump to. The list varies according to the folder you are currently looking at. For example, My Computer is often on this list, but not if you already have My Computer open.

- **Details**   Shows you some of the properties of the selected object or objects, for example, the size of a file or when it was last modified. If the selected file is an image, the Details box contains a small picture of the image (called a *thumbnail*).

> ## Where Is the Desktop Really?
>
> The Windows interface makes the desktop look as if it contains all your hard disks, floppies, CD-ROMs, and other storage devices. But the desktop is only a virtual object, not a piece of hardware; so where is the desktop folder stored?
>
> Each user has his or her own desktop folder. The shortcuts, files, and folders you move to the desktop are actually stored in the folder C:\Documents And Settings*username*\Desktop (assuming that Windows XP is installed on C:).

All of these boxes have arrows in their upper right-hand corners. An up arrow indicates that the box is currently expanded, and that you can contract it by clicking the arrow. A down arrow indicates that the box is contracted and that you can expand it by clicking the arrow.

 If the Explorer window isn't wide enough to display both the Task pane and the Explorer bar, Windows omits the Task pane, and you have to close the Explorer bar to see it.

What Is the Status Bar?

The *status bar* is the bar at the very bottom of an Explorer window (and many other windows, too). It displays information about any selected object. When a file is selected, for example, the status bar shows the file's type and size. When a drive is selected, it displays the free space and capacity of the drive. When a folder is open and no object is selected, it tells you the number of objects in the folder and how many of them are hidden. To display it, choose View | Status Bar.

When you are connected to the Internet or another network, the right end of the status bar tells you the security zone of the open folder. If the folder is on your own computer, the My Computer icon is displayed.

What is a Tool Tip?

Many objects in the Explorer window have *tool tips* associated with them. A tool tip is a small yellow or white box that appears when you let the cursor linger over an object. Figure 7-2 shows the tool tip associated with a folder named WinXP. The tool tips of files or folders give some of the same information you could find in the Details box of the Task pane. The tool tips of toolbar buttons tell you the names of the buttons.

What Is the Recycle Bin?

Files and folders deleted from your hard drives don't go away completely, at least not right away—they remain inside the *Recycle Bin*. From there, they can either be restored to the folder they were in before you deleted them or moved from the Recycle Bin to any other folder via cut-and-paste or drag-and-drop.

The Recycle Bin icon lives on the desktop and looks like a wastebasket. When you open the icon, Windows Explorer shows you the files and folders that were deleted since the Recycle Bin was last emptied.

Recycle Bin

The Recycle Bin is a hybrid object that behaves like a folder in some ways, but not in others. Like a folder, it contains objects, and you can move objects into and out of the Recycle Bin, just as you do with any other folder. Unlike a folder, even an unusual folder like the desktop, the Recycle Bin is not contained on a single drive. Instead, each of your computer's hard drives (or partitions of hard drives, if your drive is partitioned) maintains its own Recycle Bin.

Folders that have been sent to the Recycle Bin aren't considered part of the folder tree: They don't appear in the Folders Explorer bar, and they can't be opened. If you want to examine the contents of a folder in the Recycle Bin, you first must move the folder to another location. Likewise, files in the Recycle Bin cannot be opened, edited, or worked on otherwise.

The intention of the designers is clear: the Recycle Bin is not to be used as a workspace. Instead, it is a last-chance repository. You can put things in the Recycle Bin or take things out—that's all.

Working with the Recycle Bin under the default settings is covered in section "Retrieving Files and Folders from the Recycle Bin" later in this chapter. Reconfiguring the Recycle Bin settings is covered in the next chapter (see Chapter 8, section "Managing the Recycle Bin").

Working with Windows Explorer

When you Start | My Computer, Windows Explorer opens an Explorer window, as in Figure 7-2. Any folder you open from the desktop creates a new Explorer window. You can also run Windows Explorer by choosing Start | All Programs | Accessories | Windows Explorer. Alternatively, you can put a shortcut to Windows Explorer somewhere more convenient, such as the desktop, the Quick Launch toolbar, or top of the Start menu.

Every aspect of the Explorer window has numerous optional configurations, which are covered in the next chapter. This chapter describes how to do basic file and folder operations under the default configuration. If your computer works differently, someone has probably changed Windows Explorer's settings. If you want, you can change them back as follows:

1. Start Windows Explorer either by opening a folder on the desktop, choosing Start | My Computer, or by selecting Start | All Programs | Accessories | Windows Explorer. An Explorer window opens.

2. Select Tools | Folder Options from the menu bar. The Folder Options dialog box appears with the General tab selected.

3. Click the Restore Defaults button in the Folder Options dialog box.

4. Click OK.

Navigating the Folder Tree

Windows Explorer enables you to view the contents of any folder on your system. The process of changing your view from one folder to another is referred to as *navigating*. The Explorer window provides you with navigation tools that you will recognize if you have used a Web browser: You can go up or down in the folder tree and back or forth along the path you have taken. In addition, you can jump to any folder near the top of the folder tree by clicking its icon on the list that drops down from the Address box on the toolbar. You can also find a folder in the Folders Explorer bar and click its icon there to display its contents in the working area.

If you like to use the keyboard, you can use the UP-ARROW and DOWN-ARROW keys to move up and down a column of folders, or use the LEFT-ARROW and RIGHT-ARROW keys to move back and forth in a row. You can select a folder by typing the first letter of its name.

Viewing the Folder Tree with the Folders Explorer Bar

The Folders Explorer bar, shown in Figure 7-3, is a map of the folder tree. You can expand or contract this map to whatever level of detail you find most convenient. (Naturally, your folder tree will not have exactly the same folders as Figure 7-3.)

The folder tree is displayed outline-style in the Folders Explorer bar. At the top of the tree, displayed flush with the left edge of the window, is the Desktop icon. Below Desktop, and indented slightly to the right, are the folders contained in the desktop: My Documents, My Computer, My Network Places, Recycle Bin, and (in this example) Unused Desktop Shortcuts.

A folder that contains other folders has a small box next to it, called a *plus box* if it contains a plus sign and a *minus box* if it contains a minus sign. A plus box indicates that the folder has subfolders, but that they are not shown. A minus box next to a folder indicates that its subfolders are listed below and slightly to the right of folder. In Figure 7-3, My Documents contains My Music, My Pictures, and WinXP. The WinXP folder, in turn, contains Files, Fun, Publisher, and Sample Folder. My Computer and My Network Places contain subfolders that are not shown.

If the subfolders of a folder are not shown, you can display them (i.e., expand or open the folder) by clicking the plus box next to the folder's name. Clicking the minus box next to a folder's name removes its subfolders from the list (contracts or closes it, in other words). Any portion of the folder tree can be expanded as much or as little as you like.

The plus and minus boxes enable you to look at the overall structure of your files without losing sight of the folder whose contents are displayed in the working area.

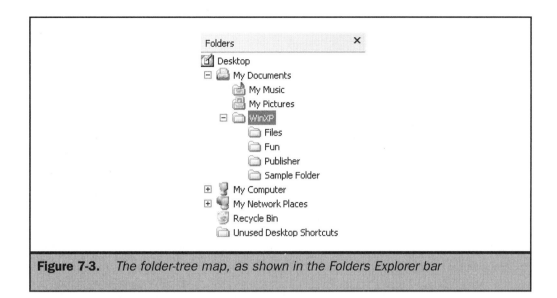

Figure 7-3.   *The folder-tree map, as shown in the Folders Explorer bar*

Opening a new folder in the working area automatically expands the folder tree in the Folders Explorer bar to show you the new folder. If you use the plus boxes in the Explorer bar to contract a folder that contains the currently open folder, that folder is closed and the working area changes to display the contents of the folder you just contracted.

You can also use the arrow keys with the Folders Explorer bar. The UP-ARROW and DOWN-ARROW keys move the cursor up and down the list of folders, while the RIGHT-ARROW and LEFT-ARROW keys expand and contract the currently selected folder.

When the folder tree expands beyond the limits of the left pane, scroll bars appear. If you want to see the full width of the folder tree, drag the border between the right and left panes to the right.

Navigating by Using the Address Box

The Address box on the Toolbar displays the name of the folder whose contents appear in the working area. An abbreviated folder-tree diagram drops down from the Address box. It shows only the top layers of the folder tree, together with the folders between the open folder and the drive that contains it. You can use this diagram to jump to a new location in the folder tree by clicking any of the icons shown.

Going Up and Down the Folder Tree

Under the default settings, the Up button on the toolbar (or the equivalent View | Go To | Up One Level command) "moves" the window up one level of indentation in the folder tree. The window then shows the contents of the folder containing the previously viewed folder. For example, if a window displays the contents of the

C:\Windows folder and you then click the Up button, a window displays the contents of the C drive. Click Up again, and you see the contents of My Computer. Wherever you begin, if you click Up enough times, you reach the desktop.

To move the window one step down the folder tree, open a subfolder of the currently open folder.

Going Back and Forth on the Folder Tree

Under the default settings, the Forward and Back buttons on the toolbar (or the equivalent commands View | Go To | Forward and View | Go To | Back) move the window back and forth among the previously displayed folders. The Back button returns to the previous open folder. Clicking the Back button again returns to the folder before that, and so on. The Forward button undoes the Back button: Clicking Back, and then clicking Forward leaves you where you started. Until you have clicked Back, there is no place to go forward to, so the Forward button is gray, indicating that nothing will happen if you click it. Similarly, once you have returned to the first folder you opened, the Back button turns gray.

Lists of folders to which you can go back or forward drop down when you click the arrows next to the Back and Forward buttons. Jump to any folder on the list by clicking its name.

Jumping to Somewhere Else Entirely

The arrow at the right end of the Address box pulls down a diagram showing the path that connects the open folder to the desktop, as well as the layers of the folder tree immediately under the desktop and My Computer. Open any of these folders by clicking its name in the list.

Jumping is particularly easy when you display the Folders Explorer bar (choose View | Explorer Bar | Folders). Just find the folder you want to view on the folder-tree map and click it.

Making and Working with Files and Folders

The basic file and folder operations—creating, selecting, naming, and opening—are relatively unchanged from earlier versions of Windows.

Creating Files and Folders

New folders and files of certain types can be created on the desktop or in Windows Explorer. On the desktop, right-click any empty area and choose New on the shortcut menu. In Windows Explorer, click the folder in which you want to create the new object and then choose File | New (or right-click any empty spot in the working area and choose New on the shortcut menu). All of these actions produce a submenu that lists the new objects you can create: folders, shortcuts, and a variety of types of files. Select an element of this list, and Windows creates the appropriate object. You can also create shortcuts by using this method (see Chapter 8).

You can create files of types other than the types listed from within application programs.

Selecting Files and Folders

Files and folders are represented on the desktop and in Windows Explorer by icons, with the name of the file or folder printed underneath or beside its icon. A *file icon* is a rectangle that looks like a piece of paper. The rectangle bears the design of the default program that opens the file. A Word file icon, for example, looks like this:

A *folder icon* looks like a manila folder. A compressed folder icon looks like a folder icon with a zipper on it.

Under the default settings, you select a file or folder by clicking its icon, and you open it by double-clicking. If you don't like all this clicking (or you're afraid of getting repetitive stress syndrome), you can adjust Windows Explorer so resting the cursor on an icon selects the corresponding object, and single-clicking opens the object (see Chapter 8, section "Replacing Double Clicks with Single Clicks").

To select more than one object, select the first object, and then press the CTRL key while you select others. (If you don't press CTRL, selecting one object deselects all the others.)

If the objects you want to select are close together, move the cursor to an empty spot nearby, hold down the left mouse button, and drag the cursor. A rectangle forms, and any object inside the rectangle is selected. When you release the mouse button, the rectangle disappears, but the objects it contained continue to be selected. You can get the same effect by using the SHIFT key instead of dragging the mouse: Select an object, and then hold down the SHIFT key and select another object. All objects in an imaginary rectangle containing the two selected objects are also selected.

More complicated patterns of objects can be selected by combining the two methods:

1. Drag out a rectangle that contains most of the objects you want to select (and perhaps some others). That is, click in one corner of an imaginary rectangle, hold down the mouse button, and drag the mouse pointer to the opposite corner of the rectangle.

2. Release the mouse button and press CTRL.

3. While pressing CTRL, deselect unwanted objects (if any) by clicking them.

4. Keep pressing CTRL, and select any additional objects you want by clicking them.

To select all the items in a folder, open the folder and choose Edit | Select All from the Explorer window's menu bar or press CTRL-A on the keyboard. To select all but a few objects in a folder, choose Select All, and then hold down CTRL while you deselect those few objects.

You can also use the keyboard to select multiple files. To select consecutive files in a single list or column, select the first file, then hold down the SHIFT key while pressing the DOWN-ARROW key until you reach the last file. To select all the files in a rectangular grid, select the file in one corner of the rectangle, then hold down the SHIFT key while pressing arrow keys until you reach the opposite corner.

To select files that aren't listed together, select one file, hold down the CTRL key, press the arrow keys to move to the next file you want to select, and press SPACEBAR to select it. Continue holding down the CTRL key, moving, and pressing SPACEBAR until you select all the files you want.

If you want to select most of the files in a folder, select all the items you don't *want to include. Then choose Edit | Invert Selection to deselect the selected items and to select the deselected ones.*

Naming and Renaming Files and Folders

Newly created folders and files are given default names, such as New Folder and New Microsoft Word Document. To rename a file or folder, select its icon and choose the Rename This File (or Rename This Folder) option from the Task pane, or right-click the icon and choose Rename from the shortcut menu. In either case, a box appears around the current name, and the entire name is selected. Type the new name in the box and press ENTER.

You can also rename by selecting an object and then clicking the name next to the icon. Again, a box appears around the current name and you proceed as before. Be sure to pause slightly between selecting the object and selecting its name—otherwise, you open the object.

If the new name is only a minor change from the old one, edit the old name instead of typing the new one. Click inside the name box at the place where you want to begin typing or deleting.

Changing a File's Extension

Changing a file's extension changes its file type. Don't do this unless you know what you're doing. If you assign the file a type that Windows doesn't recognize, it won't know how to open the file. If you assign the file a type Windows does recognize, whenever you open the file, Windows uses the application associated with that file type. Unless you prepare the file in such a way that is appropriate for that application, the opening fails. (Consider, for example, the Paint program trying to open an audio file—it doesn't work.)

Before you rename a file, check whether Windows Explorer is displaying the file extensions. (Just look at some files and see whether their names end with a period and three or four letters.) If file extensions are hidden, you can't change them when you rename a file. If they are displayed, you can change them. When you rename a file whose extension is displayed, you must include the extension in your renaming or else the file type is lost. Conversely, if you type in a file extension when the extension is hidden, you wind up with a double extension, like report.doc.doc. (It's perfectly legal to name a file report.doc.doc, but you could confuse yourself.)

  Windows always *displays file extensions that it doesn't recognize. You can tell that Windows doesn't recognize a file's extension if the file has a generic icon like this:*

If you change a file's extension (and, thus, its file type), Windows gives you a warning that the file may become unusable and asks you to confirm your decision. This feature, although annoying, may save you from making an occasional mistake.

Opening Files and Folders

You can open a folder by double-clicking its icon. The folder contents are displayed in an Explorer window.

Double-clicking a file icon opens the file using the default application for that file type. You can open a file in some other compatible application by right-clicking the file icon and selecting an application from the Open With menu, by dragging-and-dropping the icon onto an application's icon, or by using the File | Open command from the application's menu.

You can change the settings of Windows Explorer so only a single-click is required to open a file or folder (see Chapter 8, section "Replacing Double Clicks with Single Clicks").

Opening a File with the Default Application

If a file has a file type that Windows recognizes, double-clicking the file icon in an Explorer window opens the file with the application associated with that file type.

If you open a file in an Explorer window and Windows doesn't recognize its file type, or if that file type has no associated application, an Open With box appears, asking you to identify an application to use in opening the file.

Some file types may have more than one application associated with them (see Chapter 3, section "Associating a Program with a File Extension"). To check, right-click the file icon and see if a command like Edit appears under Open in the shortcut menu. For example, in the default configuration image files open with Image Preview but are edited with Paint.

Opening a File from the Open With Menu

At times, you might want to open a file with an application other than the one associated with its file type. For example, Windows by default associates HTML files (with extension .htm or .html) with Internet Explorer; but, if you want to open an

HTML file with Netscape Navigator instead, you can right-click the file's icon in an Explorer window (or the desktop) and select an application from the Open With menu. The Open With menu lists the applications that Windows knows can open the selected type of file. Initially, these are probably only Microsoft applications like WordPad or Paint. But if you don't see the application you want, select Open With | Choose Program to see an Open With dialog box and a larger list of applications. If you still don't see the application you want, click the Browse button in the Open With dialog box. A Browse window appears, allowing you to find the icon of the application you want.

When you have found and selected the application you want to use to open the file, click the Open button in the Browse window. You return to the Open With dialog box, and the application you found is now listed and selected. If you want this application to become the new default application for this file type, check the Always Use The Selected Program To Open This Kind Of File check box. Whether you have checked this box or not, click OK to make the Open With dialog box disappear and open the file.

This may seem like an arduous process just to open a file, but fortunately you only have to do it once. Now that you have used the Open With menu to open a file of this type with this application, the application should appear on the Open With menu for any file of this type. In addition, the application appears in the Open With dialog box for files of any type.

Opening a File by Dragging and Dropping

If both the file icon and the application icon (or shortcuts to either) are visible on your screen, drag-and-drop the file icon onto the application icon. If you do this frequently with a particular application, put its icon on the Links bar (see Chapter 8, section "Configuring the Links Toolbar"). Or, you can also create a shortcut to the application on the desktop (see Chapter 8, section "Making Shortcuts").

Opening a File from Within an Application

If an application is open, choose File | Open from its menu bar. The Open window appears and enables you to indicate which file to open.

Where Did My Buttons Go?

Previous versions of Windows Explorer had Move To, Copy To, Copy, Cut, and Paste buttons on the Standard Buttons toolbar. If you miss these buttons, you can put them back on the toolbar (see Chapter 8, section "Configuring the Standard Buttons Toolbar"). Meanwhile, you haven't lost any functionality—all these commands still appear on the Edit menu.

Rearranging Files and Folders

The quest for the perfect system of file organization is endless—you frequently need to move or copy files and folders to somewhere other than where they were originally created. You can rearrange your files and folders by using the following:

- Options on the Task pane
- Commands from the menus
- Drag-and-drop techniques

The commands corresponding to the options on the Task pane are also on the menus, the only difference being how the commands are issued, not what they do. This section first examines the Task pane and menu commands, and then the drag-and-drop techniques.

Moving and Copying Files and Folders

When a file or folder is selected in an Explorer window, the Task pane contains the options Move This File (or Folder) and Copy This File (or Folder). When several items have been selected, the options change to Move The Selected Items and Copy The Selected Items. If the Task pane isn't displayed, you can use the Edit | Move To Folder and Edit | Copy To Folder commands instead.

The Move To option is similar to cut-and-paste, and it has the effect of moving objects from a source folder to a target folder (see Chapter 5, section "Cutting, Copying, and Pasting"). The Copy To procedure resembles copy-and-paste, and it leaves separate copies of the objects in the source folder and the target folder.

Moving and Copying with One Explorer Window

To move (or copy) a file or folder, follow these steps:

1. Open the source folder.

2. Select the objects to be moved (or copied) from the working area of the Explorer window.

3. Click the Move (or Copy) option from the Task pane or select Edit | Move To Folder or Edit | Copy To Folder from the menu. A Move Items (or Copy Items) window opens, as shown in Figure 7-4.

4. Select the target folder in the Move Items (or Copy Items) window. This window and its plus boxes behave just like the Folders Explorer bar.

5. Click the OK button in the Move Items (or Copy Items) window.

Moving and Copying with Two Explorer Windows

If both the source and target folders are already open in their own Explorer windows, you can move and copy files and folders more easily without using the Move or Copy

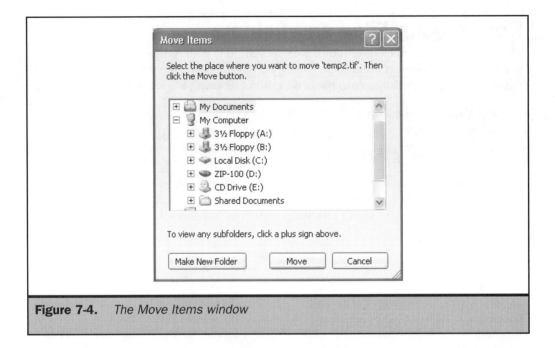

Figure 7-4.   *The Move Items window*

commands. You can drag-and-drop objects from the source window to the target window, or you can do the following:

1. Select the objects to be moved (or copied) from the source folder's window.
2. Select Edit | Cut (or Edit | Copy). Ghostly images of the objects remain in their original places until the objects are pasted elsewhere. (An alternative method is to select the objects with the right mouse button and then choose Cut or Copy from the shortcut menu.)
3. Click the spot in the target folder's window where you want to place the objects.
4. Select Edit | Paste button, or right-click an empty spot in the Explorer window and choose Paste from the shortcut menu.

Moving and Copying with the Folders Explorer Bar

When you see the Folders Explorer bar, you can use the icons it displays as target folders for either the cut-and-paste techniques described in the previous section or the drag-and-drop techniques described in the next section. If you want to move or copy entire folders, you can cut or drag them from the Folders Explorer bar into the working area, into other folders on the Explorer bar, or into other Explorer windows.

Dragging and Dropping Files and Folders

Drag-and-drop is often the simplest way to move or copy objects from one drive or folder to another or between a folder and the desktop (see Chapter 5, section "What Is

Drag-and-Drop?"). You can also delete objects by dragging and dropping them onto the Recycle Bin icon.

To drag and drop files or folders:

1. Set up window(s) so you can see both the source and the target folders (remember, the desktop itself is a kind of "window"). Our preference is to have the source folder open in the working area of an Explorer window, and the target folder visible in the Folders Explorer bar, but you can also have the source and target folders open in two separate Explorer windows.

2. Select the icons of the objects you want to move or copy.

3. While holding down the left mouse button, drag the icons to the target. (You can also drag with the right mouse button. This is discussed in the following paragraphs.) If the target is an open window, drag the icons to an open space in the window. If the target is a folder icon in an open window, drag until the cursor rests over the icon. The target icon changes color when you have the cursor in the right place.

4. Drop by releasing the mouse button.

Drag-and-drop has one unfortunate aspect. If you experiment, you soon notice it doesn't do the same thing in all circumstances—sometimes it moves an object, sometimes it copies it, and sometimes it makes a shortcut. The reason for this behavior is that the programmers at Microsoft have gone a bit overboard in trying to be helpful. Windows does what it guesses you intend to do, based on the file type of the objects being dragged, the locations of the source and target folders, and a few other things we haven't figured out.

Here's what happens when you drag-and-drop

- ■ **Objects to the same disk**   If you drag objects (other than programs) from one folder to another folder on the same disk, the objects are moved. They disappear from the source folder and appear in the target folder. Windows reasons that you are probably just rearranging your files. (Remember, the desktop is a folder on the C drive. Anything else on the C drive is considered on the same disk as the desktop.)

- ■ **Objects to a different disk**   If you drag objects (other than programs) from one folder to another folder on a different disk, the objects are copied. Separate copies exist in both the source and target folders. The rationale is that you are probably making a backup copy on another disk or making a copy to give someone else.

- ■ **Programs**   If you drag a program, it may behave like any other object but, for some programs, Windows makes a shortcut in the target folder and leaves the program file where it was in the source folder. We haven't come up with a firm rule describing this, although, in general, the more complex the program, the more likely it is that dragging and dropping it will create a shortcut. So, for example, you'll get a shortcut if you drag-and-drop Windows Media Player, but not Calculator.

Windows at least tells you what it's going to do with the objects you drop. When the object icons are in a droppable position, a tiny + appears next to them if they're going to be copied, while a tiny curved arrow (the same arrow that appears on shortcut icons) appears if a shortcut is going to be created. If nothing appears, the files are going to be moved.

If you want to use drag-and-drop, but you neither want to memorize how it works nor trust Windows to guess your intentions, drag with the right mouse button rather than the left mouse button. When you drop in the target folder, select the action you intended from the shortcut menu.

You can also control drag-and-drop behavior by using the keyboard: If you left-drag with the SHIFT key pressed, the objects are moved when you drop them. Left-dragging with the CTRL key pressed copies the objects when you drop them. You can easily remember this by noting Copy and CTRL both begin with C, or you are "shifting" a file from one location to another.

Using the Send To Menu

Send To is a menu found on the File menu of Explorer windows and on the shortcut menu when you right-click a file or folder. The Send To menu enables you to copy files to preselected locations quickly and easily. To use Send To for this purpose

1. Open a folder that contains files you want to copy.

2. Select the file(s) and folder(s) to copy (see "Selecting Files and Folders").

3. Choose File | Send To from the menu bar, or right-click the item(s) you selected and choose Send To from the shortcut menu. Either way, a menu of possible destinations appears. The Windows installation program creates a default Send To menu that varies according to the resources available to your computer. Here is a sample Send To menu:

4. Choose a destination from the Send To menu. The files are copied to the destination.

Send To is useful only if you want to move files to a destination that is on its menu. To add a new destination to the Send To menu, create a shortcut to that folder or disk in the folder C:\Documents And Settings*your username*\SendTo assuming that Windows XP is installed on C: (see Chapter 8, section "Making Shortcuts").

To delete an item from the Send To menu, delete the corresponding shortcut from C:\Documents And Settings*username*\SendTo.

 By default, the SendTo folder is hidden. To access it you must display hidden files and folders (see Chapter 8, section "What Are Hidden Files and Folders?").

Deleting Files and Folders

To delete a file, folder, or collection of files and folders in a single Explorer window

1. Select the objects to be deleted.

2. Do any of the following four actions: Click the Throw Away This File option on the Task pane, choose File | Delete from the menu bar, right-click the object and select Delete from the shortcut menu, or press the DELETE key on the keyboard. A dialog box appears that asks whether you really want to send the objects to the Recycle Bin (if they are deleted from your computer's hard drive) or delete the objects (if they are on a removable disk).

3. Click Yes in the dialog box.

Under the default settings, objects deleted from your computer's hard drives go to the Recycle Bin, from which they can be recovered. You can reset your preferences so objects are deleted immediately and don't go to the Recycle Bin (see Chapter 8, section "Streamlining the Deletion Process"). Objects deleted from floppy drives or other removable disks don't go to the Recycle Bin. For this reason, be especially cautious when deleting objects from floppies or other removable disks.

 You can delete files or folders directly, without sending them to the Recycle Bin, if you are certain you won't change your mind. To delete a file or folder irrevocably, select it, press SHIFT-DELETE, and then click Yes when the confirmation box appears.

Making Your Own CDs

All CD drives on computers can read CDs, but many can write CDs as well. Windows XP includes software for creating CDs.

What Are CD-R and CD-RW?

You can create two different kinds of CDs:

■ **CD-R** (compact disk recordable) disks can be written on once (they are *WORM*, or Write Once, Read Many). They can't be changed after they are written (though you can write on them many times until they are filled up). You can read CD-R disks in normal computer CD-ROM drives, as well as in audio

CD players, so CD-R is the type of CD to use when creating music CDs or CDs to distribute to lots of people. Blank CD-Rs are relatively cheap (we've seen them for as little as ten cents apiece in the United States).

■ **CD-RW** (compact disk rewritable) disks can be written and rewritten many times, like a floppy disk. CD-RW disks can be rewritten about 1,000 times. You can use them as removable storage for sets of files that you want to update regularly (as a backup media). However, they are only readable in other CD-RW drives, and sometimes only by the same model drive. So, for example, you might put all your documents on a CD-RW and conveniently carry them to the other side of the world, where you could read and update them on another computer with a compatible CD-RW drive.

Both types of writable CDs hold approximately the same amount of data: about 650MB for 74-minute disks and about 700MB for 80-minute disks. CD-R drives can write only CD-R disks, not CD-RW disks. CD-RW drives can write both types of disks.

CD-Burning Basics

To create (or *burn*) a CD-R or CD-RW, you collect a group of files that you want to save on the CD, and then write them in one *session*. You can write multiple sessions to both CD-R and CD-RW disks, but not all CD-ROM drives will be able to read them: Audio CD players usually see only the first session on a CD-R disk, and data CD-ROM drives usually see only the last session. (Multisession CDs, packet-writing, and other more advanced CD topics are covered in the excellent CD-Recordable FAQ by Andy McFadden, on the Web at **http://www.cdrfaq.org**.)

Previous versions of Windows required third-party software to save files on CD-Rs and CD-RWs. If you do a lot of work with CD-Rs and CD-RWs you may still find it convenient to get software like Easy CD Creator (**http://www.roxio.com**) or Nero Burning (**http://www.ahead.de**). However, Windows XP integrates CD into Windows Explorer. When you put a CD-R or CD-RW disk into your CD-R or CD-RW drive, Explorer recognizes what kind of disk it is and integrates it into the folder tree.

Before you store files on a CD, you decide what files to include in the session and how you want them arranged before you write any of them to the disk. For this reason, Windows provides a staging area on your hard drive that has the same capacity as the CD you plan to write. As you move files to and from the icon of your CD-R or CD-RW drive, the files are not actually written to the CD, but instead are copied to the staging area.

Burning CDs from Windows Explorer

Once you know what you want to store on a CD, and whether you have a CD-R or CD-RW drive, follow these steps to create a CD-R or CD-RW disk:

1. Buy some blank disks from your local computer store or mail-order or online catalog. Be sure to check whether you are getting CD-R or CD-RW disks.

2. Place the disk in the CD-R or CD-RW drive and close the drawer. Windows indicates that it has detected a CD by flashing a CD-ROM icon next to your mouse pointer. After Windows scans the disc and determines that it is indeed blank, an Explorer window for the disk opens.

3. Drag or copy all items that you wish to store on the disk into the new window and arrange them into folders as you like. For audio disks, arrange the files into the order in which you want the tracks to appear. Your data will appear on the disc in exactly the same way you arrange it.

4. Click the Copy Files To CD button in the Task pane. You see the CD Copy Wizard.

5. Follow the wizard's instructions and wait. In approximately 12–15 minutes you have a freshly burned CD. The more information you are writing on the CD, the longer it takes to complete.

6. Try out the CD in the type of drive in which you want it to work (audio CD player, computer CD drive, CD-R drive, or CD-RW drive).

Fixing Your Mistakes

Even the most experienced computer user occasionally clicks the mouse, and then stares at the screen in horror, asking, "What did I just do?" Fortunately, the horror needn't be lasting—Windows provides tools for recovering from many common errors.

Fixing Big Mistakes

Computers have been known to start misbehaving after you install new software, add a hardware device, or otherwise change delicate settings. Understanding exactly what has gone wrong and fixing it can be a laborious and unrewarding process, and sometimes you just don't care. You just want to put things back the way they were and forget this ever happened.

Windows XP contains a powerful tool for addressing these situations, System Restore (see Chapter 35, section "Returning Your System to a Predefined State with System Restore"). Using System Restore, you can return your computer's hardware/software configuration to the way it was on some previous date—when it presumably worked better than it does now.

Reversing Your Last Action Using the Undo Command

Windows Explorer has an Undo command that allows you to recover quickly from simple mistakes like deleting or moving the wrong file. Just press CTRL-Z on the keyboard or select Edit | Undo from the menu. Repeat either of these commands to step back through your recent actions. If you find yourself undoing mistakes frequently, you may want to add an Undo button to the Standard Buttons toolbar (see Chapter 8, section "Configuring the Standard Buttons Toolbar").

Retrieving Files and Folders from the Recycle Bin

If you change your mind about deleting a file or folder and it's too late to use the Undo command described in the previous section, you can still retrieve it from the Recycle Bin—if it was deleted from a hard drive and you haven't emptied the Recycle Bin in the meantime.

Emptying and configuring the Recycle Bin is discussed in the next chapter (see Chapter 8, section "Managing the Recycle Bin").

Opening the Recycle Bin

The easiest place to find the Recycle Bin is on the desktop, where its icon looks like a wastebasket. You can also find the Recycle Bin on the folder tree directly under the desktop, below your computer's disk drive and other devices.

Searching the Recycle Bin

If you know exactly what file or folder you are looking for, any view will do. But if the Recycle Bin is crowded and you need to do some real detective work to determine which objects you want to retrieve, the Details view (shown in Figure 7-5) is best. Choose View | Details from the menu bar. The working area becomes a list with columns showing the following:

- The name and icon of the file or folder
- The address of the folder from which the object was deleted
- The date and time the object was deleted
- The size
- The file type
- The date and time the object was last modified

Clicking the column header sorts the list according to that column's attribute. For example, if you know the date when you deleted the file, click the Date Deleted header to put the objects in the order in which they were deleted. All objects deleted on the same date you deleted the file appear together. If you remember the name of the file, but know you deleted several versions of it, clicking the Name header arranges the list alphabetically by name. All the versions appear next to each other, and you can easily see which is the most recent version.

Recovering Objects from the Recycle Bin

The simplest way to recover an object from the Recycle Bin is to follow these steps:

1. Open the Recycle Bin.
2. Select the object (or collection of objects) you want to recover.
3. Choose File | Restore from the menu bar.

You can also right-click the item you want to recover and choose Restore from the shortcut menu.

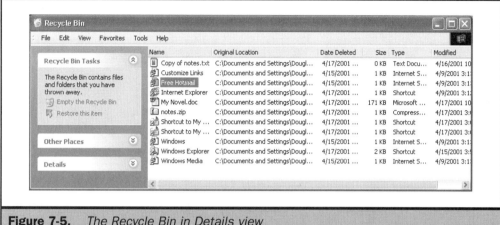

Figure 7-5. *The Recycle Bin in Details view*

The object returns to the folder it was deleted from—the address given in the Original Location column of the Details view. If the object is a folder, all its contents return with it. You can use Restore even if the object was deleted from a folder that no longer exists. A folder of the appropriate name is then created to contain the restored object. You can restore everything in the Recycle Bin to its original location by clicking the Restore All Items option on the Task pane.

To recover an object, but to put it in a new place, you can either cut-and-paste from the Recycle Bin to the new location, or do the following:

1. Open the Recycle Bin.
2. Expand the folder tree in the Folders Explorer bar so the target folder icon is visible.
3. In the working area, select the object(s) you want to recover.
4. Drag-and-drop to the target folder on the Explorer bar.

Retrieving Files with Third-Party Tools

When a file or folder is emptied from the Recycle Bin, Windows doesn't immediately do anything rash like overwrite the corresponding disk space with zeroes. Windows simply removes the file from its file allocation table, so the disk space the file occupied is no longer reserved. If that disk space is needed for something else, Windows writes over it but, until then, the information stays on the disk. (Think of a restaurant with a lazy busboy; the tables don't get cleared until more customers come.)

A number of applications have been written to recover this information and reassemble the file, but none are part of Windows XP. Two of the best known are Norton Utilities by Symantec (on the Internet at **http://www.symantec.com**) and McAfee Utilities (at **http://www.mcafee.com**). Unfortunately, these programs work only if you have installed them *before* you delete the files you want to retrieve.

The
Complete
Reference

Chapter 8

Managing Files
and Folders

The previous chapter explained what you need to know to start working with files and folders: creating and deleting them, opening them, seeing what's in them, naming them, and moving them from one place to another. This chapter discusses issues that may not come up immediately as you work with files and folders, but that you should know about if you are going to have a long-term relationship with your computer.

To a beginner, having a lot of choices is more of a burden than a convenience, but as users become more familiar with their computers, they develop their own ideas about how things should work. For this reason, Windows has default settings that cause the system to work automatically in the way the designers believe is simplest for beginners. A large number of Windows' behaviors are reconfigurable, however, so more advanced users can make their own choices.

The longer you work with your computer, the more files you create. At some point, putting them all in My Documents, or splitting them into two folders called Work and Home, is no longer adequate. You need to come up with a system that organizes your files into smaller, coherently related piles. Discussing organizational systems goes beyond the scope of this book, but you should know about one valuable organizational tool: the shortcut. Shortcuts enable you to access the same file or application from many different points in the folder tree, without the disadvantages that come with having several copies of the same file.

You should also know about compressed folders, which save the same files in a smaller amount of disk space, at the cost of some functionality.

Even the best-organized people occasionally forget where they put something, so you need to know how to use the Search Explorer bar. You can also speed up your searches with the Indexing Service.

Being able to retrieve deleted files from the Recycle Bin (described in the previous chapter) is a convenience; but, in time, the bin becomes crowded with long-forgotten files that take up disk space for no purpose. You need to know how to manage the Recycle Bin so it continues to be useful without unduly burdening your hard drive.

Finally, files and folders have properties (see Chapter 1, section "What Are Properties?"). The Properties dialog box for a file or folder contains much useful information and lets you make certain choices regarding the object's properties and attributes.

What Is a Shortcut?

Technically, a *shortcut* is a file with a .lnk extension. Less technically, a shortcut is a placeholder in your filing system. A shortcut has a definite position on the folder tree, but it points to a file or folder that is somewhere else on the folder tree.

The purpose of a shortcut is to allow an object to be, for most purposes, in two places at once. For example, you usually should leave a program file inside the folder where it was installed, so you don't mess up any of the relationships between it and its associated files. At the same time, you might want the program to be on the desktop, so you can conveniently open files by dragging them to the program's icon.

Solution: Leave the program file where it is, but make a shortcut pointing to it, and place the shortcut on the desktop. When you drag a file to the shortcut icon, Windows opens the file with the corresponding program.

Maintaining multiple copies of documents on your system is both wasteful of disk space and potentially confusing—when one copy gets updated, you could easily forget to update the others. And yet, files often belong in many different places in a filing system. If, for example, Paul writes the office's fourth-quarter report, the document may belong simultaneously in the Paul's Memos folder and in the Quarterly Reports folder. Putting the document itself in Quarterly Reports and a shortcut to it in Paul's Memos solves the problem, without creating multiple copies of the document. Clicking the shortcut icon opens the associated document, just as if you had clicked the icon of the document itself.

You can recognize a shortcut icon by the curving arrow that appears in its lower-left corner. A shortcut icon otherwise looks just like the icon of the object it points to: a document, folder, or application. A shortcut can be on your desktop or in a folder. A shortcut to the Word document To Do List.doc looks like this:

Meg and Zac
at beach.tif

You can create, delete, move, copy, and rename shortcuts from Explorer windows, just as you would any other kind of file (see "Working with Shortcuts").

Note *Windows also has shortcut keys and shortcut menus, which have nothing to do with shortcuts (see Chapter 2).*

What Are Properties of Files and Folders?

Like almost everything else in Windows, files and folders have *properties*—information about a file or folder you can access and, perhaps, change without opening the file or folder.

To view this information and make changes, select the file or folder in Windows Explorer, and then choose File | Properties (or right-click the file or folder and select Properties from the shortcut menu). The Properties dialog box appears, with the General tab selected (see Figure 8-1).

The General tab of a file's Properties dialog box displays the file's

- Name and icon
- File type (see Chapter 7, section "What Are Extensions and File Types?")

- The default application that opens files of this type (see Chapter 3, section "Associating a Program with a File Extension")

- Location in the folder tree (see Chapter 7, section "What Is the Folder Tree?")

- Size (including both the actual size of the file and the slightly larger amount of disk space allocated to the file)

- Date and time of creation, most recent modification, and most recent access

- Attributes (see the next section)

Depending on a file's type, it may have additional tabs of properties that you can access by clicking them individually. The properties of most image files, for example, include a Summary tab where you can enter the kind of information people write on the backs of photographs: who took the picture, who the people in the picture are, and so on.

Because a folder is technically a special kind of file, the General tab of its properties dialog box contains much of the same information: icon, name, type (File Folder), location, size (the number of bytes taken up by the folder and all its contents, including the contents of subfolders), date created, and attributes. The General tab has one

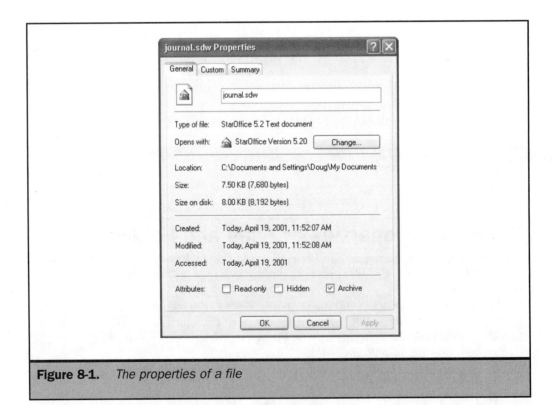

Figure 8-1. *The properties of a file*

additional item: Contains, which reports the number of files and folders contained in the folder and all its subfolders.

For some folders (such as folders that people or programs create, rather than folders that come with Windows), the Properties dialog box includes a Customize tab, which enables you to control what the folder looks like, both when it appears as an icon and when you open the folder. The Customize tab includes these settings:

- Use This Folder Type As A Template, with a list of predefined folder templates (see "What Is a Folder Template?"). The default template is Documents. If the folder will contain pictures or music, choose one of the other options so that Windows can include Picture Tasks or Music Tasks in the Task pane when you open the folder. You can click the Also Apply This Template To All Subfolders if the folder contains subfolders with the same types of files.

- Folder pictures and folder icons enable you to control how the folder's icon looks. If you have a picture that you would like to appear as part of the folder icon in Thumbnails view, click Choose Picture and select it. To control how the folder icon looks in other views, click the Change Icon button and choose another icon.

If your computer is on a local area network, folders also have a Sharing tab, with information about whether the folder (and the files and folders it contains) is shared on the network (see Chapter 29, section "Sharing Your Disk Drives and Folders with Others"). Folders may also have a Security tab to control who may see its contents.

> **Tip** *To find the total size of a group of files and folders, select them all, and then right-click anywhere in the selected filenames. Choose Properties from the shortcut menu. Windows displays the total number of files and folders, as well as their combined size. Note that you can't select multiple folders in the Folder Explorer bar—display the list of files and folders in the working area of the Explorer window.*

What Are Attributes?

The *attributes* of a file or folder include these settings, which can be selected or deselected for each file or folder:

- **Read-only**   You can read and even edit this file or folder; but when you try to save your changes, Windows reminds you this is a read-only file, and asks you to save your new version as a different file. If you try to delete a read-only file or folder, Windows reminds you it's read-only, but deletes it if you insist.

- **Hidden**   A file or folder that doesn't usually appear in Explorer windows, but can be made visible if you want to see it.

- **Archive** This setting may mean the file or folder has been changed since the last time it was backed up, depending on which backup program you use. Windows XP comes with Microsoft Backup (see Chapter 9). To see this attribute on an NTFS (NT File System) partition, click the Advanced button to see the Advanced Attributes dialog box, where it appears as the File Is Ready For Archiving attribute (see Chapter 32, section "What Is a File System?").

- **Indexed** Determines whether the file will be included in the Windows Indexing Service index, which is used when searching for files. You can set this attribute on for files stored in an NTFS partition.

- **Compressed** Compressed to save space, available only on NTFS partitions. Compressed files and folders cannot be encrypted. This type of compression is different from the compressed folders described in the next section.

- **Encrypted** Encrypted (encoded) so that only the user who created the file can open it later (see Chapter 6, section "Can Windows XP Keep Files Private?"). The encryption attribute is only visible (and settable) for files and folders on NTFS partitions.

The attributes of a file or folder appear at the bottom of the General tab of the Properties dialog box. For files and folders stored on NTFS partitions, click the Advanced button to see additional attributes.

What Are Compressed Folders?

Compressed folders are folders whose contents are stored in such a way as to conserve disk space. The amount of disk space you can save by storing a file in a compressed folder varies depending on the kind of file it is; a Word document of 100K, for example, might only take up 40K in a compressed folder, while an Acrobat document of 100K might still take up 80K in a compressed folder.

Windows XP actually has two types of compressed folders: *NTFS compressed folders* and *ZIP compressed folders*. NTFS compression, which is available for both files and folders, works only on NTFS partitions, and is completely invisible in operation. You compress or uncompress an NTFS compressed folder (or file) by changing its Compress Contents To Save Disk Space attribute on the Advanced Attributes dialog box (right-click the folder or file, choose Properties from the menu that appears, click the General tab, and click the Advanced button to see this attribute). A ZIP compressed folder, unlike an ordinary folder, is actually a file—in this case, a ZIP file (with the extension .zip). All the files in this type of compressed folder are actually stored in the ZIP file. ZIP compressed folders are "virtual folders"—files that masquerade as folders in Windows Explorer. Most other programs see ZIP compressed folders as single files, though, and can't read or write the files contained in compressed folders.

The icon representing a ZIP compressed folder is a folder icon with a zipper on it:

stuff.zip

You pay a price for compression: files in ZIP compressed folders are harder to work with. They take longer to open than an identical uncompressed file, and most applications can't open them directly. If you open a document by single- or double-clicking its filename in an Explorer window, Windows makes an uncompressed copy of the file and runs the program associated with that type of file, but the copy is opened as a read-only file. Most applications can't save files in ZIP compressed folders at all. If you want to edit the document and save your changes, you must give the file a new name and save it in an ordinary folder. You can move the file into the ZIP compressed folder later, using Windows Explorer.

Given their virtues and vices, ZIP compressed folders are best for archiving information that you don't access or change often. ZIP compressed folders are also useful for sharing information with other people; being smaller than normal folders, they take less time to transmit and occupy less disk space. (For example, large files that you download from the Internet are frequently in .zip format.) The recipients can read the files, though, only if they have Windows XP, Windows Me, or a third-party utility like WinZip. If you want ZIP files to look like folders in Explorer windows, including opening and saving directly from ZIP files (compressed folders), get ZipMagic (**http://www.ontrack.com/zipmagic**), which combines the power of WinZip and the convenience of Windows compressed folders.

A more detailed description of the techniques for working with ZIP compressed folders is given later in this chapter (see "Working with Compressed Folders"). Windows XP refers to both NTFS and ZIP compressed folders as compressed folders, and in the rest of this chapter, when we talk about compressed folders, we mean ZIP compressed folders.

Compressed folders can also be encrypted (stored in a secret code). You can attach a password to the folder so no one else can open any of the files in the folder without knowing the password.

What Are Hidden Files and Folders?

Windows contains a number of files a beginner might find confusing and that you don't want to delete or change accidentally. As a safety feature, these files are *hidden*, which means, by default, they don't show up in Windows Explorer and can't be opened, deleted, or moved in Windows Explorer unless you choose to make them visible. For example, the folder C:\Windows\Spool keeps track of technical information regarding your printers—stuff you mostly don't want to mess with. But if you open My Computer, the C drive, and then the Windows folder, you won't find it. If you want to see C:\Windows\Spool (and all the other hidden files and folders), follow these steps:

1. Choose Tools | Folder Options from the menu bar of any Explorer window. The Folder Options dialog box appears. (You can also open Folder Options from the Control Panel. It's part of the Appearances And Themes category.)

2. Click the View tab in the Folder Options dialog box. The Hidden Files section contains two radio buttons: Do Not Show Hidden Files And Folders and Show Hidden Files And Folders.

3. Click the Show Hidden Files And Folders radio button.

4. Click OK.

When hidden files and folders are shown, their icons appear as ghostly images like this:

Normal folder   Hidden folder

To hide them again, repeat the preceding procedure, but select the Do Not Show Hidden Files and Folders radio button in step 3.

Hidden files and folders usually don't play a significant role in the everyday life of the average computer user. For that reason, we recommend you leave them hidden whenever you are not working with one. This policy minimizes the chances you will alter or delete something important by accident.

Nonhidden files and folders contained in a hidden folder have an in-between status: they retain their original attributes and show up in Explorer windows if you move them to a nonhidden folder. But they are hidden in practice as long as they stay inside the hidden folder, because the path that connects them to the top of the folder tree includes a hidden link.

Caution   *A hidden file or folder shouldn't be considered secure. The Search command not only finds hidden files and folders, but anyone who finds your file by using this command can open it directly from the Search window (see "Searching for Files and Folders"). Also, you can see from the preceding discussion that viewing hidden files is not difficult. If other people use your computer and you don't want them to find particular files, you should encrypt those files, store them in your My Documents folder (assuming that your Windows user account has a password), or move them to a floppy disk you keep hidden in a more conventional way. See Chapter 6 for how to set up a password-protected user account with a private My Documents folder, and Chapter 31 for a description of Windows' other security features.*

You can hide a file or folder by following this procedure:

1. Select the file or folder.

2. Click the Properties button on the toolbar, or right-click the file or folder and choose Properties from the shortcut menu. The Properties dialog box appears.

3. If it is not already selected, click the General tab. Near the bottom of the General tab is a list of attributes, one of which is Hidden.

4. Select the check box next to Hidden. A check appears in that box.

5. Click OK to make the Properties dialog box disappear.

To unhide the file, repeat the same steps, but deselect the Hidden check box.

What Is a Folder Template?

Some folders look and behave differently from others. A folder of pictures or music, for example, can be set up to have special links in the Task pane or special display properties so that it is easy for you to find the file you want and do what you want with it. A *folder template* is a predefined set of properties that you can choose to apply to a folder. Windows XP comes with six folder templates: documents, pictures, photo album, music, music artist, and music album.

The default folder template is for documents. You can choose a different template from the Customize tab of a folder's Properties dialog box.

Configuring Windows Explorer

You can configure many facets of Explorer windows to your own taste. Some of the basic choices were described in the previous chapter. At the simplest level, you can resize and move the windows themselves just like any other windows. You can choose which Explorer bar (if any) to display by clicking a toolbar button or using the View | Explorer Bar menu. You can display or hide the Standard Buttons, Address Bar, or Links toolbars by using the View | Toolbars menu, and the Status Bar by checking or unchecking View | Status Bar. (If you are wondering what any of these objects are, see the previous chapter.)

You can also make more complex changes in Windows Explorer's behavior, the information it displays, and how that information is presented.

In addition to changing the look and behavior of Windows Explorer in general, you also can add features to individual folders. You can choose a special icon for a folder or select a picture that appears when you look at the folder in Thumbnails view.

Changing the Behavior of Explorer Windows

The Explorer windows of Windows XP are descended from two parents: the folder windows of Windows 95 and the browser windows of Internet Explorer. The default

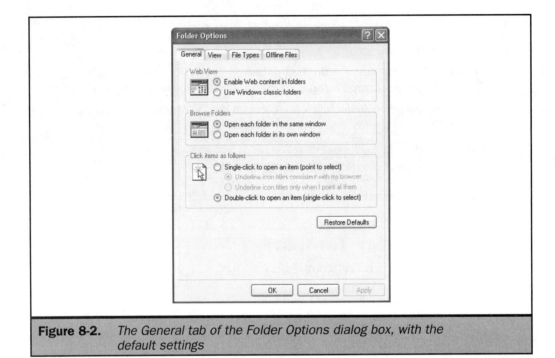

Figure 8-2. *The General tab of the Folder Options dialog box, with the default settings*

settings of the Explorer windows borrow a little from each parent. If you don't like this compromise, you can change your settings from the Folder Options dialog box, shown in Figure 8-2. To open this dialog box, choose Tools | Folder Options from the menu of Windows Explorer, or open the Control Panel and choose Folder Options from the Appearances and Themes category.

If, after experimenting with new settings, you decide the designers of Windows XP had it right after all, you can return to the Folder Options dialog box and click the Restore Defaults button.

Opening a New Window for Each Folder

The default setting of Windows Explorer is for a window to "navigate" up and down the folder tree, like a Web browser: when you open a subfolder of the currently displayed folder, the contents of the currently displayed folder vanish from the working area and are replaced by the contents of the subfolder. However, you still have the option of choosing the original Windows 95 behavior: the new folder can open in a new window, leaving the old window unchanged. If you do, the Windows Explorer's Forward and Back buttons stop working.

The new behaviors only apply to windows you create by opening folders on the desktop, however, or opening folders displayed in windows that already have this behavior. If you start Windows Explorer by choosing it from the Programs menu, for example, it behaves in the default (that is, the Web browser) way.

Replacing Double Clicks with Single Clicks

Under the default settings, a single mouse click selects a file or folder, and a double click opens it. If all that clicking seems like too much work, you can change the settings so a file or folder is selected when the mouse pointer hovers over it and is opened by a single click, as in Web browsers.

To make the change, choose Tools | Folder Options to open the Folder Options dialog box, shown in Figure 8-2. Then click the Single-Click To Open An Item radio button. To change back, click the Double-Click To Open An Item radio button in the Folder Options dialog box.

Restoring the Folder Tree's Dotted Lines

In earlier versions of Windows, the Folders Explorer bar had dotted lines that connected a folder to its subfolders. In designing the look of Windows XP, Microsoft decided that the Folders Explorer bar was too cluttered for novice users, so it created a new default setting without the dotted lines, which is called the *simple folder view*.

We think that the dotted lines make it easier to see how the folder tree is structured, so we recommend putting them back into the Folders Explorer bar as follows:

1. Open the Folder Options dialog box by choosing Tools | Folder Options from the menu of any Explorer window.

2. Click the View tab of the Folder Options dialog box.

3. Uncheck the Display Simple Folder View In Explorer's Folders List check box, and then click OK to close the Folder Options dialog box.

Getting Rid of the Task Pane

The Task pane comes in handy now and then, but it also takes up a lot of space (see Chapter 7, section "What Is the Task Pane?"). If you display both the Task pane and an Explorer bar, there isn't much room left for the working area.

The simplest way to make the Task pane go away is to shrink the size of the Explorer window. At some point Windows decides on its own that the Task pane is a waste of valuable space and stops displaying it.

To make the Task pane go away for all Explorer windows of all sizes, choose Tools | Options to open the Folder Options dialog box, and then click the Use Windows Classic Folders radio button. To reenable the Task pane, click the Enable Web Content In Folders radio button in the Folder Options dialog box.

Changing the Toolbars

In addition to making the toolbars appear and disappear, as described in the previous chapter, you can rearrange the order of the toolbars and choose which buttons you want to have appear on the Standard Buttons or Links toolbars.

Moving the Toolbars

The menu bar, Standard Button toolbar, Links bar, and Address toolbar can be displayed in any order you like. You may, for example, decide to put the Address toolbar on top of the Standard buttons, or put the menu bar and the Links bar side by side.

Before rearranging the toolbars, you must first unlock them by making sure that View | Toolbars | Lock the Toolbars is unchecked. When the toolbars are unlocked and ready to move, each toolbar has a column of dots on its left edge. When the toolbars are locked the dots vanish.

To move a toolbar, do the following:

1. Move the cursor to the left end of the toolbar, just to the right of the column of dots.

2. Hold down the left mouse button. If you have hit the right spot, the cursor turns into four crossing arrows.

3. Drag the toolbar where you want it to go, and release the mouse button.

If two toolbars are on the same level, you can adjust the amount of space given to each toolbar by dragging and dropping the separator (the vertical line next to the column of dots on the left edge of the rightmost bar) between them. If the Explorer window isn't wide enough to contain all the toolbar elements you put on one level, a >> appears at the right edge. Click it to see a menu of the buttons that have fallen off the edge of the window.

Configuring the Standard Buttons Toolbar

The six Standard Buttons discussed in the previous chapter are not the only ones you could have on your toolbar. In fact, you can choose from a total of 21 buttons, and you can display any collection of them in any order you want. This rearranging takes place in the Customize Toolbar dialog box, shown in Figure 8-3. To open this dialog box, select View | Toolbars | Customize, or right-click the toolbar itself and choose Customize from the shortcut menu.

The Customize Toolbar dialog box is well designed. The buttons you are currently displaying are listed in the Current Toolbar Buttons (right-hand) window, and the ones you are not displaying are in the Available Toolbar Buttons (left-hand) window. To add a button, select it in the left-hand window and click the Add button. To remove a button, select it in the right-hand window and click the Remove button.

You can change the order of the buttons you display as follows: select a button in the right-hand window, and then click the Move Up or Move Down buttons. The top-to-bottom order of the buttons in the Current Toolbar Buttons window is the left-to-right order of the buttons on the Standard Buttons toolbar. Group buttons together by inserting a separator. You can have as many separators on your toolbar as you like; the separator is the only item in the left-hand window that doesn't vanish when you move it to the right-hand window.

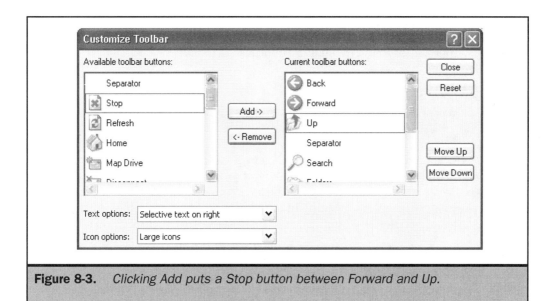

Figure 8-3. *Clicking Add puts a Stop button between Forward and Up.*

The amount of space the buttons take up on the toolbar is determined by the size of the button's icon and the text label. You can change either of these with the two drop-down lists at the bottom of the Customize Toolbar dialog box. The combination No Text Labels and Small Icons enables you to put a lot of small buttons on the toolbar, while Show Text Labels/Large Icons gives you a few big buttons.

The default settings are Selective Text on Right and Large Icons. The "selective text" labels enough buttons that you can probably guess the rest. For example, labeling the Back button gives you enough information to figure out where the Forward button is.

Configuring the Links Toolbar

The Windows Explorer Links toolbar contains buttons that can link to the Web sites or files or programs that you use most often (see Chapter 7). However, to get much use out of the Links toolbar you'll need to customize it, because the Links that Microsoft puts on the toolbar for you aren't very interesting.

To eliminate a link button, right-click it and choose Delete from the shortcut menu. To add a new link button of your own choosing, drag any file or folder icon to the Links toolbar and drop it where you want it. The file or folder stays where it was originally, and a shortcut is put on the Links toolbar (and in the folder C:\Windows\Favorites\Links, assuming that Windows is installed in C:\Windows). If you want to add the currently selected file or folder to the Links toolbar, you can drag the file or folder icon out of the Address box and drop it on the Links toolbar in the place where you want it to be.

To rename a link button, right-click it and choose Rename from the shortcut menu.

The contents of the Links toolbar also appear in the Links folder of the Favorites menu, so you can also customize the Links toolbar via the Organize Favorites dialog box (see Chapter 24, section "Organizing Favorites").

Changing Views

Windows Explorer can display file and folder icons in the working area in five different views: Tiles, Icons, List, Details, and Thumbnails. You can find all these options on the View menu. Folders that have been assigned special folder templates may have additional view options (see "Choosing a New Folder Template").

Tiles and Icons are graphical views that enable you to arrange the icons in any two-dimensional pattern you like. List and Details both put the objects into a list. Details view includes more information in its list and enables you to reorder the list according to various criteria. Thumbnails view displays a tiny picture of each image or HTML file.

Tiles and Icons Views

Tiles view and Icons view are both graphical ways of presenting the contents of a folder—you can drag-and-drop the files and folders in the window in any way that makes sense to you, just as you might arrange objects on a desktop, piling up some and spreading out others.

Icons is the more compact view, Tiles the more informative. In Icons view the icons are smaller, text labels are under the file and folder icons, and no additional information is listed beyond the file names and icons. Tiles view gives you larger icons than Icons, text labels are to the right of the icons, and the types and sizes of files are given in the text labels.

List and Details Views

List and Details views each are ways of putting the contents of a folder into a list. The difference between them is List gives only a small icon and a name for each file and subfolder. Details, as the name implies, gives a more detailed list that includes three more columns: the size of the file, its file type, and when it was last modified (see Figure 8-4). (The column headings are sometimes different for special folders. For example, columns in My Computer are Name, Type, Total Size, and Free Space.)

If you think Details view would be more informative if it had a different set of columns, right-click the bar that displays the column headings. The shortcut menu displays a list of possible column headings, with the currently displayed ones checked. Check or uncheck any you like. (Many of the headings are only appropriate for special types of files or folders; for other files or folders the corresponding column is empty.) The changes you make apply to the current folder only, but will be remembered the next time you open that folder. You can also change Details view for all folders (see "Changing How the View Settings Work").

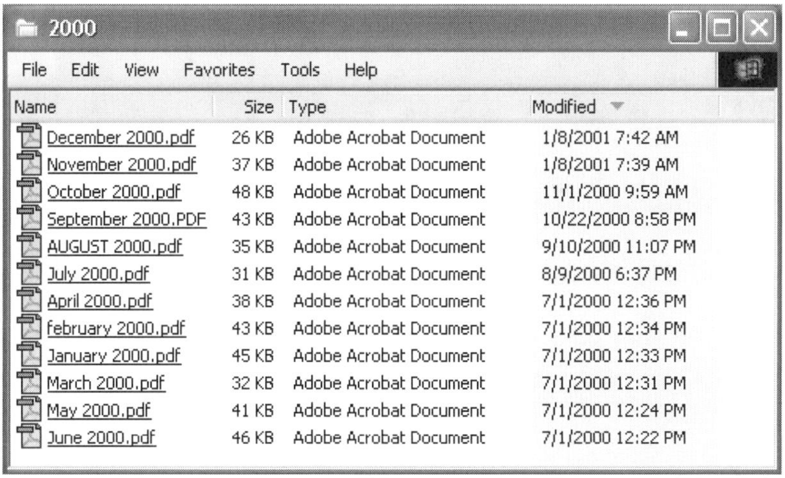

Figure 8-4.   *In Details view, you can sort by clicking any column head.*

Details view also enables you to sort the list of files and subfolders according to any column by clicking its column head. Clicking Name sorts the contents, putting them in alphabetical order. Clicking a column head twice sorts the contents in reverse order. For example, clicking the Size head once sorts from the smallest file to the largest, and clicking Size twice re-sorts from the largest file to the smallest. In Figure 8-4, clicking the column head Modified twice has sorted the contents of the folder by the date modified, from most recent to least recent. The small down arrow next to the Modified column head indicates that the list is sorted in descending order based on this column.

You can adjust the width of the columns in a Details view by dragging and dropping the lines between the adjacent column heads. You can switch the order of the columns by dragging and dropping the column heads.

Thumbnails View

If a file icon is a little picture that is supposed to tell you something about the file, and if the file itself contains a picture, then why not let a miniature version of the picture be the file icon? That's the idea behind Thumbnails view, shown in Figure 8-5. Graphics files and HTML files are denoted by miniatures of themselves, some files have been assigned special pictures, and all other files are denoted by squares surrounding their usual file icons. If the HTML documents are text, their thumbnails are too small to read, but at least you can tell whether this is the two-column document or the one-column document.

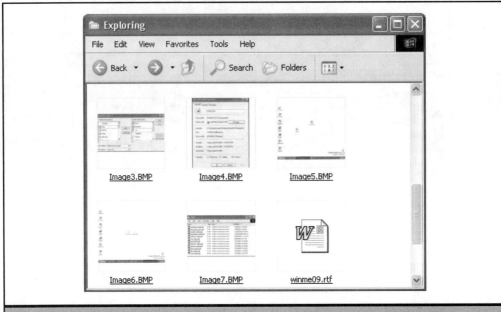

Figure 8-5. *Thumbnails view uses miniature pictures to represent image files.*

Other Views

Folders that have been assigned a special folder template may have other view options (see "Choosing a New Folder Template"). For example, a folder with the photo album template has a Filmstrip view, which you can select from the View menu as you would any other view.

Changing How the View Settings Work

By default, each folder has its own view settings. If you choose a new view from the View menu, you change the view for the currently displayed folder only. Windows remembers the new view the next time you open that folder, but all other folders are unchanged. But another method enables you to change the view for all folders in one fell swoop.

Defining One View for All Folders

If you decide you like Details or Thumbnails (or some other) view and want to use it for all your folders, you can. Here's how:

1. Configure a folder the way you want all the folders to appear.
2. With that folder open, select Tools | Folder Options. The Folder Options dialog box appears (shown in Figure 8-2).

3. Click the View tab of the Folder Options dialog box. Near the top of this tab is the Folder Views box. Inside this box is the Apply To All Folders button. Click it.

4. A confirmation box appears, asking you whether you really mean to change the default view settings. Click Yes.

5. Click OK to close the Folder Options dialog box.

If you want to reset all folders back to the default settings, follow the previous instructions, except in step 4, click the Reset All Folders button.

 Changes that you make to the layout of columns in Details view can't be extended to all folders by this technique.

Defining a View that Stays with a Window

You may also decide you want the view settings to belong to the window, not to the folder. In other words, when you switch to, say, Thumbnails view, you want every folder you open from that window to come up in Thumbnails view until you change to something else. To change window settings:

1. Select Tools | Folder Options in Windows Explorer. The Folder Options dialog box appears (shown in Figure 8-2).

2. Click the View tab of the Folder Options dialog box. The lower portion of the tab is the Advanced Settings box.

3. In the Advanced Settings box, find the line Remember Each Folder's View Settings. Uncheck the box next to this line.

4. Click OK.

To restore the default behavior, repeat the process, but check the box in step 3.

One thing you can't do is have Windows Explorer behave in different ways for different folders, such as open with a single click in one folder and open with a double click in another. Whatever decisions you make on the General tab of the Folder Options dialog box are applied automatically to all Explorer windows.

Changing View Settings

The stray odds and ends of how Explorer windows look and behave are controlled from the View tab of the Folder Options dialog box. From this tab you can tell Windows

■ Whether to display hidden files.

■ Whether to display file extensions. (If you would rather see file extensions, see the section "What Are Extensions and File Types?" in Chapter 7 for how to display them.)

You can make your experience of Windows Explorer a little more comfortable by setting its options the way you like them. To open the View tab of the Folder Options dialog box, choose Tools | Folder Options from the Windows Explorer menu bar, and then click the View tab. The View tab contains the Advanced Settings window, which is a long list of check boxes, most of which are self-explanatory. For example, the Show My Documents On The Desktop check box controls whether the My Documents folder appears on the desktop.

If you decide that whatever you changed on the View tab was a bad idea, but you can't remember exactly what you changed, go to the View tab and click the Restore Defaults button.

Sorting and Arranging the Contents of a Folder

Windows Explorer can sort the icons in an Explorer window automatically according to any column that appears in Details view. For most folders this means the icons can be sorted by name (alphabetically), by file type, by size (from smallest to largest), and by date (earliest to most recent). Even if you aren't in Details view, you can access the same choices via a shortcut menu or on the View | Arrange Icons menu. Adding a column to Details view adds the same choice to the View | Arrange Icons menu.

In any of these sortings, folders are listed before files. Thus, in Figure 8-6, the B Folder and the C Folder come before the A File. In Tiles, Icons, and Thumbnails views, the contents of the folder are sorted in rows (if the window is wide enough for more than one column). The first element in the order is located in the window's

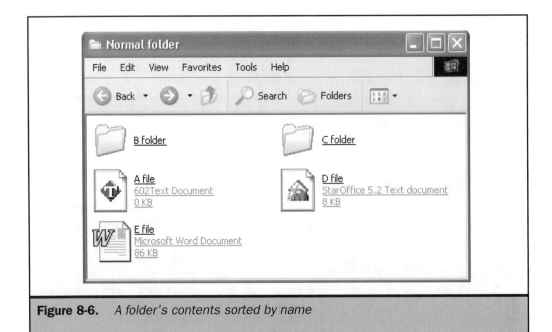

Figure 8-6. *A folder's contents sorted by name*

upper-left corner, the second is to its right, and so on. In List and Details views, the contents are sorted in a list, starting at the top of the window.

In Details view, sorting is particularly easy: click the column header to sort according to that column. Click it again to sort in reverse order (in which folders automatically go to the end of the list). The column by which the list is sorted displays a small arrowhead, which points up for a sort in ascending order and down for a sort in descending order.

In Tiles, Icons, or Thumbnails views, you can also arrange icons manually, by dragging them. Figure 8-7 shows a folder whose contents have been arranged manually—notice the irregular spacing and the overlapping icons. Metaphorically, manual arrangement is more like sorting stacks of paper on a table than sorting items in a filing cabinet. The effect can be similar to having subfolders: you can put work files on the right half of the window and home files on the left, instead of having Work and Home subfolders. If you decide you want tidy rows and columns again, select something off the View | Arrange Icons By menu.

Caution	*If you overlap an icon too closely with a folder icon, Windows will think you want to put the corresponding object inside the folder.*

You can also group files and folders automatically according to name, size, type, or date modified. Make sure that View | Arrange Icons By | Show In Groups is checked. Then choose Name, Size, Type, or Modified from the View | Arrange Icons By menu.

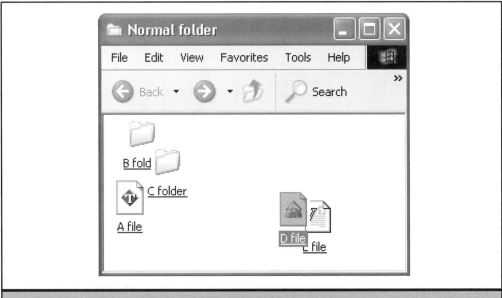

Figure 8-7. *A folder's icons arranged manually*

Customizing a Folder

Windows gives you considerable power over the appearance of a folder in an Explorer window. You can select a new folder template for the folder, choose a picture to display on the folder's icon in Thumbnails view, or select a new icon entirely to represent the folder in any view.

These changes are made from the Customize tab of the folder's Properties dialog box, shown in Figure 8-8. To display this tab, do either of the following:

- Right-click the folder's icon and choose Properties from the shortcut menu, then click the Customize tab in the Properties dialog box.

- Open the folder and then choose View | Customize This Folder.

Choosing a New Folder Template

The default template for a new folder is the document template. Windows XP also offers the option of two different templates for folders that contain images (the photo

Figure 8-8. *Customize a folder from the Customize tab of the folder's Properties dialog box.*

album and pictures templates) and three for folders that contain music files (the music, music album, and music artist templates).

A folder in photo album template is shown in Figure 8-9. Notice the virtual slide projector in the working area and the Photo Tasks box on the Task pane. The views and templates that Windows provides for graphic images are discussed in Chapter 18, while the three music templates are described in Chapter 19.

To change the template of a folder

1. Open the folder and then select View | Customize This Folder. The Properties dialog box appears with the Customize tab on top.

2. Choose the new template from the drop-down list in the What Kind Of Folder Do You Want? box on the Customize tab of the Properties dialog box.

3. Click OK.

Using a Picture as a Folder's Thumbnail Icon

The default icon for a folder in Thumbnails view is either a larger version of the ordinary yellow folder icon, or (if the folder contains image files) the first four image files from the folder arranged on the yellow folder icon like pictures pasted onto a manila folder. (You can change which four images are displayed by re-sorting the

Figure 8-9.   *The photo album folder template*

folder's contents.) You can make this icon more interesting and informative by choosing an appropriate image to be the folder's thumbnail icon. For example, if the folder contains music files from a particular album, Windows may download the album cover from the Internet and use that image as the folder's thumbnail icon.

Note   *The image on a folder's thumbnail icon doesn't have to be from an image file contained in the folder. The image can be stored anywhere on your computer or network.*

To select a picture as a folder's thumbnail icon

1. Make sure that the image you want exists as a file somewhere on your computer or your network.
2. Open the folder whose thumbnail you want to change.
3. Select View | Customize This Folder to display the Customize tab of the folder's Properties dialog box.
4. Click the Choose Picture button. A Browse window appears.
5. Use the Browse window to find the image file you want to use, then the Open button in the Browse window. The Browse window disappears and the new image is displayed in the Properties dialog box.
6. Click the OK button in the Properties dialog box.

To restore the default thumbnail icon of a folder, follow the same steps, but click the Restore Default button in step 4 instead of the Choose Picture button.

Changing a Folder's Icon

If a folder has special content or you use it for some special purpose, you can remind yourself of that by giving it a special icon. To change a folder's icon

1. Open the folder and then select View | Customize This Folder. The folder's Properties dialog box appears with the Customize tab on top.
2. Click the Change Icon button on the Customize tab. The Change Icon box appears, as shown in Figure 8-10.
3. By default the Change Icon box shows the icons contained in the file C:\Windows\System32\shell.dll, where Windows stores its icons. If you want to look in another file or folder, click the Browse button and use the Browse window to select that file or folder.
4. Select an icon in the Change Icon box and Click OK to return to the Properties dialog box, then click OK to make the Properties dialog box disappear.

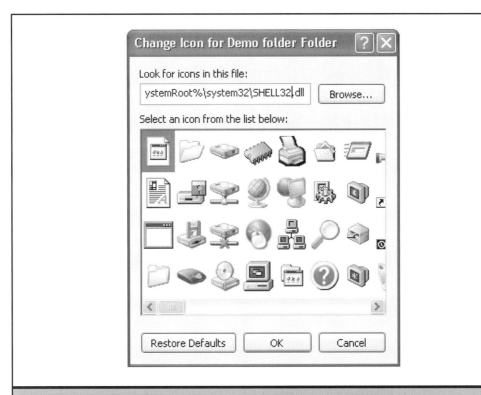

Figure 8-10.   *Windows knows hundreds of icons.*

Working with Shortcuts

Sometimes you want a file to be in two places at once: the place where it really belongs and on the desktop where you can easily get to it. Sometimes your filing system has two logical places to put the same file. Shortcuts enable you to deal with these situations, without the disadvantages that come from having two independent copies of the same file (see "What Is a Shortcut?" earlier in this chapter).

Making Shortcuts

Shortcuts are created when you

- Drag-and-drop certain applications to a new folder or to the desktop.
- Hold down the right mouse button while you drag any object to a new location, and then select Create Shortcut(s) Here from the menu that appears when you drop the object.

■ Invoke the Create Shortcut Wizard either by selecting File | New | Shortcut in an Explorer window or by right-clicking an open space on the desktop or in an Explorer window and selecting New | Shortcut from the shortcut menu.

In the first two cases, the original file or folder stays in its old location, and a shortcut to that file or folder is created in the drop location. In the third case, the shortcut is created in the folder from which the Create Shortcut Wizard was invoked.

Windows makes shortcuts automatically in certain circumstances. When you add a Web page to your list of Favorites, for example, a shortcut is created and put in the folder C:\Documents And Settings*username*\Favorites.

We find drag-and-drop techniques are the easiest way to create shortcuts. But if you prefer, you can use the Create Shortcut Wizard as follows:

1. Open the destination folder, the one in which you want to create the shortcut. If you want the shortcut to be on the desktop, make sure part of the desktop is visible on your screen.

2. Choose File | New | Shortcut in the destination folder's window. Or, if the desktop is the destination, right-click an empty place and select New | Shortcut. Either of these techniques launches the Create Shortcut Wizard.

3. If you know the address of the file or folder to which you want to create a shortcut (the target), you can type it into the Command Line box on the Wizard's first page. If you have the address written in another file, you can cut-and-paste it into the Command Line box by using CTRL-V to paste. If you use the Command Line box, skip to step 7. (If you are creating a shortcut to a folder, entering an address in the Command Line box is the only technique that works. Clicking the Browse button doesn't help.)

4. Click the Browse button. A Browse dialog box appears.

5. Use the Browse dialog box to find the target file. If you don't see the file you want (and it isn't a program), change the Files Of Type box to All Files.

6. Select the target file or folder, and then click the Open button. The Browse dialog box disappears. The first page of the Create Shortcut Wizard now contains the target's address.

7. Click Next. The second page of the Create Shortcut Wizard appears. If you don't like the suggested name for the shortcut (usually the same as the original object), type a new one in the Select A Name For The Shortcut line.

8. Click Finish.

Shortcuts can also point to Web pages on the Internet. These shortcuts have file names that end with the extension .url, and you can also make them with the Create Shortcut Wizard. The procedure is the same, except in step 3 you type the page's Internet address or URL (see Chapter 7, section "What Are Addresses?").

Using Shortcuts

For almost all purposes, a shortcut to a file or folder behaves just like the target file or folder. Opening the shortcut, dragging and dropping the shortcut, or dragging and dropping something onto the shortcut produces the same result as performing the same action with the target file or folder.

The most convenient place to put shortcuts is on the desktop. Documents you are currently working on can reside in the appropriate place in your filing system, yet a shortcut on the desktop can make them instantly available. Programs you use frequently can remain in the folders they were installed into, yet be accessible with a single click. For programs you use frequently, you can add an icon to the Quick Launch toolbar on the taskbar (see Chapter 10, section "Editing the Quick Launch Toolbar").

Working with Compressed Folders

Everyone who has packed a suitcase knows the basic idea of a compressed folder—it's a trick for getting the same quantity of information to fit in a smaller space on a disk. Windows 98 and earlier versions of Windows required that you have a third-party application such as WinZip or ZipMagic to work with compressed folders (which everyone who doesn't work for Microsoft calls *ZIP files*). In many ways, these applications are still more useful and convenient than the Compressed Folders utility in Windows Explorer. If you are going to work with ZIP files every day, you probably want to acquire ZipMagic or some similar program; for occasional use, the Compressed Folders utility in Windows Explorer works just fine.

Creating a Compressed Folder

To create a compressed folder on the desktop, right-click an empty space and choose New | Compressed Folder from the shortcut menu. To create a compressed folder inside another folder, open or select the folder and choose File | New | Compressed folder.

Either of these techniques creates a compressed folder called New Compressed Folder.zip (or New Compressed Folder if Explorer is set to hide file extensions). You may rename it as you would any other folder, though (as usual) you probably don't want to change the file extension.

To create a compressed folder with a specific file or files already inside it, select the files you want to include, right-click one of the selected files, and then choose Send To | Compressed Folder from the shortcut menu. The selected files remain unchanged, and a copy of them is created inside the compressed folder. The name and location of the folder is the same as the file you right-clicked. The name of the new compressed folder is the same name as the last of the selected files.

Working with Files in a Compressed Folder

To add a file to a compressed folder, drag the file onto the folder's icon or into its open window, and then drop it. The file remains in its original location and a copy is created inside the compressed folder. To move the file without leaving the original behind, drag-and-drop it with the right mouse button, and then choose Move Here from the shortcut menu.

To many applications, a compressed folder appears to be simply a file of a type that the application doesn't know how to open properly. You can't, for example, use the File | Open command in Word to open a Word file that lives inside a compressed folder.

You can open a file in a compressed folder by double-clicking it, but the file usually lacks its full functionality. Windows uncompresses the file into a temporary location, and then runs the program that handles the file. A Word file in a compressed folder, for example, opens in read-only mode. To regain functionality, you need to *extract* the file. The extracting process creates an uncompressed copy of the file outside the compressed folder.

To extract a file from a compressed folder, drag it from the compressed folder and drop it onto the desktop or into an uncompressed folder. One copy of the file is left behind in the compressed folder and a new, uncompressed copy appears in the new location. To extract the file without leaving a copy in the compressed folder, drag-and-drop with the right mouse button and choose Move Here from the shortcut menu.

To extract all the files in a compressed folder at once, select File | Extract All from the menu if the file is open, or right-click the folder's icon and choose Extract All from the shortcut menu. The Extract Wizard guides you in selecting a destination folder for the extracted files.

In many respects, the compressed folder and its files behave just as other folders and files. You can arrange and view the files within the folder in the usual ways, for example. However, Microsoft didn't completely integrate compressed folders into its filing system. Here is a short list of things Microsoft might want to fix:

- Compressed folders don't appear on the Folder Explorer bar.
- Compressed folders don't show up in Browse windows. So, for example, you can't save a Word document into a compressed folder by choosing File | Save As from the Word menu bar. Most programs can't open a file that's stored in a compressed folder.
- You can't customize a compressed folder.
- The columns in Details view are different for a compressed folder because there is more to know about a compressed file: the size of the compressed file, the size of the extracted file, the ratio between the sizes, whether the file is encrypted, and the method of compression.
- You can't drag-and-drop or cut-and-paste a file from one compressed folder to another unless one of the folders contains the other.

MANAGING YOUR DISK

Encrypting and Decrypting Compressed Folders

You can attach a password to a compressed folder so that Windows will ask for the password before opening or extracting any of the files in the folder. This technique encrypts the entire folder. If you want to encrypt some of the files in a compressed folder, but not other files, create a new compressed folder, move the files you want to encrypt to the new folder, and encrypt that folder. The password scheme used in compressed folders can be broken by a determined attacker and isn't a substitute for a serious encryption program, but it's adequate to deter casual snooping.

To encrypt a compressed folder, right-click its icon and select Encrypt from the shortcut menu. Or, you can open the folder and select File | Encrypt. When the Encrypt dialog box appears, type a password into the Password box, and then retype the same password into the Confirm Password box. (This retyping is to make sure you didn't mistype the password the first time, thereby creating a password that even you don't know.) Click OK to make the dialog box go away and close the folder (if it was open). The folder is encrypted.

Tip *Anyone can open an encrypted folder and look at the list of files. Windows doesn't ask for a password until you try to* open or extract *one of the files. In Details view, someone could learn the sizes and dates of the files without knowing the password. If you want even this information to be secret, put your files in another folder* inside *an encrypted folder. Then the password of the outer folder is required to open the inner folder.*

Opening and extracting files from encrypted compressed folders works exactly the same as opening and extracting files from ordinary compressed folders, except you have to type the password into the Password dialog box.

To decrypt an encrypted folder so that a password is no longer needed to access its files, right-click the folder's icon and select Decrypt from the shortcut menu, and then type the password into the Password dialog box.

Searching for Files and Folders

Even with a well-organized file system, you can occasionally forget where you put a file or even what the file's exact name is. Fortunately, Windows provides the Search Companion Explorer bar to help you. By using Search Companion, you can find a file

- By name or part of a name
- By date created, modified, or last accessed
- By file type
- By size
- By a string of text contained in the file
- By some combination of all the previous points

To start Search Companion, click the Search button on the Windows Explorer toolbar, or select View | Explorer Bar | Search from the menu. Either action causes Search Companion to appear in the Explorer Bar.

Standard vs. Advanced Search Companion

One of the new features in Windows XP is the Search Companion Wizard interface, shown in Figure 8-11. You begin by choosing an answer to the prompt What Do You Want To Search For? The multiple-choice style is maintained for as long as possible, and different responses lead to different follow-up questions. (This feature makes the interface hard for us to describe in detail.)

This behavior has the advantages and disadvantages of most Wizard interfaces: It's comfortable and nonintimidating for beginners, but it's slow and frustrating for people who know exactly what they want to do—especially people who learned how to use Search under previous versions of Windows. If the designers of the Wizard have anticipated your desires, then you find a convenient button or link that does the job for you. If not, you end up studying the options given, guessing what follow-up options they lead to, and wondering if any of them is close enough to be worthwhile.

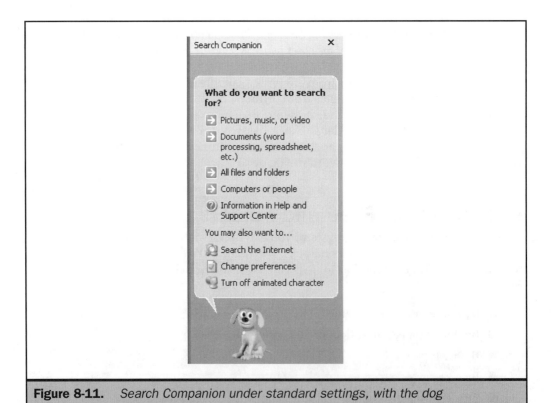

Figure 8-11. *Search Companion under standard settings, with the dog*

Fortunately, clicking the All Files And Folders option produces a window similar to the window in the old version of Search. If you like, you can skip the Wizard interface and make Search Companion go straight to this window when you start it up. In Microsoft's terminology, the Wizard interface is the "standard" version and the old interface is "advanced." If you search for files often enough to develop habits, we recommend switching to the advanced settings because they always put the same choices in the same places. To make this switch, follow these steps:

1. Choose the Change Preferences option in Search Companion. Scroll all the way down to the bottom of the Search Companion pane if you don't see this option.

2. Choose Change Files And Folders Search Behavior.

3. Click the Advanced radio button. (Do not be intimidated; you can change back whenever you want.)

4. Click OK.

If you decide to go back to the standard settings, repeat the previous steps, but click the Standard radio button in step 3.

Under the advanced settings, Search Companion has a dialog-box interface, shown in Figure 8-12. You enter information into the dialog box by typing it into boxes, checking check boxes, or selecting radio buttons. The dialog-box format allows you to see all the search criteria at once, which gives experienced users a satisfying overview, but can instill a where-do-I-start panic in novices.

Putting Out the Dog

Years ago, someone at Microsoft imagined that computers would be more friendly and less intimidating if the software included cute animated characters. The latest offering from Microsoft's cartoon studio is the animated dog in Search Companion. He serves no purpose other than to be cute, use up processing cycles, and take up screen space.

Fortunately, the dog is easier to get rid of than some of Microsoft's earlier efforts. (We can't count the number of friends and relatives who have asked us how to get rid of Clippy, the animated paper clip in Microsoft Office.) If you are using the standard Search settings, choose the Turn Off Animated Character option at the bottom of Search Companion's opening screen. Under the advanced settings, choose Change Preferences followed by Without An Animated Screen Character.

If you later decide that you can't live without his big eyes and wagging tail, you can bring the pooch back (under either the standard or advanced settings) by choosing Change Preferences followed by With An Animated Screen Character.

MANAGING YOUR DISK

Figure 8-12. *Search Companion under advanced settings, without the dog*

Starting a Search

Whether you use the standard or advanced settings in Search Companion, the overall process of searching for files and folders is basically the same. The sections that follow will describe in more detail what happens in step 2, but in general the process works like this:

1. Select Start | Search. Or, in any Explorer window, click the Search button on the toolbar or select View | Explorer Bar | Search from the menu. All of these actions give you an Explorer window with the Search Companion Explorer bar.

2. Use the Explorer bar to describe the files or folders you're looking for. In the standard settings, this part of the process consists largely of answering questions, with a box or two to fill in along the way. In the advanced settings, you fill in the form shown in Figure 8-12.

3. Click Search to start searching for all files or folders that fit the description you've given. The magnifying glass icon moves in circles while the search

continues. As matching files and folders are found, they appear in the viewing area. The number of objects found is shown in the Status bar.

4. If you aren't satisfied with the files and folders you found, change the information you entered and search again.

Remember *You can use as many different criteria as you want to narrow your search.*

When the search is done, the viewing area displays the files or folders that meet your criteria. From this window you can

- Open any of the files or folders listed.
- Copy, cut, move, or drag-and-drop any of the files or folders to the desktop or some other window.
- Sort the files or folders. If you have set the view to Details (the default, if you opened Search from the Start menu), you can sort by Name, Address, Size, and File Type by clicking the corresponding column header.

Searching by Name

The simplest kind of search is when you know the name of the file (or most of its name), but can't remember where it is located.

In the advanced settings, type the name of the file into the All Or Part Of The File Name box of the Search Explorer bar, and then click Search.

In the standard settings, begin by clicking whichever of the links best describes what you are looking for: Pictures Music Or Video; Documents; or All Files And Folders. If you aren't sure, click All Files And Folders. Each choice takes you to a somewhat different set of questions, but all of them have a box in which you can type part or all of the name of the file. Click the Search button to begin.

If you know only part of the name of a file, type that part into Search Companion. When you click Search, the viewing area displays all the files and folders whose names include that text string. (Even if you type in the full name, Search treats it as a substring, and returns all the files and folders whose names contain that text string.) For example, searching for "June" might yield the files june02.doc, Next June.txt, and 99june quarterly report.wks, plus the folders June's Recipes and Juneau Alaska.

If you don't remember much about the name of the file ("It had an *A* in it somewhere"), the resulting list of files and folders is likely to be daunting. You can make your search more specific by combining it with other criteria, or by using case sensitivity and wildcards, described in the next two sections.

Case Sensitivity

In the preceding "June" example, the search for "June" was not case sensitive—the capital *J* was not taken into account, which is why june02.doc and 99june quarterly report.wks appeared on the list. If you want your capital letters to be matched only to other capital letters, you need to find the Case Sensitive check box and check it.

Case Sensitive is classified as an Advanced Search Option, so in the standard settings you find it by clicking links that contain the phrase "Advanced Search Options" or "Advanced Options" until the Case Sensitive check box reveals itself. In the advanced settings the process is a little easier to describe:

1. Click the arrows-down button labeled More Advanced Options. The arrows on the button turn up and the Explorer bar expands to include more options.

2. Click the Case Sensitive check box.

Case sensitivity also applies to text searches (see "Searching for Text Strings").

 Case sensitivity still wasn't working in late test versions of Windows XP, but we assume Microsoft will get it fixed before shipping the commercial version.

Wildcards

The asterisk (*) and question mark (?) characters play a special role in filename searches. Neither is allowed to be part of a filename, so when you include them in a filename search, Windows knows you intend for it to do something special with them. The asterisk and question mark are called *wildcards* because (like wildcards in poker) they can stand for any other character.

The question mark stands for any single character, so you can use it when you either don't know or don't want to specify a character in a filename. If, for example, you can't remember whether a file is named Letter to Tim or Letter to Tom, search for **Letter to T?m**—either Tim or Tom will match T?m. Similarly, you can find both Annual Report 2001 and Annual Report 2002, by using "Annual Report 200?" in your search.

An asterisk stands for any string of characters. Searching for **Letter to T*m** would not only find Letter to Tim and Letter to Tom, but also Letter to Travel Management Team.

Searching for Text Strings

You can also search for documents that contain certain words or phrases. This makes for a much more time-consuming search than any of the other criteria because Windows has to search the files themselves, rather than just file properties. (If you frequently do text searches, you can speed them up by enabling the Indexing Service described in the next section.) For this reason, you should avoid using this feature if other criteria are already enough to narrow the search. But sometimes a text-string search may be exactly what you need. For example, you could generate a list of all the letters you've written to your mother by searching for the phrase "Dear Mom."

If you are using the advanced settings of Search Companion, you can add a text string to your search, type it into the A Word Or Phrase In The File line. Unfortunately, this technique works for contiguous phrases only. Unlike online search engines, you can't search for a series of keywords, such as "Mom" and "Christmas."

Under the standard settings, you also want to enter the text string into the A Word Or Phrase In The File box, but you need to click an option in order find it. If you begin by selecting the All File Types option, this box appears right away. Otherwise, you need to click the Use Advanced Search Options link to find it.

To make Windows pay attention to the capitalization in your Search, make sure the Case Sensitive box is checked on the Search Explorer bar.

Using Indexing Service

If you have ever searched through a book looking for a particular passage, you know what a difference it makes to have someone do the up-front work of making an index or concordance. That, in a nutshell, is what Indexing Service does: It is a utility that creates and maintains catalog files that keep track of the contents of the files on your computer. Having the Indexing Service enabled makes searches (especially text searches) much faster, at the cost of a certain amount of overhead: Indexing Service requires some time to construct an initial catalog, which it must update from time to time as you create new files and change old ones.

To find out whether Indexing Service is currently enabled or disabled, click the Change Preferences link in the Search Companion Explorer bar. The bar then displays the question How Do You Want To Use Search Companion? Click the response With Indexing Service or Without Indexing Service, whichever is offered. Search Companion then informs you whether Indexing Service is currently enabled or disabled, and offers you the option of enabling it or disabling it.

If you administer a large, complex file system you may find it useful to create separate catalogs for various pieces of the system, so that the users on your system can do faster, better targeted searches. Catalogs are managed from the Indexing Service icon, which is in the Services and Applications section of the Computer Management console, but this topic goes beyond the scope of this book. See the "Using Indexing Service" topic in Windows Help and Support.

Looking in the Right Place

If you know where the desired files or folders are located in the folder tree, search only that portion of the tree. That search doesn't take so long and yields fewer false "finds." The Look In pull-down list provides a number of possible limitations to the search, for example, searching only one particular drive rather than all of them. The Look In pull-down list is immediately visible under the advanced settings of Search Companion and appears when you click the All Files And Folders option in the standard settings. If you choose Documents or Pictures Music Or Video in the standard settings, you need to click Use Advanced Search Options to make Look In appear.

MANAGING YOUR DISK

To restrict your search even further, click Browse on the Look In pull-down list and a Browse For Folder window opens. In this window, select a folder to search and click OK; only that folder and its subfolders are searched. Another way to tell Windows where to search is by right-clicking the folder you want to search and choosing Search from the menu that appears.

By default, the Look In box is set to the folder that was open when you pushed the Search toolbar button, or (if you opened Search from the Start menu) your local hard drives.

Searching by Date

If you remember when you last modified a file, you can use that information to help find it. To specify date information in Search Companion, you first need to find the When Was It Modified question. Under the advanced settings, this question appears immediately, but under the standard settings you must click an option before this question appears.

When you have found the When Was It Modified question click the downward-pointing arrow button next to it. You are offered several possible answers to the question, ranging from the past week to the past year, as shown here:

If one of these options describes what you know about the file, click the corresponding radio button. You can also specify a range of dates, if you know when you most recently worked on the file (for example, some time last summer). To do this, click the Specify Dates radio button and use the From and To boxes to specify the beginning and ending dates for your search. The Specify Dates radio button also lets you base your search on the dates when the file was created or most recently accessed. Make this choice from a drop-down list.

When you are done specifying your search, click the Search button.

If all you know about a file is that you accessed it recently, you might do better to look on the History Explorer bar.

Searching by File Type

The first question you are asked under the standard settings of Search Companion is essentially a question about file type. After you choose the Documents or Pictures Music Or Video option, you have no opportunity to be more specific about file type, but in the All Files and Folders option a Type Of File drop-down list appears under More Advanced Options. (In any of the options, you can use the All Or Part Of The File Name box to enter a file extension, such as .doc for Word files.)

Under the advanced settings, click the More Advanced Options button and then choose from the Type Of File drop-down list.

Searching by Size

If you know the file you're looking for is several megabytes, don't waste time searching all those 50K files or vice versa. You can search large files only or small files only, but you can't search between two sizes. To specify a file size under the advanced settings, click the What Size Is It question. A set of radio buttons appears describing small, medium, or large files, as shown here:

Or, you can click the Specify Size radio button, choose At Least or At Most from a drop-down list, and then enter a number into the KB box to specify a limiting size in kilobytes.

Saving and Retrieving a Search

After performing a search, you can save the search parameters by selecting File | Save Search. The list of files found with that search is not saved. The parameters are saved in a *Saved Search* file (with extension .fnd). To perform the search in the future, open the Saved Search file and click the Search Now button. Once a search has been saved, you can even share it with other people in the same ways you would share any other file—by copying it to a floppy, or attaching it to e-mail. Another way to re-run a search is by double-clicking its .fnd file (which is usually stored in your My Documents folder, unless you specified another location).

Managing the Recycle Bin

Files and folders sent to the Recycle Bin may disappear from the folder tree, but Windows still stores them on your hard drive and keeps track of them. Eventually, one of four things happens:

- You eliminate things in the Recycle Bin, either by emptying it or by deleting some of the files and folders there.

- You retrieve files from the Recycle Bin and put them in some other folder (see Chapter 7, section "Recovering Objects from the Recycle Bin").

- The Recycle Bin gets full, and starts permanently deleting its oldest files to make space for new ones.

- You turn off the Recycle Bin so deleted files aren't put there anymore.

This section covers all these possibilities except the second one, which was covered in the previous chapter. In addition, this section tells you how to streamline the deleting process, if you want to do so.

Like most other things in Windows, the Recycle Bin has properties. To display them, right-click the Recycle Bin icon on the desktop, and choose Properties from the shortcut menu. The Properties dialog box for the Recycle Bin is displayed, as in Figure 8-13. The Properties dialog box contains a Global tab, plus a tab for each partition of each hard drive on your system.

Emptying the Recycle Bin

Deleting old files serves two purposes: it clears useless files away so you don't confuse them with useful files, and it reclaims the disk space they occupy. The first purpose is served by deleting a file—once it's in the Recycle Bin, you aren't going to open it or work on it by mistake. But a file in the Recycle Bin still takes up disk space: The space isn't reclaimed until the Recycle Bin is emptied.

To empty the Recycle Bin

1. Right-click the Recycle Bin icon on the desktop.

2. Choose Empty Recycle Bin from the shortcut menu. A dialog box asks you to confirm your choice.

3. Click Yes.

To purge selected files or folders from the Recycle Bin without completely emptying it, open the Recycle Bin folder and delete the files in the usual way (see Chapter 7, section "Deleting Files and Folders"). Objects deleted from an ordinary folder on a hard drive are sent to the Recycle Bin, but objects deleted from the Recycle Bin are really deleted.

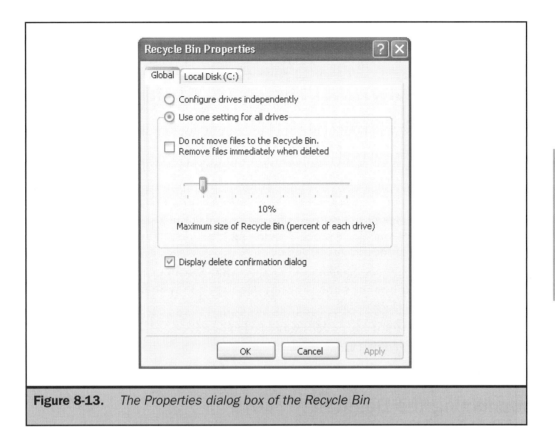

Figure 8-13.   *The Properties dialog box of the Recycle Bin*

To purge only those objects that have been in the Recycle Bin a long time:

1. Open the Recycle Bin.

2. If the window is not already in Details view, choose View I Details.

3. Click the Date Deleted header to put the objects in order of date.

4. Use the enclosing-rectangle method to select all the objects deleted prior to a certain date (see Chapter 7, section "Selecting Files and Folders").

5. Click the Delete button on the toolbar, or press the DELETE key on the keyboard.

6. When the dialog box appears, asking whether you really want to delete these objects, click Yes.

Resizing the Recycle Bin

By default, the maximum size of the Recycle Bin on any hard drive is 10 percent of the size of the drive itself. For example, a 10GB hard drive has a maximum Recycle Bin size of 1GB—a lot of space to use up for files you've decided to delete. If you delete an object that would cause the Recycle Bin to exceed that size, Windows warns you with an error message.

Having a maximum size for the Recycle Bin forces you not to clutter your hard drive with useless, deleted files, and 10 percent is as good a maximum size as any. But you may decide either to raise this limit (because you don't want to lose any of the files currently in the Recycle Bin) or lower it (because disk space is getting tight), either of which you can do by following this procedure:

1. Right-click the Recycle Bin icon on the desktop, and choose Properties from the shortcut menu. You see the Properties dialog box of the Recycle Bin (Figure 8-13).

2. The Properties dialog box contains a Global tab, plus a tab for each hard drive on your system. If you want to change the maximum size setting for all the hard drives at once, set the new maximum size of the Recycle Bin (as a percentage of total drive space) by moving the slider on the Global tab. Then click OK. Skip the remaining steps.

3. If you want to reset the maximum Recycle Bin size for only a single drive, leaving the others the same, select the Configure Drives Independently radio button on the Global tab.

4. Click the tab for the drive you want to change.

5. Set the slider on that tab.

6. Click OK.

Streamlining the Deletion Process

Many times, we've been thankful that Windows makes it so hard to eliminate a file on a hard drive. Four different actions are usually necessary: deleting the file in the first place, confirming the deletion in a dialog box, emptying the Recycle Bin (or deleting the file from the Recycle Bin), and then confirming *that* decision in a dialog box. (If you let the Recycle Bin get full, however, the oldest recycled files will be lost when new ones are recycled.) But even though this process can occasionally be a lifesaver, it can also be tedious (particularly if you are trying to get rid of sensitive files that you don't want hanging around in the Recycle Bin).

 Even deleting a file from the Recycle Bin doesn't destroy the information right away. Windows makes the file's disk space available for reassignment, but doesn't immediately write over that disk space. People with the proper tools could still read the file. To prevent this, you need file-deletion software that is not part of Windows.

Deleting Selected Files or Folders

If you want certain files and folders gone *right now*, with no shilly-shallying about confirmation dialog boxes, Recycle Bins, or Undo buttons, hold down the SHIFT key while you drag the files and folders onto the Recycle Bin icon. (Of course, you should be *very sure* you want the files and folders gone, and that you haven't dragged along any extra objects by accident.) Holding down the SHIFT key while you click the Delete button (or press the DELETE key) is almost as quick: you have to click Yes in a confirmation dialog box, but the objects are deleted for real, not just sent to the Recycle Bin.

Eliminating Confirmation Dialog Boxes

To eliminate the confirmation dialog box when you send something to the Recycle Bin

1. Right-click the Recycle Bin icon on the desktop, and choose Properties from the menu. Or, select the Recycle Bin in a Folder or Windows Explorer window and click the Properties button on the toolbar. You see the Properties dialog box of the Recycle Bin (Figure 8-13).

2. From the Global tab of the Properties dialog box, uncheck the box labeled Display Delete Confirmation Dialog.

3. Click OK.

Even after carrying out these steps, deleting something from the Recycle Bin (that is, getting rid of it for good) still requires a confirmation. If you decide later that you've made the deletion process too easy, you can reinstitute Delete Confirmation Dialog; repeat the preceding steps, but check the check box in step 2.

Turning Off the Recycle Bin

If you want to stop sending deleted files to the Recycle Bin

1. Right-click the Recycle Bin icon on the desktop, and choose Properties from the shortcut menu. You see the Properties dialog box of the Recycle Bin (Figure 8-13).

2. On the Global tab of the Properties dialog box (or on the tab corresponding to the particular drive whose Recycle Bin you are turning off, if the Configure Drives Independently option is chosen on the Global tab), check the box labeled Do Not Move Files To The Recycle Bin. Remove Files Immediately When Deleted.

3. Click OK.

After you complete this procedure, files you delete from your hard drive are gone, just as are files deleted from floppy drives. Files that were already in the Recycle Bin, however, remain there until you empty the Recycle Bin, delete them, restore them, or move them to another folder.

You can turn the Recycle Bin back on by following the same procedure, but unchecking the check box in step 2.

 If you turn off the Recycle Bin, don't forget you did. The Recycle Bin remains off until you turn it on again. A more prudent choice might be to make your Recycle Bin smaller, but to leave it on.

Chapter 9

Backing Up Your Files with the Backup Utility

The most important thing to say about backing up your files is this: Back up your files.

You can back up your files onto floppies, tapes, network servers, extra hard drives, writable CDs (CD-Rs or CD-RWs), Zip drives, Jaz drives, or whatever you happen to have. How you back up your files is much less important than that you do it. If you have only a few files or folders to back up, you can use Windows Explorer to make the copies.

A backup program called the Backup Utility (written by Microsoft and Veritas Software) is included on the Windows XP CD-ROM. It installs as part of Windows XP Professional, but not as part of Windows XP Home Edition. However, Home Edition users can install the Backup Utility separately—it is on the Windows XP Home Edition CD-ROM.

The Backup Utility makes backing up large numbers of files and folders reasonably painless. Your tape drive, Zip drive, Jaz drive, or CD-RW may come with its own backup program. Use the Backup Utility to create backup jobs (descriptions of what and how to back up) and then back them up. If a file is deleted or corrupted, use the Backup Utility to restore the file from your backup tape or disk. The Backup Utility can also create an Automated System Recovery floppy disk that you can use to restart your system if Windows won't start.

Windows XP (as with Windows 2000) includes the Removable Storage service, which manages your tapes or other backup media. The Backup Utility works with Removable Storage to keep track of what's on each tape.

What Is Backing Up?

Backing up means making copies of your files so that you can get the information back should anything happen to the originals.

Many unfortunate things can happen to files:

- A physical disaster like fire, flood, or cat hair could destroy your computer.
- A hardware failure could make your disk unreadable.
- A software problem could erase some of your files. For example, installing an upgrade to an application program might accidentally write over the folders in which you stored the previous documents that were created with that application.
- On a business computer system, a disgruntled employee might steal, erase, or corrupt important files.
- A well-meaning roommate, spouse, child, or coworker might delete or alter files without realizing it.
- You might get confused and get rid of files you meant to keep.

Any one of these possibilities might seem remote to you. (We used to think so, until we learned better.) But when you put them all together, it's amazing how often having a recent backup copy of your files turns out to be handy.

What Should You Back Up?

Ideally, you should back up everything; but (depending on the speed of your machine, the size of your hard drive, and the type of backup medium you use) a complete backup can take a considerable length of time. Once you have a complete backup to work from, updating that backup takes considerably less time.

A backup of only files that are new or have changed is called an *incremental backup*. A complete backup of all files and folders is called a *full backup* or *baseline backup*.

Backing up files is a little like flossing teeth: we all know it's good for us, but few of us do it as often as we know we should. If it takes you a month or two to get around to doing a complete backup, you should consider backing up the following parts of your system more often:

- **Documents you are working on**   Many applications put new documents in your My Documents folder or its subfolders. You may choose to put your documents anywhere you like, but for backup purposes, it is convenient to have them organized in subfolders of one easy-to-find folder.

- **Databases to which you regularly add data**   For example, if you use Quicken to balance your checkbook once a month, back up the file in which Quicken stores your checkbook data.

- **Correspondence, especially your e-mail files**   Letters and memos that you write are probably already in your documents folder(s). E-mail files, however, are usually stored in whatever folder you set up when you installed your e-mail program. Many Microsoft programs put your data in the C:\Documents And Settings*username* folder (replace *username* with your Windows user account name, described in Chapter 6).

If you back up these files frequently, a hard drive disaster is much less of an ordeal. Still, nothing beats the security of knowing that you have backups of *everything*.

Programs are not on the list of important items to back up because you (or the person who maintains your machine) should still have the CDs that you used to install the programs in the first place. Make sure you know where the CDs are, that they're in a safe place, and that the CD serial numbers are with them. If you have downloaded programs, you might want to reserve one backup tape for the downloaded installation files. If you lose your hard disk, reinstalling all of your software is a nuisance, but not a disaster. You would, however, lose all the special settings that you have made to personalize the software for yourself. If reselecting all of those settings would be an ordeal, then you need to either back up the entire program folder, or find out which specific files contain those settings.

If you like, however, you can back up all the files on your entire system, including your programs and Windows itself. If you do this, be sure to include the Windows Registry as part of the backup (see Chapter 38).

How Often Should You Back Up?

Different sources will tell you to back up your files daily, weekly, or monthly, but the real answer is that you should back up your files as soon as you have created or changed something that you don't want to lose. You need to balance the regular nuisance of backing up your files against the possible ordeal of regenerating your creative work.

If you work on a document daily, a single day's work can be a lot to lose. System files change when you reconfigure the settings of your system or when you install new hardware or software. Only you know how frequently your databases change or how much e-mail you are willing to lose in an accident. Backing up these frequently updated files need not be as involved as a full system backup (see "What Should You Back Up?").

If your machine is part of a larger network, such as an office-wide local area network, check with the network administrator to see whether your hard drive is backed up automatically, and if so, how often. If it isn't, you might consider nagging an appropriate person about it. Programs exist that allow a network administrator to back up all the hard drives on the network automatically. Many offices do this every night, relieving individuals of the need to worry about backups at all.

What Should You Do with Your Backup Disks or Tapes?

Put your backup disks or tapes in a safe place, preferably as far from your computer as practical. Backups that sit right next to your computer may be handy in a hardware or software crash—but they don't protect you at all in the event of fire, theft, or sabotage. If your backups are magnetically stored (tapes, removable disks, or hard drives—anything but CD-ROMs), keep them away from strong magnets. You may want to store an extra backup disk or tape off-site (in a different building).

What Is the Backup Utility?

The Backup Utility is an updated version of the Windows Backup program that came with Windows 2000. It is installed as part of Windows XP Professional and comes as a separate program with Windows XP Home Edition. Its purpose is to allow you to back up and recover files quickly and efficiently using file compression techniques to use as little disk space as possible in storing your backups. It can also spread your backup files across many floppy disks or other removable media without confusing itself.

The Backup Utility can make backups from all types of Windows-compatible partitions: NTFS, FAT32, and FAT (see Chapter 32). It makes a *volume shadow copy* of all the files you specify, including files that are open (many backup programs skip open files). You can continue to use your computer during a backup, even storing and editing files that are part of the backup.

Another feature of the program, Automated System Recovery, helps you save and restore the system settings and configuration files that you would need if you had to restore your system from scratch (see "Backing Up and Restoring System Information Using Automated System Recovery"). It can back up hidden system files, including the Registry (see Chapter 38).

Note   *In order to run the Backup Utility, you need to be logged into Windows as an administrative user (see Chapter 6)—Owner, Administrator, or another user account with administrative privileges. If you are logged in as a non-administrative user, you can still run the program, but you can back up only your own files, and you can store the backup only on backup media that you have permission to use.*

What Is a Backup Job?

Making a backup requires you to make a series of decisions: what files to back up, what device to store the backup files on, and a number of more technical decisions, such as whether to use compression or not. Ideally, you would make these decisions once for each type of backup that you regularly do (complete backup, document backup, mail backup, system backup, and so on), and then have the computer remember those decisions so that you don't have to go through them again every time you back up.

The Backup Utility handles this situation by maintaining a list of *backup jobs*. Its Backup Or Restore Wizard helps you define a backup job by leading you through all the necessary decisions. In the course of that process, you give the job a name. The next time you want to back up those same files and/or folders, you need only tell the Backup Utility the name of the job.

Note   *If you schedule the backup job to run later, and specify times for it to run, Backup stores your specifications as a backup job. If you tell the Backup Or Restore Wizard to run the backup job right away, it doesn't store your settings for reuse.*

Backup jobs are usually stored in the D:\Documents and Settings*username*\Local Settings\Application Data\Microsoft\Windows NT\NTBackup\Data folder (we are not making this up). They have the extension .bks (for backup specification). Backup uses Scheduled Tasks to run backup jobs on a schedule (see Chapter 2, section "Running Programs on a Schedule Using Scheduled Tasks"). Once you've created a backup job, there's no easy way to modify it—instead, you recreate it.

MANAGING YOUR FILES

What Is the Removable Storage Service?

Windows XP, as with Windows 2000, includes Removable Storage, a service that can keep track of your tapes or other large-scale removable storage (but we refer to all storage media as tapes in this section, for brevity). Removable Storage doesn't manage floppy disks or CD-ROMs, despite the name; however, it can label your tapes and keep track of which one you need to insert and when. It also works with the Backup Utility and other backup or storage programs that use removable media.

Removable Storage refers to a backup device (such as a tape drive) and its backup media (such as the tapes that work with the drive) as a *library*. A library can be robotic (with an automated media changer, like the fifty-CD changer you can get for your music CDs) or stand-alone (manually operated). Only Windows servers usually have robotic backup devices. Removable Storage organizes them in a library into these *media pools*:

- **Import media pool**   Media that have not yet been catalogued and labeled by Removable Storage. Before you can use them for backup, Removable Storage can import them into the Free media pool.

- **Free media pool**   Unused, available media. When an application (like Backup) is done with a tape, it can return it to the Free media pool.

- **Backup media pool**   Media that have been reserved for use by the Backup Utility. When you use the Backup Utility to back up onto a new tape, Removable Storage moves the tape into the Backup media pool.

Before you can back up information onto tapes, the Removable Storage system catalogues your unused tapes and moves them to the Backup media pool. You can tell Removable storage to do this automatically when you back up onto a new tape. You can also turn the service on or off, and control which users can perform backups and restores (see "Managing the Removable Storage Service").

Backing Up a Few Files or Folders

Even if you can't get around to a complete backup, you can protect yourself against the worst without too much effort by backing up your most valuable files and folders each day that you work on them.

Copying Files onto a Floppy Disk

Even on a slow system, it usually takes only a minute or two at the end of each day to pop in a floppy and copy the files you worked on that day. It's a good habit to develop.

If you typically work on only a few files each day, follow these steps:

1. Put a blank floppy disk into drive A: (the floppy drive).

2. Run Windows Explorer (choose Start | My Computer).

3. If the folder tree doesn't appear in the left pane of the Explorer window, click the Folders button on the toolbar.

4. Find the files you want to back up.

5. Drag-and-drop the files onto the floppy drive in the folder tree (see Chapter 7, section "Dragging and Dropping Files and Folders"). Or, select the files, choose File | Send To (or right-click the file and choose Send To from the menu that appears), and choose your floppy drive from the list of Send To destinations that appears.

If you work on a larger number of files, search for recently changed files to make sure that you don't miss any. Choose Start | Search to search for all files modified within the last day (see Chapter 8, section "Searching by Date"). You can drag-and-drop files directly out of the Search Results window onto a floppy disk icon in Windows Explorer. Or you can right-click any file in the Search Results window and choose Send To from the menu.

> **Tip** *If you use Search to list the files you've worked on today, construct your search in such a way as to avoid finding all the temporary files that Windows creates in the course of a day. (If you do a lot of Web browsing, there can be hundreds of them.) These temporary files are contained in subfolders of the C:\Windows folder (or whatever folder Windows is installed in).*

Copying Files onto Larger Drives

Anything you can copy onto a floppy, you can also copy onto a writable CD, a Zip drive or other removable disk, a second hard drive, or another machine on your LAN. You can drag-and-drop the files to these media in the same way you copy files to floppies. If the drive (or folder) that you use for storing backup copies isn't already available on the Send To menu, you can add it (see Chapter 7, section "Using the Send To Menu").

A larger backup drive makes it less important to be selective about what you copy. A Zip disk is approximately 70 times larger than a floppy, and a backup hard drive may be dozens of times larger yet. You probably can copy, without too much time or trouble, your entire documents folder (whether it is C:\My Documents or some other folder that you have chosen) at the end of each day. You probably can copy your entire e-mail folder as well (see "What Should You Back Up?").

Running the Backup Utility

The Backup Utility has several advantages over a more informal system of copying key files onto floppies or other storage media:

- It can copy files in a compressed form, so that they take up less disk space.

- It can spread a single backup job over several floppies or removable disks. This feature makes it possible to back up larger jobs.

- When you define a backup job, you decide once and for all what folders you want the job to back up. You don't have to go through the decision process every time you do a backup.

- It is automated. Once the job starts, all you need to do is feed it a new disk if it asks for one. If you are backing up onto a tape drive or some other medium with sufficient size, you don't need to do anything at all.

- Backup can also create an Automated System Recovery floppy disk that you can use to restart your computer in the event of a disaster.

- It can back up files that are open. The Backup Utility takes a volume shadow copy—that is, what the files contain at the moment that the backup occurs.

Installing the Backup Utility

If you don't find Backup on the Start | All Programs | Accessories | System Tools menu, follow these steps:

1. With the Windows XP CD-ROM in your CD-ROM drive, display the folder D:\Valueadd\Msft\NTBackup in an Explorer window; substitute your CD-ROM's drive letter for D: if it's not drive D:. (If the Windows XP installation window appears, click Perform Additional Tasks, then click Browse This CD to see an Explorer window showing the files on the CD.) The folder contains two files: NTBackup.msi (the Backup installation program) and Readme.txt.

2. Run NTBackup.msi. Follow the instructions on the screen to install the Backup Utility files in your C:\Windows\System32 folder. The filename of the program is Ntbackup.exe.

3. Make a shortcut for the program. Right-click the desktop, choose New | Shortcut from the menu that appears, and type **C:\Windows\System32\Ntbackup** into the box that appears. (Replace C: with the drive letter in which Windows is installed.) After you click Next, type any name for the shortcut (such as **Backup**). Click Finish, and the shortcut appears.

Running the Backup Utility

Run the Backup Utility by selecting Start | All Programs | Accessories | System Tools | Backup (if you have Windows XP Professional) or by running the shortcut you just created (if you have Windows XP Home Edition). In Windows XP Professional, all users can also start the Backup Utility in one of these ways:

- Choose Start | Run and type **ntbackup** in the Open box.
- Right-click a disk drive in an Explorer window, choose Properties to display the drive's Properties , click the Tools tab, and click the Backup Now button.

Remember that you must be logged on as an administrative user (or with a user account that is a member of the Backup Operators group) to be able to back up or restore files (see Chapter 6).

The first time you run the Backup Utility, it checks your system for devices onto which you can copy files (backup devices). Then it runs the Backup Or Restore Wizard, which steps you through backing up files or restoring from a previous backup. If you'd rather not use the Wizard, clear the Always Start In Wizard Mode check box on its first dialog box, and click the Advanced Mode link.

Believe it or not, you can run three Wizards from the Backup Utility: the Backup Or Restore Wizard, the Backup Wizard, and the Restore Wizard. You might think that running the Backup Or Restore Wizard and choosing Back Up Files And Settings would run the Backup Wizard, but it doesn't—the backup part of the Backup Or Restore Wizard is similar to the Backup Wizard, but it provides a few additional options. You can tell which Wizard you are running by the name in the title bar of its window. We recommend using the Backup Or Restore Wizard if you must use a Wizard at all—choose Tools | Switch To Wizard Mode from the Backup Utility's menu bar.

Backing Up Files with the Backup Utility

Backing up files is something you should do regularly, so it's worth taking some time to create backup jobs for the files that are the most important to you and to schedule them to run daily (or at least weekly). You can create a backup job with a Wizard or from the Backup Utility window, and you can run backup jobs you've already created.

Creating a Backup Job with the Backup Or Restore Wizard

The Backup Or Restore Wizard may run automatically when you start the Backup Utility. Otherwise, choose Tools | Switch To Wizard Mode from the menu bar in the Backup Utility window. When the program runs, choose Back Up Files And Settings from the Wizard's dialog box. Click Next to move from dialog box to dialog box, and click the Advanced button when it appears so that you have access to all the Wizard's settings. You need to make the following decisions to create a new backup job (these decisions are described in more detail in the following sections):

- Whether to back up or restore files (see "Restoring Files with the Backup Utility").

- Which files to back up (see Figure 9-1).

- Whether to back up only your files, the files of all the user accounts on the computer, or the files that you specify.

- Whether to back up all the selected files or just the ones that have changed since the previous backup.

- Where to store the backup data, and whether to replace backup jobs that are already there.

- Whether to verify the backup.

- Whether to use compression to make the backup file smaller.

- When to run the backup job—now, or at a later scheduled time.

When you click the Wizard's Finish button, if you chose to back up now, the program begins copying files. You see a Backup Progress dialog box that shows how many files will be copied, and how many have been copied so far, as shown in Figure 9-2.

When the backup is done, you can click the Report button to see a log of the files that were copied.

The following sections provide you with more detail about the choices you have to make when setting up a backup job.

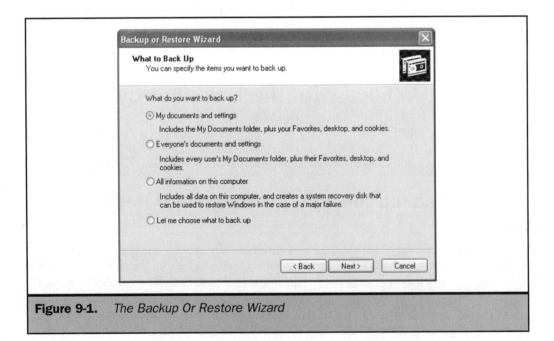

Figure 9-1. *The Backup Or Restore Wizard*

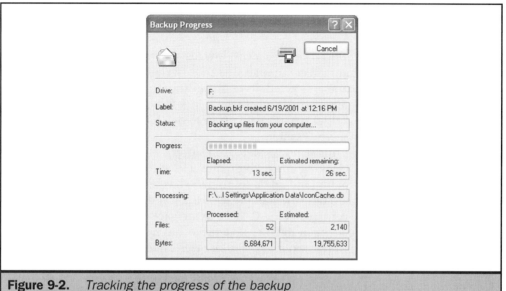

Figure 9-2.   *Tracking the progress of the backup*

Selecting Files to Back Up

The first decision you need to make is whether this backup job should be a complete backup or a backup only of selected files. You have four options:

- **My Documents And Settings**   Includes the files in your Documents And Settings folder (usually C:\Documents And Settings*username*, where *username* is your user account name). This folder includes your desktop and Start menu settings, your My Documents folder, your Favorites, and other configuration settings. If you store all your data files in your My Documents folder and its subfolders, this option is an efficient way to back up your own files—program files can always be restored from CDs.

- **Everyone's Documents And Settings**   Includes the Documents And Settings folders for all the user accounts defined on your computer (see Chapter 6).

- **All Information On This Computer**   Includes all the files from all the drives on your computer. This option backs up Windows itself and all your application programs and data. If you are running Windows XP Professional, it also creates a automated system recovery (ASR) disk —a floppy disk from which you can start your computer and restore files from the backup in case of a complete hard disk failure (see "Backing Up and Restoring System Information Using Automated System Recovery").

■ **Let Me Choose What To Back Up**   Displays a folder tree from which you can choose the files and folders you want to include.

If you choose the last option, you see a window (as shown in Figure 9-3) that works much like an Explorer window (see Chapter 7, section "What Is Windows Explorer?"). When a folder in the left pane is selected, its contents appear in the right pane. The boxes with plus or minus signs denote whether a folder is expanded. Click a plus box to see the next level of the folder tree under a given folder. Click the My Computer plus box to see the disk drives on your system.

The difference between this window and an Explorer window is that each folder has a check box next to it. Clicking one of these puts a blue check mark in the box, indicating that the entire folder (and all its subfolders) has been added to the list of files and folders to be backed up. For example, clicking the check box next to the C drive icon adds the entire contents of the C drive to the backup job.

If you want to back up some of the files on a drive, but not all of them, click the plus box next to the drive icon to expand the folder tree underneath that drive. This gives you an opportunity to decide exactly which folders to back up. Select only those files and folders that you want to be part of this backup job. A gray check mark appears in the box next to a folder from which you have chosen to back up some, but not all, of its contents.

 To back up the Registry, boot files, and other system files, choose System State from the Items To Back Up list, which appears as the last item under My Computer.

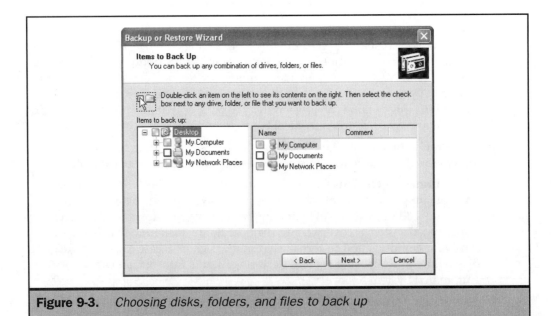

Figure 9-3. *Choosing disks, folders, and files to back up*

Choosing a Destination for the Backup File

The next screen of the Backup Or Restore Wizard asks where to store the backup files. The options you see depend on how you set the first setting, Select The Backup Type. You can set this to File or to a backup device—a tape drive or other mass storage device.

If you choose File, Backup combines the entire backup into one compressed backup file stored on the disk that you indicate. Backup files have the extension .bkf. When you restore one or more files from the backup file, the Backup Utility extracts the files you want from the backup file. When you choose File, you see these two settings, as shown in Figure 9-4:

■ **Choose A Place To Save Your Backup**   Select the drive on which to store the backup file. The drop-down box shows a list of your removable disk drives, including your floppy disk drive. (Floppy disks are convenient only when you are backing up only a few files.) You can also store a backup file on a fixed hard disk—set the box to Let Me Choose A Location Not Listed Here and click the Browse button to see your hard disks and choose a folder. (We found that you have to put a formatted floppy disk in drive A: at this point, even if you don't plan to store your backup file on the floppy.) For example, if you want to make daily backups of a few important data files, you can store the files in a Backup folder on your hard disk. However, if your hard disk dies, all your backup files will be lost. In the future, the pathname you choose appears on a drop-down list of places.

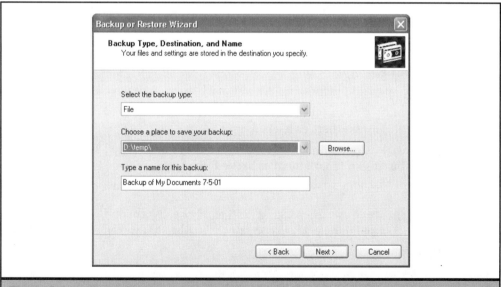

Figure 9-4.   *Choosing where to store the backup*

- **Type A Name For This Backup**   This is the name of the backup file (you don't have to type the .bkf extension). The default name is Backup.bkf (the Backup Utility adds the .bkf extension).

If your computer has a tape drive, you can choose it from the Select The Backup Type drop-down menu, which includes an option for the type of backup tape you use (for example, miniQIC or Travan). Then, you have only one other option to set: Choose The Tape You Want To Use. Set this to New to use a tape that has not been catalogued by the Removable Storage program, or choose the name of an existing tape (see "What Is the Removable Storage Service?").

Tip   *The Backup Utility doesn't work directly with CD-R or CD-RW drives. If you want to back up to a CD-R or CD-RW disk, back up to a file first, and then burn the file onto the CD. This limitation prevents the Backup Utility from creating a backup that spans several CDs. One CD-R or CD-RW can hold up to about 650MB, so if your backup file is no larger than this, you can burn it onto a CD. For larger backup files, use a CD-burning utility that can split files over multiple CDs.*

Choosing a Baseline or an Incremental Backup

After you have chosen which files to back up and where to store them, the Wizard displays the Completing The Backup Or Restore Wizard dialog box, confirming the information you have specified so far. But you're not done yet—click the Advanced button to see some other settings.

The Type Of Backup setting controls whether to back up all the files you selected, or only files that are new or changed since the previous backup. (Windows tracks which files have been created or changed since your last backup.) You have five options for this setting:

- **Normal**   Copies all the files you selected, and marks them as backed up.
- **Copy**   Copies all the files, but doesn't mark them as backed up.
- **Incremental**   Copies only files that were created or changed since the last backup, and marks them as backed up.
- **Differential**   Copies only files that were created or changed since the last backup, but doesn't mark them as backed up.
- **Daily**   Copies only files that were created or changed today.

If this is the first time you are backing up files, choose Normal. If you have recently backed up files, choose Incremental to copy only the files that weren't included in your last backup.

Choosing How to Back Up

Next, you see the How To Back Up settings, which consist of these check boxes:

- **Verify Data After Backup**   After completing the backup, the Backup Utility reads the backup and compares it to the files it backed up, to make sure that they match. This step lengthens the backup time, but it may be worth it. Verifying that the backup was successful takes only a little less time than the backup itself and may seem unnecessary, but remember: Paranoia is what backing up is all about. If you had faith that such things would always work properly, you wouldn't be backing up at all.

- **Use Hardware Compression If Available**   Some backup devices can compress the backup information as it stores it. This check box is grayed out if your backup device doesn't support this feature. (Most tape drives do.)

- **Disable Volume Snapshot**   The Backup Utility can include files that are open—files that programs are updating. If you don't want open files to be included, deselect this check box.

The next screen of the Backup Or Restore Wizard asks whether to Append This Backup To The Existing Backups or Replace The Existing Backups. For backups to tape, this setting determines what happens to the previous backup information that is already on the tape. Another option controls whether the backup is accessible only to administrative users or to all users.

If you are backing up to a new tape, the next screen of the Wizard suggests labels to use for the tape. This label is stored on the tape and appears in the Backup window on the list of available backups. You may want to write the same information on a paper label and stick it to the tape.

Choose When to Back Up

Finally, the Backup Or Restore Wizard asks whether to run the backup job Now or Later. If you choose Later, you specify the name of the backup job and when to run it, as shown in Figure 9-5. You can run the backup job once, or you can schedule it to run daily, weekly, monthly, or another schedule (see Chapter 2, section "Running Programs on a Schedule Using Scheduled Tasks").

This is the last information that the Backup Or Restore Wizard asks for. When you click Next, you see the Completing The Backup Or Restore Wizard dialog box again, with a summary window of all your settings (as shown in Figure 9-6). Click Finish to create the backup job and run it (now or whenever you specified).

If you are using a tape, you may see messages from the Removable storage program as it mounts the tape. When the backup job is finished, Backup exits.

MANAGING YOUR FILES

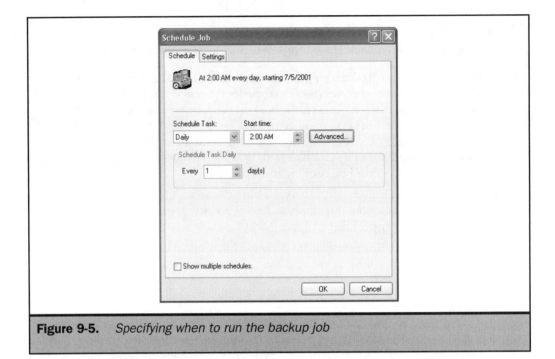

Figure 9-5. *Specifying when to run the backup job*

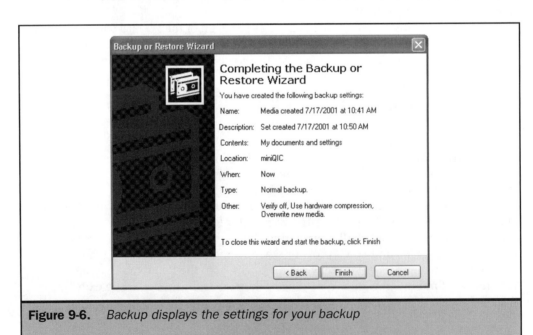

Figure 9-6. *Backup displays the settings for your backup*

If you plan to reuse these backup specifications—the files to include, the backup type, where to store the backup, and other settings—tell Backup to run the backup Later. This choice causes Backup to store the backup job so you can run it again.

Creating a Backup Job by Using the Backup Tab

You don't have to use a Wizard to create a backup job. Instead, you run the Backup Utility and click the Advanced Mode link on its opening screen. You see the main window of Backup Utility, as shown in Figure 9-7. The Backup Wizard and Restore Wizard buttons run limited versions of the Backup Or Restore Wizard that we describe in this chapter (we recommend that you run the Backup Or Restore Wizard instead, by choosing Tools | Switch To Wizard Mode from the menu bar).

 If you rarely want to use the Backup Or Restore Wizard, deselect the Always Start In Wizard Mode check box on the Wizard's opening screen.

To create a backup job, click the Backup tab just below the menu bar. You see the window shown in Figure 9-8. The upper part of the window enables you to choose the

MANAGING YOUR FILES

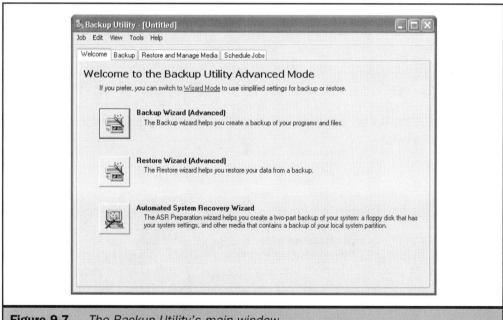

Figure 9-7.   *The Backup Utility's main window*

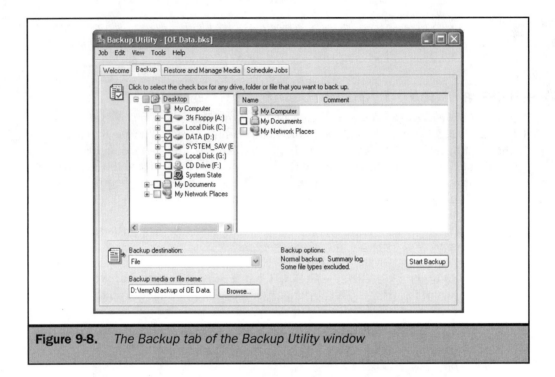

Figure 9-8.   *The Backup tab of the Backup Utility window*

files to include. The settings in the lower left corner allow you to specify where to store the backup (see "Choosing a Destination for the Backup File"). The rest of the options that the Backup Or Restore Wizard offers appear after you click the Start Backup button.

When you click the Start Backup button, you see the Backup Job Information window, shown next:

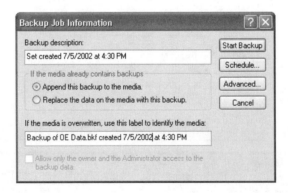

This window contains the rest of your backup options, as described in the "Creating a Backup Job with the Backup Or Restore Wizard" section earlier in this chapter.

To schedule the job to run at a specified time (or on a schedule), click the Schedule button. The Backup Utility prompts you to save your settings as a backup job, and lets you specify a name. If your user account has a password, it prompts you for the password (you have to type it twice). Then you see the Scheduled Job Options dialog box, as shown in Figure 9-5 (see "Choose When to Back Up").

For other options, click the Advanced button to display the Advanced Backup Options dialog box, shown next:

In addition to the options described in the section "Choosing How to Back Up," you see these other settings:

- **Back Up Data That Is In Remote Storage**   Includes files that are stored in a *remote storage*, a special storage device that stores infrequently used files.

- **Automatically Backup System Protected Files With The System State**   Includes the files in your C:\Windows folder (or whatever folder Windows is installed in). Choosing this option adds over 200MB to your backup job.

When you return to the Backup Job Information dialog box and click Start Backup, your backup job runs (or is stored to be run later).

Running a Backup Job

Once you have created and named a backup job, you can run it without going through the Backup Or Restore Wizard (in fact, the Wizard doesn't include a way to rerun an existing backup job). The backup job is stored as a .bks file that you can re-open and rerun.

Running a Backup Job from the Backup Utility Window

To run an existing backup job, follow these steps:

1. Run the Backup Utility. If the Backup Or Restore Wizard runs, click the Advanced Mode link on its opening window. You see the Backup Utility main window, as shown in Figure 9-7.

2. Click the Backup tab (shown in Figure 9-8).

3. Choose Job | Load Selections from the menu bar. You see the Open dialog box showing the default location of .bks files.

4. Choose a backup job and click Open. If you've already selected some files, Backup asks whether it's okay to clear the current file selections and use the ones from the backup job instead. Click Yes. Backup shows the selected drives, folders, and files on the Backup tab.

5. Follow the instructions for creating a backup job from the main window in the preceding section.

Running a Backup Job on a Schedule

When you create a backup job, you can schedule it to run daily, weekly, monthly, or on some other schedule. The Backup Utility uses the Windows Scheduled Tasks feature to handle the scheduling (see Chapter 2, section "Running Programs on a Schedule Using Scheduled Tasks ").

When you create a job using the Backup tab of the Backup Utility window, after you click the Start Backup button, click the Schedule button on the Backup Job Information dialog box to display the Scheduled Job Options dialog box (see Figure 9-5).

You can check the schedule of a backup job by clicking the Schedule Jobs tab in the Backup Utility window (as shown in Figure 9-9). Click a backup icon on a day on the calendar to see the Scheduled Job Options dialog box for that backup job. To change the schedule for the backup job, click the Properties button on the Schedule Data tab to see the Schedule Job dialog box, and click the Schedule tab. You can change the frequency, time, and day of the backups, as well as other settings (see Chapter 2, section "Configuring a Scheduled Program"). However, there's no easy way to change the files that are included—instead, open and rerun the job as described in the previous section.

Excluding Files from Backups

Some types of files don't need to be backed up, such as temporary files and files in a cache (temporary storage area). You can tell the Backup Utility not to include specific types of files by choosing Tools | Options from the Backup Utility's main window and clicking the Exclude Files tab (as shown in Figure 9-10). You can specify files that are in certain folders, files that have certain extensions, or both, and you can specify whether to exclude these files for backups made by all users, or only backups made by the current user.

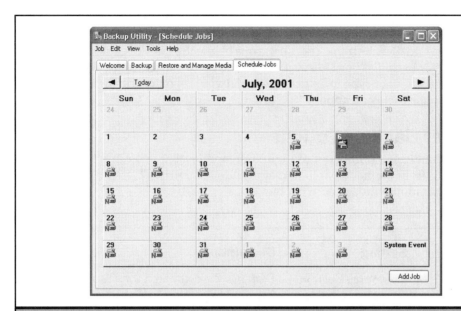

Figure 9-9. *The schedule of backup jobs*

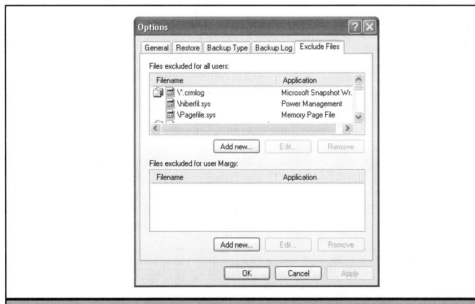

Figure 9-10. *The Exclude Files tab of the Options dialog box*

The Backup Utility is preconfigured to ignore many temporary Windows files when making backups for any user. You can add files and folders to its exclusion lists by clicking the Add New button—choose the one below the Files Excluded For All Users or the Files Excluded For User *username* box. You can choose a file type (based on filename extension) or type in an extension, and you can type or browse to the folder to which the exclusion applies.

Setting Other Backup Options

The Backup Utility has a number of configuration options that you can set by choosing Tools | Options from the menu bar in its main window (shown in Figure 9-7). Table 9-1 lists the configuration settings and what they do.

Tab	Setting	Description
General	Compute selection information before backup and restore operations	Displays the estimated total number of files and total bytes to be backed up before the backup begins (ditto for restoring).
General	Use the catalogs on the media to speed up building restore catalogs on disk	When restoring from tapes, uses the file catalogs that are stored on the tapes when creating the list of files in the entire backup. This is faster than Backup scanning the tapes for files and creating a new catalog. However, if a tape is missing or damaged, its catalog may not be available, and you may need to turn this setting off to restore files from the remaining tapes.
General	Verify data after the backup completes	Specifies that after backing up the files, Backup compares the backup copies to the original files. Files that are in use and being updated during the backup may have changed between backup and verification, so not all verification errors indicate a problem.

Table 9-1.   *Backup Utility Configuration Options*

Tab	Setting	Description
General	Back up the contents of mounted drives	For mounted drives, includes the contents of the drive (see Chapter 32, section "Assigning Pathnames to Partitions"). If deselected, Backup includes only the pathname of the mounted drive, and not its contents.
General	Show alert message when I start the Backup Utility and Removable Storage is not running	For backups to and restores from tape, displays a warning if the Removable Storage system isn't running. Backup can then start Removable Storage so you can use the tapes or other media that it manages. Select this setting if you back up to tapes. For backups to file or to removable disks (like floppies and Zip disks), this setting doesn't matter.
General	Show alert message when I start the Backup Utility and there is recognizable media available	For backups to and restores from tape, lets you know when new tapes are available. If you back up to tape, select this setting. Doesn't apply to backups to file or to removable disks.
General	Show alert message when new media is inserted	For backups to and restores from tape, lets you know when you insert a new tape. If you back up to tape, select this setting. Doesn't apply to backups to file or to removable disks.
General	Always allow use of recognizable media without prompting	For backups to tape, automatically moves a new uncataloged tape in the tape drive into the Backup media pool and then uses it for backup.

Table 9-1.   *Backup Utility Configuration Options* (continued)

MANAGING YOUR FILES

Tab	Setting	Description
Restore	Do not replace the file on my computer (recommended), Replace the file on disk only if the file on disk is older, Always replace the file on my computer	Specifies what Backup Utility does when restoring a file that already exists on your computer.
Backup Type	Default Backup Type	Specifies what type of backup appears as the default when creating new backup jobs (see "Choosing a Baseline or an Incremental Backup").
Backup Log	Detailed, Summary, None	Specifies how much information to store in the log file for backups.
Exclude Files	Files excluded for all users	For all user accounts, specifies the list of file types to skip when backing up (for example, temporary and backup files, with extensions .tmp and .bak). Click Add to add a file type to the list.
Exclude Files	Files excluded for user *username*	Ditto, for the user who is currently logged in.

Table 9-1.   *Backup Utility Configuration Options* (continued)

Running the Backup Utility from the Command Line

When you schedule a backup job, the Backup Utility creates a command line that runs the job with your settings (see Chapter 39).—where to store the backup, what to call it, and other settings. You can see the command line for a scheduled backup job by clicking the Schedule Jobs tab, clicking the icon for a backup job, and clicking the Properties button on the Scheduled Job Options dialog box that appears. You see the Schedule Job dialog box (see Chapter 2, section "Configuring a Scheduled Program"). The Run box on the Task tab shows the command line, which is something like this:

```
C:\WINDOWS\system32\ntbackup.exe backup "@C:\Documents and Settings\Margy\Local
Settings\Application Data\Microsoft\Windows NT\NTBackup\data\OE Data.bks" /a /d
"Set created 7/5/2002 at 4:12 PM" /v:no /r:no /rs:no /hc:off /m normal /j "OE
Data" /l:s /f "D:\Data\Backup OE Data.bkf"
```

To run the backup Utility from the command line (the Start | Run box, a Command Prompt window, or a shortcut), you type

ntbackup backup [systemstate] *backupjob switches*

The systemstate switch is optional (don't type the brackets if you choose to include it). Replace *backupjob* with the name of the .bks file that contains the specifications for the backup job. Replace *switches* with the appropriate switches from Table 9-2. If you are backing up to tape (or any medium that is controlled by the Removable Storage service), also use the switches described in Table 9-3.

Switch	Description
Backup	Specifies that you are performing a backup rather than a restore.
Systemstate	Backs up the system state (Registry, boot files, and other system information). Omit this switch to avoid backing up the system state.
Backupjob	Specifies the pathname of the .bks file that contains the backup job specifications.
/D "*label*"	Specifies a label for the backup set. Type the quotes around the label.
/F "*filename*"	Specifies the pathname of the backup file. Don't use this with the /G, /P, or /T switches when backing up to tape. Type the quotes around the filename.
/J "*name*"	Specifies the backup job name, which appears as the Backup Identification Label on the Restore And Manage Media tab of the Backup Utility window. It also appears in the log file for the backup. Type the quotes around the backup job name.
/L:f or /L:s or /L:n	If "f," creates a full log file. If "s," creates a summary log file. If "n," doesn't create a log file.

Table 9-2. *NTBackup Command Line Switches for All Backups*

Switch	Description
/M *backuptype*	Specifies the backup type: "normal," "copy," "differential," "incremental," or "daily" (see "Choosing a Baseline or an Incremental Backup").
/SNAP:on or /SNAP:off	If "on," includes open files, making a volume shadow copy (which used to be called a snapshot).
/V:yes or /V:no	If "yes," verifies the backup after it's finished.

Table 9-2.   *NTBackup Command Line Switches for All Backups* (continued)

Switch	Description
/A	Appends the backup to the end of the tape, rather than erasing what's already on the tape. Use with /G or /T, not with /P.
/G *"guidname"*	Specifies the tape by its GUID (globally unique identifier), and overwrites or appends to this tape. Do not use this switch in conjunction with /P. Type the quotes around the GUID.
/HC:on or /HC:off	If "on" and the tape drive supports hardware compression, uses hardware compression when backing up. If "off," doesn't use hardware compression.
/N *"newtapename"*	Specifies the name to give to the new tape used for the backup. Don't use with /A. Type the quotes around the tape name.
/P *"poolname"*	Specifies the media pool from which the tape comes. Backup uses any available tape from this pool, so you can't use /P with /A, /G, /F, or /T. Type the quotes around the media pool name.
/R:yes or /R:no	If "yes," only the user who created the tape, or administrative users, can use this tape.

Table 9-3.   *NTBackup Command Line Switches for Backups to Tape*

Switch	Description
/RS:yes or /RS:no	If "yes," includes the Removable Storage database in the backup. If "no," omits the database from the backup.
/T "*tapename*"	Specifies the name of the tape onto which to back up. Don't use with /P. Type the quotes around the tape name.
/UM	Backs up to the first available tape in the media pool that you specified with /P. Formats the tape before the backup.

Table 9-3. *NTBackup Command Line Switches for Backups to Tape* (continued)

You can run the Backup Utility from the Command Prompt window or in the Start | Run dialog box: type or copy the ntbackup command followed by the command line switches. Or create a shortcut that contains the command line: right-click the Windows desktop, choose New | Shortcut from the menu that appears, and type or copy the ntbackup command line in the Type The Location Of The Item box. Once you've made a shortcut for the ntbackup command, you can leave it on the desktop or copy it onto the Start menu (see Chapter 10, section "Reorganizing the Start Menu").

Restoring Files with the Backup Utility

To restore files that you have backed up with the Backup Utility, you can use the Restore Wizard or you can select options yourself.

 Note *The Backup Utility stores backed-up files in a special format, and you need to use Backup Utility to restore them. You can't just copy the files from an Explorer window back to where you want to use them. The Backup Utility can't restore backups made by other backup programs, either, including those made by the Windows Me/9x backup utilities.*

Restoring Files Using the Restore Wizard

To run the Backup Or Restore Wizard to help you restore one or more files, follow these steps:

1. Start the Backup Utility. If the Wizard doesn't start automatically, choose Tools | Switch To Wizard Mode from the menu bar.

MANAGING YOUR FILES

2. When the Wizard runs, choose Restore Files And Settings and click Next. You see the What To Restore window, containing two boxes: the one on the left shows the backup files and tapes available (Figure 9-11). Backups to file are listed under the File heading. Tape backups are listed under a heading that reflects the type of type (like miniQIC or Travan), and then by the tape.

3. Double-click an item on the left to see the files and folders that it contains on the right. Click the boxes next to files and folders to put a check mark by those that you want to restore. Click Next when you have finished. You see the Completing The Backup Or Restore Wizard, but you're not done.

4. Click the Advanced button to display the Where To Restore window.

5. Set the Restore Files To box to Original Location to put the files back where they came from; Alternate Location to put the structure of restored files and folders in a folder you specify; or Single Folder to put all the restored files into a single folder, without restoring the structure of the folders that they used to be in. Click Next.

6. In the How To Restore window, choose what to do if restoring a file would overwrite an existing file. Choose Leave Existing Files, Replace Existing Files If They Are Older Than The Backup Files, or Replace Existing Files. Click Next. You see the Advanced Restore Options window.

7. If you are restoring files that were stored on an NTFS partition, you can select the Restore Security Settings check box to restore the permissions and

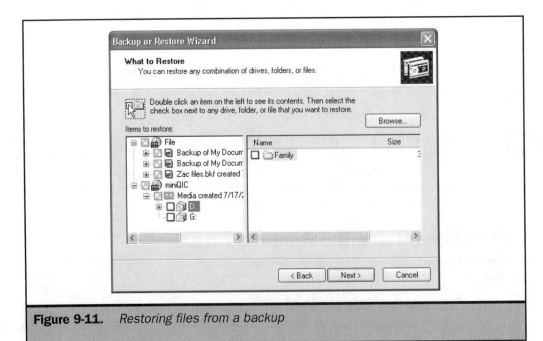

Figure 9-11.   *Restoring files from a backup*

ownership for the folders and files. (See Table 9-4 in the following section for information about the settings in steps 7–9.)

8. If you are restoring a mounted drive, select the Restore Junction Points But Not The Folders And File Data They Reference check box (see Chapter 32, section "Assigning Pathnames to Partitions").

9. If you are restoring files and folders that contain mount points for mounted drives, deselect the Preserve Existing Volume Mount Points check box. If you have already set up the mount points for mounted drives and you don't want to disturb them, select this check box. Click Next.

10. You see the Completing The Backup Or Restore Wizard window again. Click Finish to restore the files.

While the Backup Utility is restoring files, you see a Restore Progress window showing how many files have been restored and how many are yet to be restored. When it is finished, click the Report button to see the log file, or the Close button to close the window.

Restoring Files by Using the Restore And Manage Media Tab

Alternatively, you can use the Restore And Manage Media tab on the main Backup Utility window to select what to restore. Follow these steps:

1. Click the Restore And Manage Media tab in the main Backup Utility window, as shown in Figure 9-12.

2. Choose the files and folders to restore, as described in step 3 of the previous section.

3. The Restore Files To box is normally set to Original Location to restore the files and folders to the location from which they were backed up, in the same folder structure. You can change this setting to Alternate Location (to put the structure of restored files and folders in a folder you specify) or Single Folder (to put all the restored files into a single folder, without restoring the structure of the folders that they used to be in).

4. If you chose Alternate Location or Single Folder in the last step, set the Alternate Location box to the folder where you want to restore the files and folders.

5. Click the Start Restore button (you still have some other options to set). You see the Confirm Restore dialog box.

6. Click the Advanced button to choose other options for restoring files. Table 9-4 shows the advanced options available when restoring files. Click OK when you have finished.

7. Click OK to begin restoring your files and folders. If you are restoring from a tape or other removable media, Backup prompts you to put in the necessary tape or disk; do so and click OK. Then Backup restores the folders and files.

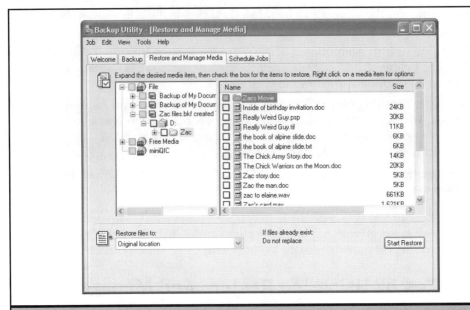

Figure 9-12. *The Restore And Manage Media tab of the main Backup window*

Setting	Description
Restore security	For files and folders that were backed up from an NTFS partition and that are to be restored to an NTFS partition, restores the permissions and ownership information with the files and folders.
Restore junction points, and restore file and folder data under junction points to the original location	When restoring files to a disk with *junction points* (which are like mount points), restores the files and folders that are stored on the hard disk to which the junction point points (see Chapter 32, section "Assigning Pathnames to Partitions"). When restoring a mounted drive, restores only the folder that contains the mounted drive (unselect this option to restore the folders and files stored on the mounted drive).

Table 9-4. *Advanced Options for Restoring Backed-Up Files*

Setting	Description
When restoring replicated data, mark the restored data as the primary data for all replicas	When restoring files that are managed by the File Replication Service (FRS), specifies that this copy of the files is the primary copy. (See *Windows .NET Server: The Complete Reference*, by Kathy Ivens, published by Osborne/McGraw-Hill, for information about FRS.)
Restore the Cluster Registry to the quorum disk and all other nodes	Not available in Windows XP Home and Professional.
Preserve existing volume mount points	Doesn't restore mount points from the backup, leaving the existing mount points. If you want to restore backed-up mount points, deselect this check box.

Table 9-4.   *Advanced Options for Restoring Backed-Up Files* (continued)

8. When Backup has finished, the Restore Progress window displays information about how many files and folders were restored. You can click the Report button to see the log file. Click Close when you are finished.

Note   *When restoring files to a FAT or FAT32 partition, Backup may warn you that not all security features are available. FAT and FAT32 partitions don't allow you to set passwords for files (only NTFS partitions support this).*

Managing the Removable Storage Service

You can see a list of the libraries set options for removable Storage by opening the Computer Management window, also known as the Microsoft Management Console. (See Chapter 35, section "The Microsoft Management Console.") Click Start, right-click My Computer, and choose Manage from the menu that appears. When you see the Computer Management window, open the Storage item, and then the Removable Storage item that it contains. You see a window that looks like the one in Figure 9-13.

You can set the Removable Storage options by clicking Removable Storage in the left pane and clicking the Properties button on the toolbar (or right-click Removable

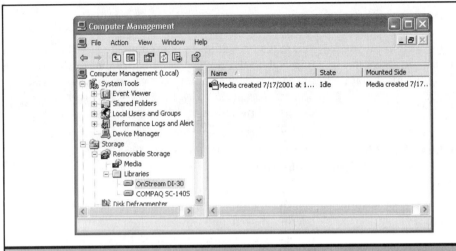

Figure 9-13. *The Computer Management window displays your Removable Storage libraries.*

Storage and choose Properties from the menu that appears). On the General tab of the Removable Storage Properties dialog box, you can set these two check boxes:

- **Display Operator Request And Progress Dialogs**   Specifies whether to display dialog boxes to let you know what's happening—we keep this selected.
- **Use Status Area Icon For Pending Requests**   Specifies whether to display an icon in the notification area of the Windows taskbar when requests are pending.

Click the Security tab to see a list of the user accounts and groups that are defined on your system, and to change their permissions. You can also change the permissions for a specific media library by right-clicking it, choosing Properties, and clicking the Security tab.

 For more information about the Removable Storage service, choose Help | Help Topics from the Computer Management window menu bar, and click Removable Storage on the list of topics in the table of contents.

Backing Up and Restoring System Information Using Automated System Recovery

Automated System Recovery (ASR) is available in Windows XP Professional, but not in Windows XP Home Edition. ASR enables the Backup Utility to back up key system information—what partitions are on your hard disks, how to start up, and other information—onto a floppy disk. You can use this floppy disk to restart your computer in the event of a disaster.

The ASR may appear to make a backup in Windows XP Home Edition, but restoring from it won't work, because Windows XP Home Edition doesn't support setups from ASR disks. You should be able to reinstall Windows XP from your Windows XP CD-ROM, and then restore the rest of the files from your backup.

Automated System Recovery doesn't recover all your files—it doesn't include all your program files or any of your data files. You need to make regular backups to have up-to-date copies of your data files. You can restore your program files from the program installation CDs or floppies.

Making an ASR Disk

Follow these steps to create an ASR floppy disk. You'll need a blank floppy disk as well as your usual backup medium for backing up the rest of the files you choose. If you plan to back up your system files to a tape, choose a blank tape or one that can be erased: the backup can't be appended to a tape with existing backups.

1. Run the Backup Utility. If the Backup Or Restore Wizard runs, click the Advanced Mode link to display the Backup Utility window.

2. On the Welcome tab, click the Automated System Recovery Wizard button (or choose Tools | ASR Wizard from the menu bar). The Automated System Recovery Preparation Wizard starts.

3. Click Next to display the Backup Destination window.

4. Set the Backup Media Type to File or another destination (such as a tape drive), and specify the filename or tape (see "Choosing a Destination for the Backup File").

5. Click Next and then Finish to start the backup. The Backup Utility backs your system files up on the destination that you chose. If the tape already contains backups, you see a message asking whether it's okay to overwrite the existing backups. Choosing No aborts the backup.

6. When Backup prompts for a blank, 1.44MB formatted floppy disk, insert it drive A and click OK.

7. When Backup is finished creating the ASR it suggests that you take the floppy out of the drive and label it. Click OK and then Close.

Keep the ASR floppy disk and backup tape (or disk with a file) in a safe place in case you need them to recover from a Windows boot failure. You can append other backups to the ASR tape.

Recovering Using an ASR Disk

If your Windows XP Professional installation won't start up, you can use the ASR floppy disk to restart Windows and restore the system files you backed up. You also need the tape or disk on which the rest of the ASR backup was made, and the Windows XP CD-ROM. Follow these steps:

1. Put the Windows XP CD-ROM in the CD-ROM drive.

2. Set your computer's ROM BIOS setup to boot from a CD-ROM. Check your computer's documentation: this step usually requires pressing F2 or some other key during system startup.

3. Restart the computer. To start from the CD, you may need to press a key or choose from a menu: consult your computer's documentation. The Windows XP installation program starts.

4. Watch for a prompt that tells you to press F2, and do so.

5. When you see a prompt to insert the ASR floppy disk into drive A, do so. Then follow the directions on the screen to restore your system files.

The Complete Reference

Part III

Configuring Windows for Your Computer

The
Complete
Reference

Chapter 10

Setting Up Your Start Menu and Taskbar

The Start menu is nothing new—it's been around since Windows 95. But the Windows XP Start menu has been completely redesigned so that the programs you run most often are most easily accessible. Windows XP has Start menu features that move frequently used commands to the "front page" of the Start menu, and hide less-often used commands. Because of the Windows XP emphasis on keeping the desktop uncluttered, you'll probably use the Start menu more and desktop icons less.

The Start menu can contain so many submenus and commands that you can lose track of what's where. Luckily, you can search the Start menu for the program you want. To make the Start menu easier to use, you might want to reorganize it, putting frequently used programs on the left side of the Start menu and demoting other programs to submenus.

The taskbar shows you which programs you're already running. Windows XP rearranges the taskbar slightly, combining the taskbar buttons for multiple windows displayed by the same program, and shrinking the notification area (located on the right end, which used to be called the system tray). The taskbar normally appears at the bottom of the screen, but you can move it, expand it, shrink it, or even make it disappear. You can also include toolbars on the taskbar—you can display any number or none at all of the four predefined toolbars, display toolbars on the desktop, and even define your own toolbars.

What Is the Start Menu?

The *Start menu*, shown in Figure 10-1, appears when you click the Start button on the taskbar. In Windows XP, the Start menu appears in two columns—the left column contains links to programs, and the right column contains links to folders, the Control Panel, online help, the search feature, and the DOS-style command prompt. If you prefer the classic style of the Start menu, you can switch back to it using the Customize Start Menu dialog box (see "Customizing the Windows XP-Style Start Menu"). If your Start menu looks nothing like the one shown in Figure 10-1, you probably have the Classic Start menu configured (the old Windows Me/98 Start menu).

The following items are usually on the Start menu (since the Start menu is customizable, your Start menu may look a little different):

- **All Programs** Displays the *Programs menu*, a menu of programs you can run. This is the Start menu option that you are likely to use the most because you can use it to find and start programs. You can change the contents of the Programs menu by changing the contents of that folder (see "Reorganizing the Start Menu").

- **Frequently used programs** Above the All Programs command, lists programs that you have used recently. Windows selects these programs based on how frequently and how recently you have run them. Click a program to run it.

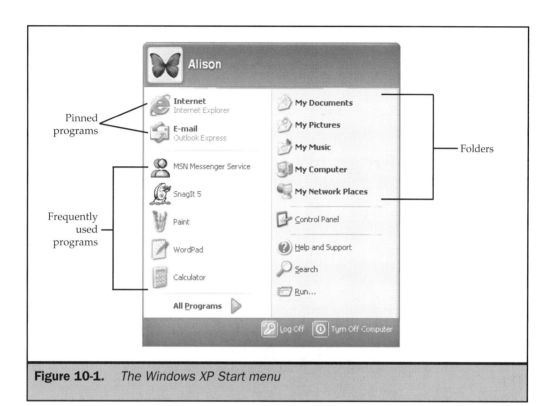

Figure 10-1. *The Windows XP Start menu*

- **Pinned programs**   At the top of the left column, lists programs that are *pinned* to the Start menu—they always appear in this position so that they are easy to run. You can remove pinned programs and add new ones so that you see the programs that you use regularly.

- **Folders (My Documents, My Pictures, My Music, My Computer, My Network Places, My Recent Documents)**   Lists these special folders. If your Start menu hasn't been customized, you can click any of these Start menu options to display the folder in an Explorer window (see Chapter 7, section "What Is Windows Explorer?"). If Start menu options have been changed, you may see a submenu displaying the contents of the folder.

- **Control Panel**   Displays the Control Panel, which helps you install software and change your Windows settings (see Chapter 1, section "What Is the Control Panel?").

- **Help and Support**   Displays online help (see Chapter 4).

- **Search**   Opens an Explorer window with the Search taskbar (see Chapter 8, section "Searching for Files and Folders").

- **Run**   Enables you to run a program by typing the name of the file that contains it (see Chapter 2, section "Starting Programs from the Run Dialog Box").

- **Log Off**   Enables you to log off from one user account and to log on using another (see Chapter 6).

■ **Turn Off Computer** Displays the Turn Off Computer options: Stand By (or Hibernate or Suspend), Turn Off, and Restart. Choose Turn Off if you are ready to turn off your computer. Choose Restart to restart your computer. Choose Stand By, Hibernate, or Suspend to put Windows in a power-conserving Standby or Hibernate mode. The power-conservation options available to you depend on whether you have turned them on and your computer supports them.

What Is the Programs Menu?

The Programs menu (also called the All Programs menu), which you display by choosing Start | All Programs, is a list of the programs you can run. This is the most commonly used part of the Start menu, and it's also the part you can customize the most. The Programs menu is hierarchical; that is, it has menus and submenus, all of which you can customize.

Figure 10-2 shows the Start menu with the All Programs option selected. In addition to the Programs menu, two submenus are open—the Accessories submenu,

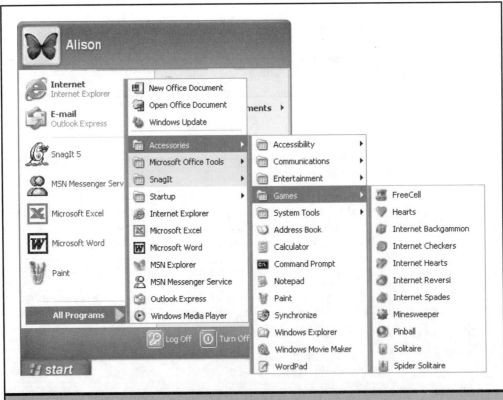

Figure 10-2. *The Start menu with many levels of menus displayed*

and the Games submenu. In this book, to open a game (say, Solitaire), we tell you to choose Start | All Programs | Accessories | Games | Solitaire—that is, click the Start button to display the Start menu, on the Start menu click All Programs, on the Programs menu click Accessories, on the Accessories menu click Games, and on the Games menu click Solitaire.

 Tip   *With Windows XP, Microsoft has abandoned the feature that shrinks the Programs menu to only those items you have used recently. However, if you miss that feature you can have it back by using the Classic Start menu.*

When you install a new program, the installation program is likely to add a folder or other item to the Start menu or (more likely) to the Programs menu. You may prefer to put such items in a submenu of the Programs menu or perhaps remove them from the Start menu completely. Newly-installed programs appear highlighted on the Programs menu.

What Can Appear on the Taskbar?

The *taskbar* is a row of buttons and icons that usually appears at the bottom of the Windows desktop. As explained in Chapter 1, the taskbar has four parts: the Start button, the toolbar(s), the task buttons (one for each running application), and the notification area (with small icons for items that need your attention). You can customize your taskbar by moving it, changing its size, and changing what appears on it. You may also see arrows on the taskbar—click them to see buttons or other information that Windows has hidden to keep the taskbar uncluttered.

Five taskbar toolbars come with Windows:

- **Quick Launch toolbar**   Usually contains three buttons, from left to right: Show Desktop (minimizes all open windows to reveal the desktop), Launch Internet Explorer Browser, and Windows Media Player. You can change which buttons appear on this toolbar (see "Editing the Quick Launch Toolbar"). Here are the standard three buttons:

  If you don't see the Quick Launch toolbar on the taskbar, see "Displaying the Quick Launch Toolbar" later in this chapter.

- **Address toolbar**   Contains a text box where you can type a URL to open a Web page or a file pathname to open a file. A drop-down list contains recently used URLs and pathnames, like this:

- **Links toolbar**   Displays a button for each of the Web pages Microsoft would like you to visit (you can remove Microsoft Web pages and add your own favorite sites). This toolbar also appears in Internet Explorer. Click a button to open the Web page. Here is an example:

■ **Desktop toolbar**   Displays a button for each icon on the desktop. If a double arrow appears, click it to display the options that don't fit on the taskbar, like this:

■ **Language bar**   Displays buttons for all installed languages and keyboard or input options that you have added using the Text Services And Input Languages dialog box available from the Control Panel (see Chapter 12, section "Changing Language Properties"). This toolbar doesn't appear as an option unless you have installed support for additional languages and keyboard layouts.

Older versions of Windows usually displayed the Quick Launch toolbar on the taskbar immediately to the right of the Start button. Windows XP doesn't by default, but you can add it to the taskbar or move it onto the desktop (see "Adding and Removing Toolbars from the Taskbar"). You can also display other toolbars on the taskbar or on the desktop.

Searching the Start Menu

If you can't find the program you want in the Start menu, you can search the menu by using the Search Results window. Follow these steps:

1. Right-click the Start button and choose Search from the shortcut menu that appears.

2. Type the name of the program you're looking for in the All Or Part Of The File Name box.

3. Click the Search button.

The files that match the text you typed are displayed in an Explorer window. Windows displays the full pathname so that you can find the item in the Start menu, or you can click or double-click the item in the Search Results list to open it. If you can't see the full path, increase the width of the In Folder column by clicking and dragging its right border to the right.

Note *When multiple users are defined for your computer, the Start Menu shortcuts are stored in two folders, both called Start Menu. One is C:\Documents And Settings\All Users\Start Menu; the other is in the folder for your profile, for example, C:\Documents and Settings\Alison\Start Menu (for a user named Alison). (If Windows is installed on a drive or partition other than C:, these folders are usually on that drive or partition.) You may need to search both folders to find the Start Menu shortcut that you are looking for.*

Customizing the Start Menu

Most of the Start menu and its submenus are customizable, except that the Turn Off Computer, Help And Support, Search, and Control Panel items on the Start menu cannot be removed or reorganized. You can, however, add items to the top of the Start menu, and you have total control over the Programs menu and submenus.

Tip *If your Programs menu has lots of submenus, getting to the item you want may take longer than you would like. If you find the Start menu cumbersome, explore the other methods of starting programs, which are covered in Chapter 2.*

Reorganizing the Start Menu

You can organize those parts of the Start menu that you are allowed to edit in three ways—you can drag-and-drop items, cut-and-paste items, or use an Explorer window to edit the Start Menu folders in the C:\Documents And Settings folder. These folders and their subfolders contain shortcuts to the programs that appear on your Start menu, and the arrangements of these shortcuts and folders define what command appears on what menu.

Here's a summary of changes you can make:

- **Add an item to the top of the left side of the Start menu** Right-click a shortcut on the desktop or in the menu, or right click a .exe file. Choose Pin To Start Menu from the menu that appears.

- **Add a program to the Programs menu** Drag a desktop shortcut or the program's .exe file to the Start button. Hold it there while the Start menu opens, hold it over the All Programs button until the Programs menu opens, and then drop it where you want it to appear. (Hold it over submenus to open them.)

- **Remove an item from the menu** To remove a program from the left side of the Start menu, right-click it and choose Remove From This List from the menu that appears. To remove a program from the All Programs menu (or its submenus), right-click the menu item and choose Delete. You can't remove items from the right side of the Start menu.

■ **Rename a menu item** Right-click the menu item and choose Rename. Type the new name and press ENTER.

If these bullet points don't cover what you need to do, or don't provide enough detail, keep reading!

Dragging and Dropping Programs to the Start Menu

You can create a Start menu entry for a program by dragging its program file (or a shortcut to the program) to the Start button. To add an item to the Start menu, drag the file, folder, program .exe file, or a shortcut to the program from an Explorer window or the Desktop and drop it on the Start button. Windows creates a new shortcut, and the new command appears in the top part of the Start menu.

To put the item further into the Start menu hierarchy, drag it to the Start button and hold it there until the Start menu appears. Then drag the item to exactly where you want it to appear (hold it on a submenu option to open the submenu). You may prefer to move the item in two steps, first dropping it on the Start button, and then dragging it within the Start menu, as described in the next section.

Dragging and Dropping Items Within the Start Menu

The easiest way to reorganize items already in the menus is to drag-and-drop the commands where you want them.

Reorganize items already in the Start menu by dragging them, like this:

1. Display the Start menu by clicking the Start button.

2. Display the menu containing the item you want to move (for instance, you might need to click All Programs to see the Microsoft Word option, which you might want to move to a submenu called Microsoft Applications).

3. Click the item you want to move and hold the mouse button down.

4. While holding the mouse button down, move the pointer in the menu. The black bar shows you where the item you are moving will appear. You can open a submenu by highlighting it, and waiting for it to open.

5. When the black bar appears in the position where you want the item to be, release the mouse button to drop the item in its new position.

Cutting and Pasting Start Menu Items

When you can see a Start menu command, you can right-click it and choose from the shortcut menu that appears. Two of the shortcut menu options are Cut and Copy—use them to move or copy a Start menu item.

To move (or copy) a command from one menu to another, right-click it and choose Cut (or Copy). Then give the command that displays the submenu into which you'd like to move the command, right-click, and choose Paste. For example, if you want to copy the Netscape Navigator command from the Start | All Programs | Netscape Communicator menu into the Programs menu, choose Start | All Programs | Netscape Communicator to display the command, right-click it, and choose Copy. Then click Start, right-click the All Programs command, and choose Paste.

Moving Commands and Submenus by Editing the Start Menu Folders

Another way to customize the Programs menu and its submenus is to use an Explorer window to add, remove, move, and rename shortcuts. (Explorer windows are discussed in Chapters 7 and 8.) You can also rename submenus and menu items and create new submenus by using this method.

The Programs menu displays the shortcuts stored in two separate folders—one contains the Programs menu shortcuts that all users see, and the other contains the shortcuts that are visible for your personal user profile. Windows combines the two sets of shortcuts and displays a single Programs menu. The C:\Documents And Settings\All Users\Start Menu folder contains most shortcuts (if Windows isn't installed on C:, substitute the correct drive letter); the other folder is in the folder for your profile, C:\Documents And Settings*username*\Start Menu (i.e., C:\Documents And Settings\Alison\Start Menu).

When you install a program that adds commands to your Programs menu, Windows asks whether you want the new menu entries to appear only in your Programs menu or on the Programs menus of all users of the computer. Adding, removing, and reorganizing the Programs menu is as simple as adding, deleting, and moving shortcuts within the two Start Menu folders. Menu items can be renamed by renaming the shortcuts.

The Start Menu folders (C:\Documents And Settings*username*\Start Menu and C:\Documents And Settings\All Users\Start Menu) contain the commands that appear at the top of the Programs menu. The Programs folder in the two Start Menu folders contain the rest of the commands that appear on the Programs menu. Each subfolder of the Programs folders corresponds to a submenu of the Programs menu. For example, the shortcuts in the C:\Documents And Settings\All Users\Start Menu\Programs\Games folder appear in the Start | All Programs | Games menu.

You can display the Start Menu folder for your user account in Windows Explorer by right-clicking the Start button and choosing Open or Explore from the menu (Open displays the C:\Documents and Settings*username*\Start Menu folder in an Explorer window; Explore displays the same window with the addition of the Folders Explorer bar—we recommend choosing Explore). To display the Start Menu folder for all users, right-click the Start button and choose Explorer All Users. Figure 10-3 shows the C:\Documents And Settings\All Users\Start Menu folder in Windows Explorer.

Figure 10-3. *Using Windows Explorer to edit the Start menu*

Notice that all the customizable choices that appear on the Start menu in Figure 10-1 also appear in the Start Menu folder: the Programs folder, the New Office Document shortcut, the Open Office Document shortcut, and the Windows Update shortcut. Commands you can't change (such as Help and Run) don't appear.

To display the contents of the Programs menu, open the Programs folder in the Start Menu folders—look both in the folder for all users and the folder for your user account. You can explore the Start Menu folders by using the same methods you use to explore all folders on your computer.

To edit any submenu of the Start menu, you can right-click it and choose Explorer. Want to make changes to the Accessories submenu? Choose Start | All Programs, right-click Accessories, and choose Explore (for your user account settings) or Explore All Users. You see the C:\Documents And Settings\username\Start Menu\ Programs\Accessories or C:\Documents And Settings\All Users\Start Menu\Programs\Accessories folder in Windows Explorer.

Because the Start menu is stored as shortcuts within folders, it can be edited in the same way you edit folders and files:

- You can move an item from one menu group to another by dragging or cutting and pasting the shortcut to another folder.

- You can create a new menu group by creating a new folder: Select the folder in which the new submenu will be stored and choose File | New | Folder from the menu bar.

- You can rename a shortcut by selecting it and pressing F2 (or right-clicking the name and choosing Rename from the shortcut menu that appears). Windows highlights the name and shows a box around it. Type a new name, or use the cursor to edit the name. Press ENTER when you finish (or press ESC if you change your mind).

Note *Although you can edit the Start menu by changing the contents of the Start Menu folder and their subfolders, the Start Menu and Programs folders are more than just regular folders. For instance, you can move the Programs folder out of its usual location, and you still see the Programs option on the Start menu (this can lead to complications that are hard to fix, though, so don't try it).*

Changing Start Menu Properties

In addition to changing the programs that appear on the Start menu and the order in which they appear, you can customize the Start menu in other ways. Right-click the Start button and choose Properties to display the Taskbar And Start Menu Properties dialog box, shown in Figure 10-4.

The Start Menu tab on this dialog box enables you to choose between the Start menu (the new Windows XP design) and the Classic Start Menu (the old Windows Me Start menu). Except for the section on the Classic Start Menu, this chapter assumes that you are using the Windows XP Start menu.

Customizing the Windows XP-Style Start Menu

To customize the standard Start menu, click the upper Customize button on the Start Menu tab of the Taskbar And Start Menu Properties dialog box to see the General tab of the Customize Start Menu dialog box, shown in Figure 10-5.

The General tab of the Customize Start Menu dialog box offers you the following options:

- **Select An Icon Size For Programs** By default, large icons are displayed in the Start menu. Choose the Small Icons option to make the first level of the Start menu take up less room on the screen.

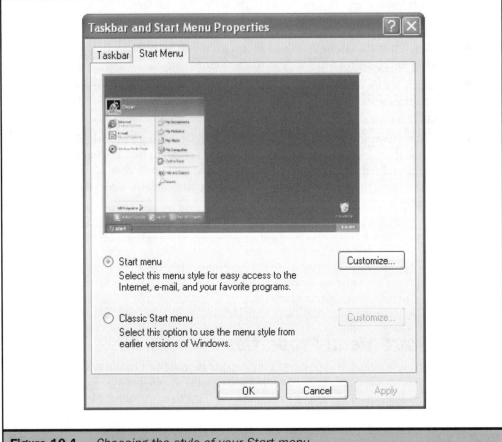

Figure 10-4. *Choosing the style of your Start menu*

- **Programs**   By default, the five programs that you use most often are displayed on the first level of the Start menu. You can change the number of programs that appear by changing this setting—choose a number between zero and thirty.

- **Show On Start Menu**   By default, a shortcut to a browser and a shortcut to an e-mail program are displayed at the top of the Start menu. You can choose to display a different program by choosing from the drop-down lists, or you can choose not to display these programs by deselecting the check box. Remember, you can put any program at the top of the Start menu by right-clicking it and choosing Pin to Start menu.

Click the Advanced tab of the Customize Start Menu dialog box to see more options, including those that allow you to choose the folder shortcuts that appear on the Start menu. The Advanced tab has the following sections:

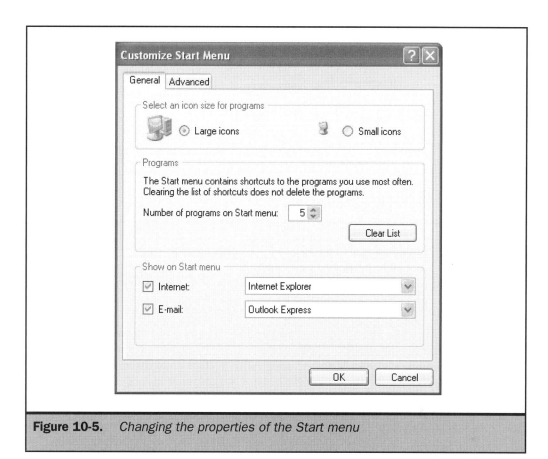

Figure 10-5.   *Changing the properties of the Start menu*

■ **Start Menu Settings**   These check boxes allow you to change Start menu behavior: You can have the Start menu open submenus when the mouse is paused over them, or, by deselecting this option, you can choose to have the submenus open only when you click on them. The other check box controls whether new programs on the Start menu are highlighted in a different color.

■ **Start Menu Items**   This box gives you control over what is displayed and how some items are displayed in the second column of the Start menu—the folder shortcuts, the Control Panel, and the Run command. (This section of the dialog box is described in more detail below.)

■ **Recent Documents**   Selecting the List My Most Recently Opened Documents check box displays the My Recent Documents submenu on the Start menu, which displays the names of recently used files. You can select a file from this list to open it in its native program. Use the Clear List button to remove the list of recently opened documents—if the check box is still selected, Windows will build a new list as you open new files. The My Recent Documents command on the Start menu is similar to the Documents item on the Classic Start menu.

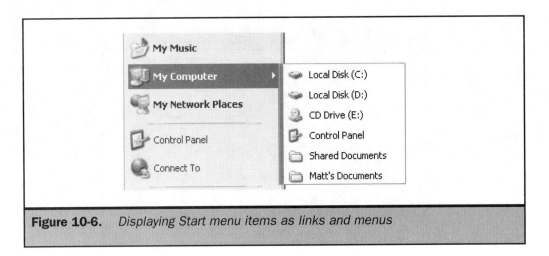

Figure 10-6. *Displaying Start menu items as links and menus*

The Start Menu Items section of the Advanced tab of the Customize Start Menu dialog box contains a list of settings that control what appears in the second column of the Start menu, and how it appears. The check boxes enable you to choose whether or not to display the menu item. Many choices in this section have three settings: Display As A Link, Display As A Menu, and Don't Display This Item. Figure 10-6 shows how these differ. My Music appears as a link: when you click My Music, you open the My Music folder in an Explorer window. My Computer appears as a menu: when you click My Computer, a submenu appears.

Here is a brief rundown of the options in the Start Menu Items box that do not appear by default on the Start menu (the default items are explained in the section "What Is the Start Menu?" at the beginning of this chapter):

- **Favorites menu** The Favorites menu displays your most frequently used files, folders, Web pages, and programs. The menu displays the contents of the Favorites folder (usually C:\Documents And Settings\All Users\Favorites or C:\Documents And Settings*username*\Favorites). The Favorites menu is easy to access, not only from the Start menu, but also from Explorer windows and most Open and Save As dialog boxes. Most people use the Favorites folder for shortcuts to frequently used files, folders, and programs, but you can also store files there (as with any other folder). Learn more about Favorites in Chapter 24.

- **Network Connections** You have two options for displaying network connections on the Start menu. You can Display As Connect To Menu, which displays Connect To on the Start menu with a submenu of your defined Internet and LAN connections (click a connection name to make the connection). The other option is Link To Network Connections Folder which displays Connect To on the Start menu as a shortcut to the Network Connections window (see Chapter 22, section "What Are Network Connections?").

- **Printers and Faxes**   This option displays a shortcut to the Printers And Faxes folder, where you can see all your defined printers and fax packages and the Add A Printer icon.

Customizing the Classic Start Menu

If you choose to use the Classic Start menu you have a whole raftload of different customization options. To display the Customize Classic Start Menu dialog box, follow these steps:

1. Right-click the Start button and choose Properties to display the Start Menu tab of the Taskbar And Start Menu Properties dialog box.

2. Select the Classic Start Menu radio button (if it isn't already selected).

3. Click the Customize button to display the Customize Classic Start Menu, shown here:

In the top half of the dialog box are five buttons. Use them to edit the programs on the Start menu. The Advanced button displays the Start Menu folder for your user account. Remember that most Start menu shortcuts are also stored in the C:/Documents And Settings/All Users/Start Menu folder. The Sort button sorts the Programs menu alphabetically when you click it.

Most of the check boxes in the bottom half of the Customize Classic Start Menu dialog box are optional menu items—use the check boxes to select which items appear on your Classic Start menu. Use the Expand Control Panel, Expand My Documents, Expand My Pictures, Expand Network Connections, and Expand Printers check boxes to display the listed item as a menu rather than as a shortcut. Microsoft also included a few options that affect how the Start menu works:

- **Enable Dragging And Dropping**   The Start menu can be edited by dragging and dropping menu commands (see "Dragging and Dropping Items within the Start Menu").

- **Scroll Programs**   Scrolls the contents of the Programs menu up and down when the list is too big to fit on the screen; otherwise, the Programs menu expands to more than one column.

- **Show Small Icons In Start Menu**   By default, large icons are displayed in the Start menu. Turn on the Small Icons option to make the first level of the Start menu take up less room on the screen.

- **Use Personalized Menus**   Displays only those commands you have used recently. Turn off this option if you want to see all commands all the time.

Customizing the Taskbar

Although most Windows users find no reason to customize the taskbar, a few do. You can move the taskbar around the desktop, and you can control its size and whether it is visible all the time. The taskbar is shown in Figure 10-7.

Enabling Taskbar Changes

You can disable and enable changes to the taskbar. Some people find they drag-and-drop items from the taskbar by accident, and they would rather have Windows prevent these changes. In fact, Windows locks the taskbar (disables changes) by default. To disable or enable editing the taskbar, right-click an unoccupied portion of the taskbar (try clicking next to the clock if you're having trouble finding an

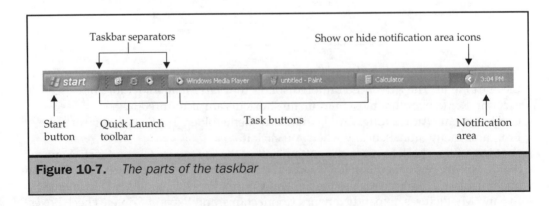

Figure 10-7.   *The parts of the taskbar*

unoccupied part) and choose Lock The Taskbar. To enable changes, repeat the same steps. When the taskbar is locked you can't edit it, move it to another edge of the screen, or change its size. You can still change the toolbars that the taskbar displays, though. (You can also lock and unlock the taskbar from the Taskbar And Start Menu Properties dialog box, which you display by right-clicking the taskbar and choosing Properties.)

Moving the Taskbar

Move the taskbar to any edge of the desktop by clicking and dragging it to the desired position. When the pointer is near an edge of the desktop, you see a gray bar showing where the taskbar will be when you release the mouse button. You have to click an unoccupied area of the taskbar—not the Start button or a program button—to drag it. An unoccupied area of taskbar is always available next to the clock.

When the taskbar appears on the left or right side of the desktop, it looks a little different than it does on the bottom, but it still has the same parts in the same order (the Start button is at the top). The taskbar doesn't cover icons on the desktop when it is moved—the icons shift to slightly new positions. The exception to this "icon shifting" rule is when the Auto-hide option is turned on (see "Hiding the Taskbar"). Then the icons don't move, but the taskbar disappears so you can see them.

Changing the Size of the Taskbar

You can change the size of the taskbar by clicking and dragging its inside edge—that is, the edge that borders the desktop. (Be sure that the taskbar is unlocked before you try this.) If the taskbar appears at the bottom of the screen, then change its size by clicking and dragging its top edge. The following illustration shows a taskbar made taller to display two rows of buttons:

A larger taskbar displays more information on each button; however, it also claims more area of the screen that could be used to display other information.

You can size the taskbar back down by clicking and dragging the inside edge back toward the edge of the screen—make sure to release the mouse button when the taskbar is the desired size. You can even decrease your taskbar to a thin stripe along one edge of the screen by dragging the edge of the taskbar to the edge of the screen. If you can't find your taskbar, try moving the mouse pointer to each edge of the screen. When the mouse pointer turns into a double-headed arrow, click-and-drag to increase the size of the taskbar.

CONFIGURING WINDOWS FOR YOUR COMPUTER

Changing Taskbar Properties

You can change some taskbar options by right-clicking an empty part of the taskbar and choosing Properties. You see the Taskbar tab of the Taskbar And Start Menu Properties dialog box, shown in Figure 10-8.

Hiding the Taskbar

You can hide the taskbar in two different ways: by decreasing its size and by using the Auto-hide option. Changing the size of the taskbar is covered in the previous section—click-and-drag the inside edge of the taskbar to the screen's closest edge. The taskbar becomes a thin blue line on one edge of the screen. The other option is to use the Auto-hide feature to hide the taskbar. Auto-hide tries to determine when you need the taskbar and displays the taskbar only when you need it.

To turn on Auto-hide, display the Taskbar tab of the Taskbar And Start Menu Properties dialog box and select the Auto-hide The Taskbar check box. When Auto-hide is on, the taskbar disappears when it isn't being used. To display it, point to the edge of the screen where it last appeared. Or, you can press CTRL-ESC or the

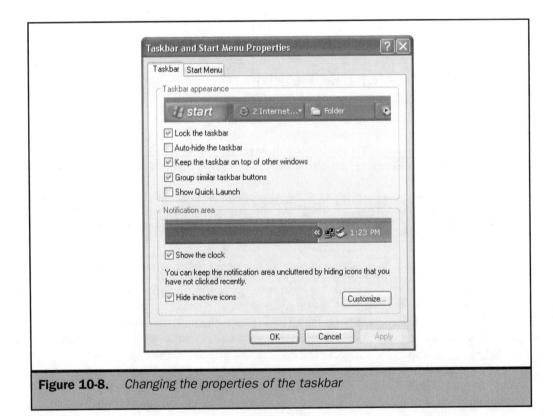

Figure 10-8. *Changing the properties of the taskbar*

WINDOWS key (a key with the Windows symbol that displays the Start menu) to display the taskbar and open the Start menu at the same time.

 If you can't find your taskbar, move the mouse pointer to each edge of the screen. If Auto-hide is on, the taskbar appears. If the taskbar is shrunk, the mouse pointer turns into a double-headed arrow—click-and-drag to increase the taskbar's size.

Allowing the Taskbar to Be Covered by a Window

You can choose whether you want the taskbar to be covered by other windows by selecting the Keep The Taskbar On Top Of Other Windows check box on the Taskbar tab of the Taskbar And Start Menu Properties dialog box. When the check box is selected, the taskbar always appears over other windows. When the option is off, windows may cover the taskbar. To use the taskbar when the Keep The Taskbar On Top Of Other Windows option is turned off, move or minimize windows until the taskbar is visible, or press CTRL-ESC or the WINDOWS key to display both the taskbar and open the Start menu (press ESC once if you want to use only the taskbar). We recommend that you leave this check box selected.

Grouping Taskbar Buttons

New in Windows XP is the option to group similar task buttons on the taskbar. This option, which is on by default, puts task buttons for files opened in the same program together on the taskbar. If the taskbar becomes crowded, the buttons are collapsed into a single button, like this (all four open Microsoft Word files appear on one task button):

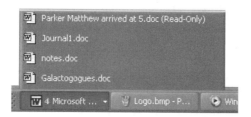

A button for grouped windows has a downward arrow on its right side. Click the button to see the individual windows, and click the window you want. You can turn this option off by deselecting the Group Similar Taskbar Buttons check box on the Taskbar tab of the Taskbar And Start Menu Properties dialog box.

 Some people don't like grouped task buttons, because it takes an extra click to switch from, say, one Word document window to another.

Hiding the Clock on the Taskbar

You can choose to display or hide the *system clock* that usually appears in the notification area of the taskbar. Display the Taskbar tab of the Taskbar And Start Menu Properties dialog box, and then select or deselect the Show The Clock check box.

Hiding Notification Area Icons

The notification area where the clock appears also holds icons for programs and processes that are running in the background (that is, running without you realizing that they are running). In previous versions of Windows, this area filled up with icons. By default, Windows XP hides inactive icons (icons that don't require your immediate attention). You can change this setting so that icons are visible all the time, by deselecting the Hide Inactive Icons check box in the Taskbar tab of the Taskbar And Start Menu Properties dialog box. You can also customize the setting by clicking Customize to see the Customize Notification dialog box, which displays a list of the icons that are currently in the notification area (whether hidden or not). Select an item and then pick from the drop-down list. For each item you can select Hide When Inactive (the default), Always Hide, or Always Show. For your settings to take effect, be sure the Hide Inactive Icons check box on the Taskbar and Start Menu Properties dialog box is selected.

Adding Toolbars to the Taskbar

You can configure the taskbar to include toolbars, or you can display toolbars elsewhere on your desktop. Taskbar toolbars give you easy access to frequently used icons: you no longer have to minimize all open programs to display a desktop icon to open a program. Instead you can use a toolbar button. Or, you can use the toolbar button Show Desktop to minimize all open programs with one click. You can even edit the buttons that appear on a toolbar or create a completely new toolbar.

Adding and Removing Toolbars from the Taskbar

Use the Taskbar shortcut menu, shown here, to add and remove toolbars from the taskbar:

You can display the Taskbar shortcut menu by right-clicking an unoccupied part of the taskbar (even on a full taskbar, an unoccupied part is on either side of the clock).

The Toolbars command on the Taskbar shortcut menu displays a menu with the available toolbars. Toolbars that are already displayed on the taskbar appear with check marks. To display a toolbar, click its name. To remove a displayed toolbar, follow the same procedure to remove the check mark.

Microsoft provides a second way to choose whether to display the Quick Launch toolbar or not. Right-click the taskbar and choose Properties to display the Taskbar tab of the Taskbar And Start Menus Properties dialog box, which includes the Show Quick Launch check box. This check box does the same thing as right-clicking the taskbar and choosing Toolbars | Quick Launch.

Moving a Toolbar

You can move the toolbar to a different position on the taskbar, or onto the desktop by clicking and dragging the toolbar handle, which looks like a vertical line of dots on the left end of the toolbar:

 Toolbar handles don't appear when the taskbar is locked. Right-click an empty spot on the taskbar and choose Lock The Taskbar to unlock (or lock) it.

To switch the order of the toolbars on the taskbar, move a toolbar by dragging its handle left or right. You may end up with a two- or three-row taskbar by the time you are done, but you can then drag the top edge of the taskbar back down to the position where you want it.

You can also control how the taskbar is partitioned. You can make each toolbar wider or narrower by dragging its handle to the left or right. When many buttons are displayed and the buttons get small, scroll buttons appear, allowing you to view all the buttons for open applications.

To move a toolbar to the desktop, drag-and-drop its handle off the taskbar. Each toolbar looks different on the desktop, but they all appear with a title bar, a Close button, and icons, like this:

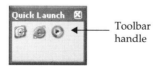

Toolbar handle

Once the toolbar is on the desktop, you can no longer make it disappear by using the Taskbar shortcut menu—instead, you can use its Close button to get rid of it. You can move and change the size of the toolbar by using the same techniques you use on any window.

You can move a toolbar from the desktop back to the taskbar, or to any edge of the desktop, by clicking and dragging the title bar—when the toolbar reaches any edge of the desktop, it changes shape to occupy the whole edge. If you move it to the edge with the taskbar, the toolbar is integrated back into the taskbar. If you move it to an empty edge, the toolbar takes up the whole edge of the desktop.

Controlling the Look of a Toolbar

You can control the way a toolbar works by using the Toolbar shortcut menu, shown here:

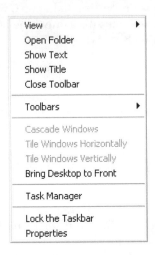

Display the Toolbar shortcut menu by right-clicking an unoccupied part of the toolbar (if you have trouble finding an unoccupied part of the toolbar, right-click the toolbar handle).

The following choices on the Toolbar shortcut menu control your toolbar (the rest of the choices that appear affect the whole taskbar):

- **View**   Allows you to display either large or small icons. The default setting is Small.

- **Open Folder**   Opens the folder where the toolbar shortcuts are stored, so you can edit the toolbar. Once the folder is open you can add and delete shortcuts to change the contents of the toolbar.

- **Show Text**   Displays text on each button. Choose this option again to display icons with no text. Turning off this option makes a toolbar take up less space.

- **Show Title**   Turns off or on the display of the name of the toolbar.

- **Close Toolbar**   Removes the toolbar from the screen.

- **Toolbars**   Allows you to display a new toolbar, hide a displayed toolbar, or create a new toolbar. This option is the same as the Toolbars option on the Taskbar shortcut menu.

When the toolbar is attached to an edge of the desktop, but not in the taskbar, you see two additional choices:

- **Always On Top**   The toolbar always appears on top of other windows.
- **Auto-hide**   The toolbar disappears when not in use. Move the pointer to the edge of the screen where the toolbar is located to display it.

These additional two options work the same as the Always On Top and Auto-hide options for the taskbar.

Editing the Quick Launch Toolbar

You can easily add and remove buttons from the Quick Launch toolbar. To remove a button, right-click the button and choose Delete. To add a button, drag a shortcut or a .exe file to the toolbar. If you want to make a copy of a shortcut from the desktop in the Quick Launch toolbar, hold down the CTRL key while you drag the shortcut from the desktop to the toolbar.

You can also edit the buttons on the Quick Launch toolbar by opening the folder that contains the shortcuts and adding and removing shortcuts. To open the folder, right-click the toolbar handle and choose Open Folder. The shortcuts for the Quick Launch toolbar are buried in the folder structure—you can find them in C:\Documents and Settings*username*\Application Data\Microsoft\Internet Explorer\Quick Launch: replace *username* with your own user name.

   Why does Microsoft store this information with Internet Explorer configuration data? Because they consider the whole desktop as a special Internet Explorer window.

Creating a New Toolbar

In addition to the existing toolbars, you can create your own toolbar to display the contents of a drive, folder, or Internet address. Depending on the options you choose for your new toolbar, it may look something like this one, which shows the contents of a folder called Consult:

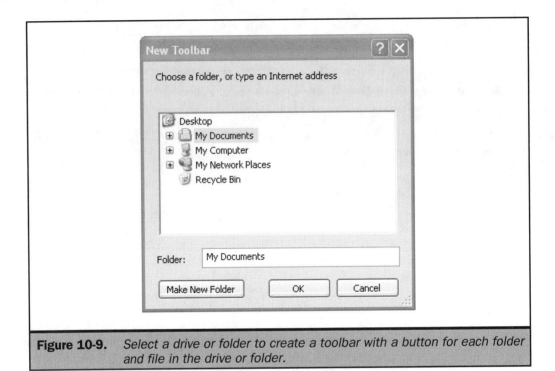

Figure 10-9.   *Select a drive or folder to create a toolbar with a button for each folder and file in the drive or folder.*

In this example, the Consult folder contains three other folders and numerous files. On the toolbar, you can see the three folders—you can display the entire contents of the Consult folder by clicking the arrow at the right end of the toolbar. Notice that the subfolders are displayed as menus, so you can open a file directly from the toolbar. Clicking a folder button opens an Explorer window for that folder; clicking a file button opens the file.

Caution   *If you create a new toolbar and then close it, it's gone. To redisplay it, you need to recreate the toolbar.*

To create a new toolbar, right-click the taskbar or a toolbar, and choose Toolbars | New Toolbar from the shortcut menu that appears. You see the New Toolbar dialog box, shown in Figure 10-9, which enables you to browse available drives and folders. Click the plus box next to a folder name to expand that branch of the folder tree. You can open any folder or drive available to you in Windows Explorer—these may include drives and folders on the Internet. Click New Folder to create a new subfolder in the highlighted folder. Select the folder you want to use to create a toolbar and click OK in the New Toolbar dialog box.

Chapter 11

Setting Up Your Desktop

When your desktop is set up in a way that is right for you, everything flows more smoothly. Files and programs are where you expect them to be. The screen is attractive and doesn't hurt your eyes. Your desktop's background and screen saver are different from everyone else's, giving your computer a familiar, homey feel. Of course, if you choose to use Windows XP's new Luna desktop theme, it may not feel quite so familiar at first.

This chapter describes how to configure your desktop to suit your own preferences, including choosing a desktop theme, background, screen saver, color scheme (using the Color dialog box), icons, other visual effects, and sound effects. Windows comes with the new Luna interface, but you can switch back to the classic Windows design if you prefer. It also describes how to set your screen resolution and how to use multiple displays at the same time, if you have the right hardware.

What Are Display Properties?

You configure your desktop and monitor by changing Windows' display properties. For example, if you want to dress up your desktop, you can change the background color or image and change the size, color, or font of the individual elements that make up the desktop. You can even incorporate a Web page or two into the background of your desktop. When you step away from your computer, you can tell it to display a screen saver until you get back.

The command center for anything having to do with your monitor or desktop is the Display Properties dialog box, shown in Figure 11-1. You can access it from the Appearance And Themes category of the Control Panel or by right-clicking any unoccupied spot on the desktop and choosing Properties from the shortcut menu.

The Display Properties dialog box has the following five tabs (your dialog box may have more tabs, if your system has any special display software):

- **Themes**   Controls desktop themes
- **Desktop**   Lets you choose icons and background pictures
- **Screen Saver**   Offers screen savers and automatic settings for turning off your monitor
- **Appearance**   Controls the color, size, and font of every standard type of object Windows uses
- **Settings**   Lets you set the size of the desktop (in pixels), number of colors displayed, and monitor performance

You can modify the settings on most of these tabs to change the way your desktop looks and acts. When you make changes on any of the other tabs of the Display Properties dialog box, the new settings are not applied until you click Apply or OK. Clicking Apply makes the change and leaves the Display Properties dialog box open. Clicking OK makes the change and also closes the Display Properties dialog box.

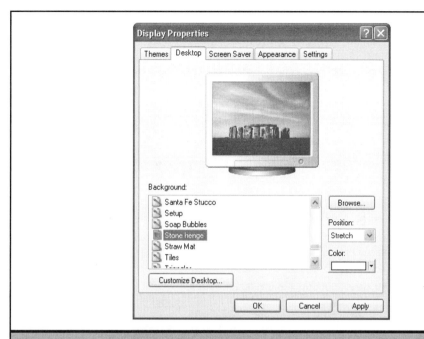

Figure 11-1. *The preview box in the center shows the effects of proposed changes before you apply them.*

Choosing a Desktop Theme

You can change the appearance of practically anything on your desktop. However, getting a collection of colors, icons, pictures, fonts, mouse pointers, screen savers, and so on, that look good together takes more time and artistic talent than most of us have. A *desktop theme* is a complete "look" for your desktop. By changing themes, you can alter everything about the appearance of your desktop in one fell swoop.

> **Note** *Windows 98 and Me had both "desktop schemes" and desktop themes. Desktop themes were separate Windows components that you could install from your Windows Me/98 CD-ROM, while desktop schemes wre selected from the Display Properties dialog box. Windows XP combines most of the elements of both into desktop themes.*

A desktop theme provides not only a system of colors and fonts, but also sounds, icons, mouse pointers, a desktop background, and a screen saver as well. Windows XP ships with two themes: Windows XP (the default Luna theme) and Windows Classic (which looks like earlier versions of Windows). Microsoft promises that you will be able to download other themes from its Web site. Also, we have confidence that themes for Windows XP will appear on third-party Web sites like C I NET's Web site (at **http://download.cnet.com**), which already has countless themes for earlier versions of Windows.

Changing Themes

To change your desktop theme, follow these steps:

1. Right-click any empty spot on the desktop and choose Properties from the shortcut menu. The Display Properties dialog box appears with the Themes tab on top, as shown in Figure 11-2.

2. Select the name of a theme from the Theme drop-down list. A preview of the theme appears in the Sample box below the Theme list.

3. Click OK. The Display Properties dialog box disappears, and Windows applies the theme to your desktop.

Creating and Saving Your Own Desktop Theme

After you choose a theme, you can modify it by changing individual elements:

■ The background image or color (see "Changing the Background")

■ The screen saver (see "Setting Up a Screen Saver")

■ The color scheme (see "Choosing a New Color Scheme")

■ The windows and buttons (see "Changing Windows, Buttons, and Fonts")

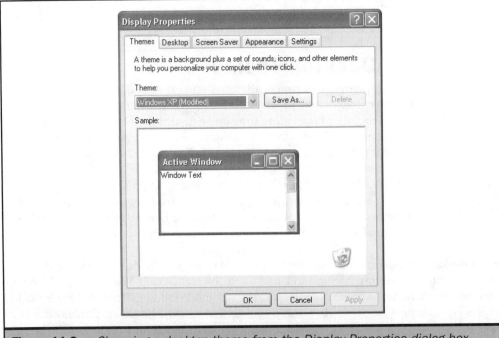

Figure 11-2.   *Choosing a desktop theme from the Display Properties dialog box*

- The font or size of text used in title bars, message boxes, menus, and elsewhere (see "Changing Fonts")

- The size or shape of icons (see "Choosing New Desktop Icons")

- Visual effects, like whether a menu fades or scrolls up after you've finished using it (see "Changing the Desktop's Visual Effects")

- Sound effects (see "Changing the Desktop's Sound Effects")

After you have modified a theme, it is listed as "modified" on the Theme drop-down list of the Themes tab of the Display Properties dialog box. To save your changes as a new desktop theme, do the following:

1. Open the Display Properties dialog box by right-clicking any empty space on the desktop and selecting Properties from the shortcut menu.

2. Click the Save As button on the Themes tab of the Display Properties dialog box. A Save As dialog box appears.

3. Use the Save As dialog box to find the folder where you want to store the file containing the new theme.

4. Type a name for the theme into the File Name box in the Save As dialog box.

5. Click the Save button.

6. Click OK to close the Display Properties dialog box.

Your new theme now appears on the Theme list in the Display Properties dialog box. To remove it (or any other theme) from the list, select it and click the Delete button.

Changing the Background

The *background* is the pattern, picture, or color that lies behind all the windows, icons, and menus on your desktop. (The background used to be called *wallpaper* before people noticed that wallpapering your desktop is a mixed metaphor.)

Your desktop background can be any color or image. Windows comes with several attractive photographs, as well as a number of abstract patterns, that you can use as a background. You can also use image files that you download from the Internet, copy from a friend, or get from your scanner or digital camera. Your background can even be a Web page.

Selecting an Image or Pattern from the Background List

Select a background image or pattern from the Desktop tab of the Display Properties dialog box (shown earlier in Figure 11-1). The Background box on that tab lists all the background image options that Windows knows about. Click a name in this list to see the image displayed in the preview box—the monitor-like graphic just above the list.

A background image is a file in an HTML or image format (with the extension .bmp, .jpg, .gif, or .tif). That image has a size, which may or may not match the dimensions of your display. If the image is smaller than the display, the Position drop-down list (to the right of the Background list) gives you three choices:

- **Center**   Puts the image in the center of the display, letting the background color of the desktop form a frame around the image. This is your best choice for photographs that are slightly smaller than the display.

- **Tile**   Repeats the image to fill the display with the image. This works particularly well with patterns such as Black Thatch or Houndstooth, which are small images designed to create intricate patterns when tiled.

- **Stretch**   Stretches the image to fill the display. Photographs end up looking like fun house mirrors, but many abstract patterns stretch well.

If the image you choose is larger than your display, Center and Tile both give you a single copy of the image, with the edges of the image off the screen. If this isn't satisfactory, you can use Paint to crop the image, or you can redefine the dimensions of your display (see "Changing the Screen Resolution").

When the preview in the Display Properties dialog box looks the way you want, click either OK (which closes the dialog box) or Apply (which applies your change but leaves the dialog box open).

Making Your Own Background Images

You aren't limited to the backgrounds that come with Windows. You can use any image file—like a digital or scanned picture of your kids—as a background. Any image file that you move to your My Pictures folder automatically appears in the Background list on the Desktop tab of the Display Properties dialog box. If the file is somewhere else on your system, you can click the Browse button and find the file in the Browse dialog box that appears.

Selecting a Background Color

Any background image you select automatically covers the background color of your desktop. This means that you see the background color of your desktop only if your background image choice is None or is centered with the background visible around the edges.

To select a new background color, follow these steps:

1. Right-click any empty area on the desktop and select Properties from the shortcut menu. The Display Properties dialog box appears.

2. Click the Desktop tab (shown earlier in Figure 11-1).

3. Click the Color button. A palette of 20 colors appears.

4. If one of the colors on the palette is what you want, click it. The background of the preview box changes to the new color.

5. If you don't like any of the colors on the palette, click Other, and follow the directions in the section "Finding the Perfect Color," later in this chapter.

6. Click Apply to change the desktop color and leave the Display Properties dialog box open, or click OK to change the color and close the Display Properties dialog box.

Using a Web Page as a Background

Rather than a static decoration, your desktop background can be a page from the Internet, or it can contain accessories regularly updated from the Internet, such as a headline ticker or a weather map. (Microsoft used to call this idea the "Active Desktop," but it seems to have dropped the term.)

In general, we recommend that you not bother with these Web-based elements if you connect to the Internet via a modem attached to an ordinary telephone line; the connection is slow, and the benefit is not worth tying up the phone. But if you connect through an office LAN or an always-on home connection like DSL or cable, you may find that you enjoy having your desktop more closely integrated with the outside world. You can also display a Web page that you've stored on your own hard drive, which doesn't depend on a connection to the Internet.

These possibilities are controlled from the Web tab of the Desktop Items dialog box, shown in Figure 11-3. Open this dialog box as follows:

1. Open the Display Properties dialog box by right-clicking an empty space on the desktop and selecting Properties from the shortcut menu.

2. Click the Desktop tab of the Display Properties dialog box (shown earlier in Figure 11-1).

3. Click the Customize Desktop button. The Desktop Items dialog box appears.

4. Click the Web tab.

Adding Web Content to Your Desktop

The Web Pages list on the Web tab of the Desktop Items dialog box offers My Current Home Page, which is the page Internet Explorer displays when it opens. Other items may appear on your Web Pages list. To display an item on your desktop, check the corresponding check box, click OK to close the Desktop Items dialog box, and then click either OK or Apply in the Display Properties dialog box. Your computer will attempt to access the Internet and find the page you chose.

You can add any Web page you want to the Web Pages list on the Web tab of the Desktop Items dialog box, as follows:

1. On the Web tab of the Desktop Items dialog box, click the New button. The New Desktop Item dialog box appears.

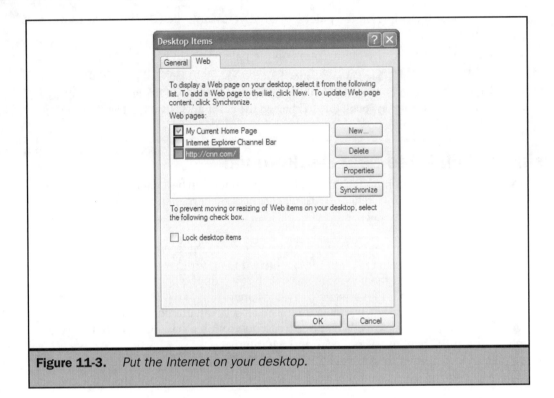

Figure 11-3. *Put the Internet on your desktop.*

2. Type the URL of the Web page into the Location box. Alternatively, choose an item from your Favorites menu by clicking the Browse button and choosing a favorite from the Browse dialog box.

3. After making your choice, click OK in the New Desktop Item dialog box. A confirmation box appears, showing the URL that you have selected. Click OK again. The new item appears on the Web Pages list with a check in its check box.

4. Click OK in the Desktop Item and Display Properties dialog boxes.

The New Desktop Item dialog box also contains a Visit Gallery button, which takes you to a Microsoft Web site containing stock tickers, weather maps, and other items that you may find interesting to have on your desktop. Instructions for installing these items can be found on the Web site.

After you have added an item to the Web Pages list on the Desktop Items dialog box, you can add it or remove it from your desktop as often as you like by checking or unchecking its check box in the Web Pages list.

If you don't want Web items to be accidentally moved or resized, select the Lock Desktop Items check box on the Web tab of the Desktop Items dialog box.

Working with Web Content on Your Desktop

Web pages that have become part of your desktop appear to have no definite boundary, especially if the background of the page matches the background of the desktop. However, if you rest the cursor at the top edge of the Web page, a small frame appears around it. You can use this frame to drag the Web page to another location or to resize it. The frame contains icons along the top border, like this:

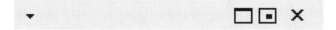

Clicking the downward-pointing arrow in the left corner displays a menu of commands you can use to change the appearance of the Web page—Microsoft calls this the Tools menu for the Web page. The Tools menu contains commands that enable you to tell Windows whether to store the Web page for use when your computer is offline, how much of the screen for the Web page to occupy, and how often to update the Web page from the Internet. You can choose Properties from the Tools menu to display the Web page's Properties dialog box, which is described in the next section.

 If you are used to working with Web pages inside browser windows, having a Web page as part of your desktop takes some getting used to. For example, the Web page stays behind any open windows on the desktop; you can't bring it to the front by clicking it.

Updating Your Desktop Web Pages

A Web page on your desktop does not stay current automatically. You must either update it by selecting Synchronize from the Tools menu that drops down from the top-left corner of its frame or by setting up a schedule to update it automatically.

To set up a schedule for Web page updating, follow these steps:

1. Choose Properties from the Web page's Tools menu to display the Web page's Properties dialog box. (Another way to display this dialog box is from the Desktop tab of the Display Properties dialog box: click Customize Desktop, click the Web tab of the Desktop Items dialog box that appears, select a Web page from the list, and click the Properties button.)

2. Click the Schedule tab of the Properties dialog box (as shown in Figure 11-4).

3. Click the Use The Following Schedule(s) radio button. If a schedule has already been defined but is not currently active, you can select it from the Schedules list.

4. If the schedule you want is not on the list, click the Add button. The New Schedule dialog box opens.

5. In the New Schedule dialog box, choose a number of days to wait before updating, a time of day when the update should happen, and a name for the schedule. A check box allows you to specify whether the computer should connect to the Internet automatically at the update time.

CONFIGURING WINDOWS FOR YOUR COMPUTER

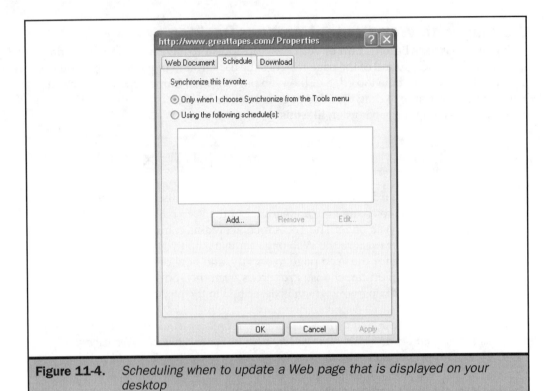

Figure 11-4. *Scheduling when to update a Web page that is displayed on your desktop*

6. When you have finished entering information in the New Schedule dialog box, click OK. The new schedule now appears on the list of schedules. Click OK in all of the open dialog boxes.

You can change or remove an update schedule by repeating step 1 in the preceding list, and then selecting the schedule and clicking the Edit or Remove button. You can make the schedule inactive by selecting the Only When I Choose Synchronize From The Tools Menu radio button in step 2.

Setting Up a Screen Saver

If you walk away from your computer and leave the monitor on, the same image might be on your screen for hours at a time. Years ago, this would tend to "burn in" the image permanently on the screen. To prevent such screen damage, developers created *screen savers*, which are programs that kick in when the display hasn't changed in a while. A good screen saver contains some kind of moving image, so no section of the screen is consistently bright or dark.

Monitor technology eventually improved to the point that burn-in is not a serious concern. In addition, many monitors now have an energy-saving feature that allows a monitor to turn off automatically if its display hasn't changed for some period of time (see Chapter 15, section "Managing Your Computer's Power").

But even though screen savers are no longer needed for their original purpose, many people continue to use them because they are pleasant to look at. They also discourage random passers-by from reading the document you're working on when you step out for coffee. If your computer is set up with user accounts, the screen saver can require you to log back in when you return, so others can't use your computer (without your password). Screen savers like Mystify Your Mind or Curves And Colors make attractive geometric patterns that can be soothing to watch; others, like 3D Maze, create a more active mood.

In offices with multiple networked computers, the screen saver can display the computer's name, suitably colorized and animated. You can also download screen savers from the Internet, enabling you to display the latest *Harry Potter* images when you're not working. Or you can use the My Pictures Slideshow screen saver to cycle through pictures of your grandchildren or your vacation in Bali.

Selecting a Screen Saver

To select and activate a screen saver, follow these steps:

1. Open the Display Properties dialog box by right-clicking any empty spot on the desktop and selecting Properties from the shortcut menu.

2. Click the Screen Saver tab of the Display Properties dialog box, shown in Figure 11-5.

3. Select a screen saver from the drop-down list. The preview box shows a miniaturized version of what the screen saver displays. To see a full-size preview, click the Preview button. Move the mouse or click a key to stop the full-size preview.

4. When you find a screen saver you like, click either the Apply or OK button.

Tip *Windows comes with a choice of several screen savers, but that's just the beginning. Additional screen savers are available over the Internet, and most of them are free. You can begin your search at C | NET's Web site at **http://www.download.com**, which lists screen savers in the "utilities" department. You can also try looking on the Web site of your favorite book, TV show, or movie to see whether there is a promotional screen saver.*

CONFIGURING WINDOWS FOR YOUR COMPUTER

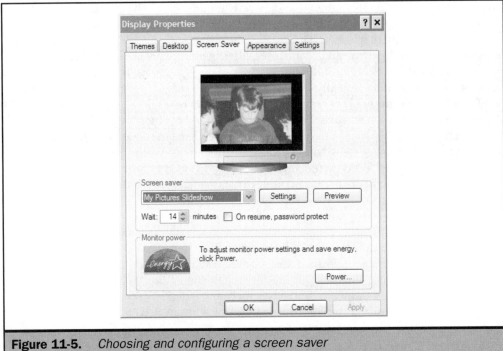

Figure 11-5. *Choosing and configuring a screen saver*

Configuring Your Screen Saver

While you have the Screen Saver tab selected, you can make a number of choices about how your screen saver functions:

■ **Change the settings.** Click the Settings button. Each screen saver has its own list of settings; some let you change a handful of parameters; others offer an entire screenful of choices. In general, the settings of your screen saver control how fast the screen saver cycles, the colors it uses, the thickness of the lines it draws, and so forth.

■ **Change the wait time.** Enter a new number of minutes into the Wait box. The *wait time* is the length of time your system must be inactive before the screen saver starts up. Windows waits this long for keyboard or mouse input before starting the screen saver.

■ **Require a password.** Check the On Resume Display Welcome Screen check box. When the screen saver is displayed and you press a key, you will see the Unlock Computer window or Welcome screen, asking for your user account name and password (see Chapter 6).

Choosing a New Color Scheme

A *color scheme* is a coordinated set of colors for all the basic desktop objects. With a color scheme, you can change the color of everything at once and wind up with colors that look good together and provide reasonable visibility. (You don't want to wind up with black text on black title bars, for example.) To change color schemes, follow these steps:

1. Right-click an empty space on the desktop and choose Properties from the shortcut menu. The Display Properties dialog box opens.

2. Click the Appearance tab, shown in Figure 11-6.

3. Make a selection from the Color Scheme drop-down list.

4. Click OK.

Note   *The color schemes that are available to you depend in part on your choice of window and button styles. If you choose Windows Classic windows and buttons, all the Windows Me color schemes are available.*

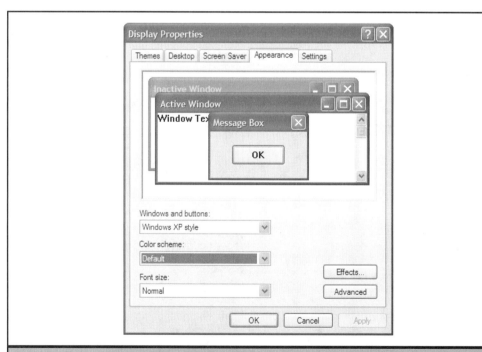

Figure 11-6.   *The Appearance tab of the Display Properties dialog box*

Finding the Perfect Color

When you choose to change the color of the desktop, the title bars, or any of the other basic objects, Windows offers a simple palette of 20 colors. If you want more choices, click Other on the color palette to display the Color dialog box, shown in woefully inadequate black and white in Figure 11-7.

The number of basic colors has now expanded to 48, shown in a palette on the left side of the Color dialog box. If the color you want is on this palette, click it and click OK. If even the 48 colors aren't enough for you, you can use the settings on the right side of the Color dialog box to get any color you want.

The currently selected color is shown in the Color | Solid box. To the right of the Color | Solid box are two different numerical systems for describing the current color: its hue, saturation, and luminescence (known as *HSV coordinates*); and its red, green, and blue components (known as *RGB coordinates*). Above the Color | Solid box and the coordinates is a graphical representation of the current color's HSV coordinates. The horizontal position of the cross-hairs in the large square represents the hue, and the vertical position of the cross-hairs represents the saturation. The position of the vertical slider next to the square represents the luminescence. Thus, the same color is represented

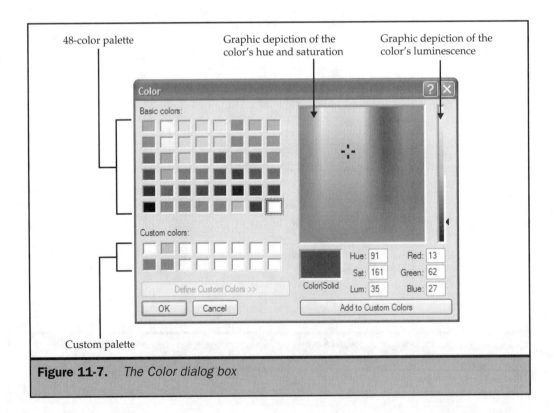

Figure 11-7.   *The Color dialog box*

three ways: as RGB, as HSV, and as a position of the cross-hairs and slider. You can select a new color by manipulating any of the three descriptions:

- Move the cross-hairs and slider with the mouse.
- Type new numbers (from 0 to 240) into the HSV coordinate boxes.
- Type new numbers (from 0 to 255) into the RGB coordinate boxes.

When you use one of these methods to specify the color, the other two descriptions (and the Color | Solid box) change automatically to match.

If you think you might want to use this color again in the future, click Add To Custom Colors. The new color appears in one of the boxes in the Custom Colors palette on the bottom-left side of the Color dialog box. If you like, you can define several custom colors, one at a time. Like basic colors, custom colors can be selected by clicking them.

When you have created all the colors you want, select the one you want to use, and click OK. The color is applied, and the Color dialog box vanishes.

 If you really want 256 colors, which Windows XP doesn't normally support, click the Settings tab on the Display Properties dialog box, click the Advanced button, click the Adapter tab, click the List All Modes button, and choose a display mode with 256 colors.

Changing Windows, Buttons, and Fonts

The Windows XP desktop theme doesn't allow many color changes—you have three color scheme choices, and you can set the background color of the desktop. However, with the Windows Classic desktop theme, you can configure the color, size, and font of almost anything—title bars, active windows, inactive windows, message boxes, and more. These choices are made all at once (along with changes in screen savers, background images, and many other items) when you choose a desktop theme (see "Choosing a Desktop Theme," earlier in the chapter). But you may want to change the windows, buttons, or fonts while leaving the rest of your desktop alone. Or you may want to change just one or two things, like the color of title bars or the font size of tool tips.

The place to make changes to the windows, buttons, and fonts in Windows is the Appearance tab of the Display Properties dialog box (shown earlier in Figure 11-6). To get to this tab, right-click any open space on the desktop, choose Properties from the shortcut menu, and then click the Appearance tab when the Display Properties dialog box appears.

Choosing Classic Style Windows and Buttons

The windows and buttons of Windows XP have a distinctive rounded look that is different from those in earlier versions of Windows. You can change back to the classic Windows look by displaying the Appearance tab of the Display Properties dialog box, shown in Figure 11-6, choosing Windows Classic Style from the Windows And Buttons drop-down list, and clicking OK. To change back to the new style, choose Windows XP Style from the Windows And Buttons drop-down list.

Choosing Windows Classic Style on the Appearance tab appears to us to have exactly the same result as choosing the Windows Classic theme on the Themes tab.

Changing the Appearance of Individual Items

You can edit the appearance of title bars, message boxes, and many other individual items from the Advanced Appearance dialog box, shown in Figure 11-8.

To display the Advanced Appearance dialog box, follow these steps:

1. Right-click any empty space on the desktop and choose Properties from the shortcut menu. The Display Properties dialog box appears.

2. Click the Appearance tab of the Display Properties dialog box.

3. Click the Advanced button on the Appearance tab.

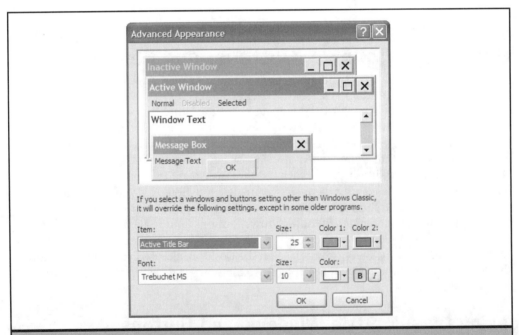

Figure 11-8. *The Advanced Appearance dialog box gives you finer control over the look of Windows.*

To change the appearance of an item, first find it on the Item drop-down list of the Advanced Appearance dialog box. (In Figure 11-8, Active Title Bar is chosen.) After you choose an item, the text boxes and buttons relevant to that item become active.

Not all of the text boxes and buttons of the Advanced Appearances dialog box are relevant to all items. For example, a scrollbar has no text, so the second line of buttons and text boxes becomes inactive when Scrollbar is the selected item.

The first line of text boxes and buttons (Size, Color1, and Color2) refer to the item itself. So, for example, for the Active Title Bar item, the Size text box on this line refers to the height of the title bar. Color1 is the color on the left side of the title bar, and Color2 is the color on the right side. The second line of text boxes and buttons (Font, Size, Color, Bold, and Italic) refers to the text (if any) displayed on the item.

As you enter the new information into the Advanced Appearance dialog box, the items in the dialog box's preview box change accordingly. When you are satisfied with your changes, click OK.

It's possible to make some dreadful choices in the Advanced Appearance dialog box. You can always go back to square one by choosing one of the built-in desktop themes (see "Choosing a Desktop Theme" earlier in the chapter).

Changing Fonts

You can fairly easily make an overall change in the size of the text that appears in menus, title bars, file labels, and other system contexts. With a little more effort, you can change not just the size, but the font as well. You also can make changes to the text used in specific contexts, rather than an overall change.

Changing the Size of Fonts

If the default fonts that Windows uses are not large enough for you, you can easily make them bigger. On the Appearance tab of the Display Properties dialog box (shown in Figure 11-6), choose Large Fonts or Extra Large Fonts from the Font Size drop-down list.

Another way to increase the size of text on your screen (as well as everything else) is to increase the magnification setting, as described in the "Changing Magnification" section, later in this chapter.

The Advanced Appearance dialog box, shown earlier in Figure 11-8, gives you much finer control over Windows' fonts. You can change the font as well as the size of text, and you can change some items while leaving others alone. For example, you could choose one font for the text in menus and another for the text in message boxes. To change the font, size, or color of the text that Windows uses for a particular type of item, display the Advanced Appearance dialog box as described in the section "Changing the Appearance of Individual Items," earlier in this chapter.

Smoothing the Edges of Fonts

Fonts have a tendency to look ragged when displayed on a monitor. Windows offers a choice of two methods for combating this tendency: Standard and ClearType. The Standard method is the default. ClearType is a relatively new technique that Microsoft invented for use in e-books. We recommend taking a look at ClearType if you think that the fonts you're seeing look ragged, especially on LCD screens.

To change from one method to the other, follow these steps:

1. Open the Display Properties dialog box by right-clicking any empty space on the desktop and selecting Properties from the shortcut menu.

2. Click the Effects button on the Appearance tab. The Effects dialog box appears, as shown in Figure 11-9.

3. Make sure that the Use The Following Method To Smooth The Edges Of Screen Fonts check box is checked.

4. Choose Standard or ClearType from the drop-down list, and then click OK in both the Effects dialog box and the Display Properties dialog box.

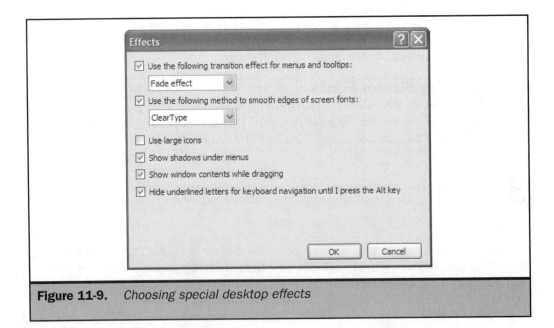

Figure 11-9. *Choosing special desktop effects*

Changing Icons

You can change the size or arrangement of the icons on your desktop. You can even define new icons for the various types of desktop objects.

Changing Icon Size

If your icons seem too small, you can switch from regular icons (32 points) to large icons (48 points), as follows:

1. Open the Display Properties dialog box by right-clicking any empty space on the desktop and selecting Properties from the shortcut menu.

2. Click the Effects button on the Appearance tab. The Effects dialog box appears (see Figure 11-9).

3. Check the Use Large Icons check box.

You can make finer adjustments in icon size from the Advanced Appearance dialog box (shown earlier in Figure 11-8). Choose Icon from the drop-down Item list in the Advanced Appearance dialog box, and then type a number between 16 and 72 in the Size box. This represents the size of icons in points. The default size is 32 points. The second row of text boxes and buttons in the dialog box controls the font and size of the labels underneath your icons.

Making your icons too large may cause them to look ragged. Rather than increase the point size of your icons, you may want to decrease the resolution of your desktop or increase the magnification setting of your display (see "Changing Magnification," later in the chapter). Icons in Explorer windows become more visible when you switch to Large Icons or Thumbnails view (see Chapter 8, section "Changing Views").

Arranging Icons on the Desktop

You can arrange your desktop icons manually by dragging and dropping them. If your system is set up for single-click opening, however, you may open the corresponding objects by mistake when you try to drag and drop icons. If you're having this problem, use right-click drag-and-drop. Select Move Here from the shortcut menu that appears when you drop the icon.

Arranging Icons Automatically

To arrange your desktop icons automatically, right-click any open spot on the desktop and choose Arrange Icons from the shortcut menu. Windows arranges the icons in columns, starting on the left side of the desktop. The Arrange Icons menu gives you the option of arranging by name, type, size, or date modified.

CONFIGURING WINDOWS FOR YOUR COMPUTER

Make sure that you really want the icons arranged in columns before you use an Arrange Icons option. There is no "undo" selection on the Arrange Icons menu.

Another option on the Arrange Icons menu is Auto Arrange. If Auto Arrange is checked, the icons are arranged in columns, and any new item is automatically ushered to the next open spot in the pattern. Auto Arrange prevents you from arranging your icons manually; any icon is whisked to the appropriate row or column as soon as you set it down.

Adjusting Icon Spacing

The spacing between icons is another of the many details controlled by the Advanced Appearance dialog box (see "Changing the Appearance of Individual Items"). To change the spacing, open the Advanced Appearance dialog box and choose Icon Spacing (Horizontal) or Icon Spacing (Vertical) from the Item drop-down list. Type a number (of points) in the Size box. Larger numbers create bigger spaces.

 Changing the icon spacing affects the icon arrangement of Explorer windows, as well as the icons on the desktop.

Choosing New Desktop Icons

You can choose new icons for any of the standard desktop objects. Make these changes from the General tab of the Desktop Items dialog box, shown in Figure 11-10.

To choose a new icon for My Computer, My Documents, My Network Places, or the Recycle Bin, follow these steps:

1. Open the Display Properties dialog box by clicking any empty space on the desktop and selecting Properties from the shortcut menu.

2. Click the Desktop tab of the Display Properties dialog box.

3. Click the Customize Desktop button. The Desktop Items dialog box appears, with the General tab displayed.

4. Select the icon that you want to change from the box of icons in the Desktop Items dialog box. Scroll left and right to see them all.

5. Click the Change Icon button. The Change Icon dialog box appears, showing you the icons available for this item. If you don't see an icon you want and know that there are other icons elsewhere on your system, you can click the Browse button and look for another file of icons.

6. When you find the icon you want, select it in the Change Icon dialog box and click OK.

7. Click OK in the Desktop Items and Display Properties dialog boxes.

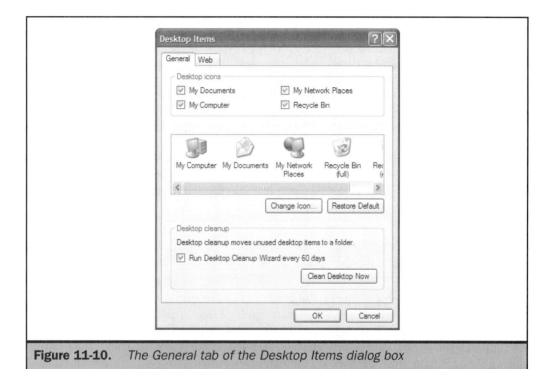

Figure 11-10. *The General tab of the Desktop Items dialog box*

Deleting and Recovering Desktop Icons

You can remove desktop icons in the same way that you delete files and folders: Select them and press the DELETE key. The only icon for which this technique fails is the Recycle Bin.

The My Computer, My Documents, My Network Places, and Recycle Bin icons represent capabilities of your system that you cannot delete; you can only stop displaying them on the desktop. The objects they represent continue to appear in Explorer windows, on the Start menu, and as links on the Task pane. To remove any of these icons from your desktop, open the General tab of the Desktop Items dialog box (Figure 11-10 in the previous section) and uncheck its check box in the Desktop Icons section. (This is the only way we know of to remove the Recycle Bin icon from the desktop.)

If you decide that you want these icons back on the desktop, you can restore them from the General tab of the Desktop Items dialog box. Select the check boxes of the items whose icons you want to have on the desktop. Then click OK to close the Desktop Items and Display Properties dialog boxes.

Using the Desktop Cleanup Wizard

The Desktop Cleanup Wizard is a handy tool for cutting down the clutter on your desktop. Run this Wizard by right-clicking any empty space on the desktop and selecting Arrange Icons By | Run Desktop Cleanup Wizard from the shortcut menu.

The Wizard shows you a list of desktop icons (other than Recycle Bin) and the date when you last used each icon. Put a check next to each icon that you want cleared away into the Unused Desktop Icons folder, which will appear on your desktop instead of those icons.

You can run the Desktop Cleanup Wizard automatically by opening the Desktop Items dialog box (shown earlier in Figure 11-10) and clicking the Run Desktop Cleanup Wizard Every 60 Days check box. Conversely, if you are annoyed by Wizards that pop up without an invitation, deselect the box.

Changing the Desktop's Visual Effects

Windows has a number of cute, but inconsequential, visual effects that create the illusion of motion or three-dimensionality on the desktop, like the thin shadow that surrounds the Start menu. You can control these effects from the Effects dialog box (shown earlier in Figure 11-9). To open this dialog box, first open the Display Properties dialog box by right-clicking any open space on the desktop and selecting Properties from the shortcut menu. Then click the Effects button on the Appearance tab.

The check boxes in the Effects dialog box are self-explanatory. The effects themselves are harmless, so don't be afraid to experiment with them.

Changing the Desktop's Sound Effects

Most actions on the desktop (closing a window, for example) are accompanied by a sound effect. You can change these sounds all at once (or turn them off entirely) by choosing a new sound scheme, or you can change only a few sounds and leave the rest alone. A *sound scheme* is a coordinated set of sounds for all the desktop actions.

Make these choices from the Sounds tab of the Sounds And Audio Devices Properties dialog box, shown in Figure 11-11. Open this dialog box by clicking the Sounds And Audio Devices icon from the Sounds Speech And Audio Devices category on the Control Panel, and then click the Sounds tab. Choose a sound scheme from the Sound Scheme drop-down list (Windows XP comes with only two sound schemes: No Sounds and Windows Default).

You can also change sounds for individual events. To choose a new sound for a type of event, select the event from the Program Events list on the Sounds tab of the Sounds And Audio Devices Properties dialog box, and then select a sound from the Sounds drop-down list. For more information about associating sounds with Windows events, see "Choosing What Sounds Windows Makes" in Chapter 19.

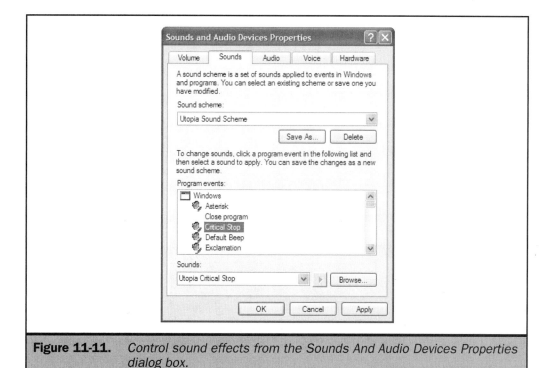

Figure 11-11.   *Control sound effects from the Sounds And Audio Devices Properties dialog box.*

Changing Display Settings

Windows gives you control over the dimensions of your desktop, the color resolution of your display, and many other properties. Most of this power resides on the Settings tab of the Display Properties dialog box, shown in Figure 11-12. Open this dialog box by right-clicking any empty space on the desktop, selecting Properties from the shortcut menu, and then clicking the Settings tab.

Changing the Screen Resolution

The Screen Resolution slider on the Settings tab of the Display Properties dialog box controls the dimensions of your desktop in *pixels*, which are the colored dots on the screen. The current dimensions are stated under the slider. Increase the dimensions by moving the slider to the right; decrease them by moving the slider to the left.

Naturally, the size of your monitor doesn't change (the number of inches on your monitor is fixed); so when you increase the number of pixels on your desktop, each pixel gets correspondingly smaller, increasing the resolution. Icons and fonts shrink as well. As you increase the desktop area, you may want to increase font and icon size to compensate. (See the "Changing Fonts" and "Changing Icon Size" sections, earlier in this chapter.)

Figure 11-12.   *The Settings tab of the Display Properties dialog box*

The range of resolutions depends on what type of monitor you use. For a 14-inch monitor, your choices may range only from 800 × 600 to 1,024 × 768. For a 17-inch monitor, you can increase the resolution up to 1,600 × 1,200. Larger monitors support even higher resolutions. If you have a monitor larger than 14 inches, consider increasing your screen resolution settings so that you'll be able to see more information on your screen. Here are our recommendations for screen resolution based on monitor size (that is, the size of the CRT tube that can display an image, measured diagonally):

Screen Size	Maximum Usable Resolution
14 inches	640 × 480
15 inches	800 × 600
17 inches	1,024 × 768
19 to 21 inches	1,280 × 1,024 or 1,600 × 1,200

Windows doesn't normally support resolutions of less than 800 × 600. However, if you really want a lower resolution, click the Settings tab on the Display Properties dialog box, click the Advanced button, click the Adapter tab, click the List All Modes button, and choose a display mode with 640×480.

Changing the Color Quality

The Settings tab of the Display Properties dialog box also controls the number of colors you display. The Color Quality drop-down list gives you choices that depend on the quality of your monitor. Your options may include 16 colors, 256 colors, high color (16-bit, or 65,536 colors), 24-bit true color (16 million colors), and 32-bit true color (even more colors). Below the list is a color bar showing the spectrum of the selected color palette.

The choice to be made is a speed versus beauty tradeoff. Displaying fewer colors or pixels is less work for your computer and may help it run faster. On the other hand, displaying more colors and pixels provides a richer viewing experience, particularly if you are looking at photographs. Using 16-bit color or higher produces much-improved image quality.

Note	*Colors and pixels also trade off against each other, because increasing either one uses more of the portion of RAM your system devotes to the display. Windows accounts for this automatically. If you increase the desktop area beyond the capabilities of your RAM, it decreases the color palette to compensate. Likewise, if you increase the color palette beyond what your RAM can handle, Windows decreases the desktop size.*

A few programs don't work properly with the new color palette until you restart your computer. In general, we recommend restarting your computer to be completely safe; but, if you change the color palette frequently, this can get to be a nuisance. You may want to experiment to see whether the software you use has any problems when you don't restart after a color change. You can set up Windows to restart automatically when you change the color palette, ask you whether to restart, or not restart (see the "Adjusting Other Monitor Settings" section, later in this chapter).

Changing Color Profiles

Subtle differences occur in the ways that different monitor and printer drivers represent a color palette. These representation schemes are called *color profiles*. For most purposes, the difference between color profiles doesn't matter. However, if you must be sure the colors you see on your monitor are exactly the colors you will get when you print, you can set the color profiles of your monitor and printer to reflect the exact way your monitor and printer render colors. Matching colors is especially important if you plan to edit and print photos.

Windows comes with profiles for many popular monitors. Its default profile, called the sRGB Color Space Profile, matches most monitors reasonably well. Unless you are a graphic artist, you probably won't notice the difference between the default profile and a perfectly tuned one. Most users do not need to change their color profiles.

To change the color profile of your monitor, click the Settings tab of the Display Properties dialog box and click the Advanced button. In the new dialog box that opens, click the Color Management tab (shown in Figure 11-13). Any profiles you have previously

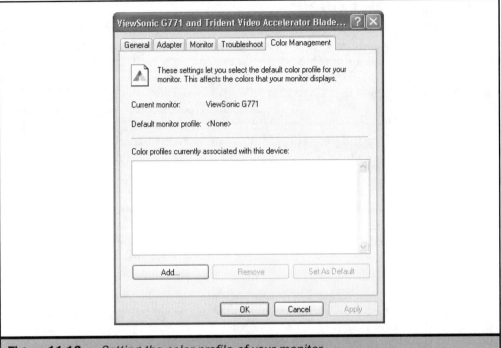

Figure 11-13.   *Setting the color profile of your monitor*

used are listed in the large window, with the current default profile in the box above the large window. To change to a new default color profile, select a new profile from the list and click the Set As Default button. To add a profile to the list, click the Add button and select from the color profiles listed. To remove a profile from the list, select it and click the Remove button.

Changing Magnification

To control font magnification, click the Advanced button on the Settings tab of the Display Properties dialog box. You see a dialog box that displays properties of your monitor. The title, tabs, and settings of this dialog box depend on the display driver.

Tip   *For higher magnification for the vision-impaired, see Chapter 16.*

For most display drivers, the settings on the General tab include a magnification setting (which may be called DPI Setting, for dots per inch). For a typical monitor, a drop-down list gives you three choices: Normal Size (96 DPI), Large Size (120 DPI), and Custom Setting. Choosing Custom Setting opens the Custom DPI Setting dialog box. From this dialog box, you can type in whatever size you want as a percentage or change the size by using the ruler as a slider.

After you've made your choice, click OK to return to the display driver's dialog box, where your chosen size is displayed under the Font Size box. If you like it, click Apply. If Windows doesn't restart your computer automatically, restart it yourself.

> **Caution**   *Be careful choosing very large font magnifications. Changing the size of fonts changes the size of everything that contains text, such as the Display Properties dialog box, for example. If you choose 200% font magnification and have an 800 × 600 desktop, the Display Properties dialog box gets so large that the Apply button goes off the bottom of the screen.*

Getting Along with Your Monitor(s)

Windows can detect and install a driver for a Plug and Play monitor with little effort on your part (see Chapter 13, section "How Do You Add Hardware to a Windows Computer?"). In addition, many newer monitors comply with Energy Star power-saving standards, enabling you to choose to have Windows turn off the monitor if you have been inactive for a certain period of time. If you have two or more monitors hooked up to your computer, your desktop can stretch across all of them, and each can have its own settings.

Using Multiple Displays

Windows can handle four screens on a single system, displaying a single desktop that spans all the screens. A pair of 17-inch monitors have considerably more screen area than a single 19-inch monitor and can be a cost-effective alternative to a single larger screen. (On the other hand, you may not have much desk space left after setting up two monitors.)

Windows XP's multiple-monitor support is based on Windows 2000's, and it is more limited than the support in Windows Me/9x. Many monitor cards that worked with Windows Me don't work with Windows XP. Either one monitor stays blank or Windows XP displays the same information on all the monitors. Older display adapters, especially those with S3 chip set, are particularly problematic.

Configuring a second, third, or fourth screen is straightforward once you install the new hardware (you need a display adapter for each screen, unless you use a special adapter). Open the Settings tab of the Display Properties dialog box, which looks like Figure 11-14 if three display adapters are installed (see Chapter 13, section "Configuring Windows for New Hardware").

To configure an additional display, follow these steps:

1. Click the picture of the new monitor to highlight it. Windows may display a message box about extending the Windows desktop over multiple monitors. Click Yes and OK.

2. Drag the pictures of the monitors so they agree with the physical arrangement of your screens.

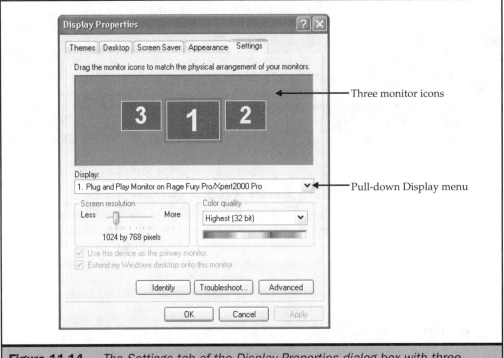

Three monitor icons

Pull-down Display menu

Figure 11-14.   *The Settings tab of the Display Properties dialog box with three monitors*

3. Configure the new display. If possible, configure all the displays to have the same number of colors and the same screen area, to avoid confusion when you move a window from one screen to another.

4. Click OK. Windows configures the new display.

Once configured, the additional display becomes part of the Windows desktop, and you can drag windows back and forth between the displays. You can even have a single window that spans multiple screens, which can be convenient for looking at spreadsheets with wide rows. If you want to change the color depth or resolution of one of the monitors, click the monitor on the Settings tab of the Display Properties dialog box, and then change the settings.

Windows considers one of your monitors to be the *primary display*, which is the monitor on which error messages and alerts appear. Some high-end DirectX graphics applications display correctly only on the primary monitor. If you have one AGP graphics card and one PCI graphics card, the PCI defaults to be the primary display, and the AGP is the secondary display.

Windows XP Professional handles dual monitors differently from Windows Me/9x. If you are upgrading from Windows Me or Windows 98, you may need to buy a new display adapter for one or both monitors. Another approach is to switch which monitor is the primary display. Check your computer's documentation for the way to tell its BIOS which monitor is primary.

Adjusting Other Monitor Settings

Depending on the capabilities of your monitor, some other configuration settings are available. When you click the Advanced button on the Settings tab of the Display Properties dialog box, you see a dialog box with a title based on the type of monitor you use, as shown in Figure 11-15. Settings may include the following:

- **After I Change Color Settings** Determines what Windows does after you change the screen resolution or color palette on the Settings tab of the Display Properties dialog box. You can choose for Windows to restart automatically or for Windows to ask you first.

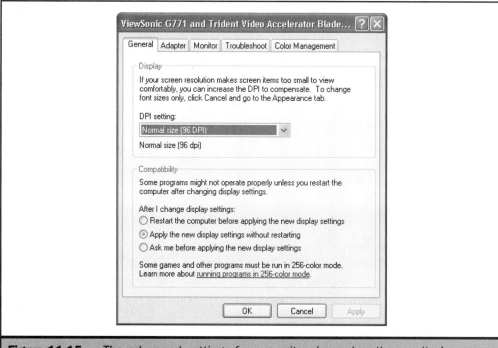

Figure 11-15. *The advanced settings for a monitor depend on the monitor's device driver.*

■ **Reset Display On Suspend/Resume**   Specifies that Windows reset the display once you resume using a computer (usually a laptop) that has been in Standby mode.

■ **Hardware Acceleration**   Specifies how fast Windows updates your screen.

■ **Color Management**   Specifies the color profiles you have defined.

The
Complete
Reference

Windows XP

Chapter 12

Keyboards, Mice, and Game Controllers

Windows XP, like all operating systems, sits between the programs you run and the computer you run them on. Whenever a program accepts input from the keyboard, mouse, or a game controller, or sends output to the screen or printer, Windows gets involved. As a result, when you configure Windows to work with your keyboard, mouse, or game controller, the settings you choose affect all the programs you run. You can choose the keyboard layout you want to use and set the sensitivity of the mouse. If you have installed a game controller or joystick, you can also check or change its settings.

Different countries use different currencies and formats for writing numbers, monetary amounts, dates, and times. Windows has regional settings that let it know about the formats used in most countries in the world (at least most of the countries where people are likely to use computers). By telling Windows which country you live in, you can cause Windows and most programs to use the date, time, and numeric formats with which you are comfortable.

Windows has a built-in calendar all programs can use. It knows the current date and time (usually displayed at the right end of the taskbar) and understands time zones, U.S. daylight saving time, and leap years. You can set the date, time, and the time zone in which you are located, so the Windows calendar will be accurate.

You can change most of these settings in the Control Panel (see Chapter 1, section "What Is the Control Panel?"). The Date And Time icon and the Regional And Language Options icon are in the Date, Time, Language, and Regional Options category of the Control Panel, while the Keyboard, Mouse, and Game Controllers icons are in the Printers And Other Hardware category.

The WINDOWS *Key*

Most new computer keyboards include a WINDOWS key, with the flying Windows logo on it. It's usually among the keys to the left of the SPACEBAR. The most convenient use of the WINDOWS key is to display the Start menu, but you can use the Windows key like a SHIFT key in combination with other keys. Here are the WINDOWS key combinations that work in Windows XP:

Key Combination	Action
WINDOWS	Opens or closes the Start menu
WINDOWS-BREAK	Displays the System Properties dialog box
WINDOWS-TAB	Makes the next application in the taskbar into the active window
WINDOWS-SHIFT-TAB	Makes the previous application in the taskbar into the active window

Key Combination	Action
WINDOWS-B	Makes the notification area active
WINDOWS-D	Shows the desktop (minimizes all windows)
WINDOWS-E	Opens Windows Explorer showing My Computer (like Start │ My Computer)
WINDOWS-F	Opens Windows Explorer with the Search pane
WINDOWS-CTRL-F	Opens Windows Explorer with the Search pane and with Search For Computers selected
WINDOWS-F1	Opens Help
WINDOWS-M	Minimize all windows
WINDOWS-SHIFT-M	Undo minimize all windows
WINDOWS-R	Opens Run dialog box (like Start │ Run)
WINDOWS-U	Opens the Utility Manager for accessibility features (see Chapter 16, section "Turning On and Off Magnifier, Narrator, and the On-Screen Keyboard by Using the Utility Manager")
WINDOWS-L	Locks the computer, with the option to switch to another user (see Chapter 6)

Configuring Your Keyboard

Configuring your keyboard can mean two subtly different things:

- **Changing the way that your keyboard produces symbols,**   for example, how long you have to press a key before it repeats. Microsoft considers these to be keyboard properties, and you control them from the Keyboard Properties dialog box.

- **Changing the way that symbols are mapped to keys,**   for example, choosing a different alphabet or a different keyboard layout. Microsoft considers these to be language properties, and you control them from the Text Services And Input Languages dialog box.

Changing Keyboard Properties

Opening the Keyboard icon from the Printers And Other Hardware category of the Control Panel (or from the Control Panel itself if you are not using the category view) produces the Keyboard Properties dialog box, shown in Figure 12-1. From here you can control these settings:

Setting	Description
Repeat delay	Delay between starting to hold down a key and when the key begins repeating
Repeat rate	How fast the key repeats once it starts repeating
Cursor blink rate	How fast the cursor blinks

Additional keyboard settings are available if you have trouble using the keyboard (see Chapter 16, section "Making the Keyboard More Accessible").

Move the sliders on the Speed tab of the Keyboard Properties dialog box to set the repeat delay, repeat rate, or cursor blink rate. You can test how your keys repeat by clicking in the text box and holding down a key.

Figure 12-1.   *The Keyboard Properties dialog box contains settings for the keyboard and the cursor.*

Changing Language Properties

You can also control which language layout the keyboard uses. Different languages use different letters and assign the letters to different locations on the keyboard. If you use more than one language, you can choose a key combination that switches between two keyboard layouts.

For some languages, Windows offers a selection of *keyboard layouts*, which define the physical organization of the keys on the keyboard. For example, if you choose U.S. English as your language, you can choose among layouts that include the standard 101-key layout, the Dvorak keyboard, and even the left-handed Dvorak keyboard.

These choices are controlled from the Text Services And Input Languages dialog box, shown in Figure 12-2.

Open this box as follows:

1. Open the Control Panel by selecting Start | Control Panel.

2. If you are displaying the Control Panel in the category view, open the Date, Time, Language, And Regional Options icon and click the Add Support For Additional Language link. If you are using the classic view of the Control Panel, open the Regional And Language Options icon. In either case, the Regional And Language Options dialog box appears with the Language tab on top.

3. Click the Details button on the Regional And Language Options dialog box.

Configuring Your Keyboard for Another Language or Keyboard Layout

The languages and keyboard layouts that are installed on your computer shown in the Installed Services box on the Text Services And Input Languages dialog box. If the Installed Services box doesn't show the language or keyboard layout you want, click the Add button. When the Add Input Language box appears, select the language you want from the Input Language drop-down list, or the keyboard layout you want from the Keyboard Layout/IME drop-down list and then click OK. The new service is added to the Installed Services box in the Text Services And Input Languages dialog box.

East Asian languages like Chinese or right-to-left languages like Hebrew might not appear, even in the Add Input Language box. In order to use these languages, you will have to do the following:

1. Open the Control Panel by selecting Start | Control Panel.

2. If you are displaying the Control Panel in the category view, open the Date, Time, Language, And Regional Options icon and click the Add Support For Additional Language link. If you are using the classic view of the Control Panel, open the Regional And Language Options icon. In either case, the Regional And Language Options dialog box appears. If the Language tab is not on top, click it.

Figure 12-2.   *You can switch among several languages and keyboard layouts.*

3. Check one of the two check boxes on the Language tab, depending on the language you want to use—either the Install Files For Complex Script And Right-To-Left Languages check box or the Install Files For East Asian Languages check box. Then click OK.

4. A confirmation box appears, listing the languages that will be added and the quantity of disk space required. (East Asian languages require 230MB of disk space, right-to-left languages only 10MB.) Click OK both in the confirmation box and in the Regional and Language Options dialog box.

5. Windows installs the necessary files. This takes a few seconds and you might need to insert your Windows XP CD-ROM. When all the files have been installed, a new confirmation box appears, asking whether you want to restart your computer. Click Yes.

6. After the computer restarts, the added languages will appear in the drop-down list on the Add Input Language box. From there you can add them to the Default Input Language drop-down list on the Text Services And Input Languages dialog box, as described earlier in this section.

To delete a language or layout you no longer plan to use, select that language or layout from the Installed Services box on the Text Services And Input Languages dialog box and click the Remove button.

Switching Languages and Keyboard Layouts

If you install more than one language or keyboard layout on your computer, you can switch from one to another in several ways. If you switch very rarely, make the switch by choosing the language you want from the Default Input Language drop-down list on the Text Services And Input Languages dialog box. Click OK and restart your computer.

Using the Language Bar   A quick way to change languages or keyboard layouts is to use the Language bar. You can display the Language bar on your desktop or a language icon on the taskbar as follows: Go to the Text Services And Input Languages dialog box (shown in Figure 12-2), and click the Language Bar button. When the Language Bar Settings dialog box appears uncheck the Turn Off Advanced Text Services check box and check the Show the Language Bar On The Desktop check box.

The Language bar is a small toolbar that sits just above the taskbar or can be dragged (by its left edge) anywhere on the desktop. (The Language bar that comes with Office XP works similarly to the one in Windows XP.) The Language bar has two buttons: one showing the keyboard's current language and the other its current layout. To change either, click the corresponding button and make a new choice from the menu that appears. The keyboard changes instantly; you do not need to restart the computer.

At the far right end of the Language bar is a small button to minimize the Language bar. If you click it, the bar disappears and is replaced by a small language icon on the taskbar next to the clock. Click the icon to change languages or restore the Language bar.

Keyboard Shortcuts for Switching Languages   You can also set a key combination for switching among languages and keyboard layouts. Your options are LEFT ALT-SHIFT (that is, the left ALT key plus the SHIFT key), CTRL-SHIFT, or none. To set up such a key combination, click the Key Settings button on the Text Services And Input Languages dialog box (shown in Figure 12-2). The Advanced Key Settings dialog box appears.

To set up or change a key combination for switching between languages or keyboard layouts, find the switching action on the Action list and select it. Then click the Change Key Sequence button. Use the Change Key Sequence box that appears to set up the desired key sequence.

Configuring Your Mouse

You can control what the mouse looks like, what its buttons do, and how fast the mouse pointer (the screen object that moves when you move the mouse) moves. You can define the shape of the mouse pointer, but not the cursor (the blinking element that shows where what you type will be inserted).

You can also choose the shape the mouse pointer assumes when used for pointing, when Windows is busy (the hourglass), when you are typing, when selecting text, when clicking a Web link, when dragging window borders, and other functions. If you choose shapes other than the Windows default shapes, you can save the set of shapes you like to use as a *pointer scheme*. Windows comes with more than a dozen predefined pointer schemes from which you can choose.

These mouse settings are controlled from the Mouse Properties dialog box, shown in Figure 12-3. Open this dialog box by clicking the mouse icon in the Printers And Other Hardware category of the Control Panel.

   Additional mouse settings are available if you have trouble using your mouse (see Chapter 16, section "Setting Mouse Accessibility Options"). You might also consider installing a trackball or other pointing device.

Defining the Mouse Buttons

Normally, you click or double-click the left mouse button to select, open, or run items on the screen. You click the right mouse button to display the shortcut menu of commands

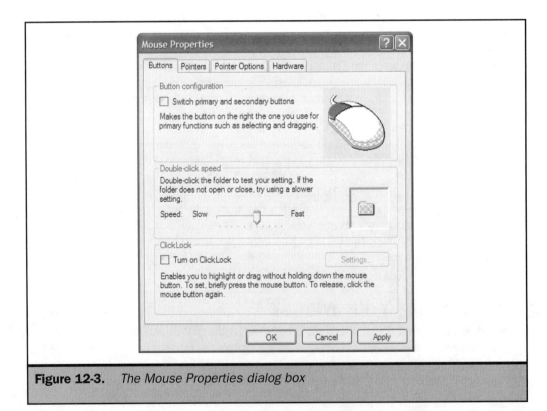

Figure 12-3.   *The Mouse Properties dialog box*

about the item you selected (see Chapter 2, section "Choosing Commands from Shortcut Menus"). Some programs use the right mouse button for other purposes.

If you are left-handed, you may find it convenient to reverse the meanings of the two buttons. In the Mouse Properties dialog box, click the Buttons tab, and check the Switch Primary And Secondary Buttons check box. To return to the default (right-handed) button configuration, uncheck the check box. Click OK to close the Mouse Properties dialog box and implement your changes.

Defining Your Double-Click Speed

Windows defines a double-click as two clicks within a specified time period, with no mouse motion during that period. That time period is called the *double-click speed*, and you can adjust it using the Double Click Speed slider on the Buttons tab of the Mouse Properties dialog box. If you have trouble clicking fast enough for Windows to realize you want to double-click, move the slider in the Slower direction. On the other hand, if you find two single clicks often get interpreted as a double-click, move the slider in the Faster direction. To test the setting, double-click the folder icon in the Double Click Speed box. If you can make the folder open and close, Windows is recognizing your double-clicks.

Configuring the Appearance of the Mouse Pointer

The mouse pointer changes shape depending on the context. For example, it appears as an arrow when you are selecting items, or as an *I* when you are editing text. You can choose the shape your mouse pointer assumes. In the Mouse Properties dialog box, click the Pointers tab to display a list of the current pointer shapes. To choose a different set of pointer shapes (mouse pointer scheme), choose a pointer scheme from the drop-down list. The pointers in the scheme are then shown in the Customize box.

You can mix-and-match to assemble your own pointer scheme. Click an item in the Customize box and click the Browse button. A browse window appears to show you the pointers in the folder C:\Windows\Cursors. This folder contains two types of pointers: static cursors (with the extension .cur) and animated cursors (with the extension .ani). Find the pointer you want and click the Open button.

If you want to go back to the default pointer for an item, click the item in the Customize box, and then click the Use Default button. When you have things the way you want them, click the Save As button and give your new pointer scheme a name.

 Tip   *Installing a desktop theme is another way to change all your pointers (see Chapter 11, section "Choosing a Desktop Theme").*

Improving Pointer Visibility

If you have trouble following the mouse pointer when it moves, you can give the pointer a *trail*. Trails are useful on laptops and other displays that redraw the screen slowly. To turn the pointer trail on or off and to set the length of the trail, click the Pointer Options tab of the Mouse Properties dialog box. Click the Show Pointer Trails check box to turn the trail on or off, and drag the Pointer Trail slider to the length you want. Click Apply or OK to implement your changes

If you have trouble finding the pointer, check the Show Location Of The Pointer When I Press The CTRL Key check box on the Pointer Options tab and click Apply or OK. When this box is checked, pressing the CTRL key causes Windows to draw a big circle around the pointer and then zero in on it with ever smaller circles.

Setting the Mouse Speed

You can adjust how far the mouse pointer moves when you move the mouse. For example, if you move the mouse in a small area of your desk, you can adjust Windows to make the mouse very sensitive, so moving the mouse one inch (2.5 cm) moves the pointer halfway across the screen. If you have shaky hands, you can make the mouse less sensitive, so small motions of the mouse result in small motions of the pointer.

On the Mouse Properties dialog box, click the Pointer Options tab and drag the Pointer Speed slider to adjust the mouse speed. To try out the new setting, click the Apply button.

 If your mouse or trackball is unresponsive, it may require a low-tech solution like cleaning. Pop the ball out and look for accumulations of dust on the contacts or the ball itself.

Setting ClickLock

ClickLock is a feature that allows you to drag objects without holding down the mouse button. To enable ClickLock, check the Turn On ClickLock check box on the Buttons tab of the Mouse Properties dialog box. After ClickLock is enabled, when you hold the mouse button down for a short time it "locks," and you can drag the selected object without continuing to hold the mouse button down.

You can adjust the length of time that you must hold the mouse button down before it locks. To make this adjustment, click the Settings button on the Buttons tab of the Mouse Properties dialog box. When the Settings For ClickLock box appears, adjust the lock time by moving the slider. Click OK to implement your changes.

Configuring Your Game Controller

Game controllers and *joysticks*—devices that enable you to play arcade-style games on your computer—come in many sizes and shapes. Windows includes drivers for many game controllers (see Chapter 13, section "What Are Drivers?").

To install a game controller, follow the instructions that come with it. Usually, you just shut down Windows, turn off the computer, plug the game controller or joystick into the game port on your computer, and turn on your computer again. Windows should recognize the new device and install it. Have the floppy disk or CD-ROM that came with the game controller handy, and insert it when Windows is looking for the driver. If you've downloaded a driver, tell Windows where the driver file is stored.

To find out whether Windows has recognized your game controller or to change the settings for a game controller, look at the Game Controllers dialog box, shown in Figure 12-4. To see this dialog box, open the Game Controllers icon from the Printers And Other Hardware category of the Control Panel.

If no devices are listed in the Installed Game Controllers box, Windows didn't recognize your game controller. Click the Add button in the Game Controllers dialog box to see the Add Game Controller dialog box, shown in Figure 12-5. Select the line in the Game Controllers list that best describes your game controller and click OK.

If none of the descriptions on the Game Controllers list fit your game controller, click the Custom button on the Add Game Controller dialog box. Fill out the form on the Custom Game Controller dialog box to generate your own description.

Displaying and Changing Game Controller Settings

To see the settings for your game controller, select it from the list in the Game Controllers dialog box and click Properties. You see the game controller's Properties dialog box, shown in Figure 12-6.

Figure 12-4. *The Game Controllers dialog box with a game controller installed*

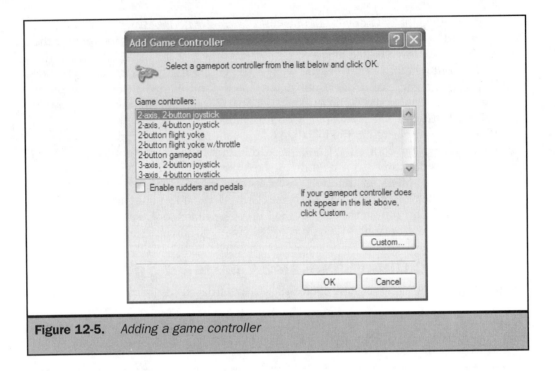

Figure 12-5.   *Adding a game controller*

One computer can have several game controllers attached. Each controller has an ID number, starting with 1. You can see and change the controller ID numbers by clicking the Advanced button in the Game Controllers dialog box.

Testing Your Game Controller

To test your game controller, select it from the list in the Game Controllers dialog box, click Properties, and click the Test tab in the game controller's Properties dialog box (see Figure 12-6). Move the joystick or yoke and see whether the crosshairs in the Axes box move. Click the buttons on the game controller and see whether the button indicators light up. If not, calibrate the game controller by clicking the Settings tab, clicking the Calibrate button, and following the instructions.

Windows' Regional Settings

Windows comes with predefined regional settings for most of the countries in the world. *Regional settings* affect the format of numbers, currency, dates, and times. For example, if you choose the regional settings for Germany, Windows knows to display numbers with dots between the thousands and a comma as the decimal point, to use Deutsch marks as the currency, and to display dates with the day preceding the month.

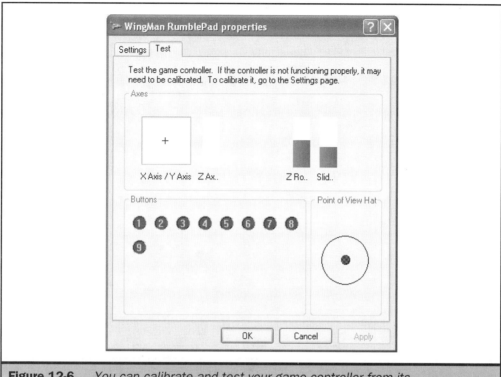

Figure 12-6. *You can calibrate and test your game controller from its Properties dialog box.*

Note *To reset your keyboard for other languages, see "Changing Language Properties" earlier in this chapter.*

To see or change your regional settings, look in the Regional and Language Options dialog box, shown in Figure 12-7. To display this box, open the Regional And Language Options icon from the Date, Time, Language, And Regional Options category of the Control Panel.

Telling Windows Where You Live

Windows has predefined sets of regional settings, so you needn't select numeric, currency, date, and time formats separately. Choose the language you speak and the country where you live from the drop-down list in the Standards And Formats box on the Region Options tab of the Regional And Language Options dialog box. The list is arranged alphabetically by language, with the country in parentheses. There are, for example, 13 English entries, including English (Belize) and English (South Africa).

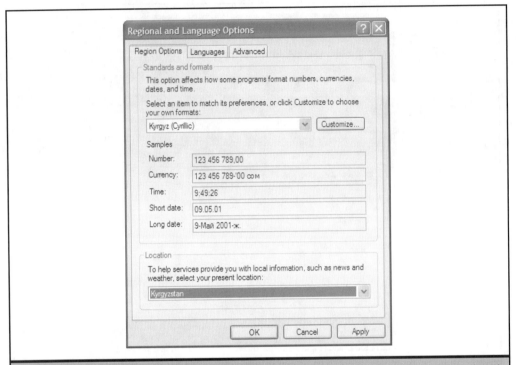

Figure 12-7. *The Regional And Language Options dialog box displaying the regional settings for Kyrgyzstan*

Setting Number, Currency, Time, and Date Formats

After you tell Windows which language you speak and where you live, it displays sample numbers, currency symbols, times, and dates on the Region Options tab of the Regional And Language Options dialog box. You will probably be happy with the way these samples are formatted. If not, you can change any of these items individually by clicking the Customize button. When the Customize Regional Options dialog box appears, click the Number, Currency, Time, or Date tab to see the corresponding settings. To change any of these settings, make another selection from the corresponding drop-down list and click the Apply or OK button.

Numbers

The following table shows the settings on the Numbers tab of the Customize Regional Options dialog box that tell Windows how you write numbers.

Setting	Description
Decimal symbol	Which character appears as the decimal point, separating the whole from the fractional portion of numbers. (In the U.S., this is a period.)
No. of digits after decimal	How many digits usually appear to the right of the decimal symbol. (The default U.S. option is two.)
Digit grouping symbol	Which character appears to group digits into groups in large numbers. (In the U.S., this is a comma.)
Digit grouping	The pattern for grouping digits in large numbers. (In the U.S., digits are grouped in threes.)
Negative sign symbol	Which character indicates negative numbers. (In the U.S., this is the minus sign –.)
Negative number format	Where the negative sign symbol appears. (In the U.S., the negative sign symbol appears to the left of the number.)
Display leading zeroes	For numbers between –1 and 1, whether to display a zero before the decimal symbol. (In the U.S., a zero is displayed; for example, 0.4.)
List separator	Which character to use to separate items in lists, for entering lists in Windows text boxes. (The Windows default for the U.S. is a comma.)
Measurement system	Whether you use the U.S. or metric system of measurements.

Currency

The following settings on the Currency tab of the Customize Regional Options dialog box control how Windows displays currency (money).

Setting	Description
Currency symbol	Symbol that indicates which currency is in use for amounts of money. (In the U.S., this is $.)
Positive currency format	How Windows formats positive amounts of money. (In the U.S., the currency symbol appears to the left of the amount with no space between the $ and the leftmost digit.)

Setting	Description
Negative currency format	How Windows formats negative amounts of money. (In the U.S., negative amounts of money are enclosed in parentheses.)
Decimal symbol	Which character appears as the decimal point in amounts of money, separating the whole from the fractional portion of numbers. (In the U.S., this is a period.)
No. of digits after decimal	How many digits appear to the right of the decimal symbol in amounts of money. (In the U.S., this is two, so dollars and cents are displayed.)
Digit grouping symbol	Which character appears to group digits into groups in large amounts of money. (In the U.S., this is a comma.)
Digit grouping	The pattern for grouping digits in large sums of money. (In the U.S., digits are grouped in threes.)

Time Formats

This table shows your options for displaying the time (the settings are on the Time tab of the Customize Regional Options dialog box).

Setting	Description
Time format	Format for displaying times. In the sample, *h* represents the hour, *hh* the hour with leading zeros, *H* the hour using the 24-hour clock, *HH* the hour using the 24-hour clock and leading zeros, *mm* the minutes, *ss* the seconds, and *tt* the A.M./P.M. symbol. (In the U.S., the format is *h:mm:ss tt*, for example, 2:45:03 PM)
Time separator	Which character separates the hours, minutes, and seconds. (In the U.S., this is a colon.)
A.M. symbol	Which characters or symbols indicate times before noon. (In the U.S., the default is A.M.)
P.M. symbol	Which characters or symbols indicate times after noon. (In the U.S., the default is P.M.)

Date Formats

The following table shows your options for displaying the date (the settings are on the Date tab of the Customize Regional Options dialog box).

Setting	Description
When a two-digit year is entered, interpret as a year between *xxxx* and *xxxx*	How two-digit years are converted to four-digit years (usually 1930 to 2029). Changing the end year also changes the beginning year.
Short date format	Short format for displaying dates. In the sample, *M* represents the month number with no leading zeros, *MM* the month number with leading zeros displayed, *MMM* the three-letter abbreviation for the month name, *d* the day with no leading zeros, *dd* the day with leading zeros displayed, *yy* the two-digit year, and *yyyy* the four-digit year. (In the U.S., this is *M/d/yyyy*, for example, 12/25/2000.)
Date separator	Which character separates the month, day, and year. (In the U.S., this is /.)
Long date format	Long format for displaying dates. In the sample, *dddd* represents the name of the day of the week, *MMMM* the name of the month, *dd* the day number, and *yyyy* the four-digit year.

Setting the Current Date and Time

Windows is good at keeping its clock and calendar correct. It knows about U.S. daylight saving time and leap years, but depending on where you live and the accuracy of your computer's internal clock, you might occasionally need to reset Windows' clock or calendar.

To display the Date And Time Properties dialog box, shown in Figure 12-8, double-click the time on the taskbar (usually displayed at the right end of the taskbar), or you can open the Date And Time icon from the Date, Time, And Language category of the Control Panel.

To set the date or time:

- **Year**   Click the year, and type a new year or click the up or down arrow buttons to move the year forward or backward. Only years between 1980 and 2099 are accepted.

- **Month**   Click the month and choose the correct month from the list that appears.

- **Day**   Click the day number on the calendar.

- **Hour, minute, or second**   Click the hour, minute, or second section of the digital clock, and type a new value, or click the up or down arrows.

- **A.M. or P.M.**   Click the AM or PM at the right end of the time, and click the up or down arrow to the right of the time.

■ **Time zone**   Click the Time Zone tab and choose a new time zone. If you want Windows to adjust the clock an hour for daylight saving time in the spring and fall, select the Automatically Adjust Clock For Daylight Saving Changes check box at the bottom of the window, so a check appears in the box.

Alternatively, you can tell Windows to update the time itself by synchronizing its clock with an Internet-based *time server*. (This feature is turned on by default.) To change this setting, click the Internet Time tab on the Date And Time Properties dialog box. The Automatically Synchorize With An Internet Time Server check box turns the feature on and off, and the Server box determines which time server you contact (the default is **time.windows.com**). Windows checks in with the time server every week and updates its clock.

If your computer communicates through a firewall (other than the firewall built into Windows XP), time synchronization may be blocked. Also, Windows doesn't update your time if the date is incorrect. If you find Windows setting your clock to the wrong time, check that the time zone is set correctly.

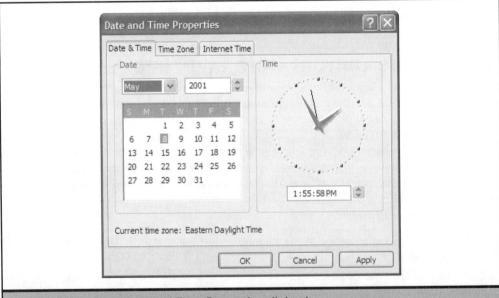

Figure 12-8.   *The Date And Time Properties dialog box.*

The
Complete
Reference

Chapter 13

Adding and
Removing Hardware

Windows XP lets you add new hardware to your computer relatively easily, but you still have a lot of details to get right. This chapter describes the general steps for installing hardware, Plug and Play, the Device Manager, the types of hardware you may want to install, how to configure Windows to work with new hardware, troubleshooting hardware, and adding memory.

How Do You Add Hardware to a Windows Computer?

Most Windows-based computers let you add extra hardware to extend your computer's capabilities. Some hardware fit inside your computer; some plug into existing connectors on the back of the computer; and some require adding a card inside your computer, into which you plug external equipment. After you add the device, you need to configure Windows to use your new hardware.

Adding hardware is a three-step process:

1. Set any switches and jumpers on the new equipment as needed.
2. If the card goes inside the computer, turn off and unplug the computer, open it up, install the card, and put the computer back together. Plug in external equipment.
3. Turn on the computer and tell Windows about the new equipment.

Tip *Before adding new hardware, make a backup of your important files, in case you can't restart your computer (see Chapter 9).*

What Is Plug and Play?

Plug and Play (PnP) is a feature of Windows and hardware that allows Windows to configure itself automatically when the hardware is installed. Windows 95 was the first version of Windows to include Plug and Play, and Microsoft has been improving the feature with each new version. *Universal Plug and Play (UPnP)* was added in Windows Me to simplify configuring network devices. If your hardware is Plug and Play, Windows notices when you install a new device, and tries to install and configure a driver for the hardware automatically.

What Is the Device Manager?

To see a list of your computer's hardware, you use the *Device Manager* window, shown in Figure 13-1. The Device Manager lists all the devices that make up your computer and lets you see and modify their configuration. If the Add New Hardware Wizard detects a device conflict, it starts the Device Manager automatically.

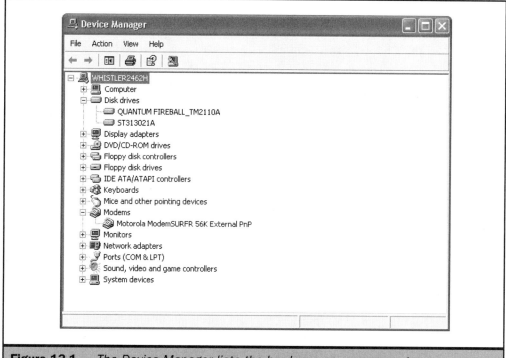

Figure 13-1. *The Device Manager lists the hardware on your computer.*

To see the Device Manager, choose Start | Control Panel, click Performance And Maintenance, click the System icon, select the Hardware tab, and click the Device Manager button. You can view devices by type or by connection; by connection is usually better for driver debugging, since it displays each connected device separately. If hardware is having trouble, Windows displays the devices listed by type, with the type of the problematic device expanded.

Another way to see the Device Manager is within the Microsoft Management Console. Click Start, right-click My Computer, and choose Manage from the shortcut menu to see the Microsoft Management Console. Then click Device Manager in the left pane of the window (see Chapter 35, section "The Device Manager").

What Types of Hardware Can You Install?

IBM-compatible computers, having evolved for over 20 years, offer numerous, often complicated, ways to attach new kinds of equipment. The details of PC hardware are beyond the scope of this book, but this section describes the basics of PC hardware that you need to know to get a recalcitrant Windows driver installed, including older types of PC components, in case you are upgrading an older computer. See Chapter 32 for more information about configuring hard disks. Chapter 11 describes how to configure your display, and Chapter 14 talks about how to print once you've installed a printer.

The system requirements for Windows XP are steep, so upgrading an older computer may not be worth the expense and trouble. Carefully weigh the costs of upgrading versus purchasing new (especially with the prices of new systems so low). Keep in mind that you may be required to completely replace everything inside the case in order to satisfy Windows XP, so keeping the old system might actually be more useful than upgrading it to XP. See the Microsoft Windows Hardware Quality Labs (HCL) Web site at **http://www.microsoft.com/hcl** *to find out whether your hardware has been approved by Microsoft for use with Windows XP. Keep in mind that lots of hardware that Microsoft hasn't gotten around to testing also works.*

Tip   *For the definitions of many hardware-related terms and acronyms, see the Dirt Cheap Drives Web site at* **http://www.dirtcheapdrives.com/tech** *and click Glossary.*

Integrated Versus Separate Peripherals

The original IBM Personal Computer contained nothing built into the computer beyond the *central processing unit (CPU)*, memory, and keyboard. Everything else, including screens, floppy disk drives, hard disk drives, printers, modems, and serial ports, was provided by separate extra-cost add-in cards. (Hardware you add to your computer, other than processors and memory, is called a *peripheral*.) Over the years, manufacturers have found that, as the functions of the computer were combined into fewer and fewer chips, it became cheaper to build the most common peripherals into the computer's *motherboard*, *mainboard*, or *system board*, the printed circuit board that carries the CPU and memory. Modern computers typically include a parallel port, one or two serial ports, two PS/2 ports for keyboard and mouse, two Universal Serial Bus (USB) ports, controllers for up to two floppy disk drives and four IDE (Integrated Device Electronics) devices (typically hard drives, CD-ROM drives, CD-R drives, or DVD drives), a 56K modem, and sound and video adapters on the motherboard. Windows usually can't tell whether these items are built-in or on separate cards, so Windows treats them all as though they are separate peripherals.

Connectors

The back of your PC is bristling with connectors for various sorts of devices (see Figure 13-2). If your computer has internal *expansion slots* holding adapter cards, each adapter card may have a connector or two, as well. Connectors to which you attach cables are also called *ports*. Most likely, the user's manual for your computer has a similar picture showing and labeling the connectors on your computer.

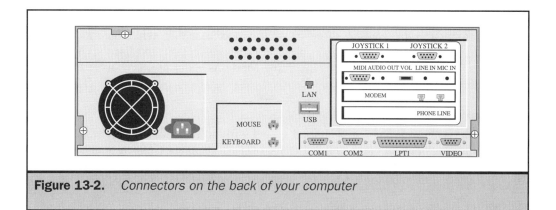

Figure 13-2.   *Connectors on the back of your computer*

Serial (Com) Ports

Most PCs have one or two *serial ports*, which are D-shaped connectors with 9 or 25 pins (sometimes referred to as *DB-9* and *DB-25*):

Most commonly, you plug an external dial-up modem into a serial port, but serial ports are also used for serial mice, computer-to-computer cabling for "poor man's networking," and occasionally for printers. If you have a UPS (uninterruptible power supply), a cable may run from the UPS to the PC's serial port so that the UPS can signal Windows to shut down when the UPS battery is almost dead.

Network Ports

Some PCs come with a built-in network adapter to enable the computer to connect to a local area network, DSL modem, or cable modem. Newer network ports have RJ45 jacks that look like phone jacks, only larger. Old network ports may have round coaxial cable connectors. See the "Buying Network Hardware" section in Chapter 27 for how to connect your computer to a network. See the "Installing Modems" section later in this chapter for more about installing DSL and cable modems.

Telephone Plugs

A *modem* connects your computer to a phone line. If you have a dial-up (analog) modem (the kind of modem that connects to a normal, old-fashioned phone line) the modem has one or two *RJ-11* telephone plugs that are identical to the plugs on the back of a U.S. telephone. (If you are outside the United States, your modem may have a different type of phone plug.) If there are two plugs, one is for the incoming phone line plugged into the wall, and the other is for a phone that shares the line with the modem. (The advantage to plugging the phone in via the modem is that, while the modem is online, the phone is disconnected, so you won't disconnect your modem call if you pick up the phone by mistake.) See "Installing Modems" later in this chapter for other types of modems.

Parallel Ports

Most PCs have a *parallel port*, a D-shaped socket with holes for 25 pins. Parallel ports are often used for printers and sometimes for other devices such as removable disk drives (such as ZIP drives).

 The 25-pin serial port is mechanically identical to the parallel port, except that the serial port is "male" and the parallel port is "female." Despite the similar connectors, you can't plug a device intended for one port into the other port.

Parallel ports can communicate unidirectionally (for sending information to a printer) or bi-directionally (for smart printers that send information back to the computer, as well as for devices that we think should never be connected to a parallel port in the first place, like Zip drives and scanners). There are two bi-directional standards: ECP (Enhanced Capability Port, used mainly by printers and scanners) and EPP (Enhanced Parallel Port, used mainly by devices other than printers). When you look at your parallel devices in Device Manager, by clicking Ports (COM & LPT), Windows shows what kind of communication each parallel port uses.

 You set the communications standard for your parallel port in the BIOS setup for your computer. If you run into trouble connecting a device (especially one that requires bi-directional information), check your computer's manual for how to configure the parallel port.

PS/2 (Keyboard and Mouse Ports)

All PCs new enough to run Windows XP have two connectors for a keyboard and a mouse and usually two *PS/2 connectors*:

The keyboard and mouse ports look identical—look at the little icons next to the connectors to determine which is which. (Nothing terrible will happen if you plug a mouse into the keyboard port, or vice versa—Windows usually complains that it can't find your keyboard or mouse.)

Display Ports

Display adapters, into which you plug your monitor, all use a 15-pin *(DB-15)* connector that is similar in size to the 9-pin serial connector.

Display adapters are identified by acronyms like SVGA, XGA, Super VGA, and Ultra XGA, depending on their maximum resolution. Don't worry about the acronyms, because each display adapter manufacturer seems to make up their own. All monitors made in recent years are compatible with almost all display adapters, at least at common resolutions. Resolutions you are likely to encounter are 800 × 600 (the minimum required for Windows XP), 1024 × 768, 1400 × 1050, and 1600 × 1200.

The video display adapters that are built into new computers can support lots of colors beyond the original 256 colors (also known as 8-bit color); most can display 16-bit High Color, 24-bit True Color, and 32-bit True Color.

Multiple Displays

Windows XP can support more than one display (screen or monitor), continuing the Windows desktop from one display to the next. You need a video display adapter for each display or a special multidisplay adapter card (see Chapter 11, section "Using Multiple Displays"). Some laptop computers enable you to use the built-in LCD screen as one monitor and an external monitor as the second monitor.

Universal Serial Bus (USB)

The *USB (universal serial bus)* is a relatively new connector for which Microsoft introduced full support in Windows 98. It is a faster and simpler alternative to serial and parallel ports, as well as for low- to moderate-speed devices such as modems, printers, sound cards, and backup tapes. Few older computers come with USB ports. Most new computers come with at least two.

The USB uses a small rectangular connector. Unlike most other connection schemes, USB lets you connect a *USB hub* to your USB port, so you can have a desk full of USB devices, even though your computer has only a single USB connector. Also remarkable is the fact that you can *hot swap* USB devices—you don't have to turn off the computer, plug in the device, and restart the computer; just plug the device in and turn it on.

USB printers and scanners are popular, and USB network adapters are a hit with high-speed Internet access installers (unlike network interface cards, USB network adapters don't require the installer to open up the computer).

  If the device you are attaching has never been connected to the computer before, Windows will likely need to install a driver for it. The vast majority of drivers for Windows XP can be used without restarting the computer, thanks in no small part to XP's Windows 2000 heritage.

FireWire

Some computers also have *FireWire* ports, also known as *IEEE 1394* or Sony *i.Link*. They are faster than USB ports, and are typically used for digital video cameras, hard disk drives, and high-speed printers. FireWire was first developed by Apple for its Macintosh computers, but is now available on many Windows-compatible PCs, too.

FireWire cables are limited to about 15 feet in length. FireWire, like USB, can be hot swapped—connected and disconnected—while the computer is running. FireWire is efficient, self-powered, flexible, and fast.

  Your FireWire port appears in the Network Connections window as a LAN port—choose Start | Control Panel, click Network And Internet Connections, and click Network Connections to see it.

Audio and Video Jacks

Most PCs have connectors for speakers or headphones, and sometimes a microphone. The speaker connector is a standard 1/8-inch stereo mini–audio jack. The microphone connector is usually also a mini–audio jack, so you have to be careful not to confuse the two. (Otherwise, your sound may play sdrawkcab. Well, not really.)

If your computer doesn't have speaker connectors, you can add an internal sound board. Many CD-ROM drives have headphone jacks so you can listen to audio CDs, even if your computer has no speakers.

Newer computers may have a digital audio jack (*S/PDIF*, or Sony/Philips Digital Interface jack) to which you can connect digital audio equipment, like a DAT (digital audio tape) machine. Most S/PDIF ports accept standard RCA connectors, the same connector used for regular audio jacks.

If you plan to use your TV to display information from your computer, check whether your PC has a TV jack or S-video jack, to which you can connect a television. Alternatively, your PC may come with a video card that includes a TV In plug so you can watch TV on your computer monitor. These video cards may include software for picture-in-picture (so that your TV picture appears in a window) and for capturing graphics from the video.

PC Cards

Laptop computers usually have one or two *PC card* slots (also known as *PCMCIA* slots). A few desktop computers have them, too. These take credit-card–sized adapter cards of many varieties, including modems, networks, and disk and tape controllers. PC cards, unlike other adapter cards, can be added to, and removed from, your computer while it's running. To add a PC card, press it firmly into the slot until it seats. To remove a PC card, press the button next to the PC card to eject the card slightly, and then pull out the card.

Before removing a PC card, you should first tell Windows, so that it can stop sending data to, or receiving data from, the card. When you have a PC card inserted, an icon for it may appear in the notification area of the taskbar. If so, click or double-click it to find a command for preparing Windows for the removal of the card.

Internal Adapter Cards

If you add a device to your computer that can't be plugged into one of the existing connectors on your computer, you have to add an *adapter card* that plugs into a slot inside the computer. As the PC has evolved over the past 20 years, the slots into which you can plug adapter cards have evolved as well.

PCI Cards

PCI (Peripheral Connect Interface) slots enable you to expand the capabilities of your computer by installing PCI adapter cards inside the computer. To install a PCI card, you need to turn off the computer, take off the cover, slide the PCI card into the slot, screw it down, replace the cover, and turn the computer back on. PCI cards include display adapters (for connecting to monitors), sound cards (for connecting to speakers), network adapter cards (for LAN and high-speed Internet connections), disk drive adapters (for connecting hard disks, CD-ROM drives, and floppy drives), and SCSI adapters (for connecting a wide variety of peripherals).

Note   *Older PCs came with ISA (Industry Standard Architecture) slots, into which you plugged ISA cards, which often required you to set jumpers and switches on the card. Later, PC manufacturers introduced EISA (Enhanced or Extended ISA) slots, an improved version of ISA. Both ISA and EISA slots have been superceded by PCI slots. Computers capable of running Windows XP are unlikely to have ISA or EISA slots.*

AGP Cards

AGP (Accelerated Graphics Port) slots are an advanced version of PCI for video cards, enabling faster screen updates. The original specification, 1x, could transfer graphics data between the card buffers and system RAM at a speed equal to the system's bus, typically 33, 50, and 66 MHz at that time. 2x and 4x varieties have since become available and bus speeds have increased 100 MHz to 200 MHz. Luckily, newer AGP cards are backwards compatible (that is, compatible with older versions). Another advanced feature of these cards is that they can use half the RAM of equivalent PCI-based cards. For example, a 4MB AGP video card is the functional equivalent of an 8MB PCI video card, because the AGP card allocates an equal amount of system RAM to that of its on-board RAM.

Other Kinds of Cards

Most computers have a few specialized slots and connectors for specific devices. There are usually two to four small slots for memory, and a connector or two for IDE or EIDE expansion disks (see "Disk Controllers: IDE, EIDE, and SCSI Devices"). Your computer's manual should list the available slots and connectors.

Hardware Parameters

Every card in your PC needs a variety of hardware parameters to be set, so that the CPU can communicate with the card reliably and without interfering with other cards. With the newer kinds of connections, such as PCI, USB, and FireWire, most—if not all—of these parameters are set automatically by Windows' Plug and Play feature; but older ISA cards and some PCI cards require manual tweaking.

To see a list of your computer's hardware, you use the Device Manager window. To display it, choose Start | Control Panel, click Performance And Maintenance, click the System icon, and select the Hardware tab (Figure 13-3 shows the hardware tab of the System Properties window on the left). Click the Device Manager button to see the Device Manager window (shown in Figure 13-3 on the right). You can choose commands from the View menu on the menu bar to see listings by type of device or by how they are connected to the computer. To see listings of the interrupts (IRQs), I/O addresses, DMA channels, and memory addresses, choose View | Resources By Type, then click the plus box to the left of each item.

 Keep a logbook for your computer, listing all the cards installed in your computer and the hardware parameters you've set on them. This makes troubleshooting a lot easier.

I/O Address

Every device attached to a PC has at least one *I/O address*, a hexadecimal number that the CPU uses to communicate with the device. All I/O addresses on a given computer must be unique; address "collisions" are the most common reason that a new I/O device doesn't work.

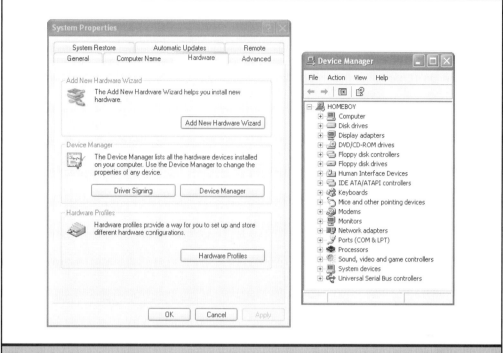

Figure 13-3.   *The System Properties dialog box and Device Manager window*

Devices on the motherboard have I/O addresses that either are permanently assigned or can be changed in the setup menus built into your motherboard (see the documentation that came with your computer). Devices on ISA cards have addresses that generally can be changed by moving jumpers on the card, while PCI cards have addresses that are set by software when you start your computer.

All traditional PC devices have well-known fixed addresses. These include up to four serial ports, a parallel port, floppy and hard disk controllers, and internal devices such as the clock and keyboard controller. Other add-in devices have more-or-less fixed addresses, depending on how popular the device is and how long it's been around. PCI cards automatically get unique addresses, but ISA cards often need jumpers to be reset.

See the troubleshooting section later in this chapter for advice on getting I/O addresses unscrambled. Luckily, with newer hardware you are unlikely to need to worry about I/S addresses.

Note   *AGP, the Accelerated Graphics Port technology from Intel, is a derivative of PCI. AGP video cards appear in the hardware list as device 1 of PCI Bus 0. This is normal, despite the name AGP.*

Interrupts (IRQs)

The PC architecture provides 15 *interrupts,* or *IRQs* (interrupt requests), channels that a device can use to alert the CPU that the device needs attention. The interrupts are numbered 0, 1, and 3 through 15. (For historical reasons, interrupt 2 isn't available, and the few devices that used interrupt 2 on early PCs use interrupt 9 instead.) PCI devices all can, and usually do, share a single interrupt, but nearly every ISA device that uses an interrupt needs a separate unique interrupt number. Motherboard devices use interrupts 0 and 1, built-in serial ports usually use 3 and 4, the floppy disk uses 6, the parallel port uses 7, the clock uses 8, a built-in mouse uses 12, the floating-point unit uses 13 (even if you don't do any floating-point calculations), and the hard disk controller uses 15—leaving 5, 9, 10, 11, and 14 for other devices. Assigning interrupts correctly on ISA cards is one of the most troublesome and error-prone aspects of hardware configuration. A few ISA cards can have their interrupt number set in software, in which case Windows sets the interrupt automatically; but most have jumpers you have to change. Fortunately, only a few ISA cards are still available commercially; everything else is PCI based.

DMA Channels

DMA, which stands for *direct memory access,* is a motherboard facility used by a few medium-speed devices. There are six DMA channels, of which the floppy disk always takes DMA 2. Some sound cards need a DMA channel, usually DMA 1. You set the DMA channel in the Properties dialog box for the device.

Memory Addresses

Each byte of memory in your computer has a unique *memory address.* A few devices, notably screen controllers and some network cards, use a shared memory region to transfer data between the CPU and the device. Those devices need a range of memory addresses for their shared memory. Screen cards generally use the ranges (expressed in hexadecimal numbers, or hex) 0xA0000 through 0xAFFFF, 0xB0000 through 0xBFFFF, and sometimes 0xC0000 through 0xCFFFF. The range from the end of the screen controller's memory to about 0xE0000 is available for other devices. PCI (and AGP) cards always have their addresses set in software.

Disk Controllers: IDE, EIDE, and SCSI Devices

A *disk controller* is a PCI adapter card or built-in board to which you connect hard disks, CD-ROM drives, or tape drives. Disk controllers present an extra configuration challenge, because you can attach more than one device to a single controller. See Chapter 32 for more information about configuring hard disks.

IDE and EIDE Device Numbers

IDE (*Integrated Device Electronics*) and *EIDE* (*Enhanced IDE,* also known as *ATA 2*) disk controllers support up to two devices, the first of which is usually a hard disk, and the second of which can be either a hard disk or a CD-ROM drive. The controller has two connectors into which drive cables are plugged, and which device is which depends on which connector each is plugged into. The first device is called the *primary* device, and the second is the *secondary* device. When the position on the cable determines which device is primary and which is secondary, this is called *cable select (CS)*. Jumpers on the devices can also determine which one is primary and which one is secondary, regardless of where they are plugged in.

Most motherboards contain two IDE or EIDE controllers, each of which can have a primary and a secondary device, for a system total of up to four devices.

SCSI Device Numbers

SCSI (Small Computer System Interface) is an older standard for connecting high-speed devices to your computer, and has largely been superceded by USB and FireWire. Few newer computers come with SCSI controllers. SCSI is still widely used in server computers for connecting disks and tapes.

Each SCSI controller can connect up to 7 devices for older controllers, or 15 devices for more recent controllers. To identify devices attached to one SCSI controller, each device has a device number from 0 to 7, or 15.

The SCSI controller itself has a device number, usually the highest possible number—7 or 15. The first disk is invariably device 0, but other numbers can be assigned arbitrarily, as long as each device has a separate number. A few devices have subunits, such as tape or CD-ROM jukebox drives that can contain several different tapes or disks.

 Due to some extremely bad planning in the early 1980s, older external SCSI devices use connectors that are physically identical to the DB-25 and Centronics connectors used on modems and printers on parallel and serial ports. Even if they fit physically, don't try connecting a SCSI device to a non-SCSI controller, or vice versa, because it won't work, and you may well cause expensive damage to the electronics.

Memory (RAM)

Memory, or *RAM (random access memory)*, is the temporary storage your computer uses for the programs that you are running and the files you currently have open. Most PCs have from two to four memory slots, and usually the computer is shipped with one or two of the four slots already containing memory. Memory comes in many different sizes, speeds, and types, so you must ensure that the memory you add is compatible with your particular computer (see the section "Adding Memory" later in this chapter). Memory chips are extremely sensitive to static electricity, so be sure to understand and follow the procedures needed to avoid static damage. (Some memory ships with an antistatic wrist strap and instructions on how to use it.)

What Are Drivers?

Many hardware devices—whether they come as part of your computer or are added later—require a *driver* or *device driver*, a program that translates between your operating system (Windows) and the hardware. For example, a printer driver translates printing requests from Windows (and through it, your applications) to commands that your printer can understand.

Windows comes with standard drivers for a wide range of monitors, printers, modems, and other devices. When you buy hardware, you usually receive a floppy disk or CD-ROM that contains the driver for the device, which you need to install during the configuring process to get the device to work with Windows. For some devices, Windows already has a driver on the Windows XP CD-ROM, so you never need to insert the driver disk. Many manufacturers provide updated device drivers on their Web sites.

Many hardware components come with one set of drivers for use with Windows 9x and Me, and another set for Windows 2000 and XP. If a device doesn't have drivers for Windows XP, try the Windows 2000 drivers.

To see information about the driver for a device, display its Properties dialog box—from the Device Manager window, right-click a device and choose Properties from the menu that appears. If there is a Driver tab, click it. Most Driver tabs contain a Driver Details button (for a list of files that make up the driver), Update Driver button (for installing a new driver), Roll Back Driver button (for reinstalling a previous driver), and Uninstall (to uninstall the driver, leaving the device with no driver).

Note *Many drivers have not been approved by Microsoft's Windows Logo testing program because it's expensive and many manufacturers don't like the idea of paying Microsoft to approve their software. When you install a driver for a new device, you may see a warning like this:*

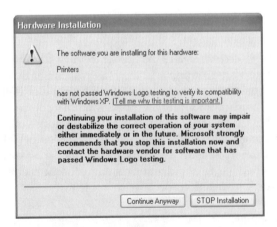

If the driver came with the device, or you downloaded it from the manufacturer's Web site, click Continue Anyway to go ahead and install it.

Configuring Windows for New Hardware

Plug and Play helps Windows XP automatically detect and configure itself for a wider range of hardware devices. Follow these steps to install new hardware and configure Windows to use it (see the next section if you are installing a PC card):

1. Install your new hardware. This can involve opening up the computer and installing a card, inserting a card into a PC card slot, or just plugging a new external device into a serial port, parallel port, SCSI adapter, USB port, or FireWire port. Follow the directions that came with the new hardware. (For USB and FireWire devices, you don't even have to turn off the computer before plugging them in.)

2. Turn on the device (if external), and turn on and start up your computer. PCI and SCSI devices usually have a BIOS setup routine that you have to enter when you turn on the computer and run one time to do low-level configuration of your new device.

3. If you're lucky, Windows notices the new device as it starts and automatically configures it for you.

4. If you're less lucky, Windows just starts up. Run the Add New Hardware Wizard, described in the next section.

5. If the new device came with a CD, put the CD-ROM into the CD-ROM drive and see what happens. If an installation program starts, follow its instructions to install the drivers and other software that the new device needs.

6. If you're unlucky, Windows doesn't start at all, or starts up in Safe Mode, and you have to figure out what's wrong (see "Troubleshooting Your Hardware Configuration").

Installing and Uninstalling PC Cards and Other Hot-Swappable Devices

You can install or uninstall PC cards without turning off your computer. For example, if you have a PC card from your digital camera with memory containing the photos you have taken, you can insert the PC card into the PC card slot of your computer at any time. Windows notices the new device within a few seconds, and you can begin using it. When one or more PC cards are installed, a Safely Remove Hardware icon appears in the notification area of your taskbar.

Before you remove the device, though, you should tell Windows that you are going to do so. Click the Safely Remove Hardware icon on the taskbar to see a list of the devices you can remove. Choose the one you are about to remove. Alternatively, right-click the icon to display the Safely Remove Hardware dialog box, as shown in Figure 13-4. Choose a device and click the Stop button. If you want to see the properties of a PC card, click the Properties button.

CONFIGURING WINDOWS FOR YOUR COMPUTER

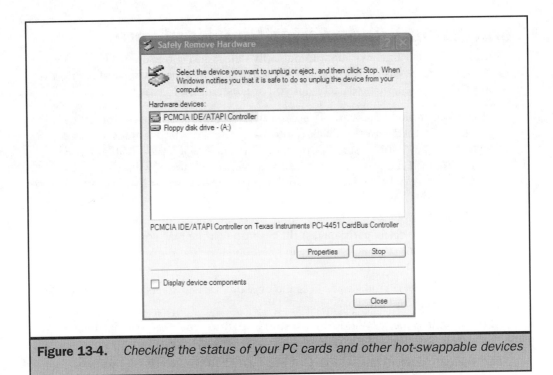

Figure 13-4.   *Checking the status of your PC cards and other hot-swappable devices*

If a device doesn't appear in the Unplug Or Eject Hardware dialog box, don't disconnect it without first shutting down Windows and turning off your computer.

 USB and FireWire peripherals don't require turning off the PC before installing or uninstalling. Your hardware vendor's driver software may impose limitations, though.

Using the Add Hardware Wizard

The Windows Add Hardware Wizard does a good job handling the details of installing new device drivers. After you've installed a new device, if Windows doesn't detect it, run the Wizard by following these steps.

1. Choose Start | Control Panel, click Printers And Other Hardware, and click Add Hardware (it's under See Also in the Task pane to the left). The Add Hardware Wizard starts.

2. The first thing the Wizard does after you click Next is search for new Plug and Play devices, devices that can communicate with Windows to provide their own configuration information. Even if you know you don't have any new Plug and Play devices, you have to wait while Windows checks for them. If the

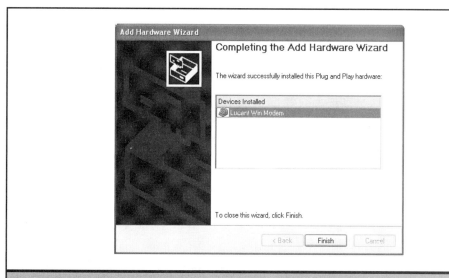

Figure 13-5.   *The Add Hardware Wizard finds a new Plug and Play device to install.*

Wizard finds new devices (or old but unused devices), it shows you a list, as in Figure 13-5. If there are no new devices to be added, you see a list of all installed hardware.

3. If Windows finds a Plug and Play device and installs and configures it, you are done—click Finish.

4. If one of the devices in the list is the one you want to install, check Yes, click the correct device, and then click Next.

5. If Windows doesn't find your new device, click the Add A New Hardware Device item at the top of the list and click Next to proceed to the next screen. Windows then offers to search for non-Plug and Play devices, which it refers to as Other Hardware. Searching for non-Plug and Play is slower and riskier than searching for Plug and Play, and it sometimes crashes the computer. If you know what you just installed, you can select Install The Hardware That I Manually Select From A List (Advanced) and select the driver yourself. If you take the automated route, Windows attempts to find any new devices, which takes a while. When it finishes, click the Next button to see a list of device categories that you can choose from (Figure 13-6).

6. Select the hardware type from the list and click Next to see a list of manufacturers and models (Figure 13-7). Sometimes it's difficult to guess which category a device falls into, so you might have to pick one category, look there, and then click Back and try another category or two before you find your device.

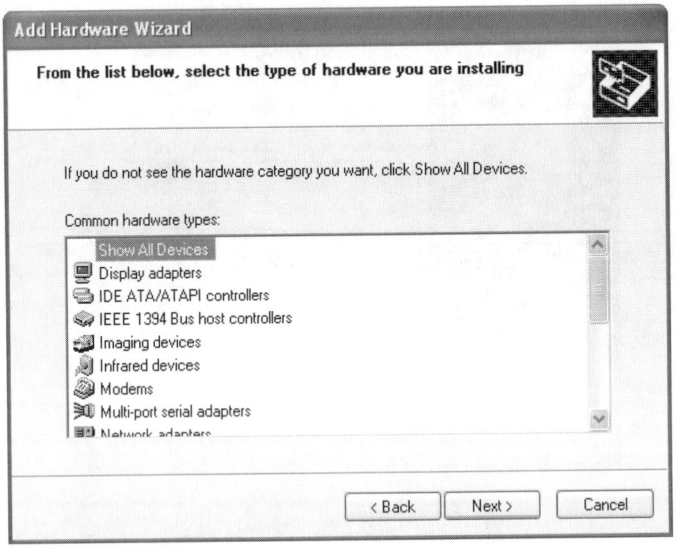

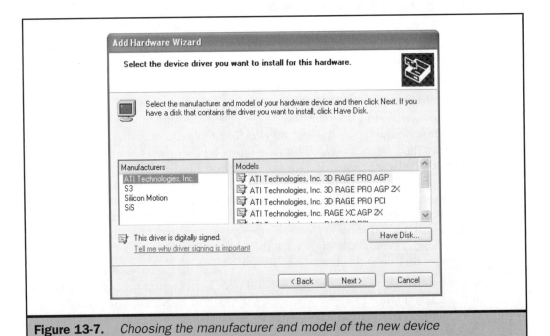

Figure 13-6.   *Adding non-Plug and Play devices*

Figure 13-7.   *Choosing the manufacturer and model of the new device*

7. Choose the manufacturer and the model of your device. If your device came with a driver on a floppy disk and you want to use that driver, click Have Disk and tell Windows which drive contains the disk, which usually is drive A. If you downloaded the driver from the manufacturer's Web site, browse the files you downloaded.

> **Tip** *Windows contains up-to-date drivers for an enormous number of devices (at least, up-to-date as of when Windows XP came out). When Windows asks for a driver, insert the floppy disk or CD-ROM that came with the hardware. Windows checks the Windows XP CD-ROM for a newer version and installs the one it thinks looks best. When in doubt, check the Web site of the hardware manufacturer for the latest driver. Look for drivers designed for use with Windows XP or 2000.*

8. Click Next, and Windows finishes installing your device. You might have to insert your Windows XP CD-ROM if the device needs drivers that haven't been used before, and you might have to reboot Windows.

At this point, unless Windows has reported a configuration problem, your device should be ready to use.

Installing Modems

Originally, all modems connected to regular phone lines, but with the advent of high-speed Internet access, you may use one of three types of modems:

- **Dial-up modem**   Connects to normal voice-grade analog phone lines. Dial-up modems may be internal (adapter cards that install inside the computer) or external (boxes that connect to the serial port).

- **DSL modem**   Connects to a high-speed DSL phone line. DSL modems may be internal or external, and external DSL modems may connect either to a network adapter or to a USB port.

- **Cable modem**   Connects to a cable TV line. Cable modems connect to either a network adapter or a USB port in your computer.

Installing Dial-Up Modems

When Windows detects that you have installed a new dial-up modem (the kind you connect to a regular phone line), it runs the Install New Modem Wizard. This Wizard also runs when you open the Modems icon in the Control Panel if Windows isn't configured to use your modem.

The Wizard asks whether the modem is a PC card (PCMCIA) modem (which can pop in or out of a laptop) or another type of modem (an internal modem that mounts permanently inside the computer, or an external modem that connects to the computer by a serial cable). The Install New Modem Wizard may call the Add Hardware Wizard

Windows Installation Glitch

Windows installation files are stored in a compressed format in *CAB* or *cabinet files* (with extension .cab) on your Windows XP CD-ROM. When you install Windows, it may copy these CAB files to your hard disk, including standard hardware drivers.

Sometimes, Windows can't find the component file that it is trying to install. When this happens, Windows says that it can't find the file where it is looking and asks for another location where the file might be. You need to find which CAB file Windows needs and tell it where to look for it.

To find the missing file, click the Details button in the dialog box that appears and find the name of the CAB file that contains the file that Windows is looking for. Then search your hard disk (or your Windows XP CD-ROM) for this CAB by choosing Start | Search. For example, if Windows is looking for a file named Winsock.dll that is supposed to be in Net4.cab, search your hard disk or the CD for files with the filename *.cab. Then tell Windows to look in that folder for the CAB file.

described in the preceding section to find the modem, or you can choose the modem manufacturer and model from a menu.

Once Windows has installed the driver for your modem, it asks for the country and area code in which you are located, any digits you need to dial to get an outside line, and whether your telephone system uses tone or pulse dialing. Windows stores this information in your default dialing location (see Chapter 21, section "Configuring Windows for Dialing Locations").

Installing DSL and Cable Modems

DSL and cable modems are installed by telephone company or cable company installers. Once the equipment is in place, see sections "Connecting to a DSL Line" and "Connecting to a Cable Modem" in Chapter 21.

Troubleshooting Your Hardware Configuration

In a perfect world, every device installation would work the first time. In the real world, something goes wrong about one time in three, and you have to fix it. The most common problem is that an I/O device address or interrupt used by the new device conflicts with an older one (see "Hardware Parameters").

In the worst case, Windows doesn't boot at all after you add your new device. Back in the old days of ISA and EISA adapter cards, this invariably meant that the settings on the card conflicted with an existing device. You'd have to turn off the computer, take out the new device, turn on the computer, and reboot. Use the Device Manager to see what addresses and interrupts are currently in use, and use the card's documentation to find out how to change jumpers to addresses and interrupts that are available (the next section describes how). Then reinstall the card and try again. However, PCI cards almost never run into this problem because few have jumpers.

If you can't tell what the conflicts are, boot the computer in Safe Mode, described in the section "Booting in Safe Mode" later in this chapter.

Solving Configuration Problems by Using the Device Manager

You can use the Device Manager to deal with configuration problems by looking at the details of how Windows communicates with the device. The settings for each device are different, depending on the type of hardware and the specific model.

Display the Device Manager by choosing Start | Control Panel, opening the System icon, selecting the Hardware tab, and clicking the Device Manager button. (Figure 13-1 near the beginning of this chapter shows the Device Manager window.) If a device has a problem, its icon appears with a red or yellow exclamation point next to it (or a red *X* over it).

To see information about a particular device, right-click that device, and click the Properties button to see the Properties dialog box for the device. Look at the General and Resources tab for information about its status (try the other tabs, too, if you can't find the information). If a device has resource conflicts, Windows displays them, as in Figure 13-8. In this case, the conflict is the interrupt number. To resolve a conflict, look at the settings that the device driver offers and try changing them.

Here are the two most common problems you can see in the Device Manager:

- **Something wrong with the driver**   If the driver for the device doesn't work with Windows or is missing, you can right-click the device in the Device Manager window and choose Update Driver from the menu that appears. The Hardware Update Wizard runs and steps you through the process of installing a driver. If the device came with a CD-ROM, choose Install From A List Or Specific Location and put the CD-ROM into your CD-ROM drive. Be sure to check the manufacturer's Web site for new drivers. If you have Windows Me/9x drivers, they may not work with Windows XP.

- **Interrupt (IRQ) conflict**   If two devices have an *X* on their icons in the Device Manager window, they may have conflicting interrupts (that is, they are both trying to use the same interrupt). Click the Resources tab on each device's Properties dialog box (if there is one) to see which IRQ the device uses to communicate with the rest of the computer—see "Interrupts (IRQs)." To see

a list of interrupts (IRQs) and which device uses each one, choose View |
Resources By Type in the Device Manager window and click the plus box by
the Interrupt Request (IRQ) item. Change the IRQ for one of the conflicting
devices, restart the computer, and see if the new setting works.

Booting in Safe Mode

Safe Mode provides minimal Windows functions by disabling all devices except the
keyboard, screen, and disk. If you are in Windows and would like to restart in Safe
Mode, restart the computer normally, but hold the CTRL key throughout the shutdown
sequence. To cold boot (turn on your computer) into Safe Mode, start your computer
normally, but watch the screen carefully. As soon as you see the Starting Windows
message, press F8 repeatedly. You should see a menu of startup options, one of which
is Safe Mode. (Other options include Safe Mode With Network Support, which you can
use if you're 100 percent sure that the problem isn't a network device, nor any other
device that might be conflicting with the hardware resources used by a network

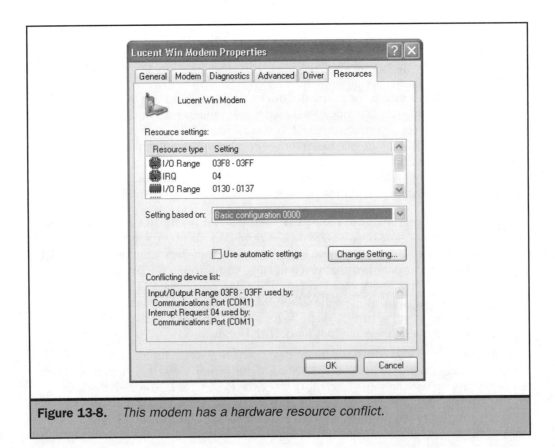

Figure 13-8.   *This modem has a hardware resource conflict.*

device.) See "Startup Modes" in Chapter 35 for more information on starting Windows in other modes.

Once you've booted in Safe Mode, you can use the Device Manager and other Windows facilities to figure out what's wrong.

To leave Safe Mode, reboot the computer normally.

Adding Memory

Adding memory is simple because no drivers are required. To add memory, follow these steps:

1. Shut down Windows, turn off and unplug the computer, open up the computer, and add the memory to available memory slots. Follow the instructions that came with your computer or with the memory.

Caution *Either use an antistatic wrist band (or a wire clipped to your metal wristwatch and the grounded metal frame); or, at the very least, touch a piece of the metal frame of the case to discharge static electricity before handling the delicate RAM, to prevent static shocks from damaging the RAM chips. You can even plug the computer back in while you are installing the memory chips, so that the third prong of the AC outlet connects your computer chassis to ground.*

2. Unplug the computer if you plugged it back in, close it up, plug it back in, and start it up. Most PCs do an internal memory test, notice that the amount of memory has changed, and possibly display a message before Windows starts.

3. If your computer complains, enter the computer's low-level configuration setup (also called *BIOS setup* or *CMOS setup*), and adjust the configured amount of memory to reflect the total now installed. Then reboot. When Windows starts, it automatically takes advantage of all memory installed in your computer.

Tip *The BIOS Setup programs of most computers can be accessed during the bootup process by pressing the DELETE or F1 keys, as instructed. If Windows doesn't accept your new memory, the RAM card may not be seated properly or may be defective. Reinsert the memory card and try again. If you have another computer, test the RAM in that computer also.*

The Complete Reference

Chapter 14

Printing and Faxing

You may not think of printing and faxing as having that much in common, but for Windows they are both ways of turning your document into a stream of dots and sending it somewhere, perhaps to a local printer six inches away, a network printer down the hall, or a fax machine in Ulan Bator.

Windows XP has a sophisticated and powerful printer management system. Setting up a Plug and Play printer is almost effortless, and even printers without Plug and Play are not that difficult. Once they're configured, you can quickly and easily print from your programs by using any printer accessible to your computer, and be confident that your printouts will look the way you want.

After your printer is installed, you can manage your print jobs from the Printers And Faxes folder, holding or canceling documents you print. You can change the printer configuration, including settings such as paper size and default fonts. If you run into printer trouble, you can use the Print Troubleshooter to find the problem (see Chapter 35, section "Diagnosing Problems Using Troubleshooters").

Windows handles the fonts that appear on the screen and on your printed pages. Windows itself comes with fonts, as do many application programs, and you can buy and install additional fonts.

"Windows XP can send faxes over a modem and phone line." You can send or receive faxes using the Windows Fax Console, or you can use other faxing clients. Some previous versions of Windows had a fax feature, although neither Windows Me nor 98 came with one.

What Is the Printers And Faxes Folder?

The command center for printing and faxing is the Printers And Faxes folder, shown in Figure 14-1. Each printer and each fax device that your computer knows about has an icon in this folder, and you start the process of adding a new printer by clicking the Add Printer link in the task pane. The default printer (the HP DeskJet in the figure) has a check next to it. The number of documents in a device's queue is shown next to its icon. (In Figure 14-1, the HP DeskJet has one document waiting to be printed, while the other printer and the fax are idle.)

You can open the Printers And Faxes folder from the Control Panel. If you are using the category view of the Control Panel, you can find the Printers And Faxes icon in the Printers And Other Hardware category. You can add Printers And Faxes to the Start menu as follows:

1. Right-click the Start button and select Properties from the shortcut menu. The Taskbar And Start Menu Properties dialog box appears (see Chapter 10, section "Changing Start Menu Properties").

2. Click the Customize button on the Start Menu tab. The Customize Start Menu dialog box appears.

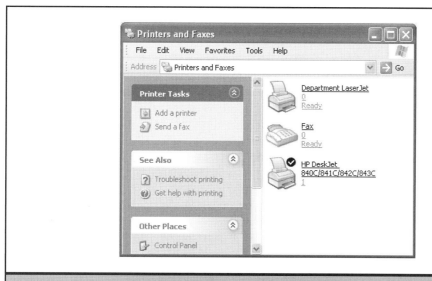

Figure 14-1.   *Windows keeps track of printers and fax devices in the same folder.*

3. Click the Advanced tab of the Customize Start Menu dialog box.

4. Check the Printers And Faxes check box. Then click OK to close each of the dialog boxes you opened.

How Does Windows Handle Printers?

Printers come in three flavors:

- **Local printers** are physically connected to the printer port or USB port of your computer. Typically, a local printer is sitting right next to your computer.

- **Network printers** are exactly what they sound like: printers that may or may not be in the same room with you, but are connected to the same network as your computer (see Chapter 29).

- **Virtual printers** aren't really printers at all, but they show up as printing options in dialog boxes and as icons in your Printers And Faxes folder. When you "print" a document to virtual printer, it doesn't put ink on paper, but it may send a fax or create a file in some compact, widely readable format like PDF. Adobe Acrobat, for example, sets up a virtual printer called PDF Writer.

Each printer installed on your system has an entry in the Printers And Faxes folder. When you print something from an application, a Windows *printer driver* (printer control program) for the current printer formats the material for that particular printer. As far as printer limitations permit, documents look the same no matter what printer they're printed on.

You can have several printers defined on your system. They may be different physical printers or different modes on the same printer. For example, a few printers handle both Hewlett Packard's PCL (Printer Control Language) and the Adobe PostScript language. You can have two printer drivers installed, one for PCL and one for PostScript. If your printer can print on both sides of the paper, you can have two drivers installed, one for single-sided printing and one for double-sided printing. To see the installed printers, open your Printers And Faxes folder.

At any particular moment, one of the printers is marked as the *default printer*. Anything you print goes to the default printer unless you specifically tell your program to use a different printer. You can make any of your printers the default by right-clicking its icon in the Printers And Faxes folder and selecting Set as Default Printer from the shortcut menu.

Windows also provides *spooling*, a service that stores document data until the printer can accept it. When you print a document from an application, the information to be printed (the *print job*) is stored temporarily in the *queue* (storage for print jobs) until it can be printed. If you print a long document to a slow printer, spooling lets you continue working with your application while the printer works in the background. (Many years ago, "spool" stood for Simultaneous Peripheral Operation On-Line, but no one thinks of it as an acronym any more.)

What Are Fonts?

Modern computer screens and printers can display text in a variety of *typefaces* and sizes, as illustrated here:

This is a sample of 12-point Times, a proportionally spaced
This is a sample of 12-point Arial, another proportional
This is a sample of 12-point Courier, a
This is very small 8-point type.

This is rather large 18-point type.

In *fixed-pitch* typefaces, all the characters are the same width, as on a typewriter. In *proportionally spaced* typefaces, different characters are different widths. (The relative widths vary from one typeface to another.) Most typefaces are available in different sizes, with the sizes measured in printer's points, 1/72 inch. The most common sizes are 10-point and 12-point, roughly corresponding to sizes of elite and pica typewriter type. Fonts are often provided in several variations, such as normal, bold, italic, and bold-italic.

Typographers use the terms *font* and *typeface* with a bit more exactness than computer people. To typographers, a *typeface* refers to the underlying design of the characters, while a *font* is the collection of all the characters in a typeface of a given size and variation. For example, Arial is a typeface and Arial italic 12-point is a font. This precision usually gets lost in computer discussions, where *font* and *typeface* are used interchangeably. Windows refers to Arial as a font, and (having noted our objections) we will do the same.

Windows comes with a small but adequate set of fonts, but many programs and printer drivers include fonts of their own. Once a font is installed, any program can use it, no matter where the font came from. Thus, a typical Windows installation may have 50 to 100 fonts available, each in a wide variety of sizes.

In addition to fonts that contain letters and numbers, Windows comes with several fonts of special characters. You can use the Character Map program to look at them and add them to your documents (see "Using Special Characters with Character Map" in Chapter 17).

What Is TrueType?

Computer printers and screens print and display characters by printing or displaying patterns of black-and-white (or colored) dots. The size of the dots depends on the resolution of the device, ranging from 72 to 100 dots per inch (dpi) on screens, to 300, 600, or even 1,200 dpi on laser printers. In early versions of Windows, each typeface was provided as a *bitmap* (dot picture) of the actual black and white dots for each character, with separate bitmaps for each size. The bitmaps were available only in a small variety of sizes, such as Courier 10-, 12-, and 18-point.

This scheme does not produce very good-looking documents, because the dot resolution of printers is rarely the same as that for a screen. In the process of printing, Windows had to rescale each character's bitmap to the printer's resolution, producing odd-looking characters with unattractive jagged corners. Even worse, if you used a font in a size other than one of the sizes provided, the system had to do a second level of rescaling, producing even worselooking characters.

TrueType solves both of these problems by storing each typeface not as a set of bitmaps, but essentially as a set of formulas the system can use to *render* (draw) each character at any desired size and resolution. This means that TrueType fonts look consistent on all devices, and that you can use them in any size.

Use only TrueType fonts in documents that you plan to print, to make your documents look their best.

How Do Printers Handle Fonts?

Older printers had one or two fonts built in, and when you printed a document, those were the fonts you got. Modern printers can print any image that the resolution of the printer permits, so they can print all the fonts that are installed on your system.

Most printers have a reasonable set of built-in, general-purpose fonts, and some printers can accept font cartridges with added fonts. Occasionally, you may want to print a document that contains fonts your printer doesn't know, and then one of the following three things happens:

■ Windows reverts to printing graphics, in effect turning your document into a full-page bitmap image that Windows can send (slowly) to the printer.

■ If your printer is smart enough (most laser printers that use PostScript and PCL5 are), Windows can send the printer all the fonts that a particular document needs. This delays the start of the print job a little, but as soon as the printing starts it proceeds at a normal speed.

■ To speed up printing, Windows uses *font substitution*, using built-in printer fonts where possible for similar TrueType fonts. For example, Microsoft's Arial font is nearly identical to the Helvetica font found in PostScript printers, so when Windows prints Arial text, it tells the printer to use Helvetica instead. This process of font substitution normally works smoothly, although occasionally on clone printers, the built-in fonts aren't exactly what Windows expects and the results can look a little off. (You can tell Windows to turn off font substitution if you suspect that's a problem.)

How Does Windows Handle Faxing?

Most dial-up modems also have the ability to send and receive faxes. You need to have a phone line connected to the modem and a fax client program installed on your computer. The client program allows you to compose, read, and archive faxes in the same way that an e-mail client handles e-mail.

The Windows XP CD-ROM contains a fax client program, Fax Console, but it isn't automatically installed. You may need to install it from the CD-ROM (see "Sending and Receiving Faxes"). Once it is installed, you need to configure it to work with your modem or whatever other fax device you have connected to your computer.

Another way to deal with faxes via your computer is to use an Internet-based fax service, like eFax (**http://www.efax.com**) or jConnect (**http://www.j2.com**). Both services will receive faxes for you and e-mail them to you at no charge, or allow you to send faxes from your computer for a monthly fee.

Setting Up a Local Printer

Setting up a local printer can be as simple as plugging it in, connecting it to your computer, and waiting for Windows to notice it (see Chapter 13, section "Configuring Windows for New Hardware"). Or, you may need to answer a few questions for the Add Printer Wizard and insert the CD-ROM or floppy disk that came with your printer.

After the printer is set up, you may decide to share it over a network (see Chapter 29).

If you have more than one user account on your computer, you'll need to install the printer from an account with administrator privileges (see Chapter 6).

Adding a Plug and Play Printer

Almost all new printers support Plug and Play, which makes them very easy to install. If Windows XP already knows a driver for your printer, the process may be effortless: We installed an HP 842C printer just by plugging one end of a cable into the printer and the other into the appropriate port on our computer. Windows found the printer on its own and installed the appropriate driver in about the time that it took us to crawl out from under the desk. (Windows Help says to turn the printer on before connecting it to the computer, but we didn't even have to do that much.) If your printer connects wirelessly via infrared, turn the printer on and point its infrared port toward your computer's infrared port.

If Windows cannot identify your printer or find a driver for it, the Found New Hardware Wizard should appear. Answer its questions and be prepared to insert the floppy or CD-ROM that came with your printer if the Wizard asks for it.

If Windows does not find your new printer at all, Plug and Play has fallen down on the job (or the printer is too old to support Plug and Play). See the instructions for installing a non-Plug and Play printer in the following section, or consult the printer's manufacturer. (see "Adding a Printer Without Plug and Play").

Adding a Printer Without Plug and Play

To add a non-Plug and Play printer, follow these steps:

1. Make sure the printer is plugged in and turned on.

2. Connect the printer to your computer. The instructions that came with your printer should tell you what cable to use and which computer port to connect it to.

3. If you have the Control Panel set up as a submenu of Start, choose Start | Control Panel | Printers And Faxes | Add Printer and proceed to step 4. Otherwise, you need to open the Printers And Faxes folder. You may be able to do this from the Start menu; if not, open the Control Panel and choose Printers And Faxes from the Printers And Other Hardware category.

4. Select Add a Printer from the Printer Tasks list, or File | Add Printer from the menu. The Add Printer Wizard opens. The first screen of the Wizard is purely informational, so click Next.

5. Answer the questions the Wizard asks. In particular, it will want to know what port you connected the printer to and the printer's manufacturer and model number. If you can't find the printer's make and model on the list the Wizard gives, click the Have Disk button and insert the floppy or CD-ROM that came with your printer.

If you have a disk for your printer, and your printer also appears in the Windows list, you have a choice to make. In general, you want to use the newest driver you can. So use the Windows driver, unless your disk is dated 2001 or later. If your printer isn't listed and you don't have a recent disk, check the printer manufacturer's Web site for up-to-date drivers that you can download and install.

Configuring a Printer

After you install your printer or printers, you configure the driver to match your printer's setup. Some simple printers have little or no setup, while laser printers have a variety of hardware and software options.

To configure a printer, open the Printers And Faxes folder either from the Start menu or from the Printers And Other Hardware category of the Control Panel. Right-click the printer of interest and select Properties from the menu that appears. You see the Properties dialog box for the printer, as shown in Figure 14-2.

The settings for the printer are organized into groups, which you can display by clicking the appropriate tab along the top of the window. Not all printers have the same capabilities, so their Properties dialog boxes are not identical. (A black-and-white

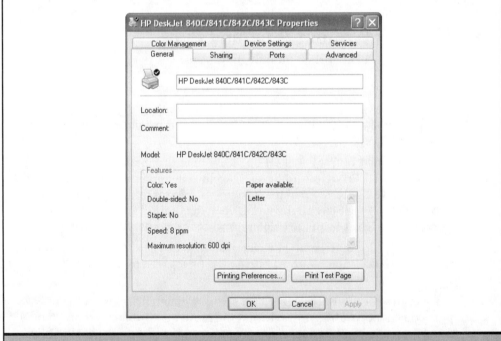

Figure 14-2.   *Configure a printer from its Properties dialog box.*

printer, for example, won't have a Color Management tab.) Commonly used tabs include the following:

- **General**   Comments about the printer and a button to print a test page.
- **Ports**   Select the network connection or printer port, and change spooler settings.
- **Color Management**   For color printers, select how color profiles work (making printed colors match screen colors).
- **Paper**   Change the size of paper the printer is using; handle options such as double-sided, portrait, or landscape print orientation; and the number of copies of each page to print. (Some printers have a Printing Preferences button on the General tab that you use for setting paper size.)
- **Graphics**   Change the dots-per-inch resolution of printed graphics (higher looks better, but prints slower); or use dithering, half-toning, and screening (techniques used to approximate shades of gray on black-and-white printers).
- **Fonts**   Change which font cartridges are in use, control font substitution, control whether TrueType fonts are downloaded to the printer as fonts or graphics (which can be useful to work around flaky print position problems). Newer printers usually don't have a Fonts tab.
- **Device Options or Setup**   Change what optional equipment the printer has, such as extra memory, envelope feeders, and other paper-handling equipment, and change among various print-quality modes on ink-jet printers.
- **PostScript**   On high-end PostScript-compatible printers, select PostScript suboptions, and control whether PostScript header information is sent with each print job (important on printers shared with other computers) or only once per session.
- **Sharing**   If your computer is on a local area network and this printer is physically connected to your computer, change whether other people on the network can share this printer (see Chapter 29).
- **Services**   Some printer drivers include procedures for maintenance, like cleaning print cartridges or aligning print heads.

After you have the properties for your printer set to your liking, you'll find that you seldom need to change the properties. For most printers, you never need to change them.

Tip   *If you find that you frequently switch between two different sets of properties, such as single- and double-sided printing, install the printer twice and configure one installation for single-sided and one for double-sided printing. Windows lets you configure single- versus double-sided printing on a dialog box, but switching "printers" is a lot easier.*

Testing and Troubleshooting Your Printer

After installing a new printer or changing its configuration, it's a good idea to print a test page. To do this, right-click the printer's icon in the Printers And Faxes folder and choose Properties from the shortcut menu. When the printer's Properties dialog box appears, click the Print Test Page button.

After sending the test page to the printer (but before the printer has had enough time to do much with it) Windows asks you how the test page came out. Wait for the page to finish printing, and click OK if it looks good. If the page either does not print or looks wrong, click the Troubleshoot button to launch the Printer Troubleshooter. You can also launch the Printer Troubleshooter without printing a test page as follows:

1. Choose Start | Help And Support to display the Help And Support Center window (see Chapter 4).

2. Click the Fixing A Problem task in the Pick A Help Topic column.

3. Click Printing Problems. The Printing Problems screen appears on the right side of the Help and Support window.

4. Click Fix A Printing Problem.

5. Click Use The Printing Troubleshooter.

The Printing Troubleshooter asks you questions about your printer problem, so that it can identify the problem. Then it makes suggestions to fix the most common printer problems, such as no printing at all, slow or garbled printing, and distorted graphics. Click the radio button that describes your problem and click the Next button to find out what Windows recommends. As with all such systems, the Printing Troubleshooter is hit-or-miss. With luck, your problem is one that the Troubleshooter addresses.

Setting the Default Printer

The default printer is the printer that Windows uses when you give a Print command without specifying a particular printer. In the Printers And Faxes folder, the current default printer is identified with a tiny check mark in the corner of its icon. You can make any printer the default printer by right-clicking the printer's icon in the Printers And Faxes folder and selecting Set As Default from the shortcut menu. Or, select the printer and choose File | Set As Default Printer from the menu bar.

Deleting a Printer

If you want to remove an installed printer, just right-click the printer's icon in the Printers And Faxes folder and choose Delete from the menu that appears. Or, select the printer and press DELETE.

Printing a Document

The simplest way to print a document is to find its icon in an Explorer window (or on the desktop), right-click it, and select Print from the shortcut menu. Windows opens the document in its default application and sends it to the printer using the default settings of that application. You have a short time in which to click a Cancel button while the document is being sent to the printer. (If you miss this opportunity, you can still cancel the job from the Printer Control window.) This technique works for some file types (such as those used by Microsoft Office), but not all (see "Pausing or Canceling Print Jobs").

If Print does not appear on the file's shortcut menu, or if you want to make some choices about how the document is printed, open the document and issue the print command from within the document's application. (Typically File | Print works, or you may find a Print icon on a toolbar.) Depending on the application, you may be able to see a preview of the printed document before giving the Print command. You can do this in Word or Internet Explorer, for example, by selecting File | Print Preview.

Choosing Printing Options

After you give the File | Print command, the Print dialog box appears. The options this dialog box presents depend on the application and on the properties of your printer, so your Print dialog box may not look exactly like the one in Figure 14-3. Some of the choices you may be offered include

- **Printer name**   The default printer is listed, but a drop-down list allows you to choose any of the printers whose icons are in the Printers and Faxes folder.

- **Pages range**   You can print the entire document, specific pages, or a range of pages.

- **Copies**   The dialog box in Figure 14-3 contains a Collate check box. If the box is checked, copies of the entire document are printed one by one. Otherwise, all the copies of a single page are printed before moving to the next page.

- **Print quality**   Low-quality printing is faster and uses less ink or toner.

- **Black-and-white or color**

- **Orientation**   Portrait orientation is taller than it is wide, while landscape orientation is wider than it is tall.

- **Paper tray**   If your printer has more than one paper tray, you can choose which to use.

- **Order of pages**   The default is to print page one first, but you may print in reverse order so that the document comes out properly ordered in the printer tray. You may also be able to choose to print only even or odd pages, which is handy if you are doing two-sided printing.

When you have made your choices, click OK to send the document to the printer.

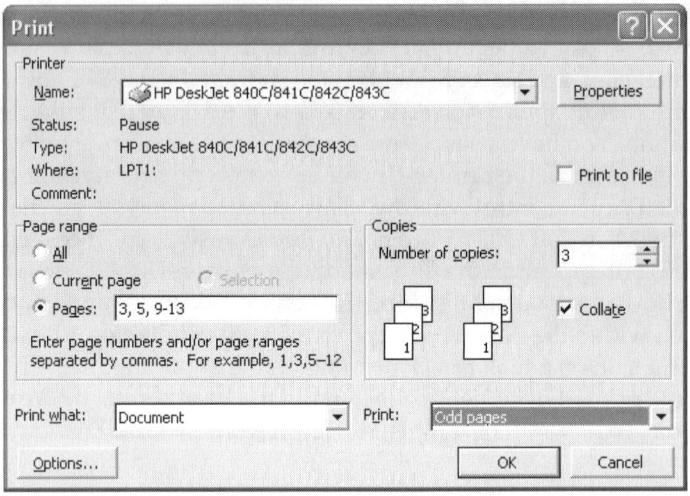

Figure 14-3. *The Print dialog box*

Printing to a File

When Windows prints a document, it first converts it into a form that the printer can understand. You can decide to capture this printer-ready form of the document in a file (and not send it to a physical printer) so that you can print it later or transport it via e-mail or a floppy disk to a printer not connected to your computer. This is called *printing to a file.* You can do this in three ways:

- From the Print dialog box
- By changing the properties of an existing printer
- By creating a new printer icon

If you are printing only a single document to a file, and will want to print subsequent documents directly to paper, issue the Print command from within the document's application, and look for a Print To File check box in the Print dialog box. (Figure 14-2 has one, but yours may be in a different place or may be absent entirely. If you can't find it, you can still print to a file by changing the printer properties.) Make whatever other choices you want in the Print dialog box, and then click OK. A Print To File dialog box appears to let you choose what to call the file and where to save it. Click OK to begin producing the file.

If you are temporarily disconnected from your printer and want to print a series of documents to files, you may find it more convenient to change the printer properties so that documents sent to that printer go to a file automatically. To do this, find your printer's icon in the Printers and Faxes folder, right-click it and select Properties. When the Properties dialog box appears, look for the tab on which the printer port is set. (In Figure 14-2 you would choose the Ports tab, but your printer's Properties dialog box may be different.) Choose File from the list of possible ports. Make a note of the port that the printer was connected to before you changed, so that you can change back.

If you frequently print to a file, create a new printer icon and choose File as its port. Follow the instructions for installing a non–Plug and Play printer (see "Adding a Printer Without Plug and Play").

Managing Printer Activity

Most print jobs don't require any management on your part: You tell your computer to print a document, it sends the job to a printer, and you pick up the printed pages after they are done. Occasionally, however, you want to communicate with a printer while it is in the act of printing. For example, you may realize that you have told the printer to print a full hundred-page document when you only intended to print one page of it. Or you may have queued several print jobs and realize that you want them printed in a different order, or that you want to cancel a job and send it to a different printer.

You deal with these situations from the printer's Print Control window, shown in Figure 14-4. Open this window by opening the printer's icon in the Printers And Faxes folder. (Or, if you are displaying the Control Panel as a menu, you can open the printer by selecting Start | Control Panel | Printers and Faxes | *printer name*.) The printer control window shows you what job is currently printing, how that job is progressing, and which jobs are waiting to be printed.

Pausing or Canceling Print Jobs

To suspend the current print job until you can figure out what you want to do with it, choose Printer | Pause Printing from the menu of the Print Control window

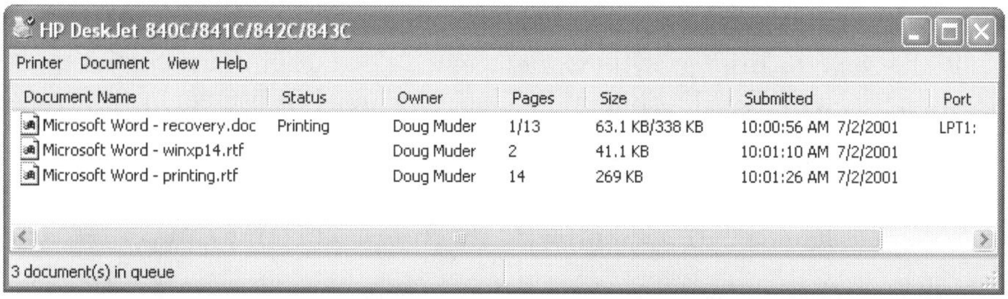
HP DeskJet 840C/841C/842C/843C
Printer Document View Help
Document Name Status Owner Pages Size Submitted Port
Microsoft Word - recovery.doc Printing Doug Muder 1/13 63.1 KB/338 KB 10:00:56 AM 7/2/2001 LPT1:
Microsoft Word - winxp14.rtf Doug Muder 2 41.1 KB 10:01:10 AM 7/2/2001
Microsoft Word - printing.rtf Doug Muder 14 269 KB 10:01:26 AM 7/2/2001
3 document(s) in queue

Figure 14-4. *The Print Control window*

(or right-click the document in the Print Control window and choose Pause Printing from the shortcut menu). To resume the job where you left off, select Printer | Pause Printing again (or right-click anywhere in the Print Control window and choose Pause Printing). To delete a particular print job, right-click the job in the Print Control window and choose Cancel from the shortcut menu that appears. To get rid of everything waiting for that printer, choose Printer | Cancel All Documents.

Changing the Order in Which Jobs Are Printed

By default, print jobs are executed in a first-in, first-out manner. However, print jobs also have priority settings and the highest priority jobs move to the front of the queue. If you are printing a number of jobs and want to move one of them in front of the others, change its priority as follows:

1. Open the printer's icon in the Printers And Faxes folder. The Print Control window appears, as shown in Figure 14-4. The jobs waiting to be printed are listed.

2. Right-click the print job whose priority you want to change and select Properties from the shortcut menu.

3. The default priority is 1, which is the setting for the least important jobs. (This takes some getting used to, as we usually think of "first priority" being the most important.) Move the priority slider to the right to raise the job's priority.

4. Click OK.

Scheduling a Print Job

If you have a very large print job that is going to take a long time, you can schedule it to print in the middle of the night or some other time when the printer is unlikely to be needed by anyone. To do this, submit your job to the printer as usual, but then do the following:

1. Open the printer's icon in the Printers And Faxes folder. The Print Control window appears, as shown in Figure 14-4.

2. Right-click the print job you want to schedule and select Properties from the shortcut menu. The Document Properties dialog box appears.

3. Click the Only From *xx* To *xx* radio button.

4. Select times from the drop-down lists so that the radio button corresponds to a complete sentence—for example: Only From 2 a.m. To 5 a.m.

5. Click OK.

If you have scheduled a large print job for a time when the printer is unattended, make sure that it has plenty of paper and a fresh cartridge of ink or toner.

Installing and Using Fonts

Windows provides a straightforward way to install and use fonts. To see which fonts you have installed, open the folder C:\Windows\Fonts in Windows Explorer (assuming that Windows is installed on drive C).

TrueType fonts have a TT icon, Open Type fonts have an O icon, and older fonts have an A icon. You can open any font to see a description and samples of the font in a variety of sizes. If you have a lot of fonts installed, choose View | Hide Variations to omit the icons for fonts that are bold or italic versions of other fonts.

 Windows can handle up to 1,000 fonts, but to avoid slowing down your applications, don't install more than 200.

Installing Fonts

To install new fonts from a floppy disk or network, follow these steps:

1. View the C:\Windows\Fonts folder in Windows Explorer (or the Fonts folder of whatever folder Windows is installed in).

2. Choose File | Install New Font. The Add Fonts dialog box, shown here, appears:

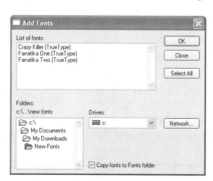

3. In the Drives and Folders boxes, select the drive and folder in which the files are located for the new font or fonts. Click the Network button if the font files are on a network drive that is not mapped to a drive letter on your computer. Windows displays the fonts it finds.

4. In the List Of Fonts box, select the font(s) you want to install.

5. Normally, Windows copies the font files into its font folder (C:\Windows\Fonts). If you are installing fonts from a networked folder, you can uncheck Copy Fonts To Fonts Folder to use the fonts where they are located, which saves space in exchange for some loss in speed.

6. Click OK, and Windows installs the fonts you want.

You can also drag font files from the install disk or folder to the C:\Windows\Fonts folder.

Deleting Fonts

To delete a font or fonts, display the C:\Windows\Fonts folder in Windows Explorer. Then select the fonts you want to get rid of and choose File | Delete. However, don't delete a font unless you are sure that none of the programs on your system use it. To be safe, move the fonts to a temporary folder for a few days to see if any programs display error messages when they try to use them. If no errors appear, then delete the fonts.

Finding Similar Fonts

Windows offers an occasionally useful "font similarity" feature that lets you look for fonts that are similar to a particular font. When viewing the Fonts folder, choose View | List Fonts By Similarity and choose the target font at the top of the Fonts window. The font similarity feature depends on special information in the font files, so older fonts without this information aren't ranked for similarity.

Sending and Receiving Faxes

Windows XP contains a Fax Console accessory for sending and receiving faxes. Fax Console is not part of the default installation of Windows XP, so you may need to add it from the Windows XP CD-ROM (see Chapter 3). Choose Start | Control Panel, click Add Or Remove Programs, click Add/Remove Windows Components, and choose Fax Services from the list of components. If Fax Console is installed, run it by selecting Start | All Programs | Accessories | Communications | Fax | Fax Console.

In order to use Fax Console, you need to have hardware capable of sending and receiving faxes. Most dial-up modems have this capability, so you may already have a fax device without realizing it. Fax Console automatically detects such hardware during installation and configures itself to send faxes via these devices. Fax Console does not automatically configure the devices to receive faxes.

Configuring Fax Console

The first time you run Fax Console, the Fax Configuration Wizard starts. It asks you to fill out the information (name, address, phone number, and so on) that you want to appear on the cover sheet of any faxes you send. If the Wizard detects that Fax Console has upgraded Personal Fax for Windows, it offers you the option of importing your fax archives.

After the Fax Configuration Wizard has run, the Fax Console window appears, as shown here:

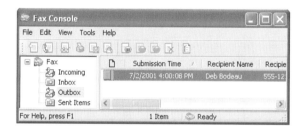

The Fax Console Window resembles Outlook Express, which is not surprising, because both programs are designed to send, receive, and keep track of messages. The Fax Console contains four folders by default: Incoming, which contains faxes that are arriving; Inbox for received faxes; Outbox for faxes that you have scheduled to be sent, but have not yet been transmitted successfully; and Sent Items for sent faxes.

Windows treats a fax device as a kind of printer and creates an icon for it in the Printers And Faxes folder. Opening this icon opens Fax Console. Right-clicking this icon and selecting Properties is equivalent to choosing Tools | Fax Printer Configuration from the Fax Console menu bar. Either action produces the Fax Properties dialog box. From here you can do the following:

- **Adjust the size and quality of the fax images you send.**   From the General tab, click Printing Preferences and make your choices from the Fax Printing Preferences dialog box.

- **Share your fax printer over a network.**   This option is not supported for all fax devices, and Windows XP Home Edition doesn't support it. Make your choices from the Sharing tab of the Fax Properties dialog box.

- **Set the properties of your fax devices.**   Use the Devices tab. This is where you configure a device to receive faxes (see "Receiving Faxes"). The options available here depend on the particular device.

- **Set the discount rate times.** One option for sending faxes is for the fax to be held until the phone rates go down. Specify the discount rate times by clicking the Properties button on the devices tab. The Properties box for your fax device appears; set the discount times there.

- **Choose where sent and received faxes are filed.** Use the Archives tab.

- **Decide how you will be notified about faxes that are sent or received.** Use the Track tab. An icon can appear in the Notification Area or the Fax Monitor window can open, as shown here:

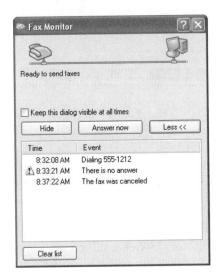

Sending a Fax

You can send a fax from within Fax Console or from within an application by selecting File | Print and choosing a fax printer from the drop-down printer list in the Print dialog box (see Figure 14-3).

Sending a Cover-Page Fax from Fax Console

You can send a cover-page fax (consisting of a cover page with a subject line and a text note) from within Fax Console by selecting File | Send a Fax from the menu. The Send Fax Wizard opens to collect the recipient information, the subject line, and the text of your note. To send a longer fax, create the document you want to send with another application and send it from that application (see "Sending a Fax from an Application").

The final page of the Send Fax Wizard is the Schedule page. Here you can choose to send the fax immediately, when discount rates apply, or during a specific time window (within the next 24 hours) that you set.

Sending a Fax from an Application

If you have a document open in an application (like Microsoft Word or Adobe Photoshop, for example) you can fax that document to someone by selecting File | Print and choosing a fax printer from the drop-down printer list in the Print dialog box (see Figure 14-3). The Send Fax Wizard appears and collects the information necessary to send the fax, such as the fax number of the recipient and the information you want to appear on the cover page of the fax. You can schedule the fax just as you would if had started the Send Fax Wizard from within Fax Console (see "Sending a Cover-Page Fax from Fax Console").

Receiving Faxes

Fax Console does not automatically configure devices to receive faxes. In order to receive a fax using a particular device, do the following:

1. Open Fax Console.

2. Select Tools | Fax Printer Configuration from the menu. The Fax Properties dialog box appears.

3. Click the Devices tab.

4. Select from the list on the Devices tab the device you want to use to receive faxes. The list tells you whether the device is already set up to receive. (If it says Yes, there is no need to continue.)

5. Click the Properties button on the Devices tab of the Fax Properties dialog box. The Properties dialog box for the device appears.

6. Click the Receive tab of the device's Properties dialog box.

7. Check the Enable Device To Receive check box.

8. Enter your called subscriber identification number into the CSID box.

9. You can make additional choices from this dialog box: You set whether the fax line should be answered automatically or manually, and whether faxes should automatically be printed or stored somewhere in addition to the Inbox folder of Fax Console.

10. Click OK in all open dialog boxes.

If you configured your fax device to receive faxes automatically, you need do nothing to receive an incoming fax. If you configured the fax device for manual receiving, select File | Receive Fax Now when a fax call is coming in.

Archiving Your Faxes

The faxes you send accumulate in the Sent Items folder and the faxes you receive accumulate in the Inbox. If you have a local fax device, the faxes stay in these folders until you delete them. For network fax devices, they may disappear after a period of time specified by the network administrator.

You cannot create additional folders for your faxes inside Fax Console, so if you want to organize your stored faxes you will have to translate them into some other format. To do this, select the Inbox (for received faxes) or Sent Items (for sent faxes) folder in the Fax Console window, then choose a message from the message list and right-click it. The shortcut menu gives you several choices. You can

- **Save the fax as a file.** Select Save As from the shortcut menu, then choose a file name and a folder in which to save your fax from the Browse window that appears.

- **Print it.**

- **Delete it.**

- **View it.** Selecting View from the shortcut menu opens the fax in a new window.

- **E-mail it.** Select Mail To from the shortcut menu. The fax appears in a message window of the default e-mail program. You can address it and send it as you would any e-mail message.

Note *Windows stores your faxes as images, with the extension .tif. You use Windows Explorer to copy these files from the Fax Console's folders into other folders. The Fax Console keeps its files in the C:\Documents And Settings\All Users\Application Data\Microsoft\Windows NT\MSFax\Inbox (if Windows is installed on C). The fax file names are cryptic: to determine which fax is which, double-click to view the fax.*

The
Complete
Reference

Windows XP

Chapter 15

Running Windows XP on Laptops

Many people use laptops—it's convenient to be able to pick up your computer, with all its data and software, and take it anywhere. But laptops have disadvantages, too, and Windows XP addresses many of them. This chapter is full of suggestions about how to make the most of your laptop, including these:

■ You can coordinate files with those on a network by using offline files and the Synchronization Manager.

■ You can coordinate files with those on a desktop computer by using the Windows Briefcase.

■ You can print a document, even when you aren't attached to a printer, by deferring printing until a printer is available.

■ You can use Remote Desktop to access your computer remotely through a LAN or the Internet.

■ You can use power management to make your battery last longer.

■ If you use a docking station to connect your laptop to desktop devices, you should know about docking and undocking and hardware profiles.

The topic is not covered in this chapter, but you may want to explore connecting to a network or another computer to use its resources when you don't have a network card by using direct network connection (with a cable between the computers) or a dial-up connection—see Chapter 27.

Coordinating Your Laptop Files

If you use files from more than one computer on a regular basis, you have two options for keeping track of files that you use on your laptop, but which are normally stored on another computer: the offline files options used together with the Synchronization Manager and Windows Briefcase. Use offline files if you usually access files from a network. If you frequently transfer files using direct cable connection or a floppy disk, Briefcase may be a better option, but few people use it. Unlike offline files, Briefcase allows you to crate multiple Briefcases to organize files.

Offline Files Options and the Synchronization Manager

Offline files allow you to use network files or files stored on another computer when you are not connected to the network or the other computer. To use files while you are *offline* (not connected), you need to store them on your own computer. By storing them on your computer using offline files, you can *synchronize* the files on your computer with the files on the network when you are online again—copy all the changed and new files from one computer to the other. If someone else changed the same file that you changed, you can choose whether to save your version or the other person's version on the network (there's no facility for merging the changes from two different versions of a file).

Note *Offline files don't work if you have Fast User Switching or the Welcome screen enabled. To turn these off, open the Control Panel, choose User Accounts, click Change The Way Users Log On Or Off, deselect Fast User Switching and Use The Welcome Screen, and click Apply Options.*

In order to use offline files, you have to enable offline files on your laptop in the following way:

1. Display an Explorer window by choosing Start | My Computer.
2. Choose Tools | Folder Options to display the Folder Options dialog box.
3. Click the Offline Files tab to display the options shown in Figure 15-1. (You must have a local drive in your Explorer window—if you are looking at a network drive you will not see the Offline Files tab.)
4. Click the Enable Offline Files option so that a check mark appears.
5. Select Create An Offline Files Shortcut On The Desktop (recommended).
6. Change any other options as needed (see the following descriptions).
7. Click OK.

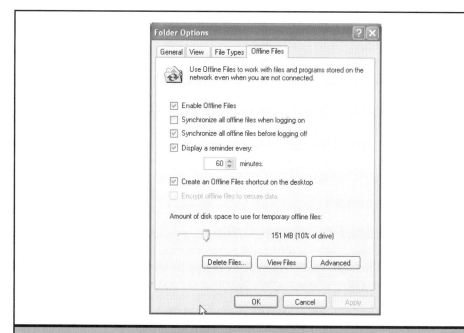

Figure 15-1. *Use the Offline Files tab of the Folder Options dialog box to configure offline files options.*

The other options in the Folder Options dialog box work in the following way:

- **Synchronize All Offline Files When Logging On**   Windows checks that the versions of offline files on your computer match those on the network as you log on.

- **Synchronize All Offline Files Before Logging Off**   Windows checks that the versions of offline files on your computer match those on the network as you log off.

- **Display A Reminder Every *xx* Minutes**   Displays a reminder that you are offline as often as specified.

- **Create An Offline Files Shortcut On The Desktop**   Displays an Offline Files shortcut on the desktop, which you can click to see your folder of offline files.

- **Encrypt Offline Files To Secure Data**   Windows encrypts the copies of network files stored on your computer. This option is not available if Windows is installed on a non-NTFS partition (see Chapter 32, section "What Is a File System?").

- **Amount Of Disk Space To Use For Temporary Offline Files**   Specifies the amount of disk space on you computer that will be used for offline files that you did not specifically request. (Your network administrator may require certain files to be included with your offline files.) This setting usually starts as 10 percent of the disk space on your Windows drive.

- **Delete Files Button**   Deletes all offline files from your computer (not from the network, though).

- **View Files Button**   Displays a list of all files available offline.

Click the Advanced button to see the When A Network Connection Is Lost option, which enables you to choose whether your computer will immediately go into offline mode when the connection is lost, or whether the computer is prevented from going into offline mode. You can use the Add button to add computers to the Exception List, which tells Windows what to do when specific computers on the network are not available.

Make a File or Folder Available Offline

Once you've configured your computer to use network files offline, you're ready to specify the files and folders that you want to have access to when you aren't connected to the network. To make a file or folder available offline, follow these steps:

1. Select the file or folder on the network that you want to make available offline in an Explorer window. (To select an entire folder and its contents, display the folder's parent directory so you can select the folder with one click.)

The shared drive must have a drive letter assigned to it (see Chapter 29, section "Mapping a Shared Drive or Folder to a Drive Letter").

2. Choose File | Make Available Offline to run the Offline Files Wizard. Or, right-click the file or folder and choose Make Available Offline from the menu that appears. The first page of the Wizard offers an explanation of offline files.

3. Click Next. The Wizard asks you if you want to automatically synchronize the offline files each time you log on or log off. Make your selection and click Next.

4. The Wizard has two options: Enable Reminders, which displays a reminder in the notification area of the taskbar when you are working offline; and Create A Shortcut To The Offline Files Folder On My Desktop, which does just that. We recommend creating an icon if you don't have one already. Choose your options and click Finish.

5. If you have selected a folder with subfolders, you see a dialog box asking if you want the subfolders available too, or just the folder that you selected. Chose the setting you want and click OK.

You see the Synchronizing dialog box while Windows moves the files or folders you selected to the Offline Folder on your PC.

Using Offline Files

The easiest way to access your offline files is to open the Offline Files shortcut on the desktop. If you did not create the icon, choose Tools | Folder Options in an Explorer window, click the Offline Files tab, and click View Files. The Offline Files Folder appears, as shown in Figure 15-2.

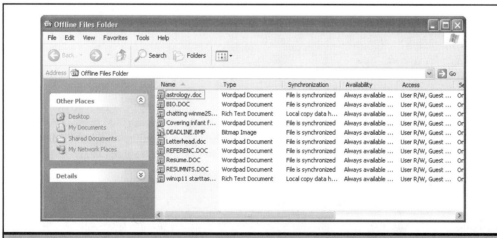

Figure 15-2.   *The Offline Files folder shows you your offline files and their synchronization status.*

You can open an offline folder from the Offline Files Explorer window. Be sure when you save it to save it back to the same location.

Synchronizing Files

If you did not choose to let Windows synchronize offline files when you log off or on, you need to use the Synchronization Manager to synchronize files. To open the Synchronization Manager, choose Tools | Synchronize from an Explorer window. Select the items you want to synchronize by using the check boxes and click Synchronize.

Making Web Pages Available Offline

You can also make Web pages available offline. Be warned, though, that sometimes having a Web page available offline can lead to frustration—the links will not work unless you have saved all the linked pages offline as well! However, having a static Web page with information that you often refer to available offline may be useful to you. To make a Web page available offline choose Favorites | Add to Favorites in Internet Explorer, then click the Make Available Offline check box and click OK (see Chapter 24, section "Using Favorites, Links, and Internet Shortcuts").

Coordinating Files with Windows Briefcase

The other way to coordinate files saved on more than one computer is to use the Windows Briefcase, a program that coordinates files you work on, so that you always use the most current version of the files. Windows Briefcase is useful if you use a laptop when you're on the road, and a desktop machine in the office, but Briefcase is useful for anyone who uses files from several computers.

The Windows Briefcase program creates and maintains *Briefcases*, which are folders containing files and subfolders that you can move between your laptop and another computer.

The easiest way to use Briefcase to coordinate files on different computers is to have the two computers connected by a network or another connection. However, you can also use Briefcase with a floppy disk or Zip disk, although that limits the total size of the files you can move from computer to computer.

You may see a Briefcase icon on the desktop. If it doesn't appear on the desktop, right-click the desktop and choose New | Briefcase from the shortcut menu (you can use this option to create multiple briefcases). The first time you open the My Briefcase window, you also see the Welcome To The Windows Briefcase window, with tips for using the program. Click Finish when you have read the tips.

Using Briefcase to Synchronize Files

The most common use of Briefcase is for transferring files from a desktop to a laptop for use while away from the office, and then transferring the updated files back to the desktop when you return. Using Briefcase to transfer files has four steps:

1. Move files to the Briefcase. Choose only the files you will use and update while you're away from your desktop computer.

2. Copy the Briefcase to the laptop.

3. Use files from the Briefcase while you are on the road using the laptop.

4. When you are ready to work at your desktop again, tell Briefcase to synchronize the files on the two computers, so both computers contain the latest version of each file in the Briefcase.

Note *Briefcase uses the system time and date to synchronize files—make sure the time and date on each computer is correct.*

These steps are somewhat different, depending on whether a local area network (LAN) connects the laptop and desktop computers. Without a LAN connection, you have to use a floppy disk (or disks) to move the Briefcase to the laptop. With a LAN, you can sit at the laptop and drag files from the desktop to the laptop's Briefcase.

Moving Files to the Briefcase

The first step is to find the files you want to have on the road and drag them to your Briefcase. The easiest way to do this is to select files in Windows Explorer and drag them to the Briefcase icon or window. You can do this in several steps as you select files in different folders on your hard disk. You can also right-click a file and choose Send To | My Briefcase from the shortcut menu.

You move files differently if the laptop and desktop computers are connected by a LAN—sit at the laptop and drag files from a drive located on the desktop computer to the laptop's Briefcase.

If you don't have a LAN, you need to complete two extra steps:

1. Sit at the desktop and drag the files you need to the Briefcase icon on the desktop, or the Briefcase window if it's open.

2. Drag the Briefcase to a floppy drive or right-click the Briefcase and choose Send To | Floppy (choosing the drive where you want to move the Briefcase).

Caution *Make sure to drag actual files to the Briefcase, not shortcuts to files.*

Copying the Briefcase to the Laptop

If your desktop and laptop computers are connected by a LAN, the Briefcase with the files you need is still on the desktop computer, where it will do you no good when you leave the office. If you have a LAN, skip this section, because the Briefcase with the files you need is already on the laptop. Also skip this section if you want to use the Briefcase files from the floppy disk. However, using a floppy instead of the hard disk will slow you down noticeably if you are using large files.

To copy the Briefcase with its files to the laptop's hard drive, follow these steps:

1. Take the disk to which you copied the Briefcase, insert it in the floppy drive of the laptop, and view the contents of the drive. You see the Briefcase icon.

2. Drag the Briefcase from the floppy drive to the laptop's desktop.

 If the laptop already has an icon on the Desktop called My Briefcase, and that is the name of the Briefcase you are copying, rename the old My Briefcase, so the two don't have the same name.

Using Files in a Briefcase

While you're on the road (or not using your desktop computer), make sure to use the files from the Briefcase. To do so, simply open the Briefcase window (as shown in Figure 15-3) and double-click a file you want to use, just as you would a file in any other folder. You can use Explorer window commands to control how files in the Briefcase window appear (see Chapter 8, section "Changing Views").

If you use an application's File | Open command, display the files in the Briefcase by clicking the Up One Level button in the Open dialog box until you can't go up any more levels—the Briefcase is on your computer's desktop. Open the Briefcase to see the files it contains.

When you save a file from the Briefcase, use the Save button to make sure you save it back to the Briefcase. If you don't save the file back to the Briefcase, the Briefcase won't be able to synchronize files for you.

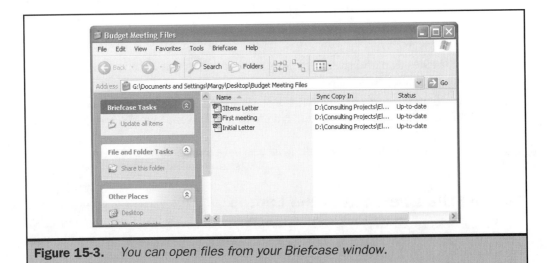

Figure 15-3. *You can open files from your Briefcase window.*

| **Note** | *You should edit a file on only one computer before you synchronize the files with Briefcase. If you edit a particular file while you're on the road and someone at the office edits the same file, you won't be able to keep all the changes unless the program the file uses can show you what they are. Briefcase gives you the option to keep only one of the two files. However, if someone at the office edits a file you took with you in your Briefcase but you didn't edit it, you can keep the most current version of the file.* |

Here are other things you can do in the Briefcase window:

- You can see the update status of each file in the Status column in the Briefcase. You can also check the status of a file in the Briefcase by selecting it in the Briefcase window and choosing File | Properties from the menu bar, or right-clicking the file and choosing Properties from the menu that appears. When you see the Properties dialog box for the file, click the Update Status tab.

- If you drag a file from another location into the Briefcase, you can find the original copy of this file. In the Properties dialog box for the file on the Update Status tab, click the Find Original button. Windows displays the folder containing the original file in an Explorer window.

- You can sever the connection between the original file and the copy of the file in the Briefcase—for example, if the copy in the Briefcase has changed sufficiently that you also want to keep the original copy. Select the file in the Briefcase window and choose Briefcase | Split From Original from the menu bar. You can also right-click the filename, choose Properties from the menu that appears, click the Update Status tab, and then click the Split From Original button.

Synchronizing the Edited Files in a Briefcase

When you return to your desktop PC, you need to synchronize the files on your laptop and your desktop. Follow these steps to synchronize the files:

1. Reestablish the connection between the two computers. If you have a docking station that supports hot docking (installing or removing the computer in the docking station without turning the computer off), the Briefcase may open automatically (see "Using a Docking Station"). If you don't have a LAN, move Briefcase from the laptop's desktop back to the floppy disk, take the floppy disk to the original computer, and then move the Briefcase back to the original computer's desktop.

2. Open the Briefcase window. You see the status of each file in the Status column. (Choose View | Details if this column doesn't appear.) A file's status can be one of the following three:

    - **Orphan**   The file exists only in the Briefcase and not on the source computer (in this example, the desktop computer is the source computer).

- ■ **Up-To-Date**   The file has not changed on either computer.
- ■ **Needs Updating**   The file has changed on either the desktop or the laptop (or both).

3. Click the Update All button on the Briefcase toolbar. The Update My Briefcase dialog box appears, showing how each file needs to be updated, as shown in Figure 15-3. A file can be updated in one of the following ways:

- ■ **Replace, with an arrow pointing to the right**   This is the most common action. It means the file in the Briefcase will replace the file of the same name on the desktop computer.
- ■ **Replace, with an arrow pointing to the left**   This means the file on the desktop computer is the most recent—it will replace the file of the same name in the Briefcase.
- ■ **Skip (both changed)**   This means both files (the one on the desktop and the one on the laptop) have been changed and Briefcase can't determine which file should be used. You need to determine which version of the file you want to use.

4. If you don't want a file updated as shown, right-click the file and choose a method from the shortcut menu that appears.

5. Click the Update button to update the files.

Deferring Printing from a Laptop

One frequent problem with traveling with a computer is you rarely have access to a printer. Even portable printers add more weight and cost to your electronic carryall than most people are willing to bear. So, instead, you survive without a printer.

You can print in several ways when you're away from home: you can connect to someone else's computer (using a network card, direct cable connection, or a dial-up connection) and print on its printer; you can sit at a computer with a printer and connect to your laptop with Remote Desktop and print; you can fax your document to the nearest fax machine (assuming you have fax software and a fax modem); or, you can go ahead and give the command to print the document, taking advantage of the Windows deferred printing feature. See Chapter 14 for more information about printing from Windows.

Printing in Offline Mode

When a printer is set up but not currently attached to your computer, you can still give the command to print a document. You see a message telling you the printer isn't available and telling you the printer will be put into *offline mode*, which means files intended for the printer will, instead, be stored on your disk. When you next connect to the printer, you see a message that print jobs are waiting—you can then print or cancel the documents.

 If you have problems printing while offline, try this: display your Printers folder, right-click the printer, and choose Use Printer Offline.

If you don't see the message asking whether you want to print, when you are reconnected to a printer, follow these steps:

1. Open the Printers folder by choosing Start | Control Panel | Printers And Other Hardware | Printers And Faxes.

2. Right-click the offline printer (grayed-out printers are offline). You see a check mark next to the Use Printer Offline option on the menu.

3. Choose Use Printer Offline to remove the check mark from the menu option and put the printer online. The print jobs waiting in the print queue start to print.

Printing on a Different Printer

If you want to print your queued documents using a printer other than the one you usually use, you can temporarily change the printer. If the printer's drivers were included on the Windows XP CD-ROM, Windows can probably find it because Windows copies most of its files to your hard disk. If your printer's drivers aren't included with Windows (if you installed them from a CD or floppy disk that came with the printer), you might need to insert that CD or floppy when changing printer descriptions.

 If you use a wide variety of printers, you might want to install the Generic printer driver on your laptop to give you a basic printing option, no matter what kind of printer you're using.

Follow these steps to change the description of a printer temporarily:

1. Open the Printers folder by choosing Start | Printers and Faxes, or by choosing Start | Control Panel | Printers and Other Hardware | Printers and Faxes.

2. Open the printer you printed to (the printer appears grayed-out to indicate it is offline). You see the Printer window with all your print jobs listed.

3. Right-click the printer window and choose Properties from the menu that appears. You see the Properties dialog box for the printer.

4. If necessary, change the port on the Ports tab.

5. On the Advanced tab, choose the Driver you need. If the printer you have available isn't listed (because you haven't used it before), click the New Driver button to choose the kind of printer you do have.

6. Close all the dialog boxes. You may be asked for your Windows XP CD-ROM.

7. If you change the driver for the printer, you need to repeat the preceding steps to change it back when you return to the office and connect to your regular printer.

Windows uses a single driver for a variety of similar printers. If you already have a printer defined that's similar to the one you want to use, you'll probably find you can define the new printer and Windows won't need any extra files.

Accessing Other Computers with Remote Desktop

Remote Desktop allows you to have access to the desktop of one computer while you are running another. Not only can you see and use all the files on the remote computer, you can actually see the desktop and run programs as if you were sitting in front of the remote computer. If the remote computer is running Windows .NET, 2000, or NT Server, more than one person can use the remote computer at the same time.

Note
*You can also access a computer remotely using NetMeeting. If you're familiar with NetMeeting, and your needs are not sophisticated, it might be a simpler solution. Other remote-access programs have been available for years, including pcAnywhere (at **http://www.symantec.com/pcanywhere**) and the freeware VNC (Virtual Network Computing, at **http://www.uk.research.att.com/vnc**).*

Remote Desktop uses a LAN, a VPN (virtual private network), or the Internet to access the remote computer—the speed of response will depend on the speed of your connection.

The *server* is the computer that you will be taking control of from a remote location. Usually, the server computer in the Remote Desktop application is the computer on your desk—the one that you will not be taking with you. You can also use Remote Desktop to connect to a Remote Access Server (RA Server) on a Windows .NET, 2000, or NT machine. The *client* computer is the one that you will use while you are away to see the desktop of the server computer.

Remote Desktop comes in two flavors—regular Remote Desktop and Remote Desktop Web Connection. The first requires that you install software on the client computer (the computer that you use to access the computer back on your desk). The second needs only Internet Explorer, but it requires more setup on the server computer (the computer that you access from another location).

Note
A computer running Windows XP Home Edition can't act as a Remote Desktop server. That is, you can't remotely access a computer running Windows XP Home Edition. However, you can use a computer running Home Edition as the Remote Desktop client.

Before you leave the computer you want to access remotely (the server), get Remote Desktop configured and working—you should also test it before you leave. For example, if you want to be able to use your office desktop computer remotely while you are traveling, be sure to configure it for Remote Desktop before you leave on your trip. This step is necessary whether you use either regular Remote Desktop or Remote Desktop Web connection.

Configuring the Server for Remote Desktop

To gain access using Remote Desktop, you specify one or more user accounts on the server computer to which you want remote access. The user accounts must have passwords, so as not to leave your system open to hackers. If you normally do not use a login password, create a password for your user account or create a new user account with a password solely for the purpose of using Remote Desktop (see Chapter 6, section "Creating, Modifying, and Deleting User Accounts"). When you configure the Remote Desktop server (as described in the next section), you type the user account name when Windows asks for the Object Name in the Select Users dialog box. If you are using Remote Desktop over a domain-based LAN, you can connect using a user account on any computer on the LAN.

Note *Microsoft discourages you from using an administrative user account in situations where there is a security risk. They recommend that you use a non-administrative user account when logging in remotely. Make a new user account and add it to the Remote Desktop Users group (see Chapter 6).*

Configuring the Server for Remote Desktop

If you plan on using Remote Desktop, follow these steps to configure the server computer for access by you or others:

1. Display the System Properties dialog box by choosing Start | Control Panel | Performance And Maintenance | System.

2. Click the Remote tab.

3. Select the Allow Users To Connect Remotely To This Computer check box in the Remote Desktop section of the dialog box. If you see a warning box about user accounts without passwords, click OK.

4. Click the Select Remote Users button to display the Remote Desktop users dialog box. Users with administrative accounts are automatically given access, and you can add other users.

5. Click Add to display the Select Users dialog box shown in Figure 15-4. User accounts have three identifiers: Object Type, Location, and Name.

6. To specify a user account from the computer you are sitting at, leave the Select This Object Type box set to Users, and type an account name in the Enter The Object Names To Select box. To specify a user account from another computer

on a domain-based LAN, click the Locations button and choose the domain before you specify the user account name.

> **Note**   *An object type is nothing mysterious—it specifies the type of resource, user account, or group account for which you want to establish remote access. To give a user account remote access, leave the Object Type box set to Users. Other types are Computers, Printers, and groups of users, computers, and printers. The entry in the From This Location box is also simple, though the name is rather misleading. The location does not describe the physical place that another computer inhabits, but is the name of that computer. To allow a user from another computer access to your computer, you type the other computer's name. In the Enter The Object Names To Select box, you can type* **computername\username** *to specify a user account on that computer (for example, SOLARIA\Rima Regas or DELL8100\Margy Levine Young).*

7. Click Check Names. Windows replaces the name using the form it needs (*computername\username*).

8. Click OK. The Remote Desktop Users dialog box displays the user you added. To add another user, repeat steps 5–8.

9. Click OK to close the Remote Desktop Users and click OK again to close the System Properties dialog boxes.

> **Note**   *If the computer you will be accessing is protected by a firewall, make sure that the firewall allows remote connection traffic (see Chapter 31).*

Configuring the Server for Remote Desktop Web Connection

The Remote Desktop Web Connection is part of Microsoft's Internet Information Services (IIS) component of Windows, which comes with Windows XP Professional (but not Windows XP Home Edition). When you install it, Windows copies the necessary

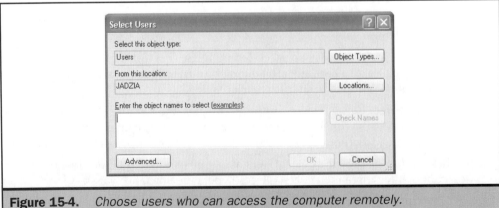

Figure 15-4.   *Choose users who can access the computer remotely.*

files to your C:\Windows\Web\TSWeb folder (assuming that Windows is installed on C:)—*TSWeb* stands for Terminal Services Web.

If you want to use Remote Desktop Web Connection you also need to complete these steps, which ensure that the Windows components are installed and running. These steps seem unnecessarily arcane to us, but they work. You must be logged in with an administrative user account to do the following:

1. Choose Start | Control Panel | Add Or Remove Programs.

2. Click Add/Remove Windows Components. You see the Windows Components Wizard window.

3. Select Internet Information Services from the list of optional Windows components and click Details; select World Wide Web Service and click Details; select Remote Desktop Web Connection and World Wide Web Service. Click OK to close dialog boxes until you return to the Windows Components Wizard.

4. Click Next in the Windows Components Wizard window to install the new components. You may need to insert the Windows XP CD-ROM during the installation. (If the Windows XP installation menu appears, click the Exit button to close it.) Installation may take several minutes. Click Finish to close the Wizard.

5. Close the Add Or Remove Programs window.

6. Open Computer Management by clicking Start, right-clicking My Computer, and selecting Manage.

7. Click the plus box to the left of the Services And Applications item in the left pane of the Computer Management window. If the component was correctly installed, you see the item Internet Information Services.

8. Click the plus box to the left of the Internet Information Services, and to its subentries, to display Internet Information Services*computername*\\Web Sites\\Default Web Site\\tsweb. (*Computername* is the name of your computer.)

9. Right-click the Tsweb folder and select Properties to display the Tsweb Properties dialog box.

10. Click the Directory Security tab.

11. Click the Edit button in the Anonymous Access And Authentication Control section of the dialog box. You see the Authentication Methods dialog box.

12. Select the Anonymous Access check box.

13. Click OK.

Configuring the Client Computer for Remote Desktop

If you are using the regular Remote Desktop (without the Web Connection), then the computer that you will use while you are away (the client computer) must have the

Remote Desktop Connection program installed. To check for this command, choose Start | All Programs | Accessories | Communications | Remote Desktop Connection. (Windows XP Professional and Home Edition both normally install Remote Desktop Connection.)

Note *If the command isn't there, install Remote Desktop Connection from your Windows XP CD-ROM—insert the CD, click Perform Additional Tasks on the Welcome page, and then choose Set Up Remote Desktop Connection to run the Remote Desktop Connection InstallShield Wizard. You get to choose who can use the remote connection: anyone on the computer, or just the logged-in user. Then the Wizard takes over. Once the Wizard has finished, you can close the installation program.*

If you are using Remote Desktop Web Connection, the client computer that you use to access the computer on your desk must have a TCP/IP connection to the LAN or the Internet, and it must have Internet Explorer 4.0 or higher (Windows XP comes with Internet Explorer 6). No other configuration is necessary for Remote Desktop Web Connection.

Connecting to the Remote Computer with Remote Desktop

Once you have completed the necessary setup tasks you are ready to test Remote Desktop. Make sure that the server machine is on and working and connected to whatever network you will use to access it—usually the Internet or a LAN (obviously, you need to do this before you leave). Sit at the client machine—that is, the computer that you will have wherever it is you are going. The next two sections describe connecting with the regular Remote Desktop and with the Remote Desktop Web Connection. Read the section for the type of connection for which you configured your computers.

Note *Although many users can log into a Windows XP Professional server computer remotely, if the computer is being used as a remote server, no one can be logged in locally. That is, one or more people can log in to the server computer using its own screen and keyboard, or one or more people can log in remotely, but not both. In fact, if someone is logged in locally when you try to log in remotely you see a message that lets you know that if you want to connect, the local user has to disconnect. The server also displays a message allowing the local user to prevent the remote connection, but if the person does not respond, the connection proceeds. This system enables you to log in remotely even if you forgot to log off before you left. Windows .NET Server can act as a multiple-user server.*

Connecting with Remote Desktop Connection

Start Remote Desktop Connection on the client computer (the one you will take with you) by following these steps:

1. Choose Start | All Programs | Accessories | Communications | Remote Desktop Connection. You see the Remote Desktop Connection window:

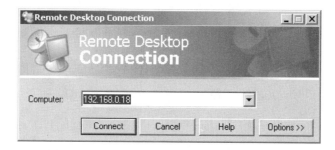

2. Select the name of the server computer from the Computer drop-down list, or enter the computer name or IP address. If no computer names appear on the drop-down list, choose Browse For More to see the available computers in your domain or workgroup—only computers that you have configured for remote access appear.

   To discover a computer's IP address, choose Start | My Network Places, click View Network Connections, right-click your LAN or Internet connection (whichever connects you to the network over which you will remotely access the server), choose Status, and click the Support tab. Or open a Command Prompt window and run the ipconfig program (see Chapter 28, section "Checking Your TCP/IP Address").

3. Click Connect.

4. Enter your name and password in the Log On To Windows window: type the user account name and password that you use on the server computer. Click OK.

5. You see the remote desktop, such as the one in Figure 15-5. Notice the special toolbar at the top of the window—you can use it to minimize, restore or close the Remote Desktop Connection window. (Click the restore or minimize button if you want to work on the client computer, but then return to the server computer.) Clicking the pushpin icon locks the menu open.

You're ready to work on the server computer.

CONFIGURING WINDOWS
FOR YOUR COMPUTER

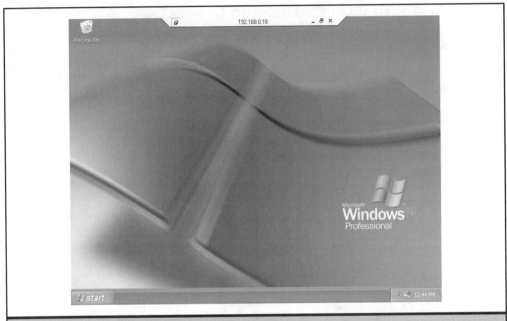

Figure 15-5. *The Remote Desktop appears on your screen—notice the special toolbar at the top.*

Connecting with Remote Desktop Web Connection

If you are connecting with Internet Explorer and Remote Desktop Web Connection you can sit at any computer, provided that it has Internet Explorer 4.0 or greater and the appropriate network connection. Access the server computer by following these steps:

1. Open Internet Explorer.

2. In the Address box, type the URL for the home directory of the Remote Desktop computer. Generally, this URL takes the following form: **http://** *servercomputer/path*. Replace *servercomputer* with the address of the server computer, and *path* with the path containing the Remote Desktop Connection files (the default location is C:\Tsweb, if Windows is installed on C:). The computer address can be the name on the LAN, or the computer's numeric IP address. You can usually omit the **http://**. For instance, if you are connecting over a LAN to a server computer named Jadzia, type **Jadzia/Tsweb** in the Address box.

 Note *To avoid typing this address again, add it to your Internet Explorer Favorites by choosing Favorites | Add To Favorites from the menu (see Chapter 24, section "Using Favorites, Links, and Internet Shortcuts").*

3. Press ENTER to see the Remote Desktop Web Connection page (shown in Figure 15-6).

4. Type the server computer's name or numeric IP address in the Server box.

5. Choose the Size for the Remote Desktop window: Full Screen, or one of the other available sizes. Remote Desktop is easier to use if the resolution of the client computer's screen is greater than size you choose (for example, you choose to display the server's screen at 800×600 on a client computer screen with a resolution of 1024×768).

6. Click Connect. The first time you use this feature, Windows may ask you whether you want to install and run the Microsoft Terminal Services Control program: if it does, click Yes. You see the Remote Desktop Connection Security Warning dialog box shown in Figure 15-7 with the following options:

   ■ **Connect Your Local Disk Drives To The Remote Computer**   Makes the drives on the local (client) computer available on the remote computer. So, for instance, if you are using Remote Desktop and opening a file in Word, you can see files on your local hard drives, network drives, and floppy drives. This option is automatically available in Remote Desktop Connection.

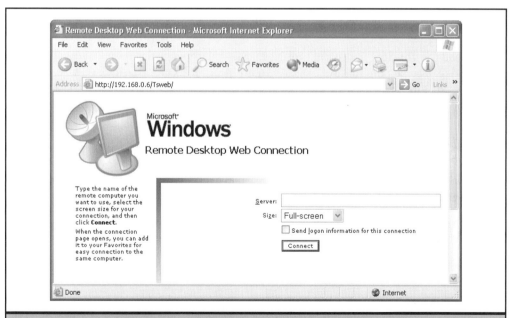

Figure 15-6.   *Logging into a remote PC using Internet Explorer*

CONFIGURING WINDOWS
FOR YOUR COMPUTER

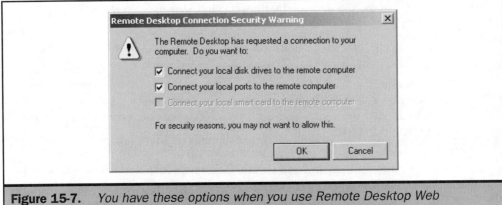

Figure 15-7. *You have these options when you use Remote Desktop Web Connection.*

- **Connect Your Local Ports To The Remote Computer** Makes the ports on the local (client) computer available on the remote computer in the Remote Desktop Web Connection window.

7. Select or deselect check boxes as needed and click OK.

8. Log in to the server computer by typing the user name and password that you use on that computer.

You see the window shown in Figure 15-5 if you chose full screen. If you chose another size, you see the remote desktop in an Internet Explorer window. Use the Minimize, Restore, or Close buttons to control the Remote Desktop Connection window. When you are done using the server computer, close the Internet Explorer window.

Using the Remote Desktop Connection

Once you have established the Remote Desktop Connection, you can work as if you were working on the server computer. You can also combine the capabilities of the remote server computer with the local client computer in the following ways:

- **Cut-and-paste** You can cut information from the Remote Desktop window and paste it into an application on the local computer.

- **Use local files in the remote session** If you are using the Remote Desktop Connection program, this option is available automatically. If you are using

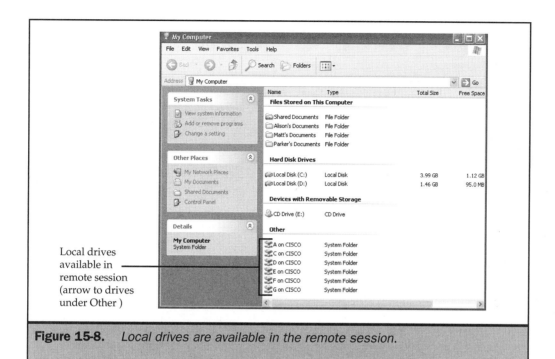

Local drives available in remote session (arrow to drives under Other)

Figure 15-8.   *Local drives are available in the remote session.*

Remote Desktop Web Connection, you need to select Connect Your Local Disk Drives To The Remote Computer when you log in. Local drives appear in My Computer under Other, as shown in Figure 15-8. They will also appear in Open and Save dialog boxes in applications.

■ **Use a local printer in the remote session**   When you print while you are using Remote Desktop, the print job automatically goes to the default local printer if the printer driver is available on the server computer.

Other Remote Desktop Options

When you connect to a computer using Remote Desktop, you see the Remote Desktop Connection dialog box (see "Connecting with Remote Desktop Connection"). You can click the Options button to see a larger version of this dialog box with many additional options, as shown in Figure 15-9. Table 15-1 lists the options.

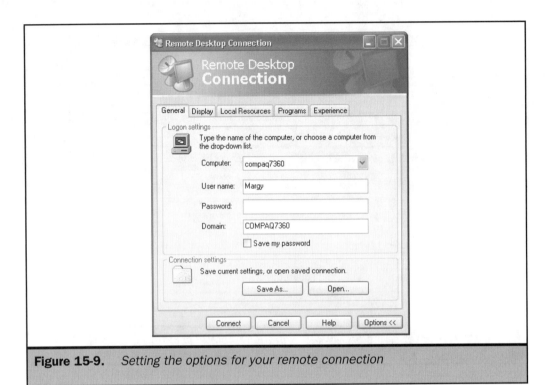

Figure 15-9.   *Setting the options for your remote connection*

Dialog Box Tab	Setting	Description
General	Save my password	Specifies whether you have to type your user account password each time you connect.
Display	Remote desktop size and colors	Selects the size and color depth of the Remote Desktop window on your screen.
Local Resources	Remote computer sound	Specifies whether to play the sounds that the other computer would make on your computer instead.

Table 15-1.   *Settings on the Remote Desktop Connection Dialog Box*

Dialog Box Tab	Setting	Description
Local Resources	Keyboard	Specifies whether ALT- key combinations apply to the local computer or the remote computer.
Local Resources	Local devices (Disk drives, Printers, and Serial ports)	Specifies which devices on the remote computer you connect to automatically.
Programs	Start the following program on connection	Runs a program automatically when you connect to the remote computer, and specifies which program.
Experience	Choose your connection speed to optimize performance	Specifies the speed of your connection to the remote computer.
Experience	Allow the following (Desktop background, Show contents of window while dragging, Menu and window animation, Themes, and Bitmap caching)	Specifies which desktop features appear in your Remote Desktop window. Deselect items to improve performance, especially if you have a slow connection.

Table 15-1.   *Settings on the Remote Desktop Connection Dialog Box* (continued)

Tip   *Once you have configured the settings for your Remote Desktop connection, you can save them with a name by clicking the Save As button on the General tab of the Remote Desktop Connection dialog box. The next time you want to use these settings, click the Open button.*

Managing Your Computer's Power

If you often use your laptop when it isn't plugged in, you probably have had a battery die before you finished your work. Windows and some applications support power management, which eases this problem without actually solving it. Windows supports two power management standards: *Advanced Power Management* (*APM*) and *Advanced*

CONFIGURING WINDOWS FOR YOUR COMPUTER

Configuration and Power Interface (ACPI). To take advantage of Windows power management features, however, you must have a computer with hardware that supports one of these standards. (The computer needn't be a laptop).

> **Tip** *The most power-hungry component of your computer system is the monitor. Turning off the monitor when you won't be using it for several hours saves energy, in exchange for the relatively minor inconvenience of waiting a few seconds for it to come on again when you're ready to go back to work.*

Most laptops support Standby Mode, in which the disks stop spinning, the screen goes blank, but the memory and CPU continue to run, using much less power than full operation. To switch to Standby Mode, choose Start | Turn Off Computer, and then choose Stand By.

Many laptops (and some desktops) also support hibernation, in which the computer stores the contents of its memory in a temporary file on your hard disk and then shuts itself down completely, so it stops using power. When you reopen the laptop, click the computer's power button and press keys or move the mouse. The computer wakes up again, restoring the contents of its memory from the temporary file. If your computer supports Hibernate Mode, the Power Options Properties dialog box includes a Hibernate tab. Click it and select the Enable Hibernation Support check box. The dialog box shows how much disk space will be required to store the contents of your computer's memory during hibernation, as well as the amount of free disk space currently available. When hibernation is enabled, an additional choice—Hibernate—appears when you choose Start | Shut Down.

Your computer can switch to Standby or Hibernate Mode automatically after a specified number of minutes of inactivity. Power management is handled from the Power Options Properties dialog box, displayed in Figure 15-10. To display the Power Options Properties dialog box, open the Performance And Maintenance icon on the Control Panel, then click Power Options. The options displayed on your Power Options Properties dialog box depend on what type of power management your hardware supports.

> **Tip** *Many laptop manufacturers add extra power management drivers to take advantage of special power-saving features—such as running the CPU slower when the computer is working on batteries than when it's plugged in, or turning off serial and parallel ports when you're not planning to use them. Consult your laptop's documentation to see whether your computer has any extra features you can enable.*

You can choose a *power scheme*, which is a group of settings that define when and if Windows should turn off the power to parts of your computer, or switch to Standby or Hibernate Mode. Power schemes enable you to create and use different power management profiles for use under different circumstances.

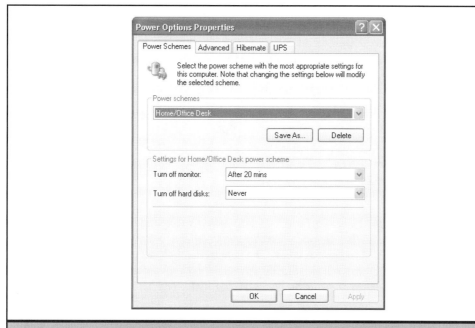

Figure 15-10.   *Manage how your laptop (or desktop) uses power by using these settings.*

Click the Power Schemes tab in the Power Options Properties dialog box and then click the Power Schemes drop-down list (the topmost setting). Choose the power scheme that reflects the type of hardware you're using:

- **Home/Office Desk**   Turns off the monitor after 20 minutes. On battery, goes into power-saving mode in less than half an hour.
- **Portable/Laptop**   Goes into power-saving mode fairly quickly whether plugged in or on battery.
- **Presentation**   Monitor never turns off. Goes into power-saving mode when running on battery without turning off monitor.
- **Always On**   Turns off monitor and hard drives (when on battery) but never goes into Standby or Hibernate.
- **Minimal Power Management**   Similar to Home/Office Desk, but takes much longer to hibernate.
- **Max Battery**   Goes into power-saving modes very quickly, especially when running on the battery.

CONFIGURING WINDOWS
FOR YOUR COMPUTER

You can see the specifics by selecting the power scheme. Once you've chosen the scheme that most closely matches your needs, you can edit the power management settings. If you've made changes you can save the settings as a new power scheme by clicking the Save As button, typing a new name for the power scheme, and clicking OK.

Note *The Advanced tab may have some additional settings for laptop power management.*

To see the status of an individual battery in your computer, click the Power Meter tab in the Power Options Properties dialog box, make sure the Show Details For Each Battery check box is selected, and click the battery icon. You can also set alarms to beep when your battery charge drops to a preset level: click the Alarms tab on the Power Options Properties dialog box to set alarms.

Tip *You can display the Power Meter in the notification area of the Windows taskbar. Click the Advanced tab on the Power Options Properties dialog box and select the Always Show Icon On The Taskbar check box. The Power Meter shows whether the computer is connected to AC power or is running on batteries. Double-clicking the Power Meter in the notification area displays the Power Meter dialog box, which shows the status of your batteries.*

Using a Docking Station

Docking stations enable laptop users to avoid resource limitations that most laptops have. A docking station lets you connect to a better monitor, a real mouse, a full-sized keyboard, and possibly a network. Some docking stations give you access to additional hardware, such as a hard drive or CD-ROM drive. In addition to these resources, docking stations are convenient—by simply clicking the laptop into the docking station, you have access to these additional resources, without having to plug cables into the laptop.

Note *Port replicators are a kind of simple docking station that contain no resources except additional ports. A port replicator can be used to give you immediate access to a full-sized screen, keyboard, mouse, printer, and network connection, without having to plug each cable in separately. Port replicators don't have hard drives or other internal resources.*

Windows provides some features that are useful to users of docking stations:

- **Hot docking**   If your hardware supports it, you can plug your laptop into its docking station *without turning off the laptop* and gain access to the additional resources provided by the docking station.
- **Hardware profiles**   Enables you to create profiles so your laptop works properly, whether it's connected to the docking station or not.

Docking and Undocking

If your laptop supports hot docking, you can usually undock it by choosing Start | Eject PC. Windows automatically adjusts to the change in hardware, notifying you of open files, and loading or unloading any necessary drivers. When you're ready to dock the laptop again, simply put it in the docking station. Windows again adjusts automatically to the change in hardware. Some laptops support hot docking, but no Eject PC command appears on the Start menu.

If your laptop doesn't support hot docking (check the laptop's manual or online help to find out for sure), you need to shut down Windows and turn the laptop off before docking or undocking. You can benefit from creating two hardware profiles—one to use when the laptop is docked, and one to use when you work away from the docking station. Multiple hardware profiles can save you time. When you undock your laptop, you needn't change each hardware setting that needs to be changed; instead, you can choose the correct hardware profile when the machine boots.

Creating and Using Hardware Profiles

A *hardware profile* is a description of your computer's hardware resources. Creating multiple hardware profiles gives you an easy way to tell Windows to what hardware the computer is connected. If the laptop is attached to a network, you want to be able to use the network printer. If it's in a docking station, you want to be able to use the docking station hardware—extra drives or sound card—and you may want to change your screen resolution to take advantage of a regular monitor. Hardware profiles can save information about the available hardware and the drivers used by the hardware. You create one hardware profile for each hardware configuration you use.

Hardware profiles store information about printers, monitors, video controllers, disk controllers, keyboards, modems, sound cards, network cards, pointing devices, and ports.

Hardware profiles are useful when you have more than one way you commonly use a computer. Your computer might sometimes be connected to a network, and use shared drives and printers. At other times, your computer might be disconnected from the network and not have access to the network's shared resources. Or, you may have a laptop you sometimes use with and sometimes use without a docking station. Hardware profiles easily enable you to load and unload the drivers needed for the resources to which your computer has access.

Creating a New Hardware Profile

The following are the steps for creating a new hardware profile. We recommend that you first configure your hardware to get all your peripherals and network connections running (see Chapter 13). Also, it's a good idea to make a copy of your original profile in case you have trouble with the new profiles.

CONFIGURING WINDOWS FOR YOUR COMPUTER

Follow these steps to create a new hardware profile:

1. Open the System Properties dialog box by choosing Start | Control Panel | Performance And Maintenance | System. (Or, click Start, right-click My Computer, and choose Properties.)

2. Click the Hardware tab and then the Hardware Profiles button to see the options shown in Figure 15-11.

3. Select the hardware profile that is current. (At this point you may want to use the Copy button to create a copy of the working profile.)

Note *Making a copy of the original configuration profile is a good idea. Leave the original configuration profile as is, in case you have problems with the other profiles.*

4. Click the Copy button to display the Copy Profile dialog box.

5. Type the new profile name in the To box. Use a name that is descriptive, such as "Networked," "No Network," or "Not Docked" as the name of the profile. Click OK.

Figure 15-11. *Creating additional hardware configurations for your computer*

6. Select the Hardware Profile that you are going to edit—in other words, the profile that will be used for the computer when hardware connections are different than when you initially set the computer up.

7. Click OK to close the Hardware Profiles dialog box.

8. Click the Device Manager button on the Hardware tab of the System Properties dialog box to see the tab shown in Figure 15-12.

9. Expand the category that you want to change in the selected profile, and look for the hardware device(s) you want to disable

10. Right-click the device and select Properties to see the properties for the device. The dialog box you see looks like the one displayed in Figure 15-13.

11. At the bottom of the General tab, choose Do Not Use This Device In The Current Hardware Profile as the Device Usage setting. When Remove is selected, the hardware is removed from Device Manager.

12. Repeat steps 10 and 11 as necessary to disable or remove additional hardware from this profile.

13. Click OK.

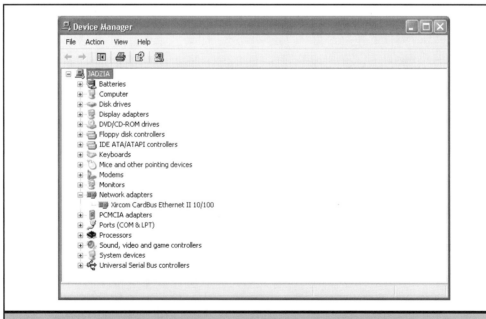

Figure 15-12.   *The Device Manager tab shows the hardware components of your computer.*

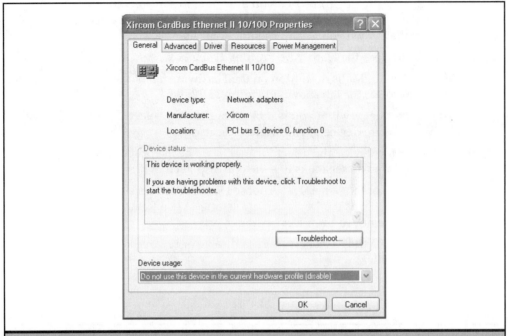

Figure 15-13.   *Disabling hardware in the current profile in the Properties dialog box*

Switching Hardware Profiles

When the computer reboots—and whenever it starts from now on—you see a menu similar to the following:

```
Windows cannot determine what configuration your computer
is in.
Select one of the following:
1. Original profile
2. Networked
3. No Network
```

The menu lists the hardware profiles you created. Pick the configuration you want to use.

Modifying and Deleting Hardware Profiles

If you decide not to use a hardware profile any more, you can delete it by selecting it on the Hardware Profile tab of the System Profiles dialog box and clicking Delete.

To re-enable a hardware device in a hardware profile, start the computer using the hardware profile. Then, open the Add New Hardware icon in the Control Panel to add the drivers for this device to the hardware profile.

CONFIGURING WINDOWS FOR YOUR COMPUTER

The
Complete
Reference

Chapter 16

Accessibility Options

ike previous versions of Windows, Windows XP includes a number of options to help people who have disabilities that make using a computer difficult. In some cases, people without disabilities may also find the accessibility options useful. The options include settings for your keyboard, sound, display, and mouse.

To set your accessibility options, you can use the Accessibility Wizard, described in this chapter. (You may need to install the options from your Windows XP CD-ROM first.) After you set your options, you can turn them on and off by using the Accessibility Options dialog box, the icons that appear in the notification area on your taskbar, or the Utility Manager. Internet Explorer (Windows' Web browser) has additional accessibility options.

What Accessibility Options Are Available in Windows XP?

Windows includes the accessibility options for people who have difficulty typing, reading the screen, hearing noises the computer makes, or using a mouse.

Keyboard aids for those who have difficulty typing include

- **StickyKeys**   Enables you to avoid pressing multiple keys by making the CTRL, WINDOWS, SHIFT, and ALT keys "sticky"—they stay in effect even after they have been released.

- **FilterKeys**   Filters out repeated keystrokes. Good for typists who have trouble pressing a key once briefly.

- **ToggleKeys**   Sounds a tone when the CAPS LOCK, SCROLL LOCK, and NUM LOCK keys are activated.

- **On-Screen Keyboard**   Displays a keyboard on the screen that enables you to type by using your mouse.

For sloppy typists of all abilities (and for those with small laptop keyboards), ToggleKeys can be convenient to guard against accidentally pressing CAPS LOCK and typing capitalized prose by mistake.

Visual translation of sounds for those who have difficulty hearing include

- **SoundSentry**   Displays a visual warning when the computer makes a sound.

- **ShowSounds**   Displays a caption when the computer makes a sound.

Display options for those who have trouble reading the screen include

- **High Contrast**   Uses a high-contrast color scheme and increases legibility wherever possible.

- **Cursor Options**   Makes the cursor easier to see.

- ■ **Magnifier**   Displays a window that magnifies part of the screen.
- ■ **Narrator**   Reads text on the screen aloud.

Mouse options for those who dislike or have trouble using a mouse or trackball include

- ■ **MouseKeys**   Enables you to use the numeric keypad to control the pointer.
- ■ **SerialKey**   Turns on support for alternate input devices attached to the serial port.

Installing Accessibility Options

Most of Windows accessibility options are found on the Accessibility Options dialog box. Choose Start | Control Panel | Accessibility Options, and then click the Accessibility Options icon.

You can also use the Accessibility Wizard to guide you through the accessibility settings that make using a computer easier for you. All the accessibility options changed by the Accessibility Wizard appear on the Accessibility Options dialog box and are covered in detail in the rest of this chapter. To run the Accessibility Wizard, choose Start | All Programs | Accessories | Accessibility | Accessibility Wizard. Or, choose Configure Windows To Work For Your Vision Hearing And Mobility Needs on the Accessibility Options screen of the Control Panel.

Making the Keyboard More Accessible

Most of the options to change the way the keyboard accepts input are found on the Keyboard tab of the Accessibility Options dialog box, shown in Figure 16-1. Choose Start | Control Panel | Accessibility Options, run the Accessibility Options program, and click the Keyboard tab if it's not selected.

Do Applications Use the Windows Accessibility Settings?

Although accessibility options are built into the Windows operating system, software applications must be designed to work with them. Microsoft maintains standards, including standards for accessibility, that developers must meet to put the Designed for Windows logo on their product. The standards include support for high-contrast and enlarged displays, keyboard use with a single hand or device, adjustable timing for the user interface, and keyboard-only operation. If you need to use accessibility options with new software, make sure the software supports Windows accessibility options before you buy. Microsoft maintains an accessibility Web site at **http://www.microsoft.com/enable**.

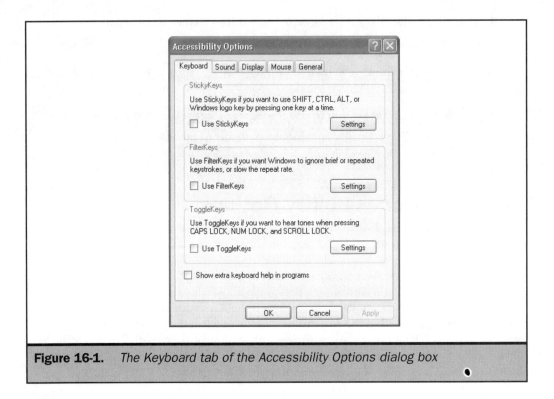

Figure 16-1.   *The Keyboard tab of the Accessibility Options dialog box*

Other keyboard settings, including character repeat settings and language, are available on the Keyboard Properties dialog box (see Chapter 12, section "Configuring Your Keyboard"). To ask programs to display all available help information about the keyboard when you use their online help systems, select the Show Extra Keyboard Help In Programs check box on the Keyboard tab of the Accessibility Options dialog box.

Making Your Keys Stick

If you have trouble holding down two keys at once, activate *StickyKeys*, so you can press the keys separately and still get the same effect. When StickyKeys is on, you can save a document (for instance) by pressing the CTRL key, and then pressing the S key—you needn't press them at the same time. Pressing a second key turns off (or unsticks) the first key. StickyKeys works only with the *modifier keys*: SHIFT, WINDOWS, CTRL, and ALT.

The ALT key is sticky all the time—to choose a command from a menu bar, you can press and release the ALT key before you press the letter for the command.

To turn on StickyKeys, select the Use StickyKeys check box on the Keyboard tab of the Accessibility Options dialog box. Then, click the Settings button to see five check boxes that define exactly how StickyKeys works:

- **Use Shortcut**   Turns StickyKeys on or off when you press SHIFT five times.

- **Press Modifier Key Twice To Lock**   Lock on a modifier key when you press it twice. Turn off the key by pressing it once again.

- **Turn StickyKeys Off If Two Keys Are Pressed At Once**   If two keys are pressed at once, StickyKeys turns off. To make a modifier key sticky again, StickyKeys must be turned on again by using the shortcut (if the Use Shortcut option is selected) or by displaying the Keyboard tab of the Accessibility Options dialog box and selecting the Use StickyKeys option. This option can be annoying if you ever want to press two keys at the same time.

- **Make Sounds When Modifier Key Is Pressed**   Beeps when a modifier key is struck. This is particularly useful when the previous option is turned on—it lets you know when StickyKeys is turned off.

- **Show StickyKeys Status On Screen**   Displays a small graphic to the left of the time in the notification area of the taskbar, as shown in the following illustration.

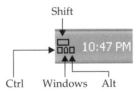

Shift

Ctrl   Windows   Alt

The four blocks represent the four modifier keys: SHIFT at the top, CTRL at the bottom left, WINDOWS in the bottom middle, and ALT at the bottom right. When a modifier key is stuck, its block is shaded on the diagram. You can double-click the icon to display the Accessibilities Options dialog box and make changes to your settings. When StickyKeys is off, the diagram is removed from the taskbar.

Filtering Out Extra Keystrokes

If you have trouble typing each letter only once, you may want to turn on *FilterKeys*—which "filters out" extra keystrokes—rather than spending time editing them out yourself. You can configure FilterKeys to ignore repeated keystrokes repeated too quickly and to slow down the repeat rate (the rate at which a character is repeated when a key is held down).

To turn on FilterKeys, select the Use FilterKeys check box on the Keyboard tab of the Accessibility Options dialog box. Then, click the Settings button to define exactly how FilterKeys works:

- **Use Shortcut**   Turns FilterKeys on or off when you hold down the right SHIFT key for eight seconds.

- **Ignore Repeated Keystrokes**   Ignores keys repeated without a sufficient pause (sometimes called *BounceKeys*). When you choose this option, click the Settings button next to it, and then define the interval within which repeated keys should be ignored. Getting the right interval is crucial to avoiding frustration, so use the Test Area box to type words with repeated letters to see whether the setting works for you.

- **Ignore Quick Keystrokes And Slow Down The Repeat Rate**   This option enables features called SlowKeys and RepeatKeys. *SlowKeys* enables you to filter out keys that are pressed only briefly. When SlowKeys is on, you must type more methodically, but Windows ignores keys touched lightly or quickly. *RepeatKeys* enables you to change the way keys are repeated (see Chapter 12, section "Changing Keyboard Properties")—normally, if you hold down a key, it repeats at a certain rate after it has been held down for a certain interval. The settings for SlowKeys and RepeatKeys are on the same dialog box. Choose the radio button and click the Settings button next to it to configure them—if holding down a key causes it to repeat; if so, after what interval and at what rate should it repeat; and how long a key should be held down to register.

- **Beep When Keys Pressed Or Accepted**   Tells Windows to beep when a key is pressed, and beep again when a key is accepted.

- **Show FilterKey Status On Screen**   Displays a small graphic to the left of the time on the system tray, as shown in the following illustration:

You can double-click the icon to display the Accessibilities Options dialog box and make changes to your settings. When FilterKeys is off, the diagram is removed from the taskbar.

Hearing when a Toggled Key Is Pressed

ToggleKeys is useful if you accidentally press keys that change the behavior of the keyboard. When ToggleKeys is turned on and you press CAPS LOCK, NUM LOCK, or SCROLL LOCK, a tone sounds—a high-pitched tone when you turn CAPS LOCK, NUM LOCK, or SCROLL LOCK on, and a low-pitched tone when you turn it off.

To turn on ToggleKeys, select the Use ToggleKeys option on the Keyboard tab of the Accessibility Options dialog box. Click the Settings button to turn on the Use

Shortcut setting, which enables you to turn ToggleKeys on or off by holding down the NUM LOCK key for five seconds.

Displaying the On-Screen Keyboard

If using the mouse or other pointing device is easier for you than typing on the keyboard, Windows can display a picture of a keyboard on the screen. You can use a mouse, joystick, pointing stick, or other pointing device to choose characters from the On-Screen Keyboard:

To display the On-Screen Keyboard, choose Start | All Programs | Accessories | Accessibility | On-Screen Keyboard. The program displays an explanatory dialog box along with the On-Screen Keyboard. After reading it, click Do Not Show This Message Again, and then OK to dismiss the dialog box.

You can type by choosing the keys on the On-Screen Keyboard with your mouse in one of three ways (typing modes):

- **Click To Select**   Click an on-screen key.
- **Hover To Select**   Rest the mouse pointer on the on-screen key for the specified period of time. You can choose the amount of time the mouse pointer must "hover" before the key types.
- **Joystick Or Key To Select**   Windows automatically moves the highlight from key to key on the On-Screen Keyboard, cycling endlessly across the keys. When the highlight gets to the key you want, press a key, click the mouse, or activate the joystick to select that key. You can choose how fast the highlight moves, what key or click chooses the selected key, and how your selection device is connected to the computer.

Choose your typing mode by choosing Settings | Typing Mode from the menu bar at the top of the On-Screen Keyboard window.

The characters you "type" using the On-Screen Keyboard appear in the active window—be sure to select the window into which you want to type first. When you choose the "shft" button on the screen, it remains on until you choose the next button (for example, choose "shft" and then *a* to type a capital *A*).

You can choose

- Whether the keyboard appears "on top" of other windows that it overlaps, by choosing Settings | Always On Top

- Whether the on-screen "keys" make a sound when chosen, by choosing Settings | Use Click Sound

- What font appears on the keys of the On-Screen Keyboard, by choosing Settings | Font

- Whether to display the standard or enhanced keyboard (the enhanced keyboard includes the numeric keypad and more cursor movement keys), by choosing Keyboard | Enhanced Keyboard or Keyboard | Standard Keyboard

- Whether to arrange the keys like a real keyboard, or in a grid, by choosing Keyboard | Regular Layout or Keyboard | Block Layout

- How many keys to display, by choosing Keyboard | 101 Keys, Keyboard | 102 Keys (which adds a backslash key to the left of Z), or Keyboard | 106 Keys (which adds Japanese-language characters)

Setting Sound Accessibility Options

Windows includes options to help translate the sounds programs make for people who have difficulty hearing. The sound accessibility options don't work for all sounds, but they do work for most sounds generated by Windows and for some sounds generated by applications. The options are found on the Sound tab of the Accessibility Options dialog box, shown in Figure 16-2. Choose Start | Control Panel | Accessibility Options, run the Accessibility Options icon, and click the Sound tab.

The two sound options are SoundSentry and ShowSounds:

- **SoundSentry** tells Windows to use a flashing element on the screen to tell the user a sound has been made. Set the Choose The Visual Warning box to choose a screen element to flash. We recommend choosing either the Flash Active Caption Bar or the Flash Active Window option—otherwise, it's impossible to determine which application caused the sound.

- **ShowSounds** option displays a caption on the screen each time Windows (and some other programs) makes a sound.

Setting Display Accessibility Options

Windows has four features that make the screen easier to read: a high-contrast color scheme, configurable cursor appearance, Magnifier (which can magnify part of the screen), and Narrator (which reads the screen out loud).

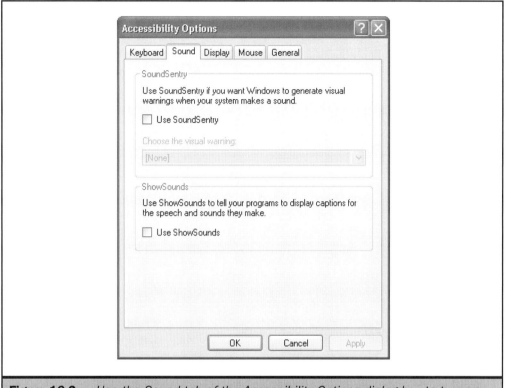

Figure 16-2. *Use the Sound tab of the Accessibility Options dialog box to turn on the accessibility options for the hearing impaired.*

Note *Other display settings—including colors and fonts—are available on the Display Properties dialog box (see Chapter 11, section "What Are Display Properties?").*

Displaying in High Contrast

High Contrast changes the Windows color scheme and increases legibility wherever possible, often by increasing font sizes. Not every program uses font sizes controlled by Windows, so not everything on the screen gets bigger. You control High Contrast from the Display tab of the Accessibility Options dialog box, shown in Figure 16-3. Choose Start | Control Panel | Accessibility Options, run the Accessibility Options icon, and click the Display tab.

Turn on the High Contrast feature by clicking the Use High Contrast check box. Click the Settings button to turn on the Use Shortcut setting, which enables you to turn High Contract on or off by pressing LEFT ALT-LEFT SHIFT-PRINT SCREEN (that is, hold

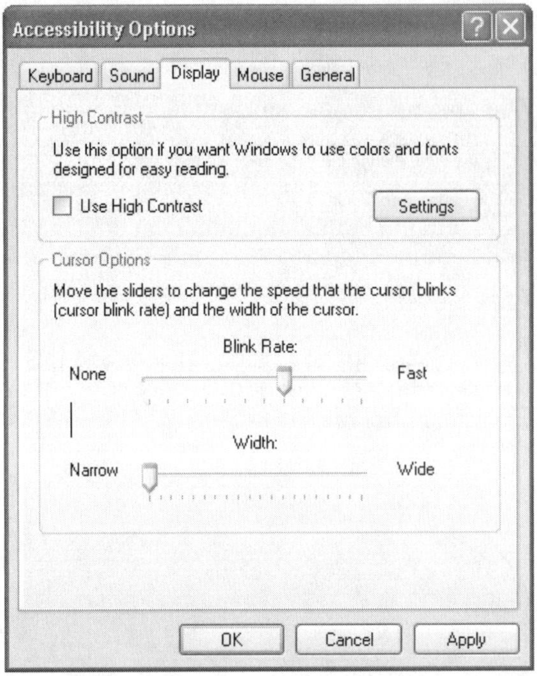

Figure 16-3. *Turn on the High Contrast option by using the Display tab of the Accessibility Options dialog box.*

down the ALT and SHIFT keys that appear on the left side of the keyboard near the X and Z keys, and also press the PRINT SCREEN button). You can also choose a color scheme.

When High Contrast is on, your screen looks like Figure 16-4—the High Contrast White (Large) color scheme is shown. (High Contrast Black is the default, but the white version is more readable when printed in this book.) Using bigger fonts results in less information fitting on the screen, so you see more scroll bars than usual. Also, the different color scheme may take some getting used to.

Controlling the Cursor's Size and Blink Rate

The Display tab of the Accessibility dialog box (shown in Figure 16-3) also contains the Cursor Blink Rate and Cursor Width settings. Move the sliders to control how quickly the cursor blinks and how wide it appears on the screen.

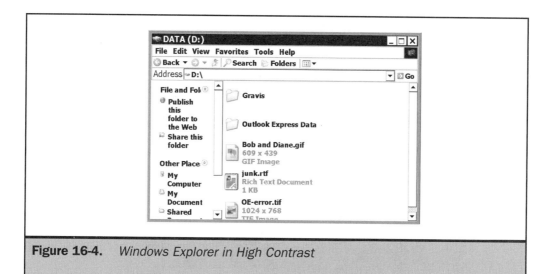

Figure 16-4. *Windows Explorer in High Contrast*

Magnifying the Screen

The Magnifier is an alternative to High Contrast mode—it enables you to magnify only a part of the screen at a time. One section of the screen (usually a strip along the top of the screen) shows a highly magnified version of one area of the screen—the area where you are working.

Turn on Magnifier by choosing Start | All Programs | Accessories | Accessibility | Magnifier. (From the keyboard, press WINDOWS or CTRL-ESC to display the Start menu, press *R* to choose Run, type **magnify**, and press ENTER.) Windows displays an explanatory message the first time you run Magnifier: Click the Do Not Show This Message Again check box after you've read it, and click OK. You see the magnification window at the top of your screen and the Magnifier Settings dialog box, as shown in Figure 16-5.

You can control the magnification level, which part of the screen is displayed in the magnification window, its color scheme, and its location on the screen:

- **Magnification Level** Determines how much larger things appear in the magnification window. Use the Magnification Level setting on the Magnifier Settings dialog box. The larger the level, the more the contents of the magnification window are magnified.

- **Tracking** Determines what part of the screen is shown in the magnification window. You can choose to Follow Mouse Cursor, Follow Keyboard Focus, and Follow Text Editing. These three options are not mutually exclusive—if you select all three, the display in the magnification window is determined by what you are currently doing—in other words, Windows does its best to display the part of the screen you're working with in the magnification window.

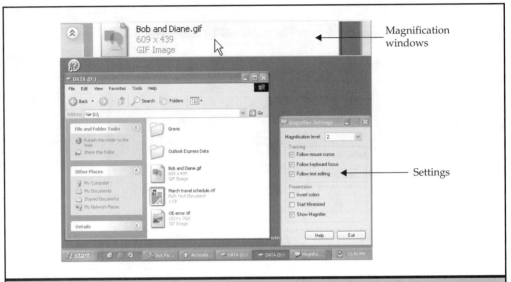

Figure 16-5.   *The Magnifier dialog box and the Magnification window at the top of the screen*

- **Colors**   Controls colors in the magnification window. Click the Invert Colors check box to use the opposite of the colors in the rest of the screen. Inverted colors make it easier to see that the magnification window is a special part of the screen, but they may also make the display more confusing.

- **Size and Location**   You can change the size of the magnification window by dragging the lower window border up or down. You can change the position of the window by clicking inside the window and dragging. You can "dock" the window along any edge of the desktop or put it somewhere in the middle of the screen. If the magnification window appears as a window rather than a wide border, you can control its size and position in the same way you'd change them for any window. Your ideal magnification window may be a small square near one corner of the screen. The magnification window always appears on top—it cannot be covered by another window.

When you have adjusted the settings in the Magnifier Settings dialog box, click its Minimize button to shrink it to a button on the taskbar. (You may want to select the Start Minimized check box first, to tell Windows to minimize the Magnifier Settings dialog box whenever you start Magnifier.) Don't click Exit unless you want to stop seeing the magnification window on your screen. You can redisplay the Magnifier Settings dialog box by right-clicking the magnification window and choosing Options from the shortcut menu or by clicking its button on the taskbar. Close the magnification window by closing the Magnifier Settings dialog box or by right-clicking the magnification window and choosing Exit.

 Deselect the Show Magnifier check box to turn off the magnification window temporarily; click it again to display the window again.

Listening to Microsoft Narrator Read the Screen Out Loud

For vision-impaired users, a screen reader can be the best way to find out what's on the computer display. Windows XP comes with a rudimentary screen-reading program called Microsoft Narrator. Narrator is designed to work with most parts of Windows XP itself, but may not work with other programs. The program says the items in the active window, including text, buttons, lists, and other things, using a computer-generated voice.

To start it, choose Start | All Programs | Accessories | Accessibility | Narrator. (From the keyboard, press WINDOWS or CTRL-ESC to display the Start menu, press *R* to choose Run, type **narrator**, and press ENTER.) Read (or listen to) the explanatory dialog box, select the Do Not Show This Message Again check box, and click OK. You see (and hear) the Narrator dialog box, shown here:

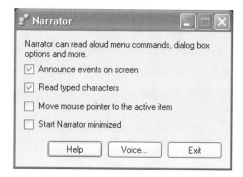

You can control these aspects of Narrator from the Narrator dialog box:

■ **Voice** Click the Voice button to choose which preprogrammed voice to use and how fast, high, and loud the voice speaks.

■ **What to read** Select the Announce Events On Screen check box to hear when something changes on the screen and the Read Typed Characters check box to hear what you type.

■ **Mouse movement** Select the Move Mouse Pointer To The Active Item check box to make the mouse pointer follow the "focus" (that is, what item on the screen is active).

You can also use the following keyboard shortcuts with Narrator:

Keyboard Shortcut	Action
CTRL-SHIFT-ENTER	Hear information about the active item.
CTRL-SHIFT-INSERT	Hear details about the active item.
CTRL-SHIFT-SPACEBAR	Hear all the information in the active window.
ALT-HOME	Hear the title bar of the active window.
ALT-END	Hear the status bar of the active window. (This feature does not work for all programs).
CTRL	Silence the Narrator.

Useful Keyboard Shortcuts

If you prefer using the keyboard to the mouse, you may want to try the following key combinations, which many but not all programs support:

- **ALT-SPACEBAR** Displays the system menu, from which you can choose to close, minimize, restore, maximize, or move the current window.
- **ALT-F4** Closes the current program.
- **ALT-TAB or TAB** Switches to another running program. Keep pressing TAB or ALT-TAB to cycle through all the programs that are running.
- **CTRL-C** Copies the selected information to the Clipboard.
- **CTRL-V** Copies the current contents of the Clipboard to the current position of the cursor.
- **CTRL-A** Selects all the information in the window.
- **CTRL-F4** Closes the current window. CTRL-W performs the same task in some programs.
- **SHIFT-F10** Displays the shortcut menu (the same menu you would see if you right-clicked at the current position of the mouse).
- **ESC** Cancels the current dialog box (the same as clicking the Cancel button).
- **ENTER** Clicks the currently selected button.
- **WINDOWS or CTRL-ESC** Displays the Start menu.
- **WINDOWS-L** Locks the computer.
- **WINDOWS-U** Displays the Utility Manager (see "Turning On and Off Magnifier, Narrator, and the On-Screen Keyboard by Using the Utility Manager").

Once you have Narrator configured as you like it, select the Start Narrator Minimized check box in the Narrator dialog box to minimize it in the future. Also take a look at the "Useful Keyboard Shortcuts" sidebar.

Setting Mouse Accessibility Options

If you have difficulty using a mouse or other pointing devices, if your pointing device is broken, or if you don't like to use it, turn on MouseKeys. If you have trouble using a keyboard and mouse for input, you can let Windows know you use an alternative input device. Windows also includes a number of keyboard shortcuts for giving commands from the keyboard (see "Useful Keyboard Shortcuts").

 Note *Other mouse settings—including button configuration, double-click speed, and mouse pointer speed—are available on the Mouse Properties dialog box (see Chapter 12, section "Configuring Your Mouse"). See Chapter 13 for information on installing other pointing devices.*

Controlling the Pointer by Using the Number Pad

MouseKeys enables you to control the mouse pointer by using the numeric keypad on your keyboard. The regular mouse or other pointing device continues to work as well. To turn on MouseKeys, choose Start | Control Panel | Accessibility Options, run the Accessibility Options icon, click the Mouse tab, select the Use MouseKeys check box, and click the Settings button to display the Settings For MouseKeys dialog box, shown in Figure 16-6. You can set these options:

- **Use Shortcut** Turns MouseKeys on or off when you press LEFT ALT-LEFT SHIFT-NUM LOCK (hold down the ALT and SHIFT keys that appear on the left side of the keyboard near the *X* and *Z* keys, and also press the NUM LOCK key). When you turn MouseKeys on using the keyboard shortcut, Windows displays a little dialog box.

- **Top Speed** Sets the pointer's top speed when you hold down keys to move it.

- **Acceleration** Sets the speed at which the pointer accelerates when you hold down a key to move it. A faster rate of acceleration means the pointer reaches its top speed sooner.

- **Hold Down Ctrl To Speed Up And Shift To Slow Down** Gives you more ways to control the speed of the mouse pointer. When this option is selected, you can hold down CTRL when you want the pointer to move in big jumps across the screen, and hold down SHIFT when you want the pointer to move in smaller-than-usual increments.

- **Use MouseKeys When NumLock Is On/Off** Determines when the number pad keys move the mouse pointer—when NUM LOCK is on or off. If you choose

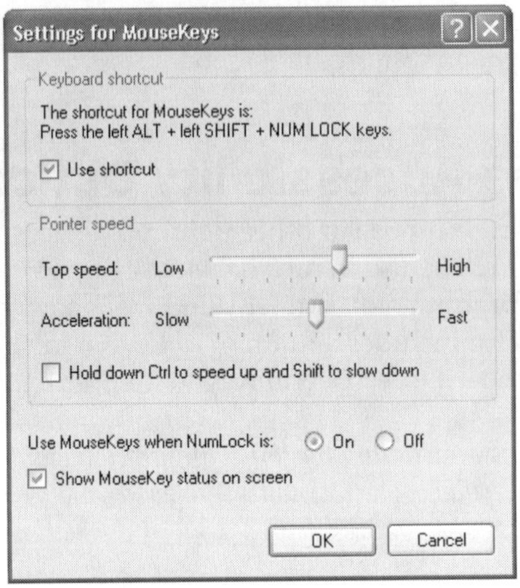

Settings for MouseKeys

Keyboard shortcut

The shortcut for MouseKeys is:
Press the left ALT + left SHIFT + NUM LOCK keys.

☑ Use shortcut

Pointer speed

Top speed: Low |————————⊔————————| High

Acceleration: Slow |———————⊔———————| Fast

☐ Hold down Ctrl to speed up and Shift to slow down

Use MouseKeys when NumLock is: ⦿ On   ○ Off
☑ Show MouseKey status on screen

[OK]   [Cancel]

Figure 16-6.   *The Settings For MouseKeys dialog box*

the Off setting, then you can enter numbers by using the number pad when NUM LOCK is on. However, you need another set of arrows to move the cursor. (Most keyboards have a separate set of cursor motion keys.)

■ **Show MouseKeys Status On Screen**   Displays a small graphic in the notification area on the taskbar to the left of the time, as shown here:

The following list shows how to use the number pad to control the pointer when MouseKeys is on (be sure to use the keys on the numeric keys, not the equivalent keys elsewhere on your keyboard):

■ Press the arrow keys to move the pointer.

■ Press the – key to set MouseKeys to click the right mouse button whenever you press the 5 key.

■ Press the / key to set MouseKeys to click the left mouse button whenever you press the 5 key.

■ Press the * key to set MouseKeys to click both mouse buttons whenever you press the 5 key.

- Press the 5 key to click (with left or right mouse button, depending whether you last pressed – or /) whatever the pointer is on.

- Press the + key to double-click whatever the pointer is on.

- Press the 0 or INSERT key to begin dragging (the equivalent of holding down the mouse button). Move the item by pressing the arrow keys on the number pad. Drop the item (release the mouse button) by pressing the "." or DELETE key.

Configuring an Alternative Input Device

If you're using an alternative input device (something other than the keyboard and a mouse), and you want to connect that device to a serial port, turn on the Use Serial Keys option on the General tab of the Accessibility Options dialog box (shown in Figure 16-7). Choose Start | Control Panel | Accessibility Options, run the Accessibility Options program, and click the General tab if it's not selected. Use the Settings button to choose the serial port and baud rate for the device.

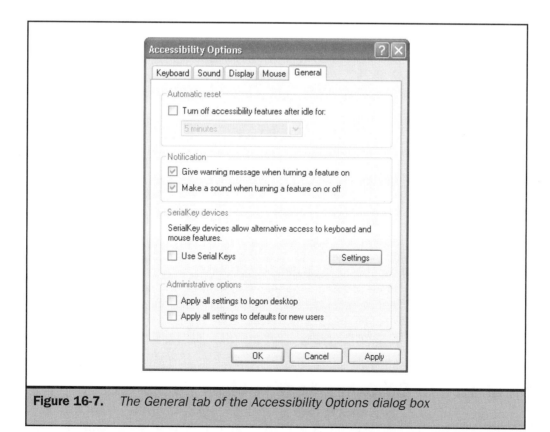

Figure 16-7.   *The General tab of the Accessibility Options dialog box*

Turning Accessibility Options Off and On

In general, you probably want to turn on whichever accessibility options you find useful, and leave them turned on but, if you share your computer, you may want the capability to turn them on and off easily.

Turning On and Off Magnifier, Narrator, and the On-Screen Keyboard by Using the Utility Manager

Windows XP has a new way to turn the Magnifier, Narrator, and On-Screen Keyboard on and off: the Utility Manager. Press WINDOWS-U to see it:

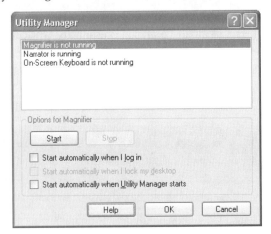

You can also start the program by choosing Start | All Programs | Accessories | Accessibility | Utility Manager. You can turn on your accessibility options by pressing WINDOWS-U when you see the Welcome To Windows logon screen, before you even log on.

The Utility Manager shows which of the three programs are running. You can stop or start a program by clicking it and clicking the Start or Stop button. You can also use check boxes in the Utility Manager window to start each of the three programs when you log on, when you lock the desktop (by pressing WINDOWS-L), or whenever you run the Utility Manager. Click a program, and then select the options for that program.

Narrator is usually configured to start automatically when you open the Utility Manager window, so don't be surprised when your computer starts reading the screen to you.

Turning On and Off Other Accessibility Features

The General tab of the Accessibility Options dialog box (shown in Figure 16-7) has some options for turning accessibility options off and on. Choose Start | Control

Panel | Accessibility Options, run the Accessibility Options program, and click the General tab if it's not selected.

■ **Turn off after the computer is idle** If more than one person uses the computer, you may want the accessibility options turned off when it has been idle for a certain interval. The Turn Off Accessibility Features After Idle For option on the General tab enables you to choose how long the computer must be idle before all accessibility options are turned off. If you always want accessibility options to remain on, make sure this option is not selected.

■ **Beep when settings change** You may also want notification when accessibility options are turned on or off. The Notification options enable you to see a message when an accessibility feature is turned on and to hear a sound when an accessibility option is turned on or off.

■ **Turn on accessibility options for Welcome logon screen** If you need accessibility options, you'd probably like them to be available during Windows logon (unless you don't use a logon screen—see Chapter 6 for logging onto a multiuser computer, and Chapter 27 for logging onto networks. You must be logged on with an administrative account to change this setting.

■ **Apply settings to new users** If your computer is set up for multiple users, apply the same accessibility settings to any new accounts. You must be logged on with an administrative account to change this setting.

After you activate an accessibility option and enable its shortcut by using the Accessibility Options dialog box, you can turn the option on and off by using these keys:

Setting	How to Toggle On and Off
FilterKeys	Hold down SHIFT for eight seconds
High Contrast mode	Press LEFT ALT-LEFT SHIFT-PRINT SCREEN
MouseKeys	Press LEFT ALT-LEFT SHIFT-NUM LOCK
StickyKeys	Press SHIFT five times
ToggleKeys	Hold down NUM LOCK for five seconds

Making Internet Explorer Accessible

Internet Explorer 6.0, which comes with Windows XP, has additional accessibility features you can use:

■ **Keyboard** Press TAB and SHIFT-TAB to cycle among the active parts of the Internet Explorer window, including links and buttons. The selected item is highlighted with a dotted-line box.

CONFIGURING WINDOWS
FOR YOUR COMPUTER

■ **Display**   Internet Explorer can use the font sizes and formatting you choose, even if they are different from those specified in the Web page (see Chapter 24, section "Choosing Fonts").

To choose other accessibility options, choose Tools | Internet Options on the Internet Explorer menu bar and click the Advanced tab. In the list of settings that appears, you can select or deselect these settings:

■ **Always Expand ALT Text For Images**   (in the Accessibility section) Turn this setting on to display the entire ALT (alternative) text supplied on some Web pages as captions for pictures, so a screen reader can read the caption.

■ **Move System Caret With Focus/Selection Changes**   (in the Accessibility section) Turn this on so the cursor moves along with the mouse pointer and a screen reader or magnifier program can read or display the right part of the Internet Explorer window.

■ **Enable Page Transitions, Use Smooth Scrolling**   (in the Browsing section) Turn these off to make screen readers and voice recognition programs work better.

■ **Play Animations In Web Pages, Play Videos In Web Pages, Show Pictures**   (in the Multimedia section) Turn these off if your vision is impaired and you want to speed up Web browsing.

■ **Play Sounds In Web Pages**   (in the Multimedia section) Turn this off if sounds are annoying or interfere with your screen reading program.

■ **Print Background Colors and Images**   (in the Printing section) Turn this off for clearer printouts.

The Complete Reference

Windows XP

Part IV

Working with Text, Numbers, Pictures, Sound, and Video

The Complete Reference

Chapter 17

Working with Documents in Windows XP

lthough word processing isn't glamorous, it is, and probably forever will be, one of the most popular uses for a computer. Windows XP comes with two tools for working with text documents—the first is the unsophisticated Notepad, and the second is the surprisingly powerful WordPad. This chapter discusses both.

This chapter also covers two other useful utilities: Calculator and Character Map. The Calculator provides all the scientific functions you may need from a calculator, and Character Map gives you access to a variety of special characters.

Reading Text Files with Notepad

Notepad is a holdover from Windows 3.0. Back in the Windows 3.0 era, configuration information was stored in text files that regularly needed to be edited, and Notepad could edit those files. In subsequent releases of Windows, editing configuration files has become a task more often done either automatically by installation programs or manually by system administrators and hackers than by people simply trying to make their computers work the way they want.

Notepad, however, remains available in Windows XP and using it is the simplest way to edit a *text file* (also called an *ASCII file*)—that is, files that contain only letters, numbers, and special characters that appear on the keyboard. Sure, you can use a full-fledged word processor, but doing so is often more trouble than it's worth. Notepad can't format your text with bold, italics, or anything else pretty, but we've been known to use Notepad to edit Web pages, and it's invaluable for storing little snippets of text you might need later.

Running Notepad

To run Notepad, choose Start | All Programs | Accessories | Notepad. (Or, you can choose Start | Run to display the Run dialog box, and then type **notepad** and press ENTER.) Notepad looks like Figure 17-1: just a window with a menu.

The following sections offer some information about Notepad and tips on using it.

Copying, Moving, and Pasting Text

You can copy or move text to or from the Windows Clipboard using the Edit | Copy, Edit | Cut, and Edit | Paste commands (see Chapter 5, section "Cutting, Copying, and Pasting").

Document Settings

To change the setup of the document when you print it, choose File | Page Setup (this command isn't available if you haven't installed a printer in Windows). Use the Page Setup dialog box (shown in Figure 17-2) to change margins, page orientation, and paper size. (In the Orientation box, Portrait prints on paper in the usual way.

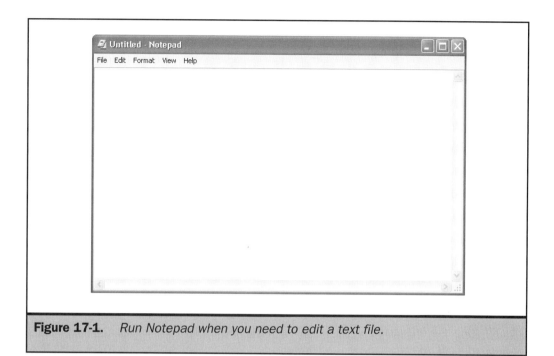

Figure 17-1.   *Run Notepad when you need to edit a text file.*

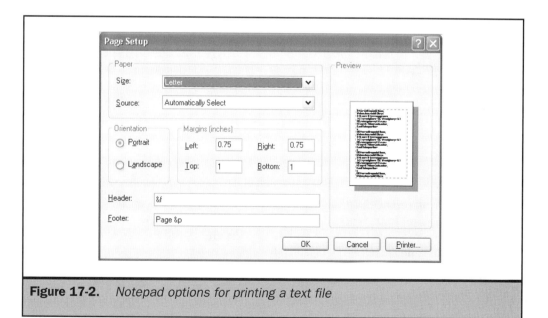

Figure 17-2.   *Notepad options for printing a text file*

Code	Meaning
&f	Displays the name of the file
&p	Displays the page number
&d	Displays the current date
&t	Displays the current time
&&	Displays an ampersand
&l	Left-justifies the text after this code
&c	Centers the text after this code
&r	Right-justifies the text after this code

Table 17-1.   *Header and Footer Codes in Notepad*

Landscape prints sideways on the page, with the lines of text parallel to the long edge of the paper.) If you have more than one printer, you can select the one to use. Use the Header and Footer text boxes to add headers and footers to your documents. You can type plain text, or you can use the codes in Table 17-1.

File Types

Choose File | Open to see the Open dialog box. Change the Files Of Type option to All Files if the file you want to open does not have the .txt extension.

Fonts

Notepad normally uses a fixed-pitch font to display text files. You can change the font by choosing Format | Font to display the Font dialog box and then setting the font, style, and size.

Log Files

Create a log file by typing **.LOG** in the top-left corner (the very beginning) of your Notepad file (be sure to use capital letters). Each time you run Notepad and open the file, Notepad enters the current time and date at the end of the file. You can then type an entry for that time and date.

Printing

Print the text file by choosing File | Print. Notepad prints the file with the filename at the top of each page and a page number at the bottom, unless you choose File | Page Setup and change the Header and Footer settings.

Saving Files

Save the text file you are editing by choosing File | Save. To save it with a name you specify, choose File | Save As to display the Save As dialog box (see Chapter 2, section "Open, Save As, and Browse Dialog Boxes").

Searching for Text

You can search for a string of text by choosing Edit | Find or press CTRL-F to display the Find dialog box, and then typing the string you're looking for into the Find What text box. Click the Match Case check box if you want Notepad to find only text that matches the capitalization of the text you typed. You can also specify whether to search forward or backward in the file by clicking the Up or Down radio button. Start the search by clicking the Find Next button. To search for the same string again, press F3 or choose Edit | Find Next.

If you want to replace text, choose Edit | Replace or press CTRL-H to display the Replace dialog box. Type the string you're looking for into the Find What text box, and type the string you want to use as the replacement in the Replace With text box. Click Find Next to find the first instance of the string. You can replace all occurrences by clicking Replace All, or you can pick and choose by clicking Replace (if you want to replace the text) or Find Next if you want to skip an instance. The Replace dialog box, like the Find dialog box, provides a check box to use if you want to match the case of the Find What and Replace With strings.

Moving Around Text Files

You can move quickly through a large file by using the Go To option—choose Edit | Go To or press CTRL-G to display the Go To Line dialog box. Enter the line number that you want to go to and either click OK or press ENTER. The dialog box disappears, and the cursor moves to the specified line.

If you want to know where you are in a document, you may find the status bar useful—it displays the cursor position in lines and columns (Ln 4, Col 6 is the sixth character on the fourth line in the document). Display the status bar by choosing View | Status Bar.

Time and Date

You can insert the current time and date (according to your computer's clock) at the cursor by choosing Edit | Time/Date, or by pressing F5.

Undo

If you make a mistake, you can reverse your last edit by choosing Edit | Undo or pressing CTRL-Z.

Word Wrap

As you work with a document, you might want to turn on the *Word Wrap*, so that Notepad breaks long lines to fit in the Notepad window. When Word Wrap is off, each paragraph appears as a single long line (unless it contains carriage returns). Turn on (or off) Word Wrap by choosing Format | Word Wrap. Notepad then wraps lines the way a word processor wraps lines, so no line is wider than the Notepad window. The Notepad Word Wrap feature doesn't add carriage return characters to the text file when you save it and it doesn't affect the way the file appears when printed.

Files You Can Edit with Notepad

The standard file extension for text files is .txt. When you click or double-click a .txt file in Windows Explorer, Windows runs Notepad to view the file.

Windows associates a number of other types of files with Notepad, too, because these files contain only text and are usually small enough for Notepad to handle. These file types include

- Configuration files, such as files with the extension .ini (see Chapter 37, section "Windows Initialization Files")
- Log files, such as the logs that the Backup program creates (see Chapter 9)
- Log files, with the extension .log, which many housekeeping programs create
- Setup information files, which come with many installation programs and have the extension .inf

Taking Advantage of Free Word Processing with WordPad

WordPad is a great little word processor if your needs are modest—and the price can't be beat! Open WordPad by choosing Start | All Programs | Accessories | WordPad. (Or, you can choose Start | Run to display the Run dialog box, type **wordpad**, and press ENTER.)

WordPad (shown in Figure 17-3) does not offer many of the advanced features that you get in Microsoft Word or Corel's WordPerfect—notably missing is a spell check—but WordPad does offer many of the formatting tools you need to create a spiffy letter, memo, or essay. Many of the commands and keyboard shortcuts are the same as those in Microsoft Word, which makes them easy for many people to remember. The version of WordPad that comes with Windows can open documents created by versions of Word up through Word 2002 (Word 10). And, because WordPad is a small program, it loads quickly.

 Display WordPad online help by pressing F1 when WordPad is open.

Opening and Saving Files with WordPad

With WordPad you can open and edit a document that is saved in any one of a variety of formats, including documents saved with Word 97, 2000, and 2002 (WordPad cannot preserve all of Word's formatting, however). To open a document, choose File | Open,

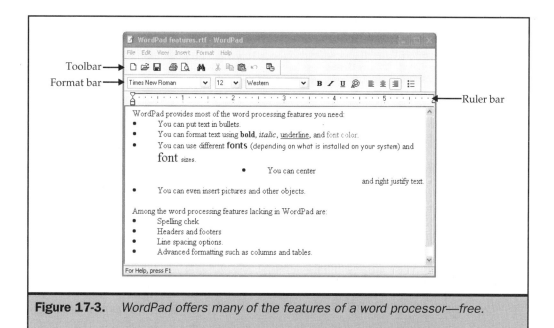

Toolbar

Format bar

Ruler bar

Figure 17-3.   *WordPad offers many of the features of a word processor—free.*

and use the Files Of Type option on the Open dialog box to choose the type of document you want to open.

When you save a document to pass on to a friend or coworker, choose File | Save to use the existing filename, or choose File | Save As to specify the filename. Be sure to save the document in a format that your friend's or coworker's software can open. Here's a rundown of the file formats WordPad can use to save a document:

- **Rich Text Format**   If you want to preserve any formatting you've done in your WordPad document, save it in Rich Text format. *Rich Text Format (.rtf)* is compatible with just about anything.

- **Text Document**   When you save a file in text format (with the extension .txt), you lose all formatting, but you preserve all text in the *ANSI* character set (a standard set of codes used for storing text).

- **Text Document—MS-DOS Format**   When you save a file in MS-DOS text format (also with the extension .txt), you lose all formatting, but you preserve all text in Microsoft's extended ASCII character set, which includes various accented characters and smiley faces. Use this format only if you want to use the text in a Windows or DOS application, but not if you plan to send the file to a Mac, UNIX, or other non-Microsoft system.

- **Unicode Text Document**   *Unicode* enables you to use characters from practically every language on Earth, from Latvian to Japanese. But make sure your recipient has a Unicode-compatible program before you save Unicode documents.

Formatting with WordPad

Use the options on the format bar (the row of buttons below the toolbar) to format a document in WordPad. If you don't see the format bar (or WordPad's other bars—the toolbar, ruler bar, or status bar), use the View menu to display them.

Formatting in WordPad works like this:

- Select the text you want to format, using your mouse. Or, choose Edit | Select All (or press CTRL-A) to select the entire document.
- Click the button or give the command for the type of formatting you want to apply.

The following sections describe some of the formatting options in WordPad.

Bullets

To format a paragraph with a bullet, click anywhere in the paragraph and click the Bullets button at the very end of the format bar, or choose Format | Bullet Style. To format more than one paragraph, select the paragraphs before clicking the Bullets button.

Indents

To indent a paragraph, click in the paragraph (or select several paragraphs) and choose Format | Paragraph to display the Paragraph dialog box. You can type a measurement from the left or right margin, or for the first line only. You can also specify that the paragraph is left aligned, right aligned, or centered. When you click OK, the margin indicators on the ruler bar move to show the current margins for the paragraph in which your cursor is located.

Tabs

You can set tab stops by clicking the ruler bar. If the ruler bar isn't already displayed, choose View | Ruler to display it. Be sure to select the text for which you need the tabs (press CTRL-A to select all text in the document) before you create tabs, because the tabs you create only apply to the paragraph the cursor is in if no text is selected. To set tab stops, click the ruler where you want a tab stop. L-shaped markers appear at each tab stop. Drag the L-shaped tab markers left or right on the ruler bar to adjust the tab stops. To delete a tab stop, drag it down off the ruler bar.

Alternatively, choose Format | Tabs to display the Tabs dialog box. Set a tab stop by typing a measurement from the left margin and clicking the Set button (if you're not sure what to use, every 0.5 of an inch is pretty standard). The tab stop appears on the list of tab stops that are set for the current position in the document. Type additional measurements from the left margin and click Set to set more tab stops. To delete a tab stop, select it from the list and click the Clear button. When you click OK, little L-shaped tab indicators appear on the ruler bar to show the location of tab stops.

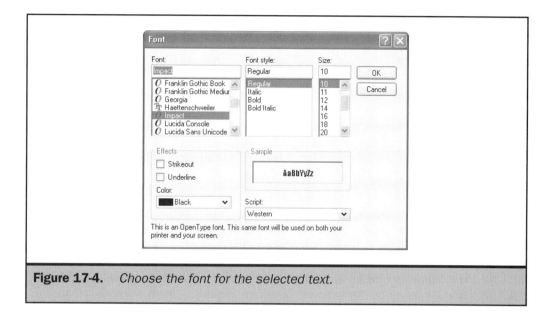

Figure 17-4.   *Choose the font for the selected text.*

Text: Fonts, Size, and Color

To change the font, font size, or color of the selected text, click the Font or Font Size box on the format bar and choose the font or font size from the list that appears. Or, choose Format | Font to display the Font dialog box, shown in Figure 17-4. Choose the font, font size, color, and whether you want the text to be bold, italic, underlined, or struck out. If you have installed multilanguage support, you can also choose the script (alphabet). Then click OK. You can also choose settings from the Font dialog box without selecting text, before you type the text you want to format; use the Font dialog box again to turn the formatting off.

You can also format text by using keystroke combinations: CTRL-B to bold, CTRL-I to italicize, and CTRL-U to underline. You can use these keystrokes after you select text or before you type the text you want to format (press the key combination again to turn off the formatting).

Printing Your WordPad Document

To print your document, click the Print button (the fourth button on the toolbar) or choose File | Print or press CTRL-P. You see the Print dialog box, in which you can select the printer, which pages to print, and the number of copies.

You may want to preview (see exactly what it will look like on paper) the document before you print it so you'll know exactly how it will look on paper. To preview your document, click the Print Preview button (the fifth button on the toolbar), or choose File | Print Preview. The WordPad window shows approximately how the

WORKING WITH TEXT, NUMBERS, PICTURES, SOUND, AND VIDEO

printed page will look. You can click the Zoom In button to get a closer look, click Print to begin printing, or click Close to return to the regular view of your document.

You can also format the page by choosing File | Page Setup to display the Page Setup dialog box. Use the Page Setup dialog box to change margins, paper orientation, and paper size.

WordPad Extras

WordPad has a few additional features you may find useful.

Copying, Moving, and Pasting Text

Use the Windows Clipboard to copy and move text within WordPad, and between WordPad and other applications (see Chapter 5, section "Cutting, Copying, and Pasting"). Choose Edit | Copy, click the Copy button on the toolbar, or press CTRL-C to copy selected text to the Clipboard. Choose Edit | Cut, click the Cut button on the toolbar, or press CTRL-X to move selected text to the Clipboard. Choose Edit | Paste, click the Paste button on the toolbar, or press CTRL-V to copy information from the Clipboard to the current cursor location. If you are pasting information other than text into your document, choose Edit | Paste Special to choose how the information should appear.

Date and Time

Insert the current date and time into your document by clicking the Date/Time button, the last button on the toolbar, or by choosing Insert | Date And Time. The Date And Time dialog box appears, from which you can choose the format for the date, time, or both.

Inserting Objects

Insert an object (such as a picture) into a WordPad document by

- Dragging the object into the WordPad window from Windows Explorer
- Using Insert | Object and choosing the type of object you want to insert
- Pasting an object from the Windows Clipboard

You can see the properties of an object by clicking the object and choosing Edit | Object Properties, or by pressing ALT-ENTER. If you insert a picture, you can use WordPad's simple graphic editing commands by double-clicking the picture; the annotation toolbar appears at the bottom of the WordPad window. You can also move an object in your document by clicking and dragging it to a new location.

Searching for Text

You can search for text by using the Find (binoculars) button on the toolbar, by choosing Edit | Find, or pressing CTRL-F. Use the options on the Find dialog box to find only the whole word, or to match the case of the contents of the Find What text box. To search for the same information again, press F3, click the Find button, or choose Edit I Find Next. You can leave the Find dialog box open while you edit the document—click the document once to keep the found text selected; double-click to put the cursor where you click. Then, when you need the Find dialog box again, simply click it.

Replacing Text

You can replace specific text with other text throughout your document by choosing Edit I Replace or pressing CTRL-H. You see the Replace dialog box. In the Find What box, type the text to be replaced. In the Replace With box, type the text to be inserted. You can select the Match Whole Word Only and Match Case check boxes to tell WordPad which instances of the text to match. Click Find Next to find the next instance of the text in the Find What box, and then click Replace to replace this instance with the Replace With text. To replace all the rest of the instances in your document, click Replace All.

Undo

Undo your last action by clicking the Undo button, the second-to-last button on the toolbar, by choosing Edit I Undo, or by pressing CTRL-Z.

Setting WordPad Options

You can configure WordPad by choosing View I Options to display the Options dialog box (shown in Figure 17-5). Five tabs of this dialog box, the Text, Rich Text, Word, Write, and Embedded tabs, have the same options. Choose the tab for the type of document you're editing—most likely, Word, Rich Text, or Text. Use the Options tab

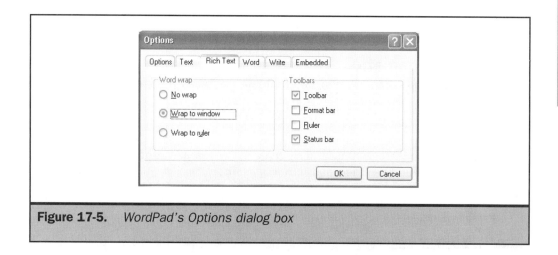

Figure 17-5.   *WordPad's Options dialog box*

to choose measurement units and automatic word selection. WordPad knows what kind of document you are editing based on the type of file you open.

Using Calculator

The Windows Calculator is actually two calculators: the unintimidating Standard Calculator that does simple arithmetic, and a more complicated Scientific Calculator. To use either of them, choose Start | All Programs | Accessories | Calculator. Switch from one calculator to the other by using the View menu.

Note
Calculator usually installs as part of Windows. If Calculator doesn't appear on the Start | All Programs | Accessories menu, you can install Calculator from the Windows XP CD-ROM (see Chapter 3, section "Installing and Uninstalling Programs that Come with Windows"). Calculator is in the Accessories And Utilities category, in the Accessories subcategory.

You can enter numbers into the calculator by clicking its buttons or by typing the numbers using the keyboard. If you misenter a digit, click the Calculator's Backspace button or press BACKSPACE on the keyboard. The CE button stands for Clear Entry (clear the current entry) and the C button stands for Clear (clear the current calculation).

You can use cut-and-paste to copy numbers from a document into the Calculator, do a calculation, and paste the result back into a document (see Chapter 5, section "Cutting, Copying, and Pasting").

Using the Standard Calculator

The Standard Calculator (which you switch to by choosing View | Standard) adds, subtracts, multiplies, divides, takes square roots, calculates percentages, and finds multiplicative inverses. It has a one-number memory.

Performing Arithmetic

To perform an arithmetic calculation, enter the calculation as you would type it, left to right, as in

    3 + 5 =

To compute a percentage, make the percentage the second number in a multiplication and don't use the equal sign. For example, to figure 15 percent of 7.4, enter

    7.4 × 15%

The $1/x$ button computes the multiplicative inverse of the displayed number.

Storing Numbers in Memory

The four buttons on the left side of the Standard Calculator control its memory. To store the currently displayed number in the memory, click the MS (memory store) button. An *M* appears in the box above the MC button to show the memory is in use. The memory holds only one number, so storing another number causes the calculator to forget the previously stored number. Clicking MC (memory clear) clears the memory. To recall the number stored in memory, click MR (memory recall). Clicking the M+ button adds the displayed number to the number in memory and stores the result in the memory.

 Use the memory to transfer a number from the standard to the scientific calculator or vice versa. The current display is cleared when you switch from one calculator to the other, but the memory is not cleared.

Using the Scientific Calculator

The Scientific Calculator (shown in Figure 17-6) is considerably larger, more powerful, and more complex than the Standard Calculator. Switch to it by choosing View | Scientific. Anything you can do on the Standard Calculator works exactly the same way on the Scientific Calculator, except the Scientific Calculator has no % or sqrt button. (Compute square roots by clicking x^2 when the Inv box is checked.) In addition, you can perform calculations in a variety of number systems, do logical operations, use trigonometric functions, and do statistical analyses.

Why Don't All the Buttons Work?

Some buttons on the Scientific Calculator only make sense in certain situations; in other situations, they are grayed out and clicking them does nothing. For example, the A–F

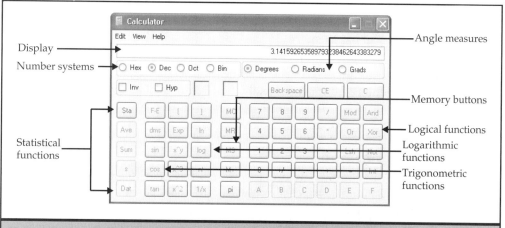

Figure 17-6.   *The Scientific Calculator displays a big piece of pi.*

WORKING WITH TEXT, NUMBERS, PICTURES, SOUND, AND VIDEO

buttons are numbers in the hexadecimal number system, so they don't work unless the Hex radio button is selected. The hexadecimal, octal, and binary number systems are set up for whole number calculations only, so the trigonometric function buttons are grayed out when the Hex, Oct, or Bin radio buttons are selected. The statistics buttons are grayed out when no data is loaded in the statistics box.

Number Systems and Angle Measures

The Scientific Calculator can work in Dec (decimal, the default), Bin (binary), Oct (octal), or Hex (hexadecimal) number systems. Choose among number systems by using the radio buttons on the left side of the top row. When you are working in the decimal number system, you can use the radio buttons just to the right of the number-system buttons to choose among the different ways of measuring angles: degrees (the default), radians, and gradients. When using degrees, the DMS button converts a decimal number of degrees into degrees-minute-seconds form. To convert back, check the Inv box and click DMS again.

When you are working in the binary, octal, or hexadecimal number systems, the radio buttons just to the right of the number system buttons enable you to select the range of whole numbers with which you will work. (In geek terms, this is the register size.) The choices are Byte (from 0 to 255, or 8 bits), Word (16 bits), Dword (double word, or 32 bits), and Qword (quadruple word, or 64 bits). The arithmetic in these systems is modular, so in hexadecimal with Byte register size

$2 - 3 =$

yields the answer FF rather than –1.

The F-E (fixed-exponential) button toggles between fixed-point notation and scientific notation. When entering a number in scientific notation, click the Exp button before entering the exponential part.

Trigonometric Functions

Trigonometric functions are computed with the Sin, Cos, and Tan buttons. Use the Inv and Hyp check boxes to compute inverse or hyperbolic trigonometric functions. The pi button (below the memory buttons) enters the first 32 digits of π. Because trigonometric functions almost never yield whole numbers, these buttons are grayed out in any number system other than decimal.

Logarithmic Functions

The Ln and Log buttons compute natural logarithms and base-10 logarithms, respectively. The Exp button *does not* compute exponentials. (It is used for entering numbers in scientific notation.) Compute exponentials by using Ln with the Inv box checked.

Statistical Functions

To use the statistical functions of the calculator, you must first enter a list of numbers, which constitutes the data. To enter a data list

1. Enter the first number in the calculator display.

2. Click the Sta button. The statistics buttons are activated and a statistics box opens.

3. Click the Dat button. The number in the calculator display appears in the statistics box.

4. Enter the rest of the data, clicking Dat after each entry.

Once you enter a data list, Ave computes the average of the entries, Sum computes their sum, and S computes their standard deviation.

You can see the statistics box at any time by clicking Sta. To edit the data list, use the buttons at the bottom of the statistics box: LOAD copies the highlighted number back to the calculator display, CD deletes the highlighted number from the data list, and CAD clears the data list.

Logical Functions

When the Bin radio button is chosen, the calculator works in the binary (base-2) number system and the buttons And, Or, and Not perform the bitwise logical operations their names suggest. The Xor button does exclusive or, and Lsh does a left shift. Perform a right shift by clicking Lsh with the Inv box checked.

Other Functions

The Int button finds the integer part of a number. When Inv is checked, the Int button finds the fractional part of a number.

Compute squares and cubes with the X^2 and X^3 buttons. Compute other powers with the X^y button.

The N! button computes factorials of integers. If the displayed number has a fractional part, N! computes a gamma function.

The Mod button does modular reductions, for example:

12 Mod 5 = 2

Getting Help

In addition to the Help Topics on the Help menu, you can find out what any button on the calculator does by right-clicking it and selecting "What's This?" from the menu that appears.

WORKING WITH TEXT, NUMBERS, PICTURES, SOUND, AND VIDEO

Using Special Characters with Character Map

Do you need to use unusual characters, like Æ, Ö, or ✺? The Character Map accessory can help you find them. Open Character Map by choosing Start | All Programs | Accessories | System Tools | Character Map. You see the Character Map window shown in Figure 17-7.

Note *If Character Map doesn't appear on the Start | All Programs | Accessories | System Tools menu, you can install Character Map from the Windows XP CD-ROM (see Chapter 3, section "Installing and Uninstalling Programs that Come with Windows"). It's in the Accessories And Utilities category, in the Accessories subcategory.*

To use a character from the Character Map

1. Select a font from the Font list. The characters available in this font appear in the Character Map window, arranged in a 20-column grid.

2. Double-click the character you want to use; or single-click it and click Select. The selected character is magnified and a copy of it appears in the Characters To Copy box.

3. When you have displayed all the characters you want from this font in the Characters To Copy box, click Copy. Character Map copies the characters to the Windows Clipboard (see Chapter 5).

4. Paste the characters into a document using a command in the program you use to edit that document. (Most programs use Edit | Paste or CTRL-V to paste from the Clipboard.)

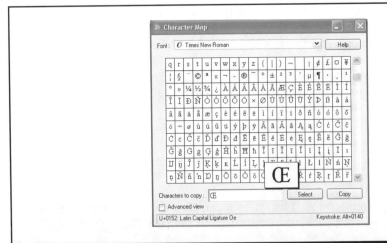

Figure 17-7. *The Character Map lets you use unusual characters.*

You can remove characters from the Characters To Copy box by clicking in the box and either backspacing over the characters or deleting them.

Another way to use many unusual characters is to select them in Character Map and notice the keystroke notation in the bottom-right corner of the Character Map window. Once you know this notation, you can produce the character in any document without running Character Map. For example, using the information in Figure 17-7 you could type a Œ character in any document as follows:

1. Open the document in a word processing program.

2. Set the font to Times New Roman.

3. Press the NUM LOCK on your keyboard.

4. While holding down the ALT key, type **0140**.

Chapter 18

Working with Graphics

431

Windows provides many tools for working with pictures and other images. This chapter tells you how to use these tools to view images on your monitor; add information to the images; create or edit image files; download images from digital cameras or scanners and print them, order prints of them over the Internet, publish them to the Web, or e-mail them to friends.

How Do Computers Handle Images?

For a computer to display, edit, or otherwise work with an image, that image has to be represented as data and stored in a file. In general, this is done by transforming the image into an array of small rectangles called *pixels*. Each pixel has only one color. If the pixels are small enough, the human eye doesn't notice this transformation, but if the rectangular components are visible the image is said to be *pixelated*. A number can represent the color of each pixel, and the list of all these numbers is then turned into a file.

A file created in this way is very large, but fortunately much of this information is redundant. (Very often, for example, pixels next to each other have similar colors.) This fact allows an image file to be compressed into a smaller file from which a computer can recreate the original image file when needed. This compression can be done in a variety of ways, depending on whether the purpose of the compression is to create the smallest possible file, to represent the image most accurately, or to perform the compression as quickly as possible. Each compression method produces a different image file format. The most popular image formats are .bmp, .pcx, .gif, .jpg, and .tif.

What Tools Does Windows Provide for Working with Images?

Windows XP gives you more tools for working with images than any previous version of Windows.

- **My Pictures folder** is a subfolder of My Documents. It is the natural place in the Windows filing system to keep digital photos, pictures, graphics, and other images. Microsoft has preconfigured the viewing options in the My Pictures folder to make it easy for you to sort through pictures.

- **Windows Picture And Fax Viewer** is the default application for viewing image files (see "Looking at Images with the Windows Picture And Fax Viewer"). You can also use it to annotate images stored in .tif files.

- **Microsoft Paint** is an application for drawing and coloring (see "Creating and Editing Images with Microsoft Paint"). It also allows you to crop photos or transform images from one file format to another.

■ **Scanner And Camera Wizard** sets up Windows to work with a scanner or digital camera (see "Downloading Images from Digital Cameras"). This Wizard starts automatically when you plug a digital camera into your computer's USB or other port.

■ **Photo Printing Wizard** leads you through the process of printing pictures on a printer (see "Printing Your Pictures at Home"). It produces pictures in all the standard photo sizes and arranges them on a page so that you get as many pictures as possible on each sheet of paper. Start this Wizard by selecting Print Pictures from the Picture Tasks section of the Task pane of the My Pictures folder, by right-clicking any image file and choosing Print from the shortcut menu, or by clicking the Print button on the toolbar of the Windows Picture And Fax Viewer.

■ **Web Publishing Wizard** helps you upload your pictures (or other files) to a free Web site where your friends and family anywhere in the world can view them (see "Sharing Your Pictures over the Internet"). Start this Wizard by displaying the file(s) you want to publish in an Explorer window and then selecting Publish This Folder To The Web from the Folder Tasks list on the Task pane.

■ **Online Print Ordering Wizard** leads you through the process of choosing an online photo service, sending them your image files, and placing an order for prints (see "Ordering Prints of Your Pictures via the Web"). Start this Wizard by selecting Order Prints Online from the Picture Tasks list of the Task pane of the My Pictures folder or any folder containing the pictures you want made into prints.

Viewing Images on Your Computer

Windows gives you two ways to view images: inside Explorer windows and using the Windows Picture And Fax Viewer.

Viewing Images in an Explorer Window

It is typically very hard to identify an image file by its name, especially if the name was assigned to the file automatically by a digital camera or scanner. Even if you rename the files yourself, the name seldom captures enough information to uniquely identify a single photo from, say, your Hawaiian vacation. For this reason, Explorer windows have two views that are much more convenient for examining folders of image files: Thumbnails view and Filmstrip view. Either can be selected from the View menu of an Explorer window.

Thumbnails view resembles the Tiles or Icons view, except that the icon that represents an image file is a small version of the image itself. These small images are themselves called *thumbnails*, which is how the view gets its name. Folders that contain images are represented by a folder icon surrounding four (or fewer) images from the folder, like this:

Moosehead Lake 2001

Filmstrip view is the default choice for the My Pictures folder. As the name suggests, this view arranges the files in a folder as if they were a filmstrip. As shown in Figure 18-1, thumbnail images of the folder's files appear in a linear order at the bottom of the screen, and the selected file is displayed in a larger window above. The two blue buttons below the selected image move the display forward and backward through the filmstrip. The other two buttons rotate the currently selected image 90 degrees clockwise or counterclockwise.

 If you want to use an image as your desktop background, right-click its icon in an Explorer window and select Set As Desktop Background.

Figure 18-1. *Filmstrip view is convenient for reviewing a folder of pictures.*

Figure 18-2. *The Windows Picture And Fax Viewer*

Looking at Images with the Windows Picture And Fax Viewer

Unless you have installed other graphics applications that have claimed image file types as their own, Windows opens image files using the Windows Picture And Fax Viewer, shown in Figure 18-2. The image resembles what you would see in the Filmstrip view in an Explorer window, but is larger and inside its own window. You also have a few more toolbar buttons to work with.

Picture And Fax Viewer can open files in a large number of formats: bitmap (.bmp), tagged image file or TIFF (.tif), JPEG (.jpg), GIF (.gif), Fax (.awd), PCX (.pcx), DCX (.dcx), XIF (.xif), and WIFF (.wif).

Changing What You See

Windows Picture And Fax Viewer gives you several tools to help you examine an image.

■ **The Zoom In and Zoom Out tools** (represented on the toolbar by magnifying glasses) adjust the magnification of the image. To use one of these tools, click its tool button. The cursor changes into a magnifying glass. Click in the image. The Zoom Out tool decreases the magnification of the image, while the Zoom In tool increases magnification and re-centers the image at the point where you clicked.

- **The Best Fit tool** (represented by a rectangle with arrows pointing outward from its corners) adjusts the size of the image to the size of the window. The image is made as large as possible within the bounds of the window. Adjusting the size of the window automatically adjusts the size of the image.

- **The Actual Size tool** (represented by a rectangle with arrows pointing inward to its sides) makes each pixel of the image equal a pixel on your monitor. This gives you the most accurate view of the image file. If the whole image does not fit within the window, scrollbars appear at the side of the window.

- **The Rotate Clockwise and Rotate Counterclockwise tools** are the most difficult icons to interpret. They are represented by a pair of triangles with a clockwise or counterclockwise arrow above them. Clicking either tool button rotates the image 90 degrees. To turn an image upside down, click either button twice. Unlike the Zoom and Size tools, the rotation tools change the image itself, not just your view of it. If you rotate an image and then save the file, the image will be rotated the next time you open the file.

Watching a Slide Show

The best way to view series of photos is to put them all into the same folder, open one with Windows Picture And Fax Viewer, and then click the Start Slide Show button, which resembles a small movie screen. The entire monitor is used to display the image. Click the left mouse button to move to the next image, or wait for the viewer to display the next "slide" automatically. Return to the view shown in Figure 18-2 by pressing the ESCAPE key.

The right and left arrow buttons in Figure 18-2 move you forward and backward through the image files in the same folder as the one you are displaying, just as the similar buttons do in Filmstrip view in Windows Explorer.

File Operations

The toolbar contains Delete, Print, Copy To, and Edit buttons. Delete sends the file to the Recycle Bin. Print starts the Photo Printing Wizard; Copy To opens a dialog box that lets you pick a folder to copy the file into; and Edit opens the default graphics editing application, which may be Microsoft Paint.

 You can use the Copy To tool to convert an image file to a different file type, for example to change a BMP file to TIFF or vice versa. Click the Copy To icon on the toolbar (it's a picture of a floppy disk) to display the Copy To dialog box. Change the Save As Type setting to the file format you want.

Adding Information to Digital Images

For as long as people have been taking photographs, they've also been writing on the backs of their prints so that they can keep track of information, such as where and when the picture was taken, who the people are, and so on. You can't write on the back of an image file, but Windows gives you two ways to attach extra information to a digital image: You can include this information in the file's properties, or (if the image is in TIFF format) you can add annotations to the image itself.

Adding Information to an Image File's Properties

Like any file, an image file has a properties box that you can open by right-clicking its icon and selecting Properties from the shortcut menu. The General tab of the Properties dialog box contains the same kind of information that is in any file's properties: the file's name, type, size, and so on. But the Summary tab of an image file's properties contains spaces you can use to record other important details about the picture. See the example in Figure 18-3.

Your camera or scanner may already have recorded quite a bit of technical information about the image without telling you. To see this information, click the

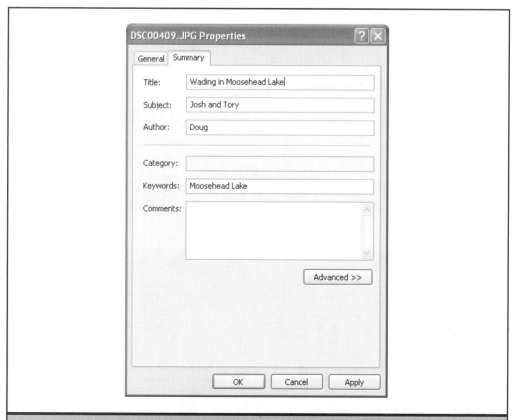

Figure 18-3.   *Typing information into the Summary tab of an image file's Properties is like writing on the back of a print.*

Advanced button on the Summary tab of the image's Properties dialog box. Return to the simple view of the Summary tab by clicking the Simple button.

Annotating an Image with Windows Picture And Fax Viewer

Windows Picture And Fax Viewer can add annotations to images in TIFF format. When you open a file of this file type in Windows Picture And Fax Viewer, the toolbar grows (as shown in Figure 18-4) to include annotation tools that let you draw on an image, highlight portions of the image, and add text comments. While you are annotating, the toolbar works exactly as described earlier in this chapter (see "Changing What You See").

The Select Annotation (arrow icon), New Freehand Annotation (curved line), and New Straight Line Annotation (straight line icon) tools are almost identical to the corresponding Paint tools.

Windows Picture And Fax Viewer has three rectangle-making tools: New Highlight Annotation (highlighter icon), which produces a translucent rectangle; New Frame Annotation (rectangle outline icon), which makes a hollow rectangle; and New Solid Rectangle Annotation (solid rectangle icon), which makes a filled rectangle. Figure 18-4 contains an example of a hollow rectangle.

Figure 18-4.   *Adding annotations to your pictures*

Two tools add text annotations: New Text Annotation adds text with a transparent background, and New Attached Note Annotation adds text with a colored background. Both work similarly to the Text tool of Paint: Click the tool button, then drag a rectangle on the image to create a box in which the text will appear. Click inside the box and start typing. The note in Figure 18-4 was made with the New Attached Note Annotation tool.

The annotations that Windows Picture And Fax Viewer adds to an image can be moved, edited, or deleted, even after they have been saved to a file. To change an existing annotation, click the Select Annotation (arrow icon) button on the Windows Picture And Fax Viewer toolbar, and then click in the annotation. A box appears around the annotation and the cursor changes to four crossing arrows. You may use the cursor to drag the annotation to another location on the image, or to resize the annotation by dragging a corner of the surrounding box.

To edit a Text or Attached Note annotation, select the annotation using the Select Annotation tool as in the previous paragraph. When the annotation has been selected, click inside the surrounding box to make an editing cursor appear.

Creating and Editing Images with Microsoft Paint

Microsoft Paint is to images what WordPad is to text documents—a simple but versatile tool for creating and editing files. You can use it to make diagrams for presentations or to crop your online vacation photos; your five-year-old can use it as a coloring book, or your ten-year-old can use it to draw moustaches on the Mona Lisa.

For more advanced editing of image files, as well as for converting files to different graphics formats, we recommend Paint Shop Pro, a shareware program you can download from the Internet (from **http://www.jasc.com**). Other graphics editing and conversion programs are available from the Consummate Winsock Applications Web site at **http://www.stroud.com**.

Note *If Paint doesn't appear on the Start | All Programs | Accessories menu, you can install Paint from the Windows XP CD-ROM (see Chapter 3, section "Installing and Uninstalling Programs that Come with Windows").*

To run Paint for the first time (or for the first time in a while) choose Start | All Programs | Accessories | Paint. Depending on how your file system is set up, Paint may be the default application for .bmp files or other image files. If so, Paint runs whenever you open one of these files. Figure 18-5 shows the parts of a Paint window.

The toolbar buttons are labeled with shapes that suggest their use. For example, the button that draws lines has a line on it. When the cursor passes over a tool button, a short description of the tool appears on the status bar.

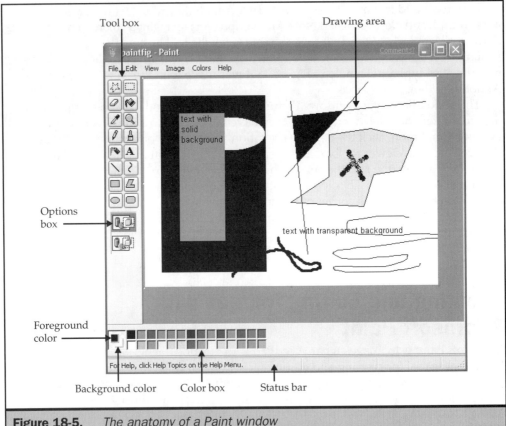

Figure 18-5.   *The anatomy of a Paint window*

Opening and Saving Files

Paint works with only one document at a time. Opening a file or creating a new one automatically closes whatever file Paint had been working on previously. Paint opens files in most popular image formats, including bitmap (.bmp), TIFF (.tif), JPEG (.jpg), and GIF (.gif). Files created or edited by Paint can be saved as bitmap files in a variety of color schemes (monochrome, 16 color, 256 color, and 24-bit color), as well other image formats.

Note   *By default, most image file types open in Windows Picture And Fax Viewer. Even if you have just created a file in Paint, opening its icon will open it in Windows Picture And Fax Viewer. To open an image file in Paint, right-click its icon and select Open With | Paint from the context menu.*

By default the File | Save command saves new files in the My Pictures folder inside My Documents, and it saves other files to the location from which they were opened. To save elsewhere, choose File | Save As.

Selecting Objects

With the Select tool chosen (by clicking the dotted rectangle button in the Tool box), you can select objects inside the drawing area, just as you select objects inside an Explorer window: by enclosing them in a rectangle. Move the pointer to one corner of the rectangular area that includes the objects you want to select, hold the mouse button down, move to the opposite corner of the area, and release the mouse button.

The Free-Form Select tool (the dotted star button in the Tool box) enables you to select objects and parts of objects inside a region of any shape. Drag the cursor to trace out any shape. Either close up the shape, or Paint closes it up automatically with a straight line. The enclosed region is now selected, and can be moved by dragging or copied by cutting-and-pasting—useful for creating repeated patterns.

Magnifying and Enlarging

To magnify the objects in your drawing, or zoom in on a portion of the drawing area, click the Magnifier tool (the magnifying-glass button in the Tool box). A rectangle appears in the drawing area, which represents the portion of the drawing that will be visible after magnification. Position the rectangle to enclose the area you want to zoom in on, and then click. The portion of the drawing that was inside the rectangle now fills the entire viewing area. To zoom back out, click the Magnifier tool again, and then click anywhere in the viewing area.

When the Magnifier tool is selected, the Options box displays four magnification levels: $1x$, $2x$, $6x$, and $8x$. The current level of magnification is highlighted. To change to another level of magnification, click that option in the Options box.

To enlarge or shrink the drawing area (the "sheet of paper"), drag its corners.

Drawing Lines and Curves

Clicking with the Line tool (the straight line button in the Tool box) nails down one end of a line; the other end moves with the cursor. When the line is where you want it, click again to fix the other end. To make a curved line, click the Curve tool (the wiggly line button in the Tool box) and begin by drawing a straight line, as you would with the Line tool. Then, click-and-drag a point on that line to make a curve. You have the option of dragging a second point to make another kink in the curve.

When the Line or Curve tools are selected, different line thicknesses appear in the Options box, just below the Tool box. Select a new thickness by clicking the line thickness you want.

WORKING WITH TEXT, NUMBERS, PICTURES, SOUND, AND VIDEO

When you click with the left mouse button, the Line and Curve tools draw in the foreground color. To draw lines and curves in the background color, use the right mouse button.

Drawing Freehand

Paint has four tools in the Tool box that make freehand marks as you drag them: Pencil, Brush, Spray Can, and Eraser. Pencil makes thin lines, Brush makes thick lines, and Spray Can sprays a pattern of dots. You can choose among three densities of Spray Can dot patterns by clicking the pattern you want in the Options box. As its name suggests, the Eraser erases anything in its path, replacing it with the background color.

Making Shapes

These four tools in the Tool box make shapes: Ellipse, Rectangle, Rounded Rectangle, and Polygon. The simplest shape to make is a rectangle:

1. Click the Rectangle tool (the solid—not the dotted—rectangle button).
2. Click in the drawing area where you want one corner of the rectangle located.
3. Drag to where you want the opposite corner of the rectangle located. When you release the mouse button, Paint creates the rectangle.

You use the Ellipse and Rounded Rectangle tools in a manner similar to the Rectangle tool.

The Polygon tool makes figures with any number of sides:

- Click the Polygon tool (the L-shaped polygon button).
- Click inside the drawing area where you want one corner of the polygon located.
- Each click defines the next corner of the polygon. For the first side, you must click-and-drag; for subsequent sides, just click.
- Double-click the last corner. Paint closes up the polygon automatically.

Coloring Objects

Control the colors of objects by using the Color box at the bottom of the Paint window. The two colored squares at the far left of the Color box show the current foreground and background colors, with the foreground square on top of the background square. Any object you construct using the left mouse button has the foreground color, whereas objects made using the right mouse button have the background color.

To choose a new foreground color, left-click the square of the new color in the Color box. To choose a new background color, right-click the square of the new color. You can match the color of any object in the drawing area by using the Pick Color tool (the eyedropper button in the Tool box). Select the tool, and then click the object whose color you want to match. Left-clicking changes the foreground color to match the object; right-clicking changes the background color to match the object.

To color within an outlined area, such as a rectangle or an ellipse, select the Fill With Color tool (the tipped paint can button), and click within the area. Right-click to fill with the background color. Using the Fill With Color tool on an area that is not outlined colors the whole "sheet of paper"—the area outside of any enclosed region.

Changing the foreground or background color does not change the color of objects already created. To change an object to the new foreground (background) color, select the Fill With Color tool and click (right-click) the object whose color you want to change. You can invert the colors in a region (that is, make a negative of the original) by selecting the region choosing Image | Invert Colors.

Adding Text

Click the Text tool (the button with the *A*), and drag across the part of your picture where you want the type to appear. Paint displays a rectangular text box for you to type in. A font selection box appears above the text box so you can select the font, size, and style of the text. The color of the text is the foreground color. Click inside the text box and type. Click outside the text box when you are done typing.

The Options box below the Tool box gives two choices for using the Text tool. The top choice makes a solid background for the text box, using the background color. The bottom choice makes a transparent background.

Flipping, Rotating, and Stretching

Commands on the Image menu flip, rotate, or stretch the entire image or a selected part of the image. Choosing Image | Flip/Rotate opens a dialog box from which you can choose to flip the image horizontally or vertically, or you can rotate it by any multiple of 90 degrees. Choosing Image | Stretch/Skew opens another dialog box from which you can stretch the image horizontally or vertically by any percentage, or slant it by any number of degrees.

Elements that you add to a flipped, stretched, slanted, or rotated drawing are normal. This feature allows you to mix elements of various types in a single drawing, as in Figure 18-5.

Cropping Images

You can crop an image—remove unwanted material around the edges of a picture. To crop an image, use the Select tool to enclose the area of the image that you want to keep. To save the selected area as a new file, choose Edit | Copy To. Type a new filename and click Save. The original image is unaffected.

Working with Digital Cameras and Scanners

From a user's point of view, scanners and cameras have little to do with each other. It would never occur to you, for example, to point your scanner at the Grand Canyon. But to a computer, scanners and digital cameras are very similar: Both turn visual information into image files. This is why these two types of devices share a Control Panel icon (Scanners And Cameras, which lives in the Printers And Other Hardware category) and a Wizard (the Scanners And Cameras Wizard) for installing them.

Setting Up a Scanner or Digital Camera

In order to work with a scanner or digital camera, Windows needs to have a driver program that tells it how to communicate with the device (see Chapter 13, section "What Are Drivers?"). Windows XP comes with drivers for most popular devices, so your installation process may be as simple as plugging your scanner or camera into the appropriate port (usually a USB or serial port), turning it on, and waiting for Windows to notice it. Installing a Sony DSC-S70 camera was just this easy when we tried it; Windows noticed the camera immediately and had it ready to go in less than a minute.

If the plug-in-and-wait technique doesn't work with your camera or scanner, put the CD that came with the camera or scanner into your CD-ROM drive and see whether a program runs that steps you through installing the drivers and related software.

If you still don't have drivers installed, try this:

1. Open the Scanners And Cameras icon from the Printers and Other Hardware category of the Control Panel.

2. Select Add An Imaging Device from the Imaging Tasks section of the Task pane. The Scanner And Camera Installation Wizard starts.

3. The Wizard asks you the manufacturer and model of your camera or scanner. If you can't find your camera or scanner on the Wizard's list, click the Have Disk button and be prepared to insert the floppy or CD that came with your hardware.

4. Tell the Wizard which port the device is connected to. The rest of the installation happens automatically. You may have to restart the computer before using your device.

You can test your scanner or digital camera by clicking its entry in the Scanners And Cameras window, clicking the Properties button, and then clicking the Test Scanner Or Camera button.

Many cameras and scanners come with additional software, beyond the drivers needed to allow Windows to work with the device. These additional programs may provide a "front panel" for the device (one of our scanners comes with a program that looks like the front of a photocopying machine) or graphics editing. You usually don't need this additional software to use your camera or scanner: you do need the drivers.

Even after you install your scanner or digital camera and it works fine, the Scanners And Cameras icon may not appear in the Control Panel. If you open the Scanners And Cameras window, your scanner or camera may not appear in the list of installed devices, either. The device may appear, however, in your System Properties dialog box: Choose Start | Control Panel | Performance And Maintenance | System, click the Hardware tab, and click the Device Manager button to display the Device Manager window (see Chapter 13, section "What Is the Device Manager?"). Look down the list of all installed devices—scanners and cameras appear in the Imaging Devices category. Older cameras and scanners may not be on the list, and you can't add them.

Downloading Images from Digital Cameras

A digital camera is also a disk drive in disguise. As you take pictures, the image files are stored on some device like a CompactFlash card, a floppy disk, or a Memory Stick. When you connect the camera to your computer, Windows assumes you want to do something with the files the camera is holding, so it displays the following box:

The default choice is to open the Scanner And Camera Wizard, which helps you download the pictures to a folder on your computer. If you want the Wizard to start automatically whenever you connect your camera to the computer, check the Always Do The Selected Action check box.

The Scanner And Camera Wizard takes you through the process of selecting which pictures to download and what folder to store them in. You can tell the Wizard to automatically delete the pictures from the camera after you download them, or you can leave them on the camera and deal with them later. After the pictures have been downloaded, you are given a choice to close the Wizard, publish the pictures to the Web using the Web Publishing Wizard, or order prints over the Web using the Online Print Ordering Wizard (see "Sharing Your Pictures over the Internet"). If you don't want to go straight into another Wizard, you will get the same publishing and ordering options when you open the folder that you downloaded the prints to.

If you would rather avoid the Scanner And Camera Wizard, you can select the Take No Action option when you plug in the camera. Instead, open My Computer; the camera should be listed among your disk drives. You can open its icon and move files to and from the camera as you would any other disk drive.

If you're on the road with nothing but a laptop and a digital camera, you can use the camera as a disk drive to back up a few important files. Strange, but true!

Downloading Images from Scanners

When you first connect your scanner to your computer, you may see the illustration shown in the preceding section, asking what you want Windows to do with images that arrive from the scanner. The preceding section also describes how you can use the Scanner And Printer Wizard to copy files from your scanner to your computer.

Alternatively, graphics programs can use your scanner to create images. Most scanners come with a *TWAIN* driver that adds an Acquire command to your graphics editor (for example, the Paint Shop Pro program gains a File | Import | TWAIN | Acquire command after you install a scanner driver). You can give this command to bring information from the scanner or camera into the program.

Run your favorite graphics editor (but not Microsoft Paint, which doesn't support TWAIN) and check whether it can acquire pictures directly from a scanner. Some programs start scanning as soon as you give the command, others display a dialog box in which you can set scanner parameters before you click a Scan button. When the scanner finishes, the picture appears on your screen. Use the graphics program's usual commands to edit and save the scanned image.

Linking Your Scanner or Digital Camera to a Program

In addition to graphics programs, some other types of programs accept digital graphic information directly from a scanner or camera. For example, a database program may accept a digital picture of a person for storage in a personnel database, and pressing the button on the camera can send the picture directly into the database. If both your scanner or camera and your program support this feature, you can tell Windows to run a program whenever you scan an image or take a digital picture. Follow these steps:

1. Display the Scanners And Cameras window (see "Setting Up a Scanner or Digital Camera").

2. Click the device and then the Properties button to display the Properties dialog box for that scanner or camera, as shown in Figure 18-6. Click the Events tab. (If the Events tab does not appear, your scanner or digital camera does not support linking to programs.)

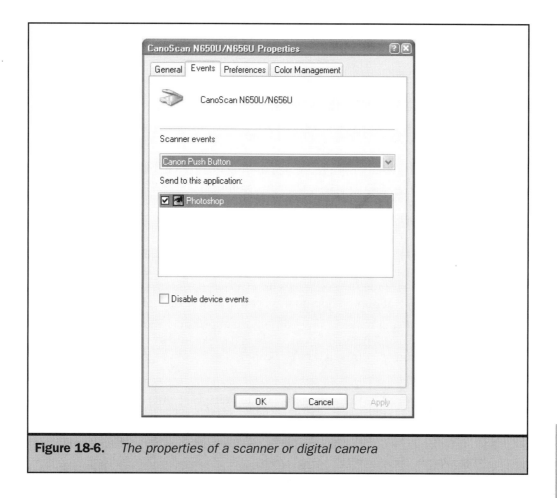

Figure 18-6. *The properties of a scanner or digital camera*

3. In the list of events to which the camera or scanner can respond, click an event.

4. In the Start This Program box, click the name of the program that will receive the image from the scanner or camera. Only programs that can accept digital images appear on the list.

5. Click OK.

Turning Images into Prints

A digital image file is convenient in many ways, but it's not very satisfying to carry one around in your wallet. For some purposes you still can't beat printing a picture on paper. An ordinary color printer can produce adequate pictures, especially if you use paper made for photographs. If you print a lot of photos and want high quality, you can get a special photo printer. Or, you can send your image files to a photo shop to be printed. You can even use the Online Print Ordering Wizard to order your prints over the Web.

Printing Your Pictures at Home

You can use any local or network printer to print your pictures. The quality of your prints depends on three factors:

- **The image file**   Paper is a more demanding medium than a computer monitor. Flaws in your pictures that don't seem significant on the screen are much more visible when you print. A rule of thumb is that you need about 2 million pixels (2 megapixels) to make a high-quality 5 × 7 print, and about 3 million to make an 8 × 10.

- **The printer**   Printers that do a perfectly good job on documents may not be adequate for pictures. A good general-purpose color printer will print your photographs reasonably well, but won't rival the prints you get from a photo shop. If you want photo-shop quality, you need a special photo printer.

- **The paper**   Paper makes a huge difference in printing photos, particularly if you have an ink-jet printer. Ink spreads as it soaks into low-quality paper, and that makes your pictures fuzzy. You can find good photographic paper at any camera store.

Windows includes a Photo Printing Wizard to help you print your pictures. Start the Wizard in any of these three ways:

- Right-click the icon of an image file in an Explorer window and choose Print from the shortcut menu,

- Select an image file in an Explorer window and choose Print This Picture from the Picture Tasks area on the Task pane, or

- Display an image with the Windows Picture And Fax Viewer and click the Print button on the toolbar.

The Photo Printing Wizard leads you through a process of selecting which pictures to print, choosing a printer (or installing one if none is installed), setting the number of copies to make of each picture, selecting print size, and laying out the pictures on the pages you print. Figure 18-7 shows how the Wizard arranges pictures on a sheet of paper.

Ordering Prints of Your Pictures via the Web

The most obvious way to get photo-shop quality prints is to order them from a photo shop. Many photo shops will print your pictures if you bring in a disk, but you can also

Figure 18-7.   *The Photo Printing Wizard arranges your pictures to use each sheet of paper efficiently.*

use the Online Print Ordering Wizard to order prints from an online photo service. The Wizard leads you through the process of selecting the pictures you want, then connects you with one of several online photo-printing services so that you can complete your order. The cost of the prints (plus a shipping fee) is charged to your credit card, and the prints are mailed to you or delivered by a courier service.

To order prints online, first assemble the pictures you want printed in a single folder. Then open that folder and select Order Prints Online from the Picture Tasks section of the Task pane. (We don't know of any way to start this Wizard if you don't have the Task pane displayed.)

The Wizard leads you through the following steps: selecting which pictures in this folder you want printed, choosing a printing service, and connecting you to that service. (You probably will have to choose between Kodak and Fuji, and all the prices we checked were the same.) You select the number and size of prints you want, give a mailing address and a credit card number. The image files are then uploaded to the service's computer.

Note   *Digital image files can be large, and upload speeds are not that fast. Even using a DSL Internet connection, it took us 10 minutes to upload 15 pictures taken with a 3.3 megapixel camera.*

WORKING WITH TEXT, NUMBERS, PICTURES, SOUND, AND VIDEO

Kodak also has an excellent photo-sharing and -printing service on the Web. Go to **http://www.ofoto.com** to sign up. As of fall 2001, you get 15 free prints when you open an Ofoto account.

Sharing Your Pictures over the Internet

The Internet is a great way to share photos. Making print copies of photos for all your friends and relatives can be terribly expensive, but it costs nothing to e-mail an image file to 20 people or to upload a picture to the Web where anyone who is interested can see it.

E-mail and the Web each have their advantages as a way of sharing pictures. In general, if you have a picture that you know a few people will want to see, e-mail it to them. On the other hand, if you have many pictures that many people may or may not want to see, put the pictures on a Web site and e-mail the Web address to people who you think are interested.

Be careful about sharing sensitive or confidential pictures over the Internet. When you give someone else a digital copy of a picture, for all practical purposes, you lose control of it. Your picture can spread like a rumor, and you have no way of knowing who ultimately will see it.

Publishing Your Pictures on the Web

You can store pictures or other files on Web servers and use a Web browser to retrieve them from any computer that is online. You can also give the Web address (and possibly a password, if the files are password protected) to other people so that they can see the files also.

You can get a small amount of Web storage space free from MSN. X-Drive offers storage, but it's not free. Kodak's Ofoto service (at **http://www.ofoto.com**) also provides free password-protected photo sharing along with its photo-printing services.

To upload files to the Web, do the following:

1. Collect the files and move or copy to a single folder.
2. Open that folder and click Publish This Folder To The Web in the File And Folder Tasks section of the task pane. The Web Publishing Wizard starts.
3. Answer the Wizard's questions.

The Wizard leads you through the process of choosing a Web hosting service for your files, and setting up how others will access them. Each service does this differently, and it goes beyond the scope of this book to describe how to use each service.

E-mailing Pictures to Your Friends

You don't need Windows XP to e-mail pictures to friends. You can use your e-mail program to create a message and then attach the picture to the message (see Chapter 23, section "What Are Attached Files?"). But Windows XP has a neat feature that can compress one or more pictures into a single file and e-mail it. Follow these steps:

1. In an Explorer window, select a picture or a folder of pictures. Or, select some pictures from a folder (click the first picture and CTRL-click the other pictures to add them to the selection).

2. In the File And Folder Tasks section of the Task pane, click E-mail This File, E-mail This Folder, or E-mail The Selected Items. Or, right-click the file(s) or folder and choose Send To | Mail Recipient from the shortcut menu that appears.

3. You see the Send Pictures Via E-Mail dialog box, asking whether you want to compress the files so that they transfer more quickly over the Internet:

4. Click Make All My Pictures Smaller if you are sending the files over a dial-up line, if the recipient uses a dial-up line, or if you are sending a lot of pictures. Otherwise, click Keep The Original Size.

5. If you want to choose the exact size of the pictures, click Show More Options and click a size.

6. Click OK. If you chose to resize or compress the files, Windows does so. If you are sending a folder, Windows compresses the files into a compressed folder (see Chapter 8, section "What Are Compressed Folders?").

7. Windows passes the files to your default e-mail program (Outlook Express or another e-mail program) and you see a new, blank message with the file(s) attached.

8. Address the message, type a subject line and text, and send the message as usual.

The Complete Reference

Windows XP

Chapter 19

Working with Sound

Early PCs weren't equipped to work with audio data, but since about 1998, most computers sold have come with a sound board and speakers, and some with a microphone. Like Windows Me/9X, NT, and 2000, Windows XP contains built-in support for audio devices—hardware that enables your computer to record and play sounds. In addition to better drivers for audio devices, Windows comes with Windows Media Player 8, which enables you to record or play audio and video files or disks.

This chapter provides an introduction to audio file formats, with instructions for configuring Windows to work with sound, using Windows Media Player, and using the older Sound Recorder. Chapter 13 describes how to install hardware, including audio hardware; this chapter explains how to configure and use these devices.

How Does Windows Work with Sound?

Almost all new computers come with a *sound board*, an adapter board inside the computer that lets you connect a microphone and either speakers or headphones to your computer for audio input and output or similar functions already on the computer's system board. Many programs use sound to alert you to events, like the musical snippets that you may hear when Windows starts or shuts down. You need sound capabilities to participate in Internet phone and voice chats and to listen to sound clips on the Web.

Windows plays sounds when certain events occur. You can associate a sound with a new event, or change the kind of sounds Windows plays, as described in the next few sections of this chapter. You can also play and record sounds by using the Sound Recorder or Media Player programs and play an audio CD in your CD-ROM by using the CD Player component of Windows Media Player.

What Are Common Sound File Formats?

For Windows to be able to save, edit, or play sound, it must be able to store audio information in files. Table 19-1 lists the most commonly used file formats for audio data.

To see the properties of any audio file, right-click the filename and choose Properties from the menu that appears. You see a Properties dialog box like the one shown in Figure 19-1.

The information on the General tab parallels that provided for almost any file: type, size, and attributes. The Summary tab displays the bit rate, audio sample size, and other formatting information.

What Is the My Music Folder?

Windows XP comes with a folder called My Music in your My Documents folder. The idea is for you to store your music files there for replay with Windows Media Player. The folder can contain subfolders for different types of music—Windows Media Player automatically creates new folders when you copy sound files from audio CDs. When

Medium	Input Device	Output Device	File Extensions for Popular Formats
Audio	Microphone, MIDI keyboard, synthesizers, line input	Speakers, headphones	.wav, .mp3, .m3u, .asx, .wax, and .wvx
Streaming audio	Microphone, MIDI keyboard, synthesizers, line input, usually downloaded from the Internet	Speakers, headphones	.ram, .ra (for RealAudio files), .asf, and .asx (for Advanced Streaming Format files)
MIDI	MIDI-compatible instrument	MIDI-compatible instrument, speakers, headphones	.mid, .midi, or .rmi

Table 19-1.   *Audio Devices and File Formats*

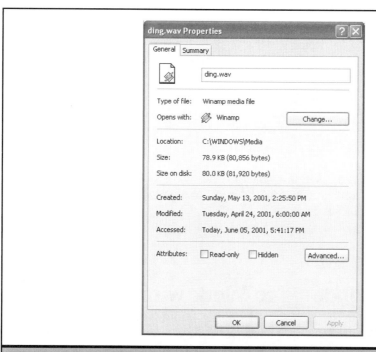

Figure 19-1.   *The properties of an audio file*

you display the My Music folder in an Explorer window, the Task pane includes two links just for sound files:

- **Play All**   Plays all the music in the folder (or just the selected files).
- **Shop For Music Online**   Displays the shopping section of Microsoft's WindowsMedia.com Web site in Internet Explorer. The site contains links to selected music e-tailer's Web sites.

What Is Streaming Audio?

Streaming audio is audio stored in a format for use over the Internet. When you want to play a streaming audio file over the Internet, your computer can start playing the file after downloading only the beginning of the file, and can continue to play the audio while the rest of the file downloads—optimally, downloading stays a step ahead of the player (the audio yet to be played is stored in a *buffer*. To play streaming audio files from the Internet, run Windows Media Player (see "Playing Sound Files with Windows Media Player"). For instructions for playing video files, see the next chapter.

The most popular streaming audio format is RealAudio (with either the .ra or .rm file extension). You can download the RealPlayer program for free from the Real.com Web site at **http://www.real.com**; this program works with your Web browser to play both RealAudio and RealVideo files from the Internet. Microsoft has its own streaming format, called Advanced Streaming Format (ASF), which Windows Media Player can play.

What Is MIDI?

A specialized type of audio data is called *MIDI* (Musical Instrument Digital Interface), a format for transmitting and storing musical notes. MIDI devices are musical instruments or recording devices that have digital inputs and outputs and can transmit, store, and play music using the MIDI language. For example, if you connect a MIDI keyboard to your computer, you can view the music you play on the MIDI keyboard on your computer screen and hear it on your speakers. Data from MIDI devices is stored in MIDI files. Windows includes software that can "play" MIDI files; that is, software that can translate the musical notes in the files into sound that can be played through speakers or headphones.

Windows Media Player can play MIDI files. You need additional MIDI software to edit and mix MIDI inputs.

Configuring Windows to Work with Sound

Many applications, particularly games, have built-in sound. Those programs automatically take advantage of your system's sound card, speakers, and microphone, once Windows is configured to work with them.

Choosing and Configuring Audio Input and Output Drivers

When you install sound equipment, Windows usually configures itself automatically to use the proper sound drivers. If you need to tell Windows which sound drivers to use, or choose settings for your audio devices, including voice, you can configure Windows in the Sounds And Audio Device Properties dialog box. This dialog box has tabs for configuring when Windows plays sounds and which drivers Windows uses to play and record sounds. You can also use this dialog box to display the properties of all your audio and video devices. Follow these steps:

1. Choose Start | Control Panel, click Sounds, Speech, And Audio Devices, and click Sounds And Audio Devices. You see the Sounds And Audio Devices Properties dialog box.

2. Click the Audio tab, as shown in Figure 19-2, if it's not already selected.

3. Choose the driver used to play sounds by selecting the device from the list of available devices in the Sound Playback section of the Audio tab.

4. Tell Windows more about your speakers or headphones by clicking the Advanced button in the Sound Playback section of the Audio tab. You see the

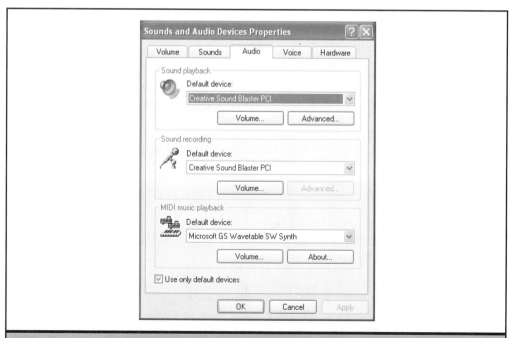

Figure 19-2. *Choosing devices for playing and recording sound and voice*

WORKING WITH TEXT, NUMBERS, PICTURES, SOUND, AND VIDEO

Advanced Audio Properties dialog box, as shown in Figure 19-3. (You can also display it by clicking the Advanced button in the Speaker Settings part of the Volume tab.)

5. Click the Speakers tab if it's not already selected. Click the Speaker Setup box and choose your computer's arrangement of speakers or headphones.

6. To set the amount of computing power your computer devotes to playing audio, click the Performance tab. Then, set the Audio Playback Hardware Acceleration slider and Sample Rate Conversion Quality slider. If your computer has a fast processor, move the sliders toward the Full and Best settings; otherwise, move them leftward to sacrifice sound quality for performance. Click OK.

Note *Microsoft is developing handwriting recognition software one language at a time. To check whether your language is supported, choose Start | Control Panel and click Date, Time, Language, And Regional Settings. Then click Regional And Language Options to display the Regional And Language Options dialog box (see Chapter 12, section "Windows' Regional Settings"). Click the Details button on the Languages tab and click your language on the list of installed languages. Click the Add button and see whether Handwriting Recognition is listed as an option.*

7. To control the volume of your speakers or headphones, click the Volume button in the Sound Playback section of the Audio tab of the Sounds And Audio Devices Properties dialog box. You see the Volume Control window

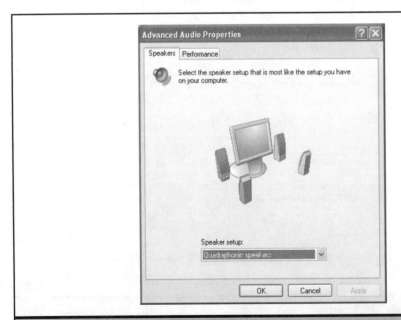

Figure 19-3. *Use the Advanced Audio Properties dialog box to set the properties of your speakers or headphones.*

(see "Controlling the Volume and Balance"). Close the window when you've adjusted the volume.

8. Choose the driver used to record sounds by clicking in the Default Device box in the Sound Recording section of the Sounds And Audio Devices Properties dialog box and choosing a driver from the list that appears—to record sound from a microphone, choose the driver for the sound card into which the microphone is plugged.

9. To set the amount of computing power your computer devotes to recording audio, click the Advanced button in the Sound Recording section of the Audio tab (unless it appears gray—some sound cards don't support advanced settings). Then set the Audio Recording Hardware Acceleration slider and Sample Rate Conversion Quality slider. Click OK.

10. To control the volume when recording, click the Volume button in the Sound Recording section of the Audio tab. You see the Recording Control window (see "Playing and Recording WAV Sound Files with Sound Recorder"). Close the window when you've set the recording volume.

11. If you use voice applications (for example, to dictate into a voice-recognition system such as Dragon Naturally Speaking, or to talk to other people over the Internet), click the Voice tab on the Sounds And Audio Devices Properties dialog box. You see sections for Voice Playback and Voice Capture, which you can set as described in steps 3–10.

12. Click OK to save your changes and exit the Sounds And Audio Devices Properties dialog box.

 If you have trouble getting sounds to play, try the Windows Sound Troubleshooter (see Chapter 35, section "Diagnosing Problems with Troubleshooters").

Displaying the Status of Your Audio Devices

To see all the audio devices installed on your system, choose Start | Control Panel, click Sounds Speech And Audio Devices, and click Sounds And Audio Devices. You see the Sounds And Audio Devices Properties dialog box. Click the Hardware tab to see the dialog box shown in Figure 19-4.

To display or change the settings for some devices, click the device and click the Properties button. Many of the devices are software only, notably the audio and video codecs (compressing and decompressing schemes) that determine the scheme used to encode sounds in audio and video files (see Chapter 20, section "How Does Windows Work with Video Data?").

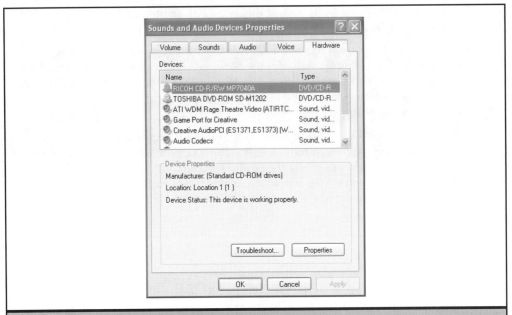

Figure 19-4. *The Hardware tab in the Sounds And Audio Devices Properties dialog box displays audio devices with their properties.*

Controlling the Volume and Balance

You can control the volume and balance of the sound that goes into your microphones and comes out of your computer's speakers or headphones. You can also choose to mute (suppress) the sound for any audio device. You can display a Volume icon (a little gray loudspeaker icon) in the notification area on your taskbar: open the Sounds And Audio Devices Properties dialog box as described in the preceding section, click the Volume tab (if it's not already selected), and select the Place Volume Icon In The Taskbar check box so that a check appears.

To adjust the volume of your speakers, click the Volume icon on the taskbar once; you see a Volume slider and a Mute check box:

Drag the Volume slider up for louder volume or down for softer volume. Select the Mute check box to suppress audio output completely (such as when you are using your laptop on a train). Click outside the window to make it disappear.

To adjust the volume and balance of any audio device, double-click the Volume icon. You see the Volume Control window:

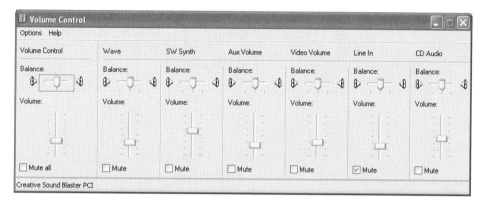

Another way to display this window is by clicking any of the Volume buttons on either the Audio or Voice tab of the Sounds And Audio Devices Properties dialog box.

The Volume Control window can display a volume, balance, and mute setting for each audio input and output device on your computer, depending on your sound card's capabilities. To choose which functions are included in the window, choose Options | Properties from the Volume Control menu bar to display the Properties dialog box, as shown in Figure 19-5. Click the Playback setting to include audio output devices, the Recording setting to include audio input devices, or the Other setting to include other audio devices. (The only other audio device is Voice Commands, which allows you to use software that interprets your voice input as commands to control programs.) You can also click check boxes for individual audio devices in the Show The Following Volume Controls list. Leave the Mixer Device setting alone—it's usually a feature of your audio card. Then click OK to return to the Volume Control dialog box.

Some sound cards come with their own mixer application. To use all of the features of your installed device, use the mixer program that comes with the sound card.

When you display volume controls for playback devices, the window is called Volume Control; when you display recording devices, it's called Recording Control.

If your speakers or headphones have a physical volume control knob, it's generally simpler to leave the Windows volume set fairly high, sending a strong signal through the wires, and just turn the knob to change the volume.

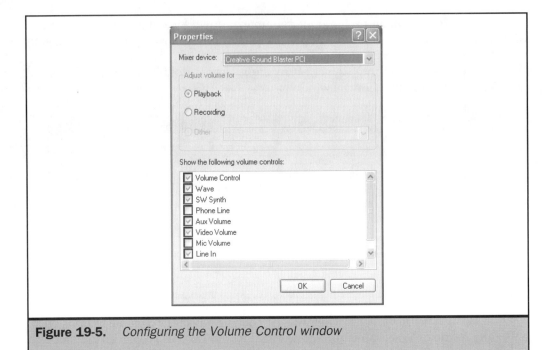

Figure 19-5. *Configuring the Volume Control window*

Choosing What Sounds Windows Makes

Windows comes with an array of sounds that it makes when certain *events* (Windows operations) occur. When you start Windows, for example, a rich, welcoming sound occurs; however, you might prefer the sound of a friend yelling "Hello!" You can control which sounds Windows plays when specified events occur by opening the Sounds And Audio Devices icon in the Control Panel. Click the Sounds tab of the Sounds And Audio Devices Properties dialog box to see the dialog box, as shown in Figure 19-6.

The Program Events box lists all the events that you can associate with a sound, including events that happen in Windows and other programs that use sound, such as Windows Messenger. If an event has no speaker icon to its left, no sound is currently assigned to that event. To change the sound for an event:

1. Click the event name in the Program Events box.

2. Click the down-arrow button at the right end of the Sounds box and choose a sound stored in a WAV file on your computer. You see a list of the sounds that come with Windows XP. Click the Browse button to find other WAV files, such as the ones you recorded yourself (see "Playing and Recording WAV Sound Files with Sound Recorder"). To assign no sound to an event, choose (None) from the Sounds list.

3. To test out the sound, click the right-pointing triangle Play button to the right of the Sounds box.

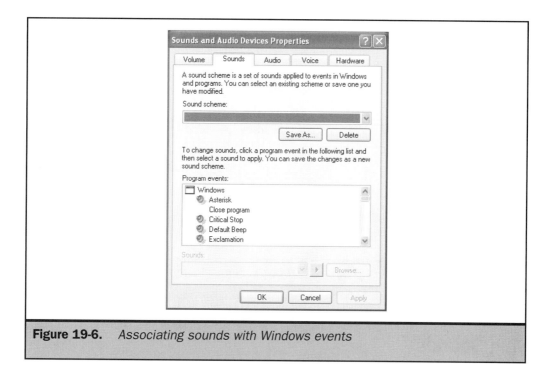

Figure 19-6.   *Associating sounds with Windows events*

The list of sounds in the Sound box is the list of WAV files (with extension .wav) in the C:\Windows\Media folder (assuming that Windows is installed on C:). You can also test sounds in the Open dialog box that you see when you click the Browse button. Select any sound that appears in the window and click the Play button at the bottom of the dialog box—the sound plays. If the sound is too long, click the black square to stop it.

You can save the set of sound associations as a *sound scheme*. Windows comes with a Windows Default sound scheme, which associates sounds with many events, and a No Sounds sound scheme, in which no sounds are associated with events. You can create your own sound schemes, too; simply associate the sounds you want to hear with the events that you want to prompt those sounds and click Save As.

Playing and Recording WAV Sound Files with Sound Recorder

To play or record WAV files (with the extension .wav), you can use the built-in Sound Recorder program. Choose Start | All Programs | Accessories | Entertainment | Sound Recorder. You see the Sound Recorder window, as shown in Figure 19-7. (It's the same program that came with Windows Me/9x.)

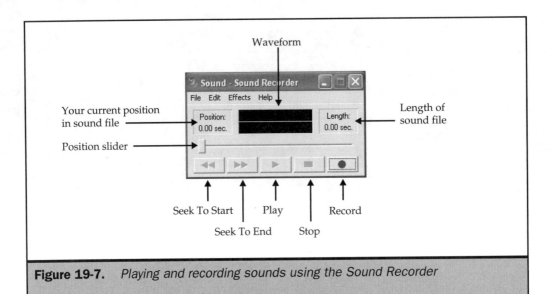

Waveform

Your current position in sound file

Length of sound file

Position slider

Seek To Start   Play   Record

Seek To End   Stop

Figure 19-7. *Playing and recording sounds using the Sound Recorder*

Playing Sounds

To play a sound file, choose File | Open, choose the filename, and click Open. Sound Recorder opens the file, displays the filename on the title bar, the waveform of the first part of the sound file, and the length of the sound in seconds. Next, click the Play button. Use the Stop button to stop playback.

The Position slider tracks your current position in the sound. To change your current position, drag the Position slider left or right to move forward or backward in the sound file. For example, to hear the second half of the sound, drag the Position slider to the middle and then click the Play button.

To discover other interesting ways that you can play back a sound (such as slower or backward), see the section "Editing Sounds" later in this chapter.

 Some sound files come with information about who created the sound; choose File | Properties to see the properties of the file.

Windows comes with lots of sounds in WAV files in C:\Windows\Media folder (assuming that Windows is installed on C:). To play these sounds, you can also use Windows Media Player (see "Playing Sound Files with Windows Media Player").

Recording Sounds

If your computer has a microphone, you can record sounds and store them in WAV files. Follow these steps:

1. Choose File | New to record a new sound file. If you are editing a sound file and haven't saved your changes, Sound Recorder asks whether you want to save them now.

2. Arrange the microphone so that you are ready to record.

3. Click the Record button in the Sound Recorder window.

4. Start the sound you want to record (for example, start talking).

5. When the sound you want to record has finished, click the Stop button.

6. Play back the sound by clicking the Play button.

7. Edit the sound as necessary (see "Editing Sounds").

8. If you want to save your recording, choose File | Save As, type a filename, and click Save.

If a file is already open in Sound Recorder when you record a sound, the recorded sound records over part of the existing sound or is added to the end of the existing sound, depending on the location of the Position slider. To add on to the end of a sound, move the Position slider to the right end (or click the Seek To End button) and then record. To replace part of any existing sound, move the Position slider to the beginning of the sound you want to record over and record.

Editing Sounds

Once you've opened or recorded a sound file, you can fool around with it in the following ways:

- **Copy**   To copy the entire sound to the Windows Clipboard so that you can paste (insert) it later, choose Edit | Copy or press CTRL-C.

- **Insert**   To insert another sound file into your existing sound, move the Position slider to the point at which you want to insert the file, choose Edit | Insert File, and choose the filename. To insert a copy from the Windows Clipboard, choose Edit | Paste Insert or press CTRL-V.

- **Mix**   To mix another sound file with your existing sound, move the Position slider to the point at which you want to mix the other sound, choose Edit | Mix With File and choose the filename. To mix a sound from the Windows Clipboard, choose Edit | Paste Mix. Sound Recorder mixes the two sounds together so you hear both at the same time. For example, you can record your voice several times and then mix the sounds together to sound like a crowd.

- **Cut**   You can omit parts of the sound, either from the beginning of the sound to your current position, or from your current position to the end of the sound. Move the Position slider to the point before or after the part that you want to delete. Then, choose Edit | Delete Before Current Position or Edit | Delete After Current Position. Click OK to confirm that you want to delete part of the sound.

- **Speed up or slow down**   To speed up the sound, choose Effects | Increase Speed. Sound Recorder plays the sound in half the time and raises the pitch. To slow down the sound, choose Effects | Decreases Speed; the sound plays in twice the time at a lower pitch.

- **Change volume**   To make the sound 25 percent louder, choose Effects | Increase Volume. To make the sound softer, choose Effects | Decrease Volume.

- **Add special effects**   To play the sound backward, choose Effects | Reverse. To add an echo, choose Effects | Add Echo.

 You can't edit a sound if it is stored in compressed format. You can tell that a sound is stored in a compressed format, because no green waveform appears in the Sound Recorder window.

Editing a sound changes the sound in memory but doesn't affect the sound file; to save your changes, choose File | Save or File | Save As. Until you save a sound, you can choose File | Revert to return to the previously saved version of the sound.

Converting Sounds to Other Formats

WAV files can use one of many different formats, which offer tradeoffs between audio fidelity and disk space, and are designed for different kinds of sounds, such as music or voice. You can also change the attributes of the sound, such as the sampling speed in Hertz (Hz), the number of bits used to store each sample, and whether the sound is stereo or mono. Some formats are compressed; if you convert a sound to a compressed format, you can't edit the sound in Sound Recorder. Confusingly, all of these formats are stored in files with the extension .wav.

To change the format of your WAV file, choose File | Properties to display the Properties dialog box for the file, as shown in Figure 19-8. The top half of the dialog box shows information about the sound, including its format. In Figure 19-8, the format is PCM, the format that Sound Recorder uses when recording sounds from your microphone.

The Format Conversion section of the Properties dialog box for a WAV file enables you to convert the sound to a different format; however, all the available formats are still stored as WAV files. Click the Convert Now button to see the Sound Selection dialog box, shown here:

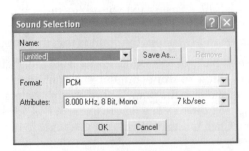

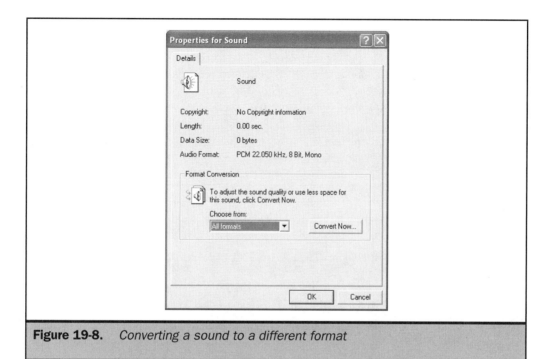

Figure 19-8. *Converting a sound to a different format*

You can choose the format and the attributes you want to use by clicking in the Format and Attributes boxes and making a selection in each. The list of Attributes changes based on the Format you choose. Some widely used combinations of formats and attributes have names to make them easier to select; click in the Name box to choose a named combination of format and attributes. Then click OK twice to convert the sound. Choose File | Save or File | Save As to save the converted sound in a file.

  You can also change the format when saving a file. Choose File | Save or File | Save As and type or select the filename. Click the Change button to display the Sound Selection dialog box, and then perform the conversion as described in this section.

Playing Sound Files with Windows Media Player

Another program that can play sound files, and many other types of files, is Windows Media Player, recently updated to version 8.0 and touting some new features. Start Windows Media Player by choosing Start | Windows Media Player (if the program appears on the left side of the Start menu, as it does when you first install Windows), choosing Start | All Programs | Windows Media Player, or clicking the Windows Media Player icon on the Quick Launch toolbar (if it appears on your taskbar). You see

WORKING WITH TEXT, NUMBERS, PICTURES, SOUND, AND VIDEO

the Windows Media Player window shown in Figure 19-9. When it starts, no image appears on its "video screen" (the gray box in the middle of its window).

 Strangely, the program doesn't update its video screen until a file is loaded, and the video screen might end up displaying bits and pieces of the windows and dialog boxes that you have displayed in that area. Don't worry—the Windows Media Player program is fine.

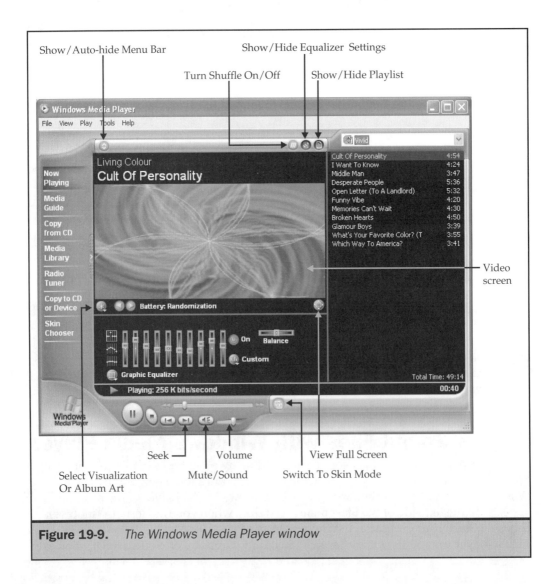

Figure 19-9. *The Windows Media Player window*

To play a sound file, choose File | Open, set the Files Of Type box to Audio File (to skip other types of files, such as video files), choose a file, and click Open. Windows Media Player loads the file and starts playing it. When it's over, you can click the Play button in the lower-left corner of the Windows Media Player window to play the sound file again. You can stop playback by clicking the Stop button near the bottom of the window.

Note   *See the section "Playing Video Files with Windows Media Player" in the next chapter for details about playing video files with Windows Media Player.*

The Windows Media Player Window

The program has buttons on the left, top, and bottom of the Windows Media Player window. The area in the center of the window is the "video screen" on which videos and other pictures appear. You can also choose to display other information on the video screen. Playlists or lists of Internet radio stations may appear on the right side of the window.

Windows Media Player has its own toolbar that runs down the side of the window. (The program calls this the Features Taskbar, but we reserve the term "taskbar" for the Windows taskbar.) If the Windows Media Player window isn't tall enough to display all the buttons, double-chevron buttons appear at the top and bottom of the toolbar so that you can scroll the toolbar buttons up and down. You can hide the toolbar by clicking the tiny left-pointing arrow button in the middle of the right side of the toolbar.

The toolbar contains these buttons:

- **Now Playing**   Displays the currently loaded file. If the file is a video, it appears on the video screen. If an audio file is loaded, you see a visualization of the music (see "Playing Audio Files Stored on Your Computer").

- **Media Guide**   Connects to the Windows Media Web site over the Internet, from which you can view video files content that is updated on a daily basis (see "Playing Streaming Audio Files from the Internet").

- **Copy from CD**   Plays sounds from an audio CD inserted in your CD-ROM drive (see "Playing Audio CDs").

- **Media Library**   Enables you to organize your audio and video files (see "Creating and Editing Playlists").

- **Radio Tuner**   Plays Internet radio stations (see "Listening to Internet Radio Stations")—that is, radio stations that are available over the Internet as streaming audio files.

- **Copy to CD or Device**   Enables you to move audio files to and from a portable audio player or create audio CDs (see "Moving Files to and from Portable Players and Other Devices").

- **Skin Chooser**   Enables you to choose a different look (appearance and controls) for the program (see "Customizing the Windows Media Player Window").

Windows Media Player has an Auto Update feature that tells you when updates to the program are available from Microsoft over the Internet. When you exit Windows Media Player, a dialog box may appear offering to download and install updates. Read the information about the update and decide whether you want it. You can check for updates any time you are online by choosing Help | Check For Player Updates from the menu bar.

Playing Audio Files Stored on Your Computer

To play a file on your computer or on a shared drive on a LAN, choose File | Open and choose the filename. (If you don't see the menu bar, click the Show/Auto-hide Menu Bar button above the upper left corner of the video screen part of the Windows Media Player window.) Windows Media Player can play sound files in a variety of formats, including WAV, MIDI, and streaming audio files.

Click the Now Playing button on the toolbar to see the video that goes with the audio. If the file you are playing doesn't include video images, Windows Media Player creates them for you. As the music plays, the video screen shows *visualizations*, graphical representations of the sound. Forty-six kinds of visualizations come with Windows Media Player—all are interesting, and some are positively mesmerizing. You can change the visualization that appears by clicking the small gray arrow buttons underneath the visualization. The name of the visualization appears to the right of the buttons. You can also surf through them all by choosing View | Visualizations from the menu, selecting the name of a group of visualizations, and choosing the specific visualization.

 You can remove visualizations that you never watch, change the properties of some visualizations, or add new visualizations that you download from the Internet. Choose Tools | Options from the menu and click the Visualizations tab to display a list of the available visualizations.

You can add other information to the video screen by using three buttons that always appear along the top of the Windows Media Player window (we list them as they appear from left to right):

- **Turn Shuffle On/Off**   Click this to tell Windows Media Player whether to play the available tracks randomly (on) or in order of appearance (off).

- **Show/Hide Equalizer And Settings In Now Playing**   Displays controls along the bottom of the video screen when Now Playing is selected (see "Adjusting Volume, Graphic Equalization, and Other Sound Settings").

- **Show/Hide Playlist In Now Playing**   Displays your current playlist down the right side of the Windows Media Player window.

Organizing Your Audio Files into a Media Library

Windows Media Player includes the Media Library, a storehouse for all of your audio and video files (Figure 19-10). To organize your audio and video files (also called tracks, as on an audio CD), Windows Media Player can search your drives (local and shared network drives) for files. It organizes them into lists of audio files, video files, and the addresses of radio stations on the Internet. You can then organize the files into playlists, described in the next section.

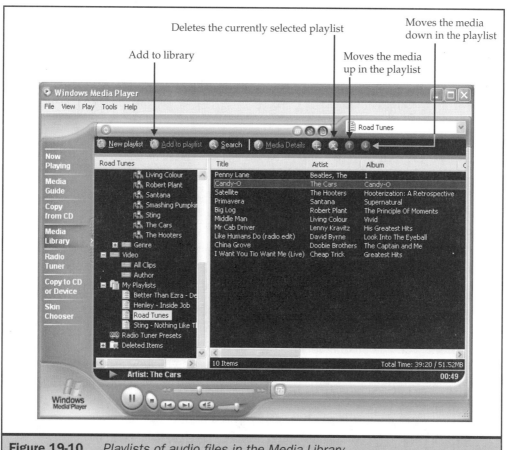

Figure 19-10. *Playlists of audio files in the Media Library*

The first time you click the Media Library button, Windows Media Player offers to perform the search, or you can follow these steps at any time:

1. Choose Tools | Search For Media Files from the menu (or press F3). You see the Search For Media Files dialog box:

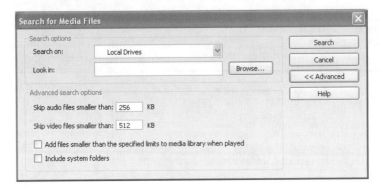

2. In the Search Options section, specify whether to search Local Drives (disk drives on your own computer), Network Drives (shared drives on a LAN), All Drives, or a list of individual drive letters. If you select a specific drive by drive letter, you can choose a folder to start in (the program searches only that folder and its subfolders).

3. Click the Advanced button to display the Advanced Search Options section of the dialog box.

4. The previous version of Windows Media Player had the annoying habit of including the small sound event files that come with Windows. Now you can specify that small files be skipped and not added to your media library—just leave the Skip Audio Files Smaller Than xx KB settings large enough to skip the small "beep" and "ding" event sounds (256KB, the default, works fine).

5. Unless you want to include the audio files that come with Windows (unlikely, if you are making a catalog of music files), leave the Include System Folders check box deselected.

6. Click Search. A dialog box appears telling you the progress of the search. When it has finished, it tells you how many files it found. Click Close.

7. Click Close again to dismiss the Search For Media Files dialog box

8. Click the Media Library button (if it's not already selected) to see all your audio and video files.

The list on the left shows the files by category, and the list on the right shows the contents of the selected category. The five major categories are Audio, Video (described in the next chapter), My Playlists (described in the next section), Radio Tuner Presets (for

Internet radio stations, described in the section "Listening to Internet Radio Stations" later in this chapter), and Deleted Items. The Audio category lists these subcategories:

- **All Audio**   Displays all audio files in alphabetical order, no matter where they are stored.

- **Album**   Displays audio files by the album of which they are a part (if any). Windows Media Player identifies albums by information from audio CDs (see the next section) or from the MP3 ID3 tags, for MP3 format files.

- **Artist**   Displays audio files by artist. If you have songs from more than one album by a single artist, the albums appear as sub-subcategories.

- **Genre**   Displays audio files by genres and styles. Since genres and styles are primarily determined by personal taste (ever argue with someone as to whether Steely Dan is jazz, rock, or progressive?), this can be an unreliable way to sort music—unless you go through each album and assign each album to the genre where you think it belongs.

You can click a file to play it and the files that follow it on the list. Windows Media Player can keep track of lots of information about each file—use the horizontal scrollbar at the bottom of the list of files to see the title, artist, computer, genre, length, file size, file format (type), creation date, file pathname, and other items. To see more information about a file, right-click it and choose Properties from the menu that appears. If you don't want a file to appear anywhere in your Media Library, right-click it and choose Delete From Library from the shortcut menu that appears.

You can also update the information about a file. Right-click a piece of information about a file and choose Edit. Windows Media Player enables you to edit the field you clicked (this feature doesn't work on all fields). You can also make the same change to the information about a group of files (for example, change the Genre of a group of files). Select a group of files, click a field (like Artist or Genre), choose Edit Selected, edit the text, and press ENTER. Windows Media Player makes the change to all the files you selected.

You can also click the Search button along the top of the video screen to search for a field by a word or phrase in its title, as shown here:

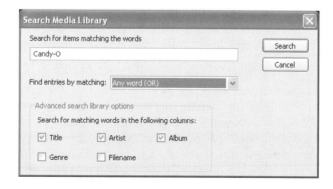

WORKING WITH TEXT, NUMBERS, PICTURES, SOUND, AND VIDEO

Click the Media Details button along the top of the video screen to ask Windows Media Player to get details, if any, about the selected file.

You can configure other Media Library settings. Choose Tools | Options from the menu and click the Media Library tab to set them:

- **Access Rights Of Other Applications**   Sets the level of access other programs have to your Media Library and playlist information.

- **Access Rights Of Internet Sites**   Sets the level of access that Web sites have to your Media Library and playlist information.

- **Media Files**   If you uncheck this check box, Windows Media Player asks whether you want the program to manage that media or not. This setting is only useful if you use other digital media applications, such as Liquid Audio.

Creating and Editing Playlists

A *playlist* is a set of audio files that you plan to play as a group. You can create a playlist, give it a name, and put audio (or video) files into it. Then you can play that group of files any time, either in the order in which they appear on the playlist or in random (shuffled) order.

Click the Media Library button on the toolbar to see, create, and edit playlists. In the list of categories on the left side of the video screen, one category is My Playlists. Windows comes with one playlist, named Sample Playlist, which contains several audio files.

To create a new playlist, click the New Playlist button at the top of the video screen area. Type a name for the new playlist and click OK. Windows Media Player adds your new playlist to the My Playlists category.

You can add files to a playlist in several ways:

- Click the Add To Playlist button at the top left of the video screen when the Media Library button is selected. You see a menu of your playlists.

- Click the unlabeled Add To Playlist button at the top right of the video screen (the one with a plus sign). You can choose among adding a file from your computer, adding a file from the Internet, or (if you are playing a CD) adding a file from the CD.

- Right-click a file (or select a group of files and right-click it), and choose Add To Playlist from the shortcut menu that appears.

- Drag the file (or files) to the name of the playlist in the My Playlists category on the left side of the video screen when Media Library is selected.

When you add a file to a playlist, Windows Media Player doesn't copy the file to the playlist—the audio file remains where it is stored. Instead, it creates a shortcut to the file. This capability allows you to include one file in many playlists. When you delete a file from a playlist, Windows doesn't delete the audio file; it just deletes the shortcut to the file from the playlist. To delete a file from a playlist, right-click the file and choose Delete From Playlist from the shortcut menu that appears (or click the Delete Media From Playlist Or Library button along the right top of the video screen).

You can adjust the order of the files in the playlist by dragging them up and down the list. Or, select a file and click either the Moves The Media Up In The Playlist button or the Moves The Media Down In The Playlist button along the right top of the video screen. Click the Turn Shuffle On button along the top of the Windows Media Player window to play the files in random order.

You can also save your playlists in files in various formats, including the uncommon Windows Media types (with extensions .asx, .wax, and .wvx), as well as the ubiquitous WinAmp format (.m3u). To export a playlist, do the following:

1. Click the Media Library button.

2. Click the My Playlists item to show your available playlists on the right.

3. Select a playlist.

4. Choose File | Export Playlist To File to open the Save As dialog box.

5. Type a name for the file in the Save As box.

6. Add one of the file extensions to have it saved as a particular type (usually .m3u).

7. Click Save.

 To play a playlist you've heard recently, choose it from the drop-down list in the upper-right corner of the Windows Media Player window.

Playing Audio CDs

Every audio CD has a serial number that identifies the artist, album title, and the list of tracks (songs) on the CD. These serial numbers are stored in a database called the *Compact Disc Database* or *CDDB*, which is accessible over the Internet. The CDDB began as a cooperative effort of the community of music lovers, entering information about their CDs, but has since become a commercial venture.

When you insert an audio CD into your CD-ROM drive, the Windows Media Player program runs automatically. If AutoPlay is turned on, the music begins playing. Windows Media Player reads the number from the audio CD and sends that number to the CDDB over the Internet. If the audio CD number is in the CDDB, the list of songs and artists is usually already in the CDDB, unless you have a truly obscure album. Windows Media Player downloads this information to your computer automatically. The list of tracks appears in the playlist that appears when you click the Now Playing or CD Audio button. If the CD is not in the CDDB database, then you have the option to type the titles of the tracks in yourself (do so—as a public service).

To play a specific track, double-click a song title, or right-click a song title and select Play; or select the song title and click the Play button at the bottom of the window. You can edit the information about a CD track the same way you edit information about a track in a playlist: right-click information about the track and choose Edit from the shortcut menu that appears; or, select a group of tracks, right-click the information about one track, and choose Edit Selected to make the same change to all the selected tracks. For more information about a track, right-click it and choose Properties.

You can change the order in which Windows Media Player plays the tracks on the CD. Right-click a track and choose Move Up or Move Down from the shortcut menu, or simply drag them up or down with the mouse. A gray line tracks your movement, indicating where the track will be placed when you let go. Click the Shuffle button along the top of the Windows Media Player window to play the files in random order. (The check boxes to the left of the tracks are used for selecting tracks when copying a CD; they don't affect which tracks Windows Media Player plays.)

When you are playing an audio CD and you click the Copy From CD button on the toolbar, these buttons appear across the top of the video screen:

- **Copy Music** Copies the selected tracks to the Windows Media (WMA) digital format at 128 Kbs (a format that includes most of what the human ear can discern from digital music, but is far more compact than purely raw audio data). By default, the program copies the files to a new folder in your My Music folder, where you can play them later. Copying tracks from a CD can take a while, but Windows Media Player can continue to play the CD while it's copying: click the Stop Copying button to interrupt copying. Windows Media Player automatically includes these new files in your Media Library.

- **Get Names** Checks the CDDB to see whether your CD is in the database. If there is only one match, Windows Media Player downloads the list and stores it for reuse later. If there is more than one match, you see a list of the located matches in the lower part of the Windows Media Player window and you can select the best one. If the CD doesn't appear in the database, Windows Media Player asks if you would like to contribute that data to the database for others to see.

- **Album Details** Displays a comprehensive look at the particular title you have in your CD-ROM drive, if available. You may see an album cover, a list of songs, and possibly even a review. Click the Hide Details button to remove this information from the window.

To see a visualization of the music, click the Now Playing button and choose a visualization (see "Playing Audio Files Stored on Your Computer").

Windows Media Player includes several configuration settings for audio CDs. Choose Tools | Options, click the Devices tab, select your CD drive from the list, and click Properties to control how audio CDs play. (Click the Show Menu Bar button above the upper-left corner of the video screen if the menu bar doesn't appear.) The Audio tab shows these settings:

- **Playback** If your CD-ROM drive supports it, select Digital for a clearer sound. You can also turn on error correction, which increases the amount of RAM used to buffer the audio data.

- **Copy** For some CD-ROM drives, you can set the quality level that you want to use when copying music from CDs to your hard disk—the higher the quality, the bigger the file.

If you have a CD-R or CD-R/RW drive on your system (either the only CD drive or in addition to a CD-ROM or DVD), its Properties dialog box includes a Recording tab where you can control the new Windows XP CD burning capabilities. On the Recording tab are these settings:

- **Enable CD Recording On This Drive**   Governs whether you can use the drive to create CDs or not. This option is purely subjective, because if the drive were not capable of recording, then the Recording tab would not have appeared in the first place.

- **Drive Selection**   Allows users with multiple disks to select which disk Windows Media Player uses to store a copy of the CD to be written before actually writing it.

- **Speed Selection**   Controls how quickly Windows can write to the drive. You can't select a speed that is faster than your drive actually supports. If you are using older CD blanks that support only slower speeds and you have trouble getting CDs that play well, burn the CDs at a slower speed than the drive is capable of handling.

- **Automatically Eject The CD After Writing**   Most CD burning software does this by default, with exception of WinOnCD.

Using Another Audio Player

The first time you insert an audio CD into your CD-ROM drive, you may see a dialog box like this:

You can decide whether to use Windows Media Player or another program to play your audio CDs.

Playing Streaming Audio Files from the Internet

If you know the exact URL of an audio file on the Internet, choose File | Open Location and enter the URL of the file to play it. However, it's usually easier to use the Media Guide button to help you find the file you want.

When you click the Media Guide button, the program connects to Microsoft's Windows Media site at **http://www.windowsmedia.com**. This site, as shown in Figure 19-11, usually has to do with television, movies, or new music, and often has neat stuff to look at or listen to.

Windows Media Player's Media Guide feature acts like a Web browser to show you the Windows Media home page, which you can also view with Internet Explorer. The pages have Back and Forward links in the upper-right corner of the display that allow you to move about with a modicum of the ease you get in your Web browser. Some links may display pages in your browser rather than on the Windows Media Player's video screen.

If your PC connects to the Internet through a firewall, you might not be able to use Windows Media Player's Media Guide or Radio Tuner buttons. The port numbers used when connecting to streaming audio material on Web sites aren't standard, and the

Figure 19-11.   *Microsoft's Media Guide Web site*

system that connects your LAN to the Internet might not be configured to handle them. If you have a problem, choose Tools | Options to display the Options dialog box. The Network tab controls how the program communicates over the Internet:

- **Protocols** Defines which network access protocols the program uses to communicate with servers and (optionally) which ports to use (useful if you communicate with the Internet through a firewall).

- **Proxy Settings** Specifies whether your PC communicates with the Internet over a LAN, using a proxy server program (see Chapter 30). The default is not to use a proxy server. If your PC connects to the Internet over a LAN, get the configuration information from your LAN administrator.

Listening to Internet Radio Stations

Many radio stations use the Internet to broadcast their signal to parts of the world that their antennas could never reach. In addition to large-scale commercial stations, hundreds of little operations are cropping up (although some have had to stop broadcasting due to issues of artist royalties). Window Media Player brings all of the stations that use the Windows Media streaming technology to you in the form of a searchable database.

An example of Internet radio on a small scale is radioIO (at **http://www.radioio.com**), where a single person handles all aspects of the operation of one streaming station. On the other end of the scale is Live365 (at **http://www.live365.com**) which has 100 streaming stations all going at the same time. Both are professionally programmed radio stations.

To listen to Internet radio, click the Radio Tuner button. Windows Media Player shows the list of presets and radio stations shown in Figure 19-12. You see information from the WindowsMedia.com Web site.

The left side of the video screen lists your preset stations (these stations also appear when you click the Media Library button in the Radio Tuner Presets category). A number of presets are already there, but you can remove or edit them. Those presets appear in the Featured Stations preset list. Click an entry to see your options: Add To My Stations (that is, to your My Stations preset list), Visit Website (the radio station's Web site), or Play. You can make your own preset list using My Stations.

To find stations that aren't on a preset list, click Find More Stations. Set the Browse By Genre box to a category, or type a name or keyword into the Search box and click the arrow button to its right.You can also search by ZIP code to find stations in your area. Windows Media Player searches for stations that match. The stations that Windows Media Player finds appear in the Search Results list. To listen to a station, click it and click Play. You may have to wait a minute or two until the music (or talk) begins. You may see a dialog box asking whether to install a downloaded codec (compressing and decompressing schemes).

Figure 19-12.   *Tuning in to Internet radio stations*

If you like a radio station, you can add it to your My Stations lists. Highlight the station and click the Add To My Stations button.

Two configuration settings affect the quality of streaming files from the Internet. Choose Tools | Options and click the Performance tab to set them:

- **Connection Speed**   You can either let Windows Media Player detect the speed at which your computer communicates with the Internet, or, if you know for sure, you can set it yourself.

- **Network Buffering**   Defines how much data is stored in RAM before it actually plays. If you have trouble with getting smooth playback, click the Buffer radio button and put up to 60 seconds in the field (30 to 45 seconds is typically adequate).

- **Video Acceleration**   Allows you to set how much of the video rendering is performed by your video card. Cryptically advanced controls and options are available by clicking the Advanced button, but we do not recommend altering anything unless specified by a technical support agent or other experienced source.

Adjusting Volume, Graphic Equalization, and Other Sound Settings

If you want to adjust how your audio files sound, click the Show Equalizer And Settings In Now Playing button at the top of the Windows Media Player window and then click the Now Playing button. The equalizer and settings appear in the bottom part of the video screen. Click the Show Equalizer And Settings In Now Playing button again to remove these tools from the screen. You can also start or stop displaying these tools by choosing View | Now Playing Tools from the menu, and choosing the tool.

Several sets of tools can appear in this area. The gray menu button in the lower-left corner of the area selects which of the following tools appears.

- ■ **SRS WOW Effects**   Includes several special effects: TruBass, WOW Effect, SRS WOW Effect, and Speakers. TruBass adds more bass to your music the farther to the right you slide it. WOW Effect adds more separation between the stereo channels. The On/Off button enables or disables all these effects. Clicking the SRS logo takes your Web browser to the SRS WOWcast.com Web site at **http://www.srswowcast.com**, in case you are interested in files that use the SRS WOW technology. The Speakers button switches among Normal Speakers, Large Speakers, and Headphones.

- ■ **Graphic Equalizer**   Enables you to adjust the treble and bass balance, and left and right speaker balance. The ten vertical sliders adjust the volume of the high treble notes (at the right end) through the low bass notes (at the left end). The On/Off button enables or disables the effects of any modifications you make to the equalizer. Turning it off means you get the sound exactly as it was recorded. Rather than setting them individually, you can click the button below the On/Off button, which cycles through preset bass/treble settings that work for many common musical genres. The Balance slider adjusts the relative volume of the left and right speakers. If you like to adjust the equalizer yourself, the three buttons on the left end of the controls define whether you can adjust each frequency individually, adjust them in a loose group, or adjust them in a tight group.

- **Video Settings**   Enables you to control the color and brightness of the video images.
- **Media Information**   Displays any information that the program can glean about tracks or albums you are listening to. If it's available, it even shows a picture of the album cover. When you are playing MP3 files downloaded from the Internet, no information appears.

Note *MP3 files have their own way of identifying the file's contents to MP3 players. They are called ID3 tags, and they embed the information about artist, album, title, length, genre, track number, and notes.*

- **Captions**   Displays captions, if the file includes them.
- **Lyrics**   Displays song lyrics if the file includes them or if they are available via the CDDB.
- **DVD Controls**   Displays the other controls that Windows Media Player needs if you are playing a DVD. These additional controls include the Variable Play Speed slider, Rewind, Play, Fast Forward, and Next Frame buttons. Even more controls are available during playback by right-clicking the video.

Moving Files to and from Portable Players and Other Devices

Portable MP3 players and personal CD players are quite popular, as are handheld devices that can play music, like PocketPCs. The portable digital music machines of today are small and can hold a few hours worth of digital music (in the case of the Sony MC-P10 Music Clip). Others can play up to 100 hours and take up no more room than a portable CD player (for example, the Creative Labs Nomad Jukebox comes with a 6GB hard disk). A number of portable CD players can play CD-R and CD-RW media in either White Book format (the same as a standard audio CD) or MP3 files.

Note *Some portable CD players can play CD-R/RW discs only if they were burned in the same format as standard audio CDs. Others have the ability to see and playback MP3 and WMA files from a CD-R/RW. A typical 640MB or 700MB CD-R can hold much more music than a 74- or 80-minute audio CD. For example, the average audio CD recorded at 128Kbps takes up 60 to 80MBs of space. That means that a 700MB CD-R can hold an average of 10 complete CDs.*

It's easy to copy music from your PC to a portable device or CD-R by using Windows Media Player. Here's how:

1. Make playlists of all the music you want to copy.

2. Click the Copy To CD Or Device button. The tracks on a playlist appear on the left side (Music To Copy). If you are using a portable device, any tracks appear on the right side (Music On Device). Otherwise, the CD burner appears, indicated by drive letter.

3. Select which files will be copied by checking or unchecking the tracks on the Music To Copy list. If no tracks appear, choose or create a playlist.

4. When you have selected all of the tracks to copy and they do not exceed the storage capacity of your device or CD-R, click the Copy Music button in the upper-left corner of the window.

The serial connections with which many portable music players connect to the PC are slow, but many portable music players come with USB connections that are much faster. CD recording is limited by the speed at which your drive can operate. This is not to say that if you can playback CDs at 40x that you will be able to record at that speed. Typical speeds are from 2x to 12x, and slower for rewriting.

You can control how Windows Media Player copies files to portable players—choose Tools | Options and click the Device tab of the Options dialog box to see a listing of your devices. If a device you have does not appear, then it is either not supported or not installed.

Licensing Issues for Digital Music

In order to protect music transferred from audio CDs or the Internet from being copied, Microsoft has integrated some protection features which prevent you from copying *unsigned* files to a portable device. A file is *signed* if you copied the music from an audio CD using Windows Media Player. When you copy music from an audio CD, Windows Media Player assumes that the music is licensed to you to use at your discretion (as long and you don't resell it or otherwise misrepresent the media to the general public). All files that you copy are encoded in Microsoft's proprietary .wma format by default, so you need a device that can play them (a PocketPC, WinJam, or other digital music systems) You can also get signed music files by buying and downloading them from the Windows Media Web site.

Note: You are fairly safe from getting improperly licensed music from unknown online sources as long as you patronize the Windows Media Web site (and maybe a few select partners). Any music purchased through the Windows Media site or from one of its partners is likely to be properly licensed.

WORKING WITH TEXT, NUMBERS, PICTURES, SOUND, AND VIDEO

Customizing the Windows Media Player Window

WinAmp, a popular shareware MP3 player, popularized the ability to *skin* an application—that is, offer a variety of user interfaces so that you can choose among a number of window, menu, and button designs (or even create your own). In a complete turnaround from Microsoft's typical functional look, the company had integrated skins into Windows Media Player. Full mode has only a single look; but in Skin mode, customization can run rampant.

When you run Windows Media Player, it appears in Full mode, with all the buttons and controls we've described so far. The other option is Skin mode, in which you see one of the included skins.

To switch from Full mode to Skin mode, click the Switch To Skin Mode button that appears at the right end of the Seek slider. How the Windows Media Player window looks depends on which skin you chose. You usually see something like this:

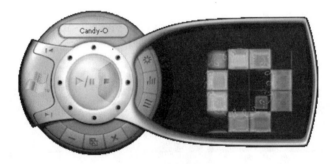

Caution *Changing skins changes the locations of all the controls and the overall appearance of Windows Media Player, often drastically. Don't try changing the program's skins until you feel confident with the application as a whole. If you do get stuck, click the large Windows Media logo button that appears in a floating window and choose Switch To Full Mode from the menu that appears:*

To switch to another skin:

1. Click the Skin Chooser button on the toolbar that runs down the left side of the window. In the video screen, you see two lists: on the left is a list of available skins and on the right is a picture of the selected skin (see Figure 19-13).

2. Select a skin name from the list on the left side. An image appears in the right pane showing you what the skin really looks like.

3. Click the Apply Skin button at the top of the list to activate the skin and switch to Skin mode. If you want to change skins without changing modes, just leave the new skin selected and click a different button on the toolbar.

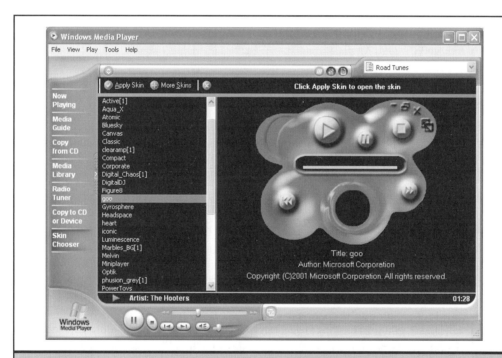

Figure 19-13.   *Choosing a different skin for Windows Media Player*

You can get more skins from the Windows Media Web site at any time. Skins are stored in files with the extension .wmz in the C:\Program Files\Windows Media Player\Skins folder (assuming that Windows is installed on C:). Click the More Skins button at the top of the list and your Web browser goes to a set of pages on the Microsoft Windowsmedia.com Web site. When you click the picture showing the skin, Windows Media Player downloads it and asks if you would like to activate your new skin now.

Switching back from a new skin can be trickier, since the new controls may be unrecognizable. Hover your mouse pointer over anything that looks like it might be a button until you find one with the label Return To Full Mode. If nothing appears familiar or your hover search reveals no clues, you may also right-click anywhere on the skin and select Full Mode from the menu that appears.

Some skins consume lots of memory. If your computer's performance slows when you are using Windows Media Player, switch back to the default skin.

You can configure Windows Media Player by choosing Tools | Options to display the Options dialog box. The Player tab of the Options dialog box controls the program itself:

- **Automatic Updates**   Specifies how often you want Windows Media Player to check the Microsoft Web site for updates. You can also enable or disable automatic codec downloads.

- **Internet Settings**   Controls whether your player is individually recognized on the Internet and whether to get media licenses. The first option allows Web sites to store something like a media cookie on your PC.

- **Player Settings**   Specifies how Windows Media Player looks when it starts.

Specifying Which File Formats Windows Media Player Plays

You can choose which file formats Windows Media Player plays (which file formats the program is associated with). Choose Tools | Options from the Windows Media Player menu bar and click the File Types tab to see a list of audio and video file formats. If you want another program to play files of a specific format, uncheck the check box for that format. If you can't live without Windows Media Player, click the Select All button to make it the default player for practically everything.

How Windows Handles Speech

Text-to-speech (*TTS*) enables the computer to speak text out loud. Conversely, *speech recognition* (*SR*) enables the computer to convert the sound of speech into text stored in the computer. Windows has built-in configuration settings that TTS and SR applications can use. Microsoft Narrator uses these settings to do text-to-speech (see Chapter 16, section "Listening to Microsoft Narrator Read the Screen Out Loud"). For speech recognition, you need to install an additional program, many of which are listed on Microsoft's Third Party Products page at **http://microsoft.com/speech/thirdparty**.

To see the speech settings, choose Start | Control Panel, click Sounds, Speech, And Audio Devices, and click Speech. You see the Speech Properties dialog box shown in next. You can choose a voice (Windows comes only with Microsoft Sam, who sounds rather robotic) and speed.

Chapter 20

Working with Video

Computers have been able to handle video data for decades—after all, when you use a computer you are already sitting in front of a video screen. Windows XP supports video output on the screen, and video input if you add the necessary hardware to your computer. This chapter describes what formats video data is stored in, how to play video files using Windows Media Player, and how to make your own video files using the Windows Movie Maker program. The new version of the Windows Media Player that comes with Windows XP can also play DVDs.

How Does Windows Work with Video Data?

You can use various *video capture* devices, such as digital video cameras, to get video information into your computer. See Chapter 13 for instructions on how to install video capture devices. To display video, Windows uses your screen, and to play the accompanying audio it uses your sound board and speakers.

Because the amount of data coming from a digital video camera is so immense, your computer can't process and store it fast enough. Instead, video data is compressed on its way into the computer from the camera and is then stored in a compressed format. A very fast *DSP* (*digital signal processor*, a kind of specialized computer) chip in your video capture hardware does the actual compression. Windows comes with a number of *codecs*, programs for video compression and decompression, so that it can decompress and recompress video data when you want to display or edit it. Windows also includes *DirectX*, a feature that enhances video playback. Windows stores most video in *AVI files*, files with the filename extension .avi. Other popular formats for video files are QuickTime (.qt) and MPEG (.mpg).

To see a list of your installed video capture devices, along with a list of the available codecs, choose Start | Control Panel; click Sound Speech And Audio Devices; click Sounds And Audio Devices; and click the Hardware tab. You see the list of audio and video devices your computer can use (see Figure 19-4 in the previous chapter). To see a list of video capture devices, click the Legacy Video Capture Devices entry, click the Properties button, and click the Properties tab. To see a list of codecs that are available, click the Video Codecs list item, click the Properties button, and select the Properties tab.

Playing Video Files with Windows Media Player

As described in the previous chapter, the Windows Media Player program that comes with Windows can play many different types of multimedia files, including video files.

To start Windows Media Player, choose Start | All Programs | Windows Media Player, choose Start | Windows Media Player (if the program is on your Start menu), or click the Windows Media Player icon on the Quick Launch toolbar on the taskbar (if your taskbar includes this toolbar).

For the details on the new interface for Windows Media Player 8, turn to the section "Playing Sound Files with Windows Media Player" in Chapter 19.

Windows Media Player can't play all types of video files. To play Apple QuickTime files (.qt), you'll need the QuickTime viewer, available at **http://www.apple.com/quicktime**. Windows Media Player can play the popular MPEG format.

Playing Video Files from Your Hard Disk

You have several options for selecting a file to play. The easiest is for you to have Windows Media Player scan your disk drives for audio and video files of all types (see Chapter 19, section "Creating and Editing Playlists"). If you have already scanned for files, click the Media Library button, click Video in the list of categories, and click the All Clips subcategory. Windows Media Player displays all available video files. When you double-click a file in the Media Library, Windows Media Player plays the file, followed by the rest of the files on the list. If the file requires a codec to tell Windows Media Player how to read its format, the program connects to the Windows Media Web site (at **http://www.windowsmedia.com**) and tries to locate the appropriate codec.

 If you access the Internet via a dial-up connection, Windows Media Player tries to connect. If you are already connected, Windows Media Player connects to the Windows Media Web site through the existing connection. You may be required to validate the installation of the new codec.

To play a video file that is not in your Media Library, choose File | Open from the Windows Media Player menu bar, or press CTRL-O. In the Open dialog box that appears, navigate to your video file and click Open. You can also drag the video file (or any multimedia file) from the desktop or an Explorer window into the Windows Media Player window.

 Make sure to set the Files Of Type box to All Files, so that you see all types of video files.

When you open a file, either by choosing File | Open or by using the Media Library, Windows Media Player loads the video file, switches to the Now Playing view, and displays the video in the video screen part of the Windows Media Player window. If it's not already playing, click the Play button to start the video, which appears in the video screen (middle) section of the Windows Media Player window.

While you are playing a video file, you can also perform these actions:

■ Stop the video by clicking the Stop button.

■ View the image full-screen by pressing ALT-ENTER or by choosing View | Full Screen from the menu bar. To return from full-screen display, press ESC.

WORKING WITH TEXT, NUMBERS, PICTURES, SOUND, AND VIDEO

■ Move forward or backward in the file by clicking the Skip Forward, Skip Backward, Fast Forward, or Rewind buttons (the VCR-style buttons along the bottom of the window); or by dragging the Position slider.

■ Adjust the volume by clicking and dragging the Volume slider or by choosing Play | Volume from the menu bar.

If you are experiencing video problems and suspect your video card, you can change your acceleration setting. Choose Tools | Options from the menu and click the Performance tab, as shown in Figure 20-1. Reduce the Video Acceleration (that is, slide it to the left) to solve some hardware-based video problems.

Playing Streaming Video Files from the Internet

Video files tend to be huge because each frame of a video requires many thousands of bytes of information. Viewing video over the Internet can involve long waits

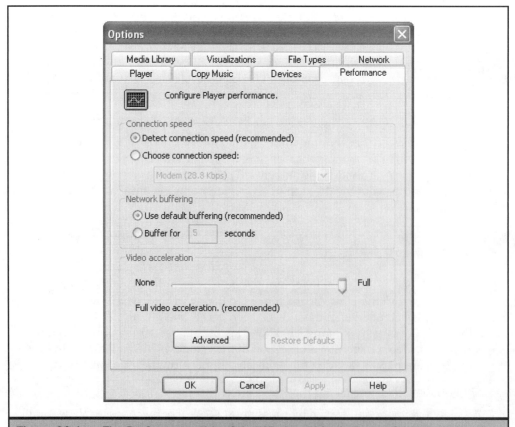

Figure 20-1. *The Performance tab of the Windows Media Player Options dialog box*

for video files to complete downloading. The advent of streaming video improved matters: you can begin playing a streaming video file after only a portion of the file has arrived. The streaming video player continues to receive parts of the file at the same time that it is playing earlier parts. As long as the program can receive information at least as fast as it can play it, you see uninterrupted video. Streaming audio files and players work the same way.

The most popular streaming video format is RealVideo (with extension .rv). You can download the RealPlayer program for free from the Real Web site at **http://www.real.com**; this program works with your Web browser to play RealAudio and RealVideo files from the Internet.

Microsoft has its own streaming video format, called *Advanced Streaming Format*, or *ASF*. Files in this format have the extension .asf or .asx. *ASF files* with the .asf extension contain the actual streaming video data. *ASX files* with the .asx extension contain a single line of text, with the URL of a continuously updating video newsfeed. Windows Media Player can play both ASF and ASX files. Normally, Windows Media Player runs automatically when you start to download an ASF or ASX file from the Internet. You can also run Windows Media Player and then open the streaming file by choosing File | Open URL from the menu.

When you see a link on a Web page for an ASF or ASX file, click the link. Depending on how your Web browser is configured, you may see a message asking whether to open the file or save it; choose to open the file. Your browser downloads the first section of the file, runs Windows Media Player, and begins to play the file. The video may appear in your browser window or in a separate window.

You can use the Stop, Pause, and Play buttons to stop and start the video. When you are done playing the video, close the Windows Media Player window if it remains open. If you started viewing the video by clicking a link in your Web browser, the browser window is probably still open where you left it.

   Strangely, if you use the Media Guide button and the Windowsmedia.com Web site to find streaming video, your browser window may pop up to play the video, rather than Windows Media Player displaying the video.

To find video to watch on the Internet, you can use the Media Guide button on the Windows Media Player toolbar, as shown in Figure 20-2 (see Chapter 19, section "Playing Streaming Audio Files from the Internet").

Creating and Editing Video Files with Windows Movie Maker

Windows Movie Maker is essentially the same program that came with Windows Me. It enables you to edit graphical, audio, and video files into movies that are stored in video files that you can play with Windows Media Player.

Figure 20-2.   *The Media Guide button offers links to online video—some appear in the Windows Media Player window, but most play in your browser.*

Windows Movie Maker creates files called *projects*, with the extension .mswmm. Each project can contain one or more *collections*, which are lists of items to include in the movie. A collection contains *clips*, which can be video, audio, or still-graphics files. Information about your collections is stored in your My Videos folder, which is in your My Documents folder. Once you've created your movie, you can save it as a video file in Windows Media format with the extension .wmv.

The Windows Movie Maker Window

To open Windows Movie Maker choose Start | All Programs | Accessories | Windows Movie Maker. The Windows Movie Maker window has four areas and several toolbars, as shown in Figure 20-3. The parts of the window are

- **Collections list**   Lists the collections in this project. One collection is selected.

- **Clips**   Shows icons for each clip in the currently selected collection. Clips can include graphics files, audio files, or video files. For graphics files, you see a small version of the file (a thumbnail). For audio files, you see a speaker icon. For video files, you see a thumbnail of a scene from the video.

■ **Monitor** Displays the current clip, if it's a graphic or video file. If the current clip is an audio file, you see a speaker icon. Below the Monitor are VCR-style buttons to play the current clip.

■ **Workspace** Displays the timeline or storyboard of your movie, as explained in the section "Composing Your Movie," later in this chapter.

If you've already been working on a movie, Windows Movie Maker opens the last project you opened. You can open any existing project by choosing File | Open Project from the menu or clicking the Open Project icon on the toolbar.

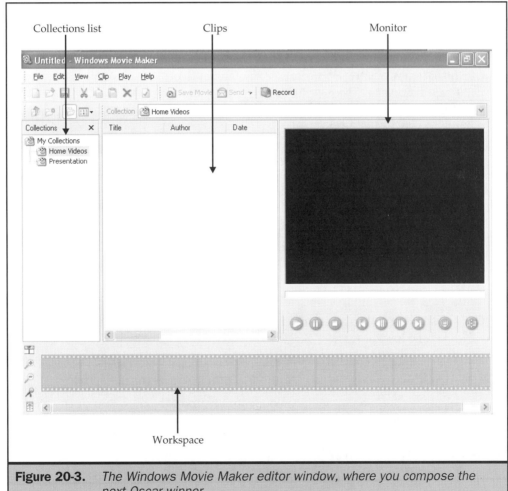

Figure 20-3.   *The Windows Movie Maker editor window, where you compose the next Oscar winner*

We've had a lot of trouble getting Windows Movie Maker to work properly on computers with limited memory. It sometimes can't export your project as a movie that you can play with Windows Media Player, and other times it can't reopen files that it saved only moments before.

Importing Files

Before you can create a movie, you need to import video, audio, and graphic information with which to make the movie. Depending on where your picture, sound, and video information come from, you need the appropriate hardware or access to get that information onto your computer. The three types of information you can import are

- **Video** Some video equipment stores can copy your videotapes to CD-ROM, which you can then import into Windows Movie Maker. If you want to import your own video from a video camera or VCR, you need a video capture card. Both ATI (**http://www.ati.com**) and Creative Labs (**http://www.creativelabs.com**) make reasonably priced video capture cards. You can also acquire video through a FireWire port by connecting it to a digital video camera. Windows Movie Maker can import .wmv, .asf, .avi, .mpg, and other video format files.

- **Audio** You can capture audio with your computer by running the Sound Recorder program, or you can use Windows Media Player to capture music from audio CDs (see Chapter 19, section "Playing and Recording WAV Sound Files with Sound Recorder"). Windows Media Player can import .mp3, .asf, .wma, .wav, and other format audio files.

- **Still pictures** You can use a digital camera or scanner to capture still pictures in graphics files (see Chapter 18). You can also create drawings or titles using Microsoft Paint or another graphics editor (see Chapter 18, section "Drawing Pictures with Microsoft Paint"). Windows Movie Maker can import .gif, .jpg, and other types of graphic files.

Once you have graphic, audio, or video files, you can import them into Windows Movie Maker. Follow these steps:

1. Run Windows Movie Maker and open your project if it's not already open. To create a new project, choose File | New | Project from the menu bar.

2. Select the collection into which you want to import the files. You can create a new collection for them by selecting the top-level collection (My Collections) and choosing File | New | Collection from the menu.

3. Choose File | Import or press CTRL-I. You see the Select The File To Import dialog box.

4. Select the file or files to import. You can select more than one file by holding the SHIFT or CTRL keys while selecting files.

5. After a potentially grueling wait, the files are added to the active collection.

Another way to import files is to drag-and-drop them into the Windows Movie Maker window.

After you import information into the program, Windows Movie Maker shows each clip as a little icon in the current collection. You can find out more about any clip by right-clicking it and choosing Properties from the shortcut menu that appears. To play a single clip, select it and click the Play button on the VCR-style buttons just below the Monitor (the leftmost button).

When you import a video file, Windows Movie Maker automatically breaks it into clips, based on where it thinks the scenes start and end. To turn this feature off, choose View | Options and deselect the Automatically Create Clips option.

You can organize your clips into collections by dragging the clips from one collection to another, or by using cut-and-paste (CTRL-X to cut and CTRL-V to paste).

If you don't have any video, just place all of your still pictures in a collection and make a slide show with still pictures and a soundtrack or narration.

Composing Your Movie

The Workspace area at the bottom of the Windows Movie Maker window displays either the Storyboard or the Timeline. To create a movie out of your clips, you drag them to the Storyboard or Timeline in the order that you want them shown.

The *Storyboard* is like a book, in which each blank square is like the page of a book, and you decide what appears on each page and in what order. Find the first clip—either video or graphic file—and drag it to the first space in the Storyboard. This clip becomes the first page of your story, and the first part of your movie. Continue dragging video and graphic clips to the Storyboard in the order in which you want them to appear. You can always switch the order later. With clips, the Storyboard looks like this:

To move clips around after you've placed them in the Storyboard, just drag them left or right. When a line appears between the clips where you would like to place the clip to be reordered, drop it.

The *Timeline* gives you another view of the same movie. Display it in the Workspace area by clicking the Timeline icon at the left end of the Workspace (switch back to the Storyboard by clicking the Storyboard icon that takes the Timeline icon's place), or choose View | Timeline from the menu (View | Storyboard takes you back to the Storyboard). The Timeline shows the timing of the clips in the movie, displaying how many seconds each clip takes:

You can add, delete, and rearrange the clips on either the Storyboard or the Timeline—the effect is the same. If you delete a clip from the Storyboard or Timeline, it disappears from the movie, but remains in the project available for reuse. If you don't think you'll use a clip after all, you can delete by selecting it in the Clips area and pressing the DELETE key—this action deletes the information from the project.

Adding Sound

To provide a soundtrack, you can drag an audio clip to the Timeline (not the Storyboard). The audio clip runs along the bottom of the Timeline, showing where the audio starts and ends. You can control the balance between the sound portion of the video clips and of the audio soundtrack by choosing Edit | Audio Levels from the menu and sliding the slider between Video Track and Audio Track:

You can record a narration to go with your slide show or video. The idea is to synchronize what you're saying with what's appearing on the screen. (Note: Your computer needs a working microphone to record the narration.) Follow these steps:

1. Choose File | Record Narration to display the Record Narration Track dialog box.

2. If you want to mute the audio track during the playback of the movie, click the check box marked Mute Video Soundtrack.

3. When you're ready, click the Record button. Be prepared—as soon as you click the Record button, Windows Movie Maker begins recording and playing the video at the same time.

4. Talk along with the movie.

5. When you're finished, click the Stop button. Windows Movie Maker prompts
   you to save your narration and imports it into your project.

 *Run through your video a few times, clicking Pause and making some notes. Then spend
some time rehearsing. Don't try to be Marlin Perkins, but you'll gain appreciation if you
do a well-timed job.*

Previewing Your Movie

After you add the clips for your movie, you can see how it looks. Choose Play | Play
Entire Storyboard/Timeline from the menu, or right-click the Storyboard or Timeline
and choose Play Entire Storyboard/Timeline from the shortcut menu that appears. You
can also play a section of the movie by selecting a series of clips from the Storyboard
and clicking the Play button below the Monitor. Or, select all of the clips on the
Storyboard (right-click any clip and choose Select All) and then click the Play VCR
button below the Monitor. The VCR-style controls look like this:

Editing Your Movie

Windows Movie Maker includes many commands for editing your movie. Here are a
few neat things you can do:

- **Slide shows** If you put a graphic file in your movie, Windows Movie Maker
  shows it for five seconds. You can make a good-looking slide show that you
  can send to people through e-mail, just by adding your still photos to the
  Storyboard of a movie. You can change the five-second length to speed up or slow
  down your slide show. On the Timeline, select the clip for the still photo. A pair
  of triangles appears along the top of the clip, one on each end. Drag the right-hand
  triangle to the right to add time to the clip, or to the left to subtract time from it.

- **Transitions** You can create a fading transition from one video or picture to the
  next. Click the first clip of the pair. A pair of triangles appears along the top of the
  clip. Drag the right triangle into the next clip, so the clips appear to overlap:

The wider the overlap, the longer the transition will be. The resulting fade-in looks
like Figure 20-4.

Figure 20-4. *Overlapping two clips results in a fade-in.*

> **Note** *Windows Movie Maker does not have integrated transition effects as other consumer-grade video editors do. You can't add special transitions other than the fade effect.*

■ **Titling** Windows Movie Maker does not have commands to create titles (as some other video edition programs do). To add titles, choose Start | All Programs | Accessories | Paint to run Microsoft Paint (see Chapter 18, section "Drawing Pictures with Microsoft Paint"). Choose Image | Attributes and change the document size to a width of 320 pixels and a height of 240 pixels. Add anything to your title page or pages that you like. A basic black background with white lettering goes well with video presentations and is also easy to read. Save your document or documents using descriptive filenames in a folder to import them into Windows Movie Maker.

Saving Your Movie

Once your movie shines, click the Save Movie button on the toolbar or choose File | Save Movie from the menu. You see the Save Movie dialog box. The Setting box in the Playback Quality section gives you four choices for quality. They are

■ Low Quality

■ Medium Quality (Recommended)

■ High Quality

■ Other (then choose a format in the Profile drop-down menu)

As you set the Play Quality Setting, the File Size shows how large the resulting movie will be. The default is Medium Quality, which gives reasonable clarity and excellent sound. A collection of photographs and music that runs 30 seconds took a mere 791Kb of space at High Quality. It was 94Kb at Low Quality and 343Kb at Medium Quality, all of which are reasonable sizes when sending movies via e-mail. If you plan to make large movies with video, be aware that they can take up anywhere from several megabytes to several hundred megabytes of disk space.

Fill out the other information on the dialog box with as much or as little detail as you wish and click OK. In the Save As dialog box that appears, enter a name for the file. Windows Movie Maker saves the movie in a file with the .wmv extension.

Tip *If you have a CD-R or CD-RW drive, create a CD-ROM to send your family and friends, rather than e-mailing huge files.*

You can e-mail your movies or send them to your Web server directly from Windows Movie Maker. To send a movie via e-mail or the Web, click the Send button on the toolbar or choose File | Send Movie To from the menu. Select E-mail or Web Server from the menu that appears. Choose the quality for the resulting video and fill out the other information on the dialog box. When you click OK, Windows Movie Maker asks which e-mail program to use. Select either Default E-mail Program at the top of the list or the name of the program you typically use from the items below. If you plan to send the videos using a different program another time, leave the Don't Ask Me Again item unchecked. Click OK. Your e-mail program opens and a new message appears, waiting for you to enter the addresses of those you wish to send it to.

Tip *Be sure to check that your intended recipients have Windows Media Player before sending them a movie.*

Playing Video Disks (DVDs)

A *DVD* (*Digital Versatile Disk* or *Digital Video Disk*) is like a large CD—it's a digital disk that can contain video material. If you buy movies on DVDs and you have a DVD drive connected to your computer, you can play DVDs on your computer by using the Windows Media Player program (previous versions of Windows came with a separate DVD Player program). Before you try this, make sure that your DVD drive has the appropriate decoder card and software drivers to play DVDs.

Caution *You cannot play a DVD movie with just a DVD drive and a disc. You must also have a decoder, either built in to the drive, on a separate card (or integrated into your systems video card), or from a software package like WinDVD or PowerDVD. Windows comes with the program—Windows Media Player—but not with the decoder. The next section includes a source for decoders if your DVD drive didn't come with one. Your DVD player may have come with its own player program that you can use for playing DVDs—you don't have to use the Windows Media Player program.*

Configuring Your DVD Decoder

If your computer has a DVD drive, you probably got it in one of two ways: preinstalled in your computer or as a third-party add-on. If the DVD drive was part of your computer system, it should have been tested and properly configured from the get-go, so no additional configuration should be needed.

If, you installed a third-party DVD drive, you need a decoder to read the DVD media. There are two kinds of DVD decoders: hardware and software. Hardware decoders are uncommon (we were only able to locate a single PCI-based DVD decoder card in two hours of searching). Software decoders, however, are easy to find and inexpensive. WinDVD (**http://www.intervideo.com**) is the most popular package, retails for $30 and ships with various third-party DVD drives, and installs in seconds. We found it capable and easy to use, though we recommend at least a 500 MHz Pentium III with 128MB of RAM for reasonable playback performance (an 800 MHz Pentium III with 256MB of RAM and an 8MB video card works about as well as a hardware DVD player).

Another option is PowerDVD from CyberLink (**http://www.gocyberlink.com**). At $49.50 it's not as cheap as WinDVD, but it does have some compelling pluses, such as smoother playback and better color even on slower machines. An 800 MHz PC becomes a powerful multimedia center when PowerDVD is at the helm.

Note	*Either WinDVD or PowerDVD installations allow Windows Media Player to play DVD titles, as they provide the decoder. However, the DVD support in Windows Media Player has resulted in crashes and in most cases does not work as well as the third-party player.*

Needless to say, with such high entrance stakes, DVD on the desktop has not taken off. (Another reason, of course, is that most people prefer to watch movies on larger screens in the comfort of their living rooms, rather than on computer screens at their desks—although they are great for long trips.)

Playing a DVD with Windows Media Player

To play a DVD, insert the DVD in your DVD drive, and Windows Media Player starts automatically. If it doesn't, choose Play | DVD Or CD Audio from the menu bar. If you have more than one CD drive (i.e., CD-RW, DVD, CD), you see a list. Select the drive letter assigned to your DVD player.

When you are playing a DVD, the Windows Media Player works like a VCR (as shown in Figure 20-5). Additional controls may appear for the advanced features that a specific DVD offers: consult the DVD itself. These advanced features may play video clips, alternative edits, different endings, or the ever-popular outtakes. Windows Media Player has a few added DVD interface options. To view them, click Now Playing on the toolbar and make sure that the Equalizer And Settings pane is

Figure 20-5. *Windows Media Player playing a DVD—it's like an onscreen VCR.*

displayed. Click the Select View button and select the DVD Controls item. If there is a problem with your DVD drive's installation or if you are missing a DVD decoder package, this item doesn't appear.

Controlling Rated Movies

One popular feature with parents is Parental Control, which is amazingly simple and effective. The Parental Control feature uses the already existing and well-established MPAA ratings system. Each DVD movie has a lot of additional information encoded into the DVD, including the movie's rating, so the decoder software can tell a G-rated movie from an NC17-rated movie.

Before you can use parental controls, you must set up user accounts for yourself and other users of the computer (see Chapter 6). Assuming that you are a parent, give yourself and other adults administrative user accounts, and make any children's accounts limited-user accounts. Once you set a maximum DVD rating in Windows

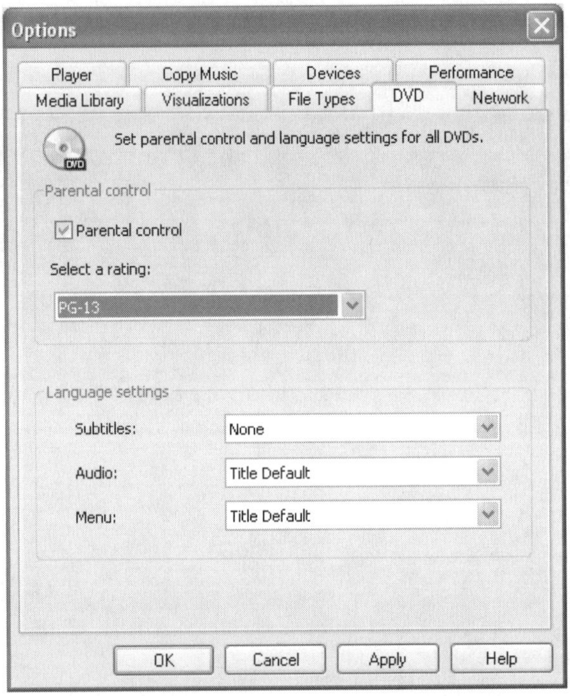

Figure 20-6.   *Parental Control in Windows Media Player*

Media Player's parental controls, only administrative users can play DVDs with higher ratings.

To control which DVDs people can play on Windows Media Player, choose Tools | Options from the menu, and click the DVD tab (shown in Figure 20-6). Select the Parental Control check box, and select the highest rating that you want nonadministrative users of the computer to be able to play.

The
Complete
Reference

Part V

Windows XP on the Internet

The Complete Reference

Chapter 21

Configuring Windows to Work with Your Modem

Before you connect to the Internet (or any other computer) using a modem, you must install your modem, whether you use a conventional modem and phone line, or a high-speed *broadband* DSL (Digital Subscriber Loop) line, cable modem, or ISDN (Integrated Services Digital Network) line (see Chapter 13, section "Installing Modems").

Once your modem is installed, you're ready to read Chapter 22 to sign up for a new Internet account or set up Windows to connect to an existing account.

Note *If you connect to the Internet over a local area network (LAN) rather than by using a modem, contact your LAN system administrator. If you are the system administrator, see Chapter 30.*

If you use a dial-up modem (with a regular or ISDN line) with a laptop, you may want to set up a dialing location for each telephone line from which you dial, so that Windows knows when to dial 1 and the area code. If you charge the cost of your calls to a telephone calling card, you can configure Windows to dial the digits to charge your calling card automatically.

Configuring Windows to Use Your Dial-Up Modem

Since the 1990s, the most common way to connect to the Internet has been via a dial-up modem that attaches to a regular phone line (or via a local area network, for computers in large organizations). Windows needs to know exactly which make of dial-up modem you have, so it can send the appropriate commands. You can also tell Windows from which area code you usually dial, from what other locations you make calls (if you have a portable computer), and to which calling cards you want to charge your calls.

What Does Windows Know about Your Modem?

When you install a modem, Windows either determines what kind of modem it is, or it asks you. Windows installs a *modem driver*, a small program that usually comes with the modem (Windows comes with modem drivers for many popular modems) (see Chapter 13, section "Installing Modems").

You can look at or change your modem configuration settings by choosing Start | Control Panel, clicking Printers And Other Hardware, and then clicking Phone And Modems Options. (If Windows doesn't know you have a modem, the Add New

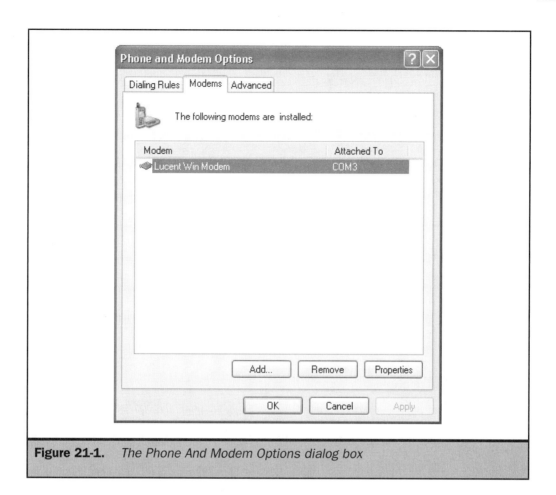

Figure 21-1.   *The Phone And Modem Options dialog box*

Hardware Wizard runs. If your modem is external, make sure it is turned on, and then follow the Wizard's instructions to set up the modem.)

You see the Phone And Modem Options dialog box. Click the Modems tab to see a list of the installed modems, as shown in Figure 21-1. Select the appropriate modem from the list, and then click the Properties button to see the Properties dialog box for the modem, shown in Figure 21-2. (The exact appearance of the dialog box depends on which modem driver you select.) To find out which modem driver Windows uses for your modem, click the Driver tab in the modem's Properties dialog box.

Table 21-1 lists the modem properties that appear in the Properties dialog box for most modems. Table 21-2 shows additional settings that appear on the Default Preferences dialog box for the modem, which you display by clicking the Advanced

WINDOWS XP
ON THE INTERNET

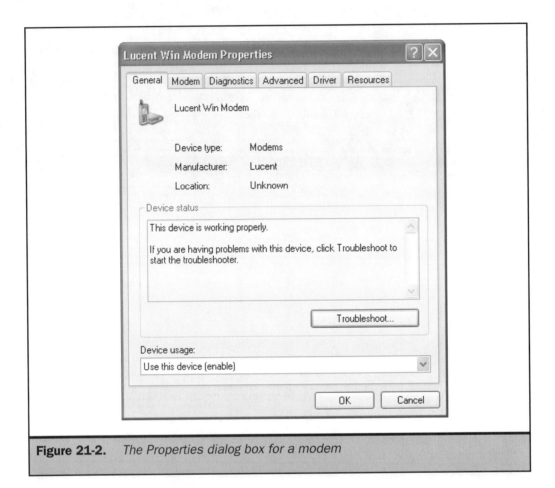

Figure 21-2.   *The Properties dialog box for a modem*

tab on the modem's Properties dialog box, and then clicking the Change Default Preferences button. Except where noted, don't change these settings unless you are sure your modem is configured incorrectly. Most people never have to change these settings except in consultation with their modem manufacturer, communications software publisher, or Internet service provider.

> **Tip**   *You can also display your modem's Properties dialog box from the Device Manager: select the modem and click the Properties button on the toolbar.*

Windows displays another dialog box about your modem—the Modem Configuration dialog box (see Chapter 22, section "Changing Your Dial-Up Connection Settings")—when you click the Configure button from the Properties dialog box of a dial-up connection. The settings on the Modem Configuration dialog box control how the modem works when used for that dial-up connection.

Dialog Box Tab	Setting	Description
General	Device usage	Enables or disables the modem. For example, if your computer's built-in modem is broken, you can disable it and use an external modem.
Modem	Port	Specifies how your modem is connected to your computer. PCs have serial communications ports named COM1, COM2, COM3, and COM4 (most PCs come with only COM1 and COM2), or your modem may connect to a USB or FireWire port. Even if your modem is internal (installed inside the computer), it is assigned a port.
Modem	Speaker volume	Specifies how loud the modem's speaker is set, or how loud the system speaker plays modem sounds.
Modem	Maximum Port Speed	Specifies the maximum speed at which your modem can communicate over the cable to your computer (not over the phone to another modem), in *bps (bits per second)* (usually 115,200 bps).
Modem	Wait for dial tone before dialing	Specifies whether to wait for the modem to detect a dial tone before sending commands to dial; if the modem can't detect a dial tone, this should be deselected. Outside North America, many modems require this to be deselected.
Diagnostics	Modem Information	Displays identifying information about your modem, such as its serial number. Click Query Modem to see the responses to standard modem commands (refer to your modem's manual for the meanings of the commands and responses).
Diagnostics	Append to Log	Specifies whether to store information sent to and from the modem in a log file—usually in C:\Windows\Modemlog_*modemname*.txt. The log file is useful for troubleshooting; to see the log file, click View Log.

Table 21-1.   *Modem Properties on the Properties Dialog Box*

WINDOWS XP
ON THE INTERNET

Dialog Box Tab	Setting	Description
Advanced	Extra initialization commands	Lists additional commands to send to your modem after Windows sends the standard initialization commands. Consult your modem's manual for a list of commands your modem understands.
Driver	Driver Provider, Driver Date, Driver Version, Digital Signer	Displays information about the software driver for the modem. Click Driver Details for more information, including the names and locations of the driver files. Click Update Driver to install a new driver. Click Roll Back Driver to reinstall a previously installed driver. Click Uninstall to remove the driver.

Table 21-1.   *Modem Properties on the Properties Dialog Box* (continued)

Dialog Box Tab	Setting	Description
General	Disconnect a call if idle for more than *xx* min.	Specifies whether to hang up the phone connection if no data is transmitted for a specified number of minutes (usually not selected). Choose this setting if you want to avoid leaving the phone off the hook when you remain online by accident.
General	Cancel the call if not connected within *xx* sec.	Specifies whether to time-out after this number of seconds if no connection occurs (usually selected, with a time-out period of 60 seconds).
General	Port speed	Same as the Maximum Port Speed in the modem Properties dialog box (see Table 21-1).
General	Data Protocol	Specifies what type of error correction to use. Removing error correction may allow modems to make a connection, but may make the connection less reliable.

Table 21-2.   *Modem Properties in the Default Preferences Dialog Box*

Dialog Box Tab	Setting	Description
General	Compression	Specifies whether to compress data before transmitting it (usually enabled). Not all modems support data compression, and the modem to which it is communicating must also support it.
General	Flow control	Specifies whether to use a system of *flow control* to control the flow of data between your modem and your computer. If selected, you have two options: Xon/Xoff or Hardware (preferred).
Advanced	Data bits	Specifies the number of *data bits*, the number of bits of information included in each byte sent (must be eight bits).
Advanced	Parity	Specifies whether the modem uses *parity*, which means the modem sends an error-detection bit as the eighth bit of each byte; and, if so, which type of parity (usually None).
Advanced	Stop bits	Specifies how many extra *stop bits* are sent after each byte (must be one bit).
Advanced	Modulation	Specifies the *modulation*, which is how your modem converts the digital information from your computer into analog "sound" information for transmission over the phone.

Table 21-2.   *Modem Properties in the Default Preferences Dialog Box* (continued)

Troubleshooting Your Modem

If you have trouble getting your modem to connect, here are some things to check:

- **Make sure the correct modem driver is installed.**   Look on the Modems tab of the Phone And Modems Options dialog box to make sure the correct modem is listed. Remove any modems that are no longer installed. If the wrong modem is listed, click Add to run the Add New Hardware Wizard and install the correct driver.

- **Make sure the modem driver is enabled.**   Choose Start, right-click My Computer, choose Manage, and choose Device Manager from the list at the left side of the Computer Management window. Choose View | Devices By Type,

and then click the plus (+) sign next to the Modems entry on the list of devices.
Your modem should appear in the list: if it appears with an exclamation point
or *X* on it, something is wrong. Click it and click the Properties button to
display the Properties dialog box for the modem. On the General tab, make sure
that Device Usage is set to Use This Device (Enabled).

- **Make sure the modem is connected to the correct port.**   Display the
  properties dialog box for the modem as described in the preceding paragraph.
  On the Modem or General tab, check that you see the port to which the modem
  is connected (see Chapter 13, section "Connectors").

- **Make sure the modem speed is right.**   On the Modem tab in the Properties
  dialog box for the modem, check the Maximum Port Speed setting. Choosing
  a lower speed may solve your connection problem.

You can also use the Windows XP Modem Troubleshooter to help pinpoint the
problem. To start the troubleshooter, click the General tab in the modem's Properties
dialog box, and then click the Troubleshoot button. Follow the instructions in the Help
And Support Center window that appears.

> **Tip**   *If you have an external modem, be sure the modem is turned on.*

Configuring Windows for Dialing Locations

If you have a laptop computer, you may connect to the Internet or your online service
from different locations using different phone numbers. Windows enables you to
define one or more dialing locations so that Windows knows from what area code you
are calling and can dial numbers appropriately.

What Is a Dialing Location?

A *dialing location* defines a location from which you use your modem. Windows stores
information about the area code and phone system from which you are dialing,
including whether to dial extra digits to get an outside line. It also remembers whether
the phone line at that location uses *call waiting*, a phone line feature that beeps when
another call is coming in on the line. The call waiting beep disrupts most modem
connections, so you should tell Windows to turn off call waiting before dialing the
phone if you don't want your online session interrupted.

You can use dialing locations when connecting to Internet accounts via dial-up
connections (explained in the next chapter).

Displaying Your Dialing Locations

To define or change your dialing locations, choose Start | Control Panel, click
Printers And Other Hardware, and click Phones And Modem Options. On the

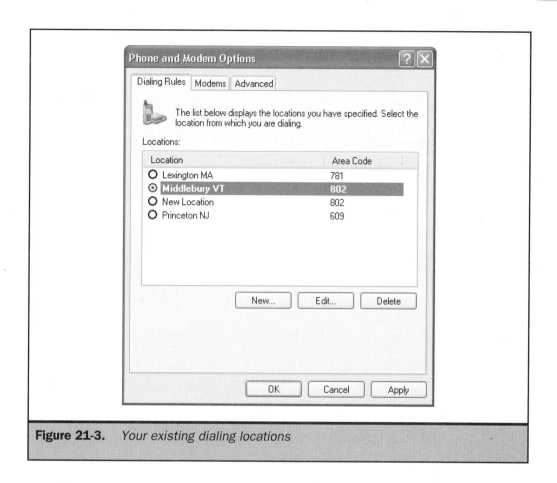

Figure 21-3.   *Your existing dialing locations*

Phone And Modem Options dialog box that appears, click the Dialing Rules tab
(if it's not already selected), which lists your existing dialing locations, as shown
in Figure 21-3.

The Dialing Rules tab enables you to create area code rules to tell Windows when
to dial 1, and enables calling card definitions to tell Windows the access number,
account number, and PIN you use when charging phone calls to a calling card.

Creating a Dialing Location

To make a new dialing location, follow these steps:

1. Click the New button in the Dialing Rules tab of the Phone And Modem
   Options dialog box. You see the New Location dialog box, shown in
   Figure 21-4. (If this is the first dialing location you create, you can skip this
   step and edit the New Location dialing location that already appears.)

2. Type a name for the dialing location in the Location Name box (using any name you'll find helpful), choose the country from the list, and type the area code or city code from which you are dialing.

3. If you need to dial extra digits before dialing local or long-distance phone numbers, type the digits into the two To Access An Outside Line boxes.

4. The Use This Carrier Code To Make Long-Distance Calls/International Calls boxes are rarely used.

5. If the phone line has call waiting (that is, if incoming calls cause a beep on the phone line), select the check box to disable call waiting and select the number to disable it. (Check with your phone company if you are unsure.)

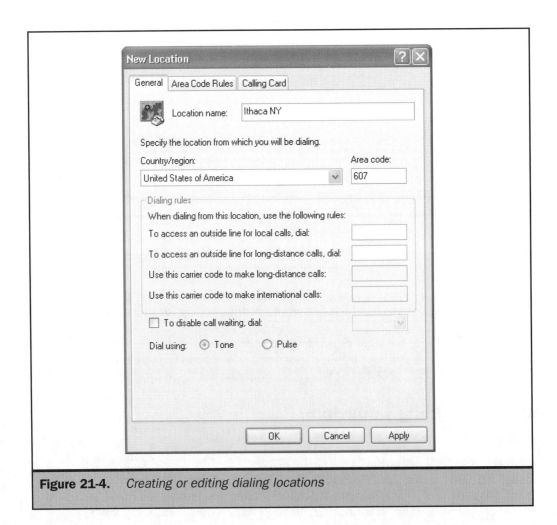

Figure 21-4.   *Creating or editing dialing locations*

6. If your phone doesn't accept tone dialing, set Dial Using to Pulse.

7. If you have to dial 1 and the area code for some exchanges in this area code, or if you have to dial 1 and the area code for all exchanges—even in your own area code—click the Area Code Rules tab to tell Windows exactly what to dial (see "Setting Up Area Code Rules").

8. If you use a calling card to charge the calls made from this phone line, click the Calling Card tab to select a card (see "Configuring Windows to Use Calling Cards").

9. Click OK to return to the Phone And Modem Options dialog box, where your new location appears.

To delete a dialing location, choose the dialing location from the Locations, and click Delete.

Setting a Default Dialing Location

Before you exit from the Phone And Modem Options dialog box, select the dialing location you use most often, so that a dot appears in the radio button to its left. Windows displays this dialing location in dial-up connections, and Fax Console as the default dialing location.

When you go on a trip and arrive at your destination, create a dialing location for the phone from which your computer will be dialing. Select this dialing location before exiting the Phone And Modem Options dialog box to make this location the default. When you return from your trip, display the Phone And Modem Options dialog box again, select the dialing location for your home or office, and click OK. This resets the default to your usual dialing location.

Using Dialing Locations

Dialing locations come in handy when connecting to the Internet and when sending faxes.

■ **Dial-up Internet connections**   You can use dialing rules when calling your ISP with a dial-up connection. In the Connect dialog box, you select your dialing location by clicking the Properties button to display the properties of the dial-up connection, clicking the Use Dialing Rules check box, clicking the Dialing Rules button, and choosing another location (see Chapter 22, section "Dialing the Internet Manually").

■ **Sending faxes**   In the Windows Fax Console, you can use dialing locations when sending a fax (see Chapter 14, section "Sending and Receiving Faxes"). In the Send Fax Wizard, select the Use Dialing Rules check box and choose a dialing location.

Setting Up Area Code Rules

You can configure Windows to dial 1 and the area code automatically when necessary, but not to dial it for local calls.

What Are Area Code Rules?

In the old days, you probably had to dial 1 and the area code only for numbers outside your own area code. Now, you may have to dial 1 and the area code for some or all phone numbers, even within your own area code. You can tell Windows exactly when it has to dial what numbers, so when you type a phone number to dial, Windows can dial the correct sequence of digits. Windows stores this information as an *area code rule*, which defines what Windows should dial when calling from one dialing location to one area code (for example, when dialing 617 area code numbers from your Lexington, Massachusetts dialing location).

Creating Area Code Rules

To tell Windows the dialing rules for an area code

1. Choose Start | Control Panel, click Printers And Other Hardware, and click Phones And Modem Options. On the Phone And Modem Options dialog box that appears, click the Dialing Rules tab (if it's not already selected), as shown in Figure 21-3.

2. Choose the dialing location for which you want to create area code rules, click the Edit button to display the Edit Locations dialog box (shown in Figure 21-4), and then click the Area Code Rules tab. You see a list of the area code rules that apply to calls made from dialing location (the list starts out empty).

3. Click the New button. You see the New Area Code Rule dialog box, shown in Figure 21-5.

4. Type the area code to which this rule applies (that is, Windows follows this rule when dialing numbers in this area code from this dialing location).

5. In the Prefixes section, specify whether the rule appears to all numbers in the area code or only to certain prefixes (or exchanges; that is, the three digits that come after the area code). If the rule applies to certain prefixes, click Add and type the prefixes.

Note   *You can't tell Windows that a rule applies to all prefixes except the ones you list (which would be handy in some area codes).*

6. If you must dial 1 (or another set of digits) for these phone numbers, click the Dial check box and type the digit (usually 1, which already appears there).

7. If you must dial the area code for these phone numbers, click the Include The Area Code check box.

8. Click OK to return to the Edit Locations dialog box, where your rule now appears. Click OK again to return to the Phone And Modem Options dialog box.

You can change an existing area code rule (or delete it) by selecting the dialing location to which it applies from the Dialing Rules tab of the Phone And Modem Options dialog box, clicking Edit, clicking the Area Code Rules tab of the Edit Location dialog box that appears, clicking the area code rule, and clicking Edit or Delete.

Configuring Windows to Use Calling Cards

If you use a telephone calling card to charge your phone calls, especially when you are away from your home or office, Windows can dial all the extra digits for you.

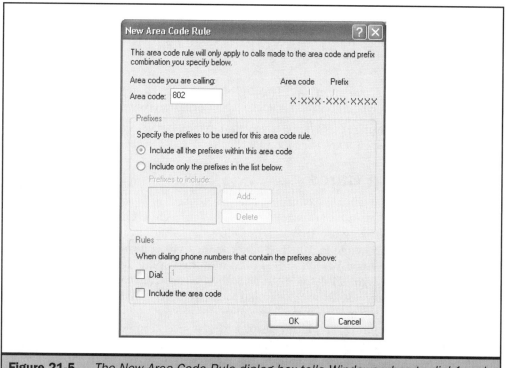

Figure 21-5. *The New Area Code Rule dialog box tells Windows when to dial 1 and the area code.*

What Is a Calling Card?

A *calling card* is a telephone credit card to which you charge toll calls. To use a calling card, you dial several series of digits in addition to the phone number you want to call, usually including some digits to identify your calling card account. Windows can store information about your telephone calling cards; so when you need to connect to an Internet account via a calling card, Windows can dial the special digits for you.

Windows needs to know the following to place calls using a calling card:

- **Account number**   The number you dial to identify yourself to the calling card company. Windows predefined calling cards don't use the account number at all, so we recommend leaving this box blank unless you are setting up your own calling card.

- **Personal ID Number (PIN)**   The number that identifies you to the calling card company, usually your phone number plus four additional digits.

- **Long-distance access number**   The digits you dial to connect to your calling card company before you dial the phone number you want to call or your calling card number. Windows doesn't let you type punctuation, such as dashes—just the digits to dial. For example, to use AT&T from most locations in the United States, you dial 10288, followed by 0; so you would type **102880**. You can also include pauses to wait for a prompt from the calling card company.

- **International access number**   The digits you dial to connect to your calling card company when you want to place an international call.

- **Local access number**   The digits you dial to connect to your calling card number when you want to place a local call.

Setting Up Calling Cards

To create, edit, or delete your list of calling cards, Choose Start | Control Panel, click Printers And Other Hardware, and click Phones And Modem Options. On the Phone And Modem Options dialog box that appears, click the Dialing Rules tab (if it's not already selected), as shown in Figure 21-3. Choose the dialing location for which you want to work with calling cards, click the Edit button to display the Edit Locations dialog box shown in Figure 21-4, and then click the Calling Card tab. You see a list of the calling cards you can use from this dialing location (Figure 21-6). Windows comes with calling cards for the major phone companies predefined.

Windows already knows about dozens of widely used calling cards, including their access numbers and the sequence of numbers to dial when placing a call. To set up a calling card that Windows already knows about, choose it from the Card Types list. Windows displays the default properties for that type of calling card. Only the Account Number and Personal ID Number (PIN) boxes are blank; you must type these numbers before Windows can use the calling card. Also check that the access numbers are right (these are the numbers that Windows tells your modem to dial when making

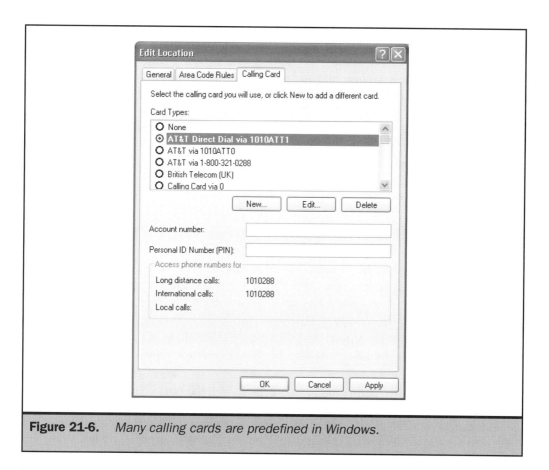

Figure 21-6. *Many calling cards are predefined in Windows.*

long-distance, international, and local calls using the calling card). When you click OK, you return to the Phone And Modem Options dialog box.

Creating a New Type of Calling Card

If your calling card doesn't appear on the Calling Card tab of the Edit Location dialog box for your dialing location, you can create one. You need to know not only the access numbers, account number, and PIN number, but also in what order to dial them and how long to wait between them. The standard set of steps for dialing a calling card number is

1. Dial the access number.

2. Wait for a moment (10 seconds is usually enough).

3. Dial the PIN.

4. Wait a moment more (about 5 seconds).

5. Dial the area code and phone number that you want to call.

When setting up a new calling card, you tell Windows what to dial and when to pause. Follow these steps:

1. Make a note of what you dial and what you wait for when you place a call by hand. If you dial your PIN (phone number plus four extra digits), followed by the number you want to dial, that's all you have to enter. But if there are additional steps, with additional prompts, make a note of them so you can tell Windows how to follow the same steps.

2. In the Edit Location dialog box for the dialing location, click the Calling Card tab and click the New button. You see a dialog box that looks like Figure 21-7. The settings for a new calling card are blank, so you have to enter them.

3. Type the name of the calling card, your account number (if your calling card uses one—most don't, so you can leave it blank), and your PIN (usually your phone number followed by a four-digit number).

4. Click the Long Distance tab (shown in Figure 21-8), in which you tell Windows the sequence of steps to follow when dialing a long-distance number using the calling card. Each step includes dialing a number or pausing for a prompt.

5. In the Access Phone Number For Long Distance Calls box, type the digits you would dial, omitting any punctuation (Windows allows only digits in this box).

6. Consult the notes you made in step 1, then click the button in the lower part of the dialog box to indicate what Windows should do first when dialing the number. For most calling cards, this usually means dialing the access number you typed in step 5, so click Access Number. The step appears in the Calling Card Dialing Steps box.

7. Continue clicking buttons to specify what to dial or how long to wait. If Windows needs to wait before continuing to dial, click Wait For Prompt and specify whether to wait for a dial tone, wait for a message to play, or wait for a specific number of seconds. Each step you specify appears in the Calling Card Dialing Steps box. If you enter a step by mistake, remove it by selecting the step and clicking Delete. You can also change the order of the steps by selecting a step and clicking Move Up or Move Down.

8. When the series of steps looks right, click the International tab to see an identical dialog box for specifying how to dial international calls with the calling card. Then click the Local Calls tab to specify how to dial local calls.

9. Click OK to save all the sequences of steps for the calling card.

If your calling card *does* appear but the access numbers or other information is wrong, you can change it by selecting the calling card and clicking Edit on the Calling Card tab. You see the Edit Calling Card dialog box with the same settings as the New Calling Card dialog box.

Deleting a Calling Card

To delete a calling card, choose the calling card you no longer want to use from the Edit Location dialog box for the dialing location, and then click Delete.

 Don't delete the standard calling cards that come with Windows. You might want to use one again later, and losing all the specifications of that type of calling card would be a shame.

Using Calling Cards

When placing calls using a dial-up connection, in the Properties dialog box for the connection, click the Use Dialing Rules check box, click the Dialing Rules button, choose a dialing location, click Edit, click the Calling Card tab, and choose a calling card to use (see Chapter 22, section "What Are Network Connections?").

When sending a fax with the Windows Fax Console, you can use calling cards when dialing the call (see Chapter 14, section "Sending and Receiving Faxes"). In the Send Fax Wizard, select the Use Dialing Rules check box, choose a dialing location, and

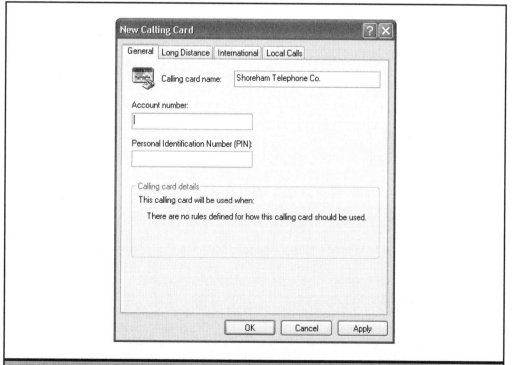

Figure 21-7.   *Entering information about a new calling card*

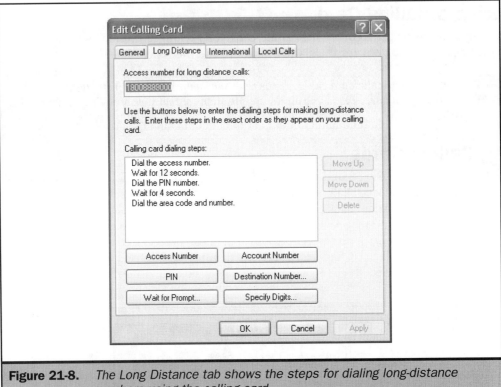

Figure 21-8.   *The Long Distance tab shows the steps for dialing long-distance numbers using the calling card.*

click the Dialing Rules button to see or change the calling card used when making calls from that dialing location.

Connecting to a DSL Line

A *DSL* (*Digital Subscriber Line* or *Digital Subscriber Loop*) is a special phone line that communicates digitally. With a dial-up phone line, your modem converts the digital information from your computer into an analog signal for transmission. At the other end, another modem converts the analog signal back into digital information. Along the way, your phone company may perform additional conversions. With a DSL line, your digital information never has to be converted. Unlike dial-up lines, DSL lines stay connected all the time—there's no waiting for your computer to connect. Data transmission is also much faster than on a dial-up line: downstream (downloading) speeds range from 384 Kbps to 8 Mbps, and upstream (uploading) speeds range from 90 Kbps to 640 Kbps. Some DSL lines support simultaneous computer and voice use.

DSL comes in several varieties:

■ **ADSL**   Asymmetric DSL, because it downloads faster than it uploads

■ **SDSL**   Symmetric DSL

■ **IDSL**   ISDN (Integrated Services Digital Network) emulating DSL

■ **HDSL**   A modern replacement for a T1 line

ADSL, the most common type of DSL line, supports faster communication to your computer (downloading) than from your computer (uploading), which matches the way most people use the Internet. When people talk about DSL, they usually mean ADSL.

There are two ways that your PC can connect to the Internet using your DSL line:

■ **DHCP (Dynamic Host Configuration Protocol)**   Your computer is online all the time, with a numeric IP address assigned to you by your ISP's DHCP server (a server computer that issues IP addresses as needed (see the section "How Does TCP/IP Work?" in Chapter 28).

■ **PPPoE (PPP over Ethernet)**   Your computer must log on each time you want to use the Internet, as if you were dialing in. Once you log in, your ISP issues your computer a numeric IP address that works until you log out (or the connection times out).

Which method you use depends on your DSL provider; you don't get to choose. Windows XP can work with either method. You can find out more about DSL from the xDSL Web site at **http://www.xdsl.com**.

 Because DSL is high speed, it's well suited for allowing a LAN (like a group of networked computers in a home or small office) to share one Internet account (see Chapter 30).

Getting DSL

DSL is not available from all phone companies, but its use is growing. Prices and speeds vary. You can call your local phone company for pricing and availability in your area. Better yet, call your ISP and ask them to order the DSL line for you. You may also be able to get a DSL line from a third-party provider.

To connect your computer to a DSL line, you need a *DSL modem*. DSL modems may be internal or external, and external DSL modems may connect either to a network adapter or to a USB port. Order the DSL line from your ISP when you check whether they offer DSL service; your ISP can probably order the line for you from your phone company. Ask for the phone company or ISP to provide the DSL modem, too—some phone companies don't support DSL modems purchased elsewhere. If the DSL modem requires a network adapter

---

Two-Way Satellite Connections

A new option for connecting to the Internet is by two-way satellite. For example, Starband (at **http://www.starband.com**) and DirecPC (at **http://www.direcpc.com**) offer a satellite dish, satellite modem, Internet account, and optional satellite television service. It's more expensive to install than a DSL or cable Internet, but it's available anywhere in the continental United States where you can see the southern sky.

The satellite dish mounts on your roof, and connects using a coaxial cable and a satellite modem to either the USB or network adapter on your computer. A Starband or DirecPC installer does the installation of both the disk and the modem.

(network interface card, or NIC), get one from a computer store and install it in your computer before the installer arrives (see Chapter 13, section "Network Ports"). The ISP or phone company should provide the software and instructions for configuring Windows to work with the DSL modem. Your phone company or other DSL provider usually installs the DSL modem and configures your computer to use it. They usually configure your network interface card to work with the cable modem.

 Not all DSL modems work with all DSL lines. Get your DSL modem from your phone company or ISP. If you already have a DSL modem, check with your DSL provider to find out whether it will work with their phone lines or not.

Configuring Windows for DSL

To see your DSL configuration, choose Start | My Network Places, click View Network Connections in the Task pane, right-click your DSL connection, and choose Properties to see the Properties dialog box. Click Internet Protocol (TCP/IP) and click the Properties button to see the configuration for the connection. Don't change the settings without information from your phone company or ISP.

 On the Properties dialog box for the DSL connection, make sure that neither the Client For Microsoft Networks nor the File And Printer Sharing For Microsoft Networks check boxes are selected. If they are, deselect them—otherwise, you may be giving other people on the Internet access to your files and printer!

Connecting to a Cable Modem

Some cable television companies offer *cable Internet accounts*—cable connections to the Internet over the same cable that your television uses. Not all cable companies can do so—they must have cables that support two-way transmissions. (A few older cable

Internet systems require a phone line to dial in for uploading information; the cable connection is for downloading only.) Downloading speeds can be fast, although the more people in your neighborhood who are using the cable, the slower transfers go. Uploading usually isn't as fast, but cable connections are almost always faster than dial-up lines. Cable Internet accounts have several advantages over dial-up Internet accounts:

- **Speed**   Cable modems can communicate much faster than dial-up modems. Expect downloading speeds of 1 to 2 Mbps or more, and uploading speeds of between 500 Kbps and 1 Mbps.

- **Separate line**   If you use a cable account, you don't tie up your regular phone line. If you currently pay for a separate phone line for your Internet connection, the cost of a cable Internet account won't be much more (depending on the phone and cable rates in your area).

Call your local cable company to find out if it offers an Internet service. A few cable companies still offer one-way cable with dial-up return—downloading occurs over the cable connection, but you use a regular phone line for uploading. This system is far less convenient than a two-way cable connection because it ties up your phone line, but downloading speeds are an improvement over a regular dial-up line.

Getting Connected

To connect your computer to the cable system, you use a *cable modem*. It connects to a network interface card (also used for connecting to a LAN—see the section "Buying Network Interface Cards (NICs)" in Chapter 27) or (less commonly) to a USB port. Your cable company usually supplies the modem, along with the software and instructions for installing the cable modem and configuring Windows to use it. Some cable companies let you buy or lease the cable modem; consider leasing, because cable modem failure rates are reported to be high. As prices fall and quality improves, buying will eventually become more advantageous. The cable installer usually configures your network interface card to work with the cable modem.

Configuring Windows for a Cable Modem

When your cable installer connects your PC to the cable modem, she usually also configures Windows to work with the cable modem. Windows communicates with the cable modem using the TCP/IP networking protocol, which you can configure. Choose Start | My Network Places, click View Network Connections, right-click your cable Internet connection, and choose Properties to see the Properties dialog box. Click Internet Protocol (TCP/IP) and click the Properties button to see the configuration for the cable connection. Don't change the settings without information from your cable company.

On the Properties dialog box for the cable Internet connection, make sure that neither the Client For Microsoft Networks nor the File And Printer Sharing For Microsoft Networks check boxes are selected. If they are, deselect them—otherwise, the other people in your neighborhood with cable Internet accounts may have access to your files and printer!

Connecting to an ISDN Line

ISDN (Integrated Services Digital Network) is an all-digital phone line that is less widely used in the United States, but quite common, for example, in Europe, where an ISDN line is typically cheaper than two analog phone lines. The type of ISDN service for residential customers is Basic Rate Interface (BRI). A BRI consists of two 64 Kbps (or 56 Kbps on some older systems in the United States) channels, each of which can be used independently for phone, fax, or data connections. Both channels can be combined (bundled) in a single data connection, allowing you to connect at 128 Kbps, over twice the speed of a fast dial-up line (at the cost of being unable to make or receive phone calls over the ISDN line for the duration of the bundled connection). Unlike DSL and cable modems, ISDN is not connected directly to the Internet, but rather to the telephone network, so you connect to the Internet by making a phone call to an ISP which offers ISDN access.

 If your phone company offers DSL, choose it over ISDN, as DSL delivers higher speeds than ISDN, is usually cheaper, and usually lacks a per-minute charge. In the United States, ISDN lines are usually priced with a monthly charge that includes a base number of minutes of usage, plus a per-minute charge if you use the line for additional minutes.

For more information about how ISDN works, see the ISDN Zone Web site at **http://www.isdnzone.com**.

Getting ISDN

You can order an ISDN line from your local telephone company, but you should call your ISP first to confirm they can also provide ISDN service. ISDN lines are more expensive than normal phone lines, and not all phone companies can provide them. Even companies that do provide ISDN lines often have trouble installing them correctly; so if your ISP can arrange to set up the line, order it through them.

You also need an *ISDN terminal adapter* (also called an *ISDN adapter, ISDN TA*, or *ISDN modem*) to connect your computer's serial port to the ISDN phone line. Better yet, get an external ISDN TA with a USB (Universal Serial Bus) interface or an internal ISDN adapter card that installs inside your computer for faster communications (external ISDN adapters that connect to the serial port are limited by the 115 Kbps speed of the serial port). Your ISP (or whatever computer you are connecting to) must have ISDN phone numbers for you to connect to (see Chapter 22, section "Internet (PPP) Accounts").

Configuring Windows for Your ISDN Adapter

Your telephone installer usually installs the ISDN adapter and configures Windows to use it, but here is information about how to do so yourself. See Chapter 13 for how to install an internal ISDN adapter. If you have an external ISDN adapter that connects to the serial port, connect its serial cable to a serial (COM) port on your PC (shut down Windows and turn your PC off first). If you have an external USB ISDN TA, plug it into a free USB connector on your PC (you don't have to turn off your PC first).

When you turn your PC back on or when you plug in an USB ISDN TA, Windows should detect the new hardware and run the Add Hardware Wizard automatically. If it doesn't, choose Start | Control Panel | Printers And Other Hardware and choose Add Hardware from the See Also list. If the Wizard doesn't detect the ISDN adapter, choose Add A New Device.

When Windows has installed the drivers for the ISDN adapter, you (or your telephone installer) configure Windows to use it. The Add Hardware Wizard usually displays a dialog box asking for configuration information: if it doesn't, choose Start | Control Panel | Printers And Other Hardware and choose System to display the System Properties dialog box. Click the Hardware tab and click the Device Manager button. (You can also see the Device Manager from the Computer Management window.) Your ISDN adapter appears in Modems if it is external or Network Adapters if it is internal. Right-click the ISDN adapter and choose Properties from the menu that appears. Click the ISDN tab and select the Switch type or D-channel protocol your phone company uses (ask your phone company for this information). Then click the Configure button and enter the requested information, which you need to get from your phone company or ISP:

- **Phone Number**   The phone number(s) of your ISDN line for U.S. and Canada switch types. Your ISDN line may have one or two phone numbers.

- **Service Profile Identifier (SPID)**   Your ISDN phone number, plus a few extra digits that identify the type of ISDN switch. SPIDs are generally used only in the United States and Canada.

- **Multi-Subscriber Numbers (MSN)**   The phone number(s) of your ISDN line for European ISDN (DSS1)—this has nothing to do with MSN, Microsoft's ISP. European ISDN allows multiple phone numbers on an ISDN line. You only need to enter the MSN(s) you actually intend to use with your computer—the MSNs you want to your computer to accept calls for, and the MSN to which you want outgoing calls to be billed. Note that outgoing calls you make with your computer will be billed to the first MSN in the list, which will always be the lowest number, since Windows sorts the list. If you enter no MSN, the calls will be billed to the primary MSN of your line.

 You must be logged on using an administrator account to configure your ISDN adapter.

See "Creating a Network Connection for an ISDN Line" for how to create and configure a dial-up connection for your ISDN line.

The Complete Reference

Chapter 22

Connecting to the Internet

Once your modem is installed (as described in the previous chapter), you need to configure Windows XP to work with the account. How you connect depends on the type of account. Windows can have network connections to dial-up, ISDN, DSL, and cable Internet accounts as well as connections to local area networks (LANs).

If you don't already have an Internet account, the New Connection Wizard can help you sign up for one. If you have an account, this Wizard can create a network connection for the account. Once created, you can configure, copy, or delete the network connection manually. Then you can connect to and disconnect from the Internet manually, or configure Windows to connect automatically when you request information from the Internet.

If your computer is connected to a local area network, you can connect to the Internet over the LAN if another computer serves as an Internet gateway. If you have a small LAN at home or in a small organization, Windows XP comes with a program called Internet Connection Sharing that allows a computer running Windows to act as an Internet gateway for all the computers on the LAN (see Chapter 30).

If you dial in to your Internet account, you can tell Windows either to dial direct or use a telephone calling card, and you can specify whether to dial the area code or not (see Chapter 21).

For all types of accounts, the built-in Ping, Tracert, and Netstat programs can help you test your connection. This chapter describes all these programs.

To What Types of Internet Accounts Can Windows Connect?

To connect to the Internet, you can use one of several types of accounts: Internet PPP accounts (using a dial-up, ISDN, or DSL line), cable Internet accounts, or online services. You can also use an old-fashioned text-based account (see the "UNIX Shell Accounts and Bulletin Board Systems" sidebar in this chapter). Cable Internet accounts are described in "Connecting to a Cable Modem" in Chapter 21.

If you use America Online (AOL), you must use the software that AOL provides—you can't use Windows network connections. AOL connection software may come with your Windows XP installation (as it has with previous versions of Windows). If you use a UNIX shell account (where you type UNIX commands), bulletin board system, or other text-based system, you can connect to the Internet by using HyperTerminal, the Windows terminal program (see Chapter 26, section "Logging into Text-Based Systems with HyperTerminal").

Internet (PPP) Accounts

A *PPP (Point-to-Point Protocol)* account is an Internet account that uses the PPP communications protocol. PPP is the most popular type of Internet account because the most popular software—Internet Explorer, Netscape Navigator, Outlook Express, Eudora, and other programs—is designed to work with PPP accounts. Occasionally, you may run into a *SLIP* (Serial Line Internet Protocol) or *CSLIP* account (Compressed SLIP), which are older, less-reliable protocols than PPP, but which work the same way. This book refers to PPP, CSLIP, and SLIP accounts as *dial-up Internet accounts*.

An *Internet service provider (ISP)* is an organization that provides Internet accounts, usually PPP accounts, but occasionally UNIX shell accounts. All ISPs provide dial-in accounts using regular phone lines, and many also provide ISDN and DSL connections.

Previous U.S. versions of Windows came with sign-up programs for ISPs, but Microsoft appears now to be pushing Microsoft Network (MSN) instead—their own ISP. The New Connection Wizard offers to set you up with an MSN account. You can also use the Wizard to call the Microsoft Referral Service to find out about ISPs in your area. The New Connection Wizard is described in the "Signing Up for a New Account" section in this chapter.

Dial-Up Internet Accounts, Including ISDN

To connect to an Internet account over a dial-up phone line, you need a PPP-, CSLIP-, or SLIP-compatible communications program, which is built into Windows (see "What Are Network Connections?"). Windows Network Connections can dial the phone by using your modem; connect to your ISP; log into your account by using your user name and password; and then establish a PPP, CSLIP, or SLIP connection, so your computer is connected to the Internet. While connected, you can use a variety of Winsock-compatible programs to read your e-mail, browse the Web, and access other information from the Internet. When you are done, you tell Windows to disconnect from your Internet account. You configure your network connection by using the New Connection Wizard (see "Running the New Connection Wizard"). You can also create and edit network connections manually (see "Changing Your Dial-Up Connection Settings").

What Is TCP/IP?

TCP/IP is the acronym for Transmission Control Protocol/Internet Protocol, the way computers communicate with each other on the Internet. All Internet accounts use TCP/IP. Windows XP also uses TCP/IP for communication over local area networks (see Chapter 22, section "What Is TCP/IP?").

Dial-up connections that appear in the Network Connections window were called Dial-Up Networking (DUN) connections in previous versions of Windows.

ISDN phone lines are a high-speed type of dial-up line; see the section "Connecting to an ISDN Line" in Chapter 21 for instructions on how to configure Windows to connect to an ISDN line. Then see "Creating a Network Connection for an ISDN Line" later in this chapter.

You can have several network connections on one computer. For example, your laptop computer might have one network connection for the DSL account you use at home and another for the national ISP you dial into when you are traveling.

DSL Accounts

If you want to use a high-speed Internet account, check with local and national ISPs to find out which ones offer DSL in your area. If your ISP offers ISDN or DSL accounts, they can work with your telephone company to get the high-speed phone line installed and tell you the type of ISDN or DSL modem you need. See the section "Connecting

---

UNIX Shell Accounts and Bulletin Board Systems

Before the advent of PPP and SLIP accounts, most Internet accounts were text-only *UNIX shell accounts*. You run a *terminal-emulation program* (a program that allows your PC to pretend it's a computer terminal) on your PC to connect to an Internet host computer. Most Internet hosts run UNIX, a powerful but frequently confusing operating system, and you have to type UNIX commands to use a UNIX shell account. To send and receive e-mail or browse the Web, you run text-only programs, such as pine (the most popular UNIX e-mail program) and Lynx (the most widely used UNIX Web browser). UNIX shell accounts don't let you see graphics, use a mouse, or easily store information on your own computer.

Some ISPs give you both a PPP account and a UNIX shell account; you use the PPP account for your regular Internet work, and the UNIX shell account only when you need to change your account's password.

A *bulletin board system (BBS)* is another type of text-based account to which you dial in directly. Like UNIX shell accounts, you usually connect to BBSs with a terminal emulator. Most bulletin board systems have migrated to the Internet, but a few are still independent, including the card-catalog systems of some small libraries.

Windows comes with HyperTerminal, a terminal-emulation program you can use to connect to UNIX shell accounts and BBSs (see Chapter 26, section "Logging into Text-Based Systems with HyperTerminal").

to a DSL Line" in Chapter 21 for how to configure Windows to work with a high-speed account.

Cable Internet Accounts

With a cable Internet account, your cable television company is your ISP, and you connect to the Internet over your cable. Contact your cable company to find out whether it offers Internet accounts. If it does, sign up to open an account. The monthly fee usually includes the rental of a cable modem. See "Configuring Windows for a Cable Modem" in Chapter 21 for an explanation of how to configure Windows to work with a cable Internet account.

Online Services

An *online service* is a commercial service that enables you to connect and access its proprietary information system. Most online services also provide an Internet connection, e-mail, access to the Web, and sometimes other Internet services. Online services usually require special programs to connect to and use your account. Previous U.S. versions of Windows came with signup programs for some online services.

The two most popular online services in the United States are America Online (AOL) and CompuServe (CIS), which is owned by AOL. The Microsoft Network (MSN) started out as an online service, but has been relaunched as an ISP (see "The Microsoft Network (MSN)"). AOL and CompuServe let you use some Winsock-compatible programs while you are connected to the account. For example, you can use the Internet Explorer or Netscape Navigator Web browsers with any of these accounts. However, AOL doesn't support standard e-mail programs—you have to use their software (or their Web site) to read your mail.

AOL is available in the United States, Canada, and the U.K., with other countries being added. The latest version of the America Online software (as of 2001) is 6.0 but 7.0 is on the way. To sign up for an AOL account, install and run the AOL software. Download the software from the AOL Web site, if you haven't already received it on

---

The Microsoft Network (MSN)

Microsoft Network (MSN) was Microsoft's entrant in the world of online services in 1995. Although MSN has gained a lot of users because of the easy-to-click icon on the Windows 95, 98, and Me desktops, it's never been as highly rated as AOL or CompuServe. Microsoft has changed MSN from an online service to a regular Internet service, so you now use network connections to connect to MSN and Winsock programs to access its services.

When you start Internet Explorer, you usually start at the MSN portal Web site **http://www.msn.com**, which is accessible no matter what kind of Internet account you use.

What Is Winsock?

Winsock (short for *Windows Sock*ets) is a standard way for Windows programs to work with Internet connection software. Any Winsock-compatible program can work with any Winsock-compatible connection software. Windows network connections are Winsock-compatible; if you use them to connect to your Internet account, you can use almost any Winsock-compatible program with your account. Most popular Internet programs are compatible with the Winsock standard.

The key file for Winsock is named Winsock.dll. Windows comes with a Winsock.dll file in the C:\Windows\System32 folder. The connection software for some online services (such as America Online) also provide Winsock.dll files, so you can use Winsock-compatible software with their services.

Windows comes with many Winsock-compatible programs, including Internet Explorer (see Chapter 24) and Outlook Express (see Chapter 23). See Chapter 26 for descriptions of other Winsock-compatible programs.

a CD-ROM bound into a magazine or in a direct mail solicitation. Windows XP may come with the AOL software preinstalled, especially if you buy a computer with Windows XP preinstalled. The program steps you through connecting to AOL using an existing account, or signing you up for a new one.

What Are Network Connections?

A *network connection* tells Windows how your computer is connected to another computer, whether over the phone or via a cable. Windows supports these types of network connections:

- **Dial-up connection**   Connection using a modem and phone line, either a regular phone line or an ISDN line. Dial-up connections to the Internet are described throughout this chapter. Dialing one computer from another is described in section "Connecting Two Computers by Using a Dial-Up Connection" in Chapter 27.

- **Local area network (LAN) connection**   Connection over a cable or wireless LAN adapter to other computers in the same building. LAN connections are described in Chapter 28. DSL and cable Internet accounts usually appear as LAN connections, because they don't have to dial in.

- **Virtual Private Network (VPN) connection**   Connection to a private LAN over the Internet. See Chapter 27 for details.

- **Direct network connection**   Connection to another computer over a cable or infrared link. See the section "Connecting Two Computers with Direct Network Connection" in Chapter 27.

- **Incoming connection**   Connection that allows other computers to dial in to your computer (or connect via a cable, infrared link, or over the Internet as part of a VPN) (see Chapter 27, section "Connecting Computers Without a LAN").

- **Gateway connection**   Connection through another computer. For example, if you connect to the Internet via Internet Connection Sharing on another computer on a LAN, you see a Residential Gateway connection on your computer (see Chapter 30).

To see network-related tasks you can perform, such as creating and editing network connections, display the Network And Internet Connections window shown in Figure 22-1 by choosing Start | Control Panel | Network And Internet Connections. You also use this window to manage your LAN connections, as described in Chapter 28.

To see your existing Internet and LAN connections, click the Network Connections icon to display the Network Connections window, shown in Figure 22-2. (You might

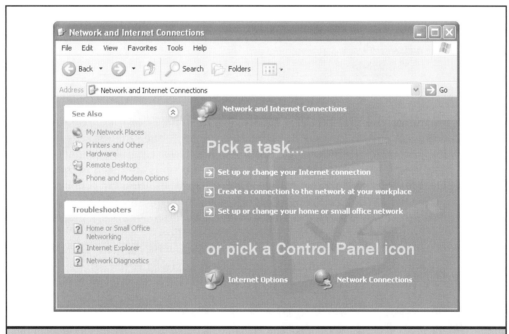

Figure 22-1.   *The Control Panel's Network And Internet Connections window*

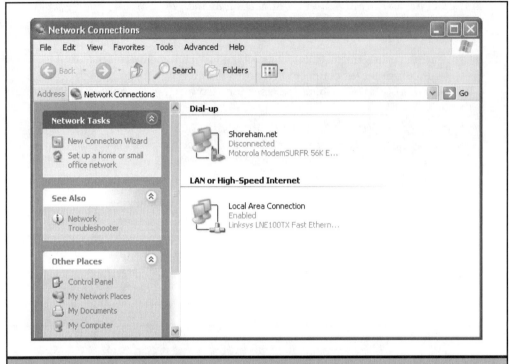

Figure 22-2.   *The Network Connections window shows both Internet and LAN connections.*

think to click the Internet Options icon instead, but the dialog box that this icon displays pertains mainly to Internet Explorer rather than connecting to the Internet.) The Network Connections window lists every way that your computer connects to other computers: LAN, cable Internet, and DSL connections are listed in the LAN Or High-Speed Internet section and dial-up connections (including ISDN connections) are listed in the Dial-Up section. You can right-click a connection in the Network Connections window and choose Properties from the menu that appears to see or change the properties for that LAN or Internet connection.

You can also display the Network Connections window by choosing Start | Connect To | Show All Connections (if Connect To appears on your Start menu) or Start | All Programs | Accessories | Communications | Network Connections.

To add a Network Connections command to your Start menu, see the sidebar "Displaying the Network Connections Window" in Chapter 27. Then you can display the Network Connections window by choosing Start | Network Connections.

Signing Up for a New Account

We recommend that you choose an ISP by talking to people you know and determining which ISP your friends and coworkers are most satisfied with. However, you can also use the New Connection Wizard to look for ISPs with phone numbers in your area or sign up for an MSN account. Whether you have already chosen an ISP or want use the Microsoft Internet Referral Service to select an ISP, you start by running the New Connection Wizard.

Running the New Connection Wizard

The New Connection Wizard starts automatically when you run an Internet application (such as Internet Explorer or Outlook Express) with no Internet connection configured. You can also start the New Connection Wizard by clicking Create A New Connection in the Task pane of the Network Connections window, or by choosing Start | All Programs | Accessories | Communications | New Connection Wizard. The New Connection Wizard gives you four choices (shown in Figure 22-3):

- **Connect to the Internet** Helps you sign up for a new Internet account and configures a network connection to connect to it. The rest of this chapter describes how to use this option.

- **Connect To The Network At My Workplace** Helps you create a Virtual Private Network connection via the Internet (see Chapter 27, section "Connecting Computers with Virtual Private Networking").

- **Set Up A Home Or Small Office Network** Runs the Network Setup Wizard to help you set up a LAN (see Chapter 28, section "Configuring Your LAN Connection by Using the Network Setup Wizard").

- **Set Up An Advanced Connection** Helps you create an incoming connection so that other people can connect to your computer, or a direct network connection for a computer that is directly cabled to yours (see Chapter 27, section "Connecting Computers Without a LAN").

Choose Connect To The Internet and click Next to move from screen to screen. The next two sections describe how to use the Wizard to sign up for an Internet account.

 Previous versions of Windows came with the Internet Connection Wizard, which has been replaced with the New Connection Wizard. If the Internet Connection Wizard is still lurking on your system (for example, if you upgraded from Windows 9x/Me), close this Wizard if it runs, and use the New Connection Wizard instead. The only time we find the Internet Connection Wizard useful is when Outlook Express runs it to set up your e-mail account.

WINDOWS XP
ON THE INTERNET

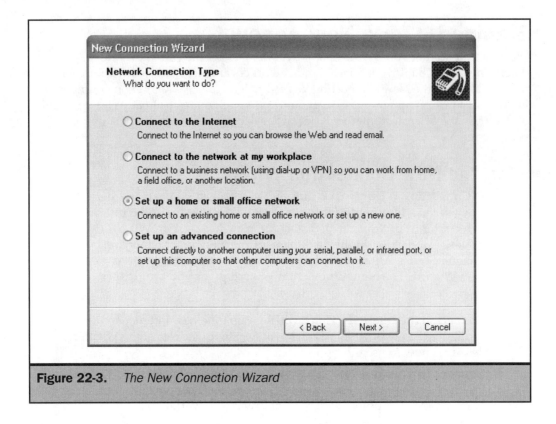

Figure 22-3.   *The New Connection Wizard*

Letting the Microsoft Internet Referral Service Recommend an ISP

Follow the instructions in the previous section to run the New Connection Wizard. Make these choices, click Next after each:

- **Network Connection Type**   Click Connect To The Internet.
- **Getting Ready**   Click Choose From A List Of Internet Service Providers (ISPs).
- **Completing The New Connection Wizard**   Click Select From A List Of Other ISPs. The Wizard dials a toll-free number (if you are in the United States) to connect to the Microsoft Internet Referral Service.

After a delay, you see a window that lists its suggested ISPs and online services. You can read about each ISP or online service by clicking its name. If you want to sign up for an account with one of these ISPs, click Next. Otherwise, click Cancel.

Microsoft's list of ISPs includes only a few of the large national ones, but no local ISPs. In fact, Microsoft may choose to make a deal with one or two big ISPs and recommend only those ISPs to everyone. The ISPs listed don't necessarily have local numbers in your area, even though you told Microsoft your area code and exchange. Before you choose an ISP, look for ads in the business section of your local newspaper to see what local ISPs are available. A small, local ISP usually gives better service and support than a large one, along with having a better selection of local numbers. If you travel frequently with a laptop, consider a national ISP, or stick with a small, local ISP and use a national ISP when you're on the road.

If you choose to create a new account by using one of the ISPs listed by Microsoft, the Wizard asks you to provide information about yourself, including a credit card to which you want to charge your account. The sign-up procedure varies by ISP. During the sign-up, be sure to write down all the information the sign-up program displays, including technical support phone numbers, account numbers, and passwords.

 Before using your account, find out whether the number your modem will be dialing to connect to the account is a local call for you. If not, you should probably cancel the account, because the long-distance charges for using the account will be many times more than the cost of the account itself. Instead, find a local ISP with a local phone number and configure a network connection for the account.

Signing Up for an MSN Account

The New Connection Wizard gives you the option of signing up for an MSN account. Follow the instructions in the section "Running the New Connection Wizard" earlier in this chapter to start the Wizard. Click the Next button to move from screen to screen, answering its questions:

- **Network Connection Type**   When the Wizard asks what you want to do, choose Connect To The Internet.
- **Getting Ready**   To get help choosing an ISP, click Choose From A List Of Internet Service Providers (ISPs).
- **Completing the New Connection Wizard**   Choose Get Online With MSN.
- **Use MSN Explorer?**   The Wizard offers to set up MSN Explorer as your Web browser and e-mail program (see Chapter 24).
- **Welcome to MSN Explorer**   Whether you choose Yes or No, MSN Explorer runs and steps you through setting up an MSN account.

Creating a Network Connection for an Existing Account

To create a new network connection to a dial-up Internet account, you use the New Connection Wizard. For ISDN accounts, see "Creating a Network Connection for an ISDN Line" later in this section. For DSL accounts, your DSL installer should already have set up Windows to work with your account: some DSL accounts appear as dial-up connections in the Network Connection window, and you use this connection to log in.

 If you installed Windows XP, the Setup Wizard may have created a network connection for your Internet account during Windows setup. Check the Network Connections window to find out.

Creating a Dial-Up Connection

The New Connection Wizard can create a network connection, with much more straightforward questions. Run it by following the instructions in the section "Running the New Connection Wizard" earlier in this chapter. Click Next to move from screen to screen and answer the following questions:

- **Network Connection Type**   Choose Connect To The Internet.

- **Getting Ready**   Choose Set Up My Connection Manually.

- **Internet Connection**   Choose the type of phone line (or cable Internet connection) you use.

- **ISP Name**   Type the name that you want to use for this connection. It doesn't have to be your ISP's name—it's the name that Windows will assign to the connection icon.

- **Phone Number**   (for dial-up accounts only) Type your ISP's access phone number.

- **Internet Account Information**   Type the user name and password for the account (your ISP provides this information).

- **Use This Account Name And Password When Anyone Connects To The Internet From This Computer**   If you want all user accounts on your computer to be able to use this Internet account, leave this check box selected.

- **Make This The Default Internet Connection**   If you want to use this network connection to connect to the Internet whenever you run an Internet program and you're not already online, leave this check box selected.

- **Turn On Internet Connection Firewall For This Connection**   Unless you have a specific program (for example, a chat program or interactive game) that doesn't work through a firewall, leave this check box selected (see Chapter 31, section "Enabling the Internet Connection Firewall Between Your PC and the Internet").

- **Add A Shortcut To This Connection To My Desktop**   A shortcut to your ISP connection used to be handy, but no longer. Now Windows can connect to your account automatically when you run your Web browser, e-mail program, or other Internet program, so you rarely need to start your Internet connection yourself.

The Wizard creates a new icon in the Network Connections window, and you see the Connect window described in "Connecting to Your Account" later in this chapter.

Creating a Network Connection for an ISDN Line

To create a dial-up connection for an ISDN line, run the New Connection Wizard by following the instructions in the section "Running the New Connection Wizard" earlier in this chapter. Click Next to move from screen to screen, and answer the following questions:

- **Network Connection Type**   Choose Connect To The Internet.
- **Getting Ready**   Choose Set Up My Connection Manually.
- **Internet Connection**   Choose Connect Using A Dial-Up Modem.
- Windows shows a list of available devices that contains the individual ISDN channels of your ISDN adapter, as well as an entry named All Available ISDN Lines Multi-linked, which is selected by default.
- Keep this selection if you want to bundle both channels of your ISDN line (for 128 Kbps speed), or clear it and select only one of the channels if you always want to connect with a single channel at 56/64 Kbps.

The Wizard creates the dial-up connection for the ISDN line. Now you can configure the ISDN line type to use. Follow these steps:

1. Right-click the dial-up connection icon in the Network Connections window. Choose Properties from the menu that appears. You see the Properties dialog box for the ISDN connection.
2. On the General tab, select the ISDN channel that you want to configure. Click the Configure button to display the ISDN Configuration dialog box.
3. Set the Line Type, Negotiate Line Type, and other settings according to the instructions you receive from your phone company or ISP.

Tip   *Some phone companies charge "data" calls by the minute, while "voice" calls are free. For that reason, some ISPs allow you to connect with the "56K Voice" line type, which disguises the connection as a "voice" call" to the phone company. This method is called Data Over Voice (DOV).*

If you create a multilinked ISDN connection that bundles both of your ISDN channels, you can also configure the bundling. Click the Options tab of your dial-up connection's Properties dialog box and select the bundling behavior under Multiple Devices:

- **Dial Only First Available Device**   Uses only the first free ISDN channel and leaves the other one available, so you can still make or receive phone calls.

- **Dial All Devices**   Creates a "static" 128 Kbps connection that uses both ISDN channels all of the time.

- **Dial Devices Only As Needed**   Allows dynamic use of the ISDN channels, which you can configure by clicking the Configure button. With this setting, Windows initially uses only one ISDN channel, and starts using the second one when you fully exploit the bandwidth of this channel for an extended time period (for example, when you start downloading a big file). When the download is finished, Windows automatically disconnects the second ISDN channel again.

(Thanks to Robert Schlabbach for these instructions.)

Changing Your Dial-Up Connection Settings

Once you have used the New Connection Wizard to create a network connection, you can change its settings, copy it, rename it, or delete it. You can also choose which network connection is the default for connecting to the Internet.

Note   *Previous versions of Windows didn't come with TCP/IP (the communications protocol used on the Internet) preinstalled. Instead, you chose it from a list of popular network protocols. Windows XP comes with TCP/IP installed, and you can't uninstall it. (It's unlikely that you'd want to do so, since TCP/IP is used for both the Internet and LANs!)*

To configure a network connection or to change an existing connection's configuration, open the Network Connections window by choosing Start | Connect To | Show All Connections (if Connect To appears on the Start menu), choosing Start | Network Connections (if Network Connections appears on the Start menu), clicking View Network Connections from the Task pane of the My Network Places window, or choosing Start | Control Panel | Network And Internet Connections | Network Connections. Right-click the icon for the connection and choose Properties from the menu that appears, or select the connection icon and choose File | Properties. Either way, you see the Properties dialog box for the network connection. Different types of connections display different properties dialog boxes. Figure 22-4 shows one for a dial-up connection, and Table 22-1 lists dial-up connection properties. For the properties of LAN connections (including DSL and cable

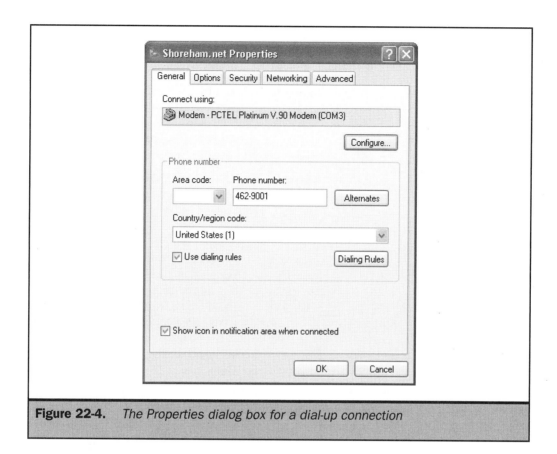

Figure 22-4. *The Properties dialog box for a dial-up connection*

Internet connections), see section "Installing and Configuring Network Components" in Chapter 28.

You can set a few more items by clicking the Configure button on the General tab of the Properties dialog box for the connection: you see the Modem Configuration dialog box. Most of the settings on this dialog box are the same as the settings in the modem's Properties dialog box (see Chapter 21, section "What Does Windows Know About Your Modem?"). One is not: the Show Terminal Window setting specifies whether Windows displays a terminal window before dialing, to enable you to type modem commands.

Caution *Make sure that file and printer sharing are not enabled for your Internet connection, unless you want to allow everyone on the Internet to access the files on your computer. On the Networking tab of the Properties dialog box for your Internet connection, make sure that the check boxes are not selected for these two components:*

- File And Printer Sharing For Microsoft Networks
- Client For Microsoft Networks

WINDOWS XP ON THE INTERNET

Tab in Properties Dialog Box	Setting	Description
General	Connecting using	Specifies which modem to use to connect. Click the Configure button to check or change the configuration of the modem (see Chapter 21).
General	Phone number	Specifies the phone number your computer dials to connect to the account. Composed of the area code, telephone number, and country code (you choose from a list of countries). Click the Alternates button to enter additional phone numbers. Select the Use Dialing Rules check box to use area code dialing rules and calling cards (see Chapter 21, section "Setting Up Area Code Rules").
General	Show icon in notification area when connected	Specifies whether to display an icon at the right end of the taskbar. You can click the icon to see the status of the connection.
General	All devices dial the same number	Appears only for multilink connections (which use multiple phone lines for the connection). Specifies whether the same phone number is dialed when additional phone lines are used for this connection.
Options	Display progress while connecting	Specifies whether to display the Connection dialog box, which shows whether Windows is dialing or verifying your user name and password before the connection is made.

Table 22-1.   *Settings for a Dial-Up Connection*

Tab in Properties Dialog Box	Setting	Description
Options	Prompt for name and password, certificate, etc.	Specifies whether to display a dialog box that prompts for your user name and password (or other security information if your account requires it) before connecting.
Options	Include Windows logon domain	Specifies that if the preceding check box is selected, Windows also prompts for your logon domain. This setting isn't used by most ISPs.
Options	Prompt for phone number	Specifies whether to include the phone number in the Connect dialog box displayed before connecting to the account. This setting allows you to check or change the phone number each time you dial the account.
Options	Redial attempts	Specifies how many times Windows redials the connection if it can't connect.
Options	Time between redial attempts	Specifies how long Windows waits before dialing again.
Options	Idle time before hanging up	Specifies whether Windows disconnects if the connection is idle for a specified length of time. Choose Never to disable auto-disconnect.
Options	Redial if line is dropped	Specifies whether Windows reconnects if the connection is lost (for example, if the ISP hangs up).
Options	X.25	Displays the X.25 Logon Settings dialog box, in which you specify the X.25 network provider and the X.121 address of the server to which you are connecting.

Table 22-1.   *Settings for a Dial-Up Connection* (continued)

WINDOWS XP
ON THE INTERNET

Tab in Properties Dialog Box	Setting	Description
Security	Validate my identity as follows	Specifies how your ISP determines who you are. For most ISPs, choose Allow Unsecured Password (that is, passwords are sent unencrypted). For corporate networks, you may need to choose Require Secured Password or Use Smart Card.
Security	Automatically use my Windows logon name and password (and domain if any)	Specifies what user name and password to use (available only if you set the preceding setting to Require Selected Password or Use Smart Card). Usually not selected for Internet accounts.
Security	Require data encryption (disconnect if none)	Specifies that the computer to which you are connecting must support encryption for all information transmitted, and to disconnect otherwise (available only if you set the preceding setting to Require Selected Password or Use Smart Card). This setting is rarely used.
Security	Advanced (custom settings)	Click the Settings button to display the Advanced Security Settings dialog box, on which you can specify EAP (Extensible Authentication Protocol) or other advanced protocols, if your ISP supports them.
Security	Show terminal window	Specifies whether to display a terminal window that shows the interaction between the network connection and the account while the logon script is running. During debugging, select this setting so you can see the terminal window.

Table 22-1.   *Settings for a Dial-Up Connection* (continued)

Tab in Properties Dialog Box	Setting	Description
Security	Run script	Specifies the name of the file containing the logon script for this connection (see "Creating and Using Logon Scripts"). Click Edit to edit a script file or Browse to select an existing file.
Networking	Type of dial-up server I am calling	Specifies the type of account; all ISPs now provide PPP. Your other choice is SLIP. Click Settings to display the PPP Settings dialog box, in which you can choose whether to use LCP (Link Control Protocol) extensions, which are not supported by older PPP accounts; whether to enable software compression, which enable most PPP accounts to speed up throughput; and whether to use *multilink* negotiation (that is, use multiple phone lines for the connection if they are available).
Networking	Components checked are used by this connection	Specifies how to communicate over the network. Most connections use TCP/IP and QoS Packet Scheduler. See Chapter 28 for information about other protocols.
Advanced	Protect my computer and network by limiting or preventing access to this computer from the Internet	Specifies whether to use the Internet Connection Firewall when connected (see Chapter 31, section "Enabling the Internet Connection Firewall Between Your PC and the Internet"). We recommend that you select this option if it has been disabled.

Table 22-1.   *Settings for a Dial-Up Connection* (continued)

WINDOWS XP ON THE INTERNET

Tab in Properties Dialog Box	Setting	Description
Advanced	Allow other network users to connect through this computer's Internet connection	Specifies whether to run Internet Connection Sharing on this PC, allowing other computers on the LAN to access the Internet through your connection (see Chapter 30).

Table 22-1. *Settings for a Dial-Up Connection* (continued)

Configuring a TCP/IP Connection

For a connection to an Internet account, you may also need to configure the TCP/IP protocol. On the Properties dialog box for the connection, click the Networking tab, select Internet Protocol (TCP/IP) in the list of components, and then click the Properties button. You see the Internet Protocol (TCP/IP) Properties dialog box, shown in Figure 22-5.

When your computer is connected to the Internet using TCP/IP, it has its own *IP address* (*IP* is the acronym for Internet Protocol). An IP address is in the form of *xxx.xxx.xxx.xxx*, where each *xxx* is a number from 0 to 255. (That is, an IP address consists of four eight-bit numbers.) An example of an IP address might be 204.71.16.253.

In addition to IP addresses, computers on the Internet have *domain names*, alphanumeric names like **www.microsoft.com** or **net.gurus.com**. A *domain name server* or *DNS* is a computer on the Internet that translates between domain names and numeric IP addresses. Your ISP usually provides two DNS servers (one is in case the other one breaks down).

On the Internet Protocol (TCP/IP) Properties dialog box, make these entries:

■ **Your IP address** Ten years ago, when you signed up for an Internet account, your ISP assigned you a static IP address (see "What Is TCP/IP?" in Chapter 28)—an IP address that never changed. Now, almost all ISPs assign you a temporary IP address when you connect, so choose Obtain An IP Address Automatically unless your ISP has given you a static IP address (unlikely).

■ **DNS Server Address** Until a few years ago, you needed to choose Use The Following DNS Server Addresses and type the addresses in. Now most ISPs can tell Windows the DNS addresses when you connect, so choose Obtain DNS Server Address Automatically unless your ISP tells you otherwise.

Note *For more settings, click the Advanced button to see the Advanced TCP/IP Settings dialog box. Few ISPs require you to change these settings.*

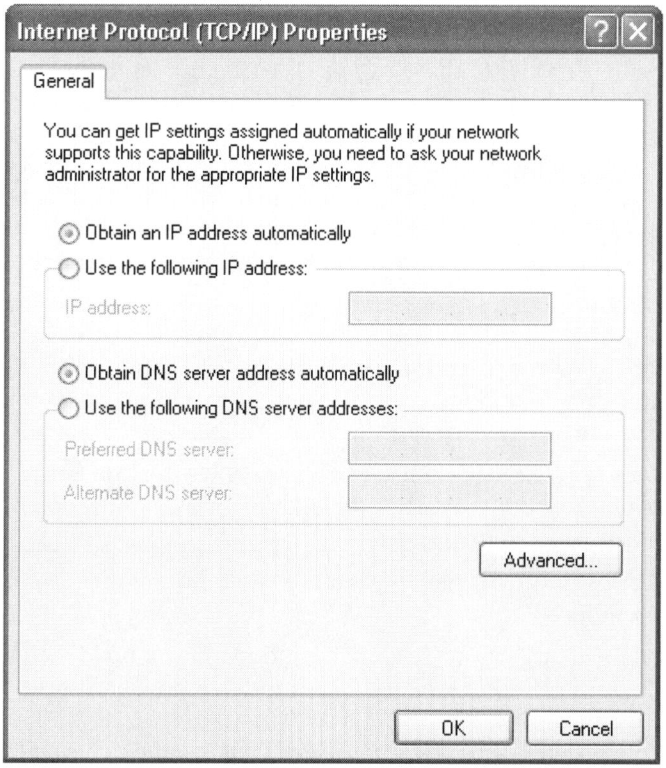

Figure 22-5. *Configuring the TCP/IP settings for a connection*

Creating and Using Logon Scripts

Windows tries to log on to your dial-up account automatically. Most accounts follow a standard series of steps: they transmit your user name and your account's password, and then receive confirmation that you are logged in so that communications can begin.

If your account uses a nonstandard dialog box for logging in, Windows can't log in automatically. You can automate logging in by creating a *logon script*, a text file containing a small program that tells Windows what prompts to wait for and what to type in response. For example, if your ISP's computer uses a nonstandard prompt to ask for your password, or requires you to type a command to begin a PPP session, you can write a script to log on for you. If your ISP uses the standard series of transmissions, you don't need a logon script. Logon scripts have the file extension .scp.

To use a logon script, follow these steps:

1. Log on manually, making notes about which prompts you see and what you must type in response to those prompts. To log in manually, you can use your network connection with a *terminal window*, which enables you to see the session and type commands to your ISP. To tell Windows to open a terminal window while connecting, click the Security tab of the Properties dialog box for the connection and select the Show Terminal Window check box. Another way to log in manually is by using HyperTerminal to connect to your ISP (see Chapter 26, section "Logging into Text-Based Systems with HyperTerminal").

2. Create a logon script by using a text editor, such as Notepad (see Chapter 17, section "Reading Text Files with Notepad"). Windows comes with a short manual about writing logon scripts in the file C:\Windows\Script.doc. (This file, and the scripting language you use in logon scripts, have remained unchanged since Windows 95.)

3. Tell Windows about the logon script by selecting the Run Script check box on the Security tab of the Properties dialog box for the connection and typing the filename in the box to its right.

4. Test the script, editing it with your text editor and viewing the results in a terminal window.

5. You can deselect the Show Terminal Windows check box when your script works, if you are tired of seeing the terminal window each time you connect.

Tip *Windows comes with a set of well-commented sample scripts. Customizing one of the sample scripts is usually easier than writing your own from scratch. These sample scripts are stored in C:\Program Files\Accessories with the extension .scp.*

Setting Additional Dial-Up Options

You might think all the properties of a dial-up connection would appear on the connection's Properties dialog box (shown earlier in the chapter in Figure 22-4), but they don't. Most of the settings on the (ill-named) Internet Properties dialog box pertain to your Web browser, rather than to your Internet connection, but a few additional settings appear on its Connections tab. (This dialog box is called Internet Options when you display it by choosing Tools | Internet Options from Internet Explorer.)

To display the Internet Properties dialog box, choose Start | Control Panel | Network And Internet Connections and run the Internet Options program. Figure 22-6 shows the Connections tab of the Internet Properties (or Internet Options) dialog box. The other tabs of this dialog box apply to using a Web browser, and are covered in Chapter 24. Most of the settings on the Connections tab control your Internet connection:

■ **Dial-up settings** Lists your dial-up connections, so you can enable those to use, disable those not to use, configure them, and set the default connection.

- **Never dial a connection, Dial whenever a network connection is not present, and Always dial my default connection**   Specify what Windows does when a program tries to connect to the Internet (for example, an e-mail program tries to connect to a mail server, or a Web browser tries to retrieve a Web page).

- **Current default**   Displays the name of the connection Windows uses unless you specify another connection. To change the default, select a connection from the Dial-Up Settings list and click the Set Default button.

Click the Setup or Add button to create a new connection: both buttons run the New Connection Wizard, but you see a different series of screen (it looks like two slightly different Wizards with the same name!). The Settings button displays a Settings dialog box (shown in Figure 22-7) that contains settings for the selected connection: you see the same settings that appear on the Properties dialog box for the connection, but arranged differently. A few items on the Settings dialog box pertain to connecting to the Internet over a LAN. The LAN Settings button displays the LAN Settings dialog box, which also contains LAN-related settings (see Chapter 30, section "ICS Server Configuration Details").

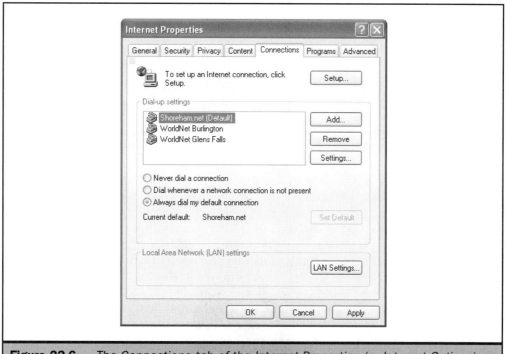

Figure 22-6.   *The Connections tab of the Internet Properties (or Internet Options) dialog box*

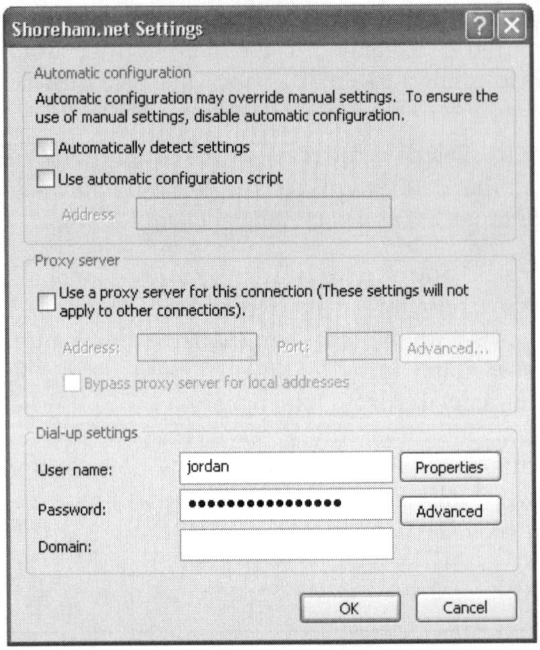

Figure 22-7.   *Settings dialog box for a dial-up connection*

Renaming, Copying, or Deleting a Network Connection

You can rename a network connection by right-clicking the connection and choosing Rename from the menu that appears. This action changes the name that appears on your computer for the connection; it doesn't change any of the information sent to the ISP.

Sometimes you want two or more versions of the same dial-up connection. For example, you might dial into your ISP from different numbers depending on where you take your laptop. To copy a connection, right-click its icon in the Network Connections window and choose Create Copy. A new icon appears. Rename the new copy and change its settings by right-clicking it and choosing Properties.

If you don't expect to connect to a particular account in the future, delete its connection from the Network Connections window by selecting the icon for the connection and pressing the DELETE key (or right-click the connection icon and choose Delete). Be sure you also delete any shortcuts to the connection.

Other Dial-Up Connection Settings

Two other settings are available for dial-up connections, although not usually used for regular Internet accounts:

- **Autodial** Windows automatically dials an Internet connection if you are not connected to the Internet and you ask for Internet information (for example, you run your browser or e-mail program, or click a Web address in a document). You can turn autodial off, or control which dialing locations it works from, by choosing Advanced | Dial-Up Preferences from the Network Connections window menu bar. Click the Autodial tab if it's not already selected, and choose which dialing locations from which you want Windows to autodial.

- **Callback** Some Internet hosts offer to call you back to continue the connection. Callbacks ensure that you are who you say you are (or at least that you are at the phone number that you're supposed to be at). If an Internet host offers to call you back, Windows usually displays a dialog box that asks whether you want to do so, but you can configure how Windows responds to the offer. Choose Advanced | Dial-Up Preferences from the Network Connections window menu bar and click the Callback tab.

Streamlining Your Internet Connection

Your Internet connection uses TCP/IP, not NetBEUI (Microsoft's file- and printer-sharing protocol) or IPX/SPX (Netware's protocol). You can speed up the process of connecting to your ISP, and make sure that your computer isn't open to intruders, by following these steps:

1. Display the Network Connections window.

2. Right-click the connection you use to connect to your ISP. Choose Properties from the shortcut menu that appears. You see the Properties dialog box for the connection.

3. Click the Networking tab. If NetBEUI or IPX/SPX appear among the installed components, make sure that their check boxes are cleared.

4. On the Networking tab, deselect the File And Printer Sharing For Microsoft Networks check box and the Client For Microsoft Networks check box. These are not needed (or wanted!) on dial-up Internet connections.

5. Click the Options tab. Deselect the Include Windows Logon Domain check box, unless your computer is on a domain-based LAN (check with your LAN administrator).

6. Click OK.

7. Connect to your ISP to make sure that changing these settings doesn't prevent you from connecting. (If so, repeat the steps and reverse your changes.)

WINDOWS XP ON THE INTERNET

Connecting to Your Account

You can tell Windows to connect to your Internet account automatically when a program asks for information from the Internet, or you can tell Windows when to connect.

 Some Internet connections, such as many DSL and cable Internet connections, are connected all the time, so you don't need to connect—you're online all the time.

Dialing the Internet Automatically

What happens if you aren't connected to the Internet and you tell your e-mail program to fetch your mail, or you ask your Web browser to display a Web page? Windows usually tries to dial up and connect to your Internet account automatically when you request Internet-based information.

To set Windows to connect automatically, follow these steps:

1. Choose Start | Control Panel | Network And Internet Connections | Internet Options (or choose Tools | Internet Options from Internet Explorer) to display the Internet Properties (or Internet Options) dialog box, shown earlier in this chapter in Figure 22-6.

2. Click the Connections tab and make sure the Always Dial My Default Connection setting is selected. (If your computer is sometimes connected to the Internet over a LAN, choose Dial Whenever A Network Connection Is Not Present instead.)

3. Click the dial-up connection you want to use and then click the Set Default button to make this connection the one Windows will use.

4. With the dial-up connection still selected, click Settings to display the settings dialog box for the connection (see Figure 22-7).

5. In the Dial-Up Settings part of the dialog box, type your user name and password.

6. Click the Advanced button to display the Advanced Dial-Up dialog box, shown here:

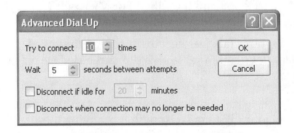

7. Set the number of times to try to connect, how long to wait between dialing attempts, whether to disconnect if the Internet connection has been idle, and whether to disconnect when the program that originally triggered the connection exits.

8. Click OK to dismiss the Advanced Dial-Up dialog box and OK again to dismiss the Internet Properties dialog box.

When you use an Internet program and Windows detects you are asking for information from the Internet, Windows dials your default connection. You don't see anything at all if you have configured the connection not to display the progress of the connection (using the Display Progress While Connecting check box on the Options tab of the Properties dialog box). If the connection is configured to display its progress, you see this Connecting dialog box, which displays the progress of your connection:

The dialog box displays messages as it dials, connects, and logs in to your Internet account using the information in the Dial-Up Settings dialog box.

Automatically dialing the Internet can be annoying, too. For example, if you are reading your e-mail offline and open a message that contains a link to the Web, you might not want your computer to dial into the Internet. If you no longer want Windows to connect automatically to the Internet, display the Internet Properties (or Internet Options) dialog box, click the Connections tab, and click the Never Dial A Connection option.

Dialing the Internet Manually

Usually, Windows connects to the Internet automatically (as described in the preceding section). However, you can also tell Windows to dial in, by following these steps:

1. Display the Network Connections window (see "What Are Network Connections?"). Then run the connection icon (click or double-click it, depending on how Windows is configured). If a connection icon appears on your desktop, you can run it instead. You see the Connect dialog box, shown in Figure 22-8.

WINDOWS XP
ON THE INTERNET

2. If the user name, password, or phone number doesn't appear, fill it in. (See "Configuring Windows for Dialing Locations" in Chapter 21 for instructions on how to set up dialing locations, if you use a laptop computer in more than one location.)

3. Unless you are worried about someone else using your computer to connect to your account, select the Save This User Name And Password For The Following Users check box so you needn't type your password each time you connect. Choose whether Windows saves this information only for when you are logged into the computer, or for all user accounts (see Chapter 6).

4. Click the Dial button. Windows dials your account and logs in. You may see a window telling you that you're connected to the account.

Tip *If you see a window confirming that you are connected, Click the Do Not Display This Message In The Future check box, so you needn't see this confirmation dialog box each time you connect to the Internet.*

5. Click the Close button.

While you are connected, the dial-up connection icon—two overlapping computer screens—may appear in the notification area at the right end of the taskbar. (It appears if you have selected the Show Icon In Notification Area When Connected check box on

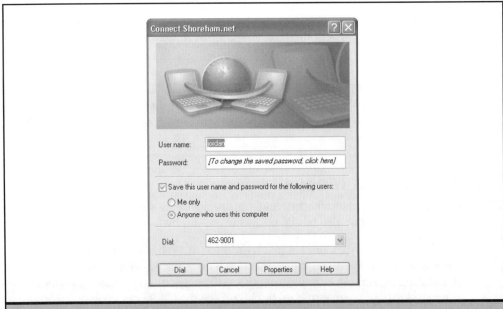

Figure 22-8. *Dialing up a network connection*

the General tab of the Properties dialog box for the connection.) Move the mouse pointer to the icon (without clicking) to see the name of the connection, your connection speed, and how many bytes have been sent and received. Click the icon to see more details, as shown here:

Click the Details tab on the status dialog box to see the modem name, connection type, IP address, and other information.

 If you need to make an operator-assisted call to connect to the Internet (for example, from a hotel phone), choose Advanced | Operator-Assisted Dialing from the menu in the Network Connections window. Open (click or double-click) the connection as usual, pick up the phone, and talk to the operator as necessary. Click Dial on the Connect dialog box when you are done. Don't hang up the phone until you hear the ISP and your modem exchange tones. Choose Advanced | Operator-Assisted Dialing again to turn off this feature.

Disconnecting from Your Account

When you are done using the Internet, you can disconnect. Or you can configure Windows to disconnect automatically when the connection isn't being used.

Disconnecting Manually

You can disconnect your Internet connection in several ways:

- If a dial-up connection icon appears in the notification area of the taskbar, right-click it and choose Disconnect from the menu that appears.
- Click the dial-up connection icon in the notification area to display the status dialog box for the connection and click the Disconnect button.

■ Choose Start | Connect To and choose the dial-up connection to display its status dialog box. Click Disconnect.

Disconnecting Automatically

If you are connected to your Internet account and don't use it for a while (usually 20 minutes), Windows or your ISP may disconnect you automatically. You may see a dialog box asking whether you want to disconnect. You can't control whether your ISP hangs up on your after a period of inactivity, but you can configure Windows whether and when to disconnect. Follow these steps:

1. Choose Start | Control Panel | Network And Internet Connections | Internet Options (or choose Tools | Internet Options from Internet Explorer) to display the Internet Properties (or Internet Options) dialog box, shown earlier in this chapter in Figure 22-6.

2. Click the Connections tab.

3. Click the dial-up connection for which you want to configure auto-disconnection and click the Settings button. You see the settings dialog box for the connection.

4. Click the Advanced button to display the Advanced Dial-Up dialog box.

5. To tell Windows to hang up after a specific time during which no information is transmitted, select the Disconnect If Idle For *xx* Minutes check box and set the number of minutes.

6. To tell Windows to hang up when no Internet programs are running, select the Disconnect When Connection May No Longer Be Needed check box.

7. Click OK three times to dismiss all the dialog boxes.

Testing Your Connection

After dialing up a network connection, you can use the Windows Ipconfig command to find out the IP address of your computer. The Ping program can test whether packets of information can make the round trip from your computer, out over the Internet to another computer, and back to your computer. You can use the Tracert program to trace the route packets take to get from your computer to another computer, and you can use the Netstat program to find out to which computers your computer is talking.

Some of these commands are usually run from the Command Prompt window (see Chapter 39). Open a Command Prompt window by choosing Start | All Programs | Accessories | Command Prompt.

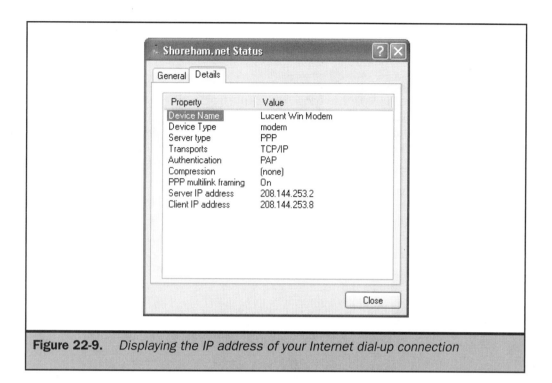

Figure 22-9.   *Displaying the IP address of your Internet dial-up connection*

Displaying Your IP Address

Your computer can have more than one IP address at the same time: each network connection can have a separate IP address. For example, your computer can have the address 204.135.25.67 on the Internet (via a dial-up, cable, DSL account, assigned by your ISP) and the address 192.168.0 on your LAN (see Chapter 27 for how IP addresses are assigned on the LAN.

There are three easy ways to display the IP address of your Internet connection:

■ **Dial-up connection icon**   For a dial-up connection, click the dial-up connection icon on the notification area of the taskbar (described earlier in this chapter, in the section "Dialing the Internet Manually"). In the status dialog box that appears, click the Details tab, as shown in Figure 22-9.

■ **View Status Of This Connection**   For all connections, display the Network Connections window (shown in Figure 22-2). Select the connection, and click View Status Of This Connection in the Network Tasks section of the Task pane. You see the status dialog box for the connection. For dial-up connections, click the Details tab (shown in Figure 22-9). For LAN connections, click the Support tab.

- **Ipconfig program**   The Ipconfig program displays information about your TCP/IP connection. To run Ipconfig, open a Command Prompt window by choosing Start | All Programs | Accessories | Command Prompt. Type **ipconfig** and press ENTER. You see a listing of your network connections that communicate using TCP/IP (including dial-up Internet connections, DSL and cable Internet connections, and most LAN connections), like this:

```
Windows IP Configuration

Ethernet adapter Local Area Connection:

        Connection-specific DNS Suffix  . :
        IP Address. . . . . . . . . . . : 192.168.0.1
        Subnet Mask . . . . . . . . . . : 255.255.255.0
        Default Gateway . . . . . . . . :

PPP adapter Shoreham.net:

        Connection-specific DNS Suffix  . :
        IP Address. . . . . . . . . . . : 208.144.253.8
        Subnet Mask . . . . . . . . . . : 255.255.255.255
        Default Gateway . . . . . . . . : 208.144.253.8
```

The IP address of your Internet connection is likely to change each time you connect to your ISP, because most ISPs assign IP addresses dynamically.

Testing Communication with Another Computer by Using Ping

Sending a small text packet on a round-trip is called *pinging*, and you can use Windows' built-in Ping program to send one. (Imagine that your computer sends the message "ping" and the other computer replies "pong.") To run Ping, open a Command Prompt window by choosing Start | All Programs | Accessories | Command Prompt and type the Ping command, as follows:

```
ping system
```

Replace *system* with either the numeric IP address or the host name of the computer you want to ping. Choose any Internet host computer that you're sure is online, such as your ISP's mail server. Then press ENTER.

To see a listing of all the command-line options for the Ping program, type **ping /?** *at the DOS prompt.*

For example, you can ping the Yahoo! Web server (a Web search engine and directory) by typing

```
ping www.yahoo.com
```

Ping sends out four test packets (pings) and reports how long the packets take to get to the Internet Gurus computer and back to yours, like this:

```
Pinging net.gurus.com [208.31.42.79] with 32 bytes of data:

Reply from 208.31.42.79: bytes=32 time=204ms TTL=248
Reply from 208.31.42.79: bytes=32 time=220ms TTL=248
Reply from 208.31.42.79: bytes=32 time=200ms TTL=248
Reply from 208.31.42.79: bytes=32 time=210ms TTL=248

Ping statistics for 208.31.42.79:
    Packets: Sent = 4, Received = 4, Lost = 0 (0% loss),
Approximate round trip times in milli-seconds:
    Minimum = 200ms, Maximum = 220ms, Average = 208ms
```

For each packet, you see both how long the round-trip takes in milliseconds and summary information about all four packets' trips. If ping doesn't receive the response it is waiting for within a time limit, you see an error message.

Ping has a number of options, which are listed in Table 22-2. Ping has other arcane options, not listed here.

First try Ping with a numeric IP address (for example, 216.32.74.50 for a Yahoo! Web server, or 208.31.42.79 for our Web server), to see whether packets get out to the Internet and back. Then try Ping with a host name, to see whether you successfully contact your DNS to convert the name into an IP address. If the first test works and the second doesn't (failing with an "Unable to resolve target system name" error), your connection isn't set up properly to contact a DNS.

Option	Description
-a	Reports numeric addresses rather than host names.
-f	Specifies that packets contain a Do Not Fragment flag, so packets aren't fragmented en route. (Useful to test very slow dial-up connections.)
-i *ttl*	Specifies the *Time To Live* for the packets (how many times the packet can be passed from one computer to another while in transit on the network).
-n *n*	Specifies to send *n* pings. (The default is four.)
-r *n*	Specifies the outgoing and returning packets should record the first *n* hosts on the route they take, using the Return Route field; *n* is a number from 1 to 9.
-t	Specifies to continue pinging until you interrupt it. (Otherwise, it pings four times.)
-w *n*	Specifies a time-out of *n* milliseconds for each packet.

Table 22-2.   *Options for the Ping Program*

Tracing Packets over the Internet

Packets of information don't usually go directly from one computer to another computer over the Internet. Instead, they are involved in a huge game of "whisper-down-the-lane," in which packets are passed from computer to computer until they reach their destination. If your data seems to be moving slowly, you can use the Tracert (short for *trace route*) program to follow your packets across the Internet, from your computer to an Internet host you frequently use. The technique Tracert uses doesn't always work, so it's quite possible running Tracert to a remote computer can fail, even though the computer is working and accessible.

To run Tracert, open a Command Prompt window by choosing Start | All Programs | Accessories | Command Prompt. Then type the Tracert command:

```
tracert system
```

Replace *system* with either the numeric IP address or the Internet name of the computer to which you want to trace the route. Then press ENTER.

Tip   *To see a listing of all the command-line options for the Tracert program, type **tracert** at the DOS prompt, with no system address.*

For example, you can trace the route of packets from your computer to the Internet Gurus Web directory at **net.gurus.com** by typing

```
tracert net.gurus.com
```

You see a listing like this:

```
Tracing route to net.gurus.com [208.31.42.79]
over a maximum of 30 hops:

  1    *         *         *       Request timed out.
  2   148 ms    149 ms    139 ms  rtr.shoreham.net [208.144.253.1]
  3   149 ms    149 ms    149 ms  shoreham253.greenmountainaccess.net
[208.144.253.253]
  4   149 ms    139 ms    149 ms  richmond-1.greenmountainaccess.net
[208.144.252.13]
  5   190 ms    179 ms    189 ms  sl-gw20-nyc-6-1-0-TS8.sprintlink.net
[160.81.215.241]
  6   216 ms    189 ms    229 ms  sl-finlak-7-0.sprintlink.net
[160.81.228.18]
  7   220 ms    199 ms    219 ms  208.31.47.5
  8   229 ms    199 ms    209 ms  net.gurus.com [208.31.42.79]

Trace complete.
```

The listing shows the route the packets took from your computer to the specified host (sometimes Tracert reports a different host name from the one you specified, which means the host has more than one name). For each hop (stage of the route), Tracert sends out three packets and reports the time each packet took to reach that far. It also reports the name and numeric IP address of the host.

Table 22-3 shows the options you can use with the Tracert program (type them before the host name or address). A few other arcane options are not listed here.

Displaying Internet Connections Using Netstat

Netstat is a network diagnostic program you can use for any TCP/IP connection—Internet connections or LANs. You can run Netstat to see which computers your computer is connected to over the Internet—not the ISP to which you dial in, but other Internet hosts to or from which you are transferring information.

Option	Description
-d	Specifies not to resolve addresses to host names, so the resulting list of hosts consists only of numeric IP addresses
-h *n*	Specifies a maximum number of *n* hops to trace before giving up
-w *n*	Specifies that the program wait *n* milliseconds for each reply before giving up

Table 22-3.   *Options for the Tracert Program*

To run Netstat, open a Command Prompt window by choosing Start | All Programs | Accessories | Command Prompt (see Chapter 39). Then type the following:

```
netstat
```

When you press ENTER, you see a listing of the Internet connections currently running, like this:

```
Active Connections

Proto   Local Address          Foreign Address            State
TCP     inspiron7000:4683      ftp1.us.dell.com:ftp       ESTABLISHED
TCP     inspiron7000:4684      wx.iecc.com:pop3           SYN_SENT
TCP     inspiron7000:4687      pop.vip.sc5.yahoo.com:pop3 TIME_WAIT
TCP     inspiron7000:4689      smtp.america.net:smtp      ESTABLISHED
TCP     inspiron7000:4690      books.iecc.com:http        SYN_SENT
TCP     inspiron7000:4431      msgr-ns9.msgr.hotmail.com:1863
                                                          ESTABLISHED
```

This listing shows that the computer is connected to other computers for receiving Web pages (the 80 or http at the end of the address signifies the port commonly used for Web page retrieval), for file transfer (ftp), for sending mail (smtp), for receiving mail (pop3), and for instant messaging.

 *To see a listing of all the command-line options for the Netstat program, type **netstat /h** at the DOS prompt.*

The Complete Reference

Chapter 23

E-Mail and Newsgroups Using Outlook Express

The most popular use of the Internet is to send and receive messages from other Internet users. Windows XP comes with Outlook Express 6, Microsoft's free e-mail and newsreading program. You can also install and use any number of mail and newsreading applications, whether they are Microsoft products or not. Windows XP also comes with an Address Book for keeping track of names, addresses, e-mail addresses, or whatever information you happen to have about people.

This chapter describes how to use Outlook Express to send and receive e-mail messages, organize the messages you decide to keep, and read and post messages to Usenet newsgroups. If you correspond with people whose software can read messages written in HTML (the language in which Web pages are written), you can compose messages using Outlook Express. This chapter also describes how to use Address Book, both with or without Outlook Express.

> **Tip**   *If you'd like to test your e-mail program, get news about updates to this book, or just say "Hi" to the authors, send a message to **winxptcr@gurus.com** (our mail robot will send an automatic response, and we read all our mail).*

Should You Use Outlook Express?

If you are a happy user of Eudora, Netscape Messenger, or another e-mail program, Outlook Express doesn't contain any gotta-have features that would make you want to switch. The hassle of importing your messages (which never seem to come through perfectly) isn't worth it. However, if you are a new user who doesn't have a lot of message files, or if you have used other e-mail programs and have been unhappy with them, Outlook Express is worth a try.

The case for using Outlook Express gets a little better with each new version. Outlook Express has a number of advantages: It's free, already installed, and easy to use; it has a nice collection of features for handling e-mail and newsgroups; it lets you import messages and addresses from most other popular e-mail programs; and it works well with Hotmail, Microsoft's free Web-based e-mail provider.

In the past, the main reason not to use Outlook Express was security. Outlook Express 6 includes some new features for handling attachments safely and avoiding spreading e-mail viruses to others. These features help resolve Outlook Express's most obvious security problems. However, the sheer popularity and ubiquity of Outlook Express (along with its cousin Outlook, which is part of Microsoft Office) makes it an inviting target for hackers. The people who write viruses (like the people who write any other kind of software) want to write for the largest possible market, so they target Microsoft products. And the problem is exacerbated by Microsoft itself, which has historically taken a lax attitude toward security.

> **Tip**   *Our favorite e-mail program, Eudora, is available at **http://www.eudora.com**. If you use Netscape Navigator as your Web browser, you may want to use its e-mail program, Netscape Messenger, which comes as part of the Netscape Communicator set of programs. See Netscape's Web site at **http://home.netscape.com/products**.*

Windows assumes that Outlook Express is your *default e-mail program* (the program that runs when another program tells Windows that you want to send e-mail). If you install another e-mail program, its installation program usually asks whether to make it the default e-mail program. If you plan to use it regularly to send and receive e-mail, choose Yes.

For news and tips about Outlook Express, check out Tom Koch's Web site at **http://www.tomsterdam.com**.

How Does E-Mail Work?

Oversimplifying somewhat, the process works like this:

1. Using an e-mail program, such as Outlook Express, the sender creates a message and decides who the recipients should be.

2. At a designated place at the beginning of the message, the sender lists the e-mail addresses of all the recipients. (The sender can specify a long list of recipients, but for simplicity, we'll pretend there is only one.) An *e-mail address* specifies two things: a computer on the Internet on which a recipient receives mail (called an *incoming mail server*), and the name that the incoming mail server uses to designate the mailbox of the recipient. So, for example, the e-mail address **president@whitehouse.gov** specifies the incoming mail server whitehouse.gov and a mailbox on whitehouse.gov called president.

3. The sender connects to an *outgoing mail server*, a computer connected to the Internet (usually a computer owned by the sender's Internet service provider) that runs a mail-handling program that supports *SMTP* (Simple Mail Transfer Protocol), which is used for Internet mail. These servers are usually called *SMTP servers*. The message is sent from the sender's computer to the outgoing mail server.

4. From the outgoing mail server, the message is passed across the Internet to the recipient's incoming mail server.

5. The recipient's incoming mail server files the message in the recipient's *mailbox*, a file or folder containing all the messages that the recipient hasn't downloaded to her own computer yet.

6. Using an e-mail program (which need not be the same as the one the sender used to create and send the message), the recipient looks for new mail by logging in to the incoming mail server. Incoming mail servers use one of three protocols for receiving mail: *Post Office Protocol 3* (abbreviated *POP3* or *POP*), *Internet Message Access Protocol (IMAP)*, or *Hypertext Transfer Protocol (HTTP)*. The incoming mail server uses POP, IMAP, or HTTP to deliver the message to the recipient's computer, along with any other messages that may have arrived since the recipient last checked for mail.

7. The recipient uses the e-mail program to read the message.

Every e-mail message consists of a *header* (lines containing the address, the return address, the date, and other information about the message) and a *body* (the text of the message).

To send messages right away to people who are logged in at the same time you are, and receive answers in seconds, use an instant messaging program like Windows Messenger (see Chapter 25, section "Chatting Online with Windows Messenger").

What Is Hotmail?

Hotmail (at **http://www.hotmail.com**) is a Web-based e-mail account that you access by visiting a Web site with your Web browser, rather than with the e-mail program installed on your computer. A notable exception is that Microsoft has set up Outlook Express to work conveniently with its Web e-mail service, Hotmail. After you identify yourself by giving a user name and a password, the Hotmail Web site shows you your messages and allows you to send e-mail to other people. You can access a Hotmail account through a Web browser or through Outlook Express.

Many other free Web-based accounts are available: the most popular is Yahoo Mail, at **http://mail.yahoo.com**. In general, Hotmail is as good as any other Web-based e-mail service, and has the advantage that Outlook Express supports it. Using Hotmail together with Outlook Express can help you avoid many of the usual aggravations of Web-based e-mail, because your e-mail interface resides on your own computer rather than on a Web site. You can conveniently work with your downloaded mail when you are offline. However, when you are away from your usual computer, you can work with your e-mail through a Web browser and leave the messages on the Hotmail computer.

What Are Attached Files?

Sometimes when you write e-mail you want to send more than just a message; you want to send files that the recipient can use with an application on her computer. For example, if you are working on a Word document with someone, you don't just want to talk about the document in your e-mail, you want to send revised versions of the document back and forth. *Attached files* (or *attachments* for short) are files that you send along with an e-mail message. The recipient can save the files on their own computer system and/or use them with their own applications. See "Attaching a File to a Message" later in this chapter for how to attach files to e-mail messages.

How Do E-Mail Viruses Work?

E-mail viruses are computer viruses—rogue programs that hackers write to do mischief on other people's computers—that spread by e-mailing copies of themselves to other computers. (Technically, such programs are *worms*, not viruses, but the popular press does not usually make this distinction.) If an e-mail virus gets into your computer, it may try to send infected e-mail to everyone in your Address Book.

The e-mail sent will look like it is coming from you—which won't make you popular with the people in your Address Book.

The most common (but not the only) way for e-mail viruses to spread is through file attachments, especially attachments that are executable (.exe) files or that invoke powerful applications like Visual Basic. The text of the message is a lure to get you to open the attachment. (Remember: the message comes to you from someone who has you in his address book. So it looks like your good friend Bob has sent you a mysterious attachment with a message saying something like "Try this. It's fun.") Once you open the attachment, your computer is infected.

Outlook Express is vulnerable to viruses, both because it is widely used and because it can automatically run programs that arrive attached to e-mail messages. However, you can decrease your risk of getting e-mail viruses: see the section "Protecting Yourself from E-Mail Viruses" later in this chapter. For more about viruses in general and what you can do to protect your system, see the section "Protecting Your System from Viruses and Worms" in Chapter 31.

What Are Newsgroups?

Newsgroups provide another way for you to use your computer and the Internet to communicate with the outside world. Unlike e-mail, however, a newsgroup is a public medium. When you send a message to a newsgroup, the message is available to anyone who wants to look at it—it's as if you have tacked up a notice on a public bulletin board. You never know who—if anyone—reads your message. The Internet-based system of newsgroups is called *Usenet*.

Newsgroups are organized by topic. Because there are tens of thousands of newsgroups, topics can be very specific. When you have something to say about the topic of a newsgroup, you can use a *newsreading program,* such as Outlook Express, to compose a message (which may be many pages or only one line) and send it to your *news server*, a computer on the Internet that supports *NNTP (Network News Transfer Protocol)*, which makes your message available to other news servers. People who want to read the recent contributions to this newsgroup (including your message) can use a newsreading program (not necessarily the same as yours) to download messages from their own news servers.

Getting Started with Outlook Express

To begin using Outlook Express, choose Start | All Programs | Outlook Express. If Outlook Express is your default mail program, you can choose Start | E-mail to run it.

When you run Outlook Express for the first time, you may be greeted with a dialog box asking if Outlook Express should be your default e-mail client. In other words, should Windows launch Outlook Express whenever you give a command to send mail from some other application (such as Internet Explorer or Address Book)? Choose Yes

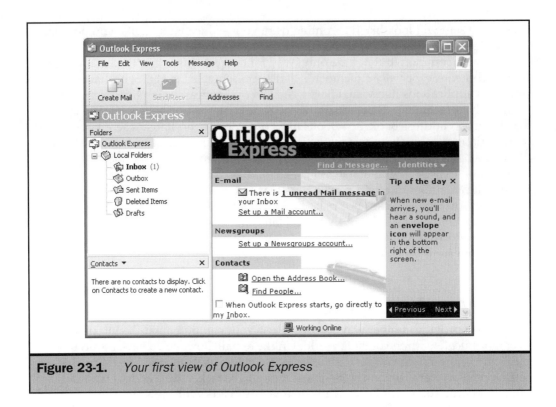

Figure 23-1. *Your first view of Outlook Express*

or No. If you intend to choose No, uncheck the Always Perform This Check When Starting Outlook Express check box so that you are not nagged. If Outlook Express is your default e-mail program, you can choose Start | E-mail.

Next, the Internet Connection Wizard may start to help you set up a mail and/or newsreader account. (If you installed Windows XP as an upgrade to some earlier Windows operating system, and if you used Outlook Express on that system, your accounts should already be set up.) If you choose to set up your accounts right away (you can always do it later), skip to "Setting Up Your Accounts" later in this chapter. Otherwise click Cancel, click Yes when the verification box asks if you are sure, and then the Outlook Express window appears, as shown in Figure 23-1.

Working with the Outlook Express Window

The Outlook Express window, as shown in Figure 23-1, resembles an Explorer window. At the top is a menu bar, with a toolbar underneath it. Below the toolbar, the window is divided into three panes. The right pane contains links that you can click to do the things that the text describes, such as set up a newsgroup account or create a new mail message. The upper-left pane is a folder list, similar to the left pane in an Explorer window. Outlook Express is at the top of the list and is highlighted, indicating that it corresponds to what is currently shown in the right pane.

The folders immediately beneath Outlook Express on the folder list are necessary parts of the mail system:

- **Inbox**   Where Outlook Express puts the incoming messages that it downloads from your incoming mail server. The messages remain there until you delete them or move them to another folder.

- **Outbox**   Contains the outgoing messages that you have completed and chosen to send, but have not yet been sent. For example, you might complete and choose to send several messages while you are offline. Those messages wait in the Outbox folder until the next time your computer is connected to your outgoing mail server.

- **Sent Items**   Contains messages that you have sent. Messages remain in this folder until you delete or move them.

- **Deleted Items**   Contains the messages (both incoming and outgoing) that you have deleted. Like the Recycle Bin, it is a last-chance folder that gets unwanted messages out of the way, but from which they still can be retrieved. Outlook Express can be set up to clean out the Deleted Items folder automatically, or you can delete messages from it manually (see "Saving and Deleting Messages"). Outlook Express cannot retrieve messages deleted from the Deleted Items folder.

- **Drafts**   Contains unfinished messages that you have chosen to save and work on later. Any time you are composing a message, you can choose File | Save to save the message in the Drafts folder.

As you begin sending and receiving messages, you can set up other folders to keep track of your correspondence (see "Organizing Your Correspondence"). You don't have to do so, but if you plan to keep copies of messages, they will be easier to find if you sort them into folders by topic or by correspondent.

Setting Up Your Accounts

Before Outlook Express can send or receive mail, or allow you to interact with newsgroups, you need to tell it what accounts you have and how it can access them. Have the following information handy:

- **The name you want attached to any message you send**   Do you want to be known as Johnny Public, Jonathan Q. Public, or by some nickname?

- **Your return e-mail address**   If people want to reply to your messages, where should the replies go?

- **The names of the servers your account deals with** For a *news account* (which lets you read newsgroups), this is an NNTP server with a name like *news.serviceprovider.com*. For an e-mail account that is not Web based, you provide two names: one server for incoming mail (a POP or IMAP server) and one server for outgoing mail (an SMTP server). (Your ISP—Internet service provider—should have given you this information—if you don't have it, check their Web site or call them.) Outlook Express can deal with Web-based e-mail accounts if they either offer public HTTP mail access (so far, Hotmail is the only one that does), or if they also have POP or IMAP servers. For Yahoo! Mail, enter **pop.mail.yahoo.com** for your incoming mail server and **smtp.mail.yahoo.com** for your outgoing mail server.

- **Your user name and password (if any) for logging into the servers** This information also comes from your ISP.

Once you have assembled this information, you need to tell Outlook Express. You configure Outlook Express for your e-mail account in two ways:

- From the Outlook Express window (see Figure 23-1) you can choose the appropriate task, Set Up A Mail Account or Set Up A Newsgroups Account, from the right-hand pane.

- From the Outlook Express menu bar choose Tools | Accounts. When the Internet Accounts dialog box opens, click the Add button and select the type of account you want to define: mail, news, or directory service. Choose Mail for an e-mail account.

You have to go through this process once for each account you want to establish. Outlook Express runs the Internet Connection Wizard, which collects the necessary information about your e-mail account.

Importing Messages from Other Mail Programs

If you've been using e-mail for a while, your message files are an asset. Continuity can be an important reason to stay with whatever mail program you've been using. Outlook Express 6 lets you convert your message files from these other mail programs:

- Previous versions of Outlook Express.

- Eudora Pro or Eudora Light, versions 1 through 3. For later versions, the import program runs but the results may be inaccurate. (When we imported messages from Eudora Pro 4.1 plain text messages appeared with HTML codes embedded.) In previous versions of Outlook Express, the importation program got the messages right, but sometimes garbled the dates.

- Microsoft Exchange, Outlook, Internet Mail for Windows 3.1, or Windows Messaging.

- Netscape Mail or Netscape Messenger (part of Netscape 6 or Netscape Communicator).

Tip   *Migrating into a Microsoft product is easier than migrating out of one. The Outlook Express export feature only exports to other Microsoft e-mail clients. If you decide to go back to your old e-mail client later on, you'll be relying on that client's ability to import Outlook Express messages. If you plan to try Outlook Express for a few days before choosing between it and your old mail program, set Outlook Express to leave your incoming messages on your incoming mail server, and collect your mail using both programs until you make up your mind. Choose Tools | Accounts, click the Mail tab, select your e-mail account, click Properties, click the Advanced tab, and select the Leave A Copy Of Messages On Server check box. Above all, you should inspect your imported files for completeness before throwing away the originals, or just archive the originals somewhere.*

To import messages from one of these mail applications, select File | Import | Messages from the menu, and then answer the questions asked by the Outlook Express Import Wizard. The Wizard needs to know the application from which it is importing, and where the files are located. If your old e-mail program isn't installed, you may need to install it for the import to work (for example, if are moving your e-mail files to a new computer).

Folders of imported messages show up in the Outlook Express folder list, from which you can move them into whatever folders you like (see "Organizing Your Correspondence"). The imported folders retain their names and structure. For example, say you import a folder from Eudora named People At Work, with subfolders Bob and Jenny. When it arrives in Outlook Express it should still have the subfolders it contained, and those subfolders should contain all the messages they had in Eudora. (However, in our experience, subfolders don't always import correctly.)

Importing Addresses from Other Mail Programs

Outlook Express can import addresses in these formats:

- Eudora Pro or Eudora Light address books, versions 1 through 3
- LDIF (LDAP Data Interchange Format) directories
- Microsoft Exchange Personal Address Book or Internet Mail for Windows 3.1 Address Books
- Netscape Address Book (from Netscape version 2 or 3) or Netscape Communicator Address Book (version 4)
- Text files created by any program, with one line per entry and fields separated by commas

To import addresses from one of these mail applications

1. If you want to import a Windows Address Book (.wab) file select File | Import | Address Book from the menu. If you are importing addresses from another program, select File | Import | Other Address Book.
2. Answer the questions asked by the Outlook Express Import Wizard.

If all goes well, the addresses wind up in the Windows Address Book (see "Storing Addresses in the Address Book").

WINDOWS XP
ON THE INTERNET

You can import your Windows Address Book from another computer. Look in the folder C:\Documents And Settings\username\Application Data\Microsoft\Address Book (replace user name with your Windows XP user account name) on the other computer to find the .wab (Windows Address Book) file that corresponds to your identity. Transfer this file to your computer, and then open Address Book and select File | Import | Address Book. When the Select Address Book File To Import From window opens, browse to find the file you want to import and click Open. If the other computer is on your LAN, you can skip the step of transferring the file to your computer, and browse through the other computer's files over the LAN.

Choosing a Layout for the Outlook Express Window

Like Windows Explorer, the Outlook Express window provides a number of features that you can choose to display or not display. When all the features are made visible, you get a busy, complicated window, as shown in Figure 23-2.

You can make any of these features (other than the working area) appear or disappear as you like. Choose View | Layout to display the Window Layout Properties dialog box, check the features that you want to have in your Outlook Express window, and click OK.

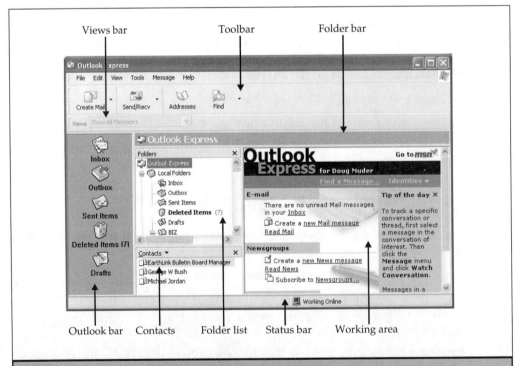

Figure 23-2. *All the features of Outlook Express, if you choose to display them*

We recommend displaying the folder list, toolbar, and status bar. You might also find the Contacts list useful. If you like the Views bar, you can drag it up to the right end of the menu bar.

Sending and Receiving E-Mail

After you set up one or more mail accounts, you can check your mail by clicking the Send And Receive button on the toolbar or choosing Tools | Send And Receive | Send and Receive All or pressing F5. After you have clicked Send And Receive, Outlook Express goes through the following process automatically.

1. Connects to your mail servers. If you are on a local area network, this part of the process may happen so quickly that it is almost invisible to you. If you connect to the Internet over a modem, however, and are not already online, Outlook Express uses your default dial-up connection to dial up your ISP. Once an Internet connection is established, Outlook Express contacts your mail servers over the Internet.

2. Sends all the messages in your Outbox. Messages you aren't ready to send should be stored in the Draft folder, not in the Outbox.

3. Downloads all the incoming messages from the server into your Inbox (or into other folders if you have defined message rules that sort your incoming correspondence). See "Filtering Your Mail with Message Rules".

By default, the Send And Receive button sends all queued messages and checks for mail in all of the e-mail accounts it knows about. If you want to be more selective, click the down arrow next to the Send and Receive button. A drop-down menu offers you the following choices:

- **Send and Receive All**   The default.
- **Receive All**   Checks for incoming mail in all known accounts, but doesn't send queued messages.
- **Send All**   Sends all queued messages, but doesn't check for incoming mail.
- **Individual Listings Of Your E-Mail Accounts**   Choosing an account sends and receives for that account only.

The same choices are available from the Tools | Send And Receive menu.

While messages are downloading, a dialog box appears. You may click the Hang Up When Finished box if you want Outlook Express to close the Internet connection when it is done.

Table 23-1 shows some of the most important configuration options for sending and receiving messages. (We omit those that are self-explanatory.) Choose Tools | Options to display the Options dialog box that shows these settings. (See Table 23-2 for settings that control how messages are composed and sent, and the section "Reading

Tab	Setting	Description
General	Send and receive messages at startup	When you start Outlook Express, sends messages in your Outbox and downloads messages from your incoming mail server.
General	Check for new messages every *xx* minutes	Specifies how often Outlook Express connects automatically to the mail servers to download incoming messages and upload outgoing messages.
General	If my computer is not connected at this time	Specifies what to do if your computer is not connected to the Internet when Outlook Express tries to check for new messages. Your options are Do Not Connect, Connect Only When Not Working Offline, and Connect Even When Working Offline.
Read	Mark message read after displaying for *xx* seconds	Specifies that Outlook Express mark a message as read after displaying it in the preview pane for the specified time.
Read	Fonts button	Enables you to set the fonts in which Outlook Express displays unformatted messages.
Receipts	Returning Read Receipts	Specifies how to process *return receipt requests* (tags attached to e-mail messages that request a receipt so that the sender knows that you've seen the message). Not all ISPs and e-mail programs support return receipts.
Send	Save copy of sent messages in the 'Sent Items' folder	Specifies that Outlook Express keep copies of your outgoing messages. You can move them from the Sent Items folder to another folder after the message is sent.

Table 23-1.   *Send/Receive Settings of the Options Dialog Box*

Tab	Setting	Description
Send	Send messages immediately	Specifies that Outlook Express connect to your outgoing mail server and send messages whenever a message is in your Outbox (see "Sending Messages").
Security	Select the Internet Explorer security zone to use	Specifies which security zone to use when deciding whether or not to let ActiveX controls and other potentially dangerous scripts and programs run (see Chapter 31, section "What Are Internet Explorer's Zones?").
Security	Warn me when other applications try to send mail as me	Stops a virus program from spreading itself via e-mail without your knowledge.
Security	Do not allow attachments to be saved or opened that could potentially be a virus	Refuses to open or save file attachments in formats used by most e-mail viruses.
Connection	Ask before switching dial-up connections	Should Outlook Express break an existing dial-up connection to use its default connection, or should it ask you what to do?
Connection	Hang up after sending and receiving	Specifies that after sending and receiving messages, Outlook Express disconnect from the Internet.

Table 23-1.   *Send/Receive Settings of the Options Dialog Box (continued)*

and Posting to Newsgroups" later in this chapter for settings that affect reading newsgroups.)

Receiving Mail

New mail accumulates in your Inbox and stays there until you delete it or move it to another folder. To see your new mail, click Inbox in the folder list of the Outlook Express window. The window has three panes, as it does when you look at any mail

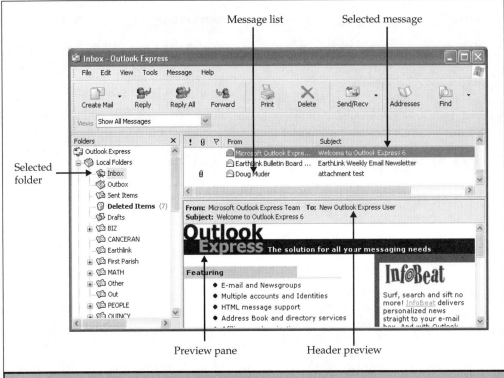

Figure 23-3.   *The folder list, the list of messages in your Inbox, and the Outlook Express welcome message*

folder: the folder list, the message list, and the selected message. (In order to call attention to the parts of the window relevant to receiving mail, we've chosen not to display the Contacts, Status Bar, Folder Bar, and Outlook Bar in Figure 23-3.) You can drag the boundaries of these three panes to reallocate the space occupied by each. The three panes are the following:

- ■ **The folder list view in the left pane**   The selected folder is highlighted. In Figure 23-3, Inbox is the selected folder.

- ■ **The selected folder's message list in the upper-right pane**   Each message receives one line in the list. The line tells who is the author of the message, what the subject line says, and when the message was received (or sent, if the message is outgoing). If the author rated the message as Urgent, an exclamation point (!) appears on the left side of its entry on the list. If the message has an attachment (a file attached to the message), a paper clip appears to the left of its entry. The currently selected message is highlighted. Unread messages have a closed-envelope icon next to them; read messages have an open-envelope icon.

- **A preview of the selected message in the lower-right pane** The bar at the top of the lower-right pane lists the sender and receiver of the message, together with the subject line. Below this bar is a scrollable window containing the full text of the message.

Customizing the Message List

To choose what columns are displayed in the message list, right-click the row of column headings and choose Columns from the shortcut menu. The Columns dialog box appears, listing the possible columns Outlook Express can display. Check the columns you want. You may also use this dialog box to rearrange the columns by selecting a column name and clicking the Move Up or Move Down button. You can switch the order of the columns by dragging the header left or right. You can use the Columns dialog box to fix the widths of the columns in the message list as well, but dragging the boundaries between the columns in the message list itself is simpler.

Sorting the Messages in a Folder

You can sort the messages in a folder according to any of the columns in the message list—just click the label above any of the columns. Click once to sort in ascending order, twice for descending order.

For example, clicking the From column label sorts the messages according to sender. The various senders appear in alphabetical order, but the program is not smart enough to recognize first names and last names, so it is alphabetical by the name as it is displayed. (Abe Zachary would come before Smith John.) Click From again to sort in reverse alphabetical order.

Reading the Messages in a Folder

To read the messages in any folder

1. Click the name of the folder in the folder list of the Outlook Express window. If the folder you want is not visible, it has either scrolled off the edge of the folder list or it's contained in another folder. Use the left pane scroll bar to look up or down in the folder list. Click the plus box next to a folder's name to see the list of folders contained inside it.

2. Find the message you want to read in the message list in the upper-right pane.

3. Double-click to read the message in its own window, or single-click to read the message in the preview pane of the Outlook Express window.

Opening Attached Files

Messages with attached files are denoted with a paper clip icon in the message list of the Outlook Express window. When the message is selected, a larger paper clip icon appears in the title bar of the preview pane. When the message is opened, attached files appear as icons just below the subject line. Images from attached image files are appended to the bottom of the message automatically; you don't have to decide to open them.

Clicking the large paper clip icon produces a list of the attached files; selecting one of the files from this list opens the file. Similarly, selecting an attached-file icon from the bottom of the message window opens the file.

    Attached files are a major source of e-mail viruses. Don't open an attachment unless you know what it is.

Protecting Yourself from E-Mail Viruses

Because Outlook and Outlook Express are so widely used, they are the most popular targets for the hackers who create e-mail viruses. Outlook Express 6 contains two new features for decreasing your vulnerability to e-mail viruses: restricting attachments and warning you if any other program attempts to send e-mail from your computer using your identity. In addition, you have a choice of whether Outlook Express uses the rules of Internet Explorer's Internet zone, or the much safer Restricted Sites zone (which we recommend). See Chapter 31, section "What Are Internet Explorer's Zones?".

These features and options are far from a panacea. The file types that are blocked are the most popular ones for e-mail viruses, but far from the only ones. And blocking HTML attachments does nothing to protect you from viruses that may be embedded in e-mail messages written in HTML. Whether you use these features or not, we recommend that you continue to be cautious: Do not open unexpected attachments from strangers, or even from friends if the accompanying message does not convince you that they are genuine.

Restricting Attachments

When you open a file attached to an e-mail message, the file is opened by the application appropriate to its file type, not by Outlook Express. In other words, if you don't know the file type of an attachment, you can't be sure what program will run when you open it. If the attachment is itself a program, opening the attachment turns the program loose to do whatever it was designed to do. Some types of files are more dangerous to open than others, because the applications that run them have the power to make fundamental changes to your system. In particular, executable (.exe) files, scripting files (such as .vbs for Visual Basic or .js for JavaScript), or files that contain links to other files that could contain executable code (like .htm or .url).

Caution *Some viruses try to disguise the file type of their attachments by giving the files two extensions (for example, Loveletter.doc.vbs). If Windows is configured not to display all extensions, you might be fooled by the filename, which would appear without the last extension (for example, you'd just see the filename Loveletter.doc). To display all extensions, choose Start | My Computer, choose Tools | Folder options from the menu bar, click the View tab, and deselect the Hide Extensions For Known File Types check box.*

Outlook Express allows you to block attachments that it judges to be of a dangerous file type. To do this

1. Select Tools | Options from the menu bar. The Options dialog box opens.
2. Click the Security tab.
3. Check the Do Not Allow Attachments To Be Saved Or Opened That Could Potentially Be A Virus check box.
4. Click OK.

To unblock all attachments, repeat these steps but uncheck the box in step 3.

When the Do Not Allow Attachments To Be Saved Or Opened That Could Potentially Be A Virus box is checked, the paper clip icon still appears to tell you when a message has attachments. Clicking the icon reveals a list of attachments, but any attachments that are blocked appear dimmed, so that they cannot be selected. If you decide that you want to open or save these attachments, go back to the Security tab of the Options dialog box and uncheck the Do Not Allow Attachments To Be Saved Or Opened That Could Potentially Be A Virus box. You can then open or save attachments normally.

Note *Even if you are blocking some attachments, image file attachments still get through and are displayed appended to the end of the message they are attached to.*

Preventing Other Programs from Sending E-Mail as You

By default, Outlook Express is set up to allow other programs to use it to send e-mail automatically. A virus program could use this feature to send itself to other people. You can alter this behavior so that Outlook Express will block such e-mail until you have confirmed that you want to send the message. Make this change as follows:

1. Select Tools | Options from the menu bar. The Options dialog box opens.
2. Click the Security tab.
3. Check the Warn Me When Other Applications Try To Send Mail As Me check box.
4. Click OK.

To undo this change, repeat these steps but uncheck the box in step 3.

Choosing Your Security Zone

Outlook Express borrows its security zones from Internet Explorer. See the section "What Are Internet Explorer's Zones?" in Chapter 31 for more details about security zones and how to change the rules that apply to them. Outlook Express offers you a choice between the two most conservative zones: the Internet zone and the Restricted Sites zone. The Restricted Sites zone is more conservative and we recommend it.

To choose your security zone

1. Select Tools | Options from the Outlook Express menu. The Options dialog box appears.

2. Click the Security tab of the Options dialog box.

3. Select the radio button of the security zone you want, and then click OK.

Composing Messages to Send

You create messages in three ways:

- **Compose a new message from scratch**   Click the Create Mail button on the Outlook Express toolbar.

- **Reply to a message you have received**   Select a message from an Outlook Express folder (such as Inbox) and click either the Reply button or the Reply All button on the Outlook Express toolbar.

- **Forward a message you have received**   Select a message from an Outlook Express folder and click the Forward button on the Outlook Express toolbar.

Any of these three actions opens a message window, like this:

The message window has two main parts: a header and a body. The body is the window into which you enter the text of your message. Use it as you would use a word processor. If you are composing a plain text message, you are limited (naturally) to plain text, but if you are composing in HTML you can use different fonts, inserted images, and other fancy formatting. (If you use HTML, make sure your recipients use mail programs that can read HTML; otherwise they may a mixture of text and HTML codes.) If you are composing a message from scratch, the body of the message window has nothing in it other than what you type. If you are forwarding a message, the text of the original message is included automatically. If you are replying, Outlook Express can be set up to either include or not include the original text (see "Including the Original Message in Your Reply").

Note   *When you reply to a message that has an attachment, the attachment is not included in the reply (because presumably the person doesn't want another copy of the file). When you forward a message with an attachment, the forwarded message includes the attachment.*

Table 23-2 shows the most important settings in the Options dialog box for composing messages. (Table 23-1 earlier in this chapter listed other settings.) Choose Tools ⎮ Options to display the Options dialog box.

Tab	Setting	Description
Receipts	Request a Read Receipt for all sent messages	Specifies that your outgoing messages include return receipt requests so you know when the person opened the message. Not all e-mail programs respond to return receipt requests, and not all ISPs process them.
Receipts	Secure Receipts	Opens the Secure Receipts Options dialog box, from which you can specify whether your outgoing messages include a request for a *secure receipt* (return receipt for a digitally signed message) and how to respond to requests for secure receipts (see Chapter 31, section "Sending and Receiving E-mail Securely").
Send	Automatically put people I reply to in my Address Book	Adds entries to your Address Book for each person to whom you send a reply (see "Storing Addresses in the Address Book"). If you reply to many messages from strangers to whom you are unlikely to write again, deselect this check box.

Table 23-2.   *Message Composition Settings of the Options Dialog Box*

Tab	Setting	Description
Send	Include message in reply	Specifies that replies contain the text of the original message in a quoted format (see "Including the Original Message in Your Reply"). Be sure to edit out the irrelevant parts of the original message.
Send	Reply to messages using the format in which they were sent	Composes replies to HTML formatted messages using HTML formatting, and composes replies to plain text messages using plain text (see "Turning HTML On and Off").
Send	Mail Sending Format: HTML/Plain Text	Specifies whether your e-mail messages are sent as HTML or as plain text.
Compose	Compose Font: Mail	Specifies how unformatted messages appear on your screen when you are composing them.
Compose	Stationery: Mail	Specifies what stationery (standard formatting) your new messages will use. Rather than specifying mail stationery here, turn it on only for occasional messages (by choosing Format | Apply Stationery when composing a message).
Compose	Business Cards: Mail	Specifies that your virtual business card (vCard) be included when you compose new messages (see "Importing Virtual Business Cards").
Signatures	Signatures	Enables you to create one or more *signatures*—a few lines of text that are appended to messages you send. Your signatures should contain your name and e-mail address, and should be no more than four lines long. Click New to create a signature, then type the text in the Edit Signature box.

Table 23-2.   *Message Composition Settings of the Options Dialog Box* (continued)

Tab	Setting	Description
Spelling	Always check spelling before sending	Specifies that Outlook Express automatically run its spell checker when you send each message (this option is available only if you have a compatible spell checker installed, such as the ones used by Microsoft Works or Microsoft Office). Other settings on this tab control whether it suggests correct spellings and which words to skip.
Security	Digitally sign all outgoing messages	Adds a digital signature to all messages that proves that you sent the messages. Click Advanced Settings to specify the type of digital signature.
Security	Encrypt contents and attachments for all outgoing messages	Encrypts (encodes) all outgoing messages so that they cannot be read unless the recipient has the encryption key. Click Advanced Settings to specify the type of encryption.

Table 23-2. *Message Composition Settings of the Options Dialog Box* (continued)

Completing the Header

The header section of the message window consists of four lines (though Bcc may not appear unless View | All Headers is checked):

■ **To** Type the e-mail addresses of the primary recipient(s) of your message. If there is more than one recipient, separate the e-mail addresses with commas. Click the open book icon to look up addresses in the Address Book. This is the only line of the header that cannot be left blank (unless you enter addresses in the Cc or Bcc lines). If you generate the message window by choosing Reply, Outlook Express puts the address of the author of the original message on this line. If you use Reply All, Outlook Express lists the addresses of the author and the other recipients of the original message. You may add more addresses or delete some of them if you want to.

- **Cc (Carbon Copy)** Type the e-mail addresses of secondary recipients (if any). If you opened this message window by clicking the Reply All button, Outlook Express uses the same Cc list as the original message. You may add to or delete from the list if you want to.

- **Bcc (Blind Carbon Copy)** Type the e-mail addresses of other secondary recipients, if any. The recipients listed in the To and Cc boxes can see the list of other recipients listed in the To and Cc boxes, but not those listed in the Bcc box. If one of the To or Cc recipients replies to your message with Reply All, the recipients on your Bcc list will not receive the reply.

- **Subject** Enter a word or short phrase to describe the subject of your message. The subject line helps both you and your recipients to keep track of the message in your files. If you are replying to another message, Outlook Express automatically uses the original subject line, preceded by Re. If you are forwarding, Outlook Express uses the original subject line, preceded by Fw.

Including the Original Message in Your Reply

One advantage e-mail has over paper mail is that you can indicate exactly what part of an e-mail message you are responding to. To make Outlook Express automatically include the original message in any reply

1. Select Tools | Options to open the Options dialog box.

2. Select the Send tab.

3. Check the Include Message In Reply check box and click OK.

By doing this, whenever you click the Reply or Reply All buttons, the body of the message window contains a divider, with the original message below the divider. The text of the original message is indented, with a > at the beginning of each line.

To remove the indentation or change the indentation character

1. Open the Send tab of the Options dialog box, as just explained.

2. If Plain Text is selected as the Mail Sending Format, click the Plain Text Settings button to open the Plain Text Settings dialog box. (If HTML is selected, see "Composing HTML Messages" later in this chapter.)

3. Check the Indent The Original Text With check box at the bottom of the Plain Text Settings dialog box to indent the original text. The drop-down list next to the Indent The Original Text With check box lets you choose a different indentation character.

You can use the original text in two ways. You can either type your message at the beginning of the message, leaving the original message at the end for reference. Or, you can edit the original message, deleting the parts irrelevant to your reply, and then type your reply in parts (each part immediately below the portions of the message to which you are responding). If don't want to include any of the original text for a particular message in your reply (but don't want to change the option), just press CTRL-A to select all the text in the message body window and then either press DELETE or just start typing your message.

Inserting Text Files into a Message

If what you want to say is already contained in a text file, you don't have to retype the text or even cut-and-paste the text out of the file. Just follow these steps to incorporate the text into your message:

1. Move the cursor to the place in the text of your message that you want the text file inserted.

2. Select Insert | Text From File.

3. When the Insert Text File window opens, browse to find the text file you want.

4. Click Open.

The complete text of the text file is now inserted into the spot where the insertion point is located.

Attaching a File to a Message

You can use e-mail to send more than just text. Any file—a picture, a spreadsheet, a formatted text document—can be sent along with your message as an attachment (see "What Are Attached Files?"). To attach a file to a message, click the Attach button on the message window toolbar or select Insert | File Attachment. When the Insert Attachment window appears, browse to find the file you want to attach, and click OK.

When sending plain text messages, Outlook Express encodes file attachments using *MIME (Multipurpose Internet Mail Extensions)*, the most widely used method of attaching files to messages. Most e-mail programs, including Netscape, Eudora, and AOL's mail program, can deal with MIME attachments. However, some e-mail programs can't do this, especially LAN e-mail programs that weren't originally designed to work with the Internet. You can switch to a different encoding method called *uuencode*: Select Tools | Options and click the Plain Text Settings button on the Send tab of the Options dialog box. Now click the Uuencode radio button in the Plain Text Settings dialog box.

When Outlook Express is set up to send HTML messages, the situation is reversed: Uuencode is the default, and you can switch to MIME using the HTML Settings button in the Options dialog box.

If you are attaching a large file or several small ones, create a compressed folder (ZIP file) that contains the file(s) and attach the compressed folder instead (see Chapter 8, section "What Are Compressed Folders?").

Saving and Deleting Messages

Outlook Express keeps the messages that you send and receive until you tell it to delete them. Messages that you receive are stored in your Inbox folder. Under the default settings, messages that you send wind up in your Sent Items folder and remain there until you either delete them or move them to another folder (see "Organizing Your Correspondence").

Saving Messages

Even though Outlook Express saves your messages automatically, you need to be aware of four issues:

- **Outlook Express folders and the messages in them are separate from the overall filing system of your computer.** You may have a folder called Mom in Outlook Express, but no Mom folder exists on the folder tree you see in Windows Explorer. If you want a message to be a file in your computer's filing system, you have to save that message as a file. You can drag a message out of the Outlook Express window and drop it onto the desktop or into an Explorer window. Or, you can select the message in the Outlook Express message list window, and select File | Save As, and give the new file a name. Either way the message is saved in a text file with the extension .eml. To read these files on a system that doesn't have Outlook Express, use Notepad.

- **Unfinished messages are lost when you close Outlook Express unless you save them.** You don't have to start and finish a message in one sitting. If you want to put the message away and work on it later, select File | Save to save the message in your Drafts folder. If you want the unfinished message to be in an Outlook Express folder other than Drafts, save it to Drafts first, and then drag it to another folder.

- **Your mail files should be backed up as often as (or perhaps more often than) any other files on your system.** The simplest method is to back up the entire folder in which you told Outlook Express to store your messages. The default folder is called Outlook Express and lies inside the C:\Windows\Application Data\Identities*username*\Microsoft folder (*username* is your user account name, as described in Chapter 6).

- **You can prevent Outlook Express from automatically saving your outgoing messages.** Select Tools | Options to open the Options dialog box. Go to the Send tab and uncheck the Save Copy Of Sent Messages In The 'Sent Items' Folder check box.

Deleting and Recovering Messages

Delete a message by clicking it in the message list and pressing DELETE. The message is sent to the Deleted Items folder, which functions within the Outlook Express filing system as a kind of Recycle Bin.

You can still examine messages from the Deleted Items folder by opening them, and you can move them to another folder if you change your mind about deleting them. However, if you delete an item from the Deleted Items folder, it is gone permanently.

Outlook Express can be set up to empty the Deleted Items folder automatically when you exit the program:

1. Select Tools | Options. The Options dialog box appears.

2. Click the Maintenance tab and check Empty Messages From The 'Deleted Items' Folder On Exit.

3. Click OK.

You can stop deleting messages this way by unchecking the Empty Messages From The 'Deleted Items' Folder On Exit check box.

Sending Messages

Once you are satisfied with the message you've composed, click the Send button in its message window. One of the following two things then happens:

- Outlook Express connects to your ISP, finds your outgoing mail server, and sends the message.

- The message is placed in your Outbox and is not sent until you press the Send and Receive button.

To tell Outlook Express whether to send messages immediately

1. Open the Options dialog box by selecting Tools | Options.

2. Select the Send tab.

3. Select or deselect the Send Messages Immediately check box.

4. Click OK.

You can undo this decision at any time by returning to the Send tab of the Options dialog box and changing the Send Messages Immediately setting.

Even if Send Messages Immediately is selected, you can move a message to your Outbox without sending it immediately to your outgoing mail server by selecting File | Send Later. This option is handy if you are temporarily unable to connect to the Internet—if you are traveling, for example, and your computer is not currently online.

As long as the message is sitting in your Outbox, you can still intercept it:

1. Select the Outbox folder from the folder list of the Outlook Express window.

2. Select the message from the Outbox message list.

3. Press DELETE or select Edit | Delete to get rid of the message completely.
   To put the message away to edit later, drag-and-drop the message from the upper-right pane into the Drafts folder in the folder list, or select Edit | Move

To Folder and choose a folder in which to move the message. Alternatively, you can right-click the message and select Move To Folder from the shortcut menu.

Storing Addresses in the Address Book

One of the first things people did when personal computers were invented was store lists of addresses on them. It makes sense—the old-fashioned little black book quickly gets filled with scratch-outs as people move, change phone numbers, or get new e-mail addresses, and you always end up wishing you had left a little more space between Sloane and Smith.

The next good idea in address management was to make the address book into a system utility so that any program could access it. You shouldn't have to keep one list of addresses for your word processor, another for your e-mail program, and a third for your personal information manager. And you shouldn't have to wonder which list has Aunt Gertrude's new address.

The Windows Address Book is still not the perfect realization of this idea, but it is a definite step in the right direction. Address Book keeps track of almost anything you would want to keep track of; provides a space for notes; and is accessible from Internet Explorer, Outlook Express, and NetMeeting. Unfortunately, Microsoft Exchange, Microsoft's e-mail server, has its own address book, so that your addresses may be stored in two separate places.

You can use the information from the Windows Address Book in Windows Messenger; only available contacts are listed. You may be able to use Address Book from older versions of Outlook, but not Outlook XP.

Running Address Book

You can access Address Book either from another program (usually by clicking the Address Book icon or the toolbar), or by choosing Start | All Programs | Accessories | Address Book. You see the Address Book window, as shown in Figure 23-4.

The window lists the people you have entered into the address book (which the Address Book calls *contacts*) with the name, e-mail address, and phone numbers for each person. It also lists people who are on your Windows Messenger list and are logged on and available for chat.

Sharing the Address Book with Other People

Each user account has its own Address Book, with its own files of contacts. People who use the same user account access the same Address Book, but they can keep their contacts separate by defining different *identities*. You can also use identities to separate your home and work contacts. Only one identity is logged in at any given time. The different identities defined under a single user account share a Shared Contacts folder. Any contact stored in the Shared Contacts folder is available to any of the identities.

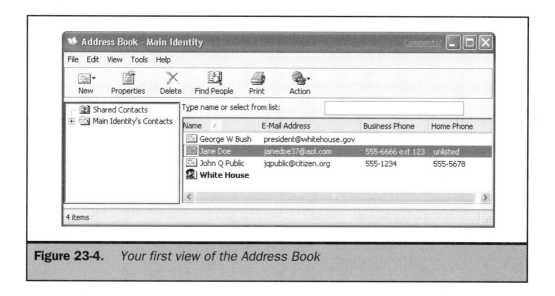

Figure 23-4.   *Your first view of the Address Book*

Switching Identities

You can tell which identity is currently logged in by looking at the title bar of the
Address Book window. In Figure 23-4, for example, the Main Identity is logged in. To
switch to a different identity, select File | Switch Identity. The Switch Identities dialog
box appears, as shown here:

Select the identity you want to switch to, enter that identity's password (if any),
and click OK.

Creating and Removing Identities

Creating, removing, and otherwise managing identities can only be done by opening
Address Book as a stand-alone application (by selecting it from the Start menu, for
example). If you open Address Book from another application, such as Outlook Express,
the Switch Identity and Manage Identity commands are not included on the File menu.

When you first start Address Book, one identity appears: the Main Identity. If you want another person to store addresses in your Address Book, create another identity by choosing File | Switch Identity, clicking the Manage Identities button to display the Manage Identities dialog box, and then clicking the New button.

To remove an identity, open the Manage Identities dialog box as before, select the identity from the list, and click Remove.

To see the entries in an identity's part of the Address Book, click that identity in the list at the left side of the Address Book window.

Securing Your Address Book Information

If you don't want the other users of your computer to access the information in your Address Book, you can secure your identity with a password. However, you should realize that the protection this provides is mainly symbolic, like putting a Keep Out sign on an unlocked door. Establishing a password prevents other people from logging in as you, but they can still examine and even change the information in your contact files by selecting File | Show All Contents.

Note   *The only real way to secure your contact files is to have your own user account and protect it with a password, as described in Chapter 6.*

To establish a password for your identity, choose File | Switch Identity, and then click the Manage Identities button in the Switch Identities dialog box. Select your identity from the Identities list in the Manage Identities dialog box and click the Properties button. Click the Require A Password box in the Identity Properties dialog box. Choose a password and type it in the Password and Confirm Password lines of the Enter Password dialog box. Click OK or Close in all the open dialog boxes.

To change the password on your identity, follow the same instructions as in the previous paragraph until you see the Identity Properties dialog box. Click the Change Password button. Enter your old and new passwords into the Change Identity Password dialog box. Type your new password a second time in the Confirm New Password line.

Entering Information into Address Book

You can get information into Address Book in three ways: importing information from your current address book program (described in the section "Importing Addresses from Other Mail Programs" earlier in this chapter), importing virtual business cards that have arrived by e-mail, capturing information automatically from Outlook Express, or entering information by hand. Once you have a list of contacts in your Address Book, you can organize them into groups. To see the entries in your address book, click the Main Identity's Contacts entry on the left side of the Address Book window. The entries appear on the right side of the Address Book window.

Importing Virtual Business Cards

Address Book can import addresses from vCards (virtual business cards), which arrive as attachments to e-mail messages in files with the extension .vcf. Select File | Import | Business Card (vCard). A Browse window opens so you can tell Address Book where your business card files are. You can also drag-and-drop vCards into the Address Book.

Capturing E-mail Addresses from Outlook Express

If you use Outlook Express as your e-mail program, you can set it up to add names and e-mail addresses to Address Book automatically whenever you reply to a message.

1. Open Outlook Express.
2. Select Tools | Options. The Options dialog box appears.
3. On the Send tab of the Options dialog box, check the box Automatically Put People I Reply To In My Address Book.
4. Click OK.

Entering Information by Hand

To enter a new contact into Address Book, click the New button on the toolbar and choose New Contact, or select File | New Contact from the menu bar. A blank Properties dialog box appears. Type in any information you want recorded, and leave blank any lines you want. To add or change information about an existing contact, select the contact on the address list and click the Properties button. The Properties dialog box appears, as shown in Figure 23-5. Enter or edit information on any of its tabs.

To add more information to an existing contact listing, choose the contact from the contact list and click the Properties button. Enter the new information on the appropriate line and tab of the contact Properties box. Notice the Properties box displays a Summary tab that you didn't see when you were entering a new contact. This tab is just for reference; each piece of information on this tab can be edited on some other tab. Any Web page listed on the Summary tab has a Go button next to it; clicking this button opens your Web browser and displays the Web page.

Address Book enables you to keep track of several e-mail addresses for a single person, with one of them specified as the default. To add a new e-mail address, type it into the E-Mail Addresses box on the Name tab of the contact Properties box. Then click the Add button. The new e-mail address appears in the list just below the E-Mail Addresses box.

To set one of a person's e-mail addresses as the default, select it from the list of e-mail addresses on the Name tab of the Properties dialog box associated with that person's name. Then click the Set As Default button.

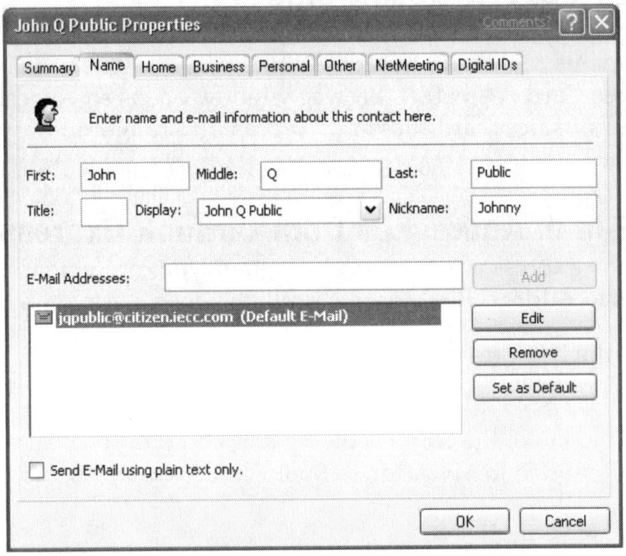

Figure 23-5. *Detailed information about a contact*

Defining Groups

Having your customers, your coworkers, and your child's piano teacher all on one big alphabetical list can be confusing. Address Book enables you to give your contact list some structure by defining groups of contacts that have something in common. An individual contact can appear in any number of groups.

To define a group

1. Click the New button on the Address Book toolbar and choose New Group from the menu that appears. A group Properties dialog box opens.

2. Type a name for the group into the Group Name box.

3. Click the Select Members button. A Select Group Members window appears. Your contacts list is in its left pane; its right pane contains the members of the new group.

4. One by one, select names in the left pane and click the Select button to add this name to the group. You can add an entire group to the new group in the same way.

5. When you have finished selecting group members, click OK to return to the group Properties dialog box. The members you have selected are listed.

6. If you want to add new members to the group, click Select Members again. If you want to remove names from the list, select the names in from the Group Members list in the Properties dialog box and click Remove. If you want to add people who aren't already in your Address Book, type the name and address into the Name and E-Mail boxes at the bottom of the dialog box, and then click the Add button. (Names that you add in this way will not be added to your contacts list as individuals, but only as part of the group.)

7. Click OK.

Looking Up Information in Address Book

When you open Address Book, the first thing you see is the contacts list, as shown in Figure 23-4.

Viewing the Contacts List

Address Book offers you the same choice of views that Windows Explorer does: Large Icon, Small Icon, List, and Details. Choose among them on the View menu. The differences among Large Icon, Small Icon, and List are fairly trivial: Large Icon uses a large index card icon and lists contacts in rows, Small Icon uses a small index icon and lists contacts in rows, and List uses a small index card icon and lists contacts in columns. Details view uses small icons and presents the name, e-mail address, home phone number, and business phone number of each contact in four columns.

Sorting the Contacts List

In any of the views, you can sort contacts according to any of the information displayed. In Small Icons, Large Icons, and List views only the name is shown, so contacts can be listed according to first or last name, in ascending or descending order. Make these choices by choosing View | Sort By.

In Details view, you can list contacts according to name, e-mail address, home phone number, or business phone number. As in the Details view in Windows Explorer, click the head of any column to list contacts according to that column in ascending order. To list in descending order, click the column head a second time. To tell Address Book whether the Name column should be ordered according to first name or last name, choose View | Sort By.

Looking Up Detailed Information

Each contact has a Properties dialog box associated with it, as shown in Figure 23-5. To view the Properties dialog box for a contact, double-click the person's entry in the contact list. The entries on the NetMeeting tab refer to the conferencing server and address used with the NetMeeting program described in Chapter 25. The entries on the Digital ID tab enable you to send and receive encrypted information from the person (see Chapter 31).

Finding People

If you have a lot of contacts in your Address Book, you don't want to have to scan the whole list to find a particular entry. To search the Address Book, click the Find People button on the toolbar. If the Address Book isn't open, you can choose Start | Search | People. Either way, you see the Find People window, shown here:

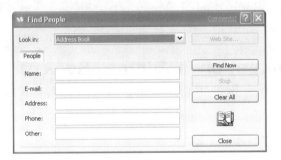

Make sure the Look In box is set to Address Book, type in what you know about the person, and then click Find Now. Any fragment of information helps to narrow down the search. If, for example, you remember the phone number has a 456 in it somewhere, enter 456 in the Phone line of the Find People box. Or, if you recall entering "wears red ties" as a note on the Other tab of the Contact Properties box, you can find the contact by typing **wears red ties** in the Other line of the Find People box.

You can also use the Find People box to search other address directories. See the section "Using Additional Directory Services."

Contacting People

To send e-mail to a person or group on your contacts list, select the recipient(s) from the address list, click the Action button on the toolbar, and choose Send Mail from the menu that appears; or, choose Tools | Action | Send Mail. (To address a message to several people, choose them by holding down the CTRL key while you select them.) Your default e-mail program should start to compose a message to the person that you selected.

Printing Information from Address Book

You can print information from the Address Book in three formats:

- **Memo**   Prints all the information Address Book has about the selected contact(s).

- **Business Card**   Prints only the information from the Business tab of the contact(s) Properties box.

- **Phone List**   Prints a list of phone numbers of the selected contact(s).

To print

1. Select contacts from the contacts list. Select blocks of names by holding down the SHIFT key while you click the names. Select individuals scattered throughout the list by holding down the CTRL key while you click the names. Select a group by clicking its name in the contacts list (not the group list). Select all contacts by choosing Edit | Select All. If you don't select any contacts, Address Book prints them all.

2. Click the Print button on the toolbar. A Print dialog box appears.

3. Select the Memo, Business Card, or Phone List from the Print dialog box.

4. Click OK.

To print addresses in any other format, export them (as described in the next section) to a database or word processing program that can print the format you want.

Exporting Names and Addresses from Address Book

You can also export names and addresses from Address Book in Microsoft Exchange Personal Address Book format, in Windows Address Book format, in a comma-delimited text file, or as vCards:

- **Windows Address Book format**   Choose File | Export | Address Book, choose the folder and filename to use (with the extension .wab), and click the Save button.

- **Microsoft Exchange Personal Address Book format**   Choose File | Export | Other Address Book and then select Microsoft Exchange Personal Address Book from the Address Book Export Tool window. Click the Export button. (If you're exporting to Outlook, you may be better off to export as vCards.)

- **Business card or vCard**   Select the person whose information you want to export, and then choose File | Export | Business Card (vCard). Specify the name and folder where you want to store the business card and click Save.

- **Text file**   Choose File | Export | Other Address Book, choose Text File (Comma Separated Values) from the list that appears, and click Export. The CSV Export Wizard runs. Specify the name of the file in which you want to store the exported addresses, and then click Next. Select the information you want to include for each person, and then click Finish.

Using Additional Directory Services

When you choose Start | Search | People, you see the Find People window. In addition to searching Address Book entries, you can search other *directory services*—listings of names, e-mail addresses, and other information. These directory services may be public, such as the Web-based services Yahoo! People Search and Bigfoot (at **http://people.yahoo.com** and **http://www.bigfoot.com**, respectively).

Or, they may be private, such as the employee directory for a large organization or the active directory used by your network logon server.

Windows XP comes with a number of public directory services already set up—click the Look In box in the Find People window to see a list. When you choose a directory service, the boxes in the Find People window adjust to match the types of entries the directory service can accept.

You can configure Windows to use other directory services, for example, for your organization. Windows can work with any LDAP-compatible directory service. (*LDAP* stands for *Lightweight Directory Access Protocol.*) To configure Windows to work with an additional directory service, run Address Book or Outlook Express, and then choose Tools | Accounts. (In Outlook Express, click the Directory Service tab.) You see the Internet Accounts window listing the directory services Windows knows about. To add a new directory service, click the Add button in the Internet Accounts window. The Internet Connection Wizard runs and asks for the information it needs to configure the new service.

To remove a directory service you no longer use, select the service in the Internet Accounts window and click the Remove button.

Organizing Your Correspondence

A mail program is more than just a way to read and write messages, it is also a filing system. Over time, the records of your correspondence may become a valuable asset. Although you can leave all of your mail in your Inbox, it's a lot easier to find messages if you file messages by sender or topic.

Outlook Express allows you to create folders and move messages from one folder to another. It also provides an Inbox Assistant utility to allow you to perform some secretarial actions automatically.

Working with Folders

The Outlook Express filing system resembles the filing system that Windows itself uses, but the Outlook Express files and folders can't be seen by other programs (see Chapter 7)—you must use Outlook Express to manipulate them.

Creating and Deleting Folders

To create a new folder in Outlook Express

1. Click the Local Folders icon in the folder list.

2. Select either File | Folder | New or File | New | Folder. The Create Folder window opens.

3. Type the name of your folder into the Folder Name line.

4. In the bottom half of the Create Folder window, select the folder into which you want to place the new folder.

5. Click OK.

To delete a folder, select it in the folder list of the Outlook Express window and select File | Folder | Delete.

Moving and Copying

To move or copy a message from one folder to another

1. Select the folder that contains the message in the folder list of the Outlook Express window. You may need to expand some folders (by clicking the plus boxes in the margin) to find it.

2. Find the message in the message list and right-click it.

3. Select either Move To Folder or Copy To Folder from the right-click menu. A window appears displaying a folder list.

4. Select the folder into which you want the message moved or copied.

5. Click OK.

You can also move a message by dragging it from the message list and dropping it onto the icon of the target folder in the folder list.

To move a folder, drag-and-drop its icon on the folder list to the location you want it to be located.

You can move several messages or folders at the same time by holding down the CTRL key while you select the items to move.

Each Outlook Express mailbox is actually a file with a .dbx extension. The Inbox, for example, is the file Inbox.dbx. One way to back up a mailbox is to make a copy of its file; you don't even need to open Outlook Express to do this. The files are a little hard to find, however, because they live many layers inside the hidden folder C:\Documents And Settings\username\Application Data. The best way to find them is to use the advanced Search option Search Hidden Files and Folders.

Finding Messages in Your Files

A filing system isn't worth much unless you can find what you put there. Outlook Express gives you a search tool that lets you search for messages based on

- The sender
- The recipient
- The subject
- A word or phrase in the message body
- Whether the message has attachments
- Whether the message is flagged
- The date received
- A folder containing the message

Begin your search by selecting Edit | Find | Message. The Find Message dialog box appears, as shown in Figure 23-6. Enter as much information as you know about the message and click Find Now. Outlook Express lists at the bottom of the window all the messages that fit the description you've given. Open any message on this list by double-clicking it.

Type any string of characters into the From, To, Subject, or Message lines of the Find Message dialog box. This restricts your search to messages whose corresponding parts contain those character strings.

To specify the date of a message, check either the Received Before or Received After check box. Enter a date in MM/DD/YY format into the corresponding line or click the drop-down arrow to locate the date you want on a calendar. (Change months on the calendar by clicking the left or right arrows at the top of the calendar.) You can use Before and After together to specify a range of dates.

The Look In box specifies a folder in which to search. Click the Browse button to locate a new folder to look in. The Include Subfolders check box does just what it says—if the box is checked, the search includes all the subfolders of the specified folder; if it is not checked, the subfolders are not included.

If the message you wanted didn't show up, check the View | Current View menu in the Find dialog box. Make sure it is set to Show All Messages.

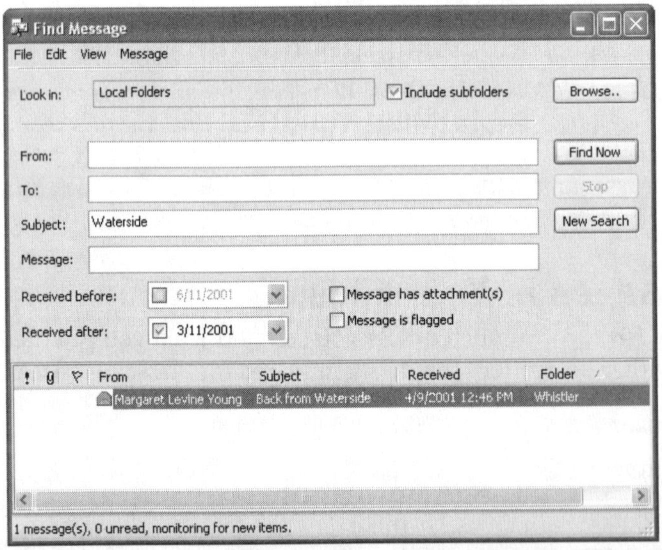

Figure 23-6.   *The Find Message dialog box*

Filtering Your Mail with Message Rules

Outlook Express can do some secretarial work to help you manage your POP e-mail messages automatically. It can do the following:

■ File messages to the appropriate folders, rather than letting them pile up in the Inbox

■ Forward messages to another e-mail address

■ Send a stock reply message

■ Delete unwelcome messages so that you never have to look at them

An easy way to delete messages from a particular person automatically is to add his or her name to your Blocked Senders list (see "Blocking a Sender").

You tell Outlook Express to do these things by establishing *message rules* or *mail rules*, which specify a kind of message and a type of action to take when such a message arrives. To establish a message rule for your e-mail, select Tools | Message Rules | Mail. The Message Rules dialog box appears, as shown in Figure 23-7. (If there

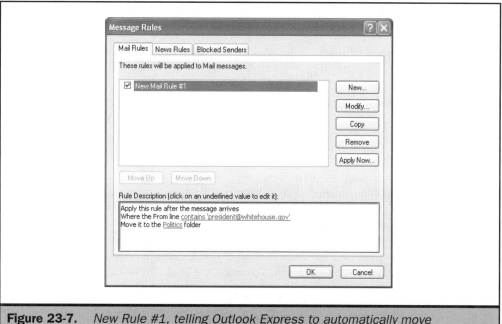

Figure 23-7.   *New Rule #1, telling Outlook Express to automatically move presidential e-mail to the Politics folder*

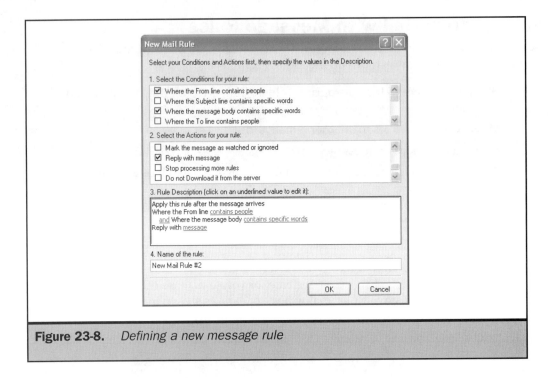

Figure 23-8. *Defining a new message rule*

are no current message rules, the New Mail Rule dialog box opens as well, as shown in Figure 23-8.)

Note *You can't use message rules with IMAP mail accounts, or Web-based mail accounts that don't also have POP servers.*

The upper portion of the Message Rules dialog box lists the rules you have created. A rule is active if its check box is checked, and inactive otherwise, so turning a rule on and off is easy. The lower portion of the dialog box gives a description of the currently selected rule. Some parts of the description are underlined in blue; these are links to other dialog boxes that allow you to edit these particular portions of the rule. In Figure 23-7, "Contains 'president@whitehouse.gov'" is linked—clicking it opens a box in which new addresses can be chosen.

To define a new rule, click the New button in the Message Rules dialog box. This opens the New Mail Rule dialog box, shown in Figure 23-8. This box has four sections.

■ **1. Select The Conditions For Your Rule** Enables you to define the messages that the rule should apply to. These conditions are vague, but you specify their details in the Rule Description section.

■ **2. Select The Actions For Your Rule** Enables you to specify what Outlook Express should do when such messages arrive. As in the first section, these actions are also vague, but are spelled out in the Rule Description section.

■ **3. Rule Description**   Gives a description of the rule as you have defined it so far; when more information is needed, the description contains a placeholder phrase that is linked to a dialog box for specifying the information. In Figure 23-8, for example, the phrases "contains people," "contains specific words," and "message" are all placeholders. Clicking these phrases opens additional dialog boxes that allow you to specify which people, which words, and what message. The word "and" is also linked; clicking it opens the And/Or dialog box, described in the next section.

■ **4. Name Of The Rule**   Enables you to specify a name for your rule. Otherwise, the rule will be numbered, such as in New Mail Rule #1 in Figure 23-7.

Defining Conditions for Message Rules

You define conditions for your message rules by checking the appropriate boxes in the Select Conditions For Your Rule section of the New Mail Rule dialog box. As you check boxes, the text next to those boxes appears in the Rule Description section, in which you click the linked phrases to specify any additional information that the condition requires.

If you check more than one box, the conditions are connected with an "and"—in other words, all checked conditions need to be true before the action you specify is taken. You can change this "and" to an "or" by clicking an "and" in the rule description and selecting the Messages Match Any One Of The Criteria radio button. There is no way to create more complicated conditions than to mix "ands" and "ors."

You can choose from 12 conditions listed in section one of the New Mail Rule dialog box:

■ **For All Messages**

■ **Where The From Line Contains People, Where the To Line Contains People, Where the CC Line Contains People**, and **Where The To Or CC Line Contains People**   Any of these four conditions requires you to specify which people the condition applies to. Click the phrase "contains people" in the Rule Description section to display the Select People dialog box. Add people to your list either by typing their e-mail addresses into the top line and clicking the Add button, or by clicking the Address Book button and selecting them from your address book. By default, the rule applies to a message in which any of the selected people are included in the specified line. You can require that the condition apply only if *all* of the people are included or if *none* of the people are included by clicking the Options button and choosing the appropriate radio button in the Rule Condition Options dialog box.

■ **Where The Subject Line Contains Specific Words** and **Where The Message Body Contains Specific Words**   Either of these conditions requires you to specify which words or phrases the rule is looking for. Click the phrase "contains specific words" in the Rule Description section. When the Type Specific Words dialog box appears, type a word or phrase and click the Add button. If you specify more than one word or phrase, click the Options button to specify whether all words/phrases must be present or just one of them.

WINDOWS XP ON THE INTERNET

- **Where the Message Is Marked As Priority, Where The Message Is From The Specified Account, Where The Message Size Is More Than Size, Where The Message Has An Attachment**, and **Where The Message Is Secure**   These five conditions require you to specify which priority, which account, what size, and what kind of security. Click the highlighted phrase in the Rule Description section and choose the appropriate radio button from the dialog box that appears.

Specifying Actions for Message Rules

By setting conditions in the Select The Conditions For Your Rule section of the New Mail Rule dialog box, you have picked out a particular class of messages. Now you need to tell Outlook Express what to do with those messages by filling out the Select The Actions For Your Rule section. Select actions by checking the check boxes. You may select as many actions as you like. You have 12 choices:

- **Move It To The Specified Folder** or **Copy It To The Specified Folder**   Either of these actions requires you to specify a folder to put the message into. Click the word "specified" in the Rule Description section and choose a folder from the dialog box that appears.

- **Forward It To People**   This action requires you to specify which people to forward the message to. Click the word "people" in the Rule Description section and enter an e-mail address into the Select People dialog box, or click the Address Book button to choose an address from your Address Book.

- **Delete It, Flag It**, **Mark It As Read**, **Do Not Download It From The Server**, and **Delete It From The Server**   These actions are self-explanatory. No highlighted words or phrases appear in the Rule Description.

- **Stop Processing More Rules**   If more than one rule applies to a message, the message may get processed twice, and may even be duplicated. If you find this happening, you add Stop Processing More Rules to the rules that are causing the problem.

- **Highlight It With Color**   After you select this check box, click the word "color" in the Rule Description section and make your choice from the Select Color dialog box.

- **Mark The Message As Watched Or Ignored**   Click "watched or ignored" in the Rule Description and choose the Watch Message or Ignore Message radio button. Outlook Express *watches* a message by displaying an icon (a pair of glasses) by it, and *ignores* a message by flagging it with the international "forbidden" icon.

- **Reply With Message**   This action requires you to tell it which message to use as your automatic reply. Click the word "message" and identify a message file when the Open dialog box appears. (Prior to defining the rule, you should compose your reply and select File | Save As to save it as an .eml file.)

Blocking a Sender

You can't stop annoying people or organizations from writing to you, but you can have Outlook Express send their e-mail messages straight to the Deleted Items folder or refuse to display their newsgroup messages. Make this happen by adding their names to the blocked senders list as follows:

1. Select Tools | Message Rules | Blocked Senders List from the Outlook Express menu bar. The Message Rules dialog box appears with the Blocked Senders tab on top, as shown in Figure 23-9.

2. Click the Add button. The Add Sender dialog box appears.

3. Enter the e-mail address that you want to block in the Address field. If you want to block all messages from an entire Internet domain (the part of the address after the @), type only the domain name.

4. Choose whether to block e-mail messages, newsgroup messages, or both by clicking the appropriate radio button.

5. Click OK. The Blocked Senders list now includes the new entry, with check boxes that say whether the blocking applies to the sender's e-mail or newsgroup messages.

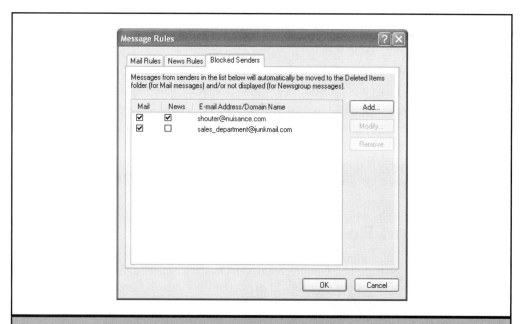

Figure 23-9.   *Blocking a few selected senders can lower your blood pressure.*

Remove a sender from your Blocked Senders list by choosing Tools | Message Rules | Blocked Senders List, selecting the sender in the Message Rules dialog box, and clicking the Remove button.

Managing Your Message Rules

All your message rules are listed by name in the upper section of the Message Rules dialog box. Outlook Express only applies rules whose check boxes are checked, so you can turn rules on and off easily by checking or unchecking their boxes. When you click a rule's name, its description appears in the Rule Description section of the dialog box. You can edit any of the highlighted phrases in the rule description, or you can rewrite the rule completely by clicking the Modify button. The Edit Mail Rule dialog box appears; it behaves in the same manner as the New Rule dialog box.

You can put the rules into a different order by selecting rules in the Message Rules dialog box and clicking the Move Up or Move Down button. To get rid of a rule completely, select its name and click Remove.

Using Message Rules to Sort Old Messages

Message rules are applied automatically to new messages as they arrive, but you can also apply message rules to the messages stored in a folder. This technique can help you organize your correspondence. To do this

1. Define a rule as described in section "Filtering Your Mail with Message Rules," or identify an already-defined rule that you want to apply.

2. If the Message Rules dialog box is not already open, select Tools | Message Rules | Mail to make it appear.

3. Select the rule you want to apply.

4. Click the Apply Now button. The Apply Message Rules Now dialog box opens.

5. Select the folder that the rule should be applied to. Inbox is the default, but if you want to apply the rule to a different folder you can click the Browse button and find the folder you want.

6. Click the Apply Now button. Outlook Express opens a confirmation box to tell you when it has finished.

Reading and Posting to Newsgroups

Before you can read and post to newsgroups with Outlook Express, you must set up a news account (see "Setting Up Your Accounts"). Once your account is set up, its folder appears in the folder list of the Outlook Express window, just below your mail folders. To begin using your news account, click its icon.

*You can read and post to newsgroups using a Web browser rather than a newsreader. The Google Groups Web site at **http://groups.google.com** gives you access to a large number of newsgroups.*

Notice that a news folder has a different icon than a mail folder, and that selecting a news folder rather than a mail folder changes the Outlook Express toolbar. Many of the news buttons resemble the mail buttons in name and function, but some do not. Left to right, the news buttons are as follows: New Post, Reply Group, Reply, Forward, Print, Stop, Send/Receive, Address Book, Find, Newsgroups, and Get Next Headers. You can choose which buttons should be on the toolbar in the same way that you can with Windows Explorer—right-click the toolbar and choose Customize from the shortcut menu.

Table 23-3 shows configuration settings that affect newsgroup reading and posting. Choose Tools | Options to display the Options dialog box that shows these settings.

Tab	Setting	Description
General	Default Messaging Programs: This application is the default News handler.	Clicking the Make Default button specifies that when you click the URL of a newsgroup, Outlook Express opens to display the newsgroup messages.
Read	Get *xx* headers at a time	Specifies how many message headers to download when you read a newsgroup.
Read	Mark all messages as read when exiting a newsgroup	Specifies that when you are done reading a newsgroup, Outlook Express marks the unread messages as read, so that they don't show up as unread the next time you read the newsgroup.
Send	News Sending Format: HTML/Plain Text	Specifies whether your newsgroup postings are sent as HTML or as plain text (see "Turning HTML On and Off"). Always set this option to Plain Text, because very few newsgroups tolerate HTML-formatted postings.
Compose	Compose Font: News	Specifies how unformatted messages appear on your screen when you are composing them.
Compose	Stationery: News	Specifies what stationery (standard formatting) your news messages will use. *Never* use stationery for newsgroup messages, because it uses HTML formatting.

Table 23-3.   *Configuration Settings for Newsgroup Reading and Posting*

Tab	Setting	Description
Compose	Business Cards: News	Specifies that your virtual business card (vCard) be included when you compose new messages (see "Importing Virtual Business Cards"). *Never* include business cards in news messages, because most newsgroups discourage attachments (except for newsgroups that specialize in trading files, which are never vCards).
Maintenance	Delete news messages *xx* days after being downloaded	Specifies whether old news messages are deleted automatically, and if so, after how many days. Because of the volume of messages in many newsgroups, you are unlikely to want to save all the messages you receive.

Table 23-3. *Configuration Settings for Newsgroup Reading and Posting* (continued)

(Tables 23-1 and 23-2 earlier in this chapter describe other settings in the Options dialog box.)

Subscribing to Newsgroups

The main thing that a newsreading application does is look at the list of newsgroups to which you subscribe and then check its news server to see whether those newsgroups have any new messages. The first step, then, in learning to use Outlook Express as a newsreader program is to find some interesting newsgroups and subscribe to them.

Downloading the List of Available Newsgroups

The first time that you click your news account icon, Outlook Express informs you that you are not subscribed to any newsgroups, and asks whether you want to download a list of available newsgroups from your news server. Be aware that there are thousands and thousands of newsgroups on most servers, so downloading the whole list takes some time. Fortunately, you have to do this only once for each news account you establish. From time to time you will want to update this list, but updating does not take nearly as long.

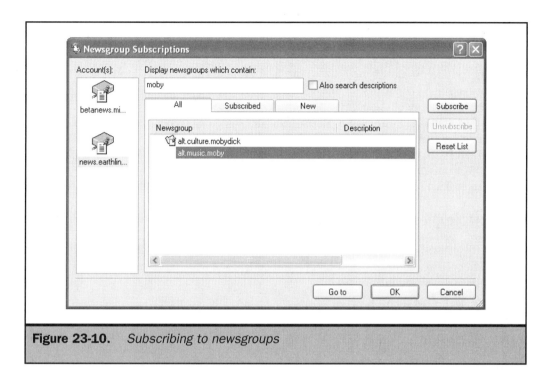

Figure 23-10.   *Subscribing to newsgroups*

Searching for Interesting Newsgroups

Once you have a list of available newsgroups, you can view it by doing the following:

1. Select a news account in the left pane of the Outlook Express window.

2. Click the Newsgroups button on the toolbar. The Newsgroup Subscriptions window appears, as shown in Figure 23-10.

In the early days of the Internet, you could choose the newsgroups to which you wanted to subscribe just by scanning the list of available groups. Now, the number of groups has grown so large that this method is like wandering through the stacks of a poorly organized library. Scrolling down the list of newsgroups can be an entertaining way to give yourself an idea of the kinds of things that are available, but it is not an efficient way to look for a particular kind of newsgroup.

Fortunately, the Newsgroup Subscriptions window gives you a few tools to aid in your search. This window has three tabs:

- **All**   Shows the complete list of newsgroups available on this server.

- **Subscribed**   Lists the (much smaller) list of newsgroups to which you have chosen to subscribe.

- **New**   Shows the newsgroups that your server has added since the previous time you updated the newsgroup list.

Above each of these tabs is the Display Newsgroups Which Contain line. When this line is blank, a tab lists all the newsgroups appropriate to it. (That is, All lists all newsgroups.) Typing something onto this line restricts the list to newsgroups containing what you have typed. In Figure 23-10 for example, the All tab lists all newsgroups that have "moby" somewhere in their names—one (alt.culture.mobydick) about the novel *Moby Dick* and another (alt.music.moby) about the musician Moby.

So, for example, if you want to know whether there is a newsgroup devoted to your favorite author or entertainer, go to the All tab of the Newsgroup Subscriptions window and type his or her last name into Display Newsgroups Which Contain. If you already did that search last week, but want to know whether there are any new newsgroups you should look at, do the same thing with the New tab.

Subscribing to a Newsgroup (or Not)

Once you have found a newsgroup you want to try out

1. Select its name in the Newsgroup Subscriptions window. (In Figure 23-10, alt.music.moby is selected.)

2. Click the Subscribe button.

The newsgroup is now listed on the Subscribed tab of the Newsgroup Subscriptions window, and a folder corresponding to the newsgroup is automatically created as a subfolder of the news account folder. Whenever the newsgroup appears in the Newsgroup Subscriptions window, it has a newsgroup icon next to it. For example, in Figure 23-10, alt.culture.mobydick has been subscribed to.

To unsubscribe, right-click the newsgroup in the folder list of the main Outlook Express window and choose Unsubscribe from the shortcut menu. Or you can select the newsgroup in the Newsgroup Subscriptions window and click the Unsubscribe button.

You can examine a newsgroup without subscribing to it by selecting it in the Newsgroup Subscriptions window and clicking the Go To button rather than the Subscribe button. Outlook Express downloads the headers of recent articles on a one-time-only basis. When you stop looking at the newsgroup, Outlook Express asks whether you want to subscribe.

Reading a Newsgroup

Outlook Express displays newsgroups in a format that is similar to the way it displays mail folders: the left pane contains a folder list, the upper-right pane contains a message list for the currently selected newsgroup, and the lower-right pane previews the currently selected message. (You can alter this layout in a variety of ways.) Most newsgroup messages are sufficiently short that the preview pane is all you'll really need (see "Choosing a Layout for the Outlook Express Window").

Unread articles are displayed in bold in the message list, and their icons are slightly brighter than the icons of messages that have been read. Newsgroups containing unread messages are displayed in bold on the folder list, with the number of unread messages in parentheses next to the name.

The message list groups all the messages that reply to a particular message. A plus box appears in the margin next to the original message; when clicked, it changes to a minus sign, and the replies are displayed underneath (and slightly indented from) the original message.

Reading a Newsgroup Online

If you are online, selecting a subscribed newsgroup from the folder list causes Outlook Express to download the headers of the messages on that newsgroup. In other words, the message list window fills up automatically. The messages themselves, however, are not downloaded until you select them in the message list. (The point of this is to save both download time and disk space on your computer.) When you find an intriguing header in the message list, click it to see its text in the preview pane, or double-click it to give the message a window of its own.

Reading a Newsgroup Offline

To read a newsgroup while spending the minimum amount of time online, download the headers as in the preceding section, and then disconnect by choosing File | Work Offline. You can then examine the headers of messages offline. When you find one you want, select it in the message window and then choose Tools | Mark For Offline | Download Message Later. The next time you are online and synchronize your new account, Outlook Express downloads all the marked messages, which you can then read either online or offline.

Using Message Rules to Filter a Newsgroup

Message rules for newsgroups work very much like message rules for e-mail (see "Filtering Your Mail with Message Rules"). They instruct Outlook Express to handle certain kinds of messages automatically. In particular, you can tell Outlook Express not to display messages written by particular people by adding them to your Blocked Senders list (see "Blocking a Sender"). Applying message rules to a newsgroup also gives you a more focused list of headers and saves download time.

Conceptually, establishing a new message rule has two basic steps: you list the criteria that define a class of messages, and you tell Outlook Express what to do with the messages in that class. More precisely, you follow these steps:

1. Select Tools | Message Rules | News. The Message Rules dialog box opens with the News Rules tab on top. (If you have no other rules defined, Outlook Express may open the New News Rule dialog box as well; if so, you can skip step 2.)

2. Click the New button. The New News Rule dialog box opens.

3. Check boxes in the Select Conditions For Your Rule section of the New News Rule dialog box. These boxes correspond to criteria that describe messages. You may need to choose several of these boxes to get the exact messages you want to act on. When you check a box, the corresponding text appears in the Rule Description section of the New News Rule dialog box. Most of the criteria need some other piece of information to make sense. For example, Where The From Line Contains People needs you to specify *which* people the rule should apply to. In these cases, the phrase that needs to be specified appears in blue. You'll insert this extra information in step 5. (A more detailed description of how to work with these criteria is contained in the section "Filtering Your Mail with Message Rules," earlier in this chapter.)

4. Check boxes in the Select The Actions For Your Rule section of the New News Rule dialog box. These boxes correspond to the actions you want Outlook Express to perform on the messages described in step 3. Like the Conditions in step 3, the Actions contain phrases that may require additional specification. For example, Highlight It With Color doesn't say which color should be used. You'll insert this extra information in step 5.

5. Examine the Rule Description section of the New News Rule dialog box. If any word or phrase is highlighted in blue, click it. A dialog box appears to allow you to insert the extra information needed to make the phrase specific.

6. When you have specified all the highlighted phrases in the Rule Description section, type a name into the Name Of The Rule section of the New News Rule dialog box.

7. Click OK. The Message Rules dialog box returns. Your new rule is included in the list of message rules.

8. Click OK.

Tip   *Mark all messages from yourself as watched so that you can easily spot replies to them.*

You can turn a message rule on or off by choosing Tools | Message Rules | News and then checking or unchecking the rule's check box in the Message Rules dialog box. To remove a rule, select it from the list in the Message Rules dialog box and click Remove. To edit a rule, select it from the list in the Message Rules dialog box and click Modify.

You can use a rule to organize newsgroup messages that you have already downloaded, in the same way that you can use a rule to organize downloaded mail messages (see "Using Message Rules to Sort Old Messages").

Saving Messages

By default, Outlook Express saves the text of downloaded news messages only for five days after you download them. When you close Outlook Express, messages older than that are thrown away, unless you save them by selecting File | Save As. Messages are saved in files with the extension .nws. Alternatively, you can tell Outlook Express to save messages longer—choose Tools | Options, click the Maintenance tab, and set the Delete News Messages *xx* Days After Being Downloaded setting.

Participating in a Newsgroup

Many people read a newsgroup for years and never respond to it in any way, neither writing e-mail messages to the authors of the messages they read, nor posting messages of their own. This is called *lurking*, and is a widely accepted practice. In fact, even if you do intend to post your own messages to a group eventually, we recommend that you lurk for a while first to learn the social norms of the group.

*To avoid asking obvious questions that a newsgroup's regular readers are sick of seeing, find out if the question is already answered in the newsgroup's Frequently Asked Questions (FAQ). You can look up the FAQs of many newsgroups at the International FAQ Consortium at **http://www.faqs.org/faqs**. A search engine at this Web site will help you find the FAQ you are looking for.*

One alternative to lurking is to examine the archives of the newsgroup, or to browse the last week or two of messages. Many newsgroups are archived at the Web site **http://starbase.neosoft.com/~claird/news.lists/newsgroup_archives.html**, at Google Groups **http://groups.google.com**, or (for a fee) at **http://www.supernews.com**.

Very few newsgroups tolerate posting HTML formatted messages or messages with attachments. Be sure to post messages as plain text.

Replying to Authors

Replying to the author of a newsgroup message is no different from replying to the author of a mail message. Just select the message and click the Reply button on the toolbar. Outlook Express opens a mail message window with the author's e-mail address entered automatically in the recipient list. You can create and edit this message just as you would any other mail message. To send your reply to the entire newsgroup rather than just the author(s), use the Reply Group button.

Posting a Message to a Newsgroup

To begin creating a newsgroup message, select a newsgroup from the folder list of the Outlook Express window, so that the Outlook Express News toolbar replaces the Mail toolbar. You may then create a message in either of these ways:

- **Composing a new message from scratch**   Click the New Post button on the Outlook Express toolbar.
- **Replying to a message**   Select a message from the message list of a newsgroup and click the Reply Group button on the toolbar. (Clicking the Reply button creates a mail message addressed to the author of the selected message and does not create a message to the newsgroup.)

In either case a New Message window opens. Like an e-mail message window, it has a header and a body, as shown here:

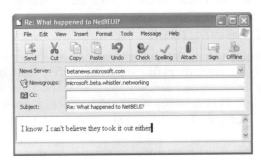

A news message header has three (or possibly four) lines:

■ **News server**   Lists the news server the message will be sent through. If you only have an account with one news server, this line does not appear.

■ **Newsgroups**   Lists the newsgroup(s) to which the message is to be posted. If you are replying to a message, Outlook Express inserts the newsgroup of the original message automatically. If you are composing a new message, Outlook Express inserts the currently selected newsgroup. If you are forwarding, this line is initially blank. To add newsgroups to the list, click the icon on the Newsgroups line of the header. The Pick Newsgroups dialog box appears. Its right pane lists the newsgroup(s) the message is currently addressed to, while its left pane lists the newsgroups you subscribe to. Clicking off the Show Only Subscribed Newsgroups button causes the left pane to list all newsgroups, not just the ones you subscribe to. The line at the upper-left of the Pick Newsgroups window is labeled Type Name Or Select From List, which is what you do. When this line contains the name of a newsgroup you want to add to the Newsgroups To Post To list in the right pane, click the Add button. Repeat this process until the right pane lists all the newsgroups to which you want to post your message.

If you change your mind about any of the newsgroups you have selected, select those newsgroups in the right pane and click the Remove button. When you are satisfied that you have just the right list of newsgroups, click OK to make the Pick Newsgroups window vanish.

■ **Cc**   If you want your message sent (as e-mail) to other people, list their e-mail addresses in the Cc line of the header. Click the index card icon if you want to choose an address from the Address Book, or type your best guess and then click the Check Names button on the toolbar, just as you would for an e-mail message.

■ **Subject** Give your message a title. If you are replying or forwarding, the subject line is automatically the same as the original message, preceded by Re or Fwd. Short, specific subject lines are the best.

After you have completed the header of your message, type the text into the body of the New Message window. You can use the Check Spelling button to check your spelling, just as you would in an e-mail message.

When you have the message exactly the way you want it, click the Send button. The message is then sent to your Outbox, where it is treated the same as your outgoing mail messages (see "Sending Messages").

Tip *If you want to test your newsgroup-posting ability, you can use a newsgroup that Microsoft set up for that very purpose. It lives on the msnews.microsoft.com news server, which (unlike most news servers) anyone can access. Set up an msnews.microsoft.com account in Outlook Express, and then subscribe to the newsgroup microsoft.public.test.here. Send your message to this newsgroup and see if it appears. You can also post test messages to the test.test newsgroup on most public news servers. Don't send test messages to other newsgroups—you'll get irate responses.*

Composing in HTML

Hypertext Markup Language (or *HTML*) is the language Web pages are written in. Outlook Express allows you to send HTML e-mail messages or newsgroup postings. This is a great idea, *but only if your recipients are set up to receive HTML messages.* If they don't have an up-to-date e-mail or newsgroup reader, your recipients will probably receive either

■ A text version of your message with the HTML version as an attachment.

■ A text version of your message either followed or preceded by a version in raw HTML—it sort of looks like text, but includes control codes that look like gibberish to the uninitiated.

At some point, HTML may take over as the dominant language for e-mail, just as it has for Web sites. But plain text is showing remarkable staying power, especially in newsgroups; so for now, we recommend using HTML *only* if you are sure that your recipient uses Outlook Express or some other e-mail program (such as Netscape Mail or Eudora Pro) that speaks HTML.

Tip *Never post an HTML formatted message to an e-mail mailing list, since you don't know whether every subscriber to the list has a mail program that can handle HTML.*

WINDOWS XP
ON THE INTERNET

If your recipient can read HTML, though, some very cool possibilities open up. You can do the following:

■ Use different fonts, sizes, and colors of text (which can be handy when replying to a message with corrections or further information)

■ Embed pictures, charts, or other graphics in your messages

■ Include links to the World Wide Web

Turning HTML On and Off

To set up Outlook Express to compose (or stop composing) messages in HTML

1. Select Tools | Options to open the Options dialog box.

2. Select the Send tab of the Options dialog box.

3. Choose either the Plain Text or HTML radio button in the Mail Sending Format box (for e-mail) and the News Sending Format box (for newsgroups).

We recommend that you set your News Sending Format to Plain Text because few newsreaders can display HTML formatting. Choose your Mail Sending Format setting based on whether most of your correspondents have e-mail programs that can display HTML formatting.

Composing HTML Messages

When Outlook Express is composing in HTML rather than plain text, the message box contains another toolbar (called the *formatting toolbar*) just below the header. Most of the tools on the formatting toolbar are familiar if you have used a word processor. From left to right, the tools are the following:

■ **Font Name**   Choose another font from the drop-down list.

■ **Font Size**   Choose from the drop-down list.

■ **Paragraph Style**   The drop-down list shows the choices of paragraph style.

■ **Bold, Italic, Underline**

■ **Font Color**   Click to see the palette.

■ **Formatting Numbers**   For making numbered lists.

■ **Formatting Bullets**   For making bulleted lists.

■ **Decrease/Increase Indentation**

■ **Align Left/Center/Right/Justify**

■ **Insert Horizontal Line**   Draws a dividing line across your message.

■ **Create a Hyperlink**   Links text in your message to Web addresses (see "Linking to the Web").

■ **Insert Picture**   Inserts any image file into your message (see "Inserting Pictures").

Linking to the Web

If your message mentions a Web page, or if a Web page reference would back up the point you are making, why not link to it? If your recipients have HTML-reading e-mail programs, they'll be able to open the page with their Web browsers just by clicking the hyperlink in your message.

To insert a hyperlink into a message you are writing in HTML

1. Select the text you want to link to the Web.
2. Click the Create A Hyperlink button on the formatting toolbar, located below the header. The Hyperlink dialog box opens.
3. Select the Web address prefix from the Type drop-down list of the Hyperlink dialog box.
4. Type the Web address into the URL box of the Hyperlink dialog box.
5. Click OK. The selected text should now appear in a different color from the rest of the message.

Inserting Pictures

You can insert photographs, diagrams, charts, or other image files into any message you compose in HTML. These objects then appear in the body of the message the way that photographs appear in a newspaper, not as file attachments.

1. Move the insertion point to the place in your message that you want the picture to be located.
2. Click the Insert Picture button on the formatting toolbar, below the header. The Picture dialog box appears.
3. Type the location of the image file into the Picture Source box or click the Browse button and find the file with a Browse window.
4. Type into the Alternate Text box the text that recipients will see if the picture (for whatever reason) is not displayed.
5. Choose the alignment from the drop-down list. This controls where the picture appears relative to the text.
6. Type a number into the Border Thickness box. This defines the width (in points) of a border surrounding the image.
7. Type numbers into the horizontal and vertical spacing boxes. These numbers define the width (in points) of a region of empty space surrounding the image.
8. Click OK. You see the image inserted into the message window.

If you want to change any of these decisions before you send the message, select the image in the message window and click Insert Picture on the formatting toolbar. The Picture dialog box opens with all your current choices. Change anything you want to and click OK.

WINDOWS XP
ON THE INTERNET

The Complete Reference

Windows XP

Chapter 24

Browsing the World Wide Web with Internet Explorer

A long with e-mail, the World Wide Web is the main reason most people bother with the Internet, and it is one of the most important reasons that people have home computers at all. Windows XP includes Internet Explorer 6, the latest version of the world's most popular Web browser, as well as an MSN-specific version called MSN Explorer. You also have the option of using other, non-Microsoft browsers.

This chapter explains some of the basic concepts of the World Wide Web and describes how to set up Internet Explorer, remember your favorite Web sites, configure it according to your tastes, use it to browse Web pages, and search for new sites. We also explain how to tell Internet Explorer to fill Web forms in automatically, set colors, set your start page, and control privacy settings. Although Windows XP doesn't come with a Web page editor, its Web Publishing Wizard can help you upload files to the Web.

What Is the World Wide Web?

The *World Wide Web* (usually just referred to as "the Web") is a collection of millions of files stored on thousands of computers (called *Web servers*) all over the world. These files represent text documents, pictures, video, sounds, programs, interactive environments, and just about any other kind of information that has ever been recorded in computer files. It is probably the largest and most diverse collection of information ever assembled.

What unites these files is a system for linking one file to another and transmitting them across the Internet. HTML codes allow a file to contain links to related files (see "What Is HTML?"). Such a *link* (also called a *hyperlink*) contains the information necessary to locate the related file on the Internet. When you connect to the Internet and use a Web browser program like Internet Explorer, you can read, view, hear, or otherwise interact with the Web without paying attention to whether the information you are accessing is stored on a computer down the hall or on the other side of the world. A news story stored on a computer in Singapore can link you to a stock quote stored in New York, a picture stored in Frankfurt, and an audio file stored in Tokyo. The combination of the Web servers, the Internet, and your Web browser assembles this information seamlessly and presents it to you as a unified whole. This system of interlinked text, called *hypertext*, was first described in the 1960s by Theodor H. Nelson, but it took thirty years for it to be widely used in the form of the World Wide Web, which was invented by Tim Berners-Lee at CERN, a particle physics lab in Geneva, Switzerland in 1990.

By following links, you can get from almost any Web document to almost any other Web document. For this reason, some people like to think of the entire Web as being one big document. In this view, the links just take you from one part of the document to another.

An *intranet* is an internal network that uses the same communication protocols as the Internet, but is limited to a specific group, usually the employees in one company.

Some organizations create private versions of the World Wide Web on their intranets so that access to their Web pages is limited to employees of that organization.

What Is HTML?

Hypertext Markup Language (*HTML*) is the universal language of the Web. It is a language for laying out pages that are capable of displaying all the diverse kinds of information that the Web contains. A Web browser, at the most basic level, is a program that reads and interprets HTML.

While various software companies own and sell HTML reading and writing programs, no one owns the language HTML itself. It is an international standard, maintained and updated by a complicated political process that so far has worked remarkably well. The World Wide Web Consortium (W3C), at **http://www.w3.org**, manages the HTML standard.

What Is a URL?

When the pieces of a document are scattered all over the world, but you want to display them seamlessly to a person who could be anywhere else in the world, you need a very good addressing system. Each file on the Internet has an address, called a *Uniform Resource Locator* (*URL*), also sometimes called an *Internet address* or *Web address*. For example, the URL of the ESPN Web site is **http://espn.go.com**. The first part of a URL (the part before the first colon) specifies the *transfer protocol*, the method that a computer needs to use to access this file. Most Web pages are accessed with the *Hypertext Transfer Protocol* (*HTTP*, the language of Web communication), which is why Web addresses typically begin with http (or its secure, encrypted versions, https or shttp). The http:// at the beginning of a Web page's URL is so common that it is assumed as the default protocol by modern browsers. If you simply type **espn.go.com** into the address window of Internet Explorer, the browser fills in the **http://** for itself. In common usage, the http:// at the beginning of a URL is left out.

The rest of the address denotes the Web page, but might not tell you where its files are actually located. Whether ESPN's Web server is in Los Angeles or Bangkok is invisible from its URL. Information about which Web server is responsible for answering requests for which URLs is contained in a huge database that the Web servers themselves are constantly updating. As users, we don't need to deal with this level of detail, and that's a good thing. The World Wide Web would be much less usable if sports fans had to learn a new set of URLs every time ESPN got a new computer.

What Are Internet Keywords?

URLs can be hard to remember, so systems of keywords have been devised to allow easier access to most popular Web sites. So, for example, you can get to CNN's Web site by typing "CNN" into Internet Explorer's Address box.

Unlike URLs, however, Internet keywords are not standardized. Netscape Navigator, another Web browser, uses a keyword system that has evolved from AOL's, while Internet Explorer uses Real Names' keywords. Other browsers might use other systems or none at all. The more popular sites usually have the same keyword in all systems, but there are occasional discrepancies. Also, no keyword system is complete. Every page on the Web has a URL, but only a (comparative) handful have their own keywords.

What Are Web Pages and Web Sites?

A *Web page* is an HTML document that is stored on a Web server and has a URL so that it can be accessed via the Web.

A *Web site* is a collection of Web pages belonging to a particular person or organization. The *home page* is the "front door" of the site and is set up to help viewers find whatever is of interest to them on that site. The URL of the home page also serves as the URL of the Web site.

For example, the URL of Microsoft's home page is **http://microsoft.com**. From the home page, you can get to Microsoft's Web pages about Windows XP at **http://microsoft.com/windowsxp**.

What Is a Web Browser?

A *Web browser* is a program that your computer runs to communicate with Web servers on the Internet so that it can download the documents you ask for and display them. At a bare minimum, a Web browser has to be able to understand HTML and display text. In recent years, however, Internet users have come to expect a lot more. A state-of-the-art Web browser provides a full multimedia experience, complete with pictures, sound, video, and even 3-D imaging.

What Are Plug-Ins?

Plug-ins are programs that are independent of your Web browser but "plug in" to it in a seamless way, so that you might not even be aware that you are using software that is not part of the Web browser. Typically, plug-ins arise when a software company develops a way to display a new type of data over the Web such as 3-D animation or streaming audio. Rather than create a whole new browser with this additional capability, the software company writes a plug-in for popular Web browsers like Netscape Navigator or Internet Explorer. Users who want to extend the capabilities of their browser in this particular way can install the plug-in, which then operates as if it is part of the Web browser.

Typically, installing a plug-in is fairly painless. Web pages that contain content requiring a special plug-in usually include instructions for downloading and installing the plug-in. The main inconvenience is the length of time necessary to download the plug-in (which is not even that long if you have a broadband Internet connection).

Installing the plug-in is usually a simple matter of clicking a few buttons and perhaps registering with the company that makes the plug-in. You can find a wide variety of plug-ins at the Tucows Web site at **http://www.tucows.com**.

As with any kind of software, downloading and installing a plug-in requires faith in whoever created and distributed it. A plug-in can introduce viruses into your system, modify files without your consent, or transmit data from your machine without your knowledge. Plug-ins from reputable software companies are as safe as any other kind of Internet software, but you should be cautious about downloading plug-ins from Web sites that you know nothing about.

What Is the Default Web Browser?

The *default Web browser* is the application that Windows uses to open a Web page when you haven't told it what browser to use—for example, when you click a Web link in an e-mail message or choose a Web page from the Favorites menu. Initially, Internet Explorer is the default Web browser, but you can choose another browser to be the default if you want (see "Changing the Default Browser").

You can, of course, open any Web browser you want and use it to browse the Web, whether it is the default browser or not. You can even have several browsers running at the same time—for example, Internet Explorer and Netscape Navigator.

What Is Internet Explorer?

Internet Explorer (IE) is Microsoft's Web browser. It intentionally resembles Windows Explorer, and it is an integral part of Windows XP—Windows uses some of the same code for displaying the Control Panel, Help And Support Center, and other pages. Having Internet Explorer doesn't depend on any decisions you might have made during installation, and you couldn't uninstall it if you wanted to, because many other Windows programs use Internet Explorer's code for displaying HTML-formatted information. You can uninstall or delete the shortcuts to Internet Explorer from your desktop, taskbar, and Start menu, but the program remains installed.

Internet Explorer 6 is the version that comes with Windows XP. It has a few new features compared to previous versions, which we spell out in the remainder of this chapter. Fundamentally, though, if you have used earlier versions of IE, you won't have much trouble figuring out how to use IE 6.

What Is MSN Explorer?

MSN Explorer is a utility that pulls together several of the free online services offered by the Microsoft Network (MSN). Its icon is a butterfly, which you can probably find on the task bar. (If not, check the Start | All Programs menu.)

When MSN Explorer is running, as shown in Figure 24-1, you are one click away from your Hotmail e-mail account, your local weather report, quotes on your stock portfolio, the appointments you have listed on MSN Calendar, and many other

Figure 24-1.   *MSN Explorer pulls together MSN's free services.*

services. You do not have to get your Internet access from MSN to use these services—
you can continue to use your existing ISP account.

*Running MSN Explorer has security implications (see Chapter 31, section "MSN
Explorer May Compromise Security"). The MSN Explorer Security Statement says:
"If you have chosen security settings that will interfere with MSN Explorer, then your
security settings are temporarily changed to allow MSN Explorer to work properly. In
addition, while MSN Explorer is active on your computer, the special settings for MSN
will apply to any Microsoft Internet Explorer window you may have open." Frankly,
the idea that some program is mucking around with our security settings behind the
scenes gives us the willies. For this reason, we do not use MSN Explorer, no matter
how cute and convenient it is.*

Should You Use Internet Explorer?

Internet Explorer 6 is the latest version of the most popular Web browser, and it has a
lot going for it. It's free. It's already installed as part of Windows XP, and because it is
the most popular Web browser, you can be sure that the people who create Web pages
will make sure they work properly with Internet Explorer.

We know of no compelling reason not to use Internet Explorer, but it does have
competitors and each competitor has its respective advantages. The most worthy
competitors, in our opinion, are Netscape and Opera.

Netscape Navigator once dominated the Web browser market, but when Microsoft integrated Internet Explorer into Windows, IE quickly became the most popular browser. Navigator lost a lot of its remaining fans when Netscape's new browser, Netscape 6, was late on the market and then was rushed out before it was ready. However, Netscape 6.1 appears to have fixed the problems of Netscape 6, and is once again worth considering. Netscape 6.1 matches Internet Explorer feature-for-feature and we like its security and privacy features better than Internet Explorer. Plus (to us, at least) it just looks cooler. It is a huge download, however, and if you don't have a broadband connection it is probably not worth the effort. You can get Netscape to send you a Netscape Navigator 4.7 or Netscape 6.1 CD-ROM for about $7. Either download or order the latest version of Netscape from the Web site **http://home.netscape.com/download**.

Rather than try to compete feature-for-feature with IE and Netscape, the Opera Web browser focuses on being small and quick. It is widely regarded as the fastest Web browser at downloading and displaying Web pages (though claims like these are hard to prove), and because it has a smaller program, it takes considerably less time to download and install than Netscape.

Opera has two main disadvantages compared to either Internet Explorer or Netscape:

■ It's not free. You either have to accept a small advertising bar or pay $39 for the advertising-free version.

■ Finding and installing plug-ins for special kinds of Web content can be tricky. In general, any plug-in that works with Netscape Navigator can be set up to work with Opera also, but the process is not always transparent.

To download Opera, go to **http://www.opera.com**. To check out dozens of other Web browsers, go to **http://download.cnet.com**.

Don't be afraid to try out a new Web browser. All browsers work more or less the same way. For an Internet Explorer user to use Netscape Navigator or Opera is about as difficult as a GM driver driving a Ford or Chrysler.

Getting Started with Internet Explorer

Internet Explorer is installed automatically when you install Windows XP. Its icon (a blue letter *e*) is not hard to find; look at or near the top of the Start menu, on the Quick Launch toolbar, or on the desktop. To run Internet Explorer click one of these icons or choose Start | All Programs | Internet Explorer.

Under the default settings, one of the following three things happens when you start Internet Explorer:

■ Internet Explorer opens displaying its start page, which Microsoft has initially set as the MSN home page **http://www.msn.com**.

- If you are not online and your start page is only available over the Internet, Internet Explorer tries to connect to the Internet. Depending on how your account is set up, this may happen automatically or you may have to enter a password into the Connect dialog box or some other connection software. If Internet Explorer succeeds in establishing an Internet connection, the start page appears. Otherwise it asks if you want to continue working offline. If you agree, it displays a blank start page.

- If you either do not have an Internet account, or have not told Windows about the one you have, the New Connection Wizard starts (see Chapter 22, section "Running the New Connection Wizard").

Elements of the Internet Explorer Window

When all of the major components of the Internet Explorer window are made visible, it looks like Figure 24-2. These components are identical to those of Windows Explorer, and can be hidden or reconfigured in the same way (see Chapter 8, section "Configuring Windows Explorer").

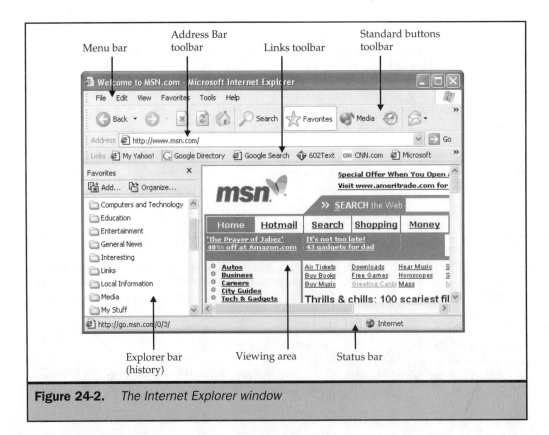

Figure 24-2. *The Internet Explorer window*

From top to bottom, it contains the following:

- **Menu bar**   Visible at all times, not configurable. You can move it to a different location in the window by clicking and dragging the handle (ridge) at its left end.

- **Standard buttons toolbar**   This is the same toolbar you see in Explorer windows, and you can customize its appearance for Internet Explorer in exactly the same way (see Chapter 7, section "What Is the Standard Buttons Toolbar?"). This is the toolbar we are referring to if we don't specify which toolbar we mean. It can be hidden or displayed with or without text labels. You can also choose what buttons to display. To hide this toolbar, uncheck View | Toolbars | Standard Buttons. To change the toolbar's appearance, select View | Toolbars | Customize and work with the Customize Toolbar dialog box (see Chapter 8, section "Configuring the Standard Buttons Toolbar"). Drag it to another location by the handle at its left end.

- **Address Bar**   Displays the URL of the currently displayed Web page or the Windows address of the currently displayed local file. Hide the Address Bar by unchecking View | Toolbars | Address Bar. Expand or shrink the Address Bar by dragging the right boundary. Drag it to another location by the handle at its left end.

- **Links toolbar**   A row of icons that you can link to files on your computer or to Web pages (see Chapter 8, section "Configuring the Links Toolbar"). Hide Links by unchecking View | Toolbars | Links. Expand or shrink this toolbar by dragging the left boundary. (You might need to unlock the toolbars first by choosing View | Toolbars | Lock The Toolbars.)

- **Explorer bar**   Displays Search, Favorites, Media, History, or Folders in a pane at the left side of the Internet Explorer window (see Chapter 7, section "What Is the Explorer Bar?"). Choose which of these to display from the View | Explorer Bar menu or by clicking a toolbar button. Hide these by selecting View | Explorer Bar and choosing the option that has a check mark to its left or by clicking the X in the upper-right corner of the Explorer bar. You can drag the border between the Explorer bar and the viewing window.

- **Viewing window**   Displays Web pages. It can't be hidden, since otherwise there would be no point in running a browser. Maximize the viewing window by selecting View | Fullscreen or pressing F11. Return to the previous (unmaximized) state by selecting View | Fullscreen or pressing F11 again.

- **Status bar**   Displays a variety of useful information. When the cursor passes over a link in the viewing window, the URL of the link is displayed in the status bar. When Internet Explorer is looking for or downloading a Web page, the status bar keeps you apprised of its progress. Hide the status bar by unchecking View | Status Bar.

Using the Standard Buttons Toolbars

The Standard Buttons toolbar has a few different buttons for Internet Explorer than it does for Windows Explorer, but several are the same and in general you use the toolbar in the same way. You can display the toolbar in several ways, and you can customize it by choosing which buttons to display and what order to put them in.

The following buttons are new to Internet Explorer, in the sense that they are not part of the default toolbar for Windows Explorer.

- **Stop** (denoted by an X) Active only when the browser is in the process of downloading a page from the Web; clicking it stops this process. The menu equivalent is View | Stop, and the keyboard equivalent is the ESCAPE key.

- **Refresh** (denoted by a document with two arrows) Asks the server to send the most recent version of the page currently being viewed. When a Web page is updated on the server, the new version is not automatically sent out to anyone who might be viewing an older version. Clicking Refresh makes sure that the scoreboard you are viewing has the latest scores, or the portfolio shows the most recent stock prices. The menu equivalent is View | Refresh, and the keyboard equivalent is the F5 key.

- **Home** (denoted by a house icon) Linked to the home or start page. The menu equivalent is View | Go To | Home Page, and the keyboard equivalent is the HOME key.

- **Media** Displays material from the WindowsMedia.com Web site in the Explorer bar, with information about audio and video downloads.

- **Mail** Opens your designated e-mail program. By default, this is Outlook Express, but if you have named another client such as Eudora on the Programs tab of the Internet Options dialog box, that program opens instead.

- **Print** Opens the Print dialog box, which is the first step in sending the current page to the printer. It is equivalent to File | Print on the menu or CTRL-P on the keyboard.

- **Edit** Opens the default HTML editing program so that you can alter a local copy of the current Web page. It's equivalent to File | Edit on the menu.

- **Messenger** Opens a Windows Messenger window for sending and receiving instant messages over the Internet (see Chapter 25, section "Chatting Online with Windows Messenger"). It is equivalent to Tools | MSN Messenger Service on the menu.

The following buttons are not part of the default configuration, but you might find them useful:

- **Related**   Produces a Related Links Explorer bar, which gives a list of Web pages that might be related to the current page. The menu equivalent is Tools | Show Related Links.

- **Full Screen**   Maximizes the viewing area by stretching the Internet Explorer window to the full size of your monitor while shrinking all the other features of the Internet Explorer window. Click it again to return to the previous configuration. It is equivalent to View | Full Screen on the menu or F11 on the keyboard.

- **Print Preview**   Shows a page-by-page view of what you would get if you printed out the current Web page. The menu equivalent is File | Print Preview.

- **Disconnect**   Breaks your Internet connection.

What Are Smart Tags?

Internet Explorer 6 was originally to have included a new feature called *smart tags*. MSN maintains a list of company names, product names, and other identifiers that IE can look for when it displayed Web pages. If smart tags are installed in IE, these terms appear with a dotted purple underline. If you move your mouse pointer to the term, a small *i* icon appears just above it—click it to see a floating window with a menu of links about that term.

Clicking a Smart Tag link displays a Web page about that company or product displayed in another IE window. It is usually a page from a Microsoft-owned site, like search.msn.com or moneycentral.msn.com. Other companies object to the smart tags feature because it directs people from other Web sites to the site defined by the Smart Tag. Microsoft removed smart tags from Windows XP and IE 6, but they are available as an add-in to Internet Explorer by choosing Start | All Programs | Windows Update or from **http://windowsupdate.microsoft.com**.

WINDOWS XP
ON THE INTERNET

Viewing Web Pages

The main purpose of a Web browser is to display Web pages. Those pages may actually be on the Web, or they may be on your own computer.

Browsing the Web

As soon as you open your first Web page, like the MSN start page in Figure 24-2, you can begin *browsing*—moving from one Web page to another, depending on what you find interesting.

On a standard Web page, text phrases that are links to other Web pages are displayed in underlined blue type. If you have recently displayed the Web page to which the text is linked, the text is displayed in maroon. When you are exploring a Web site, this feature lets you know where you've been and keeps you from going in circles. In Internet Explorer you can also define the color a link turns when the cursor is above it (the default is red). You can change these colors (see "Choosing Colors").

When you pass the mouse pointer over a linked object (including a linked text phrase), the pointer changes from an arrow to a hand, and the URL of the Web page that the object is linked to is displayed in the status bar of the browser window (if you have the status bar enabled). Not all links on a page are obvious; a small picture, for example, might just be an illustration, or it might be linked to a larger version of the same picture. Passing the mouse pointer over an object is the easiest way to tell whether it is linked.

While files are being downloaded to your Web browser, the mouse pointer changes to an hourglass. However, it is still functional—you can push buttons or scroll the window with an hourglass pointer. Most important, you can use it to click the Stop button if a link is taking longer to download than you're willing to wait.

 Try right-clicking items on Web pages—Internet Explorer provides shortcut menus of useful commands. Shortcut menus are available for links, images, backgrounds, and other parts of Web pages.

Opening Files on Your System

You can use Internet Explorer to view HTML files that are stored on your hard drive or elsewhere on your system. You can also view images stored in several different image formats, such as JPEG or GIF:

1. Select File | Open or press CTRL-O in Internet Explorer and click the Browse button in the dialog box that appears. You see an Open dialog box almost identical to the Open dialog box of Windows Explorer.

2. Make sure that the Files Of Type line of the Open window contains the type of file you want to open. Web pages are of type HTML, and pictures, depending

on picture format, are of type JPG, GIF, or other graphics formats. If the Files Of Type line doesn't contain the file type you want to open, choose another type from the drop-down menu. If you can't find the right type, choose All Files.

3. Browse until you find the file you want to open.

4. Select the file by clicking its name. Its name then appears in the File Name line.

5. Click Open. You are returned to the Open dialog box, with the address of the file entered. Click OK.

Getting Around on the Web

You can open a Web page in Internet Explorer by using any of the following methods:

- **Entering its URL into the Address box**   The most direct way is to type the URL; but if you have the URL in a file or a mail message, you can cut it and paste it. The Paste command on the Edit menu might not work when the cursor is in the Address window, but you can always paste by pressing CTRL-V. Internet Explorer has an auto-complete feature which tries to guess what URL you are typing and finishes it for you, based on similar URLs that you've visited before. A list of its guesses appears under the Address box as you type. If one is correct, click it and press ENTER.

- **Typing its Internet keyword into the Address box**   Many Web pages have been assigned Internet keywords that you can substitute for their URLs. So, for example, you can arrive at the home page of the University of California at Los Angeles by typing **UCLA** into the Address box.

- **Selecting it from the list that drops down from the Address box**   The Address box remembers the last 25 URLs or keywords that you have typed into it.

- **Linking to it from another Web page**   The reason it's called a "web" is that pages are linked to each other in a tangled, unpredictable way. Click a link (usually underlined, blue text or icons) to see the Web page it refers to.

- **Linking to it from a mail message or newsgroup article**   Many mail and messaging programs, including Outlook Express and Windows Messenger, automatically link the URLs in a message to the corresponding Web pages (see Chapter 23). Clicking the URL opens the default Web browser, which displays the Web page. If the browser can't find the page, try copying and pasting the URL into its Address box and making sure it looks right (remove spaces and line breaks from the URL, for example).

- **Selecting it from History**   Internet Explorer maintains records of the Web pages you have viewed in the past twenty days (or as many days as you select). You can display these records and return to any of the Web pages with a click (see "Examining History").

Getting Help

Access Internet Explorer Help by choosing Help | Contents And Index. You can find what you want by looking through the table of contents on the Contents tab, seeing the topics listed alphabetically on the Index tab, or searching for particular terms on the Search tab. Clicking the Web Help button and clicking the Support Online link opens a browser window displaying the Microsoft Support Web page at **http://support.microsoft.com/directory**.

- **Selecting it from the Favorites menu**   Accessing a Favorite from the Internet Explorer Favorites menu opens it in Internet Explorer, no matter what the default browser is.

- **Opening an Internet shortcut**   Opening an Internet shortcut from Windows Explorer starts the default browser (even if another browser is already running), connects to the Internet, and displays the Web page to which the shortcut points.

Remembering Where You've Been on the Web

Internet Explorer provides a variety of ways to remember which Web sites you've already visited and how to get back to them. The Back menu keeps track of the last few Web pages you've viewed and a drop-down list from the Address box shows the most recent URLs that you've typed. There's also a History feature that you can check when you find yourself saying "I know I saw that last week."

When you find a Web page you like, you likely will want to look at it again sometime. Favorites and Internet shortcuts allow you to return easily to a Web page without having to write down or remember the page's URL (see "Using Favorites, Links, and Internet Shortcuts").

Using the Back Menu

The Back button has a drop-down menu of the last several Web pages you have looked at during the current session. To access this menu, click the arrow on the right side of the Back button.

Covering Your Tracks and Tracking Others

If other people use (or are authorized to look at) your user account, you need to be aware of the privacy implications of the History folder, the Address box, and the Back menu. These features (especially the History folder) provide a trail that someone else can follow to see what you've been viewing on the Web. Conversely, you may examine the History folder to see what other people (your children, for example) have been viewing on the Web.

If you want to erase that trail, do the following:

1. Select Tools | Internet Options to open the Internet Options dialog box.

2. Click the Clear History button on the General tab.

3. Click Yes when you are asked to confirm. IE deletes the history and the list of URLs that you have typed in the Address box.

4. Click the Delete Files button to erase the files in your Temporary Internet Files cache.

5. Click OK when asked to confirm.

6. If you just walk away from the computer at this point, the Back menu could still give you away, so exit Internet Explorer. This clears the Back menu.

Using the Address Box

If you remember the beginning of the URL you are looking for, start typing it into the Address box. As you type, Internet Explorer's autocomplete feature generates a menu of URLs, based on the URLs you have visited recently. If the URL you want appears, you can choose it from the menu.

In addition, Internet Explorer maintains a drop-down list of the last 25 URLs that you have typed into the Address box. You can select an entry off the drop-down list, and the browser fetches the corresponding Web page.

Examining History

Internet Explorer keeps track of the Web pages that you have accessed recently. This information is stored as Internet shortcuts inside a hierarchy of folders capped by the History folder. You can turn History off, wipe the History folder clean, or edit it selectively, removing only the Web pages you don't want recorded.

WINDOWS XP
ON THE INTERNET

Clicking the History button on the toolbar (the one with the turn-back-the-clock icon) or selecting View | Explorer Bar | History opens the History Explorer bar, shown here:

Clicking the History button again causes the History pane to disappear.

The History folder is organized into subfolders—one for each day of the current week and one for each previous week, going back 20 days. (You can use the steps listed in the following paragraphs to change the number of days History remembers.) Selecting a closed folder expands the tree to show its contents; selecting an open folder compresses the tree to hide its contents. Each day's folder contains one subfolder for each Web site visited. Inside the Web site folders are Internet shortcuts to each of the pages viewed on that Web site.

Delete a shortcut or a subfolder from the History folder by right-clicking it and selecting Delete from the shortcut menu.

To change Internet Explorer's History settings:

1. Select Tools | Internet Options. The Internet Options dialog box opens with the General tab on top (as shown in Figure 24-3). The History box is near the bottom of the General tab.

2. If you want to delete all the entries in the History folder, click the Clear History button in the History box of the General tab.

3. If you want to change the number of days that the History folder remembers a Web page, enter a new number into the Days To Keep Pages In History box.

4. Click OK.

History is subject to user accounts: each user has his/her own History folder with its own settings. This folder is located at C:\Documents And Settings*username*\Local

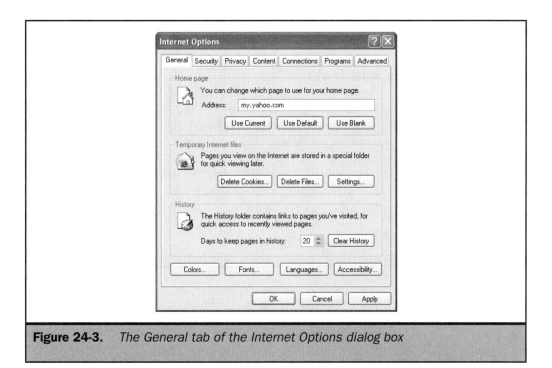

Figure 24-3.   *The General tab of the Internet Options dialog box*

Settings\History (assuming that Windows is installed on C:—replace *username* with your user account name, as described in Chapter 6). You can edit the History folder with Windows Explorer, but only if you have it set to display hidden files and folders.

Using Favorites, Links, and Internet Shortcuts

Favorites and Internet shortcuts are ways to keep track of Web sites that you think you will want to come back to.

An *Internet shortcut* is a small file (of type .URL) that contains the Internet address of a Web page. Opening an Internet shortcut causes Windows to connect to your Internet provider (if necessary), open your default Web browser, and display the Web page that the shortcut points to.

Favorites is a folder of Internet shortcuts. This folder is accessible from the Favorites menu in Internet Explorer, and you can add Favorites to the Start menu as well. Selecting an entry from the Favorites menu has the same effect as opening an Internet shortcut that points to that Web page. When Favorites are chosen from the Start menu, they open in the default browser, but choosing a Web page from the Favorites menu of Internet Explorer opens the page in Internet Explorer, even if another browser is the default browser.

The Links folder is a subfolder of Favorites. The items in the Links folder appear on the Links toolbar.

Adding Favorites and Links

Adding a Web page to the Favorites menu automatically creates an Internet shortcut pointing to that Web page. If a Web page is displayed in Internet Explorer, you can add it to Favorites by dragging its icon from the Address box to the Favorites menu or the Favorites Explorer bar, or you can invoke the Add Favorites wizard by selecting Favorites | Add To Favorites.

To add a Web page to the Links toolbar, either drag its icon from the Address box to the place on the Links bar where you want it, or drag it into the Links folder on the Favorites Explorer bar or on the Favorites menu.

Creating Internet Shortcuts

To create shortcuts in Internet Explorer, open the page to which you want to create a shortcut and choose File | Send | Shortcut To Desktop.

You can also create shortcuts in Windows Explorer or the desktop. From Windows Explorer, choose File | New | Shortcut. From the desktop, right-click and choose New | Shortcut. Either way, a Create Shortcut box opens. Type the URL of the Web page into the Create Shortcut box, or if you have copied the command line from some other document, paste it into Create Shortcut by pressing CTRL-V. Click Next. Give the shortcut a name. Click Finish.

Organizing Favorites

If you have picked out only a few Web pages, your favorites don't have to be well organized, but as time goes by, favorites accumulate like knick-knacks. It saves time to reorganize them once in a while and toss out the ones that are obsolete.

The Favorites list is actually a folder (C:\Windows\Favorites, if you haven't established user profiles on your computer; C:\Windows\Profiles*username*\Favorites, if you have), and each of the entries on the Favorites list is a shortcut pointing to the URL of the corresponding Web page. Consequently, one way to organize Favorites is to use the same techniques you would use to organize any other folder in Windows Explorer. You can choose Favorites | Organize Favorites from any Explorer or Internet Explorer window. An Organize Favorites box opens. Move, rename, or delete entries on your Favorites list by selecting the entries and clicking the corresponding buttons in the Organize Favorites box.

Importing and Exporting Favorites and Bookmarks

When you install Internet Explorer on a computer that already has Netscape Navigator, the Navigator bookmarks are automatically imported to the Favorites list. Conversely, there is no need to convert the Favorites folder to Navigator bookmarks, as long as you are using both on the same computer: The Bookmarks | Imported IE Favorites menu in Navigator displays an up-to-date list of the entries in the Favorites folder.

To import bookmarks to Internet Explorer after installation, select File | Import And Export to start the Import/Export Wizard. This Wizard provides the best way to convert between Internet Explorer's Favorites (a folder of Internet shortcuts) and Navigator's bookmarks (an HTML file of links).

Adding Favorites to the Start Menu

Having the Favorites menu appear under Start is a convenient way to eliminate one step in the process of opening a favorite Web page. Rather than starting a Web browser and then choosing the Web page, you can choose the Web page directly from the Start | Favorites menu, and the default Web browser starts automatically.

If Favorites doesn't appear on your Start menu, you can add it as follows:

1. Right-click the Start button and select Properties from the shortcut menu. The Taskbar And Start Menu Properties dialog box appears with the Start Menu tab selected (see Chapter 10). The tab contains two radio buttons: Start Menu (the default setting) and Classic Start Menu. One of the buttons is selected, and the Customize button next to this choice is active.

2. Click the active Customize button on the Start Menu tab. Either the Customize Start Menu or the Customize Classic Start Menu dialog box appears.

3. If the Customize Start Menu dialog box is open, click its Advanced tab. If the Customize Classic Start Menu dialog box is open, move on to Step 5.

4. Check the Favorites Menu check box on the Advanced tab of the Customize Start Menu dialog box, or the Display Favorites check box on the Customize Classic Start Menu dialog box.

5. Click OK in all open dialog boxes.

Searching for Web Pages

Internet Explorer gives you three ways to search the Web: Simple convenient searches can be done from the Address box; more complex searches using a variety of search engines are possible from the Search Companion Explorer bar; and you can always do your searches from the Web site of whatever search engine you like.

Searching from the Address Box

The simplest way to search the Web is to type a question mark followed by a word or phrase into the Address box and press ENTER. (Be sure to leave a space after the question mark.) By default, Internet Explorer uses the MSN search engine for Address bar searches, but you can choose a different default from the Search Companion Explorer Bar.

Using the Search Explorer Bar

The Search Companion Explorer bar allows you to search not just for Web pages, but for addresses, businesses, maps, words, pictures, and newsgroups. It is the same Explorer bar that you use to search for files and folders with Windows Explorer. The general aspects of the Search Companion Explorer bar are discussed in Chapter 8.

To look for a Web page, type a question or some keywords into the What Are You Looking For box and click the Search button in the Explorer bar.

Changing Internet Explorer's Default Search Engines

By default, Internet Explorer uses the MSN search engine for searches from either the Address box or the Explorer bar. You can change search engines as follows from the Search Companion Explorer bar. Click the Change Preferences button and then Change Internet Search Behavior. Click With Classic Internet Search and choose a new search engine from the list (we recommend Google).

*No matter what search engine Internet Explorer wants to use, you can always go to the Web site of your favorite search engine and use it directly—we like **http://google.com**.*

Interacting with Web Sites Automatically

Web sites that provide some personalized service typically ask you to fill out a registration form when you first establish a relationship with the site and to log in by giving a user name and password when you return to the site in the future. Filling out forms and typing in passwords are precisely the kinds of repetitive, mindless work that computers are supposed to do for us, so Internet Explorer provides a way to do these small tasks automatically.

You should give some thought as to whether to let the browser remember passwords and which passwords to entrust to it. Once a browser has been allowed to remember a password for a personal account on a Web site, anyone who uses your user account can get into that Web account.

Remembering Passwords Automatically

If you want Internet Explorer to remember passwords for you, do the following:

1. Choose Tools | Internet Options to open the Internet Options dialog box.
2. Go to the Content tab.
3. Click the AutoComplete button to open the AutoComplete Settings dialog box, as shown here:

4. Check the User Names And Passwords On Forms check box. This setting means that Internet Explorer will insert the user names and passwords it has memorized into the appropriate logon forms for Web pages.
5. Check the Prompt Me To Save Passwords check box. This setting means that whenever you log in to a site whose password Internet Explorer hasn't memorized, it will ask you whether you want it to memorize that password. If Internet Explorer already knows all the passwords you want it to know, leave this box unchecked.
6. Click OK in each of the open dialog boxes.

When these settings are in place, you will encounter the following dialog box every time you enter a new password:

Click Yes if you want the password remembered. Checking the Don't Offer To Remember Any More Passwords check box has the same effect as unchecking the Prompt Me To Save Passwords box on the AutoComplete Settings dialog box: Internet Explorer remembers and continues to use the passwords it knows but stops asking whether it should remember new passwords.

Occasionally you click Yes to remember the password and then later regret it. Unfortunately, there is no way to instruct Internet Explorer to forget one or two of your passwords but remember the others. If you want Internet Explorer to forget all the passwords it knows, open the AutoComplete Settings dialog box (as in the previous steps) and click the Clear Passwords button.

Using Internet Explorer's Profile Assistant

Profile Assistant is Internet Explorer's tool for filling out Web forms automatically. You fill out a profile form similar to the Windows Address Book contact form. Information from this profile is used to fill out Web forms that ask for things like your address or phone number. (No information is transmitted automatically. You have an opportunity to review forms and delete or change information before submitting forms.)

To set up your profile:

1. Open the Internet Options dialog box by selecting Tools | Internet Options from the menu bar.

2. Go to the Content tab of the dialog box and click the My Profile button. The Address Book – Choose Profile dialog box appears.

3. If you already have your own information stored as an entry in your address book, click the Select An Existing Entry From The Address Book To Represent Your Profile radio button, and do just that: select an entry from the list in the dialog box. Click OK, and your profile is established.

4. If you do not want to use an existing Address Book entry to establish your profile, click the Create A New Entry In The Address Book To Represent Your Profile radio button and click OK. A Properties dialog box opens, showing a form from the Windows Address Book. Fill out as much or as little of it as you

like, using the Name, Home, Business, and Personal tabs. Click OK, and your profile is established.

Internet Explorer can fill in Web forms with the information from the Address Book only when the names of the boxes on the form match the pieces of information that are entered in the Address Book—items like name, ZIP code, and phone.

Changing How Web Pages Look

Internet Explorer allows you to change the fonts and colors that it uses to render Web pages, and even the alphabets. You can also decide to save downloading time by telling Internet Explorer not to download pictures or other multimedia content.

These preferences are controlled from the Internet Options dialog box (shown in Figure 24-3), which you access by opening the Internet Options icon on the Control Panel or by choosing Tools | Internet Options from Internet Explorer's menu bar. (Strangely, if you open it from the Control Panel, the dialog box is called Internet Properties, but it contains the same tabs, buttons, and settings.)

 From its name, you might think that the Internet Options dialog box controls settings for any Web browser or other Internet program, but it doesn't. Changes you make in the Internet Options dialog box only affect Internet Explorer.

Choosing Fonts

To make Internet Explorer display text in a different size, use the View | Text Size menu. There are five choices, from smallest to largest. The default size is Medium, which for the Latin-based alphabet means 12 point variable-width fonts and 10-point fixed-width fonts.

To make more fundamental changes in the fonts Internet Explorer uses, click the Fonts button on the General tab of the Internet Options dialog box. The Fonts dialog box opens, shown in Figure 24-4. This dialog box has three basic elements:

- **A drop-down list of alphabets** This list is labeled Language Script and the English language script is "Latin Based."

- **Two lists specifying the Web page (or variable-width) font and the plain text (or fixed-width) font for the selected alphabet** Change either font by picking a new one from the corresponding list.

Sometimes a Web page specifies a font, and that specification overrides the choices you make in the Fonts dialog box. To make your font choices override those of the Web page, click the Accessibility button on the General tab of the Internet Options dialog box and check either the Ignore Font Styles Specified On Web Pages check box or the Ignore Font Sizes Specified On Web Pages check box.

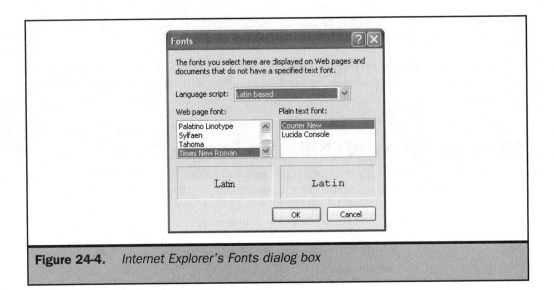

Figure 24-4. Internet Explorer's Fonts dialog box

Choosing Colors

You can change the colors Internet Explorer uses to display text, backgrounds, and links. To change the color of the text and background, click the Colors button on the General tab of the Internet Options dialog box.

The default is to use Windows colors—that is, the colors defined on the Appearance tab of the Display Properties dialog box (see Chapter 11, section "Choosing a New Color Scheme"). If you don't want to use the Windows colors, take the following steps:

1. Remove the check from the Use Windows Colors check box.

2. Click the colored button next to the Text or Background labels. A palette of colors appears.

3. Click the color you want for the Text or Background and click OK to make the palette disappear. The button next to Text or Background should now be the color you selected.

4. Click OK to close the Colors dialog box.

Changing the colors used for links is a similar process, except that you don't need to remove the check from Use Windows Colors. The Colors dialog box also allows you to define a *hover color*, a color that links change to when the cursor *hovers* over them.

 We suggest you leave the colors alone, except perhaps for making the background color white (if it's not white already).

Internet Explorer has other accessibility features for the visually impaired (see Chapter 16, section "Making Internet Explorer Accessible").

Changing Language Preferences

Some Web pages are available in multiple languages, and your Web browser picks the one that matches your preferences. To define or change your language preferences in Internet Explorer, click the Languages button near the bottom of the General tab of the Internet Options dialog box (shown in Figure 24-3, earlier in this chapter) to open the Language Preference dialog box:

The purpose of this dialog box is to maintain a list of favored languages in order, with your preferred language on top. Add a language to the list by clicking the Add button and selecting a language from the list that appears. Remove a language from the Language list by selecting it and clicking the Remove button. Reorder the Languages list by selecting a language on the list and clicking the Move Up or Move Down buttons. When you are satisfied with the list of languages, click OK.

Choosing Whether to Download Images, Audio, and Video

Many Web pages have pictures or other graphics on them. These are more time consuming to download than text, so if your connection is slow, you may decide not to bother downloading graphics. Multimedia content such as audio, video, or animation is even slower to download, and you can tell your browser to ignore them, too. To do this, go to the Advanced tab of the Internet Options dialog box, shown in Figure 24-5. Scroll down until you see the Multimedia heading. Remove the check from each box next to any type of content that you want to ignore.

WINDOWS XP
ON THE INTERNET

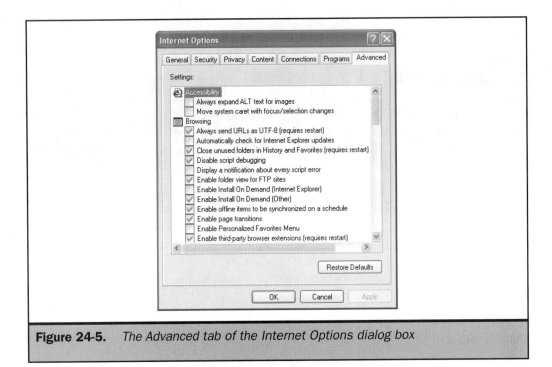

Figure 24-5. *The Advanced tab of the Internet Options dialog box*

Managing Internet Explorer's Behavior

Internet Explorer is intended to be simple enough for novice users. For this reason, most of what it does is invisible. Some choices that IE makes for you, however, have implications for your system's use of disk space or its security—implications that more advanced users may want to consider. Internet Explorer allows you some limited opportunities to "get under the hood" and make choices for yourself about your start page, blocking offensive content, caching Web pages, and the default mail and news applications. You can even decide that Internet Explorer should not be the default Web browser.

Choosing and Customizing Your Start Page

Your browser's home page (also called a *start page*) is the Web page that the browser loads when you open the browser without requesting a specific page. You can also see the browser's home page by clicking the Home button on its toolbar. (Don't confuse this use of "home page" with the home page of a Web site.)

Microsoft promotes its MSN Web site by making it the default home page of Internet Explorer. In general, this not a bad home page, and many people never change it. However, you can select any Web page or file that you want to be your browser's home page.

You aren't stuck with the MSN start page that Microsoft has chosen for you—or any other start page. To change Internet Explorer's start page, choose Tools | Internet Options to display the Internet Options dialog box with the General tab on top (as you saw in Figure 24-3). You can type the URL of the new home page into the Home Page box on this tab, or you can click one of the following buttons:

- ■ **Use Current** The page currently displayed by Internet Explorer becomes the home page. (If Internet Explorer is not open, this button is grayed out.) This can be any page on the Web, or even an HTML document on your hard drive.

- ■ **Use Default** You get a personalizable MSN homepage at **http://www.msn.com**.

- ■ **Use Blank** The home page is blank. This is handy if you want Internet Explorer to start up as quickly as possible and don't necessarily want to invoke your Internet connection.

Lots of Web sites would like to be your home page, because they can sell advertising based on the number of viewers they get. Many (including the default MSN page) allow you to customize the page to get local weather, headlines in your areas of interest, scores for your favorite teams, quotes for the stocks you own, and so on. None of them charge a fee for this service, though they do display advertising. The industry leader is Yahoo! (**http://my.yahoo.com**).

 Setting your start page to be an HTML document on your hard drive makes Internet Explorer start up more quickly than if it has to download a start page from the Internet.

Blocking Offensive Web Content

Internet Explorer includes Content Advisor, which can block access to Web sites based on their level of potentially offensive content. Unfortunately, this system does not work very well, and we cannot recommend it.

Content Advisor is based on a voluntary rating system devised by the Recreational Software Advisory Council for the Internet at **http://www.rsac.org**. It works like this: Web site managers fill out a questionnaire about their sites, and these sites then get a numerical rating for each language, nudity, sex, and violence. These ratings are attached to the Web sites with codes that browsers can read, but usually do not display. When you set up Content Advisor, you specify the numerical ratings you will accept, and Web sites that with ratings beyond your specifications are blocked.

The RSACi rating system has been in place for several years now, and it has become clear that the vast majority of Web sites (whether they contain potentially objectionable content or not) will never be rated. This leaves you with the following choice: You can block all unrated sites, which makes the Web almost useless to you, or you can allow access to unrated sites, many of which contain the kind of content you had hoped to block.

Managing Caches of Web Pages

Internet Explorer stores some of the pages that you view so that they can be redisplayed quickly if you return to them. In general, this speeds up the browsing experience, but if you are running short of disk space, you may decide to limit or eliminate these caches. They are stored in a folder named Temporary Internet Files, which is inside the hidden folder C:\Documents And Settings*username*\Local Settings.

You control Internet Explorer's cache of Web pages from the General tab of the Internet Options dialog box. Delete all these Web pages by clicking the Delete Files button. To set limits on the amount of disk space that can be devoted to temporary Internet files, click the Settings button to open the Settings dialog box. Move the slider to raise or lower the percentage of your hard drive that the Temporary Internet Files folder is allowed to use. Click OK to apply your changes.

Changing the Default Browser

When you install Windows XP, Internet Explorer is set as the default browser. After you install another browser, however, you can decide to make that browser the default. Possibly the browser's installation Wizard will ask whether it should be the default browser, or the browser itself will ask whenever you run it. If not, follow the more detailed instructions shown here.

To make Netscape 6.1 the default browser, select Edit | Preferences from Netscape's menu bar, expand the Advanced menu of the Preferences dialog box and select System. On the System tab of the Preference dialog box, click the check boxes of the protocols and file types you want Navigator to be the default program for. (The http protocol is the most important one to check.)

To make Opera the default browser, choose File | Preferences from the Opera menu bar. When the Preferences dialog box appears, select Default Browser in the left column. Check the file types and protocols you want Opera to be the default for or else just check the Check If Opera Is Default Browser On Startup check box, close Opera and restart it.

If Internet Explorer is no longer your default browser, you can easily restore it to this role. In most cases, all you have to do is open IE, and it asks whether you want it to be the default browser. If it doesn't ask, do the following: Choose View | Internet Options from the Internet Explorer menu bar. When the Internet Options dialog box appears, click the Programs tab. Click the check box labeled Internet Explorer Should Check To See Whether It Is The Default Browser. The next time you open IE it asks whether you want it to be the default browser.

You can open any browser by choosing Start | All Programs or by opening its icon on the desktop, whether it is the default or not. Once a browser is running, you can use it to open any Web page. An exception to this rule is the Microsoft Web site, which displays properly only with IE.

Setting Your Mail and Newsreading Programs

You can tell Windows which mail and newsreading programs to run with Internet Explorer; these are the programs that Internet Explorer runs when you click a mail or news link. Choose Tools | Internet Options to open the Internet Options dialog box. On the Programs tab the Mail and News boxes show the default programs that Internet Explorer runs; both are set to Outlook Express when you install Windows. See Chapter 23 for how to use Outlook Express.

Managing Internet Explorer's Security and Privacy Settings

You should keep two risk factors in mind when you use the Web:

■ Web sites may be collecting information about you and your browsing habits using small files called *cookies* that are stored on your computer.

■ The scripts and applets that allow Web sites to offer more complex content and services may also make your computer more vulnerable to viruses or hackers.

This section discusses the tools and options that Internet Explorer provides for dealing with these risks. Also see the section "Managing Which Files Internet Explorer Downloads" in Chapter 31.

Controlling Cookies

Internet Explorer 6 gives you much more control over cookies than previous versions of Internet Explorer did. Unfortunately, IE 6's privacy level settings make the situation seem much more complicated than it is, and none of them is a very good cookie policy. However, you can override Internet Explorer's automatic cookie-handling system to set up a simple, sensible cookie policy.

The next few sections explain what cookies are and how the P3P privacy protection system works. If you don't care about that and just want to know what to do, skip ahead to the "Setting Cookie Policy" section.

What Are Cookies?

A *cookie* is a small (at most 4K) file that a Web server can store on your machine. Its purpose is to allow a Web server to personalize a Web page, depending on whether you have been to that Web site before and what you may have told it during previous sessions. For example, when you establish an account with an online retailer or subscribe to an online magazine, you may be asked to fill out a form that includes some information about yourself and your preferences. The Web server may store that information (along with information about when you visit the site) in a cookie on your machine. When you return to that Web site in the future, the retailer's Web server can read its cookie, recall this information, and structure its Web pages accordingly.

Much has been written about whether cookies create a security or privacy hazard for you. If your Web browser is working properly, the security hazard is minimal. It is, at first glance, unsettling to think that Web servers are storing information on your hard drive without your knowledge. But cookies are not executable programs. They cannot, for example, search for and accumulate information from elsewhere on your system. They simply record information that you have already given to the Web server.

The privacy issue is real, however. Cookies do make it easier for advertising companies to gather information about your browsing habits. For example, a company that advertises on a large number of Web sites can use cookies to keep track of where you have seen its ads before, and which ads (if any) you clicked. In this way advertisers can learn your interests and perhaps deduce more about you than you would want them to know.

Cookies are of two basic kinds: first-party cookies and third-party cookies. (You are considered to be the second party.) The difference is in where they come from. First-party cookies are cookies that come directly from the Web site you asked for. For example, if you register with Yahoo and personalize a Yahoo start page, the cookie that Yahoo sets is a first-party cookie. Third-party cookies are cookies that come from Web servers that you may not realize you are dealing with. For example, the Yahoo start page may contain advertising placed by an agency like DoubleClick, and the cookie that the advertising agency sets is a third-party cookie.

What Is P3P?

The Platform for Privacy Preferences (P3P) is a new open standard (which Internet Explorer 6 supports) for Web sites to specify their privacy policies in a form that can be read by computers. The idea is that you can decide once and for all how high to set your privacy standards, and your Web browser can compare your decisions to the privacy policies of the Web sites you visit, warning you if your standards are about to be violated.

Here's how it works: The people who create Web sites fill out a multiple-choice form about what information their Web site collects, what it does with that information, and how long it keeps the information. Their answers get codified into tags that get attached to their Web pages—tags that browsers like IE 6 can read but typically don't display. You set one of five privacy levels that IE 6 offers, and it blocks cookies and issues privacy warnings accordingly.

The benefit of the system is that the multiple-choice questions at least pin down the Web sites. Up until now, most Web sites either have not had privacy policies or have written them in impenetrable legalese. It has been completely impractical to read the privacy policies of all the Web sites you visit and make individual judgments about them.

The system has several weaknesses, however, and at the moment it is unclear whether it will do any good. First, it's voluntary—Web sites don't have to fill out the questionnaire, and if very few do, the system will be useless. (This is what happened to the PICS system for rating the sex-and-violence content of Web sites. See "Blocking Offensive Web Content" earlier in this chapter.) Second, it's nobody's job to verify that the Web sites have answered the questions honestly. Finally, you have to count on the browser makers to implement P3P in a way that lets you do what you want to do in a simple, understandable fashion. Since Microsoft is a major player in e-commerce and Web advertising, its sympathies are at least as much with the advertisers as with you, and they have designed Internet Explorer 6 accordingly.

You can read more about the Platform for Privacy Preferences (P3P) at **http:// www.w3.org/P3P**.

How Does Internet Explorer Implement P3P Privacy Policies?

The privacy tab of the Internet Options dialog box contains a slider that you can set to one of six levels from Accept All Cookies to Block All Cookies. The default level is Medium. The descriptions of these levels are phrased using technical terms like *personally identifiable information*, *implicit consent*, *explicit consent*, and *compact privacy policy*. What follows is our interpretation of what these levels actually mean.

- **Block All Cookies**   At this level you are unable to log in to access Hotmail, or a Yahoo home page, or to use a subscription to the online *The Wall Street Journal*. You could make this setting liveable if you could create exceptions for your favorite Web sites, but Microsoft has disabled the exception-making capability for this setting.

- **High**   Cookies are only accepted from Web sites that offer P3P information, and then only if that information says that they don't make keep track of information that would identify you personally (like your name, for example, or your phone number) unless you've explicitly given them permission to do so. At this level we could log into Hotmail and Yahoo, but not *The Wall Street Journal*.

- **Medium High**   Same as High, except that first-party cookies are accepted from Web sites that use personally identifiable information without your explicit consent, if they somehow allow you to opt out of this usage. (In general, we don't like opt-out processes. They require too much alertness and diligence on your part.) At this level we could see *The Wall Street Journal*.

- **Medium**   Allows third-party cookies that let you opt out of their use of personally identifiable information. Restricts first-party cookies that use personally identifiable information without letting you opt out. (We have no idea what the difference between "restrict" and "block" is.)

- **Low**   Accepts all first-party cookies. Restricts third-party cookies from Web sites that don't offer P3P information or that don't let you opt out of their use of personally identifiable information.
- **Accept All Cookies**   Accepts all cookies without asking you.

What Is a Sensible Cookie Policy?

First we'll tell you what you don't want: You don't want to block all cookies, because you give up much of the functionality and convenience of the Web. You also don't want Internet Explorer to ask you what to do every time a Web site wants to set a cookie, because you'll spend more time deciding about cookies than you'll spend reading Web pages.

You *do* want to make a distinction between first-party and third-party cookies, because third-party cookies benefit only the advertisers, not you.

The cookie policy we'd like to have is Medium High for first-party cookies, and block third-party cookies altogether. This does not seem to be possible with Internet Explorer. Given that fact, we recommend the following policy: accept all first-party cookies and block all third-party cookies. This isn't one of the six levels on the slider, but you can configure Internet Explorer to do it.

Another reasonable option (but somewhat more difficult to set up) is to select the High level and then create exceptions for a few favorite Web sites whose cookies are blocked. This policy allows a few more third-party cookies and a few less first-party cookies than the policy suggested in the previous paragraph. However, this option stops many shopping sites from working, because the sites use shopping-cart programs hosted on third-party Web sites. (Another options is to use Netscape instead of IE, because of its more flexible cookie policies.)

Setting Cookie Policy

Cookie policy is controlled from the Privacy tab of the Internet Options dialog box. If you want one of the settings described in the previous section, move the slider to that setting and click OK.

If you want to set up our recommended cookie policy (allow first-party and block third-party cookies), do the following:

1. Select Tools | Options to open the Internet Options dialog box.
2. Select the Privacy tab of the Internet Options dialog box (see Figure 24-6).
3. Click the Advanced button on the Privacy tab. The Advanced Privacy Settings box appears.
4. Check the Override Automatic Cookie Handling box.

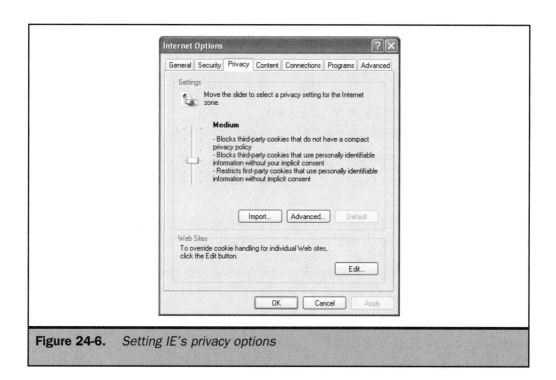

Figure 24-6.   *Setting IE's privacy options*

5. Select the Accept radio button under First-Party Cookies and the Block radio button under Third-Party Cookies.

6. Click OK in both of the open dialog boxes.

If a particular Web site is not working because its cookies are being blocked, you can choose to create an exception for it without changing your settings for other Web sites. (For reasons that escape us, Microsoft has made this option unavailable if you have chosen the Block All Cookies setting.) Do the following:

1. Select Tools | Options to open the Internet Options dialog box.

2. Select the Privacy tab of the Internet Options dialog box.

3. Click the Edit button on the Privacy tab. The Per Site Privacy Actions box opens.

4. Type the URL of the Web site into the Address Of Web Site line.

5. Click the Allow button and click OK in both open dialog boxes.

If you want to block the cookies on a particular Web site when your overall policy would allow them, do the previous steps, but click the Block button in Step 5.

WINDOWS XP
ON THE INTERNET

The first time you use MSN Explorer, the setup program requires you to move your privacy setting down to Medium. However, as soon as the setup is finished you can move your privacy settings back up. Any setting but Block All Cookies allows the great majority of MSN Explorer's features to continue working.

Managing the Cookies You Have

Windows stores your cookies in two folders:

- C:\Documents And Settings*username*\\Cookies
- C:\Documents And Settings*username*\\Local Settings\\Temporary Internet Files

Reading a cookie in WordPad or some other text program probably will not tell you much, though it may set your mind at ease to realize just how little information is there (see Chapter 17, section "Taking Advantage of Free Word Processing with WordPad"). Delete individual cookies from your system by deleting the corresponding text files, or nuke them all by clicking the Delete Cookies button on the General tab of the Internet Options dialog box.

Managing Scripts, Applets, and ActiveX Controls

Some Web pages increase the amount of interactivity they can offer by downloading small programs to run on your computer. For example, rather than transmitting the individual frames of an animation over the Internet, a Web server may send an animation-constructing program that runs on your computer. A financial Web site may download a program that displays a scrolling stock ticker. Typically, this process is invisible to the user—the interaction or the animation just happens, without calling your attention to how it happens.

While these programs are useful, they also create security issues. If Web sites can put useful programs on your computer and run them without informing you, precautions must be taken to make sure that they can't also put harmful programs on your computer. Internet Explorer takes certain precautions automatically and allows you the option to choose additional precautions.

What Are Java, JavaScript, VBScript, and ActiveX?

Java is a language for sending small applications (called *applets*) over the Web so that they can be executed by your computer. *JavaScript* is a language for extending HTML to embed small programs called *scripts* in Web pages. *VBScript*, a language that resembles Microsoft's Visual Basic, can be used to add scripts to pages that are displayed by Internet Explorer. Anything that VBScript can do, JavaScript (which Microsoft calls JScript) can do, too and vice versa.

ActiveX controls, like Java, are a way to embed executable programs into a Web page. Unlike Java and JavaScript, but like VBScript, ActiveX is a Microsoft system that is not used by Navigator or most other browsers. When Internet Explorer encounters a Web page that uses ActiveX controls, it checks to see whether that particular control is already installed; if it is not, IE installs the control on your machine.

 ActiveX controls are considerably more dangerous than JavaScript or VBScript scripts or Java applets. Java applets and JavaScript scripts are run in a "sandbox" inside your Web browser, which limits the accidental or deliberate damage they can do; and VBScript scripts are run by an interpreter, which should limit the types of damage they can do. However, ActiveX controls are programs with full access to your computer's resources.

Security Zones

Internet Explorer has different security settings for its four zones: Trusted Sites, Local Intranet, Internet, and Restricted Sites. The default settings are Low in the Trusted Sites zone, Medium-Low in the Local Intranet zone, Medium in the Internet zone, and High in the Restricted Sites zone. These zones and settings are discussed in Chapter 31.

The rules governing scripts and applets are set zone by zone on the Security tab of the Internet Options dialog box. To examine or change these settings:

1. Open the Internet Options dialog box by selecting Tools | Internet Options from the Internet Explorer menu bar.

2. Click the Security tab of the Internet Options dialog box.

3. Select the zone you want to examine or change.

4. If you want to change the security setting of a zone, move the slider on the Security tab of the Internet Options dialog box. (The slider doesn't appear if the zone has been given custom settings. To reset such a zone to one of the standard settings, click the Default Level button. When the slider reappears, you can move it to the desired setting.)

5. To see the nitty-gritty details of the current security settings for the selected zone, click the Custom Level button. The Security Settings dialog box opens.

6. If you want to change the security settings of the selected zone, scroll through the Security Settings dialog box until you see the item you want to change. Change an item by checking or unchecking its check box, or by selecting a different radio button than the current selection.

7. Click OK to close each open dialog box. Click Yes in the confirmation box that asks if you want to change the security settings.

Managing Java and JavaScript

The security settings that affect Java and JavaScript are in the Java and Scripting sections of the Security Settings dialog box. You may change what these applets and scripts are allowed to do on your computer, or even disable Java or JavaScript entirely. Follow the steps in the previous section.

Managing ActiveX Controls

We have never been big fans of ActiveX controls. They allow Web sites to have too much power over your system and are hard to monitor. If you should happen to download and install a rogue ActiveX control by mistake, it could (on its own) download and install lots more rogue ActiveX controls—which would then be permanent parts of your software environment, even when you are offline. None of this would appear the least bit suspicious to any virus-detecting software you might own, because ActiveX controls aren't viruses: They have the same status as applications that you install yourself.

Disabling ActiveX controls is one option. However, if you frequent Microsoft Web sites like MSN or MSNBC, you will be exposed to numerous temptations to turn them back on. (We finally gave in to the excellent portfolio-tracking services at MSN Moneycentral.) We suggest the following compromise: Disable ActiveX controls everywhere but in the Trusted Sites security zone. (Do this from the Security Settings dialog box, following the steps in the "Security Zones" section above.) When you find a Microsoft Web site that offers some wonderful service involving ActiveX controls, move that site into the Trusted Sites security zone. See Chapter 31 for a discussion of security zones and trusted sites.

ActiveX controls are stored in the folder C:\Windows\Downloaded Program Files. If you use Internet Explorer, you should check this file periodically to see what applications Internet Explorer has downloaded. Dispose of an ActiveX control by right-clicking its icon and selecting Remove from the shortcut menu.

Displaying a Privacy Report About a Web Page

New for Internet Explorer 6, the Privacy Report helps you determine how much information you are willing to give a particular site. It also enables you to determine what kind of information a site is storing on your computer and whether the site complies with its own privacy policy.

The primary drawback here is that Microsoft has aligned itself with TRUSTe (at **http://www.truste.org**), a self-proclaimed privacy watchdog group. However, TRUSTe predominantly sells their services as a site evaluator, only requiring sites to post a *privacy policy*. Posting a policy, no matter how good it looks, is no guarantee that it will be adhered to. Only trust those you know you can trust, and don't leave the trusting up to a third party.

Accessing the Windows Privacy Report is easy. In Internet Explorer, choose View | Privacy Report from the menu. You see a list of the objects that are loaded on the page you are looking at, typically graphics, like this:

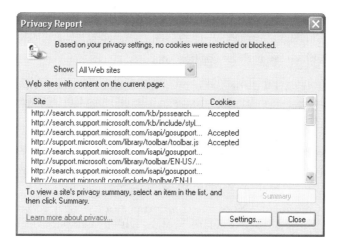

These connected objects may be on the same Web server as the page itself or might have been loaded from other Web servers. If any of the objects listed have placed a cookie on your computer, you see it listed in the column to the right.

 By using a tiny, invisible 1 pixel x 1 pixel image on many Web pages, DoubleClick (an online advertising company) can secretly install tracking cookies on your computer. These cookies, though harmless, can pass back information about where on the site you are going. This data is collected and then used to develop visitor profiles. They can also track you when you go to other sites that carry DoubleClick ads.

Click the Settings button to see the Privacy tab of the Internet Options dialog box (these options are covered in Chapter 24). The Advanced button enables you to set how cookies are dealt with. Our favorite arrangement is to allow cookies from the originating server but to refuse them from any external servers. This almost globally allows cookies that are specific to your browsing while rebuffing those that are used for external tracking and advertising information gathering.

Creating Your Own Web Pages

Previous versions of Windows came with a Web page editor called FrontPage Express. Windows XP doesn't come with a Web page editor, although you can create Web pages using Notepad if you learn all the HTML codes to include. If you have Microsoft Word or Corel WordPerfect, you can save documents as Web pages, a much easier way to make pages. Web pages created by word processors tend to be huge, including an enormous number of unnecessary codes., but they work for quick-and-dirty pages that you plan to replace later. Better options are these:

- **CoffeeCup HTML Editor**   This program is an easy way for beginners to create their first sites. Information is available from CoffeeCup Software at **http://www.coffeecup.com**. You can also download the CoffeeCup Free HTML editor from the site.

- **HomeSite**   This program is a full-featured, reasonably priced Web page editor from Allaire Software at **http://www.allaire.com/Products/HomeSite**. You can download an evaluation version.

- **Netscape Composer**   Netscape Communicator (Netscape's suite of programs that includes Netscape Navigator) comes with a Web page editor called Netscape Composer.

To make your Web pages and picture files available on the Web, you must upload files from your computer to a Web server. You can use Web Folders to drag-and-drop Web pages to your Web server, or you can use the Windows FTP program for uploading, but it uses arcane commands (see Chapter 26). Netscape Composer has a Publish button on its toolbar that makes uploading files easy. Windows XP comes with a Web Publishing Wizard, another way to upload files to a Web server.

To run the Web Publishing Wizard, put the files that you want on the Web into one folder, and click Publish This Folder To The Web from the Tasks pane. The Wizard lets you select the files from the current folder to include, select a Web server from one of the Web hosting companies which Microsoft has decided to offer (including MSN), and (for pictures) choose whether to resize the pictures to reduce their file size (see Figure 24-7). When the Wizard is finished, it displays the URL of the page you have just created. Save this URL (using cut-and-paste to a Notepad file or other file) so that you can tell other people to visit your page.

Xdrive, a widely-used Web hosting company, is one of the Web servers that the Wizard offers. Note that its Web sites are no longer free. Unfortunately, your ISP, which probably offers free Web space as part of your Internet account, might not be one of the Wizard's options.

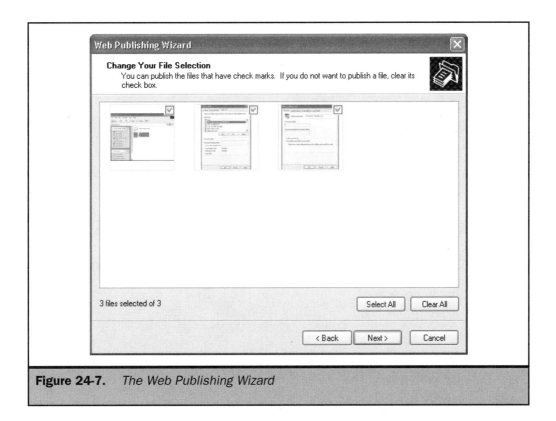

Figure 24-7.   *The Web Publishing Wizard*

The
Complete
Reference

Chapter 25

Internet Conferencing with Windows Messenger and NetMeeting

Windows XP comes with two programs for chatting and conferencing over the Internet:

- **Windows Messenger** lets you instantly communicate with anyone else online who is also using Windows Messenger. Microsoft has included audio and video features to its basic text chat capabilities, so Windows Messenger completely replaces Microsoft Chat and largely replaces NetMeeting.

- **Microsoft NetMeeting** lets you use the Internet as a long-distance phone service, including videoconferencing, typed chat, and even sharing programs over the Internet. Microsoft isn't updating NetMeeting any more, so the main reason to use it is to converse with other people who have NetMeeting but not Windows Messenger.

This chapter describes how to use both programs. You can download other Internet chat and conferencing programs from the Internet itself; Chapter 26 tells you how.

Chatting Online with Windows Messenger

Windows Messenger enables you to chat with friends or coworkers who are online at the time that you want to chat. It's quicker than e-mail, and multiple people can take part in the conversation. Windows Messenger also enables you to speak to other users and send messages to pagers.

Windows Messenger is usually loaded automatically when Windows starts up. If the Windows Messenger icon appears in the notification area of the taskbar, click it to display the Windows Messenger window. If it's not on the taskbar, run Windows Messenger by choosing Start | All Programs | Windows Messenger. Windows Messenger may ask whether you want to download updates to the program. This chapter describes the program that ships with Windows XP, but updated versions of Windows Messenger should be similar.

> **Note** *AOL Instant Messenger (AIM, available from **http://aim.aol.com**) has long been the king of instant messaging programs, and other popular instant messaging programs include ICQ (**http://www.icq.com**) and Yahoo Messenger (**http://messenger.yahoo.com**). Unfortunately, these instant messaging systems don't all talk to each other: as of late 2001, people on one system couldn't send and receive messages from the others. However, you can easily run more than one instant message program at the same time.*

Signing In to Windows Messenger with Your .NET Passport

If you haven't used Windows Messenger before, you need to establish a Microsoft .NET Passport—an ID used for Microsoft Web sites and services. (Microsoft uses

Windows Messenger as one way to get lots of people to sign up for a Microsoft .NET Passport, which will enable them to sell their .NET e-commerce services more effectively.) The .NET Passport Wizard windows pops up the first time you run Windows Messenger and steps you through the process of telling it about your existing Microsoft Passport or creating a new one:

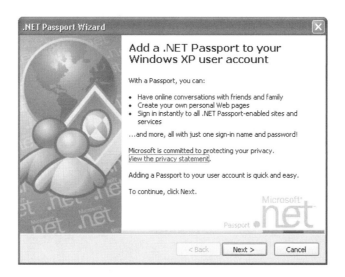

You get a Microsoft .NET Passport by creating a Hotmail account (Microsoft's Web-based e-mail service, at **http://www.hotmail.com**) or by telling it about another e-mail address. When creating a new Microsoft .NET Passport, you provide a password as well as a secret question and answer that you can use if you forget your password. You must also provide your location (country and state or province). The .NET Passport system doesn't let you log onto Windows Messenger until you have received its confirmation message (this ensures that the e-mail address that you typed is really yours).

If you use Outlook 2002, use the same address for your .NET Passport that use you with Outlook, because the programs are integrated. Also, be sure to use an address that you check often, because Windows Messenger users may send you e-mail if you aren't online when they try to send you an instant message.

If you have trouble creating a .NET Passport without creating a Hotmail account, go to MSN.com, click Passport Sign In in the top right corner, then click the Get One Here link underneath the Sign In button. (Because Web site designs change constantly, these links may move.) You can also go to **http://www.passport.com/memberservices.asp** to get help with a .NET Passport.

WINDOWS XP
ON THE INTERNET

When you have created a .NET Passport for yourself, you can sign in:

You can select the Sign Me In Automatically check box to avoid having to sign in each time you use the program.

Once you have a Microsoft .NET Passport, you see the Windows Messenger window, shown in Figure 25-1. The window lists your contacts—those who are online

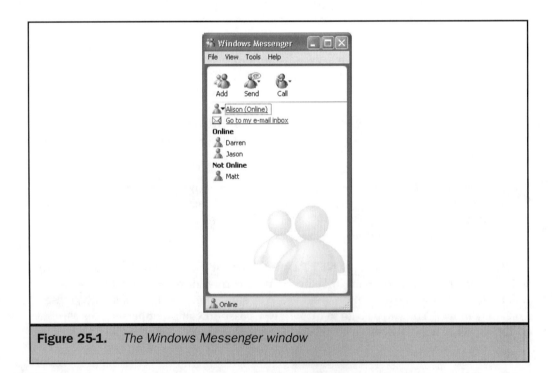

Figure 25-1.   *The Windows Messenger window*

and those who are not. Of course, if you've never used Windows Messenger, you don't have any contacts listed (yet).

The Windows Messenger window includes an entry showing how many new e-mail messages are in your Hotmail account, if you have one. If you don't have any new messages, you see a Go To My E-mail Mailbox link. To read your Hotmail messages, click the E-mail Message (or xxx New E-mail Messages) link: your browser starts and displays the Hotmail Web site. There's no way to configure Windows Messenger to display how many messages are in mailboxes other than your Hotmail mailbox (Microsoft owns Hotmail, and they are using Windows to promote it).

Telling Windows Messenger about Your Contacts

Before you can begin to chat, you have to have someone to chat with. The easiest way is to ask your friends if they use Windows Messenger and, if so, what their e-mail address is (at least, the e-mail address they use for messaging—some people use a different address to avoid getting messages at the regular e-mail address). Once you know a person's e-mail address, add it to your contacts by following these steps:

1. Open Windows Messenger.

2. Click Add on the toolbar. You see the Add A Contact dialog box, shown here:

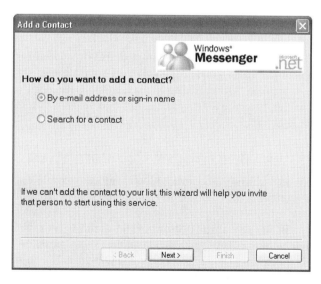

3. Choose By E-mail Address Or Sign-In Name and click Next.

4. Enter the person's e-mail address and click Next.

5. Windows Messenger adds the person to your contact list if that person has a Microsoft .NET Passport. In case the person does not have a .NET Passport, you can send them an e-mail message telling them how to get up and running with Windows Messenger.

If you think someone has a .NET Passport but you don't know the person's e-mail address, choose Search For A Contact from the Add A Contact dialog box. Enter the information you know about the person and click Next. You see a list of people who meet your search criteria—select one and click Next. If the person has a .NET Passport, Windows Messenger adds the person to your contacts.

When Someone Else Adds You as a Contact

When someone adds your e-mail address as a contact, the Windows Messenger system notifies you with a message like this:

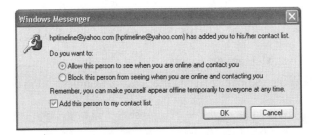

If you don't know the person (or are acquainted and don't want further contact), you can prevent him or her from knowing when you are online or from contacting you via Windows Messenger (see "Other Things You Can Do with Windows Messenger"). On the other hand, if the message is from a friend or coworker, you can add the person to your own contact list.

Starting a Windows Messenger Conversation

To exchange typed messages with a contact who is online, double-click his or her name in the Windows Messenger window. A Conversation window appears like the one in Figure 25-2.

To converse, type in the box at the bottom of the window and click Send or press ENTER. When another person is typing a response, you see a message to that effect on the status line (the bottom line) of the Conversation window. If you have a sound card, microphone, and speakers, and the person you're chatting with does also, click Start Talking to speak with them.

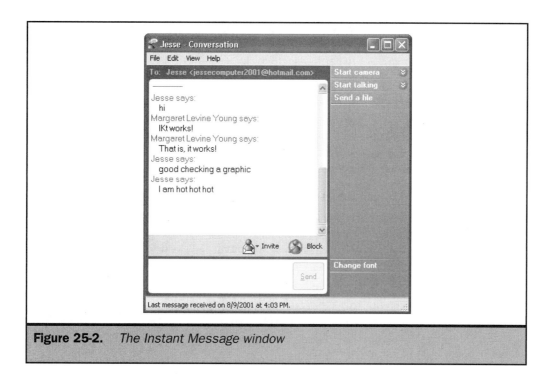

Figure 25-2.   *The Instant Message window*

When someone starts a conversation with you, a little box pops up from the notification area (right end) of the Windows taskbar, like this:

Click the box to switch to a Conversation with the person. After a few seconds, this box disappears.

You can invite other contacts to join in the chat by clicking Invite and choosing To Join This Conversation from the menu that appears. Up to five people (including you) can participate in a conversation. You can block the person you are talking to from contacting you by clicking Block. (If you want to unblock someone, right-click the person's name in your contact list and select Unblock.)

Holding Voice Conversations

Once you have opened a Conversation window with someone, you can switch to a voice chat, assuming that you and the other person have microphones and speakers attached to your computers. The first time you click Start Talking in the Conversation window, Windows runs the Audio And Video Tuning Wizard to check your microphone and speakers. Follow its instructions.

When you click Start Talking in the Conversation window (or click a contact name in the Windows Messenger window and click Call), Windows Messenger sends an invitation to the other person to have a voice conversation. The Start Talking link is replaced by these settings, which you can use to adjust your volume, mute your microphone, and end the voice conversation:

Video Conferencing

If your computer has a video camera, you can use it to transmit a picture to the person with whom you are having a conversation. Click the Start Camera link in the Conversation window to start receiving video images from the other person. The video image appears in the upper right part of the Conversation window. Click Stop Camera to stop receiving video data.

Sending Files to Others in a Conversation

To send a file to someone with whom you are having a conversation, click Send A File in the Conversation window. Otherwise, right-click the name of the contact in the Windows Messenger window and choose Send A File. Select the file and click Open. The contact has to accept the file for the transfer to occur.

When you receive a file, Windows usually stores it in the My Received Files subfolder of your My Documents folder. If you use Internet Connection Sharing you may only be able to receive files—you may not be able to send them.

Sharing a Whiteboard

You can share a whiteboard—a drawing window on which everyone in the conversation can draw—as part of a Windows Messenger conversation. Choose Invite | To Start Whiteboard. The other people in the conversation receive an invitation to start using Whiteboard. If they click Accept, you (and they) see a Sharing Session window, like this:

The Sharing Session window shows the shared items that Windows Messenger supports: Application Sharing (described in the next section) and Whiteboard.

Then you see a Whiteboard window, as shown in Figure 25-3. The whiteboard works similarly to Microsoft Paint (see Chapter 18, section "Creating and Editing Images With Microsoft Paint"). To see what a tool does, hover your mouse pointer over it. When you are finished with the drawing, close the Whiteboard window (choose File | Save As first if you want to save your joint work).

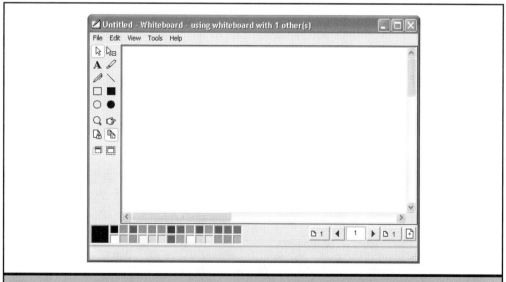

Figure 25-3. *When you share a whiteboard with Windows Messenger, everyone in the conversation can draw on it.*

Sharing Control of a Program

If you would like to show the other people in a conversation how a program works, or wordsmith a document as a group, you can use Windows Messenger's Application Sharing feature. You can let the other people take control of the program and give commands, even if they don't have the program installed on their computers.

Showing a Program on Everyone's Screen

In the Conversation window, choose Invite | To Start Application Sharing. Windows Messenger sends the other people in the conversation an invitation to share an application with you. If they click Accept, the Sharing Session window appears (pictured in the previous section), and then you see the Sharing window shown in Figure 25-4.

In the Sharing window, choose the program that you want to allow the other people in the conversation to share. For example, to edit a document as a group, choose to

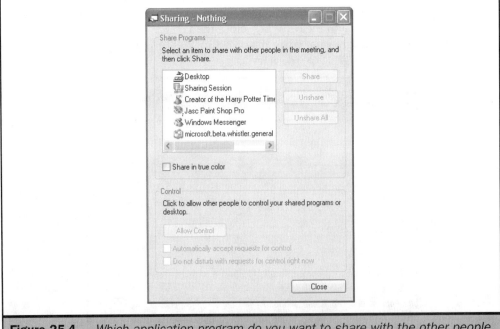

Figure 25-4. *Which application program do you want to share with the other people in your Windows Messenger conversation?*

share a word processing program that is open with the document loaded. If you want to show the other people a presentation or some Web pages, choose a presentation program or your Web browser. Then click Share.

Once you have selected a program to share, the program window appears on the screens of the other people in the Windows Messenger conversation. Bring the window to the front (that is, click in it to make it active) so that other windows don't obscure it on the other people's screens. The other people can see what you do, but can't give commands themselves.

Here are a few pointers when sharing a program:

- Before you start to share an application, be sure to agree on a screen resolution for everyone to use. Using the same resolution as the rest of the people in the conversation prevents the screen from jumping around as the cursor and mouse pointer move in the shared application.

- Others in the conversation can see only as much of the program's window as you can see on your screen; when you click another window that overlaps the window that is editing the file, the obscured part of the window disappears on everyone else's screen, too.

- Unless you and everyone else in the conversation have fast Internet connections (faster than dial-up), displaying windows with a shared program can take a long time—a minute or two. Everyone in the conversation needs to wait for the shared window to appear, or everyone's screens will get hopelessly confusing. This feature works best for users connected by a high-speed LAN.

Enabling Others to Control the Program

If you want other people to be able to control the application (giving commands and controlling the mouse), switch back to the Sharing window and click the Allow Control button. When someone else double-clicks in the window that displays your program, you see a Request Control window, indicating who wants to control the application. Click Accept or Reject to give or deny control to that person. The other person controls the mouse and keyboard for that application until you press a key. When you are finished sharing control of the application, switch back to the Sharing window and click the Prevent Control button. When you are done sharing the application, close the Sharing window (and the application, if you like).

While you are sharing control, you can select the Automatically Accept Request For Control check box in the Sharing window to skip having to accept requests for control. Alternatively, to temporarily disable control-sharing, select the Do Not Disturb With Requests For Control Right Now check box.

Note *Firewalls can prevent you from sharing applications with Windows Messenger.*

Here are some tips about sharing control of a program:

- If you share Windows Explorer, all Explorer windows are shared with the other callers, including windows that you open after clicking the Share button.

- If you are going to edit a file collaboratively, make a backup copy of the file first, just in case. When you have finished editing the file collaboratively, only the person who originally shared the file can save or print the file. If other callers want copies of the finished file, the owner of the file can send the file to the other callers.

- Each person in the call does not need to have the program that the call is sharing; mouse clicks and keystrokes are transmitted to the program owner's computer.

Other Things You Can Do with Windows Messenger

You can use Windows Messenger in a few other ways, too:

- **Block someone from calling you** Right-click a contact and choose Block.

- **Changing the way your name appears to others** Click your own name in the list of contacts and choose Personal Settings.

- **Changing other configuration settings** Choose Tools | Options from the Windows Messenger menu bar. The Options dialog box that appears contains settings that control what information other people can see about you and how the program runs.

- **Preventing Windows Messenger from running when Windows starts up** Choose Tools | Options from the Windows Messenger menu bar, click the Preferences tab, and deselect the Run This Program When Windows Starts check box.

- **Playing games** Some new Internet-based games are designed to work with Windows Messenger, and can send invitations to other Windows Messenger users to join a game.

- **Getting help with your computer** If you choose Invite | To Start Remote Assistance in the Conversation window, Windows runs the Remote Assistance program, described in "Allowing a Friend to Control Your Computer" in Chapter 4.

Note *Although you have to jump through hoops to do it, it is possible to remove Windows Messenger. To uninstall Messenger, open up C:\Windows\Inf\Sysoc.inf in Notepad (it's a hidden system file, but you can open it by typing **notepad c:\windows\inf\sysoc.inf** in the Run dialog box). Search for the line msmsgs= and remove the word "hide". Now you'll see Messenger when you run Add/Remove Programs in the Control Panel.*

Conferencing with Microsoft NetMeeting

The newest version of Windows Messenger has all of NetMeeting's features, but if you are working with someone who is not using Windows XP and Windows Messenger 4.0 you may want to use NetMeeting to chat, talk, videoconference, or share applications or a Whiteboard.

In order to connect to the other people with whom you want to meet, you have to provide a way for NetMeeting to find the person. NetMeeting uses several ways:

- **Windows Address Book**   If you use the Windows Address Book to store e-mail addresses and other information, NetMeeting can search it for the person you want to talk to.

- **Directory server**   A *directory server* stores the addresses of people who use NetMeeting. When you are logged on to a directory server, your name appears on its lists, so that anyone else can "call" you. Once you have connected to a directory server, you can call another person or several other people. Large organizations may have their own directory servers for their employees, and Microsoft maintains a public directory server called the Microsoft Internet Directory, the same server that Windows Messenger uses. You must have a Microsoft .NET Passport to connect to the Microsoft Internet Directory (see "Signing In to Windows Messenger with Your .NET Passport").

- **IP address**   If you know the person's IP address (numeric Internet address, in the format *xxx.xxx.xxx.xxx*), you can type it directly. However, most Internet users have a different address each time they connect to the Internet or restart Windows, and if you are on a LAN that connects to the Internet, you can use IP addresses only for other people on the LAN. To find out your IP address, choose Help | About Windows NetMeeting from the menu bar in the NetMeeting window, and look at the bottom of the About Windows NetMeeting dialog box that appears.

WINDOWS XP
ON THE INTERNET

If there is a firewall (like the Internet Connection Firewall) between you and the Internet, you will not be able to use many of NetMeeting's features.

NetMeeting lets you connect only with other people who use NetMeeting: it doesn't conform to any Internet conferencing standards. For example, you can't join a meeting with people who use Internet Relay Chat (IRC), CU-SeeMe, PowWow, Internet Phone, or other online chat programs.

 This section describes NetMeeting version 3.01, the same version that shipped with Windows Me. Microsoft is no longer developing NetMeeting, because Windows Messenger replaces it.

Running and Configuring NetMeeting

NetMeeting used to be on the Start menu, and we expected to see it at Start | All Programs | Accessories | Communications | NetMeeting. However, it doesn't appear on this menu as part of the regular Windows installation—you may want to add it if you plan to use NetMeeting often (see Chapter 10, section "Reorganizing the Start Menu"). Otherwise, choose Start | Run, type **conf** (for "conferencing"), and press ENTER. If you haven't already configured NetMeeting, you see a series of windows that tell you about the program and ask for the following information:

- **Your name, e-mail address, location, and comments**   You have to type your name and e-mail address, as you can see next, but you can leave the rest of the information blank.

- **Which directory server to use**   The default is Microsoft Internet Directory, which is the same directory you see when you use Windows Messenger. A number of other public directory servers are also available. You can find a list of them at the DevX NetMeeting Zone Web site at **http://www.netmeet.net/bestservers.asp**. If your organization uses NetMeeting, you may use a private directory server. You can choose the Log On To A Directory Server When NetMeeting Starts check box (the alternative is to log on manually by choosing Call | Log On from the NetMeeting menu bar). You can also choose whether you want to be listed in the directory on the server you choose—we recommend leaving the Do Not List My Name In The Directory check box checked unless you are using a private directory. If you choose a public server, you may prefer not to be listed, so that strangers don't contact you.

■ **Connection speed**   Choose the speed of your modem or specify that you are connected via a LAN (see Chapter 27). NetMeeting uses this information when sending audio or video data to you.

■ **Shortcuts**   If you use NetMeeting often, you might want to add a shortcut to the desktop or to the Quick Launch toolbar on your taskbar.

NetMeeting runs the Audio And Video Tuning Wizard to make sure that your speakers are working, for use in audio chats (don't worry if you don't have a microphone—NetMeeting is still useful). When it finishes, the configuration program displays the NetMeeting window, as shown in Figure 25-5.

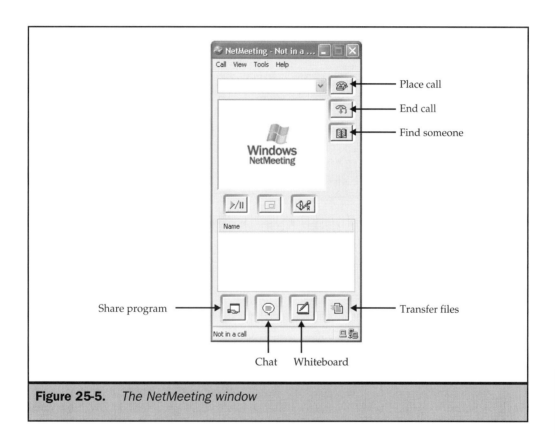

Figure 25-5.   *The NetMeeting window*

You may want to make some other changes to your configuration by choosing Tools | Options. On the Options dialog box that appears, shown next, you can set these types of options:

■ **General tab**   Make changes to the configuration information you typed when you first ran NetMeeting.

■ **Security tab**   Specify whether to accept incoming calls automatically, whether to make secure outgoing calls, and other security options.

■ **Audio tab**   Configure NetMeeting to work with your microphone and speakers.

■ **Video tab**   Specify the size and quality of video images to display.

Connecting to a Directory Server

Once you see the NetMeeting window (as shown in Figure 25-5), you can start a meeting by clicking the Place Call button (the yellow telephone) if you know the e-mail address of the person you want to talk to. However, unless you know the person's IP address or have called them before, you usually need to start the call by selecting the person from a directory.

When you click the Find Someone In A Directory button (the little open book) when you are connected to a directory server, you see the Find Someone window (if your computer isn't connected to the Internet, you see a message first: click Connect). Set the Select A Directory to the directory to which you want to connect. If you want to use the Microsoft Internet Directory, you may need to click a link to log in using your Microsoft .NET Passport name and password. Then you see a list of the people who are on your contacts list (this is the same list that appears in Windows Messenger), as in Figure 25-6.

If you want to talk to someone who isn't on your Windows Messenger contact list, you and the other person need to connect to the same directory server. See the DevX NetMeeting Zone Web site at **http://www.netmeet.net/bestservers.asp** for a list of servers to use. Choose Tools | Options from the NetMeeting window's menu bar and type the server name (usually ils.*domainname*) into the Directory box and click OK. Now, when you click the Find Someone In A Directory button, a list of people on the server appears, with a little PC icon to the left of each person's e-mail address (as shown in Figure 25-7). An icon with a blue screen and red twinkle means that the person is currently in a call, whereas a gray icon means that the person is not in a call. A little yellow speaker icon indicates that the person can communicate via audio. A little gray camera icon means that the person can communicate via video. On the listing of people, click the column headings to sort by that column; sorting by last name or e-mail address makes finding the person you want easier.

| **Note** | *When you are connected to a public server and your name is listed, you are likely to get* |
| | *unwanted calls.* |

Figure 25-6.   *You can use the Microsoft Internet Directory to see your Windows Messenger contacts.*

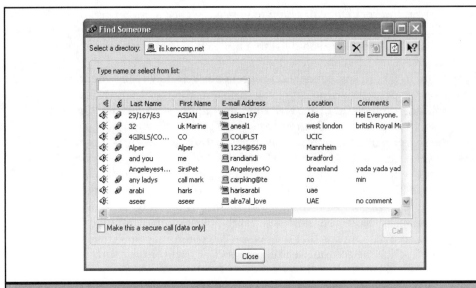

Figure 25-7. *Clicking the Directory icon displays a listing of people connected to your directory server.*

Making or Receiving a Call

To call someone, double-click the person's name on the contact or directory list, or type the name in the box and click the Call button. If you are using Microsoft Internet Directory, then the person is contacted through Windows Messenger: if they accept your invitation, Windows Messenger takes over on your computer, too. If you use another directory server, NetMeeting contacts the directory server to make the connection and displays a dialog box on that person's computer screen, asking them whether they want to connect with you. If the person accepts your call, the NetMeeting window lists the people who are in your current call, as shown in Figure 25-8.

When someone calls you, you see a dialog box asking whether you want to take the call or a message in Windows Messenger inviting you to join the meeting; click Accept in either case if you do. You see the NetMeeting window with the callers listed.

Another way to make a call is to click the Place Call button | choose Call | New Call, or press CTRL-N. You see the Place A Call dialog box, as in Figure 25-9. In the Address box, type the name of the directory server to which the person is connected, followed by a slash (/) and the e-mail address of the person you want to call. If the person you are calling uses a computer with its own computer name or IP address, you can type that instead. Then click the Call button.

When you are done with the call, click the Hang Up button. NetMeeting maintains its connection with the directory server but disconnects from the call.

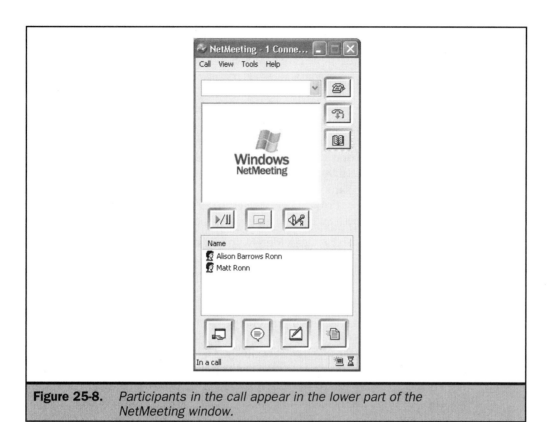

Figure 25-8. *Participants in the call appear in the lower part of the NetMeeting window.*

Figure 25-9. *The Place A Call dialog box*

Once You Are Connected

Once you are connected to at least one other person, you can communicate using most of the same features that Windows Messenger offers:

- **Text chat**   Click the Chat button to display a window in which you can type messages to the other people in the chat.

- **Voice chat**   If both of you have microphones and speakers, you can just begin talking. Speak slowly, one at a time (as though you were using a walkie-talkie—over!). Unless you have a very fast connection, you may experience "breaking up"—the sound may be interrupted and "staticky." Keep your microphone away from the speakers, or use headphones, to avoid feedback.

- **Videoconferencing**   If other people in your call have video cameras (even if you don't have one), you can see video from one of their cameras (one at a time) in your NetMeeting window. The video appears in the Remote Video window, a small box on the right side of the window when the Current Call icon is selected. If you don't see the video, click the button at the bottom of the Remote Video window. To set your video options, choose Tools | Options and click the Video tab. You can tell NetMeeting to enable your video camera automatically when you make a call; set the size of the video image; choose between faster, low-quality video and slower, high-quality video; and specify the properties of your camera. If you have a camera, be sure to light your face (or whatever the camera points at) from the front. You can't see more than one person at a time; to switch the person in the call you can see, choose Tools | Switch Audio And Video and choose the name of the person whom you want to see.

- **Sharing a whiteboard**   If you and the other participants in your call want to draw diagrams or pictures that are visible by everyone in the call, use the Whiteboard feature. When you click the Whiteboard button near the bottom of the NetMeeting window, you see a window that works similarly to Microsoft Paint (see Chapter 18, section "Creating and Editing Images With Microsoft Paint"). When anyone in the call makes a change to the Whiteboard window, everyone in the call sees the change.

- **Sending and receiving files**   Choose Tools | File Transfer or click the File Transfer button at the bottom of the NetMeeting window to open the File Transfer window. Click the Add Files button and specify which file you want to send. Alternatively, drag the name of the file from Windows Explorer onto the File Transfer window. Click the Send All button to send the files. To send a file to one caller, rather than to everyone in the call, select the person from the drop-down list at the top right of the File Transfer window. If someone sends you a file, NetMeeting automatically receives the file, storing it in the C:\Program Files\NetMeeting\Received Files folder (assuming that Windows is installed on C:). You see a window telling you about the arrival of the file. To open the file with the default application for the type of file you received, click the Open button.

Caution *Beware of viruses in executable files and of generally offensive material when receiving files from people you don't know.*

- **Sharing programs** You and the other people in your meeting can share the windows of a running program that one member has on his or her screens. For example, you could show a group around your Web site by running a browser on your machine and sharing the browser window so that the other callers can see the contents of the browser window on their screens, too. This feature works like Windows Messenger's application-sharing (see "Sharing Control of a Program").

Note *Firewalls, including the Internet Connection Firewall that comes with Windows XP, can prevent video and voice from working.*

Hosting a Meeting or Joining an Existing Meeting

In addition to calls, you can communicate in *meetings*, calls that are scheduled in advance. Hosting a meeting allows you to define some properties for the meeting. To host a meeting, let everyone invited to the meeting know when the meeting will take place and how to call you using NetMeeting. At the time the meeting is scheduled to begin, choose Call | Host Meeting, and choose the options you want from the Host A Meeting dialog box, shown in Figure 25-10. When you click OK, you return to the NetMeeting window, with only you listed as a caller. When the other callers connect, you see a dialog box asking whether they can join; click Accept or Ignore.

Because you are the host of the meeting, the meeting ends when you hang up. Other participants can come and go without ending the meeting. As the host, you can also throw people out of your meeting: right-click the person's name on the list of callers and choose Remove from the menu that appears.

To join an existing meeting, call someone who is in the meeting. You see a message that the person is currently in a meeting, asking whether you want to try to join the

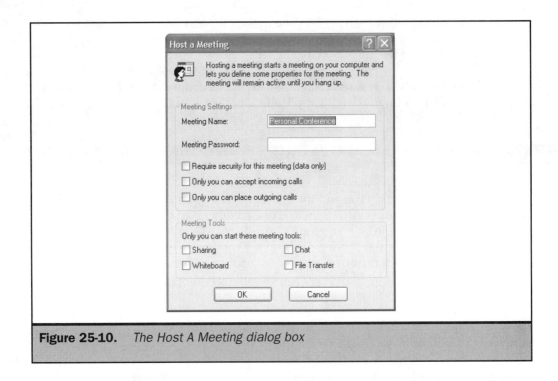

Figure 25-10. *The Host A Meeting dialog box*

meeting; click Yes. When the person you called leaves the meeting, you leave too, so it's best to call the person who is hosting the meeting.

If you don't want anyone else to join the meeting (or any NetMeeting call), choose Call | Do Not Disturb. Remember to choose the same command again when you want to re-enable receiving calls.

The
Complete
Reference

Chapter 26

Other Internet
Programs that Come
with Windows XP

Windows XP comes with lots of Internet-related programs. In addition to the automated sign-up software, the New Connection Wizard, and dial-up connections (all described in Chapter 22), you get lots of Internet applications—which are described in the other chapters in this part of the book. Windows also comes with these other useful Internet programs:

- **HyperTerminal** acts as a terminal emulator and lets you log into text-based systems, either over the Internet (like telnet) or by dialing directly.

- **Telnet** can also do terminal emulation over the Internet, faster but not as nicely as HyperTerminal.

- **Web folders** can display folders stored on FTP or Web servers, and enable you to copy, rename, and delete files using Explorer windows.

- **Ftp** lets you transfer files to or from FTP servers.

This chapter describes how to use these programs. You can download other Internet programs from the Internet itself; we recommend some programs that complement those that come with Windows and suggest where to find the programs on the Web. In fact, you can use almost any Internet program that is Winsock compatible (see Chapter 22, section "What Is Winsock?").

Logging into Text-Based Systems with HyperTerminal

HyperTerminal is the Windows terminal-emulation program. It lets your powerful Windows computer—loaded with RAM, hard disk space, and other hardware—pretend to be a dumb terminal. HyperTerminal is useful for connecting to computers that are designed to talk to terminals, including UNIX shell accounts and bulletin board systems (see Chapter 22, section "UNIX Shell Accounts and Bulletin Board Systems"). The computer you connect to by using HyperTerminal is called the *remote computer* (as opposed to your own *local computer*).

You can use HyperTerminal in three ways:

- **Dial-up connections** You can use HyperTerminal to call another computer over a modem and phone line. No other communications program or account is involved. You use this method when connecting directly to a bulletin board system, UNIX shell account, or other text-based system that works with terminals. You tell HyperTerminal what modem to use to make the connection, along with the country, area code, and phone number to dial.

■ **Direct network connections**   You can use HyperTerminal to connect to a computer to which your computer is connected by a cable. You tell HyperTerminal the communications port (COM1 or COM2) to which the cable is connected. Alternatively, you can use a direct connection in the Network Connections window (see Chapter 27, section "Connecting Two Computers with Direct Network Connection").

■ **Telnet connections**   If you have an Internet account (or other TCP/IP-based connection), you can use HyperTerminal as a Winsock-compatible *telnet* program, a terminal program that works over the Internet. First, you connect to the Internet by using a dial-up connection. Then, you connect to a computer over the Internet by using a HyperTerminal telnet connection—you "telnet in." For example, you can look up books at the U.S. Library of Congress by making a telnet connection to the library's mainframe system and using its text-only interface. You tell HyperTerminal to connect using TCP/IP (Winsock), along with the port number and host address of the computer to which you want to connect. The standard *port number* (a number that tells an Internet host computer whether you are connecting for e-mail, the Web, telnet, or another Internet service) is 23. The *host address* is the Internet host name of the computer you want to telnet in to; for example, the host address of the U.S. Library of Congress is **locis.loc.gov**.

To dial up and connect to a computer, HyperTerminal creates a *HyperTerminal connection*, a configuration file with the specifications for the connection. HyperTerminal connection files have the extension .ht.

Windows XP comes with HyperTerminal 5.1, which is very similar to the version that shipped with Windows Me/9x.

Running HyperTerminal

To run HyperTerminal, choose Start | All Programs | Accessories | Communications | HyperTerminal. If HyperTerminal isn't already your default telnet program, you see a dialog box asking whether Windows should do so. The HyperTerminal window appears, and the Connection Description window also opens to help set up a new first HyperTerminal connection.

Configuring HyperTerminal for Your Account

The first time you run HyperTerminal, it displays the Connection Description dialog box, as shown in Figure 26-1. You can also display it by choosing File | New

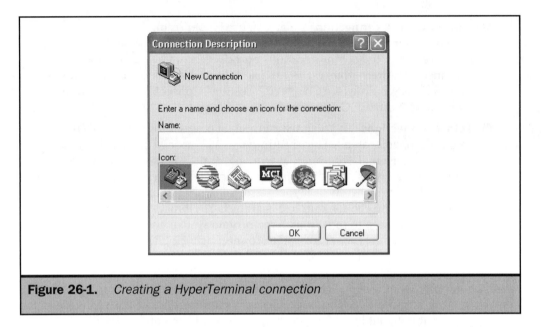

Figure 26-1. *Creating a HyperTerminal connection*

Connection or clicking the New button on the toolbar of the HyperTerminal window. When you see the Connection Description dialog box, follow these steps:

1. Type the name you want to use for the connection, choose an icon, and click OK. You see the Connect To dialog box, asking for information about how to dial the phone to connect to the computer:

2. The options you see on this dialog box depend on what you've selected for the Connect Using setting. For a dial-up connection, set the Connect Using box to the modem to use for the connection, choose the country, type the area code,

and type the phone number to dial. For a direct cable connection, set the Connect Using box to your modem or to COM1 or COM2 (the communications port to which the modem is connected). For a telnet connection, set the Connect Using box to TCP/IP (Winsock, that is, your Internet connection) and fill in the host address and port number (usually 23).

3. Click OK. For dial-up connections, you see the Connect dialog box (for telnet connections, skip to step 6):

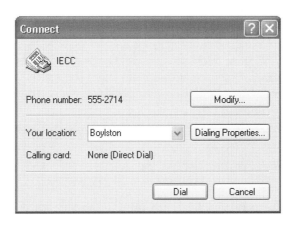

4. If you want to change your dialing location (where you are dialing from) or use a calling card, click the Dialing Properties button and use the New and Edit buttons to change the way the connection is dialed (see Chapter 21, section "Configuring Windows for Dialing Locations").

5. To connect, click Dial. (If you click Cancel, HyperTerminal remembers the connection information you entered, but doesn't make the connection.) For dial-up connections, HyperTerminal dials the phone. For telnet connections, if you're not already online, your dial-up connection may display its dialog box to get you connected to your Internet account; if so, click Connect. When HyperTerminal has established a connection with the remote computer, you see the HyperTerminal window, shown in Figure 26-2.

6. Log in and use the remote computer, typing the commands that the remote computer requires. For example, if the remote computer displays a UNIX command line, you must type UNIX commands. You can use the scroll bar along the right side of the HyperTerminal window to see the *backscroll buffer*, which stores the last 500 lines of text that have scrolled up off the top of the terminal window (you can configure the buffer to be larger).

7. When you are done using the remote computer, log off by using the commands that it requires. HyperTerminal disconnects, too. If you have trouble getting disconnected, tell HyperTerminal to hang up by choosing Call | Disconnect from the menu bar or by clicking the Disconnect icon on the toolbar.

WINDOWS XP
ON THE INTERNET

8. When you exit HyperTerminal, it asks whether you want to save the session (connection) you just created. Click Yes. (If you never plan to connect to this remote computer again, click No to throw away the connection information you entered.) HyperTerminal creates an icon for the connection in the C:\Program Files\Accessories\HyperTerminal folder.

Connecting with HyperTerminal

You can connect to a computer for which you've already created a HyperTerminal connection in two ways:

- Open the C:\Program Files\Accessories\HyperTerminal folder (replace C with the drive letter on which Windows is installed if it's not C). Then open the icon for the connection (single-click or double-click, depending on how you configured Windows).

- Choose Start | All Programs | Accessories | Communications | HyperTerminal. When the HyperTerminal window appears, click Cancel to close the Connection Description dialog box. Choose File | Open or click the Open button on the toolbar and choose the connection.

HyperTerminal runs and displays the Connect dialog box; click Dial to make the connection. If you are using a telnet connection and you are not already connected to

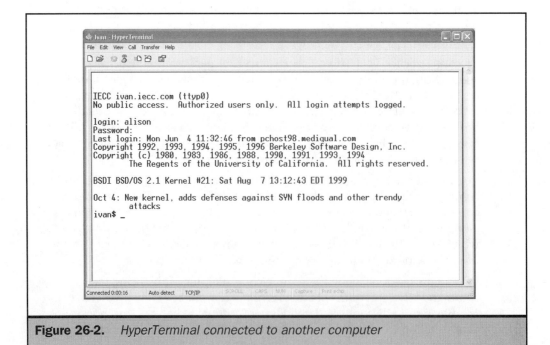

Figure 26-2. *HyperTerminal connected to another computer*

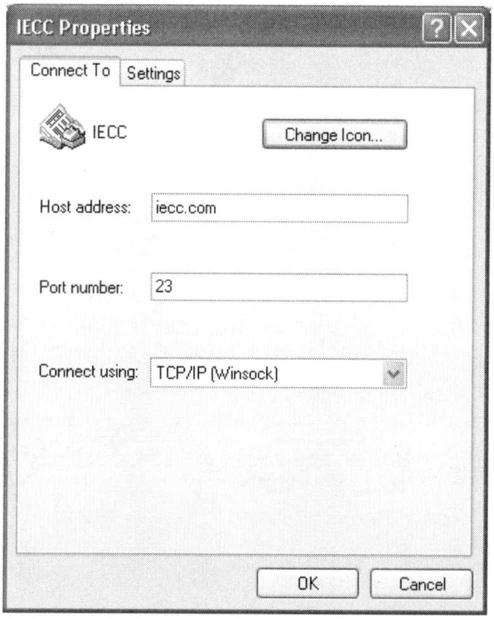

Figure 26-3. *Changing the properties of a HyperTerminal connection*

the Internet, your dial-up connection displays its window to prompt you to get online; click Connect.

When you are done using the remote computer, log off using whatever commands it requires; HyperTerminal should disconnect, too. If necessary, end the connection by choosing Call | Disconnect or by clicking the Disconnect icon on the toolbar.

Changing Information about a Connection

If the phone number for a remote computer changes or you need to change the modem (or other information about the connection), run HyperTerminal by using the connection, or choose File | Open to open the connection. Click the Properties button on the toolbar (the rightmost button) or choose File | Properties to display the connection Properties dialog box, as shown in Figure 26-3. You can also display the Properties dialog box when you are using the connection. The settings on the Properties dialog box depend on the type of connection (dial-up, direct cable connection, or telnet).

In the Properties dialog box for the connection, you can set these types of options:

- **Connect using**   On the Connect To tab, you specify the icon and how to connect: via modem, via cable (connected to your modem, COM1, or COM2 port), or via TCP/IP (for a telnet connection). For dial-up connections, you also specify the phone number. For TCP/IP connections, you also specify the host address and port number (the default is 23, telnet's usual port). If you have Virtual Private Networking installed, VPN appears as an option (see Chapter 27, section "Connecting Computers with Virtual Private Networking").

■ **What keys do**   On the Settings tab, you specify whether the function keys, cursor motion keys, and CTRL key combinations are transmitted to the other computer or are interpreted by Windows. You can also control the actions of the BACKSPACE key.

■ **Terminal emulation**   On the Settings tab, you tell HyperTerminal what type of terminal to emulate (act like). Most remote computers are configured to work with certain standard terminal types. HyperTerminal can emulate many of the most commonly used terminal types: ANSI, ANSIW, Minitel, TTY, Viewdata, VT100, VT100J, VT52, and VT-UTF8. If you set the Emulation box to Auto Detect, HyperTerminal tries to figure out what type of terminal to emulate, based on information from the remote computer. If you click the Terminal Setup button, you can further configure HyperTerminal's actions, including how the cursor looks, what keys on the keypad do, and whether the terminal window displays 80 or 132 columns.

■ **Character set**   On the Settings tab, click the Terminal Setup button to control settings that are specific to the type of terminal that you are emulating. Click the ASCII Setup button to control the characters that HyperTerminal sends and receives, including which character(s) HyperTerminal sends at the end of each line, whether HyperTerminal displays the characters you type or waits to display them until the remote computer echoes them back, and whether HyperTerminal waits a fraction of a second after each character or line it sends.

■ **Other settings**   You can specify how many lines of the text the backscroll buffer stores and whether HyperTerminal beeps when connecting and disconnecting.

Transferring Files

HyperTerminal can send files from your computer to the remote computer or receive files from the remote computer. A number of standard file transfer protocols exist; HyperTerminal can send and receive files by using the Xmodem (regular or 1K), Kermit, Ymodem, Ymodem-G, Zmodem, and Zmodem With Crash Recovery protocols. Choose a protocol that the remote computer can also handle. If you have a choice, use Zmodem With Crash Recovery.

Sending a File to the Remote Computer

To send a file to the remote computer:

1. Connect to the remote computer. If applicable, move to the directory on the remote computer in which you want to store the file.

2. If the file transfer protocol you plan to use requires you to give a command on the remote computer to tell it to expect a file, do so. For example, when transferring a file to a UNIX system by using Xmodem, you type the command **rx** *filename* on the remote computer. When transferring a file by using Zmodem (with or without Crash Recovery), no command is required; the UNIX system can detect when the file begins to arrive, and stores it automatically.

3. Click the Send button on the toolbar or choose Transfer | Send File. You see the Send File dialog box, shown here:

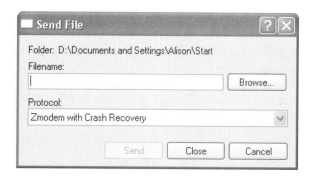

4. In the Filename box, type the name of the file you want to send or click the Browse button to select the file.

5. Set the Protocol box to a file transfer protocol that the remote computer can use when receiving files.

6. Click the Send button. You see a window displaying the status of the file transfer. How much information the window displays depends on which file transfer protocol you use. You can click the Cancel button to stop the file transfer. Click the cps/bps button to control whether you see the transfer speed in characters per second (cps) or bits per second (bps). When the window disappears, file transfer is complete.

Receiving a File from the Remote Computer

To receive a file from the remote computer:

1. Connect to the remote computer. If applicable, move to the directory on the remote computer in which the file is stored.

2. Give the command on the remote computer to tell it to send the file. For example, to tell a UNIX system to transfer a file to your system by using Xmodem, you type the command **sx** *filename* on the remote computer.

3. If you are using Zmodem (with or without Crash Recovery), HyperTerminal detects that a file is arriving and begins receiving the file automatically (skip to step 8). Otherwise, click the Receive button on the toolbar or choose Transfer | Receive File. You see the Receive File dialog box.

4. In the Place Received File In The Following Folder box, type the pathname of the folder into which you want to store the file or click the Browse button to change the pathname.

5. Set the Use Receiving Protocol setting to the file transfer protocol that the remote computer is using to send the file.

6. Click the Receive button.

7. For some protocols, HyperTerminal may need additional information. For example, when using Xmodem, the sending computer doesn't include the filename with the file, so HyperTerminal asks you what to name the file it receives. Type the additional information and click OK.

8. HyperTerminal displays a status window showing the progress of the file's transfer. You can click the Cancel button to stop the file transfer. Click the cps/bps button to control whether you see the transfer speed in characters per second (cps) or bits per second (bps). When the window disappears, the file transfer is complete.

Sending Text Files

You might want to send text to the other computer as though you were typing it. For example, if the remote computer asks a question to which you have an answer stored in a small text file, you can send the text file rather than retyping it—the remote computer doesn't realize that you are sending a file, and accepts the text as though you typed it. You can also send text that is displayed by some other program; for example, you might want to send a number that is displayed in your spreadsheet program.

You can send small amounts of text by using either of two methods:

- **Copy-and-paste it** Display the text file in another program and copy it to the Windows Clipboard (see Chapter 5, section "Sharing Data Through the Windows Clipboard"). In HyperTerminal, choose Edit | Paste To Host.

- **Transfer it** Choose Transfer | Send Text File. When you see the Send Text File dialog box, choose the file to send. (Make sure that it's a small text file; large files, or files that contain nontext information, rarely arrive intact.) HyperTerminal sends the contents of the file to the remote computer in the same way that it sends characters that you type.

Note *CTRL-C and CTRL-V may not work for cut-and-paste in HyperTerminal, depending on whether these keystrokes are used by the terminal that HyperTerminal is emulating. Choose Edit | Paste To Host from the menu bar instead, or right-click and choose Copy or Paste To Host.*

Capturing Text from the HyperTerminal Window

If the remote computer displays interesting information in the HyperTerminal window, you may want to save it. You can use these three methods to save text:

- **Copy-and-paste it**   Select the text and choose Edit | Copy from the toolbar. You can use the scroll bar to see and select text that has already scrolled up off the top of the HyperTerminal window. HyperTerminal copies the text to the Windows Clipboard (see Chapter 5, section "Sharing Data Through the Windows Clipboard"). You can paste this text into the Windows Notepad, WordPad, your word processing program, or any other program that accepts blocks of text.

- **Capture it**   Choose Transfer | Capture Text. When you see the Capture Text dialog box, type the folder name and filename of the file into which you want to store the text. (Click Browse to select the folder.) Then click Start. All the text that appears in the terminal window from this point forward is also stored in the file. To stop capturing text, choose Transfer | Capture Text | Stop. To stop temporarily, choose Transfer | Capture Text | Pause; to restart the text later and capture into the same file, choose Transfer | Capture Text | Resume. While HyperTerminal is capturing text to a file, the word Capture appears on the status bar along the bottom of the HyperTerminal window.

- **Print it**   To tell HyperTerminal to print the information as it arrives in the terminal window, choose Transfer | Capture To Printer from the menu bar. As the remote computer sends text to your computer and HyperTerminal displays it, the text is printed. To stop printing, choose Transfer | Capture To Printer again. While HyperTerminal is printing all incoming text, the message Print Echo appears on the status bar.

- **Print the whole session**   To print the entire session with the remote computer, starting at the beginning of the backscroll buffer, choose File | Print.

Other HyperTerminal Commands

Here are a few other things you can do with HyperTerminal:

- **Tell HyperTerminal to answer incoming calls**   If you are expecting a remote computer to dial into your computer, you can set your modem and HyperTerminal to answer the phone. Choose Call | Wait For A Call. The words Waiting For Calls appear on the status line. If an incoming call arrives on the phone line to which your modem is connected, your modem answers the phone, and HyperTerminal tries to connect to a computer on the other end of the phone line. To turn off auto-answer, choose Call | Stop Waiting.

- **Change the font that HyperTerminal displays in the terminal window**
  Choose View | Font.
- **Set the size of the HyperTerminal window to fit the terminal window**
  Choose View | Snap.

Logging into Other Computers Using Telnet

Windows XP also comes with a Telnet program. Unlike HyperTerminal, it can connect only over the Internet; the Telnet program can't dial the phone (see "Logging into Text-Based Systems with HyperTerminal"). If you do much telnetting, HyperTerminal is a nicer program to use because it can remember the settings for multiple host computers and transfer files, and emulate a wider variety of terminals. The only advantage of the Windows XP Telnet program is that it's faster over a LAN connection.

Running Telnet

To run Windows built-in Telnet program

1. Choose Start | Run, type **telnet**, and click OK. You see the Telnet window, shown in Figure 26-4.

2. To see the list of commands shown in Figure 26-4, type **?** and press ENTER.

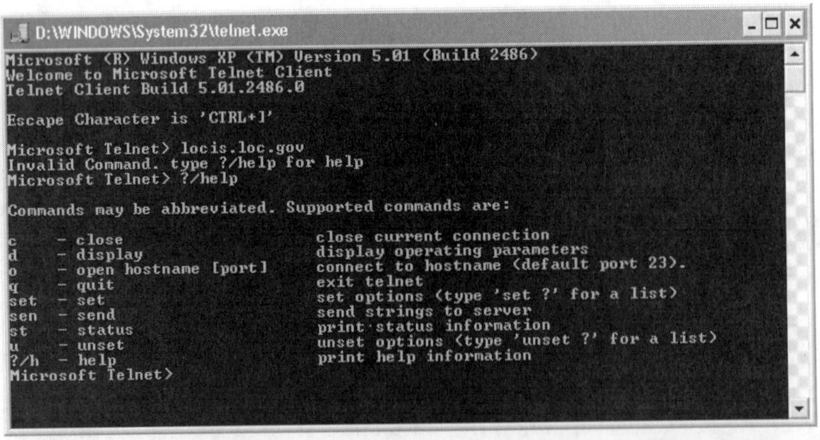

Figure 26-4. The Telnet window

Working with FTP and Web Servers Using Web Folders

FTP (File Transfer Protocol) is a system for transferring files over the Internet. An *FTP server* stores files, and *FTP clients* can log into FTP servers either to upload (transfer) files to the FTP server or (more commonly) to download files from the FTP server. To use FTP, you must have an FTP client program.

Most Web browsers, including Internet Explorer and Netscape Navigator, include an FTP client program that you can use to download and upload files (see Chapter 24). Web editors, including Netscape Composer (which is part of Netscape Communicator) include an FTP program for uploading your finished Web pages to a Web server.

Previous versions of Windows have come with an FTP client (described later in this chapter in section "Transferring Files Using Ftp"), but Windows XP has built an FTP client right into Windows Explorer. Using a feature called *Web Folders*, you can see the contents of FTP server folders in the same Explorer windows you use to manage the files on your own computer. Some Web servers also support Web Folders.

Note *To create a Web Folder for a Web server, the Web server must support Microsoft's WebDAV extensions. (All FTP servers seem to work with Web Folders.) Also, you need an account on the Web or FTP server that gives you read and write access to the folders on the server. Many sites provide you with free Web and FTP server space, including MSN Communities (at **http://communities.msn.com**), Yahoo Geocities (at http://geocities.com), and Angelfire (at **http://angelfire.lycos.com**). Not all Web servers work with Web Folders. Windows steers you toward Microsoft's service, MSN Communities, which does.*

Creating a Web Folder

To work with the files on a Web or FTP server, you create a Web Folder by adding an icon for it to your My Network Places window. Choose Start | My Network Places to open the My Network Places window, and click Add A Network from the Task pane to run the Add Network Place Wizard.

Note *If the Task pane isn't displayed, we don't know of a way to run the Wizard. Display the Task pane by choosing Tools | Folder Options from the menu bar and clicking the Show Common Tasks In Folders radio button. If you still don't see it, and the Folders Explorer bar appears, click the Folders button on the toolbar to remove the Folders Explorer bar, and the Task pane may appear.*

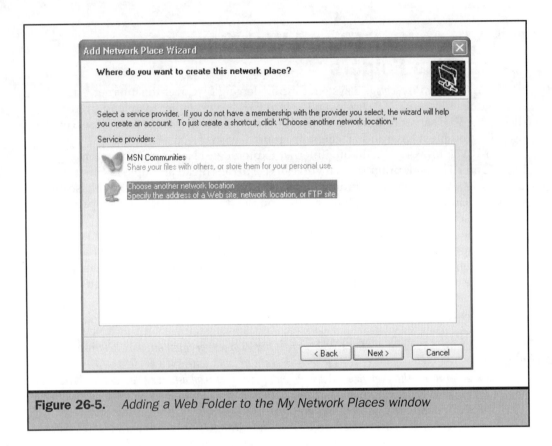

Figure 26-5.   *Adding a Web Folder to the My Network Places window*

The Add Network Place Wizard asks several questions (click Next to move to the next question):

- **Where Do You Want To Create This Network Place?**   The Wizard lists the Web servers and FTP servers that Microsoft offers (currently only MSN Communities), as shown in Figure 26-5. Click one, or click Choose Another Network Location to type the URL of an FTP or Web server. If you choose MSN Communities, you are done: the Wizard creates an MSN Communities account for you, along with a Web Folder icon with which you can access it.

- **What Is The Address Of This Network Place?**   If you choose to specify your own FTP or Web server, type the URL into the Internet Or Network Address box. The URL must start with **http://** (for a Web server) or **ftp://** (for an FTP server).

- **User Name And Password**   If you plan to download files from a public FTP server to which you don't have write access (and on which you don't have an account), leave the Log On Anonymously check box selected. If you have an account on the FTP or Web server and want to be able to upload files and use files that aren't available to the public, click the check box to deselect it. Type your account name in the User Name box.

■ **What Do You Want To Name This Place?**   Type a name for the icon that the Wizard will create for the FTP or Web server.

When the Wizard exits, the My Network Places window is divided into two sections: Local Network (with icons for shared folders on the LAN) and The Internet (with icons for Web Folders). In the latter, you see a new icon for your Web Folder.

If you chose MSN Communities, the icon is called My Communities. Windows uses your Microsoft .NET Passport user name, e-mail address, and password to create a new account for you (see Chapter 25, section "Signing In to Windows Messenger with Your .NET Passport").

Working with Web Folders

When Windows tries to display the contents of the Web Folder, you see the Log On As dialog box, as shown in Figure 26-6. (For an MSN Communities Web Folder, Windows logs you on automatically using your .NET Passport.) Type the password for the FTP or Web server. If you want Windows to remember this password so that you don't have to type it each time you view the contents of this Web Folder, select the Save

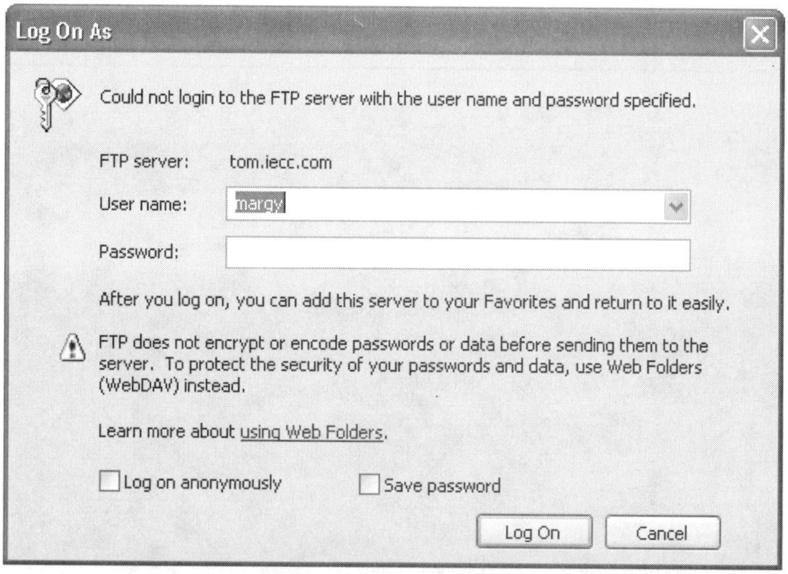

Figure 26-6.   *Logging onto an FTP server as a Web Folder*

Password check box. If you don't have an account on the server, select the Log On Anonymously check box (not all servers allow anonymous FTP). Then click Log On.

Once you are logged onto the FTP or Web server, your files on the server appear in an Explorer window. Move from folder to folder, copy, rename, delete, and view files just as you would with files on your own computer. To copy files to or from your computer, open a second Explorer window by choosing Start | My Computer, and drag files or folders from one Explorer window to the other.

Transferring Files Using Ftp

Another way to transfer files to or from an FTP server is by using a separate FTP client program. Windows XP comes with a basic command-driven FTP client program called Ftp. If you plan to do much file transfer, especially uploading, you'll want to use Web Folders (as described in the section "Working with FTP and Web Servers Using Web Folders" earlier in this chapter) or a better FTP client program, such as WS_FTP (see "Downloading, Installing, and Running Other Internet Programs").

Basics of FTP

To run the Windows XP FTP program, choose Start | Run. Type **ftp** *serverhost*, where *serverhost* is the host name of the FTP server, and click OK. If you are not connected to the Internet and you see your dial-up connection window, click Connect. You see the Ftp window, as shown in Figure 26-7.

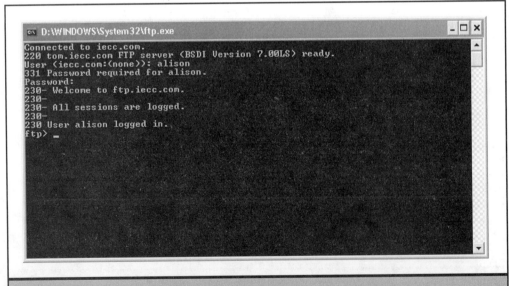

Figure 26-7.   *The Ftp window*

To connect to an FTP server, you specify the host name of the server (for example, **rtfm.mit.edu**), and then you log in. You have two choices:

- If you have an account on the FTP server, log in with your user name and password. You can access all the files that your user name gives you permission to use.

- If you don't have an account on the FTP server, the server may accept connections from guests. Connection without an account on the FTP server is called *anonymous FTP*. To use anonymous FTP, type **anonymous** for the user name and your own e-mail address as the password. Thousands of FTP servers on the Internet allow you to use anonymous FTP to download files, although some are so busy that it may be hard to get connected.

Note   *UNIX, the operating system of choice among Internet servers, is sensitive to the case of the names of files, unlike Windows. Be aware of capitalization in file names.*

Once you are connected to an FTP server, it displays lots of messages to let you know what's going on. These messages start with three-digit numbers, which you can ignore. For example, when you have transferred a file, you see the message "226 Transfer Complete."

When you transfer a file—by either uploading or downloading—you must choose between two modes:

- **ASCII mode**   When transferring text files, use ASCII mode. Different computer systems use different characters to indicate the ends of lines. In ASCII mode, the Ftp program automatically adjusts line endings for the system to which the file is transferred.

- **Binary or Image mode**   When transferring files that consist of anything but unformatted text, use Binary mode. In Binary mode, the Ftp program does not make any changes to the contents of the file during transfer. Use Binary mode when transferring graphics files, audio files, video files, programs, or any kind of file other than plain text.

Tip   *At the Ftp prompt, type ? to see a listing of the commands that Ftp can perform.*

Navigating the Folder Trees

The following are the most common ftp tasks:

- To see a list of files and subdirectories in the current directory on the FTP server, type **dir**. The exact format of the listing depends on the FTP server's operating system. Figure 26-8 shows a typical listing. You can use wildcards (*) to limit the list. If you want to see filenames only, with no other information, you can use the **ls** (list) command.

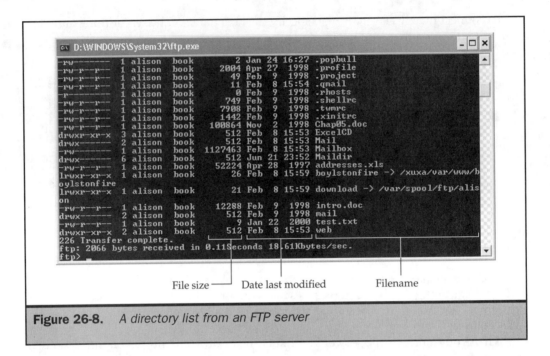

Figure 26-8. *A directory list from an FTP server*

- To change directories, type **cd** (for "change directory"), followed by the name of the directory to which you want to move.

- To find out the name of the current directory, type **pwd** (for "print working directory").

On many publicly accessible FTP servers, all the downloadable files are in a directory called pub. Here are a few tips for moving to the directory you want:

- To move to the parent directory of the current directory, type **cd ..** (that is, the **cd** command followed by a space and two dots).

- To move to the top-level directory on the FTP server, also called the root directory, type **cd /** (that is, the **cd** command followed by a forward slash). Most FTP servers run the UNIX operating system, which uses forward slashes (as opposed to the backslashes used in Windows).

- You can move directly to a directory by typing its full pathname, starting at the root; the full pathname starts with a **/** to represent the root directory.

- If the FTP server runs the UNIX operating system, capitalization is important. When typing directory or filenames, be sure to use the correct capitalization—most names use lowercase.

- To change the current local directory (the folder from which Ftp can upload files and to which it can download files), type **lcd** (local directory), followed by the name of the folder on your computer. If the pathname of the folder contains spaces, enclose the pathname in quotes. To move to the parent folder of the current folder, type **lcd ..** (the **lcd** command followed by a space and two dots).

- When you have finished transferring files, type **quit** or **bye** to disconnect from the FTP server. A message confirms that you have left the FTP server.

*If you want to disconnect from the FTP server and connect to a different server, you don't have to exit the Ftp program. Instead, type **close** or **disconnect** and press ENTER to disconnect from the FTP server. Next, type **open**, followed by a space, and then the host name of another FTP server; and press ENTER to connect to the other server.*

Uploading Files

You use the **put** command to upload the files. To upload a group of files, you can use the **mput** command.

Note

You can upload files only if you have write permission in the directory on the FTP server. Most anonymous FTP servers don't accept uploads, or they accept them into only one specific directory. Read the welcome message to find out the rules for the FTP server you are using.

To upload a file, follow these steps:

1. Connect to the FTP server, move to the directory on the FTP server in which you want to store the file, and set the current local directory to the folder on your computer that contains the files you want to upload.

2. If the file or files you want to upload contain anything but unformatted ASCII text, type **binary** to select Binary mode (see "Basics of FTP"). To switch back to ASCII mode to transfer text files, type **ascii**.

3. Type **put**, a space, the filename on your computer, a space, and the filename to use on the FTP server. Then press ENTER. For example, to upload a file named draft13.doc and call the uploaded version report.doc, you would type **put draft13.doc report.doc**.

4. You see a series of messages; the message Transfer Complete appears when the file transfer is done.

Caution

*If a file with the name that you specify already exists on the FTP server, the **put** command may overwrite the existing file with the uploaded file. You can use the **dir** or **ls** command to check for the existence of a file with the same name.*

WINDOWS XP
ON THE INTERNET

5. If you want to check that the file is really on the FTP server, type **dir** to see a listing of files in the current directory.

You can copy a group of files to the FTP server by typing **mput** (multiple put). Type **mput**, followed by a wildcard pattern that matches the names of the files you want to upload. The pattern * indicates that all files in the current directory on your computer should be copied. For example, to upload all the files with the extension .html, you would type **mput *.html**.

As it copies the files, **mput** asks you about each file. Type **y** to upload the file or **n** to skip it.

*If you don't want **mput** to ask you about each file before uploading it, type the **prompt** command first before giving the **mput** command. The **prompt** command turns off filename prompting.*

Downloading Files

To download files from the FTP server to your computer, follow these steps:

1. Connect to the FTP server, move to the directory on the FTP server that contains the file that you want to download, and set the current local directory to the folder on your computer in which you want to store the files you download.

2. If the file or files you want to download contain anything but unformatted ASCII text, type **binary** to select Binary mode (see "Basics of FTP"). To switch back to ASCII mode to transfer text files, type **ascii**.

3. Type **get**, a space, the filename on the FTP server, a space, the filename to use on your computer. Then press ENTER. (You can't use filenames with spaces.) For example, to download a file named bud9812.doc and call the downloaded version budget.dec1998.doc, the command is **get bud9812.doc budget.dec2001.doc**.

4. You see a series of messages; the message Transfer Complete appears when the file transfer is done. To interrupt the file transfer, press CTRL-C. Sometimes that doesn't work, and the only way to interrupt the transfer is to close the FTP window.

5. If you want to check whether the file is really downloaded, use Windows Explorer to see a listing of files on your computer.

You can copy a group of files to the FTP server by typing **mget**, followed by a wildcard pattern that matches the names of the files that you want to download. The pattern * means that all files in the current directory on your computer should be copied. For example, to download all the files whose names start with *d*, you would type **mget d***.

As it copies the files, **mget** asks you about each file. Type **y** to download the files or **n** to skip it.

 If you download a nontext file that is unusable, you probably forgot to issue the binary command before downloading the file.

Downloading, Installing, and Running Other Internet Programs

Once you have established a dial-up connection to the Internet, you can run any Winsock-compatible program (see Chapter 22, section "What Is Winsock?"). Although Windows comes with some good Internet applications, you can supplement (or replace) them with other programs. For example, the Ftp program that comes with Windows is not particularly powerful or easy to use; we vastly prefer the excellent shareware WS_FTP program, which shows you the contents of the local and remote directories, and lets you transfer files by clicking buttons rather than typing commands. (Read on to find out how to get it.)

Where to Get Internet Programs

Lots of Winsock-compatible Internet programs are available for downloading from the Internet itself. Some are *freeware* programs that are entirely free to use; some are *shareware* programs that require you to register the program if you decide that you like it; some are demo programs that let you try a partially disabled version of the program before you decide whether to buy the real program; and some are commercial programs that ask you to pay before downloading.

Many Web-based libraries offer all types of programs. Here are our favorites:

- **The Ultimate Collection of Windows Software (TUCOWS)** at **http://www.tucows.com**   Classifies programs by operating system and type. It has lots of mirror sites (identical Web sites) all over the globe, so it's rarely a problem to begin downloading even very popular programs. It's particularly easy to browse a long list of programs of a given type (browsers or e-mail programs, for example) and compare reviews.

- **The CWApps List** at **http://cws.internet.com**   This is the original Winsock library, and it is still excellent. Forrest Stroud set up this site when shareware and freeware Internet software were starting to become available.

- **CNET Shareware.com** at **http://shareware.cnet.com**   Offers lots of non-Internet-related programs.

- **Download.com** at **http://download.cnet.com**   Has thousands of downloadable programs organized by category.

Installing and Running Internet Programs

Once you've downloaded a program from the Internet, it's a good idea to check it for *viruses*, self-replicating programs that may infect other programs on your computer. Windows doesn't come with a virus checker, but you can download a good one from any of the software libraries in the preceding section (see Chapter 31, section "Preventing Infection by Viruses"). We like McAfee's and Symantec's Norton antivirus programs, too (commercial software downloadable from McAfee's Web site at **http://www.mcafee.com** and Symantec's Web site at **http://www.symantec.com/nav**).

Most downloaded programs arrive as self-installing files; in Windows Explorer, run the file you downloaded. The program usually installs itself, asking you configuration questions along the way. Most programs either add themselves to the Start | All Programs menu or add an icon to the desktop (or both). Other downloaded programs arrive in ZIP (compressed) files, which the Windows compressed folders feature can uncompress (see Chapter 8, section "Working with Compressed Folders").

The first time you run a program, you might need to configure it further; check any documentation files that are installed along with the program. Look for a Tools | Options command or an Edit | Preferences command, as these usually display configuration or preference dialog boxes.

The Complete Reference

Part VI

Networking with Windows XP

The
Complete
Reference

Chapter 27

Designing a Windows-Based Local Area Network

707

If you have more than one computer, you should consider connecting them with a local area network (LAN). Windows XP provides all the features needed to connect your computer to a LAN—no other software is required (although you will probably need some hardware). This chapter introduces LANs, including what a network is and why you might want one, and the two major kinds of networks. Most new networks use Ethernet technology, either with cables or wireless links. This chapter also describes what you need to do to install a LAN, including buying and installing cards and cables.

This chapter provides the background for the specifics covered in the rest of the chapters in Part V, which cover configuring Windows for a LAN (Chapter 28), sharing disks and printers (Chapter 29), sharing an Internet connection (Chapter 30), and network security (Chapter 31).

Note *This chapter covers setting up your network from scratch. However, if you are adding a Windows XP computer to an existing peer-to-peer network or upgrading a computer on a network from an earlier version of Windows to Windows XP, the steps you need to follow are also found in this chapter (see the sidebar on "Adding to an Existing Network" and "Upgrading a Computer on an Existing Network").*

In addition, this chapter provides details on alternatives if you don't need a permanent network, just a temporary connection: direct network connection with a serial or parallel cable, dial-up connections, and Virtual Private Networking.

What Is a Network and Why Would You Need One?

A network provides a connection between computing resources, a way to share hardware and files, and a paperless way to communicate. A *local area network (LAN)* is a network limited to one building or group of buildings, in which the computers are usually connected by cables. A LAN can be as useful in a small office of two or three computers as it is in a large office.

Larger networks also exist. *Wide area networks (WANs)* connect computers that are geographically dispersed, and the Internet—the biggest network of them all—is a worldwide network of interconnected networks, including LANs and WANs.

Sharing Hardware

Without a network, each *resource* (hard disk, CD-ROM drive, printer, or other device) is connected to only one computer (printers may be an exception if you have a switch box). Examples of resources in your office may include a hard drive on which the company's main database is stored, the color printer everyone wants to use, and the tape drive on which nightly backups are made. Without a network, you can use a resource only from the computer to which the resource is attached. With a network, anyone using a computer attached to the network can print to the color printer or open the database, and the computer with the tape drive can access all the hard disks on various machines that need to be backed up. You might also want to share more specialized devices, such as CD-ROM writers and Zip drives.

The cheapest way to share resources is what some techie types call *sneakernet*—take a removable disk, copy the file you need to print or share, and jog over to the computer with the printer or the person who needs to use the file. But sneakernet isn't very efficient—in the long run you save time and hassle (which of those 12 floppies or Zip disks has the current version of that file?) with a network. If you have a small office, using a network and only one printer—to which everyone can print—is more cost effective.

Sharing Files

If you want to share files without the danger of creating multiple versions, you need a network, so every person who accesses the file uses the same copy. Some software (notably database software) enables multiple users to use one file at the same time. Other software warns you when a file is being used by someone else on the network and may even notify you when the file is available for your use.

When you work with files that are too large to fit on a floppy disk, moving them to other computers is cumbersome without a network.

Sharing an Internet Connection

If everyone on the network needs to access the Internet—to send and receive e-mail, browse the Web, or other Internet applications—it's silly for each computer to have its own modem, phone line, and Internet account. Instead, one computer on the LAN can have a fast Internet connection (perhaps a DSL or cable Internet) and serve as the gateway to the Internet. Or, you can use a specialized device called a *router*, which connects a LAN to the Internet over one or more phone lines.

Chapter 30 describes how to use Windows XP Internet Connection Sharing to connect a LAN to the Internet.

What Types of Networks Exist?

Networks are either peer-to-peer or client-server. We describe these two types in the next two sections.

Understanding either kind of network requires having at least a passing familiarity with two terms: client and server. A *client* is a computer that uses resources on the network. A printer client, for instance, is a computer that uses a network printer. A *server* is a computer (or a device with a computer hidden inside) that has resources used by other devices on the network. For instance, a file server is a computer that stores files used by other computers; a print server is a computer with a printer attached to it—the print server lets other computers on the network send print jobs to the printer. The server makes a resource available to the network, and a client uses the resource.

Peer-to-Peer (Workgroup-Based) Networks

In a *peer-to-peer network*, as the term implies, all computers are equal. All computers can function as both clients and servers. Security and permissions are administered from each computer in the network. Each computer in a peer-to-peer network can both request resources from other computers and share its own resources with other computers in the network. You can also configure the network so that some computers only share their resources and others only use resources. Even in this situation, however, the network is still a peer-to-peer network because each computer on the network is administered individually.

Versions of Windows since Windows 3.11 have included support for peer-to-peer networks. Microsoft calls a group of computers on a peer-to-peer network a *workgroup*, and a the network itself a *workgroup-based* network. When you configure Windows to connect to a workgroup-based LAN, you tell it the name of the workgroup (we like to use the name WORKGROUP).

A peer-to-peer workgroup-based network is relatively easy to set up—any small office with more than one computer can create a small peer-to-peer network by using Windows to share printers and files. Only a small amount of hardware is required. The rest of this chapter explains how to choose, install, and configure the hardware to create a peer-to-peer network, and Chapter 28 describes how to configure Windows XP for a LAN.

Client-Server (Domain-Based) Networks

In a *client-server network*, server computers provide resources for the rest of the network, and client computers (also called *workstations*) use these resources. Client-server networks typically are more difficult and expensive to set up and administer than peer-to-peer networks, but they also have many advantages: they can handle more computers, they provide more-sophisticated administration and security options, and all resources are managed centrally on dedicated servers.

Client-server networks require a *network operating system (NOS)*—Windows .NET Server, Windows 2000 Server, Windows NT, Novell Netware, Linux, and UNIX are common NOSs—as well as a greater initial outlay of time and money for setup and equipment, and a network administrator to create and maintain user IDs and permissions.

Microsoft's client-server network system uses domains to organize the large numbers of computers that can be on corporate networks. A *domain* (when used in reference to Microsoft LANs) is a group of user accounts administered together. Microsoft's server versions of Windows (such as Windows .NET Server, which is based on Windows XP) includes Active Directory (AD), which provides centralized administration to the user accounts and groups in the domain. Microsoft calls a client-server network managed by Active Directory a *domain-based* network.

Table 27-1 lists differences between peer-to-peer and client-server networks. To set up your Windows computer on an already-existing Novell or Windows NT network, contact your LAN administrator. For information on creating your own domain-based network with Windows .NET Server, read *Windows .NET Server: The Complete Reference,* by Kathy Ivens (published by Osborne/McGraw-Hill).

Caution *Windows XP Home Edition cannot log into a domain-based network. If you plan to connect to a domain-based network, you need Windows XP Professional.*

	Peer-to-Peer (Workgroup-Based)	**Client-Server (Domain-Based)**
Size	Good for small networks (under 12 computers, depending on the uses for the network). Keeping track of available resources and passwords for each resource becomes difficult on a large peer-to-peer network.	Good for medium-to-large networks. Because administration of network resources is central, the user can access all available resources with only one password (more passwords may be necessary if the network has more than one server).
Hardware	No dedicated file server is needed.	At least one computer must be a server.
Operating system	Windows XP Home Edition or Professional, Me/9x, NT Workstation, or 2000 Professional on all computers.	Requires a network operating system (NOS) on the server. Workstations can run Windows XP Professional, but not XP Home Edition.
Administrator training	Little training needed for users to administer their own computers' resources for all users on the network.	System administrator must be trained.
Resource control	Each computer's user has full control of that computer's resources.	The system administrator is in control of shared resources.
Resource administration	Administered by the owner of each workstation.	Administered by network administrator.

Table 27-1. *Differences Between Peer-to-Peer and Client-Server Networks*

	Peer-to-Peer (Workgroup-Based)	**Client-Server (Domain-Based)**
Resource security	Password is assigned to each resource.	Password is assigned to each user of a server. Each user is given permission to use certain resources by the network administrator.
Security administration	The owner of each computer grants permissions.	Only one password per user is required for the use of the resources associated with one server. A network administrator manages security.

Table 27-1.   *Differences Between Peer-to-Peer and Client-Server Networks (continued)*

What Do You Need to Do?

Setting up a network consists of four major tasks:

■ Choosing the network technology (the type of cabling, cable connections, and adapter cards for your computers). These choices are described in the next few sections of this chapter.

■ Choosing and buying the hardware (see "Buying Network Hardware").

■ Installing the hardware (see "Installing Your Network Hardware").

■ Configuring Windows to use the network (see Chapter 28).

While you needn't be a network engineer to set up a small peer-to-peer network, you do need to have some knowledge about your computer. You need to be able to install a *network interface card (NIC)* in each computer that will be on the LAN (unless the NIC has already been installed), and to use Windows to configure each computer to communicate on the LAN. If you don't feel comfortable installing network cards and configuring Windows, you can hire someone to install your hardware and configure your network. Make sure you tell the installer what type of network you're expecting—a peer-to-peer, workgroup-based network. Otherwise—read on.

Choosing Between Cabled and Wireless LANs

Before you buy hardware for your network, you need to decide how to connect the computers on your network. Almost all new cabled networks use *Ethernet* cards and cabling. Although there are topologies other than Ethernet (such as IBM Token Ring), the majority of new LAN installations are some form of Ethernet because the components are

Adding to an Existing Network

If you're adding a computer to an existing network, you can skip the sections regarding choosing a network technology and a topology—someone has already made those choices for you. Find out what technology is in use on your network, and then buy the appropriate NIC for the computer you want to add to the network. Also, if no leftover cable is on hand, buy the correct kind of cable for your network. Once you've done these things, you can dive into the section "Installing Your Network Hardware" later in this chapter.

Upgrading a Computer on an Existing Network

If you are upgrading the operating system of a computer on an existing network from an earlier version of Windows to Windows XP, you may find your network works right away—open the My Network Places icon on the desktop to see whether other computers on the network appear. If your computer doesn't appear to be communicating on the network, skip ahead to Chapter 28.

widely available and cheap. Because it's so widely used, Ethernet network interface boards are relatively cheap and are also available as PC Cards that fit most laptops.

If you are setting up a new network, you need to choose between regular Ethernet cabling and Ethernet-based wireless equipment.

Ethernet Cable and NICs

There are two speeds of Ethernet. Original Ethernet has a speed of 10 Mbps (megabits/second). *Fast Ethernet* has a speed of 100 Mbps. An even faster version, *Gigabit Ethernet*, is available and can transmit data at a maximum speed of 1 Gbps (gigabits/second), or ten times the Fast Ethernet standard.

The *topology* of a network determines the pattern of cabling you use to connect the computers. In a *star topology* network, each computer is connected by a cable to a *hub*, the computer in the center of the star. One end of the cable plugs into a computer's network interface card, and the other end plugs into the hub, which provides a central connection point for the network cabling. Hubs vary in size (with different numbers of ports), and more advanced hubs can correct signal errors and amplify signals. Figure 27-1 shows a diagram of a network using star topology.

In the past, you chose from star and bus topology (see the "Bus Topology" sidebar in this chapter). However, most new peer-to-peer networks use star topology. This configuration uses more cable and more hardware than a bus topology network, but it's easier to manage and less likely to fail. Star topology is easy to set up, and the network is easier to troubleshoot than a bus network because a damaged cable affects only one computer.

The cable used in Ethernet star topology is usually *unshielded twisted-pair* (also called *Category-5* or *Cat-5*). The connectors on the ends of the cables are *RJ-45 connectors*, which look like large phone connectors.

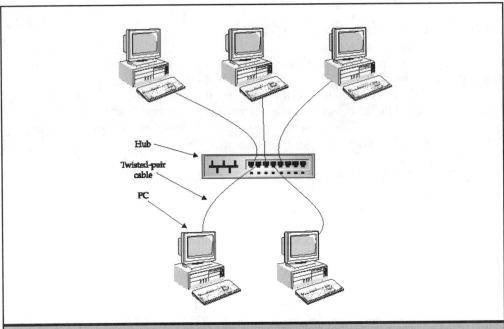

Figure 27-1.   *Star topology (with twisted-pair cable)*

Wireless LANs

In a *wireless LAN* there are no wires dedicated to network traffic. Each computer has a wireless network adapter, allowing the computers to communicate via radio waves, infrared, over the AC power wires in your walls, or over phone wires. Wireless LAN adapters enable you to put computers as far as 300 feet away from each other, depending on what walls and furniture are between them. The adapters include scrambling or encryption to prevent other computers from listening in on your data transmissions or adding themselves to your LAN.

A wireless LAN generally looks like a star topology LAN, but without the cable. The LAN includes one *access point* as the hub of the star. The access point connects to one computer on the LAN and contains a radio transceiver, hardware and software for communications and encryption, and a cable connection that lets you connect it to a cabled LAN, if you have one. The rest of the computers on the LAN have wireless LAN adapters that contain a radio transceiver, which communicates with the access point.

Two standards for wireless LANS—*IEEE 802.11b* and *Wi-Fi*—exist to ensure that wireless adapters from different manufacturers can communicate with each other. IEEE 802.11b networks can communicate at 11 Mbps, as fast as slower cabled networks. For more information about these standards, see **http://www.wirelessethernet.com**.

HomeRF is another standard based on IEEE 802.11b, but it is limited to home rather than business networks (see **http://www.homerf.org**).

Some wireless network adapters actually do use wires—they send data over the power wires in the walls of your house. These are still slower than cabled networks, though, and may be harder to troubleshoot than cabled networks. However, if you can live with the slower speeds, wireless networks can be very useful and easy to install in hard-to-cable buildings

Making the Choice

The cabling technology you choose determines the hardware you buy. Each standard has advantages and disadvantages. However, if you are starting a network from scratch, choose the cheaper and more common Fast Ethernet. If cabling would be a problem (for example, people using laptops will be moving around the building, or the architecture of the building would make cabling expensive), consider a wireless LAN.

From here on, this chapter discusses setting up an Ethernet network. However, the steps outlined here don't differ much for setting up a wireless network—instead of buying NICs, cabling, and a hub, you buy wireless LAN adapters and a wireless access point.

Bus Topology

Older networks used the *bus topology*, in which the *bus* is the main cable to which all the other computers are attached. (Communication within a computer also happens along a bus.) A *coaxial cable* (or *coax*) cable is connected from one computer to the next, in a long line, until all computers are connected. A network using bus topology looks like this:

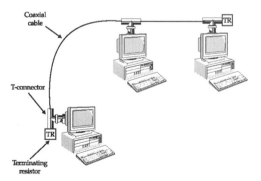

Unless you're adding computers to an existing small bus topology network, we recommend you use a star topology. Network interface cards with coaxial cable connectors are becoming hard to find.

Buying Network Hardware

You need the following hardware to set up your network:

Cabled LAN	Wireless LAN
A network interface card for each computer in the network.	A wireless LAN adapter with an antenna.
A connection among all the computers, most commonly, copper wires, but can also be fiber-optic cable, infrared, radio waves, or a mixture. The amount and type of cable you need depends on the topology you choose for your network.	Nothing.
A hub.	A wireless access point.

Note *If you are connecting only two computers with no plans to add additional computers, you may not need a hub or access point. You can use a crossover cable to connect the two computers.*

Take inventory of every computer that will be on the LAN and make a note of the type of slot each has available. You have to buy a network interface card or wireless LAN adapter that fits a slot in each computer. The easiest way to determine slot types is to check the documentation for each computer. PCI slots are most common for desktop computers. Laptops usually have PC Card slots (also called PCMCIA) that look like they fit a credit card. Both laptops and desktops may have Universal Serial Bus (USB) ports (a narrow rectangular plug) that may be used for some models of network cards, especially wireless NICs. You may be able to tell what kind of slot your computer has by taking the cover off and looking, and then describing the slot to your local computer store expert. However, it's safer to check your documentation for the type of architecture the motherboard has for each computer that will be on the LAN. You can and probably will mix cards of different slot types so long as the network type is consistent. For example, one of our networks has PCI and PCMCIA interface cards connected to a 100 Mbps Fast Ethernet.

For a cabled network, the hardware is not expensive to install—often less than $50 per PC on the network. You may be able to buy a network kit with all the hardware you need to set up a small network: network interface cards, cable, and a hub. For a wireless network, look into the wireless kits that are readily available at office supply and computer stores.

Buying Network Interface Cards (NICs)

Many new computers come with *network interface cards (NICs)* pre-installed. Check the back of the computer for a RJ-45 connector, which looks like a large phone jack. If you have to buy NICs, choose cards that

- Match the speed you chose for your Ethernet LAN—the two most common speeds are 10 Mbps and 100 Mbps. A good choice is a *10/100Base-T* card, which can handle both speeds and autonegotiates to choose the right one.

- Fit the cable you are using—usually Category-5 wire with a RJ-45 jack on the end that plugs into the computer.

- Fit the computer you buy it for—computers with PCI, ISA, PC Card, or other slots. If a computer doesn't have any available slots, consider a USB or parallel-port–based network adapter, if either of those ports is free. Contact your computer's manufacturer if you're not sure.

All the network interface cards in each computer in the network must support the same standard—in an Ethernet network, for instance, all network interface cards must be Ethernet cards. Decide whether you want a speed of 10 Mbps or 100 Mbps (or expensive Gigabyte) and buy cards that are all the same speed (most people base their decision on price). You should be able to find 10/100Base-T cards for desktop computers for under $20 and for laptops for under $50 in the United States.

Buying a Hub

If you've chosen a standard Ethernet network—star topology with Category-5 cable—you need a *hub*, a small box with lots of cable connectors. Buy a hub with enough connections for all the computers on your network. You may want a few extra connections, so you can add additional computers to the network later. Hubs are widely available with 4, 8, 16, or 24 ports. Instead of a hub, you can install a *switch*, which distributes information faster than a hub. A cheap four-port hub can cost less than $50. If you plan to connect a small LAN to a DSL line, consider a router, which combines a hub with a small computer that provides Internet connection sharing (see "Sharing an Internet Connection").

Caution *Although it's tempting, you cannot take a twisted-pair cable and connect two computers directly, unless you get a crossover cable. You need to connect the cable into a hub because the hub manages which pairs of wires inside your cable are used for transmitting and receiving data. If you try to connect two computers directly with a standard cable, the transmit and receive wires will be incorrect on one end, and your connection won't work. Even if you only have two computers, an inexpensive hub may be a good investment to ease network debugging and future upgrades.*

Buying Wireless LAN Adapters and Access Points

If you are planning a wireless LAN, you'll probably have better luck if all the computers on the LAN must use the same time of wireless LAN adapter—don't mix different wireless LAN adapters. A wireless LAN needs one access point (base station) as its hub. An access point costs about $200 and each computer's wireless LAN adapter costs from $100 to $150.

Buying Ethernet Cable

For a standard cabled Ethernet network, you need twisted-pair or Category-5 cable (as shown in Figure 27-1). The ends of these cables have RJ-45 connectors, which look like telephone cord connectors (the ones that plug into a telephone wall jack), but are about twice as big. When using twisted-pair cable, plug one end of each cable into a network interface card installed in a PC and plug the other end into the hub that's at the center of the star topology.

A general rule is not to run a cable more than 150 meters between computers (although the actual specifications for different types of cable in different types of networks may be greater). If you are connecting computers that are not close to each other, you need to do some research on how to create a network over medium distances.

To determine how much cable you need, decide where you are going to place the hub, and then measure from each computer to the hub's location. Remember to allocate extra cable to go around furniture and out of the way of office traffic, and add some slack to allow you to move the computer around—like pulling it away from the wall for repairs.

 When you buy your cable, remember string it so people don't trip over the cable. Measure carefully and allow extra—you can always hide cable that's too long. If your cable is too short, you'll have to go shopping again.

Installing Your Network Hardware

Now that you have all your parts—an NIC (or wireless LAN adapter) for each computer, enough cabling (or none, for a wireless LAN), and a hub (or wireless access point), you're ready to put it all together to create the physical network. This procedure is best done when the computers aren't in use and when you have a good chunk of time to devote to it—on a weekend.

Installing Network Interface Cards or Wireless LAN Adapters

The first step to installing your network hardware is to install a network interface card (or wireless LAN adapter) in each computer that will be on the network. Turn off each computer, take the cover off, install the NIC, and put the cover on again. For a laptop, this is usually as easy as sliding the card into the PC slot. For a desktop computer, this requires installing the card in a slot on the motherboard according to the manufacturer's installation instructions.

Once the NIC or wireless LAN adapter is installed, start the computer. Windows should detect the new hardware and ask you to install the adapter drivers for it (see Chapter 13).

Stringing Cable

For a cabled network, once the NIC and its driver are installed, you can connect the cabling. The computers can be turned on when you connect the cables.

Cabling can be a simple job or an extravagant one, depending on your needs and how much time, effort, and money you're willing to invest. A home office network that consists of two computers close together probably means cables running on the floor around the edge of the room and behind furniture. Cabling for an office probably means cables hidden by conduit, running inside walls, and running above dropped ceilings. You may want to hire someone if you have many computers to connect and want it done neatly. If you put cable inside ceilings or walls, be sure the installation conforms to fire and electrical codes.

When planning your wiring job, plan for the future. If you're wiring your office, add extra cables while the walls and ceiling are open. Put network jacks in the walls of any room that you think might have a computer in it some day. Plan your network cabling in the same manner you would plan phone extensions. Doing all the wiring now can make adding a computer to your network much easier in the future.

Run Category-5 cable from each computer to the hub. The RJ-45 jacks are easy to use—just plug the cable into the NIC and the hub as you would plug a phone wire into a phone jack.

 Don't run twisted-pair cable in a bundle with electrical power cable because the electromagnetic interference can adversely affect the network—a short-circuit between power and network cables could cause injury or fire.

Once you complete the construction phase, you need to sit at each computer and configure Windows so it knows about the network, as described in the next chapter.

Installing the Hub, Switch, or Wireless Access Point

Finally, put the hub, switch, or wireless access point in a location where it won't be disturbed. For a hub or switch, be sure to label each cable, so that when you are troubleshooting later, you can tell which cable goes to which computer. When you buy your Ethernet cable, you can choose different-colored cables.

Connecting Computers Without a LAN

While a LAN is the best way to use resources on another computer, you may find yourself in a situation where you want to share resources, but you don't have a LAN or the network card and cable needed to connect to one. Or you may be physically distant from the computer you want to connect to. If you don't have a LAN, but need to connect two computers you have two options:

- **Direct network connection**   If you are in close proximity to the computer you want to connect to, Windows allows you to connect computers using a serial or parallel cable or infrared ports (see "Designing a Windows-Based Local Area Network").

- **Dial-up connection**   You can dial into one computer from another using a regular phone line (see "Connecting Two Computers by Using a Dial-Up Connection").

- **Virtual Private Networking (VPN)**   If you are away from the other computer, you can connect using modems and phone lines (dial-up connection), using the Internet (VPN) (see "Connecting Computers with Virtual Private Networking").

These options are accessed though the New Connection Wizard, which you can display by clicking Create A New Connection in the Task pane of the Network Connections window (see Chapter 22, section "What Are Network Connections?"). See the sidebar "Displaying the Network Connections Window" for how to display it.

All three of these ways of connecting two computers require you to set up one computer to accept a connection from the other computer, by creating an *incoming connection* in the Network Connections window. An incoming connection tells Windows how the other computer can connect (by phone, by cable, or over the Internet) and who is authorized to connect (which user accounts can log in using the connection).

Connecting Two Computers with Direct Network Connection

A *direct network connection* (called a *direct cable connection* in previous versions of Windows) enables you to create a slow, but usable, network between two computers by using a serial cable or a parallel cable. You don't need a network card; all you need is the Windows XP or an earlier version of Windows that supports direct network connection. If both computers have infrared ports, you don't even need a cable.

If you need a continuous connection, you should invest in the hardware and time needed to set up a LAN as explained earlier in this chapter—the hardware isn't expensive, the setup isn't that onerous, and the performance and reliability are far better than a direct network connection. Although a direct network connection isn't a

Displaying the Network Connections Window

Because you'll be using the Network Connections window frequently if you use any of the connection options in this chapter, we recommend that you add the Connect To command to the Start menu, if it isn't there already. Follow these steps:

1. Right-click the Start menu and choose Properties to display the Start Menu tab of the Taskbar And Start Menu Properties dialog box.

2. Click the Customize button to display the Customize Start Menu dialog box.

3. Click the Advanced tab.

4. Scroll down in the Start Menu Items box until you see Network Connections. Choose either Display As Connect To Menu or Link To Network Connections Folder. Either of these options will make it easy to open the Network Connections window from the Start menu.

5. Click OK to close the two dialog boxes.

Now you can choose Start | Network Connections or Start | Connect To | Show All Connections to display the Network Connections window, depending on which option you chose in step 4.

If you choose not to add the Connect To command to the Start menu, you can open the Network Connections folder in one of the following ways:

- Choose Start, right-click My Network Places, and choose Properties from the shortcut menu.

- Open the Control Panel, click Network And Internet Connections, then click Network Connection.

- Open My Network Places and click View Network Connections. (My Network Places is one of the options in the task pane on most Explorer windows.)

good long-term solution to your network needs, it can be extremely useful when you need to transfer files between two computers. One particularly convenient use of a direct network connection is to hook up a laptop without a CD-ROM drive to a desktop machine to install new software using the desktop computer's CD-ROM drive, or to copy files to or from the laptop. Direct network connections are also useful with palmtop computers. A direct network connection can even enable you to access the network to which the host computer is attached.

When you attach two computers by using direct network connection, one computer is the *host computer*, the computer with the resources you want to use (usually a desktop computer). The other computer is the *guest computer*, the computer that needs to make use of the resources (such as reading from the CD-ROM drive or printing to the printer). The guest computer is frequently a laptop. A direct network connection is one-way: The guest computer can see and use any shared resources on the host computer, and it can access any shared network resources the host can access. However, the host computer cannot see the guest computer.

We had trouble getting direct network connections to work, but other Windows users have had better luck. If you can't get one working, consider a LAN.

Getting and Connecting Your Cable

The only piece of hardware you need for a direct network connection is a cable (direct network connection using modems is covered in the next section); however, you need the right kind of cable with the right kind of connectors on the ends. (If both computers have infrared ports, you don't need any cable.) The cable should be called a *null-modem cable*, LapLink cable, Serial PC-to-PC File Transfer cable, or InterLink cable. Before you go shopping, check for available ports on the two computers you want to connect. You can use parallel ports, but serial ports are preferable—they are probably labeled Serial, Com1, or Com2. (Serial ports are usually used for a mouse or modem; parallel ports are usually used for a printer.) If you're using parallel ports, look for a DirectParallel cable.

Serial ports come in 9-pin and 25-pin varieties (see Chapter 13, section "Serial (Com) Ports")—see what you have available on the computers you want to connect and get the cable with the appropriate connectors. If you're connecting a 25-pin serial port and a 9-pin serial port, try to get a cable with a 25-pin plug on one end and a 9-pin plug on the other. If you think you may create a direct network connection often—and with different computers—try to find an "octopus" cable with both kinds of plugs on both ends. Also check whether pins are on the port (male), in which case you need a female plug on the cable, or whether the plug on the cable needs to have pins (male). You can buy gender changers for the plugs, if necessary.

It's safer, but not absolutely required, to turn off both computers before connecting the cables. Note to which port the cable is attached—you need to know when you configure the connection. If you're using the parallel port, you must use the parallel port on both computers. If you're using serial ports, you can use either serial port: COM1 on one computer and COM2 on the other works fine.

When the cable is firmly connected to both ends, power up the two computers.

Both computers need to be members of the same workgroup. Click Start, right-click My Computer, choose Properties, and click the Computer Name tab in the System Properties dialog box to see the name of the workgroup that your computer belongs to. Click Change to change the workgroup name.

Configuring the Host Computer

The host computer needs a direct incoming connection, which you can create by following these steps:

1. Open the Network Connections window (see "Displaying the Network Connections Window").

2. Click Create A New Connection from the task pane to start the New Connection Wizard. Click Next to move from window to window. You see the options shown in Figure 27-2.

3. Choose Set Up An Advanced Connection and click Next.

4. Choose Connect Directly To Another Computer (yes, even though this is the host) and click Next.

5. Choose Host and click Next.

6. Choose the port to which the cable is connected (or select your infrared port) and click Next.

7. Select users who will be allowed to connect by clicking to display a check mark next to their user name, as shown in Figure 27-3. Click Next.

8. Click Finish to create the connection definition. An Incoming Connections icon appears in the Incoming section of the Network Connections window.

Note   *To create a direct network connection on the host computer, you must be logged on as Administrator or be a member of the Administrators group.*

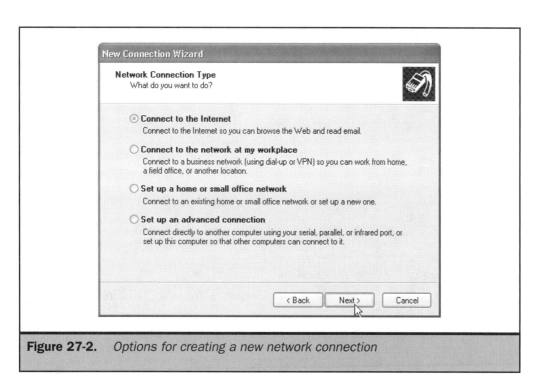

Figure 27-2.   *Options for creating a new network connection*

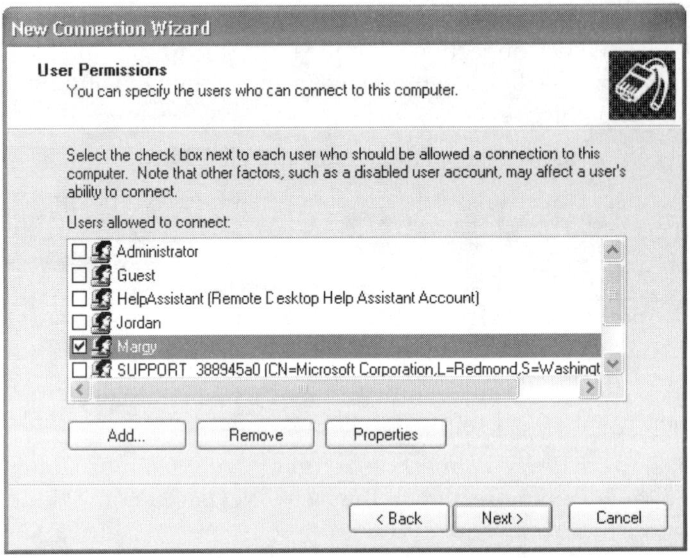

Figure 27-3. *Selecting which user accounts can use this incoming connection*

Configuring the Guest Computer

To configure the guest computer, you create a direct network connection by following these steps:

1. Open the Network Connections window (see "Displaying the Network Connections Window").

2. Click Create A New Connection in the task pane to start the New Connection Wizard. Click Next to move from window to window. You see the options shown in Figure 27-2.

3. Choose Set Up An Advanced Connection and click Next.

4. Choose Connect Directly To Another Computer and click Next.

5. Choose Guest and click Next.

6. Type a name for the connection and click Next.

7. Choose the port to which the cable is connected (or select your infrared port) and click Next.

8. If you want an icon on the desktop for this connection, click that option. Click Finish to create the connection definition. A new connection icon appears in the Direct section of the Network Connections window.

Using a Direct Network Connection

Once you have created connections on both the guest and the host computers, follow these steps to connect the two computers:

1. On the guest computer, open the Network Connections window (see "Displaying the Network Connections Window").

2. Open the icon for the cable connection.

3. Log in using a user name and password that you selected when you created the incoming connection on the host computer. Click Connect.

When the connection is established, the icon for the connection on the guest computer says "Connected." On the host machine, the Incoming Connection icon changes to show the user name. (We've also seen it change to say "Unauthenticated User," but the connection still works.)

Using the Host Computer's Resources from the Guest Computer

A direct network connection is one-way: The guest computer can see and use any shared resources on the host computer, but the host computer cannot see the guest computer. If you need to copy files from or to the host computer, do it while you're sitting at the guest computer.

To access the shared resources on the host computer from the guest computer, open the My Network Places folder. (Choose Start | My Network Places, or click the My Network Places icon in an Explorer window). Open the icon for the host computer to see available resources (to find out how to share resources and use shared resources, see Chapter 29).

If you have a direct network connection but don't see the host computer in My Network Places, try choosing Start | Run and typing \\hostcomputername. *Alternatively, you can type* \\hostIPaddress. *That command opens a window showing the shared resources on the host computer.*

Closing a Direct Network Connection

To close the connection, right-click the connection icon in the Network Connections window or in the notification area of the taskbar, and choose Disconnect.

Changing Connection Properties

You can change the properties for the connection by opening the Properties dialog box for the connection (right-click the connection icon in the Network Connections window and choose Properties).

Troubleshooting Direct Network Connections

Although a direct network connection should work if you follow the steps in this chapter, we have found the following useful to complete a successful connection:

- Check that the cable is securely attached to both computers.

- Check that each computer has a unique computer name and the same workgroup name. To change either, click Start, right-click My Computer, choose Properties, click the Computer Name tab, and click Change.

- Check that each communications port used has the same settings (bits/second, data bits, parity, stop bits, flow control). The baud rate should be 115,200 to maximize the speed of transfers.

- Install an additional protocol on both computers, such as IPX/SPX.

- Log into both computers using the same user name.

- If connecting using parallel ports, check that the BIOS parallel port settings are the same on both computers.

If you set up a direct network connection frequently between the same two computers, please build yourself a LAN: It's slightly more expensive in the short run, but more reliable, easier to work with, and much faster in the long run. You can also use a LAN to share an Internet connection.

Connecting Two Computers by Using a Dial-Up Connection

Dial-up connections are most frequently used to connect computers to the Internet (see Chapter 22, section "What Are Network Connections?"). However, you can also create one to connect your computer to another Windows computer through a modem. For example:

- If you have a desktop computer and a laptop computer, both with modems, you can use a dial-up connection to call your desktop from your laptop. (You need two phone lines.) Your laptop can share the resources (hard disks and printers) on your desktop.

- If you have a laptop computer that is usually connected to a LAN at your office, and another computer on the LAN has a modem, you can use a dial-up connection when you're away from your office to call that computer from your laptop and use facilities on the LAN. A dial-up connection is a slow way to access a LAN's resources but, in some cases, it is exactly what you need.

Note   *See Chapter 21 for information on setting up your modem. Chapter 22 has more information about dial-up connections.*

The computer you call using a dial-up connection is called the *remote access server*. The remote access server is usually a desktop computer back at the office. It has resources, such as files or a printer, that you want to use from the client computer, which is usually a laptop. Those resources must be shared. Chapter 29 discusses sharing disks and printers over a network. You cannot configure the resources for sharing from a remote location, so make sure you've shared all the necessary resources before you hit the road. You might even want to spend a day working on the laptop to discover what resources you might need to have configured for sharing while you're on the road.

When the remote access server computer is attached to a LAN, the client computer dialing in becomes a *remote node* on the network, meaning the client computer's connection to the network works exactly as it would if you were in the building and attached to the LAN—from the client computer, you can use resources on the network, and other computers on the network can see the shared resources on your computer. Of course, access from a remote node through phone lines is much slower than access from a computer that is connected to the network using cables.

Both the server and client computers must have a modem attached to a phone line (and, yes, you do need two different phone lines). Neither computer needs a network card. See Chapter 13 for instructions on how to configure Windows to work with your modem.

 If both computers are on the Internet, you can use the Remote Desktop feature of Windows XP to communicate between the two computers (see Chapter 15, section "Accessing Other Computers with Remote Desktop").

Configuring a Dial-Up Connection on the Client Computer

The client computer makes the call, using a dial-up connection. Follow these steps to create the dial-up connection:

1. Open the Network Connections window (see "Displaying the Network Connections Window").

2. Click Create A New Connection in the task pane to start the New Connection Wizard. Click Next to move from window to window.

3. Select Connect To The Network At My Workplace and click Next.

4. Select Dial-up Connection and click Next.

5. Type a name for the connection and click Next.

6. Enter the phone number for the host computer and click Next. Dashes and parentheses are not necessary, but you can use them if you wish.

7. Choose whether you want an icon for this connection on the desktop and click Finish. You see a new icon for the connection in the Dial-up section of the Network Connections window.

When you double-click the connection, Windows dials the phone, and if the host computer answers, you are asked to log in.

If you plan to call more than one remote access server, you can create additional dial-up connections by repeating these steps. If you need to change the phone number or modem, right-click the dial-up connection icon in the Network Connections window and choose Properties from the shortcut menu.

Configuring the Incoming Connection on the Dial-Up Server Computer

The remote access server must have a dial-up incoming connection, which tells Windows XP to answer the phone. Follow these steps:

1. Open the Network Connections window (see "Displaying the Network Connections Window").

2. Click Create a New Connection to start the New Connection Wizard. Click Next to move from window to window.

3. Select Set Up An Advanced Connection and click Next.

4. Select Accept Incoming Connections and click Next. You see the Devices For Incoming Connections window, as shown in Figure 27-4.

5. Choose the modem as the device for incoming calls. You can select more than one device, if you have more than one modem. Click Next. You see the Incoming Virtual Private Network (VPN) Connection window (see "Connecting Computers with Virtual Private Networking").

6. For accepting dial-up connections, it doesn't matter if you choose to allow virtual private connections or not. Click Next.

7. Select the users you want to allow to connect, as shown in Figure 27-3. Click Next.

8. You see a list of the network components that Microsoft suggests (see Chapter 28 for explanations of these components). Deselect any components that you don't want used. Generally, no change to this page is necessary. Click Next.

9. Click Finish. An icon called Incoming Connections is created in the Incoming section of your Network Connections window. If you already have an Incoming Connections icon, its properties are edited to allow dial-in access.

Once you configure a computer as a remote access server, be sure to read the section "Network Security Issues" later in this chapter.

Before you leave your remote access server computer, make sure it picks up the phone when the client computer calls in. Because this seemingly small glitch can totally ruin your plans to access network resources remotely, you might want to make a trial run before you go very far, following the steps in the next section.

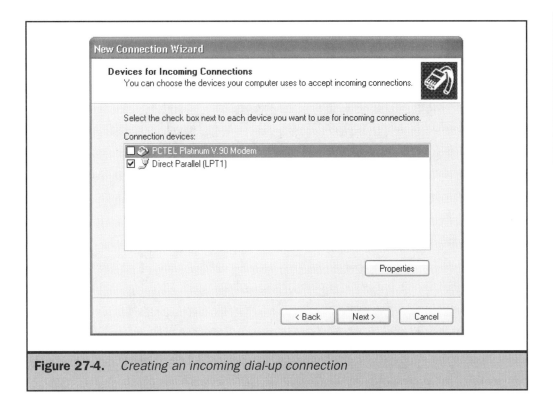

Figure 27-4. *Creating an incoming dial-up connection*

Connecting via a Dial-Up Connection

Once you configure both the client and the server computers, you can use the dial-up connection to connect the two computers. You can establish a dial-up connection by following these steps on the client computer:

1. Open the Network Connections window (see "Displaying the Network Connections Window").

2. Open the dial-up connection icon you created. You see the Connect To dialog box, shown in Figure 27-5.

> **Note** *Click the Dial Properties button to display the Dialing Properties dialog box (see Chapter 21, section "Configuring Windows for Dialing Locations"). You can use this dialog box to set properties for the different places from which you dial in.*

3. Type the password needed to access the dial-up server in the Password box.

4. Click Dial to make the connection to the dial-up server. Establishing the connection takes a few seconds. When the connection is made, you see a dialog box telling you that you are connected.

Figure 27-5.   *You see the Connect dialog box when you open your new Dial-Up Networking connection.*

Note   *When you want to close the connection, click the Disconnect button on the dialog box.*

Once you establish the connection, you can use My Network Places on the client computer to use resources on the dial-up server.

Connecting Computers with Virtual Private Networking

When you're away from your office, you may find that a dial-up connection (described in the previous section) using a regular phone line runs up large long-distance bills. You may also think that because you're connected to the Internet, and because the computer you want to access is connected to the Internet, you ought to be able to figure out a way to access resources using the Internet as your network. You are right!

Virtual Private Networking (VPN) provides a way for an authorized computer on the Internet to *tunnel* through the firewall and connect to a LAN. A VPN can allow you to connect to a single computer or to a LAN connected to the Internet.

When you are connecting to a LAN with a firewall, the firewall must support *Point-to-Point Tunneling Protocol (PPTP)*. PPTP lets VPN connect you through the firewall. Your organization's LAN administrator must have set up the firewall and a *VPN server*, the program that provides PPTP. Both the *VPN client* (the computer making the connection) and the VPN server must have Internet connections.

To connect to an existing VPN server, you don't have to worry about configuring the server. Contact your organization's system administrator to find out the host name or numeric IP address of the VPN server. However, if you are creating both the VPN client and the server, then you need to complete the steps in both of the following sections.

Note
The VPN server must have a routable IP address—that is, it must be directly on the Internet. If the computer you want to connect to shares an Internet connection, it is not accessible using VPN. Computers inside a firewall on a company LAN and those otherwise sharing an Internet connection (using ICS, for instance) do not have routable IP addresses.

Configuring the VPN Client

Follow these steps for creating a VPN connection on the client computer over the Internet:

1. Connect to the Internet.

2. Open the Network Connections window (see "Displaying the Network Connections Window").

3. Click Create A New Connection in the Network Tasks part of the Task pane to run the New Connection Wizard. Click Next to move from window to window.

4. Select Connect To The Network At My Workplace. Click Next.

5. Select Virtual Private Network Connection. Click Next.

6. Type a name for the connection in the Company Name box (like "VPN" or the name of your organization or the location of the VPN server). Click Next.

7. In the Public Network window, specify which Internet connection to use to connect to the Internet. If you'd prefer to make the Internet connection yourself, rather than allowing the VPN connection to initiate a connection, choose Do Not Dial The Initial Connection. Click Next.

8. In the VPN Server Selection window, shown in Figure 27-6, type the host name or numeric IP address of the VPN server (for example, **pptp.microsoft.com**). If you are connecting to an organization, get this information from your organization's system administrator.

To find out a computer's IP address, right-click the Internet connection in the Network Connections window, choose Status from the shortcut menu, and click the Details tab. The following blocks of IP addresses are reserved and not used on the Internet, so a computer with one of these numbers cannot be used in VPN: 10.0.0.0 through 10.255.255.255, 172.16.0.0 through 172.31.255.255, and 192.168.0.0 through 192.168.255.255.

9. You see a window confirming that you have created a VPN connection. Choose whether you want to add a shortcut for the connection to the desktop. Click Finish.

The VPN connection appears in a new Virtual Private Network section of the Network Connections window.

Now, when you want to connect to your VPN, open the VPN connection you just created. It connects to the Internet through the connection you specified in step 7 (unless you told it you wanted to make the connection yourself), and then connects to the VPN through the Internet.

 If your VPN server has a dial-in connection to the Internet, it may be issued a new IP address each session by its ISP. If so, you'll have to adjust the address on the VPN properties dialog box of the client computer before each connection.

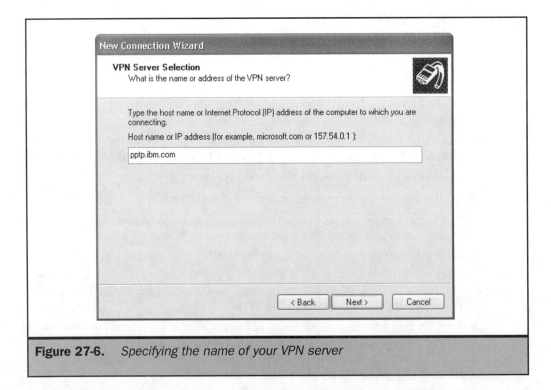

Figure 27-6.   *Specifying the name of your VPN server*

Configuring the VPN Server

To configure a computer to accept VPN connections, you must have an Incoming Connections icon in the Network Connections folder. If you already have this icon, double-click it to display the Incoming Connections Properties dialog box. Check that the Virtual Private Network option is selected (Allow Others To Make Private Connections To My Computer By Tunneling Through The Internet Or Other Network).

 Windows XP includes VPN server software that can accept only one incoming connection at a time. If you need more than one simultaneous VPN connection to your server, upgrade to Windows .NET Server.

If you do not have the Incoming Connections icon, follow these steps to create it and configure your computer to accept incoming VPN connections.

1. Open the Network Connections window (see "Displaying the Network Connections Window").

2. Click Create a New Connection to start the New Connection Wizard. Click Next to move from window to window.

3. Select Set Up An Advanced Connection and click Next.

4. Select Accept Incoming Connections and click Next.

5. The Devices For Incoming Connections doesn't include an option for the Internet, which is the actual device you'll be using. Deselect all modems and ports and click Next.

6. Select Allow Virtual Private Connections. Click Next.

7. Select the users you want to allow to connect. Click Next.

8. Deselect any protocols that you don't want used. Generally, no change to this page is necessary as long as TCP/IP is one of the selected protocols. Click Next.

9. Click Finish. An icon called Incoming Connections is created in your Network Connections window. If you already have an Incoming Connections icon, its properties are changed to support VPN.

Once you configure a computer as a VPN server, be sure to read the section "Networking Security Issues" later in this chapter.

Configuring a VPN Connection

You can display and change the settings for your VPN or incoming connection. In the Network Connections window, right-click the VPN or incoming connection and choose Properties from the menu that appears. The properties for clients and servers are different—the Properties dialog box for a VPN client connection is shown in Figure 27-7.

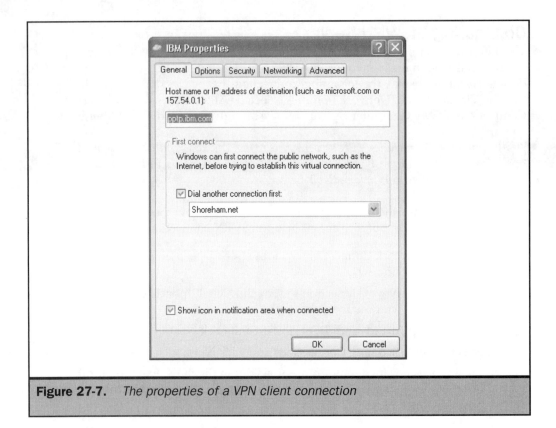

Figure 27-7.   *The properties of a VPN client connection*

On the General tab, you can change the host name or IP address of your company's VPN server or the Internet connection to use. The Advanced tab allows you to enable the Internet Connection Firewall, and to share the VPN connection.

The properties for the VPN server allow you to make changes to the options you selected with the New Connection Wizard. You can turn VPN on or off, display an icon in the notification area of the taskbar, and add and remove allowed users.

Networking Security Issues

When a computer is configured as a server that accepts dial-in or VPN connections, it is open to abuse by unauthorized users. Damage can include reading and destroying files on shared drives, as well as introducing viruses.

Be sure to disable Incoming Connections when you don't expect any. Here's how:

1. Open the Network Connections window (see "Displaying the Network Connections Window").

2. Double-click the Incoming Connections icon to display the Incoming Connections Properties dialog box.

3. Deselect the modem in the Devices box to disable dial-up networking, and deselect the Virtual Private Network option to disable VPN.

4. Click OK.

Repeat the same steps, but select the modem, to turn dial-up networking and VPN back on when you plan to use your computer as a server. Because networking does you no good when it's turned off, take some additional prudent security measures for the times you need it enabled:

- Keep your modem's phone number a closely guarded secret.

- Use passwords and change them regularly.

- Consider using the callback feature.

If your computer is a remote access server, you have the option of enabling *callback*. When callback is enabled, the caller logs in. Then, if login is accepted, the server disconnects and calls the client back.

Enable the callback feature by following these steps:

1. In the Network Connections window, open the Incoming Connections icon to display the Incoming Connections Properties dialog box.

2. Click the Users tab.

3. Select the user for whom you want to enable callback. Click Properties.

4. Click the Callback tab.

5. Choose either to Allow The Caller To Set The Callback Number, or to Always Use The Following Callback Number (and enter the number with any additional digits, such as 9, to get an outside line).

6. Click OK.

Chapter 28

Configuring Windows for a LAN

If you have a small number of computers (say, 20 or fewer), and they all run some version of Windows (any version since 3.11), you can set up a peer-to-peer local area network (LAN) using Windows as your network operating system. Read the previous chapter for how to choose a cabling technology, a cabling topology, and network interface cards, as well as how to install the necessary hardware.

Once the network interface cards are installed and the cable is strung, you still need to configure the networking software. You need to make sure that Windows' networking components are installed, and then configure the components. The easiest way to configure your computer to communicate over a LAN is usually to run the Network Setup Wizard, and then to test your network connection using the Ping program and the My Network Places window. Windows comes with some network troubleshooting tools, described at the end of this chapter. Once your computer can communicate over the LAN, read the next chapter to learn how to share folders and printers with other computers.

Note *This chapter describes how to connect your computer to a new or existing workgroup-based (peer-to-peer) LAN. If you are connecting to a domain-based LAN, contact your LAN administrator. If you are setting up a domain-based network, you'll need a computer running Windows .NET Server, Windows 2000 Server, or Windows NT Server to manage the domain—refer to* Windows 2000: The Complete Reference *or* Windows .NET Server: The Complete Reference, *both by Kathy Ivens (published by Osborne/McGraw-Hill).*

What Windows Components Are Needed for a Network?

No matter what kind of network you're attaching your Windows machine to, you must take some steps to configure it for the network (usually using a Wizard). Specifically, you must identify the client and the protocol the network uses. If you want to share your local resources (your hard drive or the printer attached to your computer, for instance), you also need to install a service. You work with these three types of network components:

- **Client** Specifies the type of network to which you are attaching: a Windows-compatible peer-to-peer network, a domain (a network managed by a Windows .NET, 2000, or NT Server), or another type of network (Novell NetWare, for example). Windows XP Home Edition doesn't support connecting to domains.

- **Protocol** Identifies the way information is passed between computers on the network. TCP/IP is the protocol used by the Internet, for example. The most commonly used protocols are described in the next section.

- **Service** Enables you to share resources on the computer (for example, file or printer sharing).

What Is a Network Protocol?

Without a protocol, the computers on your network won't know how to talk to each other. The *protocol* is the language your computer uses on the network. More than one protocol may be installed on a single computer, because computers can speak more than one language. Networks that use Microsoft software (such as the peer-to-peer network described in this chapter) usually use one of these three protocols:

- **TCP/IP (Transmission Control Protocol/Internet Protocol)**   The language spoken by computers on the Internet. Any computer using the Internet through a direct connection needs to have TCP/IP installed. Microsoft is standardizing on this protocol for all networking. See the next section for more details.

- **IPX/SPX (Internetwork Packet eXchange/Sequenced Packet eXchange)**   Used primarily by Novell in its NetWare operating system. IPX/SPX also works well for workgroup-based networks. Using IPX/SPX, rather than TCP/IP, for sharing files on networks that connect to the Internet provides more security. IPX/SPX isn't available in Windows XP 64-Bit Edition.

- **NetBEUI (NetBIOS Extended User Interface)**   Used primarily by Microsoft in its networking products. NetBEUI is fast and requires almost no configuration—it's by far the simplest protocol to use and configure. That simplicity has a drawback, however. NetBEUI is *nonroutable*, which means it works only on simple networks where routing devices aren't used to connect multiple segments of networks.

How Does TCP/IP Work?

When you use TCP/IP on a LAN, the network interface card in each computer on the LAN has an IP address on the LAN. IP addresses are in the format *xxx.xxx.xxx.xxx*, where each *xxx* is a number from 0 to 254. IP addresses are used on the Internet to identify Internet host computers and on LANs to identify the computers on the LAN. When you connect directly to the Internet, you also use TCP/IP, and your computer has an IP address to identify it to other computers on the Internet.

On a LAN that uses TCP/IP, computers usually use "private" IP addresses that are not used on the Internet. Several ranges of IP addresses have been set aside for private use. The most commonly used private IP addresses are in the format 192.168.0.*xxx*, where *xxx* is a number from 1 to 253. If one computer on the LAN connects to the Internet, that computer has the address 192.168.0.1, and the rest of the computers have addresses from 192.168.0.2 up to 192.168.0.253. Figure 28-1 shows a LAN with an IP address assigned to each computer.

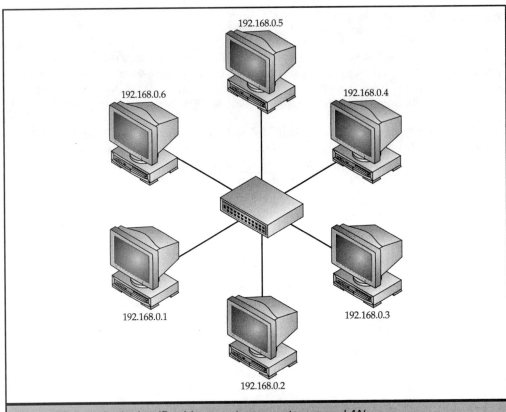

Figure 28-1.   *Assigning IP addresses to computers on a LAN*

How are IP addresses assigned? You can use one of three methods:

- **Static IP addressing**   You can assign the IP addresses yourself, using addresses in the format 192.168.0.*xxx*. You need to keep track of which addresses you've assigned, so that you don't give two computers the same address. Another problem is that ICS (Windows' Internet Connection Sharing program, described in Chapter 30) doesn't work with static IP addressing.

- **Automatic private IP addressing (APIPA)**   This Windows system assigns IP addresses to the computers on a LAN automatically (called *dynamic addressing*). The addresses are in the format 169.254.*xxx*.*xxx*, where each *xxx* can be a number from 1 to 253. You can't use APIPA addresses with ICS or on LANs that use DHCP addressing.

■ **DHCP (Dynamic Host Configuration Protocol) addressing**   A *DHCP server* is software that assigns IP addresses for the LAN. Like APIPA, DHCP assigns an IP address to your computer automatically, but it is designed to work with much larger LANs. ICS, which is part of Windows XP, includes a simplified DHCP server. Microsoft's TCP/IP networking systems generally use DHCP addressing. When you connect to the Internet over a DSL line, your ISP probably uses something like a DHCP server to assign your PC an IP address.

When you connect directly to the Internet, you don't have a choice about your address; your ISP assigns it for you. In the early days of dial-up connections, ISPs issued a static IP address with each Internet account. Now, most ISPs run DHCP-like servers that issue your computer an IP address each time you connect.

When setting up a LAN that uses TCP/IP, you must choose among these IP addressing methods. Use static addressing only for very small LANs (with fewer than 10 computers) that don't use ICS. If your network includes servers running Windows XP, 2000, NT, Linux, or Unix, it probably already uses DHCP. If you plan to share an Internet connection using ICS, it includes a DHCP server (see Chapter 30).

Note   *If your computer has more than one TCP/IP connection, it needs more than one IP address. For example, your computer might have a network interface card that connects it to the LAN, and another card that connects to a DSL modem that connects to the Internet. Each network interface card has one TCP/IP address.*

The section "Configuring the TCP/IP Protocol," later in this chapter, describes how to configure Windows to communicate using TCP/IP.

Identifying the Computer

For your computer to communicate with the other computers in your workgroup, you need to give the computer a unique name, identify the workgroup, and, optionally, provide a description:

■ **Computer name**   Naming your computer lets the users of other computers refer to your computer by name. Each computer on the LAN needs a unique name. If you are adding your computer to an existing LAN, check with the LAN administrator for the name to use. Some LAN administrators pick a convention to use to name all of their computers, such as names of cartoon characters, planets, friends, grade-school teachers, or each person using the computer. You may want to name your computers according to their primary function.

■ **Workgroup**   The *workgroup* is a group of computers on your network. The computers in a workgroup don't need to be physically close to each other, but they should be used by people who work together. The workgroup is a way to organize your peer-to-peer network's computers, similar to the way folders and subfolders organize the files on your PC. Check with your LAN administrator for the name of an existing workgroup. For a new LAN, the default name is MSHOME (although we prefer to use WORKGROUP as the name).

■ **Computer description**   Optionally, you can enter a description of the computer. Windows doesn't use this description during logon, but it does display it in the My Network Places window.

For example, a small network of five computers may all belong to the same workgroup called WORKGROUP. Within the workgroup, the computers might be named Pluto, Neptune, Jupiter, Saturn, and Mars, or Accounting, Sales, Marketing, Administration, and Shipping.

Note	*Larger networks use domains to centralize network administration and require a computer running Windows .NET Server, Windows 2000 Server, or Windows NT Server.*

When you configure your LAN using the Network Setup Wizard (described in the next section), the Wizard asks you for the computer name, workgroup, and computer description. You can also change them later (see "Changing the Computer Name, Workgroup, or Domain," later in this chapter).

Configuring and Viewing Your LAN Connections

Windows XP installs most networking components automatically, either when you install Windows or when it detects a network interface card among your computer's hardware (see Chapter 22, section "What Are Network Connections?"). The Network Setup Wizard can step you through the rest of the process of configuring your computer to communicate on your LAN, including setting up ICS (described in Chapter 30). The Wizard can also create a floppy disk containing a configuration program that you can use to configure other Windows systems to work with your network (to use this feature, you need a blank floppy disk). Once your computer is connected to the LAN, you can use the Network Connections window to see your connections and the My Network Places window to see folders on other computers (see Chapter 22, section "What Are Network Connections?").

Note	*In order to run the Network Setup Wizard or make any of the configuration changes described in this chapter, you must be logged in with an administrative user account (see Chapter 6).*

Windows XP Home Edition and Domain-Based LANs

You can use the Network Setup Wizard to connect to a domain-based LAN if you are running Windows XP Professional, but Windows XP Home Edition cannot log onto a domain. Either version can, however, dial into a company's domain-based network using a dial-up connection and your company's Remote Access Server (RAS). Or, if your office uses the Microsoft Exchange Server for e-mail, you can use Exchange's Web interface to read your mail. Check with your company's LAN administrator for instructions. Windows XP Home Edition can also connect to an Exchange server by using Outlook to send and receive mail without logging into the domain.

If you need to access files on a shared folder on your company's domain-based LAN, and if the folder is stored on a computer that has a static IP address (unlikely—ask your LAN administrator), you can map that shared folder to a drive letter on your computer and then access your files. Connect to the Internet. Then choose Start | All Programs | Accessories | Command Prompt to open a Command Prompt window (see Chapter 39, section "Using the Command Prompt Window"). Type **net use** *t: \\xxx.xxx.xxx.xxx\sharename* and press ENTER. Replace *t:* with any drive letter you aren't currently using. Replace *xxx.xxx.xxx.xxx* with the IP address of the computer on which the shared folder is stored, and *sharename* with the share name of the folder (see Chapter 29, section "Sharing Your Disk Drives and Folders with Others"). For example, you might type **net use t: \\215.26.128.137\helpdesk** to map your drive T: to the shared Helpdesk folder at work. When you see a prompt for your user name and password, type your user name and password on the domain. After a pause, during which the domain server authenticates your password, you connect. Now, drive T: (or whatever letter you used) on your computer is the shared folder on the computer at your office.

Running the Network Setup Wizard

After installing your network interface card (if it's not already installed) and attaching a cable to connect your computer to the LAN, follow these steps:

1. Connect to the Internet, if you have an Internet connection. Turn on all printers on the network, so that the Wizard can detect them.

2. Start the Network Setup Wizard by choosing Start | All Programs | Accessories | Communications | Network Setup Wizard. Alternatively, choose Start | Control Panel, click Network And Internet Connections, click

Network Connections, and click Set Up A Home Or Small Office Network in the Task pane. You see the Network Setup Wizard window.

3. Follow the instructions the Wizard displays, clicking Next to move to the next window. Tell it whether you dial into the Internet directly from this computer, you want to connect to the Internet over the LAN, or you don't connect to the Internet.

4. Provide a computer name for your computer (see Figure 28-2). On the Wizard's next screen, type the workgroup name. If you are attaching to an existing network, ask your LAN administrator for the workgroup or domain name to use. If you are setting up a new workgroup, use WORKGROUP as the workgroup (or MSHOME, as Windows XP Home Edition suggests). All computers that will share files on a small network need to use the same workgroup name.

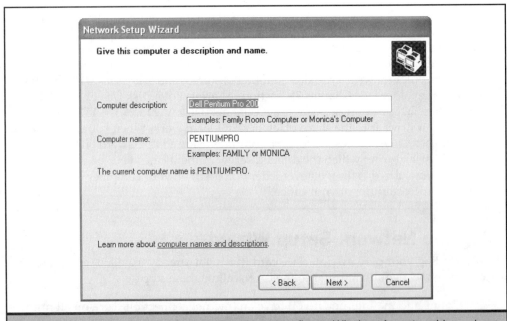

Figure 28-2. *The Network Setup Wizard can configure Windows's networking, along with Internet Connection Sharing.*

5. If you want the Wizard to create a Network Setup Disk with a LAN configuration program that you can run on Windows Me, 2000, 9*x*, and NT computers on your LAN, insert a blank floppy disk into the drive when the Wizard prompts you. Choose to create the disk if you are setting up a new network that includes computers running previous versions of Windows; otherwise, don't bother.

The Wizard installs the Client For Microsoft Networks, the TCP/IP protocol, and the File And Printer Sharing service to enable your computer to communicate on the LAN.

If you tell the Network Setup Wizard that you dial directly into the Internet and you want to share your Internet connection with other computers on the LAN, the Wizard installs ICS (see Chapter 30 for more information).

Viewing Network Resources with the My Network Places Window

When the Network Setup Wizard finishes, My Network Places should appear on the right side of your Start menu. My Network Places also appears as a choice in the Task pane of many Explorer windows and Open dialog boxes, enabling you to access shared folders on the network easily. When you choose Start | My Network Places, you see the My Network Places window, which is an Explorer window with shortcuts to network resources, as shown in Figure 28-3.

Note   *If My Network Places doesn't appear on the Start menu, Windows may not have found your network interface card. Check that it's listed and working by using the Device Manager (see Chapter 13, section "What Is the Device Manager?"). Or you may need to run the Network Setup Wizard as described in the previous section.*

The My Network Places window should list shared folders you can use. Click a shortcut to see the contents of the folder. Chapter 29 describes how to add folders on your computer to the list of folders that other people on your LAN can share, how to control who can use which folder, and how to share printers. My Network Places can also include shortcuts to Web and FTP servers on the Internet.

 Tip   *If you want a My Network Places icon to appear on your desktop, click Start, right-click My Network Places, and choose Show On Desktop from the menu that appears.*

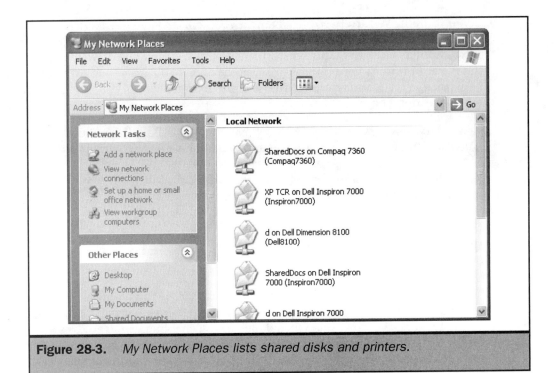

Figure 28-3.   *My Network Places lists shared disks and printers.*

Viewing Your Network Connections

To configure the network, you use the Network Connections window, shown in Figure 28-4. Choose Start | Control Panel, click Network and Internet Connections, and click Network Connections. Another way to display this window is by clicking Start, right-clicking My Network Places, and choosing Properties. Alternatively, if Connect To appears on the Start menu, choose Start | Connect To | Show All Connections.

The Network Connections window displays your LAN and Internet connections and lists network-related tasks. To check whether your computer can communicate with other computers on the LAN, click View Workgroup Computers on the Task pane. You should see a list of the other computers in your workgroup or domain.

 You also use the Network Connections window to configure Windows to communicate with an Internet account.

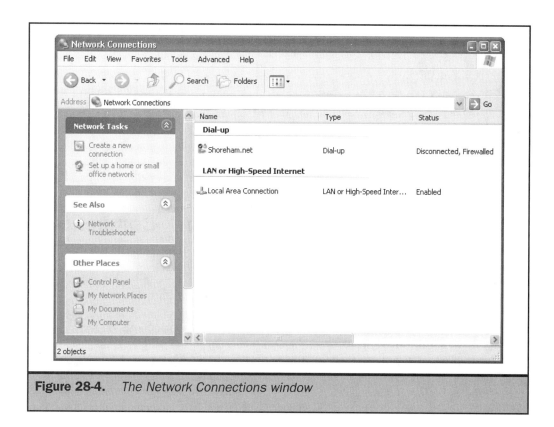

Figure 28-4. *The Network Connections window*

Running the Network Setup Wizard on Windows Me/98, 2000, and NT Systems

You can use the Network Setup Wizard to configure computers on your LAN even if they don't run Windows XP. If you created a Network Setup Disk when you ran the Network Setup Wizard (as described in the section "Running the Network Setup Wizard" earlier in this chapter), you can run the Network Setup Wizard on Windows 2000, Me, NT, or 9x computers on your LAN by putting the floppy disk in the drive, choosing Start | Run, typing **a:setup** in the Open box, and clicking OK. The Wizard may need to restart each computer after it runs.

If you didn't create a Network Setup Disk, you can run the Wizard from the Windows XP CD-ROM. Follow these steps:

1. Put the Windows XP CD-ROM in the computer's CD drive. If the Welcome To Microsoft Windows XP window doesn't appear, choose Start | Run and type **d:setup** (where *d* is the letter of your CD drive) to display it.

2. Choose Perform Additional Tasks.

3. Choose Set Up A Home Or Small Office Network.

4. Follow the Wizard's instructions, clicking Next to move from window to window.

Installing and Configuring Network Components

Running the Network Setup Wizard is usually all you need to do to set up a workgroup network or attach your PC to an existing workgroup. However, if you are connecting to a domain-based or other type of network, you may need to install, configure, or uninstall network components yourself. Talk to your LAN administrator before making any changes to your configuration.

For each networking connection listed in the Network Connections window, you can see its properties by right-clicking the connection and choosing Properties from the menu that appears. Figure 28-5 shows the properties of a LAN connection.

The Local Area Connection Properties dialog box lists the network interface card that connects your computer to the LAN. It also lists the clients, protocols, and services used for this network connection. The network interface card appears at the top, in the Connect Using box. The clients, protocols, and services are listed in the This Connection Uses the Following Items box, with icons that identify the different types of components:

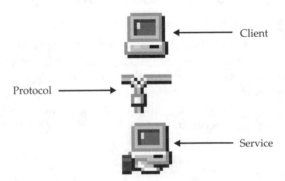

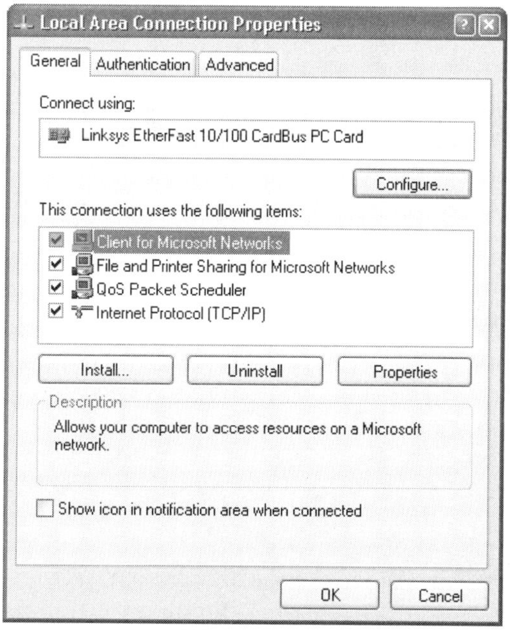

Figure 28-5.   *Properties of a LAN connection*

For a standard TCP/IP LAN, these four components should be installed (they should appear in your Local Area Connection Properties dialog box) and enabled (each check box contains a check mark):

- ■ **Client For Microsoft Networks**   Client that enables the computer to communicate with other Windows computers.

- ■ **File And Printer Sharing For Microsoft Networks**   Service that shares files and printers. This service should be enabled only on a LAN connection, not on an Internet connection.

- ■ **QoS Packet Scheduler**   Service that determines the precedence of information packets on the LAN based on Quality of Service (QoS) standards.

- ■ **Internet Protocol (TCP/IP)**   Protocol used on the Internet and many LANs.

If you have these four components and your LAN uses TCP/IP, you probably don't need to install any network components. Skip down to the section "Checking Your Network Connection," later in this chapter.

Installing and Configuring an Adapter

Chapter 13 described how to install a network interface adapter if your computer doesn't already have one. The *adapter* is the software driver that allows your PC to communicate with the network interface card in your PC. (Network interface cards are also called *network adapters*.) Every model of network interface card has its own driver, which must be installed so the client software knows how to package information and send it to the network interface card.

Your network adapter appears in the Connect Using box of the Local Area Connection Properties dialog box (Figure 28-5). Click the Configure button to see the Properties dialog box for the network interface card (see Chapter 13, section "What Are Drivers?").

Installing a Client

The next step is to install the client component, which identifies the type of network on which your computer will be. When you configure your network connection (or when Windows finds your Plug and Play network interface card), Windows also installs the Client For Microsoft Networks. If a client is installed, it appears in the This Connection Uses The Following Items dialog box in the Local Area Connection Properties dialog box (Figure 28-5).

Because you are installing a peer-to-peer Windows network, the Client For Microsoft Networks is the one you need. (It is similar to the Workstation service that came with Windows NT 4.0 Workstation.) If you mistakenly deleted your Client For Microsoft Networks, or if you need the Client Service For NetWare (which also comes with Windows XP), follow these steps:

1. Display the Local Area Connection Properties dialog box (by clicking Start, right-clicking My Network Places, choosing Properties, right-clicking Local Area Connection, and choosing Properties). Click the General tab (if it's not already selected).

2. Click the Install button. You see the Select Network Component Type dialog box:

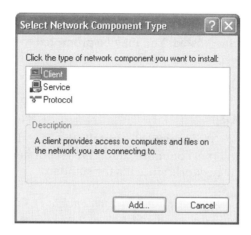

3. Select Client as the type of network component you want to install and click the Add button. You see the Select Network Client dialog box.

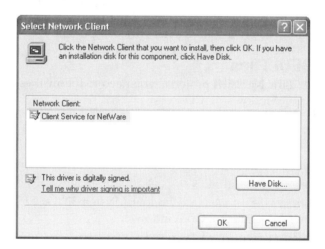

4. Choose the network client. If you have a floppy disk or CD with software for another type of client, insert it now and click Have Disk.

5. Click OK. You return to the Local Area Connection Properties dialog box, with the client you just defined listed. You may be prompted to insert the Windows XP CD-ROM.

6. Click OK to save your changes.

Installing a Protocol

When you install Windows, it automatically installs the TCP/IP protocol, in case you want to use TCP/IP for Internet communication. We recommend that you use TCP/IP if you are setting up a new network, since it's the standard.

 You can delete protocols you don't use, but don't delete TCP/IP! We did so, and ended up needing to reinstall Windows in order to get it back.

Starting with Windows XP, Microsoft no longer supports NetBEUI. If you use NetBEUI for a small network, you have two choices: install NetBEUI from the Windows XP CD-ROM, even though Microsoft no longer supports it, or upgrade all the computers on your LAN to TCP/IP. Windows XP also comes with support for NetWare's IPX/SPX protocol, which you can easily install as a network component.

Copying NetBEUI Files

Before you can install the NetBEUI protocol, you need to follow these steps to copy the files by hand from the Windows XP CD-ROM:

1. Put the Windows XP CD-ROM in the drive. Choose Perform Additional Tasks, and then Browse This CD.

2. In the Explorer window that appears, locate the Valueadd\msft\net\netbeui folder on the CD.

3. Copy the Nbf.sys file into the C:\Windows\System32\Drivers folder (assuming that Windows is installed in C:\Windows).

4. Copy Netnbf.inf into the C:\Windows\Inf folder.

After copying the files, you can install NetBEUI, as described in the next section.

Installing NetBEUI or IPX/SPX

Installing a protocol is similar to installing other network components. Follow these steps to install NetBEUI or IPX/SPX:

1. Display the Local Area Connection Properties dialog box (by clicking Start, right-clicking My Network Places, choosing Properties, right-clicking Local Area Connection, and choosing Properties). Click the General tab (if it's not already selected).

2. Click the Add button to display the Select Network Component Type dialog box.

3. Select Protocol and click the Add button. You see the Select Network Protocol dialog box, shown in Figure 28-6.

4. Select NetBEUI or NWLink IPX/SPX/NetBIOS Compatible Transport Protocol and click OK.

5. You return to the Local Area Connection Properties dialog box, with the protocol you just defined listed. You may be prompted to insert the Windows XP CD-ROM.

6. Click OK to save your changes.

Setting the Order of Your Protocols

When you install a protocol, Windows "binds" the new protocol to all the clients and services you have available—usually File And Printer Sharing For Microsoft Networks and Client For Microsoft Networks. A *binding* tells Windows to use a specific protocol with a specific client or service.

You might not want to use all of your installed protocols to work with all your installed clients and services. You can control which protocols work with which clients and services, and which protocol Windows should try first, by opening the Network Connections window (choose Start | Control Panel, click Network And Internet Connections, and click Network Connections) and choosing Advanced | Advanced Settings. You see the Advanced Settings dialog box, shown in Figure 28-7. Click the Local Area Connection

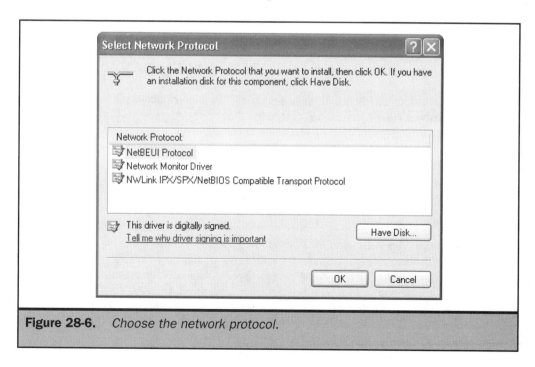

Figure 28-6. *Choose the network protocol.*

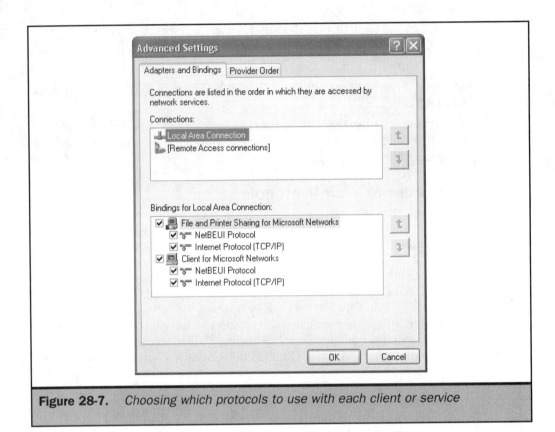

Figure 28-7.   *Choosing which protocols to use with each client or service*

in the Connections box (if it's not already selected). The lower part of the Adapters And Bindings tab shows your client and services for that connection, with your installed protocols listed under each client or service.

You can switch the order of the protocols, so that the one you plan to use most often appears first. Click the protocol and click the up- or down-pointing arrow button to move it. If you don't plan to use a protocol with a particular service, deselect the check box by the protocol.

Tip   *If you connect to the Internet through a hub or router than doesn't provide a firewall between your computers and the Internet, don't use TCP/IP for your file and printer sharing. Instead, on each computer on your LAN, install the IPX/SPX protocol, as described in "Installing a Protocol," earlier in this chapter. Then use the Advanced Settings dialog box on each computer to disable Internet Protocol (TCP/IP) for File And Printer Sharing For Microsoft Networks. Leave IPX/SPX enabled, so that all the computers can use that protocol for file and printer sharing. Leave TCP/IP installed for use by your Internet connection.*

Configuring the TCP/IP Protocol

If you use TCP/IP for communication on your LAN, you need to assign an IP address to your computer's network interface card, using static addressing or DHCP (see "How Does TCP/IP Work?"). For a laptop, you can also use an alternate configuration, for when the computer isn't connected to its regular network. Follow these steps:

1. Display the Local Area Connection Properties dialog box (by clicking Start, right-clicking My Network Places, choosing Properties, right-clicking Local Area Connection, and choosing Properties). Click the General tab (if it's not already selected).

2. On the list of network components that the connection uses, select Internet Protocol (TCP/IP).

3. Click Properties. You see the Internet Protocol (TCP/IP) Properties dialog box:

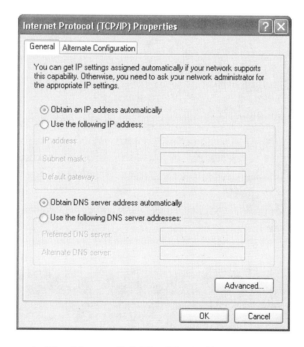

4. To assign a static IP address, click Use The Following IP Address. In the IP Address box, type the IP address you've chosen. Windows supplies the dots that separate the four parts of the address.

5. In the Subnet Mask box, type **255.255.255.0**.

6. To use DHCP or APIPA (systems that assign an IP address to your computer when Windows starts up), select Obtain An IP Address Automatically. If your

LAN has a DHCP server, Windows will get IP addresses from the server each time you start Windows. If not, Windows will assign itself an address.

7. If you have a laptop that connects to a LAN in a different way when you are not at your desk, click the Alternate Configuration tab. Your IP addressing choices are Automatic Private IP Address (APIPA) or User Configured (a static address).

8. Click OK in each dialog box.

Installing a Service

A service is the last network component you install. It also is the only optional component. Your network can work fine without a service, but no one on the network will be able to share resources, such as hard disks, CD-ROM drives, files, or printers. If you don't want to share resources, don't install any services.

Even when a service has been defined, you can add some security measures to ensure that the resources on your computer are not abused (see Chapter 29, section "Using Shared Drives and Folders with Passwords").

If you are creating a peer-to-peer network of Windows computers, you need the File And Printer Sharing For Microsoft Networks service. This service is installed automatically by the Network Setup Wizard. If you need to install it (or another service) yourself, follow these steps:

1. Display the Local Area Connection Properties dialog box (by clicking Start, right-clicking My Network Places, choosing Properties, right-clicking Local Area Connection, and choosing Properties). Click the General tab (if it's not already selected).

2. Click the Add button to display the Select Network Component Type dialog box.

3. Select Service and click the Add button. You see the Select Network Service dialog box:

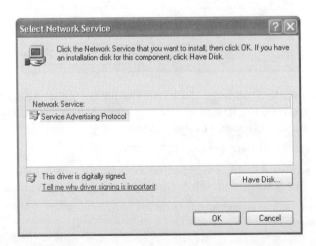

4. Select the service you want and click OK.

5. You return to the Local Area Connection Properties dialog box, with the protocol you just defined listed. You may be prompted to insert the Windows XP CD-ROM.

6. Click OK to save your changes.

Changing the Computer Name, Workgroup, or Domain

To see or change your computer's name and which workgroup or domain it is in, follow these steps:

1. Click Start, right-click My Computer, and choose Properties from the menu that appears. You see the System Properties dialog box.

2. Click the Computer Name tab, shown in Figure 28-8.

3. Type a description of the computer in the Computer Description box. This description appears in the My Network Places window.

4. To change the computer name or workgroup, click the Change button to display the Computer Name Changes dialog box:

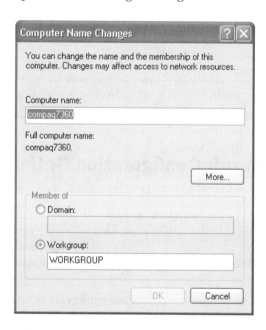

5. In the Computer Name box, type a unique name for the computer.

6. If the computer is part of a workgroup, choose Workgroup in the Member Of section of the dialog box and type the workgroup name in the box. If the computer is part of a domain, choose Domain and type the domain name.

7. Click OK. You may see a message telling you to restart Windows for your changes to take effect.

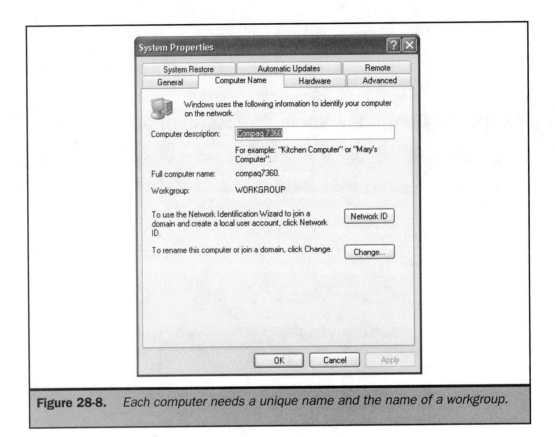

Figure 28-8.   *Each computer needs a unique name and the name of a workgroup.*

Setting Other Network Configuration Options

Here are a few other options that you can configure for your LAN connection:

- **Showing an icon in the notification area**   If you would like to see an icon for the LAN connection in the notification area (the right end of the taskbar, next to the clock), display the Local Area Connection Properties dialog box, click the General tab, and select the Show Icon In Notification Area When Connected check box.

- **Wireless networks**   Wireless LANs use radio waves rather than cables to communicate. One computer has an access point, which serves as the hub for the LAN (see Chapter 27, section "Wireless LANs"). The other computers have wireless LAN cards with antennas for communicating to the access point. If your computer has a wireless LAN connection, it appears as a local area connection in the Network Connections window (choose Start | Control Panel, click Network And Internet Connections, and click Network Connections). Right-click the connection and click the Wireless Networks tab to configure the connection.

■ **Bridging two networks**   If you have two network interface cards, and each one connects your computer to a network, your computer can *bridge* (connect together) the two networks. In the Network Connections window, select the two (or more) LANs (by clicking one and CTRL-clicking the others). Choose Advanced | Bridge Connections from the menu bar. You can't bridge a connection that has the Internet Connection Firewall or ICS enabled. Network bridges are useful for connecting a wireless LAN to your regular cable-based LAN. (Network bridging isn't available in Windows XP 64-Bit Edition.)

Caution	*Don't bridge anything to an Internet connection. Doing so would create a wide-open security hole into your LAN!*

■ **Optional network components**   Windows XP comes with several optional services that you can install, but none of them is commonly used on small peer-to-peer networks.

■ **Authentication using smart cards**   Windows can use IEEE 802.1X-standard authentication, which supports smart cards and other access controls. In the Local Area Connection Properties dialog box, click the Authentication tab.

Checking Your Network Connection

The Network Setup Wizard usually installs and configures your network components correctly. This section describes how to discover your computer's IP address and how, to try rudimentary network communication.

Checking Your TCP/IP Address

Windows can display your computer's IP address and other TCP/IP settings. In the Network Connections window (choose Start | Control Panel, click Network And Internet

Connections, and click Network Connections), right-click a connection and choose Status from the menu that appears. You see a window like this:

Click the Support tab to see your IP address:

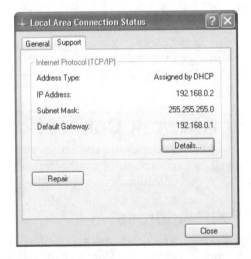

You can also see where the IP address came from (in this example, it was assigned by a DHCP server). For details, click the Details button. You can click Repair to re-request an IP address from the DHCP server.

Another way to see your IP address and other information is by running the Ipconfig program. Choose Start | All Programs | Accessories | Command Prompt to open a

Command Prompt window (see Chapter 39, section "Using the Command Prompt Window"). Then type **ipconfig /all** and press ENTER. You see a listing like this:

```
Windows IP Configuration

        Host Name . . . . . . . . . . . . : inspiron7000
        Primary Dns Suffix  . . . . . . . :
        Node Type . . . . . . . . . . . . : Hybrid
        IP Routing Enabled. . . . . . . . : No
        WINS Proxy Enabled. . . . . . . . : No

Ethernet adapter Local Area Connection:

        Connection-specific DNS Suffix  . : mshome.net
        Description . . . . . . . . . . . : EtherFast 10/100 PC Card
        Physical Address. . . . . . . . . : 00-E0-98-04-47-15
        Dhcp Enabled. . . . . . . . . . . : Yes
        Autoconfiguration Enabled . . . . : Yes
        IP Address. . . . . . . . . . . . : 192.168.0.4
        Subnet Mask . . . . . . . . . . . : 255.255.255.0
        Default Gateway . . . . . . . . . : 192.168.0.1
        DHCP Server . . . . . . . . . . . : 192.168.0.1
        DNS Servers . . . . . . . . . . . : 192.168.0.1
        Lease Obtained. . . . . . . . . . : Tuesday, July 31, 2001
        Lease Expires . . . . . . . . . . : Wednesday, August 01, 2001
```

The Dhcp Enabled line tells you whether your computer got its IP address from a DHCP server, and if so, the Lease Obtained line tells when your computer got the address. If your computer uses ICS, the Default Gateway, DHCP Server, and DNS Servers, entries are 192.168.0.1 (see Chapter 30).

Testing Your TCP/IP Connection

Once you've installed and configured the network components for a computer, you need to see whether your network works. Sit down at any of the computers on the network and follow these steps:

1. Use the Ping program to ping yourself—that is, ping your own computer's IP address (see Chapter 22, section "Testing Communication with Another Computer by Using Ping"). In the Network Connections window (choose Start | Control Panel, click Network And Internet Connections, and click Network Connections), right-click your LAN connection, choose Status, and click the Support tab to find out your own computer's IP address. If this step doesn't work, TCP/IP isn't correctly installed on your computer, or it's not getting an IP address. (The Ipconfig program described in the previous

section pings your own computer to get some of the information the Ipconfig displays.)

2. Ping another computer on the LAN to see whether information can travel from your computer to another. Follow the instructions in the previous section first to determine the IP address of a computer on the LAN to ping. (Trying pinging your default gateway, which is frequently at 192.168.0.1.) If this step fails, your LAN cable or connection may not work.

3. Open the My Network Places window (choose Start | My Network Places) to see what appears. If you are part of a small network (fewer than 32 computers), shortcuts shared folders on the other computers should appear automatically. Otherwise, you can click Add A Network Place to add shortcuts to folders (see Chapter 29, section "Using Network Drives with My Network Places"). If this step doesn't work, your workgroup name may not be set correctly.

4. If you don't see shortcuts in the My Network Places window, there's another way to connect to other computers on the LAN. Click View Workgroup Computers in the Task pane of the My Network Places window. You see the names of all the computers in the workgroup. Open an icon (click or double-click it, depending on how you have Windows configured) to see the folders and printers that are available on that computer. If you see Entire Network as an entry, open it. Then open Microsoft Windows Network, and then open your workgroup. The computers in your workgroup should appear.

5. If you still don't see icons for the other computers on the network, read through the section "Troubleshooting Your Network," later in this chapter, to find and fix the problem. If you see only your own computer in the workgroup, or the Entire Network window is blank, communication has broken down with the other computers. It could be physical, like a bad cable, or it could be a problem with your software configuration, such as using the wrong protocol.

Once your network is working, the next step is to use it to share resources (see Chapter 29).

Viewing LAN Resources with the Net Command

You can see a list of the shared resources of a computer on the LAN by using a command-line program called Net. Open a Command Prompt window by choosing Start | All Programs | Accessories | Command Prompt. Then type **net view //computername** and press ENTER. Replace *computername* with the name of a computer on the LAN. For example, the command **net view \\dell8100** might produce this listing:

```
Shared resources at \\dell8100

Dell Dimension 8100
```

```
Share name      Type        Use as    Comment
---------------------------------------------------
D               Disk
SharedDocs      Disk
PRINTER         Print
The command completed successfully.
```

If the computer has no shared resources, you see the message "There are no entries in the list." If you don't have permission to view the shared resources on that computer, you see the message "Access is denied." If you see the message "System error 53 has occurred," the computer name is wrong, the computer is not on the LAN, or File And Printer Sharing for Microsoft Networks isn't running on that computer.

You can see a list of all the shared resources on your own computer by typing **net share**.

 The Net View command works with all installed protocols. Ping works only with TCP/IP.

Viewing LAN Usage

If you are worried that your LAN is slowing down because it can't handle the volume of data, Windows can display a graph of LAN utilization. Press CTRL-ALT-DELETE to see the Windows Task Manager window (see Chapter 34, section "Monitoring System Use with the Task Manager"). Click the Networking tab to see this window:

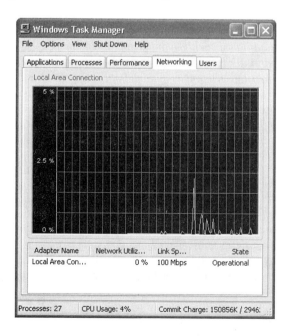

The graph shows network usage over time, as a percentage of the amount of data that it could carry. Unless you are copying huge files (for example, if you do backups over the LAN), the percentages usually stay amazingly low.

Troubleshooting Your Network

Although Windows networking generally works well, you may have trouble with one computer or all of the computers on the network, especially when you first set up the network. This section recommends some steps to take to solve your problems.

If you have trouble with the IP addresses on the LAN, use the Networking (TCP/IP) Troubleshooter. Choose Start | Help And Support, click Fixing A Problem in the Pick A Help Topic list, click Networking Problems, and click Home And Small Office Networking Troubleshooter. Another useful program is Network Diagnostics. To use it, type **Network Diagnostics** in the Help And Support Center window's Search box and press ENTER.

The solutions to some common problems and solutions follow:

- **The "Local Area Network: A Network Cable Is Unplugged" message appears**   If you see this message in a pop-up window from the notification bar of the taskbar, the message is probably right—the cable from your computer to the LAN hub is unplugged or damaged. When you fix the connection, the message goes away.

- **Computer can't log onto a domain**   You can't log onto a domain-based LAN if you use Windows XP Home Edition; only Windows XP Professional can log on to a domain.

- **Computers do not appear in My Network Places**   If a computer doesn't appear in your My Network Places window when you click View Workgroup Computers, it may have a loose cable connection, a bad cable, or a network interface card that isn't working properly. Check all of the cable connections. Occasionally, cables become damaged, so you might want to try replacing a suspect length of cable with one you know is good. Use Ping to see whether the computer can communicate (see Chapter 22, section "Testing Communication with Another Computer by Using Ping").

- **Shared folders don't appear in My Network Places**   The My Network Places window contains shortcuts to shared folders on the LAN, but these shortcuts can be deleted. If a shared folder you need doesn't appear in My Network Places, click Add A Network Place in the Task pane (see Chapter 29, section "Using Network Drives with My Network Places"). Try searching for the computer name by choosing Start | Search, and choosing Computers Or People at the What Do You Want To Search For prompt (if you don't see that prompt, click More Advanced Options and then Other Search Options).

■ **Bad or missing protocol**   A protocol may be missing or incorrectly configured. Check to see that your computer is speaking the same language as all the others. If the other computers are using NetBEUI and you are using TCP/IP, you will not be able to communicate with them. Open the Network Connections window, right-click the Local Area Connection icon, and choose Repair from the menu that appears. Windows will try to reinstall any missing components. Also, check which protocols the other computers are using to communicate, and install that protocol on the computer that is incommunicado.

■ **Network interface card problem**   You may have a hardware conflict. Use the Device Manager to see whether there's a problem with the network interface card. If the network interface card appears with a yellow exclamation point, the card isn't working properly. Check the installation instructions for your card.

■ **Password problems**   If Windows asks for a password when you try to use a shared folder or printer, you may need to find out the password for that resource or have your user account name added to the list of users who can address the resource. See Chapter 29 for more information on sharing resources.

The Complete Reference

Windows XP

Chapter 29

Sharing Drives and Printers on a LAN

If you have a LAN, you probably set it up because you have resources that you want to share. Perhaps you have three computers and only one printer. Perhaps several people use a database from different computers, and you want to make sure that they're always working with updated information. Whatever the reason, your LAN isn't much good if you don't know how to share your hardware and files.

This chapter tells you how to share disks and folders on your own computer, use shared disks and folders on other computers, and choose which of your own disk drives to make available to other people on your LAN. We also describe how to share the printers on your system and how to use printers on other people's systems.

> **Note**   *This chapter assumes that you have connected your computer to a workgroup-based LAN and have installed file-sharing and printer-sharing services (see Chapters 27 and 28). If your computer is connected to a domain-based LAN, contact your LAN administrator for information about what shared resources are available.*

Network drives (also called *shared drives*) are disk drives that have been configured to be available for use from other computers on the LAN. Similarly, *shared folders* are folders that have been configured to be usable by other computers on the LAN. For a disk drive or folder to be shared by other people on a LAN, it must be configured as sharable. Once a drive or folder is sharable, other people can read and write files on the disk drive or in the folder. Microsoft makes sharing a whole drive a little more difficult than sharing just a folder because of the security risks involved.

Enabling Hardware Sharing

To share your hardware—disk drives and printers—with others on the LAN, you need to make sure that sharing is enabled. For a workgroup-based, peer-to-peer network, see "Installing the Service" in Chapter 28 to install File And Printer Sharing For Microsoft Networks. For a domain-based network, ask your LAN administrator what you need to do.

Installing file and printer sharing does not automatically share your printer and disk drives—that could compromise security. Instead, you choose exactly which resources to share on your computer by using the commands covered in this chapter.

Using Shared Drives from Other Computers

You can access a shared drive or shared folder in one of two ways:

- If you use the drive or folder only occasionally, you can use My Network Places to access the drive.

- If you use the drive or folder frequently, you can *map* the drive or folder, which means that you assign the drive or folder a letter so that it appears on the drop-down list of drives in Open and Save As dialog boxes.

Using Network Drives with My Network Places

You can see a list of the shared drives and folders to which you have access. The My Network Places window, shown in Figure 29-1, lists *network shortcuts* to all the shared drives and folders available to you on the LAN. Choose View | Details to display all the information about each shared drive.

The name of each shared drive or folder appears, along with its UNC (Universal Naming Convention) address—the path name you use when referring to that shared drive or folder. The UNC address consists of two backslashes, the name of the computer, another backslash, and the share name of the drive or folder (see "Sharing Your Disk Drives and Folders with Others").

To display the My Network Places window, use one of these methods:

- Choose Start | My Network Places.

- Open any folder (such as My Computer or My Documents) and click the My Network Places link in the Task pane on the left.

- Use Windows Explorer (where the folder tree is showing) and click My Network Places near the bottom of the folder tree.

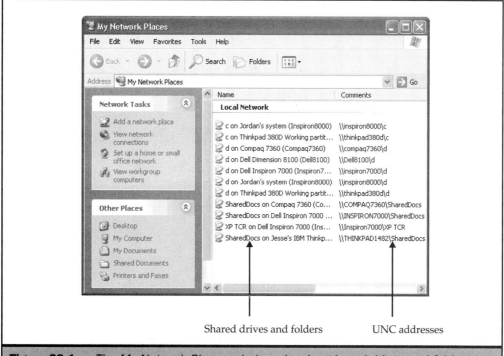

Shared drives and folders   UNC addresses

Figure 29-1.   *The My Network Places window showing shared drives and folders on the LAN*

If you don't see a list of shared folders, consider troubleshooting your network (see Chapter 28, section "Troubleshooting Your Network"). If one or two shared folders are missing, click Add A Network Place in the Task pane to add it. This command is also useful for adding Web servers and FTP servers to your My Network Places window (see Chapter 26, section "Working with FTP and Web Servers Using Web Folders").

You can change the name of a shared drive or folder as it appears on your computer. For example, if a drive appears as "data drive on Dell" and you'd rather see the name "Accounting Data," you can rename it by right-clicking the shared drive or folder in an Explorer window, choosing Properties from the shortcut menu that appears, and editing the contents of the box at the top of the Properties dialog box. Renaming a shared drive or folder on your computer doesn't change its real name on the computer on which it's stored, just how it appears in your Explorer windows.

Opening and Saving Files on Shared Drives and Folders

You can see the folders and files on a shared drive by opening the drive or folder in the My Network Places window. Once you see the drive, you can work with it as you do any drive on your own computer (see Chapter 7, section "Working with Windows Explorer").

My Network Places is also available from dialog boxes of any applications you use. It appears in the Places bar on the left side of the dialog box (see Chapter 2, section "Open, Save As, and Browse Dialog Boxes"). Figure 29-2 shows a Save Message As

Figure 29-2.   *Using a shared drive or folder by using My Network Places from an Open or Save As dialog box*

dialog box from Outlook Express, with the contents of My Network Places displayed. If the dialog box doesn't have a Places bar down the left side, click the Save In or Look In box at the top of the dialog box and choose My Network Places from the drop-down menu. Once you have opened My Network Places, move to the folder and file you want. A few programs don't allow saving to a network drive unless you assign it a drive letter, which is covered in the next section.

Mapping a Shared Drive or Folder to a Drive Letter

If you use a shared drive or folder frequently, you can assign it a drive letter. The process is easy, and when you want to find or save a file to the shared drive or folder, you don't have to spend so much time navigating through My Network Places to find it.

For example, if you frequently use files on drive D of your department's server, you can map drive letter S to that drive. Drive S appears as a disk drive on your computer, even though it's actually on the server.

Here's the easiest way to map a shared drive or folder to a drive letter:

1. Run Windows Explorer (choosing Start | My Computer is the easiest way) to display an Explorer window.

2. Choose Tools | Map Network Drive from the menu bar. You see the Map Network Drive dialog box, shown here:

3. Choose a drive letter, clicking the Drive drop-down list to see the available letters. Letters that are mapped to drives on your own computer don't appear. Letters that are already mapped to shared drives or folders appear with the name of the resource to which they are mapped.

4. In the Folder box, type the UNC address of the shared drive or folder you want to Map. Better yet, click the downward-pointing arrow at the right end of the Folder box, and choose from the UNC addresses that appear or click the Browse

button and navigate to the drive or folder. The list includes all the drives and folders on the LAN that have been configured to be sharable.

5. If you want to continue to map this drive or folder to this drive letter each time you restart Windows, leave the Reconnect At Logon check box selected.

6. Click Finish to close the dialog box. If the shared drive or folder requires a password, Windows prompts you to type it.

Note *To display a Map Network Drive button on the Windows Explorer toolbar, right-click the toolbar, choose Customize from the shortcut menu that appears, click Map Drive from the Available Toolbar Buttons list, click Add, and click Close.*

Once you have mapped a drive, it appears in the folder tree with your local drives; and in Windows Explorer, you see it when you open My Computer. You can access a mapped network drive in the same way that you access a local drive from any dialog box.

Note *To map a drive letter to a folder, the folder itself must be defined as shared. It is not enough to share the drive on which the folder resides.*

Tips for Mapping

When you map a drive letter, you only map it for only one computer at a time. If you want the drive letter mapped for other computers in the LAN, you need to sit down at each of them and repeat the steps in the preceding section. That is, if you want all the computers in your office to be able to use the drive letter F to refer to the Consulting folder on the Accounting computer, you must map the Consulting folder to the F drive on each computer in the LAN.

If you use a shared drive or folder from more than one computer, you might want to spend a moment considering which drive letter to use. You will find it more convenient if the shared network drive has the same drive letter on each computer in the LAN—that way you won't have to refer to "the C drive on the computer in the corner near the door—the one called Bambi." Instead, you can just call it the F drive (the exception, of course, is the person who uses the computer called Bambi, for whom it's just the C drive). Choose a letter that people can remember—for example, map the main disk drive on the server to drive S, or the drive that everyone in the Purchasing department uses to drive P. Before you assign the drive letter, make sure that letter is available on the other computers on the LAN (letters up to about G are frequently already occupied by hard disks, CD-ROM drives, Zip drives, and other devices).

You may have noticed the Reconnect At Logon check box on the Map Network Drive dialog box. When this option is selected, your computer checks that the shared resource is available each time you log on. Reconnecting at logon slows down the logon process slightly, but means that using the drive the first time is quicker because the drive is already connected. If you are mapping a drive only temporarily (you need

Mapping Drives and Folders with the NET USE Command

If you like to use the DOS command prompt, there's a command that maps a shared drive or folder to a drive letter. This command is useful if you want to create batch files (lists of commands) that create or delete mappings (see Chapter 39, section "Running Batch Files").

To use the NET USE command, open a Command Prompt window by choosing Start | All Programs | Accessories | Command Prompt (see Chapter 39, section "Using the Command Prompt Window"). In the Command Prompt window, type this command:

```
net use d: \\computername\sharename
```

Replace *d* with the drive letter you want to map, and *computername**sharename* with the UNC address of the shared drive or folder. For more NET USE options, type this command:

```
net use /?
```

it only for the next 20 minutes, for example), or if the computer that drive is on gets rebooted or turned off often, turn off the Reconnect At Logon option.

Unmapping a Drive

If you want to "unmap" a drive letter, you can do so by disconnecting it: right-click the drive in Windows Explorer and choose Disconnect from the shortcut menu or choose Tools | Disconnect Network Drive, choose the drive to disconnect and click OK. The drive remains accessible through My Network Places, but a drive letter is no longer mapped to it. (To make a drive inaccessible even through My Network Places, you must disable sharing from the computer that owns the resource.)

Using Shared Drives and Folders with Passwords

Sometimes a shared resource requires that you log in. When you log in, use the name and password recognized by the computer with the resource you are trying to use. If you have read-only access, you can't save, delete, or edit files on the shared drive or folder. If you try, you see an error message.

To use shared drives and folders on a domain-based LAN, connect to the drive or folder by clicking it in the My Network Places window. When it prompts you for a password, type *domainname\username* for the user name, and type your domain password. (Ask the LAN administrator of the domain if you don't know this information.) Select the Remember This Password check box so that you don't have to type this information the next time you connect.

 If you use Windows XP Home Edition, you can't use roaming profiles, login scripts, or other domain-based networking features.

Sharing Your Disk Drives and Folders with Others

You might want to share the files stored on your computer's disk drives in a number of ways. You might want to permit all the computers on the LAN to access a Zip drive, Jaz drive, or CD-ROM writer, so that you don't have to buy a drive for each computer. You can even permit other users of the LAN to read files in a certain folder on a particular hard drive. For instance, give read-only access to the folder that contains the company personnel policies, so that you don't waste space on each computer saving the same files (and time updating numerous copies of the files). You can allow some users to be able to read and write to one file, perhaps the one containing the database in which orders are entered, so that the information each user sees is always the most up-to-date information available. Maybe there is one shared folder on your hard drive that you want other people to be able to use—maybe you just want to share everything—you want to allow everyone on the LAN to read and write to your hard drive.

Before anyone else can read or write files on your disk drives, you must configure either the entire drive or specific folders as sharable. You choose a *share name* for the drive or folder—the name that you want to appear in Windows Explorer as *name* on *computer name*. For example, if your computer is named Laptop, and you share your CD-ROM (which is drive D on your computer) with the share name CD-ROM Drive, it appears as CD-ROM Drive On Laptop in Windows Explorer on other people's computers. You can provide a comment to further identify a shared drive or folder. The comment is visible only when the properties are displayed, however.

When you make a drive or folder sharable, you also decide what access to specify—at least, you can if you have Windows XP Professional (Windows XP Home Edition eliminates many security features). There are alternatives to sharing a whole drive with full read and write access:

- You can share just a folder.
- You can specify read-only rights.
- You can choose the users who can access the drive.

Enabling Security for Shared Resources

By default, Windows XP enables *Simple File Sharing*, which means that when you share a drive or folder, you share it with everyone in your network workgroup (see Chapter 6, section "What Is Simple File Sharing?"). If you want to enable any security measures, such as permitting only some users access to the drive or preventing users from writing to the drive (allowing only read permission), you have to disable Simple File Sharing. You can't disable Simple File Sharing in Windows XP Home Edition, only in Windows XP Professional.

Follow these steps to change the Simple File Sharing setting on your computer:

1. Run Windows Explorer (choose Start | My Computer, for example).

2. Choose Tools | Folder Options to see the Folder Options dialog box.

3. Click the View tab.

4. Scroll to the bottom of the Advanced Settings box to find the Use Simple File Sharing check box (see Figure 29-3).

5. Click the check box to change the setting. When Use Simple File Sharing is selected, you will not see any security options when you share a drive or folder.

6. Click OK to close the dialog box.

When Simple File Sharing is disabled, you see security options when you share a drive or folder. However, the options you see depend on whether the drive that you are sharing is formatted with NTFS or FAT32.

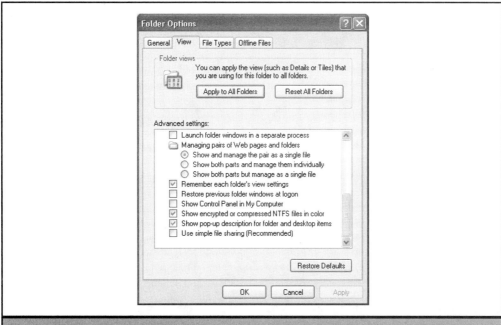

Figure 29-3. *Scroll to the bottom to see the Use Simple File Sharing check box.*

Making a Drive Sharable

Follow these steps to share a drive or folder:

1. Run Windows Explorer and display the name of the drive or folder you want to share with others.

If you open the folder you want to share, you can use the Share This Folder link in the Task pane to share it.

2. Right-click the drive or folder you want to share, and choose Sharing And Security from the shortcut menu. (If you don't see Sharing And Security, you need to install File And Printer Sharing For Microsoft Networks from the Network dialog box.) You see the Properties dialog box for the drive or folder, with the Sharing tab selected. Which options appear on the Sharing tab depend on whether you are using Simple File Sharing (shown in Figure 29-4) or not (shown in Figure 29-5). If have Simple File Sharing and you have chosen to

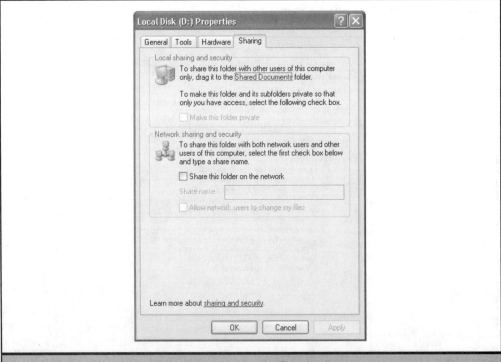

Figure 29-4.   *Sharing a disk drive with simple file sharing*

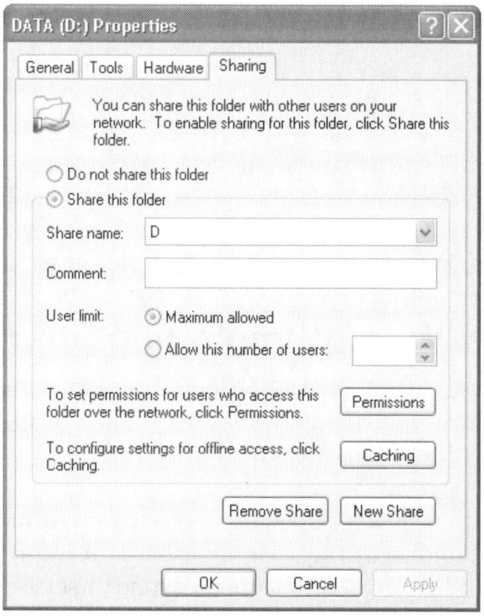

Figure 29-5.   *Sharing a disk drive with simple file sharing turned off*

share a whole drive, you will see a link warning you that sharing the root of the drive is risky.

3. Click the Share This Folder radio button or click the Share This Folder On The Network check box.

4. Type the share name into the Share Name box. A share name can be from 1 to 12 characters long, including spaces.

5. If you want the drive or folder to be available to everyone in your workgroup, click OK to close the dialog box. If you want to add some security to the shared resource, see one of the next two sections, depending on whether you use Simple File Sharing.

When you close the dialog box, you see a tiny hand as part of the drive or folder icon, signifying that the resource is shared. Other users can use your files by navigating to them through My Network Places. If they use the drive or folder often, they have the option of mapping the drive. If you decide to stop sharing of the drive, open the Properties dialog box for the drive and select the Do Not Share This Folder radio button or deselect the Share This Folder On The Network check box on the Sharing tab.

If you make a folder sharable, the shared folder looks like a whole drive from other computers on the LAN, but other people can see and use only the shared folder.

Controlling Access with Simple File Sharing Security

If you are using Simple File Sharing (if you haven't changed the option, it is on by default), you have only one security option. You can select the Allow Network Users To Change My Files check box when you share a folder or drive to make files on the shared resource read-only—other users will be able to open files, but not save changes to your drive. Leave this check box blank if you want other users to be able to save changes to files on your disk. (This setting works for Windows XP Home Edition, or for Windows XP Professional systems that are not logged onto a domain-based LAN.)

Controlling Access When Simple File Sharing Is Disabled

When Simple File Sharing is disabled, you see different options on the Sharing tab of the Properties dialog box for a drive or folder. You can control how many people can access the drive or folder, how files are saved for offline use, and which users have permission to do what.

Permissions tell Windows what a specific user account or user group is allowed to do with a specific drive, folder, or file. (See Chapter 6 for information about user and group accounts.) You can set permissions for everyone or set permissions for individual users (however, it is preferable to set permissions for groups, rather than individual users, because groups are easier to manage as individuals come and go). The permissions that you can set depend on the file system of the disk on which the shared drive or folder resides. NTFS disks (or partitions) support more security options than other formats (FAT32 and FAT). See the section "What Are FAT, FAT32, and NTFS?" in Chapter 32 for information about file systems.

Setting User Permissions for FAT32 Drives

For a shared FAT32 (Windows Me/9x-style) drive or a shared folder stored on an FAT32 drive or partition, you have limited options for setting permissions. You set permissions on the Permissions dialog box, shown in Figure 29-6, which you display by clicking the Permissions button on the Sharing tab of the Properties dialog box for the shared drive or folder. In the Permissions dialog box, select the group or user and use the check boxes in the Permissions box to turn permissions on or off. You see the following permissions options:

- **Full Control**   Allows the user or group to read, create, change, delete files, etc. Full Control allows network users to do whatever the computer owner can do with the shared folder or drive.

- **Change**   Prevents users from deleting folders and files, changing permissions, or taking ownership for a file or folder.

- **Read**   Allows users only to open and read files.

Although each option has Allow and Deny check boxes, only three options are really available: Full Control, Change, or Read. If you click a Deny check box, other

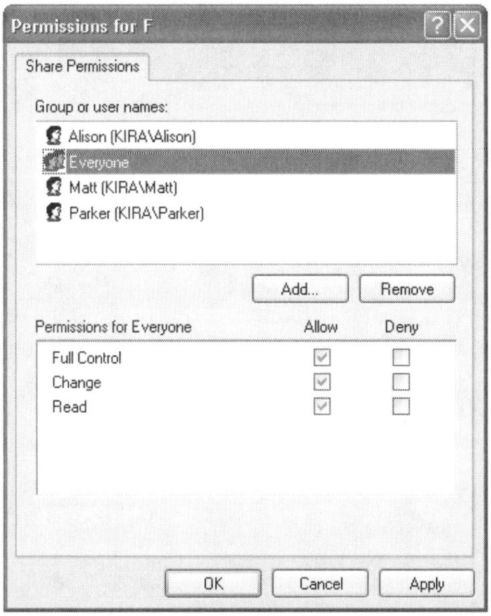

Figure 29-6. *Click the user or group in the Group Or User Names box to see the permissions for that user or group.*

settings will change to reflect the option that is denied—for instance if you deny full control, then change and read are also denied.

You can add or remove users and groups listed by using the Add and Remove buttons. When you click Add, you see the Select Users Or Groups dialog box, shown here:

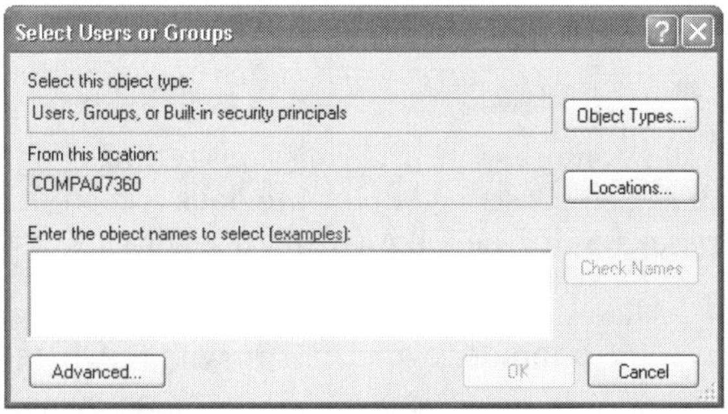

The From This Location box shows the name of your computer. Type a user account or group account name into the box at the bottom of the dialog box and click OK.

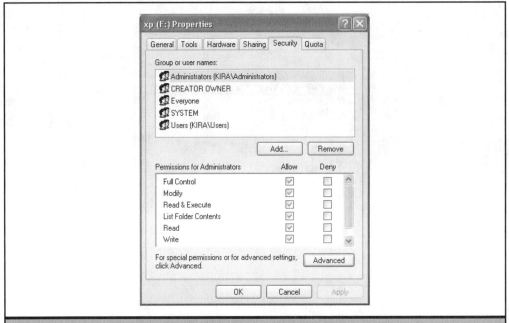

Figure 29-7.   *The Security tab of the Properties dialog box (for NTFS only)*

Setting User Permissions for NTFS Drives

For shared NTFS drives and folders that are stored on an NTFS drive or partition, you have more options when setting permissions for LAN and local users. The Properties dialog box for the shared drive or folder includes a Security tab that you can click to set permissions, as shown in Figure 29-7.

 If the shared drive is formatted with NTFS, you should set permissions on the Security tab, rather than by clicking the Permissions button on the Sharing tab.

The Security tab allows more specific permissions settings but works the same way as the Permissions dialog box described in the previous section—first select a user or group; then define permissions. The following permissions are available:

- **Full Control**   Allows the user or group to read, create, change, and delete files—whatever the computer owner can do with the shared folder or drive.

- **Modify**   Prevents users from deleting folders and files, changing permissions, or taking ownership of a file or folder.

- **Read & Execute**   Allows users to read and run files, but not to change the contents of the shared drive or folder.

- **List Folder Contents**   Allows users to see the contents of the folder.
- **Read**   Allows users to see the contents of the drive or folder, and open files but not save changes.
- **Write**   Allows users to write to the drive or folder, but not to open files or see a list of files already there.
- **Special Permissions**   Click the Advanced button to apply special permissions.

  If you need to know more about permissions on a network, see Windows .NET Server: The Complete Reference, *by Kathy Ivens (published by Osborne/McGraw-Hill), which discusses domain-based permissions. If you need complicated permissions, you probably need to think about creating a domain-based LAN.*

Limiting the Number of Users for Your Drive or Folder

In the User Limit section on the Sharing tab of the Properties dialog box for a shared drive or folder, choose Maximum Allowed (which allows as many people to connect as the network allows), or choose Allow This Number of Users and specify the number allowed at one time.

Controlling Offline Files

Caching affects how files stored on your computer are saved for offline use on another network computer. Click the Caching button on the Properties dialog box for the shared drive or folder to see the Caching Settings dialog box, shown in Figure 29-8.

Figure 29-8.   *Caching options affect files saved for offline use.*

The Allow Caching Of Files In This Shared Folder check box controls whether files are stored on the other computers for use when your computer isn't available.

If you allow caching, you can choose from one of the three caching settings:

- **Automatic Caching Of Documents**   Makes all open files in the shared folder or drive available offline automatically.

- **Automatic Caching Of Programs And Documents**   When you use this option, permissions need to be restricted to allow only Read access. This option opens files that cannot be changed without accessing the network version and thus reduces network traffic.

- **Manual Caching Of Documents**   The user must identify files for offline use (see Chapter 15, section "Offline Files Options and the Synchronization Manager"). This is the default setting.

Sharing Printers on a LAN

Sharing a printer on a LAN has two steps. First, you sit at the computer that is directly attached to the printer and configure the printer to be a *network printer* or *shared printer* so that other computers on the network can print to it. Then you configure the other computers on the LAN so that they know about the network printer—with luck, Windows on each computer automatically detects the existence of the newly sharable printer and installs the new printer driver itself.

   Not all printers come with printer drivers that work for sharing the printer on a LAN.

Making Your Printer Sharable

If you want other people on the LAN to be able to print on your printer, the first step is to install the printer on your own computer and make sure that you can print to it (see Chapter 14, section "Setting Up a Local Printer"). Once the printer is correctly installed, you can share it.

The computer that the printer is attached to is called a *print server*. The print server can also be someone's PC, the usual arrangement on a small network, or a computer that does nothing else. You give the printer a share name, the name that other people will see when they connect to the printer. The share name can be the type of printer (for example, HP1100A), the group that uses the printer (for example, Accounting), or some other name. A straightforward name makes it easier for others on the network to figure out which printer they are using.

To share the printer so that other computers on the LAN can print to it, follow these steps:

1. Choose Start | Printers And Faxes to see the Printers folder. (If this command doesn't appear on your Start menu, choose Start | Control Panel | Printers And Other Hardware | Printers And Faxes.)

2. Right-click the printer you want to share and choose Sharing from the Shortcut menu (or select the printer icon and click Share This Printer in the Task pane). You see the Properties dialog box for the printer, with the Sharing tab displayed, as shown in Figure 29-9. (Depending on what type of network you use, you might see different settings.)

3. Click the Share This Printer radio button.

4. Give your printer a share name.

5. If you have turned off Simple File Sharing, you see the Security tab on the Properties dialog box (see "Enabling Security for Shared Resources," earlier in the chapter). Click it to limit use of the shared printer by the user. Print is the default setting—it allows users to print to the shared printer. Manage Printers does not allow the user to print, but gives the user administrative control of the printer. Manage Documents allows the user to start, cancel, and rearrange the order that documents are printed.

6. Close the printer's Properties dialog box. The icon for the printer you just shared now has a tiny hand under it, indicating that the printer is shared.

To turn sharing off, open the Properties dialog box for the printer and select the Do Not Share This Printer radio button on the Sharing tab.

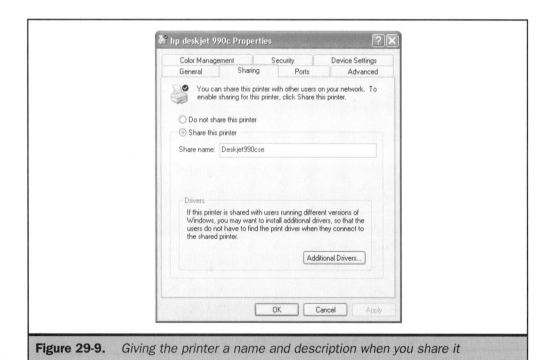

Figure 29-9.   *Giving the printer a name and description when you share it*

Printing to a Network Printer from Another Computer

 When Windows detects a shared printer on another computer on the LAN, it tries to install the printer's driver automatically. When you print from an application, check the list of available printers—the list may already include shared printers on other computers. To see the list of printers you can use, choose Start | Printers And Faxes (or Start | Control Panel | Printers And Other Hardware | Printers And Faxes) to display the Printers And Faxes folder. The icon for a shared printer has a cable beneath it.

If the printer doesn't appear on the list, you need to install a driver for the printer. Here's how:

1. Open the Printers And Faxes window.

2. Click Add A Printer. You see the Add Printer Wizard. The Wizard asks the following:

   - **Whether you're installing a local or network printer**   You're installing a network printer.

   - **The network path for the printer**   Unless you can type the path for the printer from memory, use the Browse button to find it. To find the printer, first find the computer to which it is attached by expanding the My Network Places hierarchy; click My Network Places, then Entire Network, then the computer to which the printer is attached, then the name of the printer.

   - **Which driver to install**   If you already have a driver installed for this type of printer, the Wizard asks whether you want to keep the existing driver or install a new one (one of these options will be recommended). If you don't have a driver installed, the Wizard prompts you to install one—you'll probably need your Windows XP CD-ROM or a printer driver from another source (many can be found on the Internet).

   - **What name you want to call the printer**   This should be a name that enables you to identify the printer. If you have six LaserJets on your network, you probably don't want to call it just "LaserJet"—instead, you might want to call it "Cindy's LaserJet" since it's attached to Cindy's machine. That way, when you print to this printer, you'll know where to go to pick up your printout.

   - **Whether you want this printer to be your default printer**   If you want to print automatically to this printer every time you print, then the answer is Yes. If you usually want to print to another printer, choose No.

Once you've completed these steps, you can print to the shared printer from this computer any time you want. If you defined the shared printer as your default printer, then anything you print automatically goes to that printer. If you didn't define the network printer as the default printer, then you have to choose it from the list of defined printers before you print. This is usually done on the Print dialog box of the application you are using.

   If the network printer is unavailable, any print jobs will be held on your computer until the printer is again available.

   For more information about printing, installing, and configuring a printer and changing the default printer, refer to Chapter 14.

Chapter 30

Connecting Your LAN to the Internet

If you have a LAN, connecting the whole LAN to the Internet makes more sense than connecting each individual computer on the LAN. By connecting the LAN to the Internet, all of the PCs on the LAN can share one Internet account and one phone line or cable connection. Large companies have connected their internal networks to the Internet for years, and small offices and home LANs can do the same.

For the PCs on a LAN to use the Internet, you must configure each PC to communicate using TCP/IP, the Internet's communication protocol. Then a program or device must route the TCP/IP information between the LAN and the Internet; you can use a dedicated device (a *router*) or a gateway program running on a PC (see Chapter 28, section "How Does TCP/IP Work?").

Windows XP (like Windows Me and 2000) comes with Internet Connection Sharing (ICS), a gateway program that can route information between a LAN and the Internet. This chapter describes how to configure the ICS server program on the computer connected to the Internet and the ICS client settings on the other computers on the LAN. Once ICS (or another gateway) is installed, everyone on the LAN can send and receive e-mail, browse the Web, and use other Internet programs at the same time. Windows comes with troubleshooting tools for making sure that your ICS system works.

 Neither Internet Connection Sharing nor Internet Connection Firewall is supported under Windows XP 64-Bit Edition.

Virtual Private Networking (VPN) is a system that lets your organization create a private LAN over the Internet. Windows comes with a VPN program that enables your computer to connect to a virtual private network (see Chapter 27, section "Connecting Computers with Virtual Private Networking").

How Can You Connect a LAN to the Internet?

When a computer communicates with other computers on the Internet, it sends messages in the TCP/IP protocol addressed to the other computers using their numeric IP (Internet Protocol) addresses. To share an Internet connection, the computers on your LAN must be able to communicate with TCP/IP. The computers can also communicate on the LAN with another protocol (for example, a LAN might use NetBEUI for file and printer sharing on the LAN and TCP/IP for Internet Connection Sharing).

The device or program that connects your LAN to the Internet acts as a *gateway*, passing messages between the computers on the LAN and computers on the Internet, and possibly controlling what types of information can pass.

What Does a Gateway Do?

An Internet gateway can perform the following tasks:

- **Translating between the IP address on the LAN and the IP addresses on the Internet**   Computers on a LAN usually use private, LAN-only IP addresses, frequently assigned by a DHCP server on the LAN. Computers on the Internet use publicly visible IP addresses that are usually assigned by your ISP. A gateway accepts packets (messages) from the LAN, strips off the private IP address, substitutes its own ISP-supplied IP address, and passes the packet along to the Internet. When replies return, the gateway passes the replies back to the computer that made the request. To the rest of the Internet, all packets from the LAN appear to be from the gateway, so no information leaks out about the individual systems on your LAN. This service is called *Network Address Translation* (*NAT*). All gateways to networks that use private addresses must perform this task.

- **Controlling the types of information that can flow between the Internet and your LAN**   The gateway, for example, can prevent telnet sessions (remote terminal sessions, described in the section "Logging in to Other Computers Using Telnet" in Chapter 28) from coming in from the Internet, or prevent chat sessions from going in either direction between the LAN and the Internet.

- **Caching**   The gateway can store information that has been requested from the Internet so that if a user requests the same information, the gateway can provide it without having to get it from the Internet again.

- **Logging usage of the Internet**   The gateway can log all packets that pass between the LAN and the Internet so you can have a record of who has access to your LAN from the Internet and what Internet services your LAN users have used.

Some gateway software (like ICS) provides only address translation. Other gateway programs, called *proxy servers*, provide address translation, caching, and logging. If the proxy server also provides security, controlling what information can pass between the LAN and the Internet, it's called a *firewall* (see Chapter 31, section "Enabling the Internet Connection Firewall Between Your PC and the Internet").

Devices That Can Act as Gateways

Three kinds of devices are commonly used as gateways, connecting LANs to the Internet:

- **Routers**   A "black box" that connects to your LAN hub or switch and to a phone line (dial-up, ISDN line, DSL line, or cable modem connection). Firewall software is built into the router. All you have to do is cable it to your LAN, connect your phone line or cable modem, plug it into power, and your LAN is on the Internet. Routers can be the simplest and most effective way to connect your LAN to the Internet. You connect your Internet connection (phone line or cable Internet cable) to the router, and run a LAN cable from the router to the LAN's hub or switch.

- **UNIX or Linux systems**   Because the Internet was built on UNIX systems, lots of excellent TCP/IP communication software comes with most UNIX and Linux systems. Many "black box" routers are actually computers running UNIX or Linux, but you can set up your own for less money. You can run a wide variety of firewall software, as well as Web server, POP (e-mail) server, or other Internet server software on the UNIX or Linux system. The UNIX or Linux system needs two connections: an Internet connection (phone line or cable Internet cable) and a LAN connection (cable to the LAN's hub or switch).

■ **Windows systems running proxy server software**   A Windows XP, Me, 98, 2000, or NT 4 system can act as a router, running a gateway program. The Windows system connects to the Internet over a phone line or cable connection, and the gateway program provides the IP address translation. If you run proxy server or firewall programs, the Windows system also provides security: Windows XP comes with a built-in firewall.

Software and Hardware for a Windows-Based Gateway

If you use a Windows system running NAT (Network Address Translation), proxy server, or firewall software, the system has two connections: one to the LAN (using a network interface card) and the other to the Internet (using a modem for dial-up or another network interface card or USB port for DSL or cable Internet connection).

Caution	*Even though DSL and cable Internet connections use the same cabling as a LAN (RJ45 Category-5 cable), don't plug the DSL or cable Internet cable into your LAN's hub or switch. The DSL or cable Internet must connect to a PC or router so that you have a gateway between the Internet and the LAN. (Connecting the modem to the hub is possible, but tricky and prone to error.)*

Windows XP comes with Internet Connection Sharing, which is easy to install and set up. Several Windows-based proxy server programs have been available for years, including SyGate (at **http://www.sygate.com**), WinGate (at **http://wingate.deerfield. com**), and WinProxy (at **http://www.winproxy.com**). All three of these programs have downloadable versions that you can try before buying. You install the proxy server program on the computer that is connected to the Internet and a matching client program on each of the other computers on the LAN. When the user of any computer on the LAN wants to check e-mail or browse the Web, the computer running the proxy server program connects to the Internet (if it's not already connected) and passes data from the user's computer to and from the Internet.

Tip	*Test the security of your LAN's Internet connection by going to the Gibson Research Corporation's Web site at **http://grc.com**. Follow the links to their Shields UP! service, which can check how vulnerable your computer is to attack or data theft from the Internet.*

What Is Internet Connection Sharing?

Windows XP's Internet Connection Sharing (or ICS) is a NAT program, and doesn't provide caching or logging. ICS allows one computer—the *ICS server*—to provide an Internet connection for all the computers on a LAN. The ICS host runs the ICS server program. The other computers—the *ICS clients*—on the LAN can run Windows Me, 9x, 2000, NT, older Windows versions, or other operating systems, as long as they support TCP/IP.

ICS uses private IP addresses in the format 192.168.0.*xxx*. You can't use static IP addressing (Microsoft claims that there's a way, but we haven't had any luck). ICS includes a DHCP (Dynamic Host Configuration Protocol) server, which runs on the ICS server and assigns IP addresses to the rest of the computers on your LAN automatically (see Chapter 28, section "How Does TCP/IP Work?"). DHCP assigns the address 192.168.0.1 to the ICS server itself.

Figure 30-1 shows a LAN with five computers, including the ICS server computer, with private IP addresses from 192.168.0.1 to 192.168.0.5. The ICS server has a separate

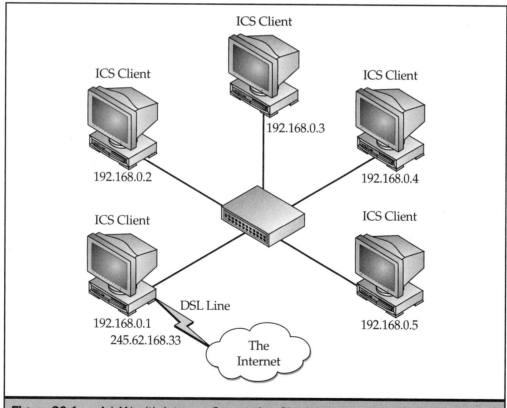

Figure 30-1.   *A LAN with Internet Connection Sharing*

IP address for communicating with the Internet over a DSL line; this address is assigned by the ISP (in the figure, it has the address 245.62.168.33).

ICS includes these components:

- **DHCP Allocator**   Assigns IP addresses to ICS client computers on the LAN
- **DNS Proxy**   Translates between IP addresses and Internet host names (like www.yahoo.com), using your ISP's DNS server
- **Network Address Translation (NAT)**   When passing packets of information between the LAN and the Internet, replaces the private IP address with the ICS server's IP address, and vice versa

The next section describes how to install ICS on the ICS server and how to configure the rest of the computers on the LAN to share the connection.

Windows also comes with an Internet Connection Firewall to provide security for any Internet connection, whether shared or not (see Chapter 31, section "Enabling the Internet Connection Firewall Between Your PC and the Internet").

Installing ICS on the ICS Server

One computer on your LAN, the ICS server, runs the ICS program. This computer must connect to the Internet with a dial-up account, ISDN line, DSL line, cable modem, or other Internet connection—make sure that you have this Internet connection working (see Chapter 22).

The Wizard can't set up your computer as an ICS server if it's not connected to the Internet or to a LAN. It also doesn't work if another computer is already acting as the Internet gateway for the LAN, running a DHCP server, or is using the IP address 192.168.0.1.

Configuring the ICS Server Using the Network Setup Wizard

The easiest way to install and configure ICS is by running the Network Setup Wizard (see Chapter 28, section "Configuring Your LAN Connection by Using the Network Setup Wizard"). The Wizard can create a floppy disk with a version of the Wizard that you can use to configure the other Windows Me, 9x, 2000, and NT computers on the LAN.

On the computer that has the Internet connection, run the Network Setup Wizard by choosing Start I All Programs I Accessories I Communications I Network Setup Wizard. Or, choose Start I Control Panel, click Network And Internet Connections, click Network Connections, and click Set Up A Home Or Small Office Network in the Task pane. As the Wizard asks you questions, make these choices:

- **Select A Connection Method**   Choose This Computer Connections Directly To The Internet. You must already have created a dial-up, DLS, ISDN, or cable connection.

- **Select Your Internet Connection**   The Wizard displays a list of the connections (both Internet and LAN connections) on your computer. Choose the connection to the Internet, as shown here:

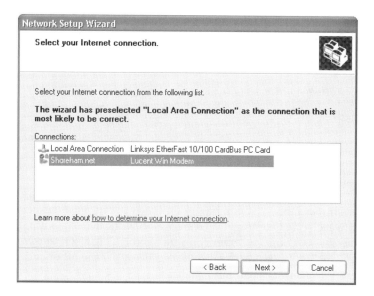

- **Give This Computer A Description And Name**   Type a description of your computer in the Computer Description box and a unique name for your computer in the Computer Name box. The boxes may already be filled in if you entered this information when you installed Windows or when you set up your LAN.

- **Name Your Network**   In the Workgroup Name box, type the name of your workgroup (for workgroup-based networks). The workgroup name must match the workgroup name of the other computers on the LAN. When you click Next, the Wizard confirms your settings, like this (the Internet Connection Firewall is turned on by default):

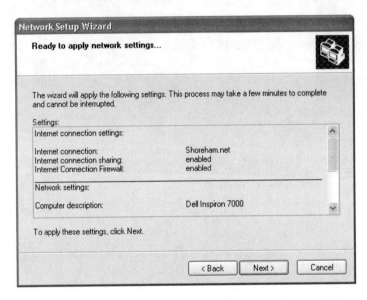

When you click Next, the Network Setup Wizard installs and enables Internet Connection Sharing and the Internet Connection Firewall.

■ **You're Almost Done**   If you haven't already set up your LAN, you need to configure each other computer on the LAN to work with the settings you've just installed (that is, your ICS server computer is the DHCP server that hands out IP addresses, as well as being the Internet gateway). If the other computers on the LAN run Windows XP, you can run the Network Setup Wizard as described at the beginning of this section. If the LAN includes computers running older versions of Windows, you can create a Network Setup Disk to run on those computers.

Configuring the ICS Server Manually

If your LAN and Internet connections both work, there's a quicker way to turn on Internet Connection Sharing. On the computer that has the Internet connection, follow these steps:

1. Open the Network Connections window (choose Start | Control Panel | Network And Internet Connections | Network Connections).

2. Click the Internet connection (not the LAN connection).

3. Click Change Settings Of This Connection in the Network Tasks listed in the Task pane. You see the Properties dialog box for the Internet connection.

4. Click the Advanced tab. You see the Internet Connection Firewall and Internet Connection Sharing settings, shown in Figure 30-2. The settings are as follows:

- **Protect My Computer And Network By Limiting Or Preventing Access To This Computer From The Network** Select this check box to turn on the Internet Connection Firewall, which we highly recommend for all Internet connections (see Chapter 31, section "Enabling the Internet Connection Firewall Between Your PC and the Internet").

- **Allow Other Network Users To Connect Through This Computer's Internet Connection** Select this check box to turn on ICS, or clear the check box to turn ICS off.

- **Establish A Dial-Up Connection Whenever A Computer On My Network Attempts To Access The Internet** Select this check box to enable dial-on-demand.

- **Allow Other Network Users To Control Or Disable The Shared Internet Connection** Select this check box to allow other people on the LAN to disconnect the Internet connection (hang up) or reconnect (if dial-on-demand is turned off).

5. Click OK to put the changes into effect.

Testing the ICS Server

To test whether your computer is working as the ICS server, try connecting to the Internet from the ICS server—you should connect as if ICS weren't installed. Browsing, e-mail, and other Internet services should be unaffected. Right-click the Local Area Network connection in the Network Connections window and choose Status to see whether the LAN is working and confirm that your IP address is 192.168.0.1.

ICS Server Configuration Details

Make sure that the dial-up connection (or other Internet connection) works. To test it, connect to the Internet and browse the Web or send and receive e-mail.

Make sure that the ICS server is set to connect to the Internet whenever it receives a request to connect. To set your Internet options to dial the Internet on demand, choose Start | Control Panel | Network And Internet Connections, and click Internet Options to display the Internet Properties dialog box (see Chapter 22, section "Setting Additional Dial-Up Options"). Click the Connections tab and choose Always Dial My Default Connection so that Windows can connect to the Internet on demand. Click the Settings button and make sure that your user name and password are entered so that the ICS server can connect to the Internet without waiting for you to type this information.

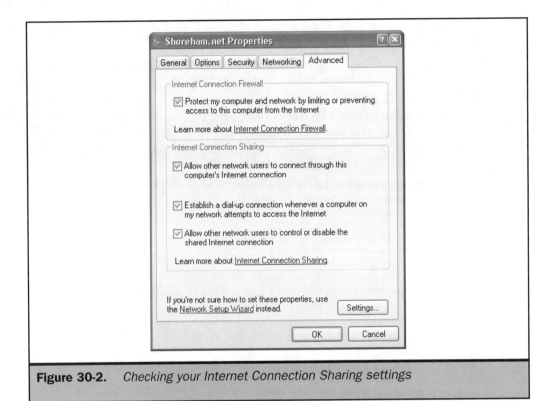

Figure 30-2.   *Checking your Internet Connection Sharing settings*

Tip   *If you ran the Network Setup Wizard, take a look at the Nsw.log file, which is stored in your C:\Windows folder (or whatever folder Windows is installed in). Navigate to it in an Explorer window and double-click it to open it in Notepad. It lists the actions that the Wizard took when installing and configuring your LAN and ICS, including searching your system for networking components and deciding which to use.*

Configuring the ICS Clients

You must configure each of the ICS *clients*—the other computers that share the ICS connection to the Internet. If you installed the ICS server using the Network Setup Wizard and you chose to create a Network Setup Disk, the Wizard created a floppy disk that contains a version of the Wizard program with which you can configure the ICS clients. The Wizard configures only computers running Windows Me, 9x, 2000, or NT 4. For ICS clients running Windows XP, you can run the Network Setup Wizard that is part of Windows.

When you configure a computer as an ICS client, you add TCP/IP as a network protocol, if it's not already installed, and set the computer to get its IP address from a DHCP server (the one that is running on the ICS server as part of ICS).

Configuring an ICS Client with the Network Setup Wizard

To configure your computer as an ICS client, insert the floppy disk that the Network Setup Wizard created, choose Start | Run, type **a:setup**, and click Open. Or, if your computer runs Windows XP, choose Start | All Programs | Accessories | Communications | Network Setup Wizard

As the Wizard asks you questions, make these choices:

- **Select A Connection Method**   Select This Computer Connects To The Internet Through Another Computer On My Network Or Through A Residential Gateway.

- **Give This Computer A Description And Name**   Type a unique name for your computer and a description (this description doesn't have to be unique and appears only in the My Network Places window).

- **Name Your Network**   Type the name for your workgroup (see Chapter 28, section "Identifying the Computer"). Use the same workgroup name you entered for the ICS server. When you click Next, the Wizard confirms your settings, like this:

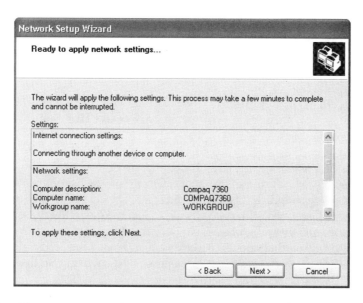

- **You're Almost Done**   After the Wizard installs your settings, it offers to create a Network Setup Disk. Choose Yes only if you need one for configuring ICS clients that don't run Windows XP.

Testing Your Internet Connection from an ICS Client

When you ask a browser or other Internet program to display a Web page or send or receive e-mail on an ICS client computer, Windows passes your Internet request along to the ICS server, which connects to the Internet on your behalf. If the ICS server was already logged into the Internet, you should see your Web page or e-mail right away; if the ICS server has to connect, there's the usual delay in logging in. Once the ICS server and clients are configured correctly, users on all ICS servers and clients can use the Internet connection simultaneously.

To test your connection from an ICS server, try these actions:

- Run Internet Explorer (or another Web browser) and try to display a Web page.
- Run the Ping program and try to ping the ICS server at 192.168.0.1 (see Chapter 22, section "Testing Communication with Another Computer by Using Ping"). If that works, try pinging a computer on the Internet, like **www.yahoo.com**.

ICS Client Configuration Details

Here are ways you can check the configuration of your ICS client.

Check that your computer is configured to communicate over the LAN using TCP/IP. Choose Start | Control Panel | Network And Internet Connections | Network Connections to display the Network Connections window. Right-click your Local Area Connection and choose Properties from the menu that appears to display the Properties dialog box for the LAN connection (see Chapter 28, section "Installing and Configuring Network Components").

On the General tab, check that Internet Protocol (TCP/IP) appears and is selected so that your computer can communicate via TCP/IP on the LAN. If the TCP/IP entries don't appear, install TCP/IP by clicking the Install button, choosing Protocol, clicking the Add button, choosing TCP/IP from the list of network protocols, and clicking OK (see Chapter 28, section "Installing a Protocol"). Also make sure that the QoS Packet Scheduler appears and is selected.

Make sure that your computer is configured to get its IP address from the DHCP server that runs on the ICS server. On the General tab of the Local Area Connections Properties dialog box, click Internet Protocol (TCP/IP) on the list of installed components and click the Properties button to display the Internet Protocol (TCP/IP) Properties dialog box (see Chapter 22, section "What Is TCP/IP?"). On the General tab, select Obtain An IP Address Automatically and Obtain DNS Server Address Automatically.

Check the TCP/IP settings on the ICS client by opening the Network Connections window, right-clicking the Local Area Connection, and choosing Status from the menu that appears. Click the Support tab, shown next:

The settings should be the same as those in this illustration, except for the IP Address, which may end with a number other than 2.

Check to see that your computer is not configured to connect to the Internet directly. Choose Start | Control Panel, click Network And Internet Options, and click Internet Options. On the Connections tab of the Internet Properties dialog box, select either Never Dial A Connection or Dial Whenever A Network Connection Is Not Present. (If no connections appear in the Dial-Up And Virtual Private Network Settings box, the Never Dial A Connection setting is gray, but it's still selected.)

Click the LAN Settings button on the Connections tab of the Internet Properties dialog box to display the Local Area Network (LAN) Settings dialog box, shown here:

These are settings you might need to use if you connect to the Internet using a proxy server other than ICS. None of the check boxes should be selected, unless your LAN administrator specifies otherwise.

Using Internet Connection Sharing

Once you've configured the ICS server and the ICS clients, ICS is easy to use. From either the server or a client, run a Web browser, e-mail program, or other program that works with the Internet. When the program sends information to or requests information from the Internet, the ICS server connects to the Internet to provide the Internet connection.

To see how many people are sharing the Internet connection on the ICS server, double-click the ICS icon on the notification area of the taskbar (or click it and choose Status from the menu that appears). A small dialog box pops up, telling you how many computers are sharing the connection, including the ICS server itself.

Troubleshooting ICS

If you can't get connected to the Internet from an ICS client computer, here are some things to try.

- Give the ICS server time to connect to the Internet, especially if it uses a dial-up phone line. The program on the ICS client may time out before the ICS server gets connected to your Internet account and ICS passes your request along.

- If you have restarted the ICS server since you restarted the ICS client, restart the client.

- Test your Internet connection from the ICS server (as described in "Testing the ICS Server," earlier in this chapter) and test your LAN connection from an ICS client (as described in "Testing Your Internet Connection from an ICS Client," earlier in this chapter).

- Run the Internet Connection Sharing Troubleshooter on the ICS server and at least one ICS client. Choose Start | Help And Support to display the Help And Support Center window, click Fixing A Problem, click Networking Problems, and click Internet Connection Sharing Troubleshooter.

The
Complete
Reference

Chapter 31

Network and Internet Security

ommunication security ensures that the data you transmit and receive through the Internet or an intranet is sent to and received from the actual systems with which you intend to communicate, as opposed to another system impersonating the desired system. It also ensures that messages are sent and received without being intercepted or spied upon.

Chances are, your Windows XP computer is connected to the Internet, and you've probably wondered how safe your computer and your personal information are. This chapter discusses viruses and how to avoid catching them, how to control what Internet Explorer downloads when you browse the Web, browsing secure Web sites, and how to send and receive secure e-mail messages. Windows XP includes an Internet Connection Firewall that you can turn on to protect your computer from malicious Internauts.

Note *User accounts and passwords are described in Chapter 6. If you are also interested in Credential Management, domain accounts, group policy, Active Directory, Security Templates, and other corporate network security systems, check out* Windows .NET Server: The Complete Reference *by Kathy Ivens, published by Osborne/McGraw-Hill.*

Protecting Your System from Viruses and Worms

One of the less appealing aspects of the Internet has been security and the potential for becoming the victim of a *virus* (a program that reproduces by infecting—or copying itself into—other files or computers). More properly, a virus is a self-reproducing program that can infect files on one computer but needs help in order to find other systems to infect (like people sharing programs), while a *worm* is a self-reproducing program that can send itself to other systems (e-mail viruses are actually worms). Some viruses and worms are just annoying, taking up space on your system or displaying an annoying message, but many others are destructive, deleting or altering files or clogging up Internet e-mail systems with thousands of unwanted messages. The sidebar "How Do Viruses Spread?" contains more information.

John M. Goodman, author of many computer books, says, "If your computer is in good health (with regular backups), a virus is annoying and can waste several days work. If your computer's health is shaky (with irregular or no backups), a virus can kill you."

Types of Virus Files

Viruses and worms can be stored in several types of files:

- **.exe, .com, .bat, .msi, .mso, or .pif (program files); scraps; or shortcuts** These viruses and worms run when they are opened (clicked or double-clicked in Windows Explorer or your e-mail program, for example). If Windows is configured not to show file extensions, you may not be able to tell easily which files have these extensions. (Tell Windows to display filename extensions by choosing

Start | My Computer, choosing Tools | Folder Options, clicking the View tab, and deselecting the Hide Extensions For Known File Types check box.)

- **.doc (Word documents), .xls (Excel spreadsheets), or .mdb (Access databases)** These files may contain viruses and worms written in Microsoft Word, Excel, or Access macro languages. The macros (customized automation instructions) usually run when you open the file. Because Word and Excel are the most popular programs that run macros, Word documents and Excel spreadsheets are the most common macro virus carriers.

- **.vbs (Visual Basic Script files)** These viruses and worms are written in Visual Basic and run when you click or double-click them. Visual Basic is a programming language used, among other things, to write macros for the Office suite of applications, including Outlook 2002.

For a more complete list of file types that might contain viruses, see article Q262631, "Information About the Outlook E-mail Security Update" in Microsoft's Knowledge Base: go to **htp://support.microsoft.com** and search for the article number.

Caution *Scraps, a Windows file type created by cut-and-paste operations, can contain executable files (including viruses and worms) that appear to be other types of (harmless) files. An article on this issue is at **http://pc-help.org/security/scrap.htm**.*

How Do Viruses Spread?

The commonly cited psychological reasons for individuals to open suspicious e-mails are fear, greed, and sex. Greed is the least enticing of the dastardly trio. While fear can cause people to open an e-mail to find out how to stop something bad from happening, sex is the most effective motivator.

The notorious Melissa worm by David Smith was started by simply being posted to the **alt.sex** newsgroup. Smith asked that the file not be circulated, so, of course, it was. That single posting to a newsgroup was the only action that Smith performed to spread his worm throughout the world, causing millions of dollars in damages and, in some cases, days of mail server downtime for some major companies.

A new tactic is to appeal to the recipient's ego. The more recent SirCam worm draws in the viewer by asking for sage advice on the "subject" included in the attached "message." The attachment is really the worm in disguise.

So, the moral of the story is this: If you receive a message from someone you don't know, or from someone you know but didn't expect to receive a file from, approach it with caution. If it has an attachment, just delete it. If you're not sure, let it sit unopened in your inbox for a few days, while you check the anti-virus and e-mail hoax Web sites. A six- or eight-hour delay in opening the ILOVEYOU virus would have been enough for most people to have heard about the danger of the virus.

Preventing Infection by Viruses

The best prevention for viruses is to avoid getting infected in the first place (practice safe computing). If you do get infected, tools are available to clean your system.

Avoiding Getting Infected

The generally accepted method of preventing viruses from successfully attacking your computer is the use of *antivirus software*—programs that detect known viruses before they run and infect your computer. Of course, there is the tried-and-true method of not downloading or opening anything that you cannot verify, validate, or otherwise determine the source of.

Note   *The Internet isn't the only way to catch viruses. If you commonly move files from one place to another using removable media (for example, floppy disks, writable CD-ROMs, Zip disks, or Jaz disks) then you need to be careful with these as well. The data on a disk, whether it be from school, office, or library, likely came from the Internet. This simple fact makes it possible for the disk to contain a virus. Office networks are typically more secure, because your LAN administrator has probably installed antivirus software, but don't take that for granted. School networks can be less secure because of insufficient staffing resources. Public access points like ones in libraries, copy shops, or cyber cafés are a mixed bag. Your best bet is to be wary of any data coming to your computer from the outside. Even commercial software has been known to be a transmission source for viruses. Trust no one. When in doubt, wait at least 24 hours before opening attachments, and check an anti-virus Web site in the meantime (see "Sources of Antivirus Information"). And back up your entire system regularly! (See Chapter 9.)*

Antivirus Programs   Take our word for it and do *not* wait until you have contracted a virus to install an antivirus program. An antivirus program can't prevent infection if it's not running. Buying and installing an antivirus application is a small price to pay, compared to losing all of your work for a week, all of your carefully collected bookmarks, the hours that you spent making all of your CDs into MP3 files, your family pictures from last year's picnic in Hawaii—whatever your most treasured files include. Here are some of the most popular and effective antivirus programs:

- **Symantec Norton AntiVirus, at (http://www.symantec.com/nav)**   Norton AntiVirus is a complete solution. You can go with the simple Norton Anti Virus or pop for the complete Internet Security Family Edition suite of security applications—the Family Edition is a particularly good deal, including a personal *firewall* application that is particularly well suited to protecting broadband (cable and DSL) users.

- **McAfee VirusScan, at http://www.mcafee.com**   McAfee has lately turned many of their programs into online applications—online information services that are updated 24 hours a day. They also offer an application update service that tracks what you have and sends you updates as they become available.

After you install an antivirus program, make sure that you arrange to get regular updates. Some antivirus programs can update themselves by downloading lists of viruses from the manufacturer's Web site automatically. You can also visit the manufacturer's Web site and download new virus lists yourself. An antivirus program won't protect you from the latest virus if your virus lists are months old.

Once you have an antivirus program installed, configured, and running according to the documentation that came with the program, the antivirus program scans all incoming files (via e-mail and Web) for viruses. For example, the antivirus program might display a dialog box while you are retrieving your e-mail, reporting that a message contains the SirCam worm and offering to delete it for you. Some antivirus programs also scan your hard disk regularly to look for viruses that might have sneaked through. If the program sees a virus, it displays a message telling you what to do.

Practicing Safe Computing Online   Here's a brief list of ways to protect yourself when you're online:

- Do not open an attachment that you either did not specifically request or that would not normally be unexpected. If a colleague sends you a file that you asked for, it's likely to be safe. However, if someone named GaToR | RoTaG or something similar sends you a file, don't touch it. Similarly, if someone you know (whose address book you are likely to be in) sends a file you aren't expecting, write back and ask about it *before* opening the file.

- Before opening an attachment, wait a few hours or days. In the meantime, check an antivirus Web site for news of new viruses and worms.

- Do not download files from sources you are not familiar with. Stick to known, reputable Web sites like ZDNet (**http://www.zdnet.com**), Tucows (**http://www.tucows.com**), Stroud's CWSApps (**http://cws.internet.com**), and C | Net (**http://www.cnet.com**), or the Web sites of well-known hardware and software manufacturers, as sources for downloadable software. Many pornographic sites require you to download a viewer program: think twice, since these programs have been known to contain dangerous viruses.

- Do not accept any file that is offered unsolicited. If you receive an e-mail notifying you that you have won a contest and you can click a URL in the message to download your prize, think again. Did you sign up for a contest? Legitimate sources invariably draw from an existing customer base and rely on word of mouth and advertising campaigns to get new customers, not random free give-aways.

- Ask friends and family not to forward too many jokes to you (or choose *one* friend to be your Internet joke source). This reduces your potential for infection, as well as cutting down on your e-mail volume.

Avoiding Outlook and Outlook Express   Many people believe that your computer can't get infected by a virus simply by opening an e-mail message that has no attachments. This used to be true, but is no longer. Formatted e-mail messages can carry viruses, too, because some versions of Outlook and Outlook Express automatically open and display attachments. Many viruses have been written specifically to exploit security holes in Outlook and Outlook Express. Microsoft has issued several security patches to close these security holes. As Microsoft finds new security problems, they usually respond quickly with patches. Be sure to use Windows Automatic Updates to download and install these patches (see Chapter 36, section "Updating Your Computer Automatically with Automatic Updates").

One simple solution to this and many other worms is not to use older versions of Outlook or Outlook Express. The most recent versions, Outlook 2002 and Outlook Express 6, respectively, have vastly improved handling of known viruses. If you use Eudora, an excellent and widely-used e-mail program from Qualcomm, Inc. (at http://www.eudora.com), you can avoid most viruses by not opening attached files.

Knowing When You're Infected   You may find out that your system is infected when you see a strange message telling you that you're a victim. Some other ways of telling are as follows (although all but the last can be signs of other Windows problems):

■ Your system slows down (especially programs loading).

■ Files disappear.

■ Programs crash unexpectedly.

■ For e-mail based viruses, people e-mail you to say that they received a virus from you.

Dealing with an Infected Windows System

If you have already been infected with a virus, follow these steps:

1. If an unfamiliar dialog box, error message, or something else unfamiliar appears, make a note of the message or other symptom. Unplug the modem or network cable, and then shut down the computer. Continuing to use an infected computer is a bad idea for several reasons. Depending on what type of virus or worm you have, additional damage can be done. With the speed of today's systems, a virus or worm can delete or write over gigabytes of data in a matter of minutes. Also, some viruses exploit functions in Microsoft Outlook and Outlook Express that can cause your computer to forward a copy of the virus to all entries in your address book.

2. Do not try to repair or otherwise contain the damage or effects of a virus or worm using software that was not specifically designed to do so. In other words, don't run Norton Speed Disk to try and solve the problem.

3. Do not install antivirus software *after* you discover a virus or worm. Unless you are sure that the virus is nondestructive, leave the computer turned off until you find out how to get rid of the specific virus that your system has contracted.

4. Locate a computer that is not infected. Go to a virus resource Web site and find out how to fix it. Try the Web site of one of the most popular antivirus programs (listed in a previous section), or one of the virus information sites listed in the next section. Look for step-by-step instructions for removing the virus. Companies like Symantec and McAfee often develop scripts that aid in the removal of recently discovered viruses, and publish the details about what that virus has done or can do, so that they can be safely removed.

5. Once you know which virus you have, follow the steps to disinfect your system (that is, remove the virus). If the virus has deleted or overwritten files, it might not be possible to get the files back, but you can at least prevent further damage to your system and infection of other systems.

6. If you can't identify the virus or find a procedure for getting rid of it, call technical support for your computer (or your local technical support person). Explain to them what happened and that you would like some assistance in removing the virus, or at least in taking steps to minimize the damage.

7. Once you are sure that the virus is gone, buy and install an antivirus program. Don't make the same mistake twice!

Another approach is to back up all your data files (but none of your programs), reformat your hard disk, reinstall Windows and your applications, restore your data files, and buy and install an antivirus program to prevent reinfection. However, leaving your computer running while you make the backups can give the virus time to delete more files.

After you have cleaned up a virus, back up, reformat, and reinstall your system. Many viruses and the resulting repairs leave your system unstable, and parts of virus files may still be lying around.

If you make regular backups, check the backups that you made within at least 72 hours of discovering the infection (see Chapter 9). Your system may have been infected for days (or longer) before you realized it.

Sources of Antivirus Information

Here is a quick list of applications and sites that you should investigate long before you need them:

■ **Doug Muth's Anti-Virus Help Page, at http://www.claws-and-paws.com/virus**
A fantastically deep collection of information regarding computer viruses with lots of helpful papers, reports, and links to additional resources. One thing that makes this site great is that it's not tied to any commercial concern.

■ **Symantec AntiVirus Research Center (SARC), at http://www.sarc.com**   An easy enough domain name to remember, especially when you need fast access to the latest virus alerts. Muth's page is great, but the SARC team is fast, which is one of the benefits of commercial relations.

■ **McAfee Virus Information Library, at http://vil.nai.com/vil** This encyclopedic listing of viruses is one of the first places you should look to get help or find out what's going on.

■ **Vmyths (formerly the Computer Virus Myths page), at http://www.vmyths.com** Myths and news about viruses and hoaxes.

Please take our advice and make sure you're covered.

Managing Which Files Internet Explorer Downloads

Internet Explorer can retrieve a wide variety of files and objects, ranging from innocuous plain text files and images to potentially destructive executable programs. Some Web pages increase the amount of interactivity they can offer by downloading small programs to run on your computer. For example, rather than transmitting the individual frames of an animation over the Internet, a Web server may send an animation-constructing program that runs on your computer. A financial Web site may download a program that displays a scrolling stock ticker. Typically, this process is invisible to the user—the interaction or the animation just happens, without calling your attention to how it happens.

While these programs are useful, they also create security issues. If Web sites can put useful programs on your computer and run them without informing you, precautions must be taken to make sure that they can't also put harmful programs on your computer. Internet Explorer takes certain precautions automatically, and allows you the option to choose additional precautions.

Internet Explorer's downloaded object security allows you to decide, based on both the Web site where an object came from and the type of object, whether to retrieve an object, and once it's retrieved, what to do with it. Internet Explorer defines three levels of object access (low, medium, and high) to give varying amounts of access to your computer. You can also define custom access permissions, if the three standard settings don't meet your needs.

What Are Java, JavaScript, VBScript, and ActiveX?

Java is a language for sending small applications (called *applets*) over the Web, so that they can be executed by your computer. *JavaScript* is a language for extending HTML to embed small programs called *scripts* in Web pages. *VBScript*, a language that resembles Microsoft's Visual Basic, can be used to add scripts to pages that are displayed by Internet Explorer. Anything that VBScript can do, JavaScript (which Microsoft calls JScript) can do, too, and vice versa.

ActiveX controls, like Java, are a way to embed executable programs into a Web page. Unlike Java and JavaScript, but like VBScript, ActiveX is a Microsoft system that is not used by Navigator or most other browsers. When Internet Explorer encounters a Web page that uses ActiveX controls, it checks to see whether that particular control is already installed, and if it is not, IE installs the control on your machine.

 ActiveX controls are considerably more dangerous than JavaScript or VBScript scripts or Java applets. Java applets and JavaScript scripts are run in a "sandbox" inside your Web browser, which limits the accidental or deliberate damage they can do; and VBScript scripts are run by an interpreter, which should limit the types of damage they can do. However, ActiveX controls are programs with full access to your computer's resources.

What Are Internet Explorer's Zones?

Internet Explorer divides the world into four *zones*:

- **Internet**   Includes all sites that are not in one of the other three zones. Objects from this zone generally are given the medium level of access to your computer.

- **Local Intranet**   Contains computers on your local network. They're usually considered fairly trustworthy, and objects are given a medium level of access to your computer.

- **Trusted Sites**   Includes the sites that you or Microsoft have listed as trustworthy. Objects from this zone generally are given the high level of access to your computer.

- **Restricted Sites**   Includes the sites that you have listed as untrustworthy. Objects from this zone are given the low level of access to your computer. Don't change the access level of this zone to grant higher access.

Downloaded ActiveX controls and other executable objects can and should be signed by their authors using a certificate scheme similar to that used for validating remote servers.

For each of the four zones into which a Web page can fall, you can set the security to high, medium, medium-low, or low. For each zone, you set exactly which remote operations you're willing to perform. To prevent downloading and running software that might infect your system with a virus, see the section "Preventing Infection by Viruses," earlier in this chapter.

Controlling Your Download Security

The rules governing scripts and applets are set zone by zone on the Security tab of the Internet Options dialog box. To examine or change these settings:

1. Open the Internet Options dialog box by selecting Tools | Internet Options from the Internet Explorer menu bar.

2. Click the Security tab of the Internet Options dialog box (as shown in Figure 31-1).

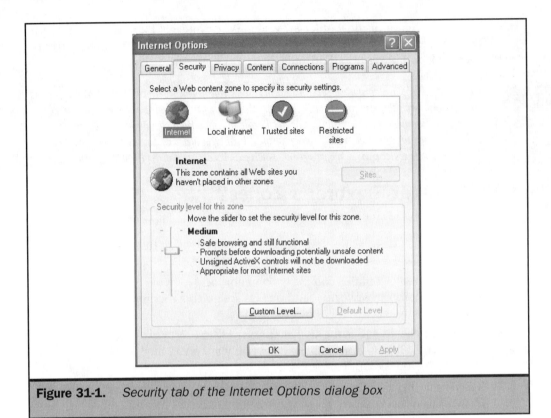

Figure 31-1. Security tab of the Internet Options dialog box

3. Select the security zone you want to examine or change. The rest of the information on the Security tab changes to show the settings for that zone.

4. If you want to change the security setting of a zone, move the slider on the Security tab of the Internet Options dialog box. (The slider doesn't appear if the zone has been given custom settings. To reset such a zone to one of the standard settings, click the Default Level button. When the slider reappears, you can move it to the desired setting.)

5. If you want to change the security settings of the selected zone, scroll through the Security Settings dialog box until you see the item you want to change. Change an item by selecting or deselecting its check box, or by selecting a different radio button than the current selection.

6. Click OK to close each open dialog box. Click Yes in the confirmation box that asks whether you want to change the security settings.

Displaying and Changing Settings for Zones

To add or delete a Web site from the Local Intranet, Trusted Sites, or Restricted Sites Zones, click the zone on the Security tab of the Internet Options dialog box. Click the Sites button. (There's no button for the Internet Zone, since it contains all the Web sites that are not contained in the other three zones.) You see a dialog box like the one shown here:

If you want to include only sites that have secure servers, leave the Require Server Verification (https:) For All Sites In This Zone check box selected. If you want to be able to add any Web site to the list of trusted sites for this zone, deselect the check box. To add a site, type its URP (including **http://** or **https://**) in the top box and click Add. To remove a site, click in the Web Sites box and click Remove.

Controlling Which Web Sites Are in the Local Intranet Zone

The Local Intranet Zone normally contains sites on your own local area network, and is set up that way by your network administrator when he or she sets up the network. When you click Add Sites on the Security tab, Windows displays the Local Intranet Zone dialog box, with these three check boxes:

- **Include All Local (Intranet) Sites Not Listed In Other Zones**   Select this check box to include all other sites on the same local area network in the Local Intranet Zone. This check box is usually checked.

- **Include All Sites That Bypass The Proxy Server**   Many organizations have a *proxy server* that mediates access to sites outside the organization. Select this check box to include sites outside your organization to which your organization lets you connect directly in the Local Intranet zone. You can see a list of the sites that bypass the proxy server by displaying the Internet Properties or Internet Options dialog box, clicking the Connections tab, and clicking the Advanced button.

■ **Include All Network Paths (UNCs)**   Select this check box to include all the sites with UNC addresses (Universal Naming Convention addresses) that apply only to computers on your LAN.

You can also click the Advanced button to add sites individually, as for Trusted and Restricted sites. See Chapter 30 for more information on how networks connect to the Internet.

Controlling Which Web Sites Are in the Trusted and Restricted Sites Zones

The Trusted and Restricted Sites zones start with no Web sites listed; you must specify the Web sites to include in these zones. To specify sites, select the zone to which you want to add sites and click Sites on the Security tab of the Internet Options dialog box. You see the Trusted Sites or the Restricted Sites dialog box, the first of which is shown in Figure 31-2. To add a new site, type its full address, starting with **http://** or **https://**, into the Add This Web Site To The Zone box and click Add. The Web site appears in the Web Sites list. To remove a site, select it in the Web Sites list and click Remove. You

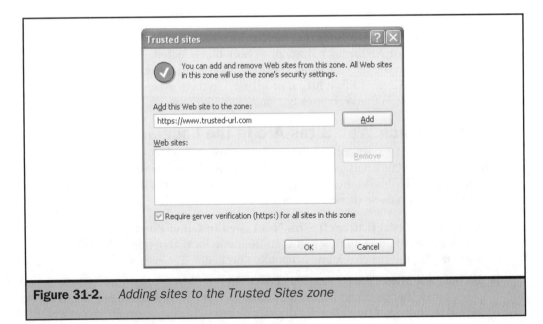

Figure 31-2.   *Adding sites to the Trusted Sites zone*

can require a verified secure connection to all sites in this zone by clicking the Require Server Verification (https:) For All Sites In This Zone check box at the bottom of the dialog box; when selected, this setting prevents you from adding any sites that don't support HTTPS, which is described in the section "Securing Your Web Communication with Encryption and Certificates," later in this chapter.

Managing Java and JavaScript

The security settings that affect how Internet Explorer deals with Java and JavaScript programs are in the Microsoft VM and Scripting sections of the Security Settings dialog box. Follow these steps:

1. On the Security tab of the Internet Options dialog box, click the zone for which you want to change or see the settings.

2. Click the Custom Level button to display the Security Settings dialog box, shown here:

3. You may change what these applets and scripts are allowed to do on your computer, or even disable Java or JavaScript entirely, by choosing Disable (Internet Explorer does not run this type of program downloaded from this zone), Enable (IE does run this type of program downloaded from this zone), or Prompt (ask before running the program).

Managing ActiveX Controls

We have never been big fans of ActiveX controls. They allow Web sites to have too much power over your system and are hard to monitor. If you should happen to download and install a rogue ActiveX control by mistake, it could (on its own) download and install lots more rogue ActiveX controls—which would then be permanent parts of your software environment, even when you are offline. None of this would appear the least bit suspicious to any virus-detecting software you might own, because ActiveX controls aren't viruses: They have the same status as applications that you install yourself.

Disabling ActiveX controls is one option, as described in the previous section. However, if you frequent Microsoft Web sites like MSN or MSNBC, you will be exposed to numerous temptations to turn them back on. (We finally gave in to the excellent portfolio-tracking services at MSN Moneycentral.) We suggest the following compromise: Disable ActiveX controls everywhere but in the Trusted Sites security zone. (Do this from the Security Settings dialog box, following the steps in the previous section.) When you find a Microsoft Web site that offers some wonderful service involving ActiveX controls, move that site into the Trusted Sites security zone.

ActiveX controls are stored in the folder C:\Windows\Downloaded Program Files (if Windows is installed in C:\Windows). If you use Internet Explorer, you should check this file periodically to see what applications Internet Explorer has downloaded. Dispose of an ActiveX control by right-clicking its icon and selecting Remove from the shortcut menu.

Securing Your Web Communication with Encryption and Certificates

Browsers store *certificates*, cryptographic data that can identify your computer to remote computers, or vice versa. Certificates are issued by *certificate authorities*, each of which has its own certificate. Internet Explorer comes with about 30 *authority certificates* that they can use to check that the certificates presented to your computer by other sites are, in fact, issued by known certificate authorities. To provide secure communication with a remote Web site, Internet Explorer uses *SSL* (Secure Sockets Layer) to provide a variation of the standard HTTP Web protocol, called *HTTPS*. Web servers that use HTTPS are called *secure servers*.

You can also acquire a *personal certificate* to use to identify yourself when your Internet Explorer or Navigator contacts a Web site. The most widely used authorities for personal certificates are VeriSign at **http://www.verisign.com** and Thawte (which is owned by VeriSign) at **http://www.thawte.com**. See RSA Data Security's list of questions and answers at their Web site at **http://www.rsasecurity.com/rsalabs/faq** for more information about certificates.

New applets usually are digitally signed by their authors, that is, each applet includes certificate information that identifies the applet's author and verifies that the applet wasn't tampered with since the author signed it. The only way that a software publisher can create an officially signed application is to participate in Microsoft's very costly and involved certification procedures, which we expect that many smaller software vendors won't be able to afford. Unfortunately, the high cost of Microsoft's certification process means that many perfectly safe applets won't be signed and will trigger a warning message when you install them.

Browsing the Web Securely

Internet Explorer handles communication security by using SSL (Secure Sockets Layer) to encrypt messages sent to and from remote servers and certificates to verify who the party is at the other end of a connection. For example, you use this type of security when you place a credit card order with a Web-based retailer that uses a secure Web server. For the most part, SSL works invisibly, with all the security validation happening automatically. Internet Explorer, by default, warns you when you switch between secure and normal pages with dialog boxes like this:

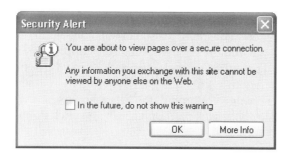

(We find these warnings annoying and turn them off.) You can tell whether the current page is secure in the following ways:

- Look at the URL for the page in the browser's Address or Location box to see whether the page's address starts with **https://** rather than **http://**.

- Look at the status bar at the bottom of the browser window to see whether a little lock icon appears, indicating that the connection is secure.

Whenever your browser opens an HTTPS connection to a server that supports SSL, the server presents a certificate to your computer. If the certificate is validated by one of the authority certificates known to your browser, and the name on the certificate matches the name of the Web site, the browser uses the connection and displays Web pages as usual. If either of those checks fails, the Web browser warns you and gives you the option to continue. You see a Security Alert or similar dialog box when your browser can't validate a remote site's certificate. If you trust the source of the file that you are downloading, you can tell Windows to continue and use the connection despite the warning.

Using Object Certificates When Downloading Files

Whenever Internet Explorer retrieves a Web page that uses a hitherto unknown ActiveX or Java applet, Internet Explorer checks to see whether your download security settings permit you to download it (see "Controlling Your Download Security," earlier in the chapter). If your settings don't permit the download, Internet Explorer warns you and doesn't download the file. You see the dialog box shown here:

Unless a site is in the Trusted Zone (in which case Internet Explorer accepts the applet without question), Internet Explorer checks the certificate with which the program is signed and displays the Security Warning dialog box, as shown in Figure 31-3. You see who the signer is and who verified the signature. If the signer is someone you're inclined to trust, such as a large reputable organization or someone you know personally, click Yes to accept the applet. If you expect always to accept applets from this signer, click the Always Trust Content From *ThisSigner'sName* check box at the bottom of the dialog box to tell Internet Explorer not to ask about signatures from this signer in the future. (If you check the box and later change your mind, the list of signers you've checked is in the Internet Properties dialog box; click the Content tab and click Publishers to examine and change the list.)

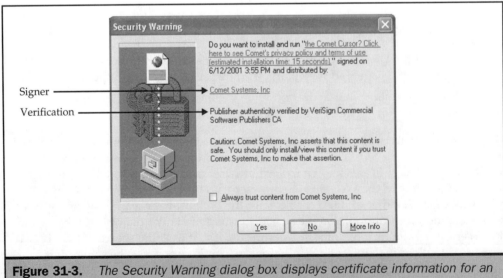

Figure 31-3.   *The Security Warning dialog box displays certificate information for an ActiveX applet.*

Managing Certificates from Certificate Publishers

If you expect to download many programs (or display Web pages that contain applets), you will end up with a collection of certificates with which Internet Explorer can verify the sources of the programs. You can see lists of the certificates that you have received. Click the Content tab on the Internet Options dialog box. Click the buttons in the Certificates section of the dialog box.

In Internet Explorer, choose Tools | Internet Options from the menu to see the Internet Options dialog box. Clicking the Content tab and then the Publishers button displays the Certificates dialog box with the Trusted Publishers tab selected, as shown in Figure 31-4. The dialog box lists certificates for software publishers that you have told your browsers to trust (by clicking the Always Trust Content From check box in the Security Warning dialog box, shown in Figure 31-3). New certificates are added when you download authenticated software from the Internet. You can delete a certificate from this list by selecting it and clicking Remove.

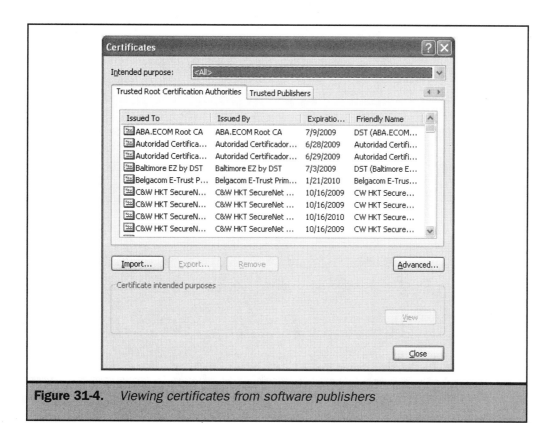

Figure 31-4. *Viewing certificates from software publishers*

Managing Your Personal Certificates

You can get your own certificate to identify yourself to secure remote Web servers that demand user certificates for identification. See "Getting a Certificate," later in this chapter, for how to get your own certificate for use both on the Web and in sending and receiving secure e-mail.

To see what personal certificates are installed in Internet Explorer, choose Tools | Options, click the Content tab, and click the Certificates button to display the Certificates dialog box with the Personal tab selected, shown in Figure 31-5. You see a list of the certificates you have installed on your computer that you can use to identify yourself.

If you receive a certificate and store it on your disk, click Import to read the certificate and include it on the list in this dialog box. Windows can read certificates stored in personal certificate files (with the extension .pfx). You can export a certificate and its associated information to a personal certificate file; select the certificate from the list on the Certificates dialog box and click Export.

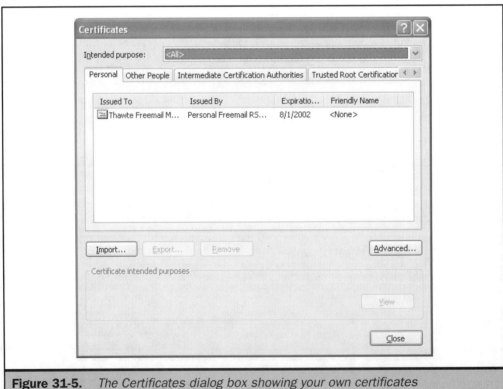

Figure 31-5. *The Certificates dialog box showing your own certificates*

If you get a certificate in Internet Explorer, you can export it to a file and then import the certificate from that file into any other certificate-capable web browser (like Netscape) or vice versa.

Enabling the Internet Connection Firewall Between Your PC and the Internet

Some people say the Internet is an evil place filled with miscreants, while other people say the Internet is one of the safest places anyone can be. Neither group is right, but are more likely to be fulfilling some politically charged agenda. While the Internet contains pornography and social aberration, it also provides clean and wholesome fun for all who want it. However, there is still a dark side to the Internet, and you need to protect your computer (and yourself) from it.

A *cracker* is a programmer whose goal is to exploit gaps in Windows security to gain access to your files, take over your computer, or simply crash it. Fortunately, Microsoft has provided some protection against such malicious programmers by adding Internet Connection Firewall to Windows XP.

A *firewall* is a program that stands between your computer (or your LAN) and the Internet. Each packet on the Internet is addressed to a specific *port number* on a specific computer. Each computer connected to the Internet "listens" to packets addressed only to certain ports. As a general rule, most people use only a few ports: 21 (for FTP, or file transfer), 25 (for outgoing e-mail), 80 (for Web pages), 110 (for incoming e-mail), 119 (for newsgroup messagess), and sometimes 443 (for secure connections).

The Internet Connection Firewall (ICF) controls what ports are open, refusing to respond to packets addressed to other ports. We recommend that you enable the Internet Connection Firewall on all your Internet connections. Follow these steps:

1. Open the Network Connections window (choose Start | Control Panel | Network And Internet Connections | Network Connections).

2. Click the Internet connection.

3. Click Change Settings Of This Connection in the Network Tasks listed in the Task pane. You see the Properties dialog box for the Internet connection.

4. Click the Advanced tab. You see the Internet Connection Firewall and Internet Connection Sharing settings.

5. Select the Protect My Computer And Network By Limiting Or Preventing Access To This Computer From The Network check box.

6. Click OK to put the changes into effect.

MSN Explorer May Compromise Security

MSN Explorer is a program that works with Internet Explorer and provides access to a bunch of MSN services like Hotmail (see Chapter 24, section "What Is MSN Explorer?"). It's pretty cute. But we found the following line in the MSN Explorer Security Statement:

> If you have chosen security settings that will interfere with MSN Explorer, then your security settings are temporarily changed to allow MSN Explorer to work properly. In addition, while MSN Explorer is active on your computer, the special settings for MSN will apply to any Microsoft Internet Explorer window you may have open.

If Internet security is important to you, you may prefer to forego using MSN Explorer.

*Once you have enabled the Internet Connection Firewall, go to Steve Gibson's Web site at **http://grc.com**, click the link to his Shields Up free firewall-testing service, and follow the directions on the Web page. Shields Up can tell you whether the firewall is working correctly.*

Sending and Receiving E-mail Securely

E-mail programs offer two kinds of security: signatures and encryption. Both depend on certificates that serve as electronic identity keys. The security system that Microsoft provides with Outlook Express, *S/MIME*, uses certificates issued by third parties, such as VeriSign and Thawte. Another popular security system, *Pretty Good Privacy* (or *PGP*), lets each user generate his or her own keys (Eudora can work with PGP keys). Both are forms of *public-key cryptography*. Each certificate consists of a *public key* (or *digital ID*), a *private key*, and a *digital signature*. You keep your private key and digital signature secret, while you provide your public key to anyone with whom you exchange secure mail, either directly or via a generally available key server.

Signatures allow you to add to your mail a *signature block*, generated with your private key, that verifies the author is indeed you and the message was not modified in transit. Anyone who wants to validate your signature can check it by using your public key. The signature is added as an extra block at the end of the message, without modifying the other contents, so that the recipient can read your message, whether he or she validates your signature or not.

Encryption scrambles a message so that only the recipient can decode it. A message encrypted with someone's public key can be decrypted only with that person's private key. You encrypt a message with the recipient's public key, and the recipient uses his or her private key to decode it. Anyone else looking at the message would see only unreadable gibberish. It's possible both to *digitally sign* and encrypt the same message, so that only the designated recipient can decode the message and the designated recipient can then verify that the message is really from you.

Mail security depends on a *key ring* of keys. On your key ring, you need your own private key and digital signature and the public key of everyone with whom you plan to exchange secure mail. Outlook Express security keeps your private key and digital signature as one of the properties of your Mail account and keeps other people's public keys in the Address Book.

Outlook Express and other Microsoft e-mail programs provide a certificate-based system (called S/MIME) for signing and encrypting mail. *Signed* mail uses your own certificate to prove to the recipient that the author of the message is you and that the message arrived without tampering (these are the same type of certificates described in the preceding sections for authenticating material you download from the Web). *Encrypted* mail uses the recipient's certificate to protect the message's contents so that only the intended recipient can read the messages. A single message can be both signed and encrypted.

Note	*For more information about encryption and signature, see RSA Data Security's Web site at* **http://www.rsasecurity.com** *and Network Associates' Pretty Good Privacy Web site at* **http://www.pgp.com**. *These sites describe how to use encryption with various e-mail programs.*

Getting a Certificate

The only source of certificates is a certificate authority, and for a certificate to be useful, the authority has to be one that is widely accepted. The best known certificate authority is VeriSign, at **http://www.verisign.com**, who also owns Thawte, at **http://www.thawte.com**. It provides a variety of certificates at various prices, usually including a free two-month trial of a personal certificate suitable for signing e-mail. The certificate authority's Web site walks you through the process of getting a certificate. Details vary, but, generally, the steps include the following:

- You enter basic information, including your e-mail address, into a form on the authority's Web site.

- Your Web browser automatically downloads your private key, part of the security information from the authority.

- The authority e-mails a confirmation code to the address you give. This ensures that the address you provide is really yours.

- You run Outlook Express and receive the message. It contains the URL of a page that will finish the registration and a unique code to identify yourself when you get there. Use Windows cut-and-paste tool to copy the code from your mail program to the browser window, rather than trying to retype it.

- The authority generates the public key that matches your private key and downloads it as well.

This process of obtaining a certificate only verifies your e-mail address, not any other aspect of your identity. VeriSign offers more secure certificates with more careful identity checks, but the vast majority of certificates in use are the simplest kind.

Sending Signed Mail

Once you have a certificate, sending signed mail is simple. While you're composing a message in Outlook Express, click the Digitally Sign Message button (the one with the little orange seal) to tell Outlook Express to sign the message as it's sent. Signed messages appear with the orange seal in the list of messages, as shown here:

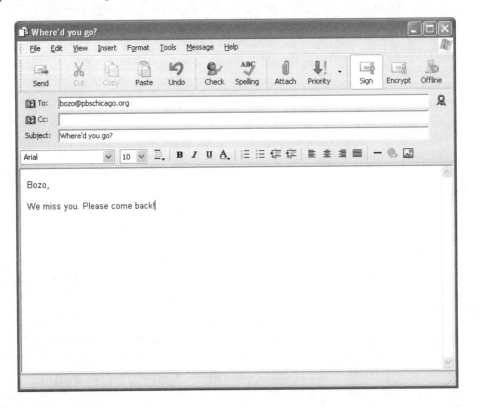

Sending Encrypted Mail

Sending encrypted mail is only slightly harder than sending signed mail. The difference is that before you can send signed mail to someone, you have to have that recipient's digital ID (public key) in your Windows Address Book (see Chapter 23, section "Storing Addresses in the Address Book"). Once you have the digital ID, create the message as usual in Outlook Express and click the Encrypt Message button (the envelope with the little blue lock) before sending the message. The encrypted mail icon looks like this:

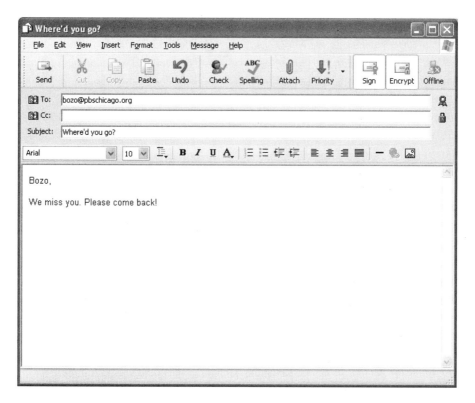

There are three common ways to obtain someone's digital ID: from a signed message he or she sent, from an online directory, or from a file obtained elsewhere, such as a Web-based lookup system.

Getting a Digital ID from Incoming Mail

Any time someone sends you a digitally signed message, you can get that person's digital ID from the message and add it to your Address Book. (Note that the digital ID is the equivalent of the sender's public key; the corresponding private key is not disclosed.) Open the message, select File | Properties, and click the Security tab; you see the View Certificates dialog box shown in Figure 31-6. Assuming that the signature is valid, click Add To Address Book. The Address Book opens, creating a new entry for your correspondent (if one does not already exist). Click the Digital IDs tab and observe that a digital ID is listed; then click OK to update the Address Book.

Getting a Digital ID Through LDAP Search

If you know that your correspondent has a digital ID and you know which certificate authority issued it, you can look it up in that authority's directory.

In Outlook Express, open the Address Book and click the Find button to open the search window, shown in Figure 31-7. In the Look In box, select the directory to search,

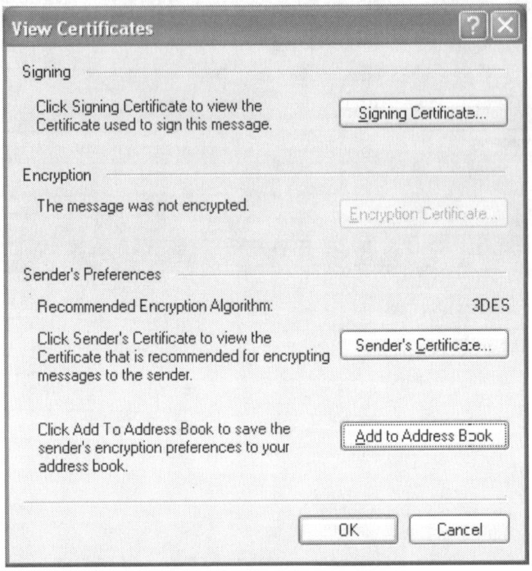

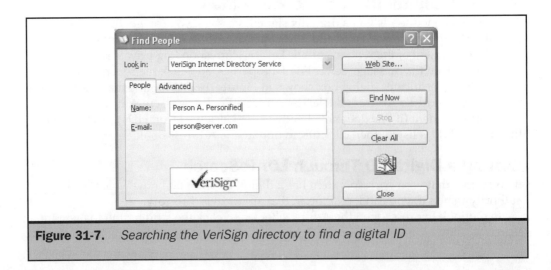

Figure 31-6. *Getting a digital ID from a mail message*

which is most likely VeriSign for personal digital IDs. Enter the person's name or e-mail address and click Find Now.

The directory returns a list of entries that match your request. Double-click any entry in the list to see the details, which are arranged like an Address Book entry, to be

Figure 31-7. *Searching the VeriSign directory to find a digital ID*

sure it's the person you want. If it is, click Add To Address Book to turn it into an Address Book entry, edit as desired (adding more personal info, usually), and click OK to update the Address Book.

Getting a Digital ID from a File

Digital IDs can be stored in certificate files, usually with the extension .cer (see "Securing Your Web Communication with Encryption and Certificates," earlier in the chapter). Someone can mail you a third party's ID as a file, or you might download the file from a Web-based search system.

To add the digital ID to your Address Book, open the Address Book and create an entry for the person, including his or her e-mail address. (The e-mail address has to match the one to which the certificate is assigned.) Then click the Address Book's Digital IDs tab, shown in Figure 31-8. Click the Import button and select the file containing the ID. The Address Book reads the digital ID and adds it to the Address Book entry.

If you want to store someone's digital ID in a file to transfer it to another computer or send it to a third person, open the Address Book entry for that person, click the Digital IDs tab, click Export, and specify the file to create.

Caution   *Don't try to export your own digital ID this way; bugs in Windows keep it from working. Remember, you can send anyone your digital ID by sending a signed e-mail message.*

Figure 31-8.   *Importing or exporting a digital ID*

Receiving Encrypted or Signed Mail

Outlook Express automatically handles incoming encrypted or signed mail. Signed messages have a little orange seal at the right end of the Security line of the message headers; encrypted messages have a little blue lock. When you open the message, Outlook Express automatically validates the signature or decrypts the message. The first time it does so, it displays a special window in place of the actual message, telling you what it did. Scroll down and click Continue to see the actual message. If you'd rather not see the special window in the future, a box above the Continue button lets you avoid the window in the future.

The
Complete
Reference

Part VII

Windows Housekeeping

The Complete Reference

Chapter 32

Formatting and Partitioning Disks

Before Windows XP can use a hard disk or a removable disk (including floppy disks), the disk must be prepared for use. Hard disks have to be *partitioned*, divided into one or more logical sections, using the Disk Management or compatible program. Both hard disks and removable disks must be formatted with a *file system*, the information that keeps track of which files are stored where on the disk. Windows XP supports three file systems: FAT (the file system used in DOS and Windows 95), FAT32 (file system introduced with Windows 95 OSR2 and used in Windows 98, 98SE, and Me), and NTFS 5.0 (the latest version of the file system designed for Windows NT/2000).

On computers with Windows preinstalled, the hard disk has already been partitioned (usually into a single large partition) and formatted. However, if you install an additional hard disk or replace the original hard disk, you have to partition and format the new disk. Some disks (both hard disks and removable disks) come preformatted and some don't. Whether or not a disk is preformatted, you can reformat it to remove any existing files and make it a "clean" empty disk.

Each disk drive, including floppy disk and CD drives, has a drive letter assigned to it by Windows, but you can change these letters, or assign drive letters to folders, if you must. You can also check how much free space is on any disk and look at the properties of a disk.

This chapter describes how to partition and format hard disks; how to decide whether to use FAT, FAT32, or NTFS (and how to convert partitions to NTFS); how to assign drive letters to disk drives; how to check for free space; and how to control the way in which Windows uses CD-ROMs. It also covers how to format and copy floppy disks.

Note *For information on dividing your hard disk into separate partitions for Windows XP and other operating systems, see the section "Creating Multiboot Installations" in the Appendix.*

What Are Partitions, File Systems, NTFS, and Drive Letters?

Partitions and file systems determine how and where Windows stores information on your disk. Drive letters refer to the various disks on your computer. Before you can decide which file system to use on your partitions, you need to know the differences among FAT, FAT32, and NTFS.

What Is a Partition?

A *partition* is a section of a hard disk. Every hard disk must be partitioned before Windows can use it. Normally, a disk is set up as a single large partition spanning the entire disk, but in some circumstances using more than one partition makes sense. When you partition a disk, you allocate a fixed amount of space to each partition.

Tip   *If your disks contain only one partition each, you can use the terms "disk drive" and "partition" interchangeably.*

Types of Partitions

Each partition on a disk is set up for a type of operating system. The partitions used by DOS and Windows have historically been called *primary partition* and *extended partition*. One disk drive can store either four primary partitions, or three primary partitions and one extended partition. An extended partition can contain many *logical drives*, which are also partitions—extended partitions provide a way to have more than four partitions on a disk. An extended partition can also contain free space, which isn't allocated to a logical drive. Disks can also contain unallocated space, which doesn't belong to any partition. Other operating systems, such as Linux and OS/2, have their own types of partitions.

When you are running Windows XP, it also designates partitions as system, boot, and active:

- **System partition**   Has the files needed to start up the computer (the most important startup file is called Ntldr, an abbreviation for "NT Loader"), stored in the root (main) folder. May be FAT, FAT32, or NTFS. For a multiboot system with Windows Me/9x, the system partition must be FAT or FAT32. The system partition can be small because only a few files are needed. The files needed to start the computer are Ntldr, Boot.ini, and Ntdetect.com.

- **Boot partition**   Has the files that contain the Windows XP operating system. May be formatted with the FAT (not recommended), FAT32, or NTFS (recommended) file system (see "What Is a File System?"). The boot partition must be large enough for the Windows XP program files and lots of extra space, since other programs usually install in the same partition and Microsoft encourages users to store data there, too.

- **Active partition**   Older term for the boot partition. You can mark a primary partition as active so that the next time you restart your computer, this partition will be used as the boot partition (see "Selecting the Active Partition").

The system and boot partitions can be the same partition, or they can be different. If they are different, the computer reads the files from the system partition first when it starts up, then switches to the boot partition to load Windows XP.

You can see what partitions your hard disks contain, what types of partitions they are, and which are your system and boot partitions, by using the Disk Management program (see "What Are the Properties of Disk Drives and Partitions?").

Note   *Windows also refers to partitions as volumes. Volumes can be disk partitions or they can be on storage media other than hard disks, such as tape drives.*

WINDOWS HOUSEKEEPING

Partitions for Multiple Operating Systems

If you run more than one operating system on your computer, you can create a partition for each operating system and then start the computer from either of the partitions, depending on which operating system you want to use. With Windows Me/9x, using multiple partitions to switch between different Windows versions was hard, because they all started from the primary partition. (PartitionMagic, a program you can purchase separately, enables you to install more than one version of Windows.) Windows NT and 2000 included the NT Boot manager, which made dual-boot systems easier to set up (see "Installing Multiple Versions of Windows with PartitionMagic").

Windows XP has partitioning built in, and its installation program can create a separate partition for it, leaving other versions of Windows alone. However, PartitionMagic is still useful for moving and resizing partitions.

What Is a File System?

A *file system* is the information that keeps track of which files and folders are stored where in a partition, and what disk space is free. The Windows file system includes a *FAT (File Allocation Table)* or *Master File Table*, which stores information about each *sector*, or physical block of storage space, on the disk.

Windows XP supports three different file systems: FAT, FAT32, and NTFS.

What Are FAT, FAT32, and NTFS?

FAT (or *FAT16*) dates back to DOS 3.0, and *FAT32* was introduced with the OSR2 update to Windows 95. *NTFS* (NT file system) is a more mature version of FAT32 that was originally designed for use with Windows NT and Windows 2000 for server applications. Each partition on a hard disk and each removable disk must be formatted with FAT, FAT32, or NTFS, but it's possible (and often desirable) to have some disks with one format and some with the other format on the same system.

Here are some facts about each of the file systems:

- **FAT** Partitions are limited to 4GB. Files are limited to 2GB. Works on floppy disks. Readable by DOS, OS/2, and all versions of Windows. Does not work with domains (server-based network security) (see Chapter 27, section "What Types of Networks Exist?"). Not recommended unless you need to share data with a DOS, OS/2, or Windows 95 system.

- **FAT32** Partitions can be from 512MB to 2 terabytes, although Windows XP can format a FAT32 only as large as 32GB. Files are limited to 4GB. Readable by Windows 95 OSR2, 98, Me, NT, 2000, and XP. Does not work with domains. Recommended for home systems with no security needs, and for systems that need to share data with a Windows 98 or Me system.

- **NTFS** Partition size can be from 520MB to 2 terabytes (larger sizes are possible, but not recommended). Files are limited only to the size of the partition. Can't be used on floppy disks. Readable by Windows 2000 and XP, and by Windows NT 4.0 with Service Pack 4 or later. Required for domains. Enables encrypted folders and files, permissions for individual folders and files, and disk quotas by user. Windows XP uses NTFS 5.0 (it was called 5.1 during product testing), a very slight upgrade from the version used in Windows 2000. Recommended for systems with security needs, large hard disks, and LAN connections.

Installing Multiple Versions of Windows with PartitionMagic

PartitionMagic is a program from PowerQuest Corporation (**http://www.powerquest.com/partitionmagic**) that allows one hard disk to include more than one primary partition. Each primary partition can contain a different version of Windows—for example, you can have one partition for Windows 98SE, one for Windows 2000, and one for Windows XP. PartitionMagic, using a small utility called BootMagic, enables you to switch among the primary partitions, using one and optionally hiding the rest. You need version 7.0 or later to work with Windows XP's NTFS partitions.

The Windows XP installation program can set up a separate partition for Windows XP, and the Windows Disk Management window can create and delete partitions, but it still can't do everything that we use PartitionMagic for, such as expanding, shrinking, copying, and moving partitions.

We like to use PartitionMagic to set up three partitions: one primary NTFS partition (which appears as drive C) for Windows XP; one extended partition (drive D) for data; and an extra, hidden primary NTFS partition for a duplicate copy of Windows XP. We use drive C for Windows and programs, and we use drive D for data—all documents, spreadsheets, e-mail, and other files that we create or edit. The hidden partition is a copy of drive C, made right after we install all the programs we usually use. Over the months, our working Windows partition (drive C) slowly fills up with junk, and Windows slows down and becomes less reliable. When Windows starts hanging, crashing, or acting funny, we copy the hidden partition to drive C using PartitionMagic, so we have a clean copy of Windows and our programs, without affecting our data. We developed this system over years of using earlier versions of Windows—we hope that Windows XP will prove to be so much more reliable that we rarely use the hidden copy of the primary partition.

Because all of our data is stored separately on drive D, backups can be smaller and faster, including only data and not programs.

Another way to keep a clean copy of your Windows partition is by using Drive Image, which can make a copy of an entire partition onto a Zip disk, Jaz disk, or writable CD-ROM. More information is available at **http://www.powerquest.com/driveimage**.

Both FAT32 and NTFS are designed for large partitions and disks and offer no significant benefits when used on smaller disks. However, with XP's rather significant system requirements it will be unlikely to see a system available with less than 10GB of hard drive space, making FAT16 largely useless.

 NTFS 5.0 was introduced with Windows 2000. The original NTFS that was used by Windows NT does not have the same features as NTFS 5.0. Partitions made with Windows NT need to be converted for Windows XP to use them. Windows XP automatically converts Windows 2000 to the slightly updated version of NTFS that it uses. Older versions of some partitioning utilities (like PartitionMagic version 6) don't work with Windows XP NTFS partitions: be sure to get the latest versions.

NTFS 5.0 offers all of the advantages of FAT32 as well as the following:

- **More efficient use of space**   NTFS can allocate as little as 2K of disk space to a file, reducing wasted disk space.

- **On-the-fly compression**   Individual files can be compressed and decompressed as needed. Entire drives can be reduced in size without affecting overall performance.

- **Encryption**   Files and folders can be encrypted with a user's password (see Chapter 8, section "What Are Attributes?").

Note *NTFS offers one big benefit to Windows XP Home Edition users: it supports password-protection of files and folders. If you have a network administrator at your workplace, consult with her before deciding which file system to use for your partitions.*

Why Divide Your Hard Disk into Partitions?

Most often, you allocate all the space on a hard disk to one partition, which Windows treats as a single logical disk drive using a single drive letter (drive C for the first hard disk). You can also allocate some of the space to the primary partition and some to an extended partition, which can, in turn, be subdivided into multiple logical disks.

As a general rule, a single partition is all you ever need. However, here are circumstances where more than one partition will be useful:

- **Compatibility with older operating systems**   If you want a disk to be usable from DOS, Windows 3.1, or Windows 95, you need to make a FAT16 partition that is less than 2GB. If you want a disk to be usable from Windows 98 or Me, make a FAT32 partition.

- **Scratch areas**   In some cases, it's useful to have a separate partition to use as a scratch area that you can quickly reformat to wipe out its contents and start fresh.

- **Multiboot systems**   The boot manager built into Windows (or PartitionMagic) can dynamically reassign active partitions so that you can effectively have more than one operating system on a large drive (see "Installing Multiple Versions of Windows with PartitionMagic").

■ **Data partitions**   We recommend creating a separate partition for your data—all your documents, spreadsheets, databases, and other files. You should back up your data partition regularly. You needn't back up your programs as often because you can restore them from your program CDs.

■ **Quotas**   You can set quotas for each user, limiting the amount of space that each user can use on a partition (see Chapter 6, section "Setting Quotas for Disk Usage").

Don't slice your disk into too many partitions—we rarely use more than three. Unlike folders, when you create a partition, you must decide in advance how much disk space to devote to that partition. You are bound to run out of space in one partition while you still have plenty of space in another.

What Are Drive Letters?

Every partition, logical drive, and removable disk available to Windows has a *drive letter*. Drive A is the floppy disk drive, and drive B is reserved for a second floppy disk. Hard disk partitions are assigned letters in order. Drive C is usually the primary partition on your first hard disk. If logical drives are in an extended partition, they are assigned letters next. Then, if you have more than one hard disk, the partitions on those disks are assigned letters. Finally, each *removable disk*, such as a CD-ROM or Zip disk, is assigned a letter, with the order of the letters being arbitrary. Any remaining letters can be used for network drives.

On a typical system, the floppy disk is A, the hard disk is C, and the CD-ROM is D.

Windows XP has an annoying habit of reassigning drive letters, so that the drive that contains the Windows program itself may not be C, and hard disk drive letters may follow CD-ROM drive letters. You can reassign drive letters if necessary (see "Choosing Your Own Drive Letters").

What Are the Properties of Disk Drives and Partitions?

Windows stores a set of properties for each installed disk drive and partition, and allows you to manage them from one program, Disk Management. Even though the option is not visible in the Windows XP Home Edition, the Disk Management utility is still there. To use the Disk Management program, you display the Computer Management window by right-clicking My Computer and selecting Manage. In the Computer Management window that appears, click the Disk Management item under the Storage heading. The Computer Management window with Disk Management selected, as shown in Figure 32-1, includes everything that you ever wanted to know about hard disks in an easy-to-read format.

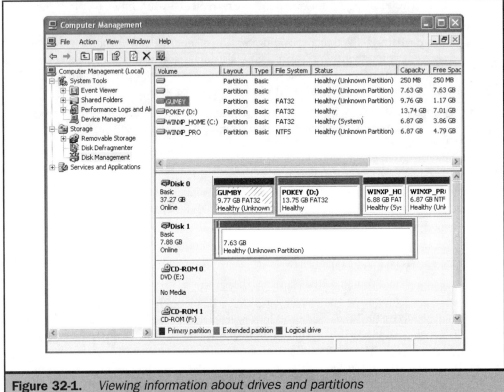

Figure 32-1. *Viewing information about drives and partitions*

Properties of Partitions (Volumes), Floppy Drives, CD-ROM Drives, and DVD Drives

The top part of the Disk Management pane (or the right half of the Computer Management window), lists the volumes (partitions and volumes stored on other devices) on your computer. It lists all disks, drives, and partitions that are loaded, mounted, and recognized by Windows XP. It doesn't include removable storage like floppies, CDs, or DVDs. The columns that run across the top of the volume list are

- **Volume** The label name applied to the volume.

- **Layout** Generally a partition. For server computers that provide large-scale storage to networks of computers, other types of volumes may be listed: *spanned volumes* (which make many disks look like a single, large volume), *striped volumes* (which store data on two or more disks in an alternating pattern), *mirrored volumes* (which duplicate the data from the volume on other disks, to minimize the possibility of losing data), and *RAID-5 volumes* (striped volumes that use three or more disks).

■ **Type**   Identifies whether the volume is Basic or Dynamic. A *dynamic disk* is formatted so that volumes can be changed on-the-fly (dynamically)—*dynamic volumes*. Dynamic disks are supported only by Windows XP and 2000. Disks on workstation computers are generally Basic.

■ **File System**   Indicates whether the volume is FAT, FAT32, or NTFS. A blank entry indicates a file system *other* than one developed by Microsoft, such as EXT2 (Linux extended), NFS (Network File System, from Sun Microsystems), or HFS (Hierarchical File System, from Apple).

■ **Status**   Shows the state of the volume and its relationship to the operating system. Typical states are Healthy, Healthy (At Risk), Initializing, and Failed. If you are using spanned volumes, you might also see Resynching, Regenerating, Failed Redundancy, or Failed Redundancy (At Risk).

■ **Capacity**   Shows the overall capacity for the volume.

■ **Free Space**   Shows the space that is free on the volume.

■ **% Free**   Shows free space in percentage format.

The last items here are for the seriously nerdy, system administrator types among you:

■ **Fault Tolerant**   Shows whether the drive is capable of protecting itself from its own errors or if the volume is a member of a fault tolerant *RAID* (redundant array of independent disks).

■ **Overhead**   Indicates the amount of space used by spanned disks. This space can only be used by the volume stripe and cannot store data.

Each item on your system with a drive letter—each hard disk partition, floppy disk, and removable disk—also has properties. You can display these properties from a Windows Explorer window (for example, open Start | My Computer); right-click the drive, and choose Properties from the menu that appears. From the Disk Management pane of the Computer Management window, right-click the partition and choose Properties. Figure 32-2 shows the Properties dialog box for a partition (the dialog boxes for floppy and removable disks look similar).

Table 32-1 lists the settings on the General and Tools tabs of the Properties dialog box for a partition. The Tools tab doesn't appear for disks you can't write on, such as CD-ROM drives. If you use a local area network (LAN) and are using Windows XP Professional, the Sharing tab appears (see Chapter 29, section "Sharing Your Disk Drives and Folders with Others"). If you have turned off Simple File Sharing, the Security and Quota tabs appear (see Chapter 29, section "Enabling Security for Shared Resources"). The Hardware tab lists disk drives. If you have installed a hard-disk housekeeping program like Norton Utilities, additional tabs may appear.

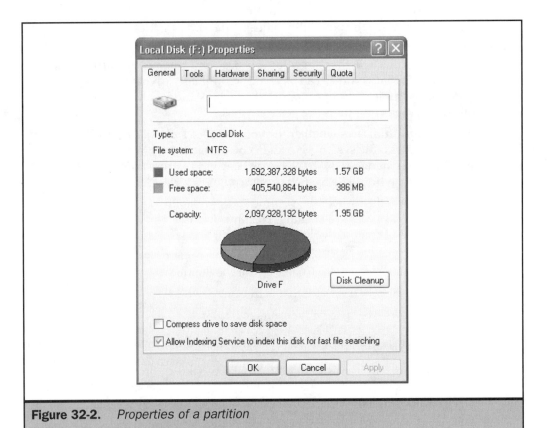

Figure 32-2. *Properties of a partition*

Tab	Setting	Description
General	Label	Specifies the name of the disk, which you can edit.
General	Type	Specifies whether this disk is a *local disk* (disk connected to your own computer), *network disk* (hard disk connected to a computer you can access over a network), floppy disk, CD-ROM drive, DVD drive, or removable disk drive.

Table 32-1. *Settings on the General, Tools, and Hardware Tabs of the Properties Dialog Box for Partitions*

Tab	Setting	Description
General	File system	Specifies the file system used on the disk. For hard disks, the types are FAT, FAT32, or NTFS. For CD-ROMs, the file system is CDFS.
General	Used space	Specifies how much disk space is occupied by files (including files in the Recycle Bin).
General	Free space	Specifies how much disk space is available for use.
General	Capacity	Specifies the total capacity of the disk drive; a pie chart shows how much is in use. Click the Disk Cleanup button to look for and delete unneeded files (see Chapter 33, section "Deleting Temporary Files with Disk Cleanup").
Tools	Error-checking	Click the Check Now button to run ChkDsk on this disk drive (see Chapter 33, section "Testing Your Disk Structure with ChkDsk").
Tools	Defragmentation	Click the Defragment Now button to run Disk Defragmenter on this disk drive (see Chapter 33, section "Defragmenting Your Disk").
Tools	Backup	Click Backup Now to run the Microsoft Backup Utility (see Chapter 9).
Hardware	All disk drives	Displays a list of all drives installed on the system, including hard disks, floppy disks, CD-ROMs, and DVDs.
Hardware	Device Properties	Shows the manufacturer, location, and status for the selected drive and offers the Troubleshoot button for device-specific troubleshooting, and the Properties button for the drive's properties.

Table 32-1.   *Settings on the General, Tools, and Hardware Tabs of the Properties Dialog Box for Partitions* (continued)

Properties of Hard Disk Drives

The bottom half of the Disk Management pane lists the hard disk, CD-ROM, CD-R/RW, and DVD drives on your computer. To the right of each disk name is a diagram of the partitions that are stored on that drive. You see the same partitions that appear in the volume list, in the approximate positions where they are stored on the drives (the sizes of the partitions aren't accurately depicted, though). This diagram includes *hidden partitions* (partitions with file systems that Windows XP can't read), even though you cannot access them or their files.

The Properties dialog box for a disk drive (shown in Figure 32-3) usually includes four tabs—General, Disk Policies, Volumes, and Driver. To display the dialog box from the Disk Management pane of the Computer Management window, right-click a disk drive from the list in the lower part of the window and choose Properties from the menu that appears. Or, choose Start | My Computer, right-click any drive or partition, select Properties from the menu that appears (you see the properties of that partition), click the Hardware tab, select the drive you are interested in, and click the Properties button. Table 32-2 lists the properties of a hard disk drive.

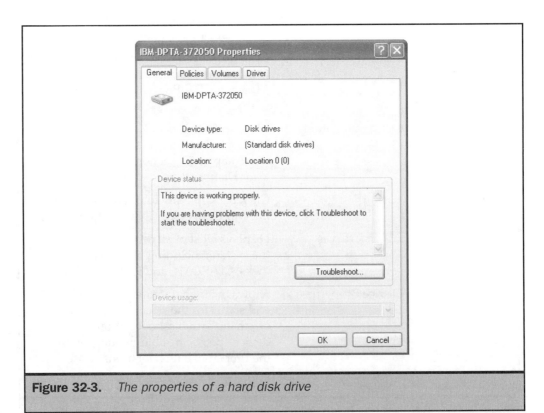

Figure 32-3.   *The properties of a hard disk drive*

Tab	Setting	Description
General	Device type	Set to "Disk drives" by Windows.
General	Manufacturer	Manufacturer of the disk drive, if known.
General	Location	How the drive is physically connected to the computer.
General	Device status	Current status of the disk drive. Click the Troubleshoot button to run the Troubleshooting Wizard.
General	Device usage	Whether the drive is enabled.
Policies	Enable write caching on the disk	When selected, enables the write cache, which on some drives improves performance.
Volumes	Disk	Disk number Windows assigns to the drive. The first disk attached to the first disk controller is disk 0. Floppy disk, CD-ROM, and DVD drives don't have disk numbers.
Volumes	Type	Drive's Type value, typically Basic. Other types are Dynamic, CDRom, Removable (for Zip, Jaz, and similar disks), and DVD.
Volumes	Status	What the drive is doing now, usually Online (working). Other statuses are Offline (not working), Online (Errors) (something is wrong), Foreign, Unreadable, Unrecognized, and No Media (no disk in the drive).
Volumes	Partition Style	How the disk is partitioned, usually MBR (Master Boot Record). Other styles are GPT (GUID Partition Table).
Volumes	Capacity	Total space available.
Volumes	Unallocated Space	Space not allocated to an existing volume partition.
Volumes	Reserved Space	Amount of space allocated to other uses other than storing data.

Table 32-2. *Properties of a Hard Disk Drive*

Tab	Setting	Description
Volumes	Volumes	List of volumes stored on the drive (click the Populate button to tell Windows to gather and display the information). Click the Properties button to see the Properties dialog box for the selected volume.
Driver	Provider/Date Version/ Digital Signer	Source and date of the driver used for this disk drive; many drivers come with Windows XP. Click the Driver Details to see details about the installed device driver. Click the Update driver to run the Update Device Driver Wizard to look for a more recent driver for your disk drive; the Wizard can look on the Windows CD (or floppies) or can connect to the Internet to look for a driver. Click the Roll Back Driver button to reinstall the previous version of the driver (if something fails after you update the driver, returning to the previous version can restore original functionality). Click the Uninstall button to remove the driver from the system, rendering the device unusable.

Table 32-2.   *Properties of a Hard Disk Drive* (continued)

Partitioning a Disk Using Disk Management

When you buy a new computer or hard disk, you receive it ready for use—already partitioned (usually with one partition) and formatted. If you are adding new unformatted, unpartitioned disk drives, or if you want to create a computer system that can run one of several operating systems—such as switching between Windows XP and UNIX or Linux—you may need to partition a disk yourself. However, formatting destroys the data in the areas of the disk it partitions, so be sure to make a backup copy of all the information on your disk before formatting a disk or partition (see Chapter 9).

 Most of the commands in this chapter are available only to users who have administrator user accounts (see Chapter 6)—user accounts that give them permission to make changes to the system itself. Before working with partitions and drives, be sure to back up the important files on your system (see Chapter 9).

Volume	Layout	Type	File System	Status	Capacity	Free Space	% Free	Fault Tolerance	Overhead
🖿	Partition	Basic		Healthy (Unknown Partition)	250 MB	250 MB	100 %	No	0%
🖿	Partition	Basic		Healthy (Unknown Partition)	7.63 GB	7.63 GB	100 %	No	0%
🖿 GUMBY	Partition	Basic	FAT32	Healthy (Unknown Partition)	9.76 GB	1.17 GB	11 %	No	0%
🖿 POKEY (D:)	Partition	Basic	FAT32	Healthy	13.74 GB	7.01 GB	51 %	No	0%
🖿 WINXP_HOME (C:)	Partition	Basic	FAT32	Healthy (System)	6.87 GB	3.86 GB	56 %	No	0%
🖿 WINXP_PRO	Partition	Basic	NTFS	Healthy (Unknown Partition)	6.87 GB	4.79 GB	69 %	No	0%

💾Disk 0				
Basic 37.27 GB Online	**GUMBY** 9.77 GB FAT32 Healthy (Unknown Partition)	**POKEY (D:)** 13.75 GB FAT32 Healthy	**WINXP_HOME (C:)** 6.88 GB FAT32 Healthy (System)	**WINXP_PRO** 6.87 GB NTFS Healthy (Unknown Pa

💾Disk 1	
Basic 7.88 GB Online	7.63 GB Healthy (Unknown Partition)

💿CD-ROM 0 DVD (E:)	
No Media	

💿CD-ROM 1 CD-ROM (F:)	
No Media	

■ Primary partition ■ Extended partition ■ Logical drive

Figure 32-4. *The Disk Management pane of the Computer Management window*

To partition a hard disk, you use the Disk Management tool, a tool straight from Windows 2000. To run Disk Management, choose Start, right-click My Computer, and select Manage from the menu that appears. When you see the Computer Management window, click the Disk Management item listed underneath the Storage heading. You then see the main Disk Management pane in the right side of the Computer Management window, as shown in Figure 32-4.

Many computer systems have only one hard disk and one CD-ROM (CD-R/RW, DVD, or what have you), which appear as Disk 0 and CD-ROM 0 in the left column of the lower pane. Figure 32-4 shows two hard disks, Disk 0 and Disk 1, and two removable storage drives, CD-ROM 0 and CD-ROM 1. Disk 0 is a 40GB drive that has three primary partitions and one logical partition; Disk 1 is an 8GB drive that has no space allocated.

Note *The Disk Management program replaces the Fdisk program that was part of previous versions of Windows.*

Creating a New Partition

If you have unallocated space (which appears as an Unknown Partition in the Disk Management diagram), you can create a new partition in some or all of that space. For example, you could create a new partition for Windows on the 8GB drive in Figure 32-4. To create a new partition, right-click the part of the diagram that represents the unallocated space (unallocated space has a black stripe running along the top), and choose New Partition from the menu that appears. To create a new logical drive in an extended partition that contains free space (free space has a light green strip along the top), right-click the free space and choose New Logical Drive from the menu that appears. Either way, you see the New Partition Wizard.

The New Partition Wizard asks you to specify the following:

- **Type**   Primary, extended, or logical partition. A disk drive can contain up to four primary partitions, or three primary partitions and one extended partition. The logical partition type is available only if you choose to create the new partition in an extended partition with some free space. Choose a primary partition if you are created a partition in which you will install an operating system (an unusual situation). Choose extended if you plan to create several logical partitions within it.

- **Size**   The Wizard displays the minimum and maximum size for the partition, based on its type and the space where it will be stored. You can use the entire available space, or leave room for other partitions. Windows XP doesn't provide a way to resize partitions later, but you can use a third-party program like PartitionMagic to do so (see "Installing Multiple Versions of Windows with PartitionMagic").

- **Drive letter or path**   The Wizard offers the next available drive letter, but you may select any unused letter. To use the Mount In The Following Empty NTFS Folder option, you must have an NTFS partition with a drive letter on the same machine. If you plan on installing more than one operating system on your computer, you may select the Do Not Assign A Drive Letter Or Drive Path option, and let Windows assign a letter later. We usually take the default drive letter assignment.

- **File system**   The default is NTFS, but you can feel good about using FAT32 as well (see "What Are FAT, FAT32, and NTFS?"). Both efficiently utilize space on large drives, but NTFS has more security features, better recovery capabilities after a crash, and file-level compression built in. If you select NTFS, you are also given the option to enable compression. Leave the Allocation unit size as Default.

- **Label**   Type a name for the partition, indicating what you will use it for.

Figure 32-5 shows the final screen of the New Partition Wizard, summarizing your choices before Windows creates the partition. Formatting a new partition can take several minutes (see "Formatting a Disk").

Selecting the Active Partition

If you partition your disk among multiple operating systems, one of the partitions is the active partition, the partition from which your computer starts. If you run Windows only, the primary partition is always active. In Windows XP you can change

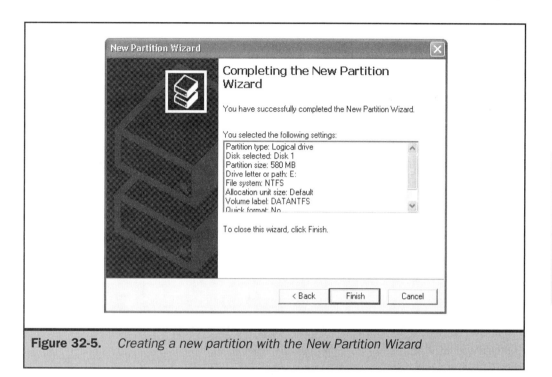

Figure 32-5.   *Creating a new partition with the New Partition Wizard*

this behavior manually by selecting another partition as active using the Disk Management pane in the Computer Management window. Right-click the disk or partition that you want to make active and select Mark Partition As Active from the menu that appears. You can only make this change to primary partitions. Extended partitions and logical drives cannot be made active. Only one partition is active at a time—and make sure it's a partition that contains a bootable operating system!

Deleting a Partition

You can delete a partition using the Disk Management pane of the Computer Management window. Right-click the partition and choose Delete Partition (for a primary or extended partition) or Delete Logical Drive (for a logical drive). If you want to delete an extended partition, you first have to delete all the logical drives in the partition.

 When you delete a partition, all the files and folders on the partition are deleted for good—they don't go to the Recycle Bin. There's no way to get them back (unless you have a backup copy).

Repartitioning a Disk

Repartitioning a disk with Windows XP is unpleasant at best. Windows can only create and delete partitions—it can't move, resize, or copy them, and converting them requires using a DOS command. To rearrange the partitions on your system using only the Windows Disk Management program, you delete the partitions that are the wrong size or in the wrong location. Then create new partitions. Follow these steps:

1. Back up all the files on the partitions that you need to delete (see Chapter 9).

2. Open the Disk Management pane in the Computer Management window—choose Start, right-click My Computer, choose Manage, and click Disk Management under the Storage heading in the Computer Management window. You see the Disk Management pane shown in Figure 32-4.

3. Delete the partitions that are in the wrong place or are the wrong size by right-clicking each one and choosing Delete Partition or Delete Logical Drive from the menu that appears.

4. Create new ones by right-clicking the unallocated space (or free space in an extended partition) and choosing New Partition or New Logical Drive from the menu that appears.

5. Reload the backed up data.

Third-party disk utilities, such as PartitionMagic, make this process safer and easier and permit many kinds of changes without backing up and reloading everything. PartitionMagic can move, copy, and resize partitions without deleting them (it's amazing, actually). Utilities such as Drive Image make it easy to create a copy of a partition so you can reload it later. If you plan to use multiple partitions, we recommend you look into third-party partitioning programs (see the section "Installing Multiple Versions of Windows with PartitionMagic" earlier in this chapter).

Converting Partitions to NTFS

Windows comes with a Convert command that can convert a FAT or FAT32 partition to NTFS (the Convert command can't convert anything to FAT or FAT32). To convert a partition to NTFS (after backing it up!), follow these steps:

1. Choose Start | All Programs | Accessories | Command Prompt to open a Command Prompt window (see Chapter 39, section "Starting DOS Programs").

2. Type **convert** *n:* **/FS:NTFS** and press ENTER, replacing *n:* with the drive letter of the partition you want to convert. If you want verbose mode, in which you see extra explanatory messages, type **/v** at the end of the command.

 If you need to convert to a file system other than NTFS, try PartitionMagic. Be sure to get the latest version, since earlier versions don't support NTFS 5.0, which is new in Windows XP.

Choosing Your Own Drive Letters

Windows assigns a drive letter to each partition, logical drive, and removable disk that it can read. Whenever possible, we recommend you use the drive letters Windows assigns (see "What Are Drive Letters?"). If you can't, (for example, you are using an antiquated program that expects files to be on certain drives or you install an application that reassigns drive letters willy-nilly like WinOnCD 3.8), you have a few options: change the letters, assign letters to folders, or assign pathnames to drives or partitions.

When assigning or changing drive letters, you can use any unassigned letter from C to Z (inclusive). Letters A and B are reserved for floppy disk drives. If a program is using the files on a drive or partition when you try to change its letter, Windows displays an error message.

Changing Drive Letters

You can tell Windows to assign different drive letters to most of your drives and partitions. You cannot, however, change the drive letter of the boot partition (the one that contains the Windows XP program files). You can alternately add new drive letter assignment or, if you're using NTFS, assign special folders to act as conduits to drives.

To change the drive letter for a partition, follow these steps:

1. Choose Start, right-click My Computer, and choose Manage from the menu that appears. In the Computer Management window, click the Disk Management item under the Storage heading (as shown in Figure 32-1 earlier in the chapter). The Disk Management pane appears in the right part of the Computer Management window.

2. Locate the partition whose letter you would like to change in the upper-right pane of the Computer Management console (the volume list) or the lower-right pane (the list of drives and the diagram of partitions on each drive).

3. Right-click the partition and select Change Drive Letters And Paths from the menu that appears. You see the dialog box shown in Figure 32-6.

4. Click the Change button to modify the existing letter assignment. You see this dialog box:

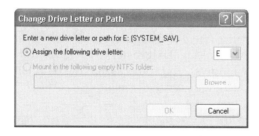

5. Type or choose a letter in the Assign The Following Drive Letter box and click OK. You return to the Computer Management window, with updated drive letters for the partition.

You can't add a second drive letter to a partition—each partition has only one drive letter at a time. You can remove the drive letter, though, by clicking the Remove button

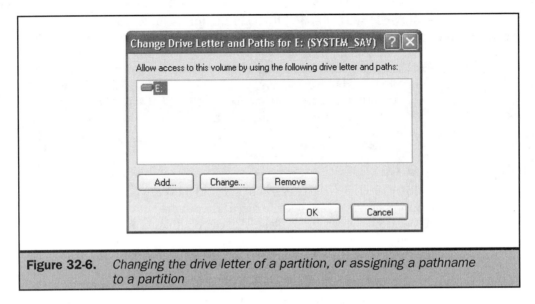

Figure 32-6. *Changing the drive letter of a partition, or assigning a pathname to a partition*

in the Change Drive Letter And Paths dialog box. Windows warns you not to proceed if the drive letter is in use. If you click the Add button, Windows assumes that you want to assign a pathname to the partition, as described in the next section.

 Don't change the drive letters of the boot partition (which contains Windows XP itself—Windows XP shouldn't allow you to, anyway). Watch out when changing the drive letter of a partition that contains programs. With a different drive letter, existing references to the program files on that partition would be wrong. Changing the drive letter does not update references to the files on that partition.

Assigning Pathnames to Partitions

You can assign a pathname—like C:\My Documents or D:\Budget Workarea—to a partition. The partition still has its usual drive letter (unless you remove it), but it also has a second name—a pathname. For example, if you want to store your documents on a second partition (which would make it easier to back up, and wouldn't fill up the partition that contains Windows), you could assign the pathname C:\My Documents to the partition D:. This technique is called *mounting a partition.*

 Any space allocated to a specific file system is called a partition, whether it is a small partition on a large drive or a single partition that takes up an entire drive.

Before you mount a partition (that is, assign it a pathname) you choose two things:

- **The partition to mount** It continues to have its original drive letter, unless you delete the drive letter. The partition can contain files and folders, which will not be disturbed by assigning a pathname to the drive.

■ **The pathname to assign to the partition** The pathname must refer to an existing, empty folder on an NTFS partition. After you assign the pathname to the partition (mount the partition), Windows will redirect references to that folder to the partition instead.

For example, rather than storing all your user's settings and files in the C:\Documents And Settings folders and their subfolders, you might want to store them on a separate partition. You could format a partition with NTFS for this purpose. Move the entire contents of C:\Documents And Settings to the new partition, and mount this partition at the pathname C:\Documents And Settings.

Caution *Be sure to empty the folder in which you are about to mount a partition. In the C:\Documents And Settings example, move the contents of C:\Documents And Settings before issuing the command to mount the partition at the pathname. After issuing the command, you won't be able to access those files and folders—Windows will redirect all requests to the new partition.*

To assign a pathname to a partition or drive, follow these steps:

1. In an Explorer window, create an empty folder (choose New | Folder from the menu) in a partition formatted with NTFS. Or, empty out an existing folder. If you have a blank NTFS partition, you can use the root folder. (In the C:\Documents And Settings example, you might use a partition currently named F:.)

2. Choose Start, right-click My Computer, and choose Manage from the menu that appears. In the Computer Management window, click the Disk Management item under the Storage heading (as shown in Figure 32-1 earlier in the chapter). The Disk Management pane appears in the right part of the Computer Management window.

3. Right-click the partition that you want to mount and choose Change Drive Letter And Paths from the menu that appears. You see the dialog box shown in Figure 32-6. (In our example, right-click the F: partition.)

4. Click the Add button to create a new pathname for the partition. You see this dialog box:

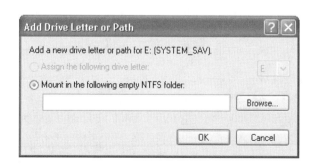

5. In the Mount In The Following Empty NTFS Folder box, type the pathname that you want to assign to the partition, or click the Browse button and navigate to the empty folder you identified in step 1. (In our example, browse to C:\Documents And Settings.)

6. Click OK.

You can also assign a drive letter to a network drive or a folder stored on a network drive (see Chapter 29, section "Mapping a Shared Drive or Folder to a Drive Letter").

Assigning Drive Letters to Folders

You can use the DOS SUBST command to assign new drive letters that correspond to folders on existing disks. Follow these steps:

1. Open a Command Prompt window by choosing Start | All Programs | Accessories | Command Prompt.

2. Type the SUBST command in the following format (press ENTER after typing the command):

   SUBST N: C:\MYAPP

   This command makes the drive letter N a synonym for the folder C:\Myapp. You can use any unused drive letter and the address (pathname) of any folder.

3. Type **exit** to close the Command Prompt window.

The new substituted drive letter is available immediately.

If the path of your folder uses long names, then in the SUBST command, you have to use the MS-DOS name equivalent, as shown by the DOS DIR command (see Chapter 39, section "What Are DOS Names?").

To disconnect a SUBSTed drive letter, type the following:

SUBST N: /D

The SUBST command lists only until you restart Windows. If you use a SUBSTed drive on a regular basis, put the SUBST command in your Autoexec.nt file so that it's available every time you start Windows (see Chapter 39).

Formatting a Disk

Every disk, including hard disks and floppies, must be formatted before you can use it. Formatting a disk writes the file system, the low-level structure information needed to track where files and folders will be located on the disk (see "What Is a File System?"). When you buy a new computer, the hard disk is typically formatted at the factory.

Figure 32-7.   *The Format dialog box*

Generally, you need to format disks only when you want to clean off a floppy disk or other removable disk (like a Zip or Jaz disk) for reuse, if you repartition your hard disk and create a new partition, or if you have a disaster with Windows and want to reinstall it from scratch.

Caution   *Formatting a disk—hard disk or removable—deletes all the information from the disk, so proceed with care!*

Formatting a Hard Disk

Before formatting your hard disk (or one partition on a hard disk), be sure you make a backup copy of any files you want to keep (see Chapter 9). To format a hard disk, follow these steps:

1. Open My Computer and locate the drive you want to format.

2. Right-click the icon for the drive and choose Format in the menu that pops up. You see the Format dialog box shown in Figure 32-7. Almost none of the fields in the window, except for the volume label, apply to hard disks—leave them with their default settings.

3. Type a drive label in the Volume Label box (if the box is blank or if you want to change the existing label) and click the Start button in the Format dialog box.

4. If the drive contains files or folders, Windows asks whether you really want to reformat the disk because existing files will be lost. Assuming you want to format the disk, choose Yes to do so. Formatting can take several minutes—the process involves reading the entire disk to check for bad spots.

You can't format the disk from which you are running Windows; Windows displays an error message saying the disk contains files Windows is using. You can't format a CD-ROM either.

Formatting a Removable Disk

Formatting a removable disk (like a floppy disk, Zip disk, or Jaz disk) is like formatting a hard disk, except more format options are available. If you only want to erase the files on a previously formatted disk without rechecking for bad spots, select Quick Format or Quick (Erase) on the Format dialog box shown in Figure 32-4. Then click the Start button in the Format dialog box.

When you format a disk, Windows may report bad sectors on the disk. Windows marks the sectors as unusable, to prevent programs from trying to write information there. If a floppy disk has any bad sectors, throw it away and use a new one—floppy disks are too cheap for you to fool around with the possibility of losing data.

To make a boot floppy disk (a floppy disk from which you can start the computer, in the event that the hard disk is corrupted), choose the Create An MS-DOS Startup Disk check box (see Chapter 35, section "The Boot Floppy Disk").

Copying a Floppy Disk

To copy a floppy disk (that is, to copy all the information from one floppy to another while erasing the previous contents of the disk you are copying into), right-click the floppy disk in an Explorer window and choose Copy Disk from the shortcut menu that appears. Click Start and follow the prompts to insert first the original disk and then the disk onto which you want to copy.

*If you copy floppy disks often, create an icon on your desktop for the Copy Disk command. Right-click a blank space on the desktop and choose New | Shortcut from the shortcut menu that appears. In the Type The Location Of The Item box on the Create Shortcut dialog box that appears, type **diskcopy a: a:** (the DOS command that copies a floppy). Click Next. In the Type A Name For This Shortcut box, type a name like **Copy Floppy**. Click Next, choose an icon, and click Finish.*

Checking Free Space

You can easily see how much free space is available on any partition. Choose Start | My Computer and select the partition (or drive). Right-click the partition or drive and select Properties from the menu that appears. You see a Properties dialog box with a pie chart like the one in Figure 32-2 (if the General tab isn't selected, click it).

 Click the Disk Cleanup button to look for and delete unneeded files (see Chapter 33, section "Deleting Temporary Files with Disk Cleanup").

Using CD-ROMs and Audio CDs

Because CD-ROMs (CDs containing software) and audio CDs (CDs containing sound) are prerecorded at the factory, no preparation is needed to use them. Just insert them in the drive, and Windows recognizes them. If a CD-ROM contains an *AutoRun* program (that is, a file named Autorun.inf in the root folder of the CD-ROM, containing instructions for what program to run), Windows runs it. On audio CDs, Windows runs the Windows Media Player application automatically, turning your computer into a CD player (see Chapter 19, section "Playing Audio CDs")—useful if you like background music while you work.

Tip *If you don't want the AutoRun program on a CD-ROM to run, or you don't want Windows to start playing an audio CD, open the drive, insert the disk, and hold down the SHIFT key while closing the drive—keep the SHIFT key down until you are sure no program has started.*

If the CD-ROM that you insert contains audio or video files (i.e., MP3 or AVI video), a dialog box appears asking what you would like to do with the media contained on the disk. Your options are to either play the files or to open an Explorer window displaying the items. Checking the Always Do The Selected Action check box causes Windows to either play or display the files for that disk.

Note *Unlike previous versions of Windows, Windows XP has no way to turn off Autorun from the CD-ROM drive's Properties dialog box. One thing you can do is hold the SHIFT key when closing the drive door. Autorun does not operate when you hold down the SHIFT key.*

WINDOWS HOUSEKEEPING

The Complete Reference

Chapter 33

Keeping Your Disk Safe

Your disk contains an incredible amount of information; the hard disks on most Windows XP machines hold anywhere from 4 to 80 gigabytes (GB). (One gigabyte is equal to 1 billion bytes). Some of the space on each disk is used to store the structure of the disk, including a table of the parts of the disk that are free (available for storing new information), a table of the files and folders on the disk, and a list of which blocks on the disk store the information in which file.

If this structural information gets corrupted, you can lose some or all of the information on the disk. It's wise to check the structure of the information on each hard disk regularly by using a Windows program called ChkDsk—which not only checks the disk structure, but can also fix most of the errors that it finds.

Another disk problem arises when you create and delete many files over a long period of time. Files are stored in a series of sectors on your disk, and the sectors are not necessarily next to each other. While this is more of a problem for FAT32 partitions, NTFS partitions can also become fragmented after time. To fix this problem, you can run the Disk Defragmenter utility that comes with Windows. Disk Defragmenter moves the information on your disk around to speed up access.

Many programs create temporary or backup files, which are not always deleted when they are no longer needed. The Disk Cleanup program can delete stale temporary files for you.

Does it sound like you have a lot to worry about to keep your Windows system tidy? Fortunately, you can schedule Windows to run these housekeeping programs for you. In fact, you can tell the Scheduled Tasks program to run any program on a regular basis. Be sure to make regular backups of your hard disk, too (see Chapter 9).

> **Note**   *If you need to restore your Windows system files to the way they were before you installed an upgrade or before your system started having problems, try the System Restore program (see Chapter 35, section "Returning Your System to a Predefined State with System Restore"). For information about your system, try the System Information program (see Chapter 35, section "System Information").*

Windows File Protection

Windows XP comes with a feature called *Windows File Protection*, or *WFP*. WFP is running whenever Windows is running, monitoring the files that make up Windows itself. Whenever a program replaces one of the Windows system files, WFP checks whether the new file was accompanied by a "signed" (verified and encrypted) file from Microsoft. If not, or if an earlier version of a file has replaced a later version, WFP replaces the file with its own copy (from the WFP collection of duplicate files at C:\Windows\System32\dllcache).

You don't have to turn WFP on, and there's no way to turn it off. WFP doesn't display any messages when it decides to replace a system file with its own version, but it may prompt you to insert the Windows XP CD-ROM to reinstall a file.

Testing Your Disk Structure with ChkDsk

The ChkDsk (Check Disk) program can both diagnose and repair errors on a wide variety of devices, including hard disks, floppy disks, RAM drives, removable disks, and laptop memory cards. ChkDsk can check the physical surface of disk drivers for bad sectors and possibly recover lost data, and it checks the file allocation table (FAT), the directory structure, and the long filenames associated with many files.

If Windows crashes or you turn off the computer without shutting down, Windows typically runs ChkDsk when you restart to check your hard disk for errors resulting from the unexpected termination. There are some occasions when ChkDsk will not run.

Running ChkDsk

Certain functions, like fixing disk errors and recovering lost sectors, are not accessible while Windows is running. This is because the repairs cannot be completed while there are open files on the disk to be fixed. When you try to run ChkDsk, Windows might need to schedule the program to run the next time you restart Windows instead.

To run ChkDsk, follow these steps:

1. Right-click the disk drive in an Explorer window and choose Properties.

2. On the Properties dialog box for the disk, click the Tools tab and click the Check Now button. You see the Check Disk dialog box:

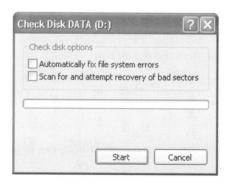

3. Select both check boxes to perform a full disk check and click Start. You usually see a message saying that Windows can't run the program until the next time you start Windows.

4. Click Yes. The next time Windows starts, you see a message that the disk check has been scheduled, and displaying the results as the program runs, which can take several minutes (depending on the size of the disk). When ChkDsk runs, you see its results before Windows displays your logon screen or desktop.

You can also run ChkDsk at the DOS command prompt (see Chapter 39, section "The Command Prompt Window"). Choose Start | Run and type **chkdsk** *at the command prompt. Then press* ENTER. *To tell ChkDsk to fix any errors it finds, type* **chkdsk /f** *instead.*

Other ChkDsk Options

ChkDsk can do a number of other things if you run it at the command prompt. To see your options at the command line, type the following at the prompt in a Command Prompt window:

```
chkdsk /?
```

or type **help chkdsk**. When you press ENTER, you see information about ChkDsk's options, which are also listed in Table 33-1. Some switches work only on NTFS partitions, and some work only on FAT32 partitions.

Switch or Argument	FAT32 Partitions	NTFS Partitions
volume	Specifies the drive to be acted on. Enter the drive letter as the letter and a colon (i.e., **c:**, **d:**, **x:**) or as a volume name (i.e., **CRUNCHY, DRV012**).	
filename	Specifies the files to be checked for fragmentation.	Not used.
/F	Fixes errors on the specified disk. If no disk is specified, ChkDsk checks the boot disk and fixes it as needed.	
/V	Displays the full filename and path of every file on the disk. This is not recommended, unless you have a lot of free time.	Not used.
/R	Locates and attempts to recover the data in lost sectors. This command also implicitly applies an /F command.	

Table 33-1. *ChkDsk Command Switches*

Switch or Argument	FAT32 Partitions	NTFS Partitions
/L:*size*	Not used.	Changes the file size of the operations log to the specified amount (in KB: 1MB = 1024KB).
/X	Causes a mounted volume to be forcibly dismounted before performing the implicit /F command. This switch cannot be used on the boot volume.	
/I	Not used.	Performs a less complete index check.
/C	Not used.	Skips checking directory structure cycles.

Table 33-1.   *ChkDsk Command Switches* (continued)

Defragmenting Your Disk

Windows stores information on your disks in sectors, which can be anywhere from 2 to 32 kilobytes (KB) in size. Files are stored in as many sectors as required to fit (for example, a 64KB file would take two sectors on a disk with 32KB sectors). These sectors do not need to remain sequential: Windows keeps track of which sectors are used for which files, no matter where they are on the disk. Sectors for a single file can be located just about anywhere on the disk.

Fragmentation occurs when you add and remove files from your computer. When you delete a file, Windows marks the sectors as available, and uses them the next time you create a file. If a file gets larger and contiguous space isn't available, Windows uses other available sectors to store the new part of the file. As you continue to use your computer, your files can become more and more fragmented. When you save a new file, if no contiguous space is large enough, Windows writes the new file using sectors that aren't together—the file is fragmented right from the start.

Fragmentation slows down your disk access and, subsequently, your computing efficiency, because Windows has to spend more time finding the parts of each file. The more chunks a file is split into, the slower Windows accesses the file, because the file system has to move all over the disk to find pieces of the file.

Fortunately, Windows comes with a program that moves the contents of files around on your hard disk so that each file is stored as one contiguous string of sectors—Disk Defragmenter. Run the Disk Defragmenter utility when you don't plan to use your computer for some time, because it can take an hour or so, and has to restart if you change any files.

In this day of ultra-cheap, gargantuan drives (80GB and beyond) with superfast access times (7,200 RPM standard and 10,000 RPM becoming more common), fragmentation doesn't affect speed nearly as much as it did on older hard disks. One reason is that newer disks read an entire *track* (concentric circle of information) at a time from the disk into the disk's buffer memory, so it matters less if the sectors of the track contain information in the wrong order.

 Even though Disk Defragmenter moves data about on your drive, no files or folders appear to move. How you organize your files and such is really an illusion anyway. Which folder you put your copy of the next Great American Novel into has nothing to do with where it's stored in the disk itself.

Running Disk Defragmenter

Follow these steps to run Disk Defragmenter.

1. Choose Start | All Programs | Accessories | System Tools | Disk Defragmenter, or right-click the disk drive in an Explorer window and choose Properties. On the Properties dialog box for the disk, click the Tools tab and click the Defragment Now button. You see the Disk Defragmenter window, shown here:

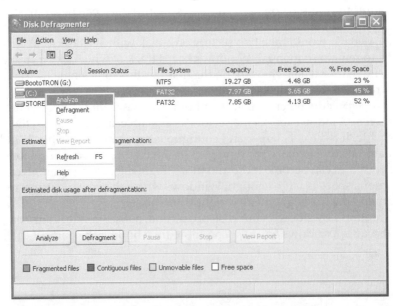

2. Choose the drive you want to defragment by right-clicking the drive from the list that appears. (They're listed by the partition's location on the drive and not by drive letter.) The list of drives includes physical drives (actual disk drives or partitions of drives) and removable drives. The list does not include networked drives on other systems (see Chapter 29).

3. Click Analyze. Disk Defragmenter starts to work and displays the results of its analysis, shown here:

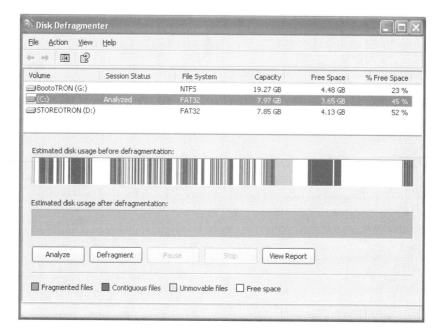

4. The colored bar in the Estimated Disk Usage Before Defragmentation box shows the usage of the sectors on the disk. The meanings of the colors are shown at the bottom of the window. If the analysis reveals that the volume should be defragmented, the same dialog box offers to start the process. Click the Defragment button if it appears; if it doesn't, your disk doesn't need defragmentation.

5. When Disk Defragmenter is done, a message asks whether you want to exit the program; click Yes.

Tips for Defragmenting

When Disk Defragmenter is running, you see two disk maps; the upper one is the analysis of your hard disk, and the lower one is an estimate of what it will look like following the defragmentation, as shown in Figure 33-1.

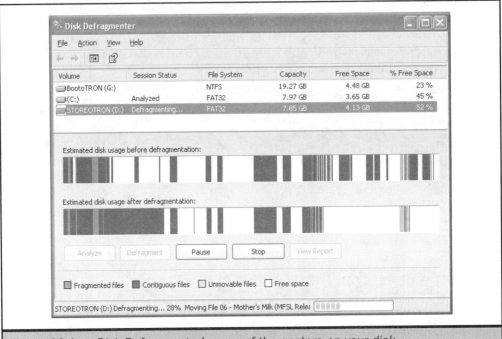

Figure 33-1. *Disk Defragmenter's map of the sectors on your disk*

Deleting Temporary Files with Disk Cleanup

Disk Cleanup is a program that can delete unneeded temporary files from your hard disk. Some programs create temporary files and then don't delete the files when they are through with them. If a program, or Windows itself, exits unexpectedly (or "crashes"), temporary files can be left on your hard disk. Deleting these files from time to time is a good idea, not only because they take up space, but also because their presence can confuse the programs that created them.

Disk Cleanup may recommend deleting files that haven't been used in months, without regard to type. Take a look at the names of the files it recommends deleting to make sure that they don't include important documents that you haven't used in months but want to keep.

Deleting Files Once

Here's how to run Disk Cleanup:

1. Choose Start | All Programs | Accessories | System Tools | Disk Cleanup.

2. The Disk Cleanup program runs and asks which disk you want to clean up. Choose a disk drive and click OK. The Disk Cleanup window, shown in Figure 33-2, tells you how much disk space you can reclaim by deleting temporary files right now. Of course, this may include temporary files that your programs are currently using!

3. Click the box for each type of temporary file you want Disk Cleanup to delete. For more information on a type of temporary file, click the description; the program displays an explanation of what the files are and what folders Disk Cleanup will delete them from.

4. For additional options, click the More Options tab. Three buttons provide other ways to free up disk space, including deleting Windows components you don't use, uninstalling programs, and reducing the amount of space used by the System Restore program (see Chapter 35, section "Returning Your System to a Predefined State with System Restore"). Click the corresponding button to try any of these methods.

5. If you want to see the names of the files that will be deleted (in a separate Explorer window), select the type of files to be deleted and click the View Files button.

6. To begin deleting files, click OK. The program asks whether you are sure you want to delete files. Click Yes.

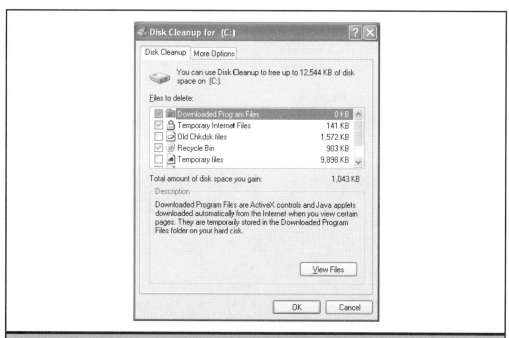

Figure 33-2. *The Disk Cleanup's list of temporary files to delete*

WINDOWS HOUSEKEEPING

The programs shown on the More Options tab that can free up disk space are one-time operations. If you schedule the Disk Cleanup program to run on a regular basis (using Scheduled Tasks), these other programs do not run.

Deleting Files Regularly

Run the Scheduled Tasks program to tell Windows to run the Disk Cleanup program regularly (see Chapter 2, section "Running Programs on a Schedule Using Scheduled Tasks"). If you use Scheduled Tasks to schedule running the program, be sure to run Disk Cleanup once following the steps in the preceding section so that you can choose the types of files to delete.

 When you run Disk Cleanup, be sure to include the Temporary Files in the Files To Delete list. Windows stores most temporary files in the C:\Documents And Settings\username\Local Settings\Temp folder, although a few may end up in the C:\Windows\Temp folder (if you installed Windows in a different folder, they are in the Temp folder wherever Windows is installed). Windows can become confused if this folder contains lots of temporary files that should have been deleted automatically but weren't.

The
Complete
Reference

Chapter 34

Tuning Windows XP for Maximum Performance

Windows XP automatically sets itself up to give you adequate performance. That performance is greatly improved over Windows Me, but you can still improve it. Several tools enable you to tune your configuration to enhance performance, primarily disk performance:

- **The Performance Options dialog box**   Shows you display, processor, and memory settings that affect performance.
- **The Task Manager program**   Displays the system resources of your computer.
- **The System Monitor**   Displays graphs of system usage.

Another important way to speed up Windows is to tune your hard disk to speed up disk access.

The Microsoft Management Console displays information about your whole system, and can display information about events, performance, devices, storage, and applications (see Chapter 35, section "The Microsoft Management Console").

Note   *In our experience, few of the tuning techniques make a noticeable difference on a balanced system with adequate memory and disk, although they do make some difference on small systems with slow disks. The best ways to improve system performance are to add more memory and a faster disk, in that order. Microsoft says Windows XP can run in only 64MB of memory (RAM), but we've tried it, and we recommend at least 128MB.*

Tuning Your Computer's Performance with the Performance Options Dialog Box

Things have changed drastically in the migration from Windows Me/9x to Windows 2000. Even the differences between Windows 2000 and Windows XP are significant. Most of the changes and additions to performance tuning are oriented toward the new interface (the Windows XP desktop theme). For slower computers and for people who like to fiddle with the details of system configuration, this is a great thing. For the rest of us, it means a lot of options that control minor aspects of the interface, such as whether a drop shadow appears under menus or whether the taskbar buttons slide instead of just appearing and disappearing.

To look at and change settings that affect Windows performance, you use the Performance Options dialog box. Click Start, right-click My Computer, and choose Properties to display the System Properties dialog box, which contains information about many aspects of your computer system. Click the Advanced tab (shown in Figure 34–1) and then click the Settings button in the Performance section (the top part). You see the Performance Options dialog box (shown in Figure 34–2).

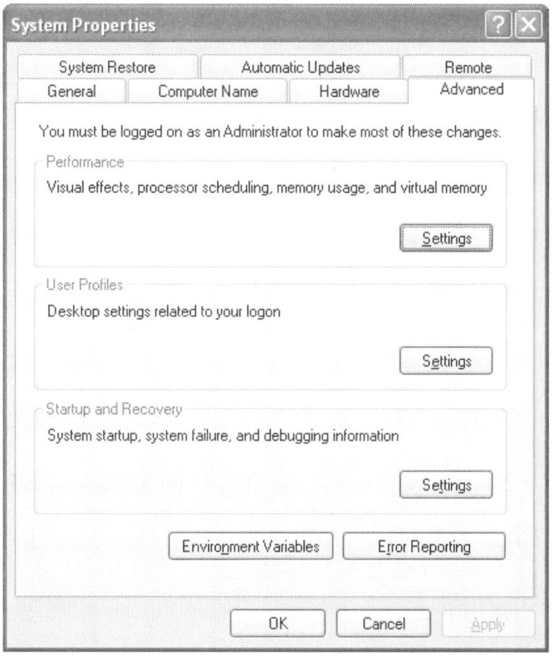

Figure 34-1. *The Advanced tab of the System Properties dialog box*

Tuning Your Display Settings

The Visual Effects tab of the Performance Options dialog box lists about a dozen effects that make your screen display look snazzy but that also require processing power almost every time your computer updates the screen. The top part of the dialog box shows four options:

- **Let Windows Choose What's Best For My Computer**   Windows decides which effects to make active (or otherwise) based on the system resources you have available. Newer, faster systems have most, if not all, effects selected.
- **Adjust For Best Appearance**   Turns all effects on.
- **Adjust For Best Performance**   Turns all effects off.
- **Custom**   Enables you to select which effects you want active.

The list of screen effects appears in the lower part of the dialog box with check boxes to show which effects are active. If you select Custom, you can override

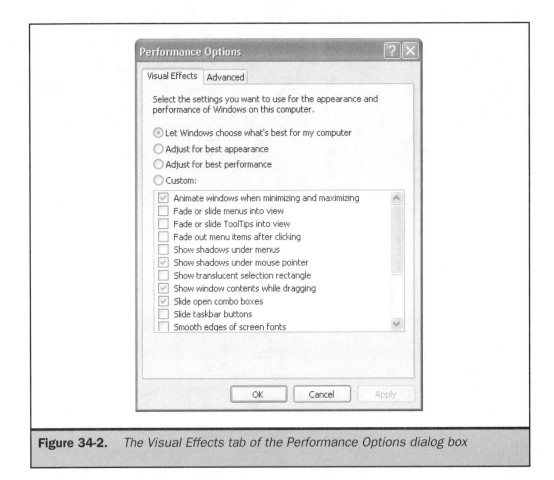

Figure 34-2. *The Visual Effects tab of the Performance Options dialog box*

Windows settings. Most of the effects do exactly what their names say they do, but two names defy comprehension:

- **Use Common Tasks In Folders** Toggles on and off the Task pane that appears by default in all Explorer windows. (We find it particularly useful.)

- **Use Visual Styles On Windows And Buttons** Toggles on and off the default Windows XP appearance. If you use a utility like WindowBlinds (**http://www.windowblinds.net**) from Stardock Corporation, be sure to uncheck this item or else the Windows XP appearance will conflict with your WindowBlinds skins.

Tuning Your Processor and Memory Settings

A few settings affect how Windows allocates its resources. These settings appear on the Advanced tab of the Performance Options dialog box (see Figure 34–3).

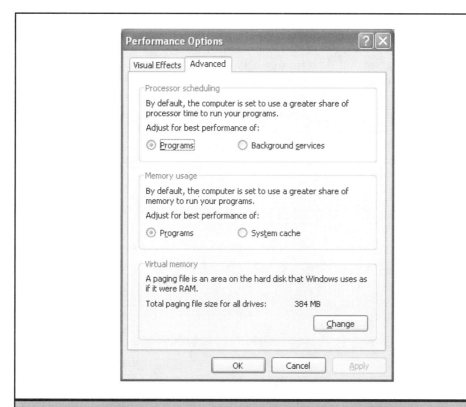

Figure 34-3. *The Performance Options dialog box showing the Advanced tab*

- **Processor Scheduling** Controls how Windows allocates processor time to processes. You can elect to favor either Programs (applications) or Background Services (processes that Windows runs behind the scenes). If your computer provides file, printing, or Internet connection services for other computers on a network, you may wish to select Background Services to give requests from other computers higher priority. Otherwise, leave it as Programs. You can use the computer even if Background Services is selected, though your programs may run slowly.

- **Memory Usage** This setting, which controls how Windows allocates your computer's memory, is interesting. Normally, leave this setting at its default, Programs, to give your programs as much memory as they need. However, if you tend to load a few applications and then run them without loading other applications, you may be better served by selecting the System Cache option. Specifically designed for Web and network servers, this setting can also assist users who frequently access large files. The System Cache has priority over the disc cache, and is faster.

Tuning Your Swap File Size

Windows automatically manages program storage by using *virtual memory*, which moves chunks of program and data storage between disk and memory automatically, so individual programs don't have to do all their own memory management.

Normally, Windows manages virtual memory automatically, but in a few cases you may want to change its parameters. Click the Change button in the Virtual Memory part of the Advanced tab of the Performance Options dialog box to see the Virtual Memory dialog box, as shown in Figure 34-4. You can specify the disk drive on which Windows stores its *swap file* (the file to which virtual memory is copied), along with the minimum and maximum sizes of the swap file. Click a drive to see the settings for any swap file stored on it.

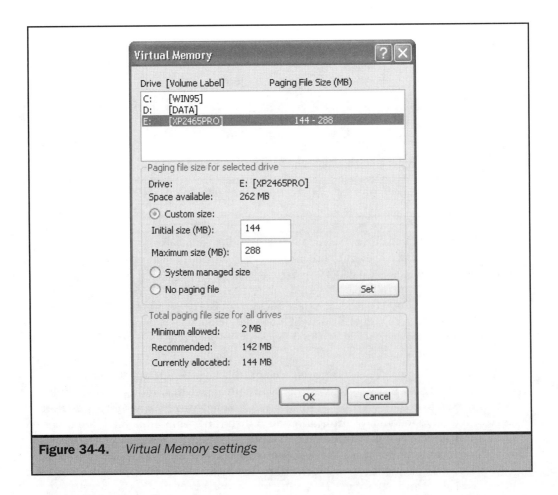

Figure 34-4. *Virtual Memory settings*

You might want to set your own virtual memory settings in two cases:

- If you have more than one disk, Windows normally puts the swap file on the boot partition (the partition or drive from which Windows loads). If you have another partition or drive that is larger or faster, you might want to tell Windows to store the swap file there, instead.

- If you are extremely short of disk space, you can decrease the amount of virtual memory and, hence, the disk space that Windows allocates. If you decrease virtual memory too far, programs may fail as they run out of memory. Generally, there's no advantage to increasing the amount of virtual memory beyond the default because extra virtual memory doesn't make the system run any faster.

You can also disable virtual memory altogether, which is usually a bad idea unless you have an enormous amount of RAM.

Tracking System Resources

To keep Windows running smoothly, it helps to know when your system resources are running low.

What Are System Resources?

Windows XP deals with *system resources*—memory used by Windows applications—on a much more sophisticated level than Windows Me/9x. Because it is based on Windows 2000/NT, Windows XP inherits its foreparents' technological edge in memory management and does not succumb to the same resource limitations as Windows Me/9x.

Windows XP runs each application in its own protected memory space. If a program crashes, XP is far more likely to be responsive than Windows Me was, because other programs and Windows itself are not affected by the crash. The protected memory space also allows you to restart a crashed application safely, which rarely worked in Windows Me/9x. Of course, Windows XP has its own liabilities.

If you push Windows XP to the limit of its resources—by running too many programs at the same time—it behaves unreliably, just as Windows Me/9x did. This is because Windows XP requires access to global system resources just like all other versions of Windows, so the benefits of protected memory do not apply in the event of a general system overload. If you only have a 64MB system but have 256MB appetites, your system will operate unreliably, if at all. The best thing to do is to monitor your system to see where your computer's cycles are going. (A *cycle* is a process in which the CPU completes one string of instructions.)

Monitoring System Use with the Task Manager

Windows, like any computer system, can monitor many aspects of its own operation, including CPU use, the software disk cache, disk operations, serial port operations, and network operations. Sometimes, when system performance is unacceptable, you can monitor key aspects and determine where the bottleneck is occurring. This helps determine whether the most effective improvements would be through software reconfiguration or a hardware upgrade, such as adding more memory. The Task Manager is a small utility that comes with Windows and displays performance data, running applications, system-level processes, and network operability (see Figure 34–5).

You can run the Task Manager by right-clicking the taskbar and selecting Task Manager, or by pressing CTRL-ALT-DEL. The Task Manager loads a small icon in the notification area of the task bar, with bars that indicate at what percentage the CPU is being used.

The Processes tab lists all the processes that are currently running. If you want to see only your applications programs, rather than all the Windows-related background

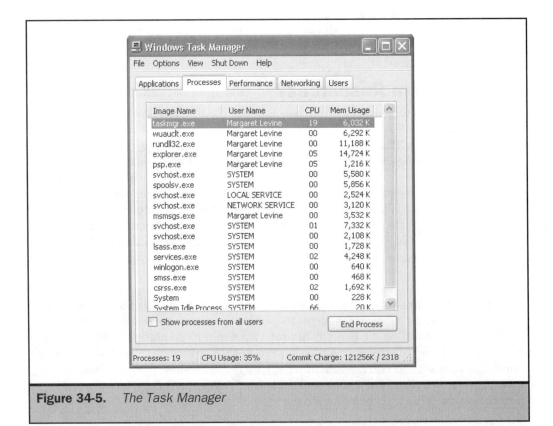

Figure 34-5. *The Task Manager*

processes that take up most of the processes list, click the Application tab. The Networking tab displays information about your network connection, if any (see Chapter 28). The Users tab (which doesn't appear if Fast User Switching is disabled) shows what user accounts are in use (see Chapter 6).

The Performance tab, as shown in Figure 34-6, reveals a plethora of technical information, the same as the equivalent tab in Windows 2000.

What does this mean to the average user? Nothing. The important item to note is the CPU Usage bar graph in the top left corner. Even when the computer is idle (meaning that no applications are doing anything significant), you still see some activity. However, if the meter spikes and mouse movement is sluggish, a culprit application is probably causing havoc. Switch to the Processes tab (as shown in Figure 34-5) and look in the CPU column. (You can click a column heading to sort by the values in that column—click the CPU heading twice to list the highest CPU values at the top of the list.) The System Idle Process item should have a number from 0 to 99 in the CPU column. If a process is using a lot of CPU cycles, try closing the program

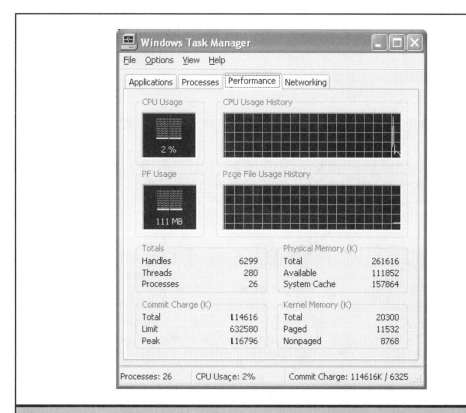

Figure 34-6. *The Performance tab of the Task Manager*

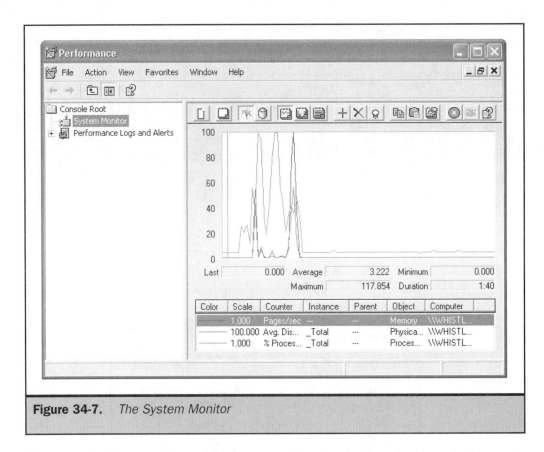

Figure 34-7.   *The System Monitor*

that created it. You can also end (kill) a process by selecting it and clicking End Process. If that doesn't work, you may be forced to shut down and restart the computer to stop the rogue process.

Viewing Graphs in the System Monitor

Older versions of Windows came with a program called System Monitor, which graphed various measures of system performance. Windows XP also has this program—its version is shown in Figure 34-7. You can run it by choosing Start | Control Panel | Performance And Maintenance | Administrative Tools and running the Performance icon. The meanings of the items on the graph are listed below the graph. You can use the toolbar buttons to change the format of the graph and add data to it.

Tuning Your Hard Disk's Performance

The most effective way to speed up most Windows systems, short of adding extra memory or a faster drive, is to optimize your hard disk. Try these two Windows utilities:

- **Disk Defragmenter**   The most important Windows tuning program is the Disk Defragmenter (see Chapter 33, section "Defragmenting Your Disk"). As it defragments your disk, this program can also rearrange your executable programs so they can start and run faster.

- **Disk Cleanup**   As time passes, your computer's hard disk gathers junk (such as unneeded files). Windows slows down and may act strangely if too many of these unneeded files have accumulated, especially if they are in your temporary storage folder (usually C:\Documents And Settings*username*\Local Settings\Temp). The Disk Cleanup utility deletes these troublesome files (see Chapter 33, section "Deleting Temporary Files with Disk Cleanup").

Tip   *The biggest space waster of the bunch is Internet Explorer, which is usually configured to occupy as much as 100MB of your hard disk with temporary files. Two options can help to reduce this waste. First, reduce the amount of space that Internet Explorer uses for its temporary files. Choose Start | Control Panel | Network And Internet Connections and open the Internet Options icon. Or choose Tools | Internet Options from the Internet Explorer menu bar. You see the General tab of the Internet Properties dialog box. In the Temporary Internet Files section of the dialog box, click the Settings button and reduce the space allocation to something more reasonable, like 50MB. Click OK. Second, click the Advanced tab and scroll down to the Security section of the settings. Select the Empty Temporary Internet Files Folder When Browser Is Closed check box to tell Internet Explorer to remove all old files automatically.*

WINDOWS
HOUSEKEEPING

The Complete Reference

Chapter 35

Troubleshooting Windows XP

Usually Windows XP works quite well, but even though it is more stable than its predecessors, it still hangs and crashes on occasion. Fortunately, Windows comes with a number of diagnostic tools that can help (most come from its Windows 2000 heritage). Microsoft has also added one new tool, Remote Assistance, which allows Microsoft technicians (or knowledgeable friends of yours) to fix your computer over the phone (see Chapter 4, section "Allowing a Friend to Control Your Computer").

This chapter describes techniques for dealing with programs that hang or crash, stopping programs from running automatically, diagnosing other problems, using the Microsoft Management Console to see what's going on, using System Restore to return to a more reliable configuration, and if all else fails, reporting problems to Microsoft for possible resolution. Be sure to set up a system of regular backups for your most important files (see Chapter 9).

We recommend leaving your computer on all the time so that Windows can run housekeeping and backup programs in the middle of the night.

What Diagnostic Tools Does Windows XP Provide?

Windows provides a wide range of diagnostic tools that you can use for different kinds of problems. In addition to the tools listed here, see "Configuring Windows Using the System Configuration Utility" in Chapter 37.

Startup Modes

The worst problems prevent Windows from starting up at all. If the Windows installation on your hard disk is intact, you can start Windows in one of several special *startup modes* that provide limited function and help diagnose problems. Windows XP, however, brings its legacy from Windows 2000 and Windows NT, decidedly more complicated operating systems than Windows 98 and Me. Because of this sophisticated lineage, Windows XP has a number of more challenging options than Windows 98/Me. Nearly every mode has a purpose and the added options give you more recourse when disaster strikes.

Press F8 during Windows startup (when you see the boot menu, if you have a dual-boot system) to see a menu of startup modes:

- **Safe Mode** Windows starts by using the simplest possible set of drivers and hardware devices. If Windows still doesn't start, try Safe Mode With Command Prompt or the Recovery Console.

- **Safe Mode With Networking** Windows starts by using the simplest possible set of drivers and hardware devices, but also includes simple networking components. If Safe Mode works and you need information from a network, try this mode.

- **Safe Mode With Command Prompt**   Windows starts by using the simplest possible set of drivers and hardware devices. It further reduces the overhead by not loading the Graphical User Interface—you communicate with it by typing DOS-style commands. This mode works the same way as the Recovery Console.

- **Enable Boot Logging**   Windows starts normally but logs all the drivers it loads in the file Ntbtlog.txt (usually stored in C:\Windows). Use this mode if you think that a device driver might be the problem.

- **Enable VGA Mode**   Windows loads the standard, super-compatible Microsoft VGA driver, which can often assist in reducing conflicts until you can fix the problem. Use this mode if your video driver isn't working.

- **Last Known Good Configuration**   Windows starts using the last configuration that did *not* to have any known problems. It uses backup copies of your Registry and device driver files (see Chapter 38).

- **Directory Services Restore Mode**   This mode is not used in either Windows XP Home Edition or Professional: it is used on Windows servers.

- **Debugging Mode**   Windows starts normally but sends debugging information through a serial cable to another computer (rarely used except by Windows system programmers).

- **Selective Startup**   This mode isn't displayed on the Windows startup menu that appears when you press F8. Instead, you enable it by using the System Configuration Utility (see "Stopping Programs from Running at Startup"). Windows prompts before loading or running each driver or program.

- **Normal Mode**   Windows starts normally.

> **Note**   *Windows XP does not support DOS, with the exception of a DOS Virtual Machine, to run legacy applications. Because of this, Windows cannot start up in DOS mode. Of course, you can still start up DOS from a floppy disk, Zip drive (if your BIOS supports it), or bootable CD-ROM (see Chapter 39). When running DOS, you can't read disks formatted with NTFS.*

Safe Mode

Safe Mode is a limited operating mode used to diagnose problems. All of Windows' basic functions are available, but the screen runs in basic VGA mode (640 × 480, 16 colors) and no devices are available beyond the screen, keyboard, and disks. See "Booting in Safe Mode" in Chapter 13 for more information.

Safe Mode With Networking

Safe Mode With Networking is the same as Safe Mode, but with some simple networking components installed. This mode is helpful if you have an immediate need to access files over a network *before* you can fix your computer, if the tools you need to fix your computer are located on a remote machine, or if you would like to be able to take advantage of the new Remote Assistance feature (see Chapter 4, section "Allowing a Friend to Control Your Computer").

Safe Mode With Command Prompt or Recovery Console

Safe Mode With Command Prompt is nothing like the modes described in the previous two sections. Instead of emerging into a pygmy version of the Windows desktop, this mode ejects you into a dark world with no comforting menus or OK buttons. This place is called the *Command Prompt* or *Command Line Interface* (*CLI*). In order to issue commands, you must know an arcane language that consists of only words and some symbols. Most DOS commands will work here, but this is not DOS.

The Command Prompt also doubles as the Recovery Console that you can start from the Windows XP CD-ROM. All of these commands apply there as well. You can enter the Recover Console by booting from the Windows XP CD-ROM (as described in the section "Booting off the Windows XP CD-ROM" in the Appendix), and pressing R when the text mode part of the setup begins. You can install the Recovery Console as a startup option by putting the Windows XP CD-ROM in the CD drive, choosing Start | Run, typing d:\i386\winnt32.exe /cmdcons (replacing d: with your CD-ROM drive letter if it's not D:) and clicking OK. Recovery Console appears as an option on the boot menu that Windows XP uses for dual-boot systems, which is described in the Appendix.

The safe Mode With Command Prompt asks you to enter your Administrator password. If you entered one when you installed Windows, you don't need one here. If you wrote down any names of files that were indicated as being corrupted or the cause of your systems recent demise, that's good. Its even better if you note any files that may be causing your system not to start up properly. Using the command prompt you can often go in and fish out these culprit files, though it's best to do this with a qualified technician (or at least the proven local nerd).

Tip   *To get a listing of all commands in the Recovery Console, simply type **HELP** at the prompt and press* ENTER.

When you see the command prompt (usually C:>), type a command and press ENTER. Here are a few useful commands:

- **DIR** (Directory)   Displays a listing of the files in the directory you are currently in. Items that have a <DIR> legend next to them are directories (folders). Type **DIR /P** to tell Windows to pause if there are more than a screenful of items. Type **DIR /W** to cause the listing to be shown in several columns. Better yet, type **DIR /P/W** for a multicolumn listing that pauses before scrolling.

You can use an asterisk to represent part of the filename. For example, to list all text files, type this:

```
DIR *.txt
```

- **CD (Change Directory)**   To move to a different directory (folder), type **CD** and a space and the name of the folder. For example, to move to the Windows folder that is contained in the current folder, type

```
CD windows
```

If you want to go deeper in one go, you add directory names, like so:

```
CD windows\system32
```

If you want to back out of a directory and return to what is called the "parent" directory of the one you are in, type the following:

```
CD ..
```

The two periods indicate one level up.

- **DEL**   Deletes the indicated file or files. Type **DEL** followed by a space and the name of the file to delete. You must indicate a file by name and extension. This can be dangerous, so be very cautious and always triple-check whatever it is you plan to delete. For example:

```
DEL filename.txt
```

You can use an asterisk to represent part of the filename. For example, to delete all Word documents, type this:

```
DEL *.doc
```

- **CHKDSK**   The Microsoft Check Disk utility has been upstaged by ScanDisk since Windows 95 first shipped, but no more. CHKDSK is far more capable these days and can even work with NTFS-based systems. To get basic info and run a simple test, type **CHKDSK** and press ENTER. Windows checks the integrity of the current partition and lists the current space usage. In order for the utility to do *all* of its magic, however, it must do so before Windows starts. Type this:

```
CHKDSK /F
```

First, CHKDSK displays an error, and then it asks whether you'd like to run it the next time Windows restarts. Press Y and ENTER. CHKDSK will run when you next boot up Windows.

The Boot Floppy Disk

Historically, one of the steps in the Windows installation process created a startup floppy disk, or *boot floppy disk*. The general idea was that if the file system on your hard disk was damaged, you could often start your computer from the startup floppy disk and repair the damage enough to make the hard disk bootable.

You can still make a boot floppy in Windows XP, but Windows now includes System Restore, a sort of time traveling utility that can take your Windows machine back in time to when it actually worked (see "Returning Your System to a Predefined State with System Restore," later in the chapter).

To make a boot floppy in Windows XP, you need a single 1.44MB floppy disk. Follow these steps:

1. Write-enable the disk and put it in the disk drive.
2. Choose Start | My Computer.
3. Right-click the 3 1/2 Floppy (A:) icon and choose Format from the shortcut menu that appears. You see the Format 3 1/2 Floppy (A:) dialog box.
4. Select the Create An MS-DOS Startup Disk check box.
5. Click Start. Windows creates a bootable startup disk.
6. Remove the disk from the drive, write-protect it, label it, and put it in a safe place.

If you use this floppy disk to start your system, you see the DOS command prompt, described in Chapter 39. No drivers are loaded, so you can't use your CD-ROM or other hardware, and you can't see your NTFS disks, only disks formatted as FAT or FAT32 (see Chapter 32, section "What Are FAT, FAT32, and NTFS?").

System Information

You can display the System Information window by choosing Start | All Programs | Accessories | System Tools | System Information. This window (shown in Figure 35-1) displays detailed information about all the devices and hardware drivers configured into your copy of Windows, and is a good place to check to see whether system components are correctly configured. We find it more efficient than poking around the various dialog boxes that the Control Panel displays. Its Tools menu lists a number of other useful diagnostic programs you can run.

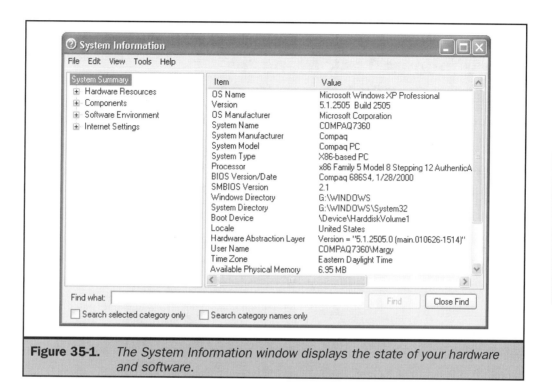

Figure 35-1.   *The System Information window displays the state of your hardware and software.*

The Windows XP Setup Wizard

The Windows XP Setup Wizard may be able to repair a corrupted Windows XP installation. Follow these steps:

1. Start the Setup Wizard from the Windows XP CD-ROM by putting the CD-ROM into your CD drive and choosing Install Windows XP. After the first reboot, the Setup Wizard should find the existing installation of Windows XP and ask whether you want to repair it (see Appendix A, section "Answering the Windows Setup Wizard's Questions").

2. Press R to attempt the repair. The Setup Wizard tries to repair the installation, and then prompts you to reboot.

3. Press F3 to restart. After you reboot back into the Windows XP Setup, you can quit the Setup Wizard without reinstalling Windows by pressing F3.

Dealing with Hung or Crashed Programs: The Windows Task Manager

Despite all the testing that software vendors do, Windows and the applications you run under it have bugs and sometimes *hang* (stop responding) or *crash* (fail altogether). When an application crashes, Windows displays a box telling you about it. There's not much you can do at that point, other than click OK. You may want to restart Windows if you're concerned that the program may have damaged files or Windows' internal operations.

If a program hangs, you generally can force Windows to stop the hung program. Press CTRL-ALT-DEL to open the Windows Task Manager dialog box, shown here:

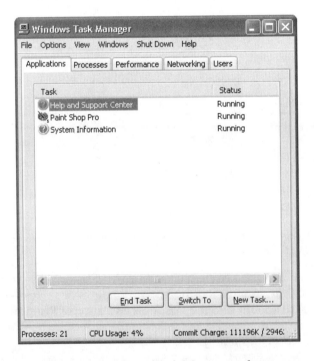

On the Applications tab of the Windows Task Manager, a hung program usually has the notation "Not responding" in the Status column. (Healthy programs are designated as "Running.") Select the name of the program and click End Task. Normally, the program then exits.

If all else fails, press CTRL-ALT-DEL to display the Windows Task Manager and then choose Shut Down | Restart from the menu bar: Windows should restart. If the hang was particularly nasty, Windows runs ChkDsk so that disk errors can be repaired (see Chapter 33, section "Testing Your Disk Structure with ChkDsk").

For more information about the Windows Task Manager, see Chapter 34.

Windows Error Reporting

Windows XP can call home when it has a problem. That is, if you have an Internet connection, when a program crashes, Windows can send an error report back to Microsoft. Microsoft promises to send you an automatic notification when they receive the error report. By collecting hang and crash information, Microsoft can fix problems with Windows more effectively.

When a program crashes or hangs, you see a dialog box asking whether to send a report. Microsoft promises that the information in the error report doesn't contain any personal information about you, just system configuration information about your computer. However, you also have the option of turning Windows Error Reporting off. Click Start, right-click My Computer, and choose Properties from the menu that appears. On the System Properties dialog box, click the Advanced tab. Click the Error Reporting button to display the Error Reporting dialog box:

You can choose whether to do any error reporting, and whether to send reports only about Windows errors or about application program errors as well.

Stopping Programs from Running at Startup

When you start Windows, other programs may start up automatically, which can be very convenient (see Chapter 2, section "Starting Programs When Windows Starts"). It's not always easy, however, to *stop* a program from running automatically when you start Windows. Here are three places to look for the entry that causes Windows to run the program:

- **Startup folder**   Make sure that a shortcut for the program isn't in the StartUp folder (Start | All Programs | Startup). If a shortcut for the program is there, delete it. (Choose Start | All Programs | Startup, right-click the item for the program, and choose Delete from the menu that appears, or drag the program item out of the folder.)

- **Win.ini**   Look for a line in your Win.ini file that runs the program (see Chapter 37, section "The Win.ini File"). The line would start with "run=" or "load=" in the windows section.

- **Registry**   Examine the Registry for an entry that runs the program (see Chapter 38, section "What Is the Registry?"). You can use the Registry Editor to remove the offending entry, after making a backup of the Registry (see Chapter 38, section "Editing the Registry"). Look in the HKEY_LOCAL_MACHINE\ SOFTWARE\Microsoft\Windows\CurrentVersion\RUN "hive" (group of Registry keys), which lists programs that are run automatically.

Alternatively, choose Start | Run, type **msconfig**, and press ENTER to see the System Configuration Utility. Click the Startup tab, shown in Figure 35-2, to see a list of the

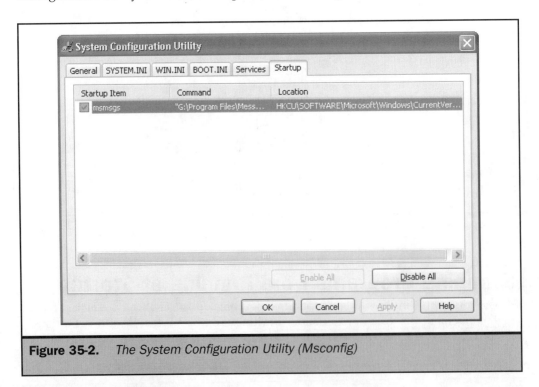

Figure 35-2.   *The System Configuration Utility (Msconfig)*

Two Handy Utilities

If you install many programs, two free utilities can come in handy. Startup and Startup Monitor were developed by a 17-year-old wunderkind named Mike Lin. You can download these utilities from his Web site (**http://www.mlin.net**) and install them in a matter of moments. Note, however, that there are two versions of Startup; one is an add-in to Control Panel and the other is a stand-alone application. They both do the same thing: choose the one you prefer.

Startup gives you convenient access to all of the places Windows hides application startup data. Poke around the tabs until you find the offending application and uncheck it. You can also add your own programs to any tab, and deleting something only causes it to be stored in the Deleted tab, in case you want it back later. Startup Monitor works with Startup and it provides one function, to warn you when a new application is being added to one of the startup locations. You are offered a choice to allow the change or not, though you should know that not all applications will work properly without whatever program you might be disabling.

An example of a potentially annoying application is Windows Messenger, which is included in Windows XP and constantly begs for your attention (see Chapter 25, section "Chatting Online with Windows Messenger"). Most people will simply give in, sign up for an account, and be done with its constant pestering, but this requires signing up for a Microsoft .NET Passport. Instead, you can turn Windows Messenger off with Startup by deselecting the MSMSGS item in the HKCU/Run tab.

programs that run at startup. You can use this program to display and edit the Win.ini file (but make a backup first). On the General tab, you can choose Selective Startup to turn on Selective Startup mode, a startup mode in which Windows asks before running each startup program. Deselecting any item on the Startup tab automatically turns on Selective Startup. Selective Startup is particularly useful for temporarily disabling startup items.

Diagnosing Problems

If Windows doesn't start, or a piece of hardware is operating strangely, you may have either a hardware configuration problem or broken hardware. The most likely culprit is the last piece of software you installed.

Diagnosing Hardware Problems

Windows XP is smart when it comes to hardware, but it's not savvy about everything. Some older hardware may simply not work because Microsoft does not have an updated driver for it. It's better to avoid potential conflicts when you install Windows by allowing the installation program to check system compatibility (see Appendix A, section

"Answering the Windows Setup Wizard's Questions"). The Microsoft Windows Upgrade Advisor notifies you of any questionable software and drivers or hardware known to be problematic.

Windows is also good at allocating resources and dealing with conflicts, either real or looming. The most likely source for hardware conflicts is from older hardware (for example, an ISA or VESA Local Bus adapter card) that is not Plug and Play.

If Windows does have a conflict with recently added hardware, the best thing to do is to locate the culprit in the Device Manager (click Start, right-click My Computer, select Manager, click the Hardware tab, and click Device Manager). If Windows is aware of the problem, it usually already has the device's listing in view and marked with an ugly-looking icon. Highlight the gizmo and click Properties. There, you can access the devices specific to Troubleshooter.

If you can't start Windows because of a device driver problem, press F8 while Windows is starting, and choose Last Known Good Configuration from the menu that appears. Windows restores the Registry and drivers from the last time that Windows started, effectively rolling back to a configuration that worked.

Diagnosing Display Problems

If your display is acting strangely, Windows offers several possible ways to fix the problem. This section describes the most common ways; also see the next section for how to use Windows' Troubleshooters.

If the screen is utterly unreadable, restart Windows in Safe Mode. After Windows is running in Safe or Normal Mode, right-click the Windows desktop and choose Properties from the menu that appears to display the Display Properties dialog box, and click the Settings tab (see Chapter 11, section "Changing Display Settings").

Your screen might not be able to handle the display resolution your adapter is using. Try setting the Screen Resolution (number of pixels displayed) to a smaller value to see whether the screen clears. (The number of colors doesn't matter—all modern screens can display an unlimited number of colors. What you actually get, however, depends on your video card's capabilities.) When choosing Color Quality, choose 16-bit or 32-bit, not 24-bit, which takes more system resources.

Your screen might be able to handle the display resolution but might not be able to handle the adapter's *refresh rate*, the number of times per second the adapter sends the image to the monitor. Click the Advanced button to display the Properties dialog box for your display adapter and then click the Monitor tab. Try setting the Screen Refresh Rate box to the slowest available refresh rate, usually 60 Hz. If that works, try faster rates until you find the fastest one that works reliably.

Note   *Once you change a setting and try to apply it, Windows makes the adjustment and then asks if you want to accept the changes. If you cannot see this query, that means that the settings are not ideal. Wait 15 seconds and the display will be returned to the currently saved settings.*

One final possibility is that the accelerator features in your display adapter aren't compatible with your computer. Symptoms typically are that the display is clear, but wrong, with lines or areas of the wrong color or pattern on the screen. Click the Advanced button on the Settings tab in the Display Properties dialog box to display the Properties dialog box for your display adapter. Click the Performance or Troubleshoot and look for the Hardware Acceleration slider ranging from None to Full. Try setting it to None; if this improves the display, try increasing the acceleration setting one notch at a time.

Diagnosing Problems with Troubleshooters

Windows includes many *Troubleshooters*, step-by-step diagnostics that look for some of the most common problems and suggest solutions. The Troubleshooters start at a basic level and walk you through the details of system configuration changes.

All of the Troubleshooters are part of the Help And Support Center (see Chapter 4). Follow these steps to run a Troubleshooter:

1. Choose Start | Help And Support to display the Help And Support Center window. (Click the Home icon on the toolbar if this window is already open.)

2. Click the Fixing A Problem topic and select the topic that most closely matches the problems you're experiencing.

3. Follow its advice. Windows asks whether its suggestion solved the problem.

4. Click Yes or No and click Next to try the rest of the Troubleshooter's suggestions.

The Microsoft Management Console (MMC)

Like Windows 2000, Windows XP collects lots of system tools into one place—the Microsoft Management Console (MMC). Strangely, the window that displays the MMC is titled Computer Management, but the program that provides the information (what is referred to as a *framework*) is the MMC, and that's what everyone calls it. The MMC can be the "frame" for a number of other "pictures." The pictures are called *snap-ins*, and each snap-in adds new capabilities to the MMC. (This is the same model that Web browsers use.)

Note *The vast majority of snap-ins are targeted at systems administrators, information technology professionals, and all-around nerds. Though an integral part of Windows and its general health, you will not commonly find yourself poking around the MMC if you have a choice between that and playing a few rounds of Solitaire.*

To display the MMC, choose Start, right-click My Computer, and choose Manage from the menu that appears. The MMC is shown in Figure 35-3.

WINDOWS HOUSEKEEPING

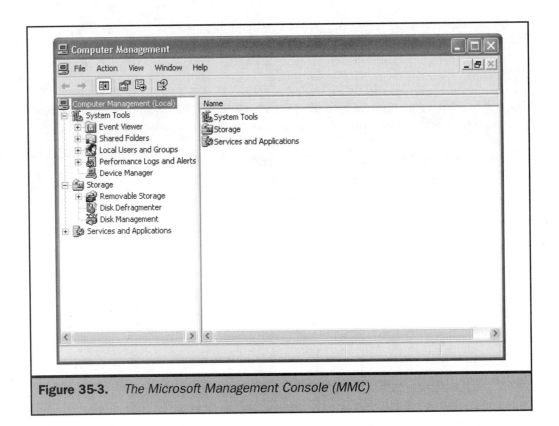

Figure 35-3. *The Microsoft Management Console (MMC)*

Several items in the Computer Management MMC are of interest to troubleshooting. The System Tools section of the Computer Management MMC includes the following tools:

- Event Viewer
- Shared Folders (see Chapter 29, section "Sharing Disk Drives and Folders on a LAN")
- Local Users And Groups (see Chapter 6, section "Setting Up a Computer for Multiple Users")
- Performance Logs And Alerts

The Event Viewer and Performanace Logs And Alerts are of interest because they provide large amounts of information about your system and its components. The Device Manager is useful for fixing hardware and driver problems.

The Event Viewer

As Windows runs it makes notes of what's going on. The Event Viewer has a venerated history, beginning with Windows NT 3.1 where it was designed to centrally locate all operational data for the person or persons that managed the server. Your Windows computer may not be a server, but this information is no less helpful, especially when diagnosing a problem. In fact, the Event Viewer may know exactly what's wrong.

In the Computer Management MMC, open System Tools and click Event Viewer. Clicking the plus box reveals three items; Application, Security, and System. Each of these items stores recorded operational data from their respective categories:

- **Application**   Logs all events generated by applications and programs. These are not system-related events, but they may be generated by components that are used by the operating system.

- **Security**   Logs security-related events, anything from the number of bad logins recorded to when and where objects were added to or taken away from the computers file system.

- **System**   Logs of events that are recorded by the operating system itself. It keeps track of events, errors, and failures that occur in the system's files and functions. It also records errors and failures that occur in the system but are generated by an external application or program.

The information contained in these logs is often helpful in determining the cause of a system instability.

Performance Logs and Alerts

Like Event Viewer, the Performance Logs And Alerts component stores information about the state of the system. It records information about how well Windows performs and what tolerances, if any, it approaches or exceeds during normal operation. The logs are stored (usually in the Perflogs folder on the same disk as Windows) and you can configure Windows to store them in text files that you can import into a spreadsheet program, a database program, or a program designed specifically for analyzing logs. *Counter logs* record system statistics at regular intervals, *trace logs* record what was happening at the time of particular events, and *alerts* send a message or run a program when a counter hits a preset value.

By default, the logging and alert functions are not configured except for one sample Counter log that is installed with Windows. Logging is useful on large networks, where one network administrator is responsible for the functioning of many computers, but individual users rarely use them.

Most people never use the MMC Performance Logs And Alerts logs, but if you do, follow these steps to create a log:

1. Open the MMC window and open the Performance Logs And Alerts item.

2. Right-click Counter Logs and choose New Log Settings from the menu that appears.

3. In the Name box, type a descriptive name for your new log (for example, type **Disk Access** if you plan to log what percentage of the time the system is active

that the disk is idle). Click OK. You see a Properties dialog box for your new log, like this one:

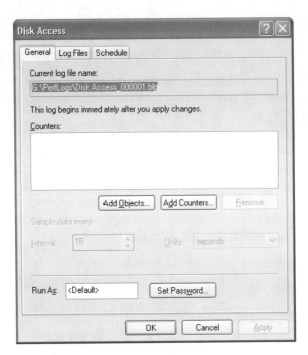

4. To determine which counter (or counters) to log, click the Add Counters button, which opens the Add Counters dialog box:

5. The Select Counters From Computer item is selected with your computer's name below it. Leave this setting, so that you are logging your own computer's performance. (Network administrators can log the performances of computers throughout the network they manage.)

6. Set the Performance Object box to Physical Disk to choose which part of your system you want to see counters about. (You can click the Explain button to get information on the selection option on this and the other lists.)

7. The Select Counters From List list displays counters about the performance object you choose. Set this to % Idle Time (that is, the percentage of the time that the physical hard disk is idle).

8. The Select Instances From List list displays Total (for the total for all the hard disks and partitions on your system) and an item that includes the individual hard disk (ours says "0 C: F: D:" to include the three partitions on our hard disk). Select the latter to see separate statistics for the individual disks and partitions.

9. Click the Add button to add this counter to your log. Click Close. Back in the Disk Access dialog box, the Counters list now includes an entry for the counter that you added—something like this:

```
\\MORTICIA\PhysicalDisk(0 C:)\% Idle Time
```

10. Logging usually stores a sample every 15 seconds. You can change that interval by changing the value in the Interval box.

11. If you want to store the log file somewhere other than in the Perflogs folder on the same disk on which Windows is installed, click the Log Files tab and change the settings there.

12. If you want to store the log file in a format that you can import into a database or spreadsheet file, click the Log Files tab and change the Log File Type. (Logging defaults to a Binary File type, which can't be imported.)

13. If you want to control when logging starts and stops (rather than just starting now and continuing indefinitely), click the Schedule tab.

14. Click OK to create your log. Now the log appears in the Counter Logs section of the Performance Logs And Alerts item in the MMC Computer Management window.

You can start and stop logging by selecting the log from the list and clicking the Stop The Selected Log button (a black box) on the MMC toolbar. To start it again, click the Start The Selected Log button (the right-pointing "play" arrow).

To view the log file after it has collected some data, you can open the log file, which is usually in C:\Perflogs and has the name you typed when you created the log, with a number at the end (for example, C:\Perflogs\Disk Access_000001.blg). Click or double- click it to open the Performance window, a version of the Performance Logs And Alerts MMC snap-in with one additional component, System Monitor. This window is a live viewer into the operations that you have selected in your log.

The Device Manager

Like the Device Manager in previous versions of Windows, the Windows XP Device Manager displays information about all the hardware on your computer (see Chapter 13, section "What Is the Device Manager?"). In Windows XP, however, you can display it as an MMC snap-in. You can also display the Device Manager in its own window by choosing Start, right-clicking My Computer, choosing Properties from the menu, clicking the Hardware tab, and clicking the Device Manager button. You can do two important things with the Device Manager: modify drivers for a device and remove a device (see Chapter 13, section "Solving Configuration Problems by Using the Device Manager").

> **Tip**   *The Windows 2000 and XP versions of the Device Manager have a little-known feature—accessing device-specific Troubleshooters from within the device's Properties dialog box. Locate the device that is giving you trouble, double-click it to open its Properties dialog box, and click the Troubleshooter button. If you look at the General tab of the Properties dialog box, Windows tells you if it thinks the device is misbehaving.*

Returning Your System to a Predefined State with System Restore

Many people run into trouble with Windows right after they install a new program, upgrade a program to a newer version, or upgrade to a new version of Windows itself. When new program files interfere with the operation of other programs, you may wish that you could undo the installation and put your system back the way it was. Another common occurrence is that Windows' operation and performance degrades over time, and you may wish that you could return it to the way it ran a few weeks or months ago.

Windows XP contains a utility called System Restore, introduced in Windows Me. This program watches your system as you work, noting when program files are installed, changed, or deleted. It keeps a log of these changes for the last one to three weeks (depending on how many changes you make). You can also tell it to take a "snapshot"—a *restore point*—of the state of the system and store it away. For example, you might want to take a snapshot right after you have installed Windows from scratch, along with all the applications you rely on. Later, if you decide that an installation or some other fault has irreparably damaged your computer's stability, you can tell System Restore that you'd rather return your system to the way it was when you took the restore point snapshot.

When you tell System Restore to create a restore point, it makes copies of the critical files that define how the system works and what applications it is registered to use (the Registry, Windows program files, and other program files). It stores these copies, which are used later to restore the system to that state, in another location on your hard drive.

*Not all files are copied, only program files. Your documents aren't stored—System Restore does not take the place of regular backups of the files you create and edit. System Restore does not take your computer back in time, as a product called GoBack from Adaptec (**http://www.adaptec.com**) claims to do. Under System Restore, all of the nonsystem changes and additions you make will still be there. Even an offending application will still have all of its files available. The important thing is that the system files, including most of the Registry, the central repository for all configuration settings in Windows, are returned to a state prior to the bad change.*

System Restore restores programs, not documents. It doesn't restore Word documents, Excel spreadsheets, Access databases, text files, Web pages, or files in the My Documents folder.

If you want to make sure that restoring from a restore point won't affect a file, move the file to the My Documents folder.

To protect against major damage to your files, be sure to make regular backups. If you use Windows XP Professional, also consider making an Automated System Recovery floppy disk, which can help in restoring your hard disk if Windows is too damaged to run System Restore (see Chapter 9, section "Backing Up and Restoring System Information Using Automated System Recovery").

Automatic Restore Points

System Restore creates a number of restore points automatically:

- **Initial system checkpoint**   Created the first time you start your computer after installing Windows XP.

- **System checkpoints**   Created every 10 hours that Windows is running or every 24 hours (or as soon thereafter as you run Windows again).

- **Program installation checkpoints**   Created when you install a new program, it records the state of the system just *before* the installation.

- **Windows automatic update restore points**   Created when you install an update to Windows, it records the state of the system just *before* the installation.

In addition, you can create a restore point whenever you like, as described in the next two sections.

Running System Restore

System Restore is installed and running behind the scenes by default all the time that Windows is running. You can do only two things with it directly:

■ Create a restore point for the current state of your system.

■ Return your system to a previously recorded restore point.

To run the System Restore program, choose Start | All Programs | Accessories | Systems Tools | System Restore. You can also run it by choosing Start | Help And Support and clicking Undo Changes To Your Computer With System Restore in the right column (under Pick A Task). If you happen to have the System Information window open (as shown in Figure 35-1), choose Tools | System Restore. No matter how you start it, you see the System Restore window, with two options: Restore My Computer To An Earlier Time and Create A Restore Point. If you've restored your system to a restore point recently, a third option also appears: Undo My Last Restoration.

Configuring System Restore

Although System Restore is running all the time by default, you can turn it off. To do so, to make sure that it's turned on, or to change its configuration, follow these steps:

1. Click Start, right-click My Computer, and choose Properties from the menu that appears. You see the System Properties window.

2. Click the System Restore tab, as shown in Figure 35-4.

3. Click the Turn Off System Restore On All Drives check box until it contains a check mark if you *don't* want to be able to use System Restore. Click it until it is empty if you want System Restore to run in the background all the time, creating restore points to which you can return. (We recommend that you leave it running—leave the check box blank.)

4. You can control how much space System Restore uses for its restore points. Click a drive in the Available Drives box and click the Settings button to display the Disk Space Usage slider for that drive. Move the slider to specify how much of your hard disk (the disk on which the Windows program file is stored, if you have more than one) may be used to store restore points.

If you have a dual-boot computer and one disk or partition is used only for the program files of another version of Windows, turn off System Restore for that disk or partition. When you are running Windows XP, you shouldn't be changing the files on that disk or partition.

5. Click OK on both dialog boxes to save any changes.

System Restore won't run if you have less than 200MB free on your hard disk (the hard disk that contains the Windows system folder, if you have more than one hard disk). It notifies you of the problem and offers to run Disk Cleanup.

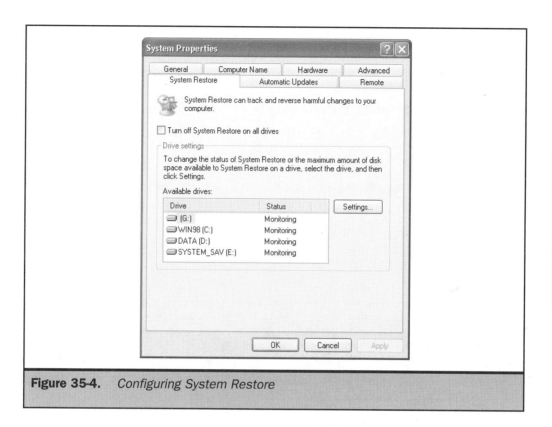

Figure 35-4.   *Configuring System Restore*

Creating a Restore Point

You can create a restore point any time you think you are about to make a change to the system that might be risky. It's a good idea to create a restore point when everything is working fine, so you can get your Windows system back to that state again later. A restore point you create is called a *manual checkpoint*. To create a restore point of your own, follow these steps:

1. Choose Start | All Programs | Accessories | Systems Tools | System Restore.
2. Select Create A Restore Point and click Next.
3. Enter a description of the save point for future reference. If you are installing software immediately after creating the save point, make note of it.
4. Click Next. System Restore creates the restore point and asks you to confirm the information about it.
5. Read the description to make sure you haven't missed anything. Click Back if you want to change the description you entered. Click OK.

That's it. You've finished. If you need to access System Restore when there's a serious problem that prevents you from restarting your computer normally, reboot into Safe Mode (see Chapter 13, section "Booting in Safe Mode").

Restoring Your System to a Restore Point

If your system starts acting strangely, if you get a virus, or if you delete a program file by accident, you can return the program files on your system to the way they were when System Restore created a restore point. Follow these steps:

1. Choose Start | All Programs | Accessories | Systems Tools | System Restore.

2. Select Restore My Computer To An Earlier Time and click Next.

3. You see a calendar of the current month. Days for which there is a restore point appear highlighted. Click a date to see a list of the restore points created on that day (as shown in Figure 35-5).

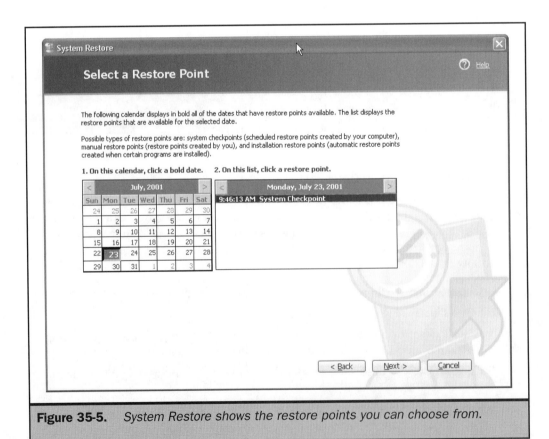

Figure 35-5. *System Restore shows the restore points you can choose from.*

4. Click the restore point to which you want to return your system and click Next.

5. System Restore reminds you to close all other programs before continuing. Do so and click OK.

6. System Restore shows the date, time, and description of the restore point you chose for your confirmation. Click Next. The restoration may take a few minutes and includes restarting Windows. When Windows is running again, you see the System Restore window, reporting whether the restore was successful.

7. Click OK.

Another way to return your system to a restore point is by starting your computer in Safe Mode (see "Safe Mode"). After you log in and before you see the Windows desktop, Windows asks whether you want to run System Restore.

Undoing a Restoration

If you return your system to a restore point and it doesn't solve the problem you were facing, you can undo the restoration by following these steps:

1. Choose Start | All Programs | Accessories | Systems Tools | System Restore.

2. Choose Undo My Last Restoration and click Next.

3. System Restore prompts you to close all other programs and confirm the operation that you want to undo. In the process of undoing the restoration, it restarts Windows.

Reporting Problems with Dr. Watson

Dr. Watson is a program that takes a "snapshot" of the system's state, including RAM usage, what tasks were running, and what programs loaded at startup. After a program fails (crashes or hangs), you can take a snapshot that the program's support department can use to figure out what went wrong. If you are having trouble with a program (including Windows itself), start Dr. Watson, and then run the troublesome program. When the program fails, immediately take a snapshot to document the current state of Windows and your programs, to aid in diagnosing the problem.

To use Dr. Watson, choose Start | Run, type **drwatson**, and press ENTER. The program doesn't open a window, but adds a small icon to the taskbar. When a program fails, immediately double-click the Dr. Watson button on the taskbar, or click it and choose Dr. Watson from the menu that appears. (If Dr. Watson detected the crash, it may appear onscreen automatically.) Dr. Watson creates a snapshot of the state of your system, reporting its progress as it does so. It then opens a report window in which it lists any possible trouble spots it noted and lets you enter a sentence or two describing what you were doing when the program crashed. If you want to make a note of what you were doing when the problem occurred, click in the lower box and type a description.

To save the information you've gathered, choose File | Save and save the report to a file. Dr. Watson creates a log file with the extension .wlg. When you contact your software vendor about the problem, they may ask you either to open the saved report and read them some of the saved information or, more likely, e-mail or upload the entire log file to them.

Tip   *You can use the information from Dr. Watson's report to research the problem yourself. Look in the first few lines of the log file for the names of the program(s) that caused the problem. Go to the Microsoft Support Web site at* **http://support.microsoft.com** *and search for those names. Microsoft may have articles about the problem programs in the Microsoft Knowledge Base.*

You can open a saved log file later by running Dr. Watson and choosing File | Open Log File from the menu (or open the .wlg file—Windows runs Dr. Watson automatically).

If you want all the information possible about what your system was doing when the program failed, choose View | Advanced from the Dr. Watson menu bar. Tabs appear along the top of the Dr. Watson window—so many that you need to click the right-arrow button at the right side of the window to see the rest of the tabs. (You can drag the right side of the Dr. Watson window toward the right to make the window wider.)

You can change how Dr. Watson works by choosing View | Options from the Dr. Watson menu bar or clicking the Dr. Watson button on the taskbar and choosing Options from the menu that appears. You can specify how many log files to save, where to store them, and whether Dr. Watson opens in standard or advanced view.

Chapter 36

Other Windows XP Resources

Microsoft updates Windows constantly to accommodate new hardware and software and to enhance features already found in the system. To stay up to date with these changes, you can run the Windows Update program to scan your system and look for outdated drivers and programs, or you can configure the Automatic Updates program to download and install updates automatically. You can also check the information that Microsoft provides on the Internet and do your own sleuthing by using resources and information available there.

This chapter explains how to update your computer by using Windows Update and Automatic Updates and how to locate information about Windows from Microsoft and other sources.

Updating Your Computer with Windows Update

Windows Update examines your computer and gives you a list of device drivers and other files that can be updated. When the scan is complete, a list of available updates is presented, and you can choose which update(s) you want to install., Windows Update includes a Restore option that returns your computer to its condition prior to the update, in case you install an update that is not what you expected or does not work properly.

You can run Windows Update at any time to see whether new updates are available. It is especially important to run Windows Update after you install a new piece of hardware or a new software program to be sure you have the drivers and files that you need on your system.

Windows Update uses a Wizard that guides you through the screens to complete the setup information. The first time you run Windows Update, you may be asked to register as a Windows user and supply some personal information, such as your name, location, and e-mail address. Windows Update uses Internet Explorer and your Internet settings to connect you to the Microsoft site on the Web. Before you start Windows Update, be sure your computer is connected or is ready to connect to the Internet. Also, close all your other programs, since some updates require restarting Windows.

To run Windows Update and update your Windows installation, follow these steps:

1. Choose Start | All Programs | Windows Update, or run Internet Explorer and choose Tools | Windows Update. The Help And Support Center home page has a link to Windows Update, too.

2. If your computer is not already connected to the Internet, you may see the Connect dialog box; if so, enter your user name and password and click Dial. Windows Update connects to the Microsoft server over the Internet and displays a Web page like the one shown in Figure 36-1. The Windows Update page shows options that you can use to update Windows, get answers to technical support questions, or send your feedback about the Update page to Microsoft. (Since this page is on the Web, Microsoft may change its design at any time, but similar options will probably be available.)

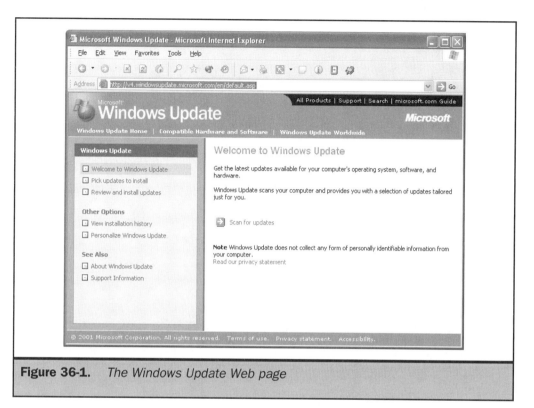

Figure 36-1.   *The Windows Update Web page*

3. Click the Scan For Updates button to check for updates. You see a catalog of available updates from which you can choose those appropriate for your system.

4. Click the Critical Updates link in the Task pane section of the Web page. Be sure to download all the Critical Update items. Windows Update lists the items it found, as shown in Figure 36-2.

5. For each update you want to download, click the Add button.

6. When you've chosen the updates you want, click the Review And Install Updates link in the Task pane section of the Web page. You see a list of the updates you've selected.

7. Click the Install Now button to download and install the updates.

8. If an update requires you to agree to a license, you see a dialog box with the license agreement. Click Accept if you agree to the license agreement.

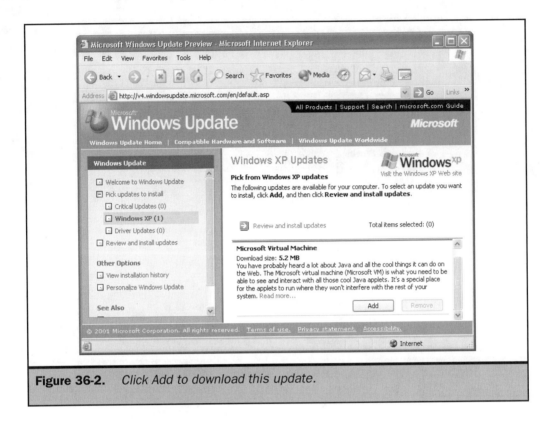

Figure 36-2. *Click Add to download this update.*

9. Windows displays a status dialog box like this, to let you know about its progress:

10. Some updates require restarting Windows: if so, Windows Update asks before restarting.

Updating Your Computer Automatically with Automatic Updates

If you've used your Windows XP for more than a few days, you may have seen a little Update Reminder balloon appear above the notification area at the right end of the taskbar, asking you to configure Windows to update itself automatically over the Internet. This message comes from Automatic Updates, a Windows feature that contacts Microsoft over the Internet, checks for Windows updates, downloads them, and installs them. You can configure Automatic Updates to ask you before downloading or installing updates.

You have two ways to configure Automatic Updates:

■ If the Automatic Updates icon or balloon appears in the notification area of the taskbar, click it to see the Updates dialog box. Click Settings to configure Automatic Updates, Remind Me Later if you want the Update Reminder Box to appear later, or choose Next to view the license for Windows Updates and to turn the feature on.

■ Otherwise, choose Start | Control Panel, click Performance And Maintenance, and click System to display the System Properties dialog box. (Another way to display this dialog box is to click Start, right-click My Computer, and choose Properties from the menu that appears.) Click the Automatic Updates tab, as shown in Figure 36-3.

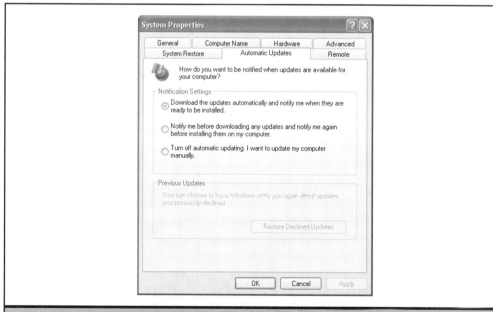

Figure 36-3.   *Configuring the Automatic Update system*

The Notification Settings give you three options:

■ **Download The Updates Automatically And Notify Me When They Are Ready To Be Installed** Enables Automatic Updates. When Automatic Updates downloads a group of updates, you can choose which ones to install, as described later in this section.

■ **Notify Me Before Downloading Any Updates And Notify Me Again Before Installing Them On My Computer** Enables Automatic Updates. Windows checks to see whether updates are available. If they are, an icon appears in the notification area of the taskbar, and a reminder box asks whether you want to download and install them, as described later in this section. Double-click the icon to see the list of updates and click the check boxes so that a check mark appears next to each update you want to download.

■ **Turn Off Automatic Updating. I Want To Update My Computer Manually** Windows doesn't do automatic updating.

If Automatic Updates are enabled, and new updates are available for you to download an install, an icon appears in the notification area on the taskbar, and a balloon might appear, like this:

ⓘ **New updates are ready to install**

Updates for your computer have been downloaded from Windows Update. Click here to review these updates and install them.

Click the icon or balloon to display the Automatic Updates Ready To Install dialog box (shown in Figure 36-4), which asks whether you want to install them. Click the Details button to see a list of the downloaded updates. Click Install to install the updates you choose. Click Remind Me Later if now is not a convenient time to install them (for example, you don't want to restart Windows).

If you decide not to install an update you've downloaded, Windows deletes it from your hard disk. However, you can decide to install it later. From the Automatic Updates tab of the System Properties dialog box, click the Restore Declined Updates button to display a list of the updates that you decided not to install. You can choose which items you want to install after all. The next time Automatic Updates checks the Microsoft site for updates, it includes the items you specify.

What Materials Are Available from Microsoft?

Other materials about Windows, besides those listed on the Windows Update Web page and the Help And Support Center window, are available from Microsoft:

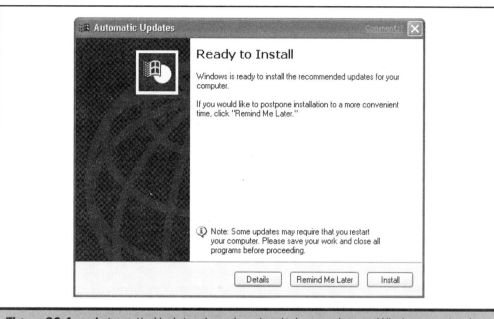

Figure 36-4. *Automatic Updates has downloaded an update to Windows and asks whether you want to install it.*

- **Microsoft Product Support Services Web site at http://support.microsoft.com** Site with support information for all Microsoft products. Use the searchable Knowledge Base to find articles about problems and solutions, known bugs, and overviews of how products work. You can also get to this page by clicking the Support link on the Windows Update Web page.

- **Windows XP home page at http://www.microsoft.com/windowsxp** A good resource for general announcements and information about Windows XP. You can also check the general Windows site at **http://www.microsoft.com/windows**.

- **Internet Explorer home page at http://www.microsoft.com/windows/ie** Each component included with Windows has its own page at the Microsoft Web site. From the Internet Explorer page, click Features to see an overview of the new features incorporated as part of Internet Explorer.

- **Outlook Express home page at http://www.microsoft.com/windows/oe** Click the Features button to see details about Outlook Express

- **Computing Central at http://computingcentral.msn.com** Microsoft's MSN-hosted Web site about computers. Click the Software link and the Operating Systems link for information about Windows.

- **Microsoft's Usenet newsgroups** Discussion groups about Microsoft products (see Chapter 23, section "What Are Newsgroups?"). Microsoft hosts over a thousand discussions on its news server, with newsgroups about its major products in a variety of languages (two-letter country codes appear in the newsgroup names, like *br* for Brazil or *fr* for France). Choose Start | Help And Support to see the Help And Support Center window, click Get Support Or Find Information In Windows XP Newsgroups, and click Go To A Windows Web Site Forum in the Task pane. Then follow the instructions on the Web page. You can also use Outlook Express to read the newsgroups. To add a Microsoft news server to your list of servers in Outlook Express, run Outlook Express. Select Tools | Accounts and click the News tab. Click Add, choose News, and follow the prompts as the wizard walks you through the steps to add the news server. The public Microsoft news server is named **msnews.microsoft.com**. After you add the server, download all the newsgroups so that you can see a list of what's available on the server. Many newsgroups discuss Windows and its components.

| Tip | *You can get online help from Microsoft by using the Help And Support window's Support button (see Chapter 4, section "Getting Help from Microsoft or from a Friend").* |

What Other Materials Are Available on the Internet?

Windows is a popular topic on the Internet. A number of Windows-related Web sites and newsgroups are not connected to or sponsored by Microsoft.

Web Sites

These Web sites provide information on a variety of computer-related issues, including Windows:

- **CNET.com at http://www.cnet.com**   Current news on all things related to computers. If you don't see an article on Windows on the home page, click Search.Com and search for Windows XP. CNET searches resources around the Web to locate pages. Click a link to visit the site and view the information.

- **Internet Gurus at http://net.gurus.com/winxptcr**   Our own Web site for readers of the book. As we find useful information about Windows, we'll post it on this Web site.

- **Paul Thurrott's SuperSite for Windows at http://www.winsupersite.com** FAQs (frequently asked questions and their answers), reviews, and news.

- **Windows Guide at http://www.zdnet.com/windows**   Prints articles on a variety of computer topics, including Windows. To search for an article from *PC Magazine*, click Search and type **Windows XP** in the Search box. The most recent articles are listed first.

Information on the Internet changes quickly. To search the Web for other Windows-related information, see "Searching for Web Pages" in Chapter 24.

Usenet Newsgroups

Newsgroups are discussion arenas on the Internet (see Chapter 23, section "What Are Newsgroups?"). In addition to the newsgroups hosted by Microsoft, many other newsgroups, unaffiliated with Microsoft, discuss Windows topics.

To find newsgroups about Windows, run Outlook Express or your favorite newsreader and search for newsgroups with **win** in the newsgroup name. Most should be in the **comp** (computing) hierarchy, but you may find them in the **alt** or other hierarchies as well.

 When you are searching for newsgroups, you can enter as few or as many characters as you like. The more characters you enter, the narrower the search. For example, a search for "Windows" will not show newsgroups with "WinXP" in the title.

If you can't find the type of discussion you want in the newsgroups listed on your ISP's news server, use the Web site **http://groups.google.com** as a resource for newsgroup information. The Google Groups Web site lets you search past newsgroup articles. You can search for newsgroup messages containing a word or phrase, or you can read messages from newsgroups that do not appear on your news server.

As of August 2001, only one newsgroup is dedicated to Windows XP—**alt.os.windows-xp**. By the time you read this, other newsgroups may have formed. You might want to start at **comp.os.ms-windows.winnt.misc**, **comp.os.ms-windows.winnt.moderated**, and **comp.os.ms-windows.winnt.setup**—these three newsgroups are for Windows NT, but most also include information about Windows 2000 and XP.

Mailing Lists

Many mailing lists discuss various versions and aspects of Windows, and Windows XP–specific lists will pop up as people upgrade to the product. To find mailing lists that discuss Windows XP, or e-mail-based "tip-a-day" newsletters with Windows XP tips, go to the Topica Web site at **http://www.topica.com** and search for "Windows" or "Windows XP." For more information about how to subscribe to and participate in mailing lists, go to the List Gurus Web site at **http://lists.gurus.com**.

The
Complete
Reference

Windows XP

Part VIII

Behind the Scenes:
Windows XP Internals

Chapter 37

Windows XP Configuration Files

Windows stores its configuration information in a variety of files of different formats, including files for configuring Windows itself, as well as for running Windows and DOS programs. Windows comes with the System Configuration Utility (or Msconfig, for short) to help make controlled changes to some of its configuration files. This chapter explains the configuration files used by Windows XP, as well as how to run the System Configuration Utility program. The last section offers some pointers for running both Windows and another operating system (such as UNIX or Linux) on the same computer.

What Kinds of Configuration Files Does Windows XP Use?

Other than the Registry (described in Chapter 38), most of Windows' control information is stored in text files that you can open with Notepad or any other text editor. Although changing these files is usually a bad idea unless you're quite sure you know what you're doing, looking at their contents is entirely safe—and provides fascinating glimpses into how Windows works.

Making Configuration Files Visible

Most of the control information is stored in hidden, system, and read-only files (see Chapter 8, section "What Are Attributes?"). Hidden and system files are like any other files, except that they don't normally appear in file listings when you use Windows Explorer to display a folder that contains them. (Any file can be hidden, but only a couple of required files in the root folder of the boot drive are system files.) Read-only files can't be changed or deleted.

You can tell Windows to show you all the hidden files on your computer. In an Explorer window, select Tools | Folder Options and click the View tab. The list of Advanced Settings includes a Hidden Files And Folders category. Click the Show Hidden Files And Folders check box so a check appears. This setting reveals hidden files in all folders, not just the current folder. Hidden files appear listed with regular files, but their icons are paler than regular files. To reveal the hidden files that Windows considers "special," uncheck the Hide Protected Operating System Files (Recommended) check box. Click Yes in the warning dialog box. Click OK when you have finished making changes in the Folder Options dialog box to make the changes active.

You can change a file's hidden or system status by right-clicking the file and selecting Properties. Click the Hidden and Read-only check boxes at the bottom of the Properties dialog box to select or deselect these attributes.

Tip   *We recommend that you leave hidden and system folders and files hidden unless you plan to look at them. They can be distracting during normal work. If you do decide to display them, you can tell hidden and system files from normal files by their dimmed appearance.*

What Is %SystemRoot%?

You may see pathnames that include "%SystemRoot%" in a dialog box setting or in a configuration file. SystemRoot is a global system variable that tells Windows where the Windows program is stored. Windows replaces "%SystemRoot%" with the current location of Windows (usually C:\Windows).

Why is this useful? Because if you create a configuration file for your computer and then give it to a friend, your friend's Windows system may be installed somewhere else (for example, F:\Windows on a dual-boot system in which the C: partition is used by a previous version of Windows). Your Windows system could be installed on C:, but theirs could be F: or L: or Z:. Using %SystemRoot% in a configuration file allows it to work on any system, regardless of circumstance.

Windows Initialization Files

Since Windows 95, Microsoft has moved most Windows initialization information into the Registry, but Windows still uses two initialization files: Win.ini and System.ini. Some Windows 3.1 applications stored their setup information in individual *INI files* (initialization files), such as Progman.ini for the Windows 3.1 Program Manager. Other Windows 3.1 programs used sections in the general-purpose Win.ini file.

All INI files have the file extension .ini, and nearly all reside in the folder in which Windows is installed (usually C:\Windows). All INI files have a common format, of which the following is a typical example (it contains configuration information for the WS_FTP file transfer program):

```
[WS_FTP]
DIR=F:\Program Files\WS_FTP
DEFDIR=F:\Program Files\WS_FTP
GROUP=WS_FTP Pro
INSTOPTS=4

[Mail]
MAPI=1
```

An INI file is divided into sections, with each section starting with a section name in square brackets. Within a section, each line is of the form *parameter=value*, where the value may be a filename, number, or other string. Blank lines and lines that start with a semicolon are ignored.

In general, editing the Win.ini or System.ini file is a bad idea, but if you need to do so, use the System Configuration Utility (see the next section, "Configuring Windows with the System Configuration Utility"). You can take a look at the contents of the files using this program, too.

While Windows may not make much use of the Win.ini and System.ini files, third-party software publishers make wide use of application-specific INI files to retain their program settings. Take a peek into the program folders for a few of your applications and you'll almost certainly find an INI file.

The Win.ini File

In Windows 3.1, nearly every scrap of setup information in the entire system ended up in the Win.ini file in C:\Windows, meaning that if any program messed up Win.ini, the system could be nearly unusable. More recent versions of Windows alleviate this situation by moving most configuration of the information into the Registry, but Win.ini is retained to offer support for 16-bit applications. You'll typically find sections for a few of your application programs in Win.ini, plus a little setup information for Windows itself.

You can use Notepad to edit Win.ini, but it's dangerous. Instead, use the System Configuration Utility to edit the Win.ini file (see the next section, "Configuring Windows with the System Configuration Utility").

The System.ini File

In Windows 3.1, the System.ini file in C:\Windows listed all the Windows device and subsystem drivers to be loaded at startup. In Windows XP the vast majority of the driver information is in the Registry, but System.ini still contains driver configuration information for 16-bit applications. Use the System Configuration Utility (rather than Notepad) to edit the System.ini file (see the next section, "Configuring Windows with the System Configuration Utility").

The Registry

The Windows Registry contains all of the configuration information not in an INI file, including the vast majority of the actual information used to control Windows and its applications. Use the Registry Editor to examine and manage the Registry (see Chapter 38, section "Editing the Registry").

Configuring Windows with the System Configuration Utility

Microsoft provides the System Configuration Utility to help you make controlled changes to the various configuration files described earlier in this chapter. To run the System Configuration Utility, choose Start | Run, type **msconfig** in the Open box, and click OK. You see the System Configuration Utility window, shown in Figure 37-1.

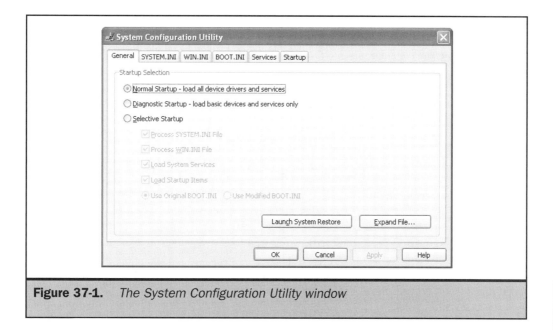

Figure 37-1.   *The System Configuration Utility window*

The System Configuration Utility includes a tab for each configuration file, along with the Startup tab, which lists information from the Registry about programs to be run at startup time. Changes you make don't take effect until the next time Windows restarts, so when you close the System Configuration Utility, it asks whether you want to save the changes you've made; if you click Yes, it offers to reboot Windows for you.

Restarting Windows with Selected Startup Options

The General tab of the System Configuration Utility window can help you restart Windows in a startup mode that helps diagnose problems (see Chapter 35, section "Startup Modes"). The three startup items are as follows:

- **Normal Startup**   The default mode. You'll not likely switch back to this if things are running smoothly.
- **Diagnostic Startup**   Essentially the same as Safe Mode. This option limits loading device drivers and system services that may interfere with normal operation.
- **Selective Startup**   Enables you to select which startup items to load. A good plan when you experience system instability is to turn all your startup items off, reboot, and then turn one on at a time. If that doesn't help, try different combinations. You'd be surprised how much instability can come from a little icon like AOL or Palm Desktop in the notification area of the Windows taskbar.

If you want to restart Windows and tell it to process only specific configuration files, click the Selective Startup setting on the General tab of the System Configuration Utility window and choose the files to process. When you click OK, Windows asks whether you want to reboot your computer. Click Yes. Windows restarts and processes only the files you specified. To save your changes without restarting Windows, click Apply (the changes to the files are saved, but don't go into effect until you reboot).

Replacing a Corrupted Windows File

Occasionally, one of the program files that make up Windows is deleted or corrupted (perhaps by a virus). The Expand File on the General tab of the System Configuration Utility window provides an easy way to extract a single file from the Windows XP CD-ROM (or any other CAB file) and replace it on your system. The program extracts a file from a CAB file (Windows Cabinet file, the format in which program files are stored on the Windows XP CD-ROM). You need to know which file is bad and which CAB file contains the replacement for the file.

If you know what file you want to replace and the location of the CAB file that contains a good copy, follow these steps:

1. Click the Expand File button on the General tab of the System Configuration Utility window. You see the Expand One File From Installation Source dialog box, shown here:

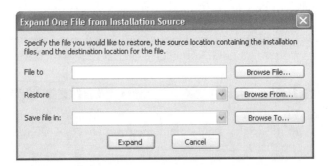

2. Click the Browse File button and navigate to the problem file. When you have it selected in the Open dialog box, click OK.

3. Click the Browse From button and select the CAB file on the CD-ROM that contains the file you want to replace.

4. Click the Browse To button and navigate to the directory that the replacement file should be stored in.

5. Click Expand.

The program doesn't give you any help in figuring out which CAB file on the Windows XP CD-ROM contains the file you need. Also, CAB filenames are not known for their readability. You may have quite a time locating something. Finally, there's no indicator that you have or have not successfully extracted the file. One way to know is to keep an Explorer window open on the desktop showing the contents of the folder into which you are storing the replacement file. If a file is added, it will appear in that folder within 30 seconds or so.

Changing Your System.ini and Win.ini Files

The System Configuration Utility window's System.ini tab, shown in Figure 37-2, and Win.ini tab (which looks similar) show a list of the sections in the System.ini and Win.ini files. To see the individual lines within a section, click the plus box to the left of the section name. To disable an entire section, deselect the check box to the left of the section name (or select it and click the Disable button). To disable an individual line, deselect the check box to its left (or select it and click the Enable button). If you want to add a new setting, select the line after which you want to add the setting and click the New button. The program adds a new blank line: type the contents (in the format *parameter=value*) and press ENTER You can also reorder the items by selecting them and clicking the Move Up and Move Down buttons.

Changing Your Boot.ini File

Windows XP, like Windows NT and Windows 2000 before it, was designed as a multiuser operating system. It was also designed to allow more than one operating

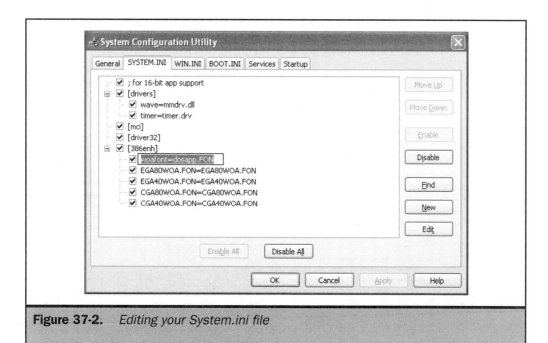

Figure 37-2. *Editing your System.ini file*

BEHIND THE SCENES: WINDOWS XP INTERNALS

system to be installed at a time on one computer. It is this capability you see when you start your computer and are asked whether you would like to boot Windows XP or another operating system in another partition (in some cases, whether or not you have another OS installed). This multiboot feature stores your list of bootable partitions in the Boot.ini file.

You can edit the Boot.ini file by clicking the Boot.ini tab in the System Configuration Utility window or by using the System Properties dialog box.

Changing Your Services and Startup Settings

The Services and Startup tabs in the System Configuration Utility window (Figure 37-3) show the services and applications that run when Windows starts up, including the startup programs listed in the Registry and the programs in your Startup folder (usually stored in the C:\Documents And Settings*username*\Start Menu\Programs\ StartUp folder). You can disable loading a service or program at startup by deselecting its check box.

 We strongly suggest that you avoid modifying the Services tab at all. When installed as a workstation or home system, most of these services are already disabled, so deselecting them results in no change of functionality anyway. The Startup tab, which lists application programs, is where you should concentrate your debugging efforts.

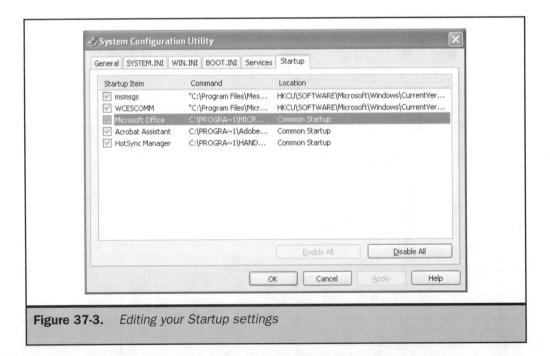

Figure 37-3. *Editing your Startup settings*

Changing Your Environment Settings

DOS and early versions of Windows used *environment variables* to store some settings. Environment variables can be changed while Windows is running by using the DOS SET command. When Window or a DOS VM start up, the variables must be *initialized* (that is, set to their initial values).

To see or set your environment variables, click Start, right-click My Computer, and select Properties from the shortcut menu. On the System Properties dialog box that appears, click the Advanced tab and then click the Environment Variables button. You see the Environment Variables dialog box (shown in Figure 37-4). The upper part of the dialog box shows user variables (which store information about the current user account). The lower part shows system variables (which store information about Windows itself).

The two default user variables are TEMP and TMP. Both define where Windows stores its temporary files. The default system variables, which you should not remove or modify, are as follows:

- **COMSPEC**   Location of the Command Prompt program (usually C:\Windows\System32\Cmd.exe). See Chapter 39 for how to use the Command Prompt program.

- **NUMBER_OF_PROCESSORS**   For single-CPU computers, 1.

- **OS**   The name of your OS. Though a bit odd for more than one reason, Windows XP's name appears as "Windows_NT."

- **PATH**   Where Windows looks for executable programs for launching applications from the command prompt (usually a list of pathnames including C:\Windows\System32 and C:\Windows.

- **PATHEXT**   Which extensions are recognized as executable when launching from the command prompt (usually a list of extensions including COM, BAT, CMD, VBS, VBE, JS, JSE, WSF, and WSH).

- **PROCESSOR_ARCHITECTURE**   Usually "x86", the types of processors designed and sold by Intel.

- **PROCESSOR_IDENTIFIER**   Description of your computer's CPU. Ours shows "x86 Family 6 Model 8 Stepping 6, GenuineIntel".

- **PROCESSOR_LEVEL**   Stepping level in the PROCESSOR_IDENTIFIER.

- **PROCESSOR_REVISION**   Revision number of the processor. Ours is "0806."

- **TEMP**   Where to store temporary files (usually "C:\Windows\Temp").

- **TMP**   Where to store temporary files (usually "C:\Windows\Temp").

- **WINDIR**   Location of the system directory (usually "C:\Windows").

Note   *Do not remove or modify these system variables.*

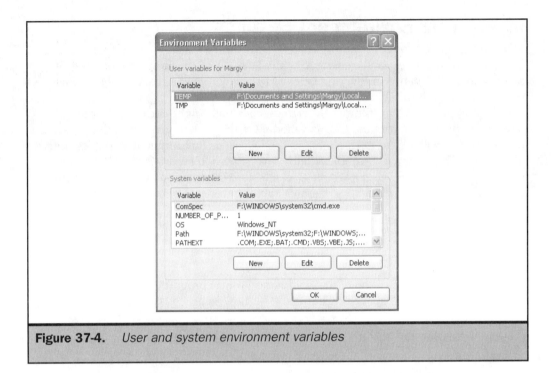

Figure 37-4. *User and system environment variables*

Changing Your International Settings

Most of the Windows international and regional settings appear in the Regional And Language Options dialog box (see Chapter 12, section "Windows' Regional Settings"). Set the Language box to the language of your choice—Windows updates the rest of the settings on the tab to match. Don't edit the individual settings unless you know what you are doing.

Configuring DOS and Older Windows Programs to Run Under Windows XP

Most previous versions of Windows ran "on top" of DOS—that is, DOS loaded first, and then Windows loaded, continuing to run DOS for basic operating system functions. Windows XP doesn't load DOS; it performs these operating system functions itself.

You rarely need to run DOS itself. All recent versions of Windows programs are designed to work directly with Windows rather than requiring DOS. However, some older *legacy programs* that were written when DOS ran "beneath" Windows require DOS to run. Legacy programs include programs written to run directly under DOS, and Windows programs that call on DOS for operating system services. (Many older games are legacy programs.) Like Windows Me, Windows XP comes with a DOS Virtual Machine (VM), which simulates DOS, displaying the DOS prompt and responding to DOS commands (see Chapter 39). See the section "Configuring the DOS Environment" in Chapter 39 for how to configure DOS and Windows 3.1 programs to run under Windows XP.

Disk Formats and Coexisting with Other Operating Systems

Windows can share a hard disk with some other operating systems. Because different operating systems format the disk differently, sharing a disk requires splitting it up into partitions.

Partitioning Disks

One way for multiple operating systems to be installed on a single hard disk is for each system to be assigned one or more partitions on the disk and use its partition(s) when running. Windows can share a disk with OS/2 or UNIX this way. Windows uses a Primary partition (which used to be called a Primary DOS partition). Most other operating systems also use a single partition. Windows can create FAT32 and NTFS partitions and respects partitions created by other systems, but cannot itself create a partition for any other system (see Chapter 32, section "Partitioning a Disk Using Disk Management").

Here are ways to partition a disk between Windows and another system:

■ *Install Windows first.* When installing Windows, tell the Setup Wizard to use only as much of the disk as you want to assign to Windows and leave the rest of the disk unassigned. Once Windows is installed, shut Windows down and install the other system, which generally creates its own partition using the rest of the disk.

■ *Install the other system first.* Most other operating systems can usually create a Primary partition for Windows at the same time they create their own partitions by using an included utility. Once the other system is installed, shut the system down and install Windows, which automatically uses the existing Primary partition.

■ *Use a partitioning program like Partition Magic to create the partitions.* There are utility programs designed for creating, modifying, and copying partitions of all types (see Chapter 32, section "Installing Multiple Versions of Windows with PartitionMagic").

A few systems offer other ways to coexist with Windows or DOS. For example, some versions of Linux (a popular clone of UNIX) can create a large file in a DOS partition and use that file as the Linux partition. This makes it possible to install Linux, even on a system that has Windows preinstalled, and assigns the entire disk to the DOS partition.

 When installing more than one operating system to a computer with one or more drives, it's important to know that if you install Windows Me/9x last, it will only boot the computer to Windows Me/9x and will ignore the existence of another operating system. The easiest way around this is to install Windows Me/9x first if you plan to install it at all, followed by UNIX or Linux. Install Windows XP last: its boot loader detects the existing operating systems and adds them to its boot menu to create a multiboot installation (see Appendix A, section "Creating Dual-Boot Installations").

Other Operating Systems and Windows Files

Windows XP can't read or write files in partitions that are formatted with any file system other than DOS FAT, FAT32, or NTFS. Fortunately, nearly every other operating system that runs on a PC can deal with Windows files. Most UNIX and Linux systems, for example, can logically mount a DOS FAT partition so that it appears to be part of the UNIX file system. Consult the documentation for your other operating system to find out how to give it access to your Windows files.

 If you are creating a dual-boot system with Windows XP and Windows Me/9x and you use NTFS for your Windows XP partition, Windows Me/9x won't be able to read the files in the Windows XP partition. Solve this problem by creating an additional FAT or FAT32 partition that contains no operating system, only data.

The Complete Reference

Windows XP

Chapter 38

Registering Programs and File Types

The Windows Registry stores configuration information about the programs you run, including which program Windows uses to open, create, and edit each type of data file. It also includes configuration information for each user account you create on your system. You can use the Registry Editor program to edit the Registry, but do so with caution!

What Is the Registry?

Early versions of Windows scattered configuration settings among dozens of different files. Many settings were stored in C:\Windows\Win.ini and C:\Windows\System.ini, but programs were as likely to use their own INI files as the standard ones, and there was no consistency in the way that INI files were created and maintained. In Windows 95, Microsoft created the *Registry*, a single centralized database in which programs keep their setup information (see Chapter 37, section "Windows Initialization Files"). The Registry contains all of the information that the INI files contained, as well as other settings from around the system. All subsequent versions of Windows store configuration information settings in the Registry, and the win.ini and system.ini files remain only for backwards compatibility with older programs.

The Registry contains configuration settings for Windows itself, as well as for most programs you have installed. It also includes user profile information and information about each hardware component.

Most of the time, the Registry works automatically in the background, but in a few circumstances, you may want to edit it yourself.

Where Is the Registry Stored?

The Registry is stored in a group of files in your C:\Windows\System32\Config folder (assuming that Windows XP is installed on C:). The files with no extension (Default, Software, System, Sam, Security, Userdiff) contain the actual Registry entries. The .sav files are copies of the corresponding files made when you installed Windows. User profile information is stored in a file named Ntuser.dat in each user's folder in C:\Documents And Settings.

 Although Registry Editor looks and works the same as the Windows Me/9x Registry Editor, the location and format of the Registry files are quite different. The Windows XP Registry system is based on Windows 2000/NT and is much larger than its Windows Me/9x equivalent.

What Are Hives and Keys?

The Registry is organized much like the Windows file system. The Registry contains a set of *hives*, which are like folders, inside of which are stored *keys*. Additional keys can be stored within keys. Each key defines a setting or behavior for Windows or an installed application. Key pathnames are written with reverse slashes between them, much like filenames, so a typical key name is

> `HKEY_LOCAL_MACHINE\System\CurrentControlSet\Services\Sysaudio`

This key is in the `HKEY_LOCAL_MACHINE` hive, which contains a key named `System`, which in turn contains a key named `CurrentControlSet`, which contains a key named `Services`, which contains a key named `Sysaudio`. Each key can have one or more *values*, each of which consists of a name, a data type, and some data. A key at any level can contain any number of values, so in the example, values can be associated with `HKEY_LOCAL_MACHINE\System\CurrentControlSet\Services` or `HKEY_LOCAL_MACHINE\System`. (In practice, most of the values are stored at the lowest level or next lowest level.)

The data type of a value can be `REG_BINARY` (a series of binary or hexadecimal digits), `REG_DWORD` (four-byte numeric value, also called a *DWORD*), `REG_EXPAND_SZ` (variable-length *string*, or text), `REG_SZ` (fixed-length string), `REG_MULTI_SZ` (list of strings, separated by spaces, commas, or other punctuation), or `REG_FULL_RESOURCE_DESCRIPTOR` (larger grouping of information for storing a resource list, usually for a hardware driver). You never change the data type of a value: you change the data. (But only if you are *sure* you know what you are doing!)

The Top-Level Hives

The Registry comes with these hives at the top level of the tree structure (directly under the My Computer entry in the Registry):

- **HKEY_CLASSES_ROOT**   File associations for file types
- **HKEY_CURRENT_USER**   Configuration information for the current user account
- **HKEY_LOCAL_MACHINE**   Configuration information about the computer, for all users
- **HKEY_USERS**   Configuration information for all user accounts
- **HKEY_CURRENT_CONFIG**   Hardware profile information for the hardware profile that your computer uses at startup

Associating File Types with Programs

In Windows, every file has a *file type*, determined by the file extension (usually three letters) after the dot (see Chapter 7, section "What Are Extensions and File Types?"). For example, My Proposal.doc has type DOC, so one usually calls it a DOC file. Every file type can be associated with a program or group of programs, so when you open a file of that type in an Explorer window (by clicking or double-clicking the file), the associated program runs automatically to process the file. Most programs associate themselves with the appropriate file types when you install the program, but in two circumstances, you may want to set your own associations:

- **Dueling programs**   When two or more programs can handle the same type of file, whichever one you installed most recently wins, unless you intervene. This problem is particularly common with graphics formats such as GIF and JPG, because both graphics editing programs (such as the Windows Picture And Fax Viewer that comes with Windows XP) and Web browsers (such as Internet Explorer) can display them. You can change the association to whichever program you prefer, and Windows XP can display a list of the programs that should be able to open a file.

- **Nonstandard file extensions**   Many files with unknown types are, in fact, known types in disguise, or close enough to known types that a program you have installed can handle them. For example, most .log files are actually text files that Notepad, WordPad, or any other text editor can read. Word processors can almost all read each other's files; for example, if you use WordPerfect rather than Word, you can associate DOC files with WordPerfect.

The Windows file association facility is complex and flexible. A file type can have several programs associated with it to do different actions, such as viewing and editing a file. The usual way to process a file is to open an application, but file associations can also use DDE (Dynamic Data Exchange), a Windows facility that enables one running program to send a message to another program (see Chapter 5, section "What Is DDE?").

To see or change the details of a file association or to create a new association, open any disk drive or folder in Windows Explorer and choose Tools | Folder Options. In the Folder Options window, click the File Types tab. (The first time you do so, Windows takes a minute to assemble a list of the registered file types.) Highlight a file type in the Registered File Types list to see information about that file type in the lower part of the dialog box. Click the Change button to display the Open With dialog box and to choose a different program to run when you open that type of file. Windows lists the programs that it recommends for handling this type of file, along with other programs that it knows can open them. You can also browse to other programs that are not listed. Or, click the Advanced button to see the Edit File Type dialog box, which contains a description of the type, the icon, the usual extension for the type, and a list of actions (see Chapter 3, section "Associating Files with Programs by Using Folder Options").

When you try to open a file from the Explorer window but the filename extension isn't associated with any program, Windows opens a dialog box explaining that it can't open the file. It offers two choices: downloading a program from the Internet, or using the Open With window to choose an application that you have on your computer. If you do not see the application you want to use, click the Browse button at the bottom of the dialog box and find the file that contains the program. You can also create a file association for this file type by entering a short description of the file type and selecting the appropriate application from the Programs list. Unless you uncheck the Always Use The Selected Program To Open This Kind Of File box, Windows saves the association.

Editing the Registry

The Windows Registry contains a great deal of information beyond the file associations discussed in the previous section. For the most part, you won't need to do any editing yourself, but occasionally, a bug fix or parameter change requires a change to the Registry, so you need to be prepared to do a little editing now and then. If you're interested in how Windows works, you can also spend as much time as you want nosing around the Registry with the Registry Editor program.

 Never make changes to the Registry without first making a backup! Better yet, include the Registry in your daily backups (see Chapter 9).

Restoring the Registry

If the Registry is damaged, you can restore it from a backup. Follow these steps:

1. Save your files and close all your programs.
2. Choose Start | Turn Off Computer | Restart. Windows shuts down and restarts.
3. When you see the message Please Select The Operating System To Start, press F8. Windows displays a list of options (see section "Startup Modes" in Chapter 35).
4. Press the UP-ARROW or DOWN-ARROW until you highlight the Last Known Good Configuration option, and press ENTER. (If the arrow keys don't work, press NUM LOCK to enable them.)
5. Choose the operating system (either Windows XP Professional or Windows XP Home Edition). Windows then restores your most recently backed up values for the HKEY_LOCAL_MACHINE\System\CurrentControlSet hive in the Registry, and restarts Windows.

If the Registry entries for an application get damaged, consider uninstalling and reinstalling the program. If restoring a backup of the Registry still doesn't fix your problem, you may have to back up your data, reformat the disk (or partition) on which Windows is installed, and reinstall Windows and all your programs.

 System Restore can also restore a previous version of the Registry (see Chapter 35, section "Returning Your System to a Predefined State with System Restore").

Running Registry Editor

Registry Editor (Regedit for short) lets you edit anything in the Registry. To run Registry Editor, select Start | Run, type **regedit**, and press ENTER. This chapter describes Registry Editor version 5.

 Registry Editor has almost no built-in checks or validation, so be very sure that you make any changes correctly. Incorrect Registry entries can lead to anything from occasional flaky behavior to complete system failure. We suggest that you export the keys that you plan to edit before making any changes, so that you can reimport them if the changes cause problems.

Finding Registry Entries

Registry Editor has a two-part window, shown in Figure 38-1, much like Windows Explorer. Each key is shown as a folder in the left pane of the Registry Editor window. When you select a key in the left pane, the name and data of each of its values appear in the right pane. You can expand and contract parts of the name tree by clicking the + and – icons in the key area. Select any key to see the names and data of the values, if any, associated with that key.

If you know the name of the key you want, you can navigate through the key names similar to the way you navigate through files in Windows Explorer.

If you don't know the name of the key, you can search for it by choosing Edit | Find (or pressing CTRL-F). You can search for any combination of keys, value names, and value data. For example, if you mistyped your name at the time you set up Windows and want to correct it, search for the mistyped name as value data. Press F3 to step from one match to the next.

 As you edit Registry entries, Registry Editor makes the changes right away—there's no Save, Cancel, or Undo command. You can edit the Registry and leave the Registry Editor window open while you check whether your changes produce the desired effect. Some programs aren't affected by Registry changes until they are restarted; others reflect the changes immediately.

When you run Registry Editor again, it displays the key that you were looking at when you last exited the program, so it's easy to continue making changes to the same key.

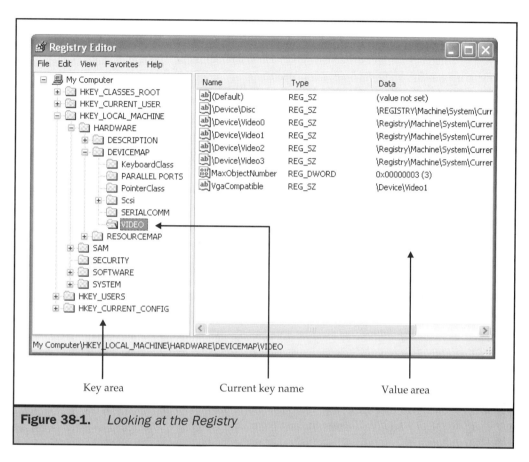

Figure 38-1.   *Looking at the Registry*

Adding and Changing Registry Entries

You can add, edit, and delete Registry entries (but be sure you back them up first):

- **Changing the data of a value**   Double-click the name of the value (in the Name column of the right pane of the Registry Editor window). Registry Editor displays a dialog box in which you can enter the new data for the value. You see the Edit String dialog box, which looks different depending on the data type of the value you are changing:

You can't change the type of a value, so you have to enter a text string, a numeric value, or a string of hexadecimal digits, depending on the type of the data.

■ **Renaming a key or a value**   Right-click its name and choose Rename from the menu that appears. (Don't rename a value that Windows or another program uses, because Windows won't be able to find the key under its new name.)

■ **Creating a new key**   Right-click the folder (key) into which you want to add the new key and choose New | Key from the menu that appears. As in Windows Explorer, the new key is created with a dummy name. Type the name you actually want and press ENTER.

■ **Creating a new value**   Right-click the key in which you want store the new value, choose New from the menu that appears, and choose the type of value (String Value, Binary Value, or DWORD). Once you've created a value, double-click the value's name to enter its data.

■ **Deleting a value or key**   Select the value or key and press DELETE.

If you're not absolutely sure about deleting a key, rename it. Add an underscore or number to the end, so that the Registry doesn't recognize it, but you will if you need to change it back later.

You can also rename and delete keys and values by using the Edit menu.

If you want to remember the name of a Registry key—or tell a friend about it—you can copy it to the Clipboard. Select the key whose complete name you want, and choose Edit | Copy Key Name from the menu bar.

Editing the Registry as a Text File

Another way to edit the Registry is to export all or part of the Registry to a text file, edit the text file, and then import the changed values back into the Registry. You can export and import the entire Registry or one "branch" of the Registry's tree of keys. Registry Editor stores the exported Registry entries in a *registration file* with the extension .reg.

A registration file consists of a series of lines that look like this:

```
[HKEY_CLASSES_ROOT\.bfc\ShellNew\Config]
"NoExtension"="Temp"
```

The first line is the name of the key (enclosed in square brackets) and the lines that follow are the values in the key, in the format *"name"="value"*.

Running Programs on Startup

You can tell Windows to start a program automatically when Windows starts up by including a shortcut to it in the Startup folder of your Start Menu (see Chapter 2, section "Starting Programs when Windows Starts"). However, there are two other ways to run a program automatically when Windows starts: lines in the Win.ini file and keys in the Registry.

The Win.ini file (which is stored in C:\Windows, assuming that Windows is installed on C:), can include lines like this:

```
run=program
load=program
```

Replace *program* with the pathname of the file that contains the program. To stop a program from running, remove this line from the Win.ini file, or add a semicolon at the beginning of the line.

Two places in the Registry can contain entries that run programs at Windows startup. Look in these two keys:

```
HKEY_LOCAL_MACHINE\Software\Microsoft\Windows\Current Version
HKEY_CURRENT_USER\Software\Microsoft\Windows\Current Version
```

These keys can contain keys named Run, RunOnce, or RunOnceEx, which contain values that start programs when Windows starts. To stop the program from running, remove or rename the key.

Note   *Windows XP (like Windows NT and 2000) exports the Registry using Unicode rather than plain text. You can't export keys from the Windows XP Registry and import them into a Windows Me/9x Registry.*

Follow these steps to edit the Registry by using a text editor:

1. Select a hive or key in the left pane, choosing one that contains all the keys that you want to edit. To export the entire Registry, select the My Computer item at the root of the Registry tree.

2. Choose File | Export to write the text file. Registry Editor asks you for the folder and filename to use for the registration file. Then it writes the data into the new file, which may take a few minutes.

3. Edit the registration file in any text editor. (Notepad works fine.) Right-click the .reg file in Windows Explorer and choose Edit from the shortcut menu that appears. Notepad runs (or another text editor, if you choose it). Make as few changes as possible to the file and save the file.

4. In Registry Editor, choose File | Import to read the edited file back into the Registry. The keys and values in the imported file replace the corresponding keys and values in the Registry. Note that if you delete a key or value in the text file, importing the file doesn't delete the key or value in the Registry.

Tip *The Registry is quite large—an exported version of the whole thing can be 30MB or more. If you do plan to edit it, just export the branch you plan to work on.*

The Complete Reference

Chapter 39

Running DOS Programs and Commands

Y ou may need to install and run older DOS programs on your Windows XP system. Some important Windows utilities must be run at the DOS prompt, like ChkDsk and Msconfig. Windows provides ways to run DOS programs and commands; cut-and-paste between DOS and Windows programs; and configure how DOS programs work with the screen, mouse, and keyboard. If you're an old hand at DOS, you may also wonder what's happened to two files that were crucial to DOS: Autoexec.bat and Config.sys. This chapter covers all of these topics.

Windows 95, 98, and 98 Second Edition (SE) had a special version of DOS (version 7.0) to run DOS applications and games. Those versions could also be rebooted into a DOS mode, where the machine became a DOS-only computer until it was rebooted. In Windows Me, Microsoft finally removed all vestiges of DOS as it is traditionally known and replaced it with the *DOS Virtual Machine* (*DOS VM*). The only real difference was the absence of a DOS mode on startup, but the vast majority of DOS programs could still run successfully in the DOS VM.

Windows XP contains a similar DOS VM, which allows you to run those old, but still fun, DOS games of yore—at least a good percentage of them. Some old games just won't work because they don't have *real* access to the hardware, as they would running under DOS.

What Is DOS?

MS-DOS (or *DOS*, Disk Operating System, for short) is a simple operating system that was the predecessor to Windows. DOS version 1.0 was created in about 1981, and later versions—through DOS 6.22—added features and supported more recent hardware. Early versions of Windows (through 3.11) were add-ons for DOS—first you installed DOS on your computer, then you installed Windows, and then you started Windows from the DOS command prompt. Windows 95, 98, 98SE, Me, and XP still have a version of DOS buried inside them, although Microsoft's engineers have integrated almost all of the DOS functions into Windows.

DOS provides only disk file management and the most rudimentary support for the screen, keyboard, mouse, timer, and other peripherals. As a result, interactive *DOS programs* (programs written to work with DOS rather than Windows) need to create their own user interfaces, usually by directly operating the hardware controllers for the screen and sometimes other devices. DOS supports only 640KB of memory, and the base functions of all DOS applications must fit inside of this limited space. Subsequently, Microsoft and other companies developed a variety of add-on drivers to allow DOS to handle larger amounts of memory, including *expanded memory* (EMS memory) and *extended memory* (XMS memory).

DOS doesn't have a graphical user interface (GUI), and usually doesn't display windows or work with a mouse. Instead, you type commands at the *DOS prompt*, a symbol that indicates DOS is waiting for you to type a *command line* (a command, optionally followed by additional information). The default DOS prompt is C:\>. This method of typing commands at a prompt is called a *command-line interface (CLI)*.

What Are DOS Names?

Each file and folder in Windows has a *DOS name*, an eight-or-fewer-character name that resembles its real name, but that is legal under the pre-Windows 95 file-naming rules. The DOS name exists for the purpose of backward compatibility; programs written for DOS or older versions of Windows might crash if Windows hands them files with long names and previously illegal characters. So, when dealing with pre-Windows 95 application programs, Windows pretends nothing has changed and gives the application the DOS name of a file rather than its real name. The DOS name is usually the first six characters of the filename, followed by a tilde (~) and a number. The extension part of the DOS name is the first three characters of the extension.

DOS names are invisible in Windows, but you still may see them if you run an older application. If the file you named My Summer Vacation.doc shows up later as MYSUMM~1.DOC, you'll know what happened.

Windows, on the other hand, provides extensive facilities to handle the screen and keyboard, as well as sophisticated memory management, which all Windows applications use. These facilities make it difficult to run some DOS programs in Windows, because the DOS programs and Windows can't both control the same hardware at the same time. The DOS VM eliminates most of those hurdles and makes it easier to run pesky DOS programs.

Using the Command Prompt Window

Previous versions of Windows could run DOS programs in two different ways: as an application running in Windows or as a stand-alone program in a DOS environment. In Windows XP, the MS-DOS mode is no longer available, although you are welcome to boot your computer using a floppy disk that has DOS on it. But if you do so, most extended DOS services will not be available unless you have taken the time to prepare a bootable DOS floppy with all the necessary DOS programs, or have a fully configured DOS hard disk and partition management software. Preparing such a floppy is a tedious process at best.

 If you have an Emergency Boot Disk for Windows 98, hold onto it. You might want to use it to start your computer in DOS mode, although when running DOS, you won't be able to read any disks formatted with NTFS.

The most convenient way to run most DOS programs is in a *Command Prompt window* (or DOS window), as shown in Figure 39-1. Windows creates a *virtual machine* for the DOS program—a special hardware and software environment that emulates enough of the features of a stand-alone environment to allow most DOS programs to

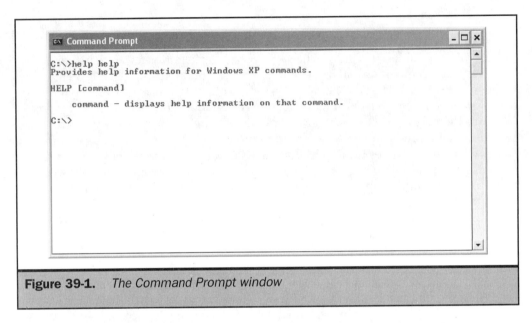

Figure 39-1.   *The Command Prompt window*

run correctly. DOS programs that don't use extensive graphics can usually run within a Command Prompt window, sharing the screen with Windows applications. Programs that require full access to the screen hardware can also take over the screen while Windows continues to run in the background.

Since Windows doesn't give the DOS program full control of the system, DOS programs running in a Command Prompt window can run side by side with Windows applications, and even with other DOS applications. Some DOS programs are *Windows aware,* so that even though they don't run as Windows applications, they can check whether they're running under Windows and handle their screen and keyboard in a way that lets them run efficiently in Windows.

Running DOS Programs

Once you run a DOS program, you can do your work and then exit. You can also adjust the way it looks on the screen, copy-and-paste material to and from the Windows Clipboard, print, and run batch files.

Starting DOS Programs

You run a DOS program the same way you run a Windows program: by clicking or double-clicking its icon or filename in the Windows Explorer window or the Start menu, or by choosing Start | Run and typing its name into the Run dialog box. For some DOS commands, you can type arguments or switches on the command line after the program name, separated by spaces. An *argument* provides additional information (for example, the DOS COPY command accepts arguments that tell it what files to copy). A *switch* specifies a program option and usually consists of a slash (/) and a letter.

You can also type DOS commands at a DOS prompt by selecting Start | All Programs | Accessories | Command Prompt (or by choosing Start | Run and typing **cmd**). You see the Command Prompt window (Figure 39-1). In this window, you can type DOS commands—such as DIR, CHDIR, MKDIR, and DELETE—as well as run programs. Just type the command (possibly followed by arguments or switches) and press ENTER.

> **Note** *Windows XP comes with two programs that display a Command Prompt window: Command.exe and Cmd.exe. Command.exe displays a Command Prompt window that cannot handle long filenames (that is, filenames longer than eight characters and extensions longer than three characters). Cmd.exe's window handles filenames the same way that Windows does. There's no reason to use Command.exe rather than Cmd.exe.*

If you run a specific program to open the window, the program name appears in the title bar. If you choose the Start | All Programs | Accessories | Command Prompt command, the window is named Command Prompt.

While the vast majority of DOS commands work, not all do, and most will not operate as expected. For a mostly complete list of commands accepted by the Command Prompt, type **help** and press ENTER.

To get help with a particular DOS command, type the command followed by **/?**. For example, type **copy /?** to get help with the DOS COPY command. To stop the help text from scrolling off the top of the Command Prompt window, add | **more** to the end of the command line, like this:

```
copy /? | more
```

> **Tip** *If you can open a file by clicking or double-clicking it in Windows Explorer, you can open the file from the DOS prompt. Type **start** followed by a space and the pathname (address) of the file. If the pathname contains spaces, enclose it in double-quotation marks. The Start program opens the file (or folder) using the Windows file association.*

Exiting DOS Programs

Every DOS program has its own command to exit. Some use a function key, some use a text command (like "quit" or "exit"), and some use a menu command starting with a slash or another character. You can also force Windows to close a Command Prompt window by clicking the Close button while the program is running. Windows may warn you that closing the program will lose unsaved information, but if you click End Now, Windows stops the program and closes the window anyway.

Adjusting the Screen

Windows normally starts each Command Prompt window as a 25 × 80 character window, choosing a font to make the window fit your screen. You can select a different font from the Command Prompt Properties dialog box's Font tab.

To switch between running in a window and using the full screen, press ALT-ENTER. Once in a full screen, ALT-ENTER is the only way, short of exiting and restarting the program, to return the program to running in a window.

Using the Mouse and Clipboard

Early versions of DOS provided no mouse support at all. Even in later versions, DOS provided only low-level mouse support, leaving it entirely up to each application which (if any) mouse features to provide. As a result, most DOS programs provide no mouse support, so the primary use of the mouse is to cut-and-paste material to the Windows Clipboard (see Chapter 5, section "Sharing Data Through the Windows Clipboard").

Using the Windows Clipboard

You can copy material from a Command Prompt window to the Clipboard. To do so, first click the System Menu button (with the C:\ icon) in the upper-left corner of the window and select Edit | Mark from the System menu that appears. Then use the mouse to highlight the area to copy and press ENTER to copy the selected area to the Clipboard.

DOS programs can place the screen (or the virtual screen emulated in a Command Prompt window) into either text mode *(which can display only text) or* graphics mode *(which can display any pattern of dots, including text). Windows copies the marked area as text if the screen is in text mode and as a bitmap if the screen is in graphics mode. Some programs, such as word processors, often use graphics mode to display text so that they can show font changes. Tell the DOS program to switch back to text mode before copying, to get text on the Clipboard.*

Windows lets you paste text from the Clipboard into DOS applications, too. The text is entered as though you had typed it on the keyboard. To paste, select Edit | Paste from the System menu.

Using the Mouse in DOS Programs

In those DOS programs that do provide mouse support, using the mouse in a Command Prompt window can be difficult. Since DOS provides no high-level mouse support, each application displays its own mouse pointer. In some Windows-aware applications, the DOS mouse pointer is synchronized with the Windows mouse pointer, but more often than not, it isn't. In the latter case, the best solution usually is to press ALT-ENTER to switch to full-screen mode, so there's no Windows mouse pointer at all.

Printing from DOS Programs

Windows provides very limited support for printing from DOS programs. It offers a pass-through scheme that receives output from DOS programs and sends it directly to the printer. DOS programs have no access to Windows printer drivers, so each DOS application must have its own driver for any printer that it prints to.

Windows intercepts the DOS output and spools the output as it does printer output from Windows applications (that is, Windows stores the output and then sends it to the printer). This provides more flexibility in printer management and avoids the possibility that a DOS program will interfere with an active print job from another program.

Determining the Printer Port

DOS programs identify your printer according to the port to which the printer is attached (LPT1, LPT2, LPT3, COM1, COM2, COM3, or COM4). To find out what port a printer is attached to, follow these steps:

1. Select Start | Printers and Faxes (or Start | Control Panel | Printers and Other Hardware | Printers and Faxes) to open the Printers and Faxes window (see Chapter 14, section "Managing Printer Activity").

2. Right-click the desired printer and select Properties to open the printer's Properties dialog box.

3. Click the Ports tab to see a list of the ports, and look down the list for the first one whose check box is selected. If the dialog box has no Ports tab, look on all the tabs—the contents of the dialog box depend on the printer driver.

4. Click OK to close the printer Properties dialog box.

Printing to a Network Printer

DOS programs can also print to network printers. Windows captures the output from a simulated printer port and then spools the printer output through the network in the same way that printer output is spooled from Windows programs.

 All printers are not created equal. Their capabilities depend both on the printer hardware and on the printer driver software. You may notice anywhere from subtle to enormous differences between the printer-related dialog boxes you see in this book and those you see on your computer. If you don't see a feature we mention here, your printer probably doesn't have it. Check your printer's manual to prevent yourself from wasting a lot of time on something that will simply not work.

To print from a DOS program to a network printer, follow these steps:

1. Determine the pathname of the printer by displaying its Properties dialog box (as described in the previous section). If you see a Ports tab, look on that tab at

the bottom of the list of ports for the pathname (you may need to drag the Port column divider to the right to make the entire name visible). The pathname is in the format *computername**printername*, where *computername* is the computer's name on the LAN, and *printername* is the printer's share name (see Chapter 28, section "Identifying the Computer").

2. Close the printer's Properties dialog box.

3. Choose Start | All Programs | Accessories | Command Prompt to open a Command Prompt window.

4. Type the following command and press ENTER. Replace *n* with the LPT number you want to use (if you already have a printer on LPT1, use LPT2), and *computername**printername* with the printer's pathname.

```
net use lptn: \\computername\printername /persistent:yes
```

5. Now you can print from your DOS program to the LPT port you specified. When you have finished printing, type this command in the Command Prompt window:

```
net use lptn: /delete
```

When you print from a DOS program to a spooled printer, either local or networked, Windows has no reliable way to tell when the DOS program has finished printing. If your program doesn't print anything for several seconds, Windows assumes that it has finished. This occasionally causes problems when an application prints part of a report, computes for a while, and then resumes printing, because Windows can interpret the pause in printing as the end of the print job. If this is a problem, use a locally connected printer and do *not* configure the printer to spool DOS print jobs.

Running Batch Files

DOS provides *batch files*, which are text files that contain a sequence of commands to be run as though they were typed at the DOS prompt. Batch files have the filename extension .bat. Windows treats a batch file as a DOS program and opens a Command Prompt window to run the batch file and any programs that the batch file runs. Since the Windows version of DOS lets you run any DOS or Windows program from the DOS prompt, you can use batch files as a low-budget scripting language, listing a sequence of programs you want to run.

For example, you can use a batch file as quick-and-dirty backup scheme for making copies of a few files on a Zip or other removable disk. Write a batch file that copies the files from their current location to the Zip disk. Then use the Windows Scheduled

Tasks program to run the batch file every night, and remember to leave a Zip disk in your Zip drive (see Chapter 2, section "Running Programs on a Schedule Using Scheduled Tasks").

Configuring the DOS Environment

Windows provides a long list of settings for customizing the environment for the Command Prompt window or for a DOS program. Nearly all the settings are parameters you can tweak to help a recalcitrant DOS program run in the Windows environment. More often than not, adjusting these settings won't be necessary.

Earlier versions of Windows put the settings for DOS programs into separate *PIF files* (program information files), and some programs still use them. Windows XP stores the settings in DOS initialization files, in Command Prompt properties, and in program properties.

Note *Although you can edit a program's properties while the program is running, most changes do not take effect until you close the program and run it again. (The main exception is changing fonts.)*

DOS Initialization Files: Autoexec and Config

Windows XP enables you to create a Config file to load drivers and an Autoexec file to run DOS commands before the program runs. Windows XP provides default versions of these DOS initialization files, called Config.nt and Autoexec.nt, which are located in the C:\Windows\System32 folder (assuming that Windows is installed in C:\Windows).

The Config file contains DOS VM configuration commands, as well as commands to load real-mode device drivers. Autoexec contains regular DOS commands to be run as soon as DOS has finished starting up. Although any DOS command is valid, the only command commonly used is SET, which defines environment variables used by some programs and drivers. Config.nt is read during the DOS startup process. Windows runs the commands from Autoexec.nt after processing Config.nt. These files can now be located anywhere, which improves DOS backward compatibility by allowing you to have several different versions of the files and selecting the one that best suits the program you want to run.

The Autoexec and Config files are text files, which you can edit with Notepad. Microsoft recommends that you leave the original Config.nt and Autoexec.nt unchanged, and create edited copies with other names, like Config.games and Autoexec.pcfile, for your various applications. See "Installing and Configuring DOS Programs," later in this chapter, for how to create your own versions of the files for the DOS program you want to configure.

Read the Autoexec.nt and Config.nt files to start learning about how they work. They are both copiously commented.

Setting Command Prompt Window Properties

When a Command Prompt window is open, you can see and set its settings by clicking the System Menu button in its upper-left corner and choosing Properties. The settings on the various tabs of the Command Prompt Properties dialog box, shown in Figure 39-2, control the appearance and some operational aspects of a DOS program. Table 39-1 lists the settings by tab (left to right).

Depending on whether you start the Command Prompt from the Start menu (by choosing Start | All Programs | Accessories | Command Prompt) or from the Run command (by choosing Start | Run, typing **cmd**, and pressing ENTER), you see a different Properties dialog box. Changing the settings for one does not affect the other.

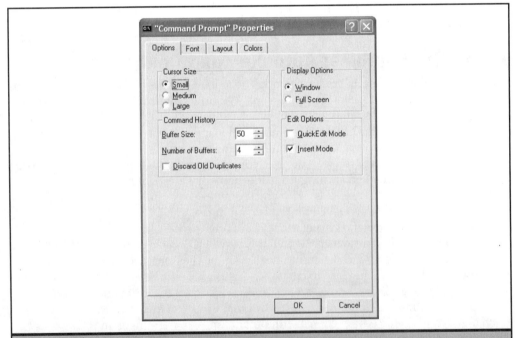

Figure 39-2. The Options tab of the Command Prompt Properties dialog box

Tab	Setting	Description
Options	Cursor Size	Specifies the size of the cursor, the flashing marker that draws attention to where your typing will appear. Small appears as a line. Medium appears as a thick line. Large is a block.
Options	Command History Buffer Size, Number of Buffers, Discard Old Duplicates	Every time you type a command, Windows stores it in a buffer. Use the UP-ARROW and DOWN-ARROW keys on your keyboard to cycle through commands. The Buffer Size setting specifies the number of command lines stored. Number of Buffers controls how many different Command Prompt windows have buffers simultaneously. Discard Old Duplicates deletes duplicate commands from the buffer.
Options	Display Options	Specifies the default window size: Windowed or Full Screen.
Options	Edit Options	Selects either QuickEdit mode (in which you use the mouse pointer to select text and move the cursor) or Insert mode (in which you can place additional text wherever the cursor is instead of overwriting what's already there).
Font	Size	Specifies the font size in pixels (dots).
Font	Font	Specifies the font.
Font	Bold Fonts	Displays the selected font in boldface.
Layout	Screen Buffer Size	Specifies the virtual size of the window.
Layout	Window Size	Specifies the physical size of the Command Prompt window. If the Screen Buffer Size is larger, scrollbars appear to allow you access to the information that doesn't fit in the window.

Table 39-1.   *Settings in the Command Prompt Properties Dialog Box*

Tab	Setting	Description
Layout	Window Position	Specifies the position of the window on the screen. Let System Position Window enables Windows to choose the position. If you want the Command Prompt window to appear in the same place every time it opens, deselect the check box and set the coordinates of the upper-left corner of the window; 0 indicates the left or top edge of the screen. The limits are determined by what resolution you have your display set to.
Colors	Screen Text, Screen Background, Popup Text, Popup Background	Allows you to select which settings appear in the Selected Color Values section and the color bar.
Colors	Select Color Values	Specifies the color of the selected item (see the previous setting). The row of colors below this setting do the same thing.

Table 39-1. *Settings in the Command Prompt Properties Dialog Box* (continued)

Choosing DOS Program Fonts

On the Font tab, shown in Figure 39-3, the Window Preview box shows you how big your window will be relative to the Windows screen, and the Selected Font box shows what the text in the window will look like. First, choose a font from the Font box, and then choose from the sizes that are available for that font.

Controlling DOS Program Window Settings

On the Layout tab, shown in Figure 39-4, you can set the virtual and actual sizes of the window. The virtual size (set using the Screen Buffer Size setting) controls the amount of text that Windows stores for the window. The Window Size setting controls the actual size of the widow on the screen. If the Screen Buffer Size is larger than the Windows Size (the default is for it to be several times taller, but the same width), you can scroll up and down the buffer using the window's scroll bars.

Setting DOS Program Colors

The Colors tab of the Command Prompt Properties dialog box, shown in Figure 39-5, controls the foreground and background colors of the text in the window. Select the

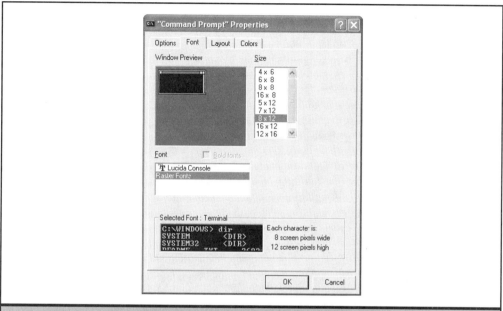

Figure 39-3.   *Setting the font for the Command Prompt window*

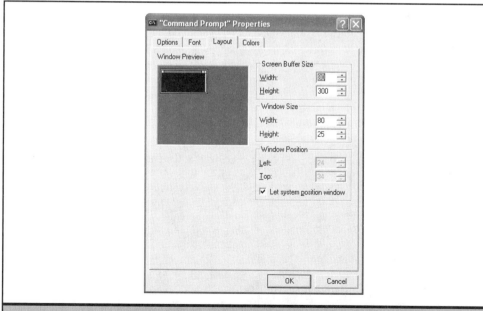

Figure 39-4.   *Specifying the Command Prompt window size and position*

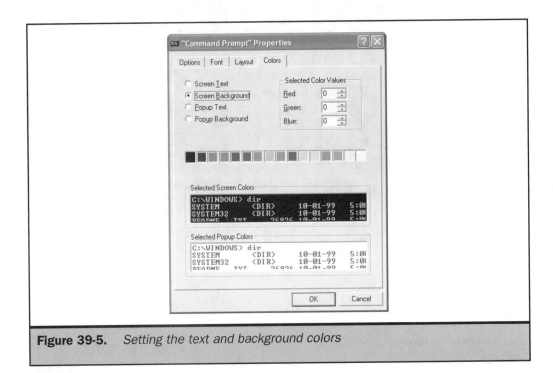

Figure 39-5.   *Setting the text and background colors*

item for which you want to set the color (Screen Text, Screen Background, Popup Text, or Popup Background), and then select a color for it from the bar of colors running across the middle of the dialog box. Your choices appear in the preview panes below. If you don't like the colors listed, you can adjust the Selected Color Values boxes to get the colors you like.

Setting Executable and Shortcut Properties

Additional options for DOS programs are set in the program's Properties dialog box. To set them, find either the executable (.exe or .com) file for the program or a shortcut to the executable file (you may need to choose Start | Search to find it). Many DOS applications, especially games, come with more than one executable file. Along with the executable file that runs the program, other executable files may uninstall or configure the program. Once you've located the executable file that runs the program (or a shortcut to it), right-click the file or shortcut and choose Properties to see its Properties dialog box. Figure 39-6 shows the Memory tab of the dialog box.

Table 39-2 lists settings in the dialog box, except for those on the Font tab, which is similar to the Font tab in the Command Prompt Properties dialog box, described in Table 39-1. The Properties dialog box for a shortcut also includes a Summary tab, which isn't used for configuring programs.

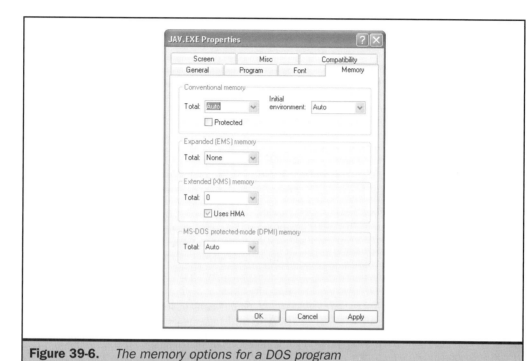

Figure 39-6. *The memory options for a DOS program*

Tab	Setting	Description
General	Attributes: Read-only, Hidden, Archive	Specifies the file attributes (see Chapter 8, section "What Are Attributes?").
Program	Cmd Line	Specifies the command line that you would type at the command prompt. The first thing on the command line must be the filename of the program. Many programs let you put parameters, switches, and filenames in the command line as well. If you type a space followed by a question mark in this box, Windows prompts you for command-line data when you start the program and replaces the question mark with the data you type.

Table 39-2. *Settings in the Properties Dialog Box for a Program or Shortcut*

Tab	Setting	Description
Program	Working	Specifies the name of the folder to use as the program's *working folder*. The program reads and writes its files from this folder unless the program specifically names a different folder.
Program	Batch File	Specifies the name of a DOS batch file to run before the program starts. This is rarely used.
Program	Shortcut Key	Specifies the key combination to start or activate the program (see Chapter 2, section "Starting Programs Using Shortcut Keys"). You can specify the CTRL or ALT key in combination with another key, or a plain function key. Any combination you specify as a shortcut can no longer be used as input by any other program running on your computer, so choose a combination that isn't commonly used.
Program	Run	Specifies whether Windows starts the program in a normal, minimized, or maximized window (see Chapter 2, section "Controlling the Size and Shape of Your Windows"). Most DOS programs can't handle a maximized window.
Program	Close on Exit	Specifies whether Windows closes the window in which the program appears when the program exits.
Memory	Conventional Memory: Total, Initial Environment	Specifies the amount of memory (RAM) in kilobytes available to the program, up to DOS's limit of 640KB. For programs run in Windows 95 compatibility mode, the Initial Environment setting specifies the amount of memory reserved for the command-interpreter part of DOS itself. For most programs, leave these set to Auto.

Table 39-2. *Settings in the Properties Dialog Box for a Program or Shortcut (continued)*

Tab	Setting	Description
Memory	Protected	Protects Windows' system memory from accidental modification by the DOS program and can keep a DOS program failure from crashing Windows. We recommend selecting this check box.
Memory	Expanded (EMS) Memory, Extended (XMS) Memory, MS-DOS Protected-Mode (DPMI) Memory	Specifies the amount of memory in kilobytes that Windows allocates as expanded, extended, or DPMI memory (three systems that DOS programs use to access more than 640KB).
Screen	Usage: Full-screen, Window, Initial Size	Specifies whether the program starts full-screen or in a window. For some programs, you can select 25, 43, or 50 text lines on the screen by setting the Initial Size box. (If you select more than 25, be sure that the program can handle the size you select.) The program may override these settings.
Screen	Restore Settings at Startup	Specifies whether Windows remembers changes that the program makes to the screen setup from one run of the program to another.
Screen	Fast ROM Emulation	Specifies whether the display driver provides video functions. Select this check box unless the screen display looks wrong.
Screen	Dynamic Memory Allocation	Maximizes the amount of memory available to other programs while this program is running.
Misc	Allow Screen Saver	Enables the Windows screen saver, even when this program is running.

Table 39-2.   *Settings in the Properties Dialog Box for a Program or Shortcut (continued)*

Tab	Setting	Description
Misc	QuickEdit	Causes any use of the mouse to mark text as though you had chosen the Mark command from the System menu first. Check this box if your program makes no use of the mouse (though often Windows is able to automatically detect whether the program can use a mouse or not and will disable the option appropriately).
Misc	Exclusive Mode	Dedicates the mouse to this program. Not recommended, since it makes the mouse unusable as the Windows pointer until the program exits. If you select it, switch the Command Prompt window to full-screen mode instead (by pressing ALT-ENTER), which makes the Windows mouse pointer vanish.
Misc	Always Suspend	Suspends this program whenever it's not the active window. Leave this box checked, unless the program does useful background activity.
Misc	Warn If Still Active	Specifies that Windows pop up a warning box if you try to close this program before it exits.
Misc	Idle Sensitivity	Specifies that Windows attempt to detect when an active DOS program is idle and waiting for keyboard input, so that Windows can give more processor time to other applications. High sensitivity makes Windows give more time to other applications. Leave this alone unless keyboard response to the program is sluggish, in which case, make the sensitivity lower.

Table 39-2.   *Settings in the Properties Dialog Box for a Program or Shortcut* (continued)

Tab	Setting	Description
Misc	Fast Pasting	Uses an optimized technique for pasting text into a Command Prompt window that fails with a few programs. If pasting doesn't work, turn this off.
Misc	Windows Shortcut Keys	Specifies which of the key combinations listed in this box perform Windows functions, even when Windows is running a DOS program. If your DOS application needs to use any of these combinations itself, uncheck the ones it needs.
Compatibility	Run This Program in Compatibility Mode For	Specifies whether to use compatibility mode. When selected, choose from Windows 95, Windows 98, Windows NT 4, and Windows 2000.
Compatibility	Run in 256 Colors	Sets the window to use 8-bit color.
Compatibility	Run in 640 × 480 Screen Resolution	Sets the window to use 640 × 480 (VGA) screen resolution.
Compatibility	Disable Visual Themes	Disables the Windows XP desktop theme for the window (see Chapter 11, section "Choosing a Desktop Theme").

Table 39-2. *Settings in the Properties Dialog Box for a Program or Shortcut* (continued)

BEHIND THE SCENES: WINDOWS XP INTERNALS

Controlling the Amount of Memory the Program Can Use

The Memory tab of the program's Properties dialog box (shown in Figure 39-6) controls how much memory is available to a program using each of the DOS addressing schemes. In nearly all cases, Windows automatically allocates an appropriate amount of each kind of memory to the program when it runs the program. A few programs fail if given as much memory as Windows makes available (at the time many DOS programs were written, most people never imagined that anyone would ever put as much as 4MB in a single PC). If this is a problem, determine the kind of memory that the program uses—expanded (EMS), extended (XMS), or MS-DOS Protected-Mode (DPMI)—and try limiting it to 8,192KB (the program's documentation or help files may specify what types of memory the program can use and the maximum amount of memory that the program can handle).

Be sure to select the Protected check box, to prevent the DOS program from inadvertently changing the part of memory used by Windows itself.

Setting the Compatibility Mode

New to Windows XP is the compatibility mode, which attempts to present an environment for software that expects to be run in a particular version of Windows (see Chapter 2, section "Running Programs in Compatibility Mode"). For example, Ignition (the classic racing game from Unique Development Studios) refuses to install on Windows XP without the Windows 95 compatibility mode. You set the program's compatibility mode on the Compatibility tab of the Properties dialog box for the executable file or shortcut, as shown in Figure 39-7.

Note   *You often must set the compatibility mode of both the installation program and the actual program for them to work properly. First, set the compatibility mode for the installation program and run it. Once the program is installed, find the installed executable program and give it the same compatibility mode. If it doesn't work the first time, try another mode.*

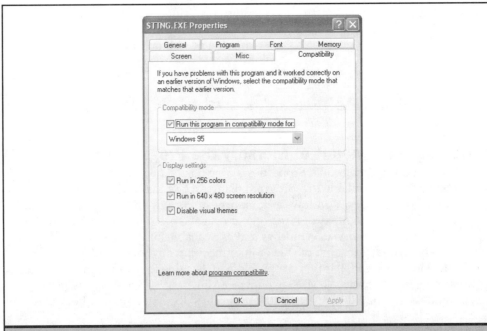

Figure 39-7.   *Configuring a program to run in compatibility mode*

DOS Programs vs. the Luna Desktop Theme

Applications written specifically for Windows XP use something called a *manifest* to work with the Luna (Windows XP) theme. A manifest is a file that describes how the application is to appear while using the Luna interface. Most recent applications that comply closely with the Win32 API (Application Programming Interface—a set of tools that define how applications work with Windows) typically work fine without a manifest, but some do not. If an application behaves unexpectedly or does not appear correctly, try selecting the Disable Visual Themes check box on the Compatibility tab of the Properties dialog box for the program. For example, Macromedia's Dreamweaver 4.0 Web site authoring program has custom toolbars that do not work well with Luna (some buttons are covered by the swoopy new interface).

Installing and Configuring DOS Programs

DOS provides no standard way to install programs. Most DOS programs include a simple installation batch file that copies the program's files from the installation disks to your hard disk. Once a program's files are installed, you can create shortcuts to the executable file and put those shortcuts in the Start menu, on the desktop, or both, just like native Windows applications (see Chapter 2 for how to create shortcuts).

Since some DOS programs require that you install DOS drivers, Microsoft has included basic drivers for both sound cards and CD-ROM drives. These are loaded when Windows starts through lines in the Config.nt or Autoexec.nt files. For certain DOS programs, you may need to make changes to these files.

If you have a DOS program (or an older Windows program) that doesn't run properly under Windows XP, you can create revised copies of the Autoexec.nt and Config.nt files for use with the program, and edit the properties of the program file (or a shortcut to it) to refer to the Autoexec and Config files you created. This method works if the documentation for the program specifies the lines that the Autoexec.bat (old name for Autoexec.nt) and Config.sys (old name for Config.nt) files need to contain. Follow these steps:

1. In an Explorer window, locate C:\Windows\System32\Config.nt and C:\Windows\System32\Autoexec.nt (if Windows is stored on another drive, substitute the drive letter for C).

2. Select each file (Config.nt and Autoexec.nt) and press CTRL-C and then CTRL-V to place a copy of the file in the same folder.

3. Scroll down to the bottom of the list of files to find the copies. Select a file and press F2 to rename it. Name the copies Config.*ext* and Autoexec.*ext*, where *ext* is an abbreviation for the program you are configuring.

BEHIND THE SCENES: WINDOWS XP INTERNALS

4. Right-click the program file or shortcut and choose Properties from the menu that appears. You see the Properties dialog box for the file or shortcut (described in the previous section).

5. Click the Program tab, which displays the name of the program file that the shortcut runs. Click the Advanced button to display the Windows PIF Settings dialog box:

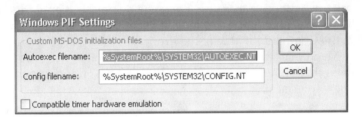

6. Change the contents of the Autoexec Filename and Config Filename boxes to the pathname of the file you created earlier. (If they are in the same folder as the Autoexec.nt and Config.nt files, change only the filename at the end of the pathname.) As you edit the filename, Windows shows you matching filenames.

7. If the program needs for the system clock to appear to run slower (that is, if it uses the computer's system clock for timing, and modern PCs make the program run too fast to be usable), select the Compatible Timer Hardware Emulation check box.

8. Click OK to return to the Properties dialog box for the shortcut.

9. For DOS programs that display information in the Command Prompt window, click the Font tab and choose a font size that looks good.

10. If the program uses expanded or extended memory, click the Memory tab and set the memory sizes, as described in the section "Controlling the Amount of Memory the Program Can Use," earlier in this chapter.

11. If you want the program to appear full-screen rather than in a window, click the Screen tab and choose Full-screen.

12. If the program needs to run in compatibility mode, so that Windows provides a software environment like a previous version of Windows, click the Compatibility tab, select the Run This Program In Compatibility Mode For check box, and select the version of Windows (see Chapter 2, section "Running Programs in Compatibility Mode").

13. Make any other changes to the properties of the file or shortcut, and then click OK to save your changes.

14. Refer to the program's documentation and make whatever changes it suggests to the Autoexec and Config files you created for the program. When the manual or help file refers to the Autoexec.bat file, make the change to your copy of the Autoexec.nt file. When instructions refer to the Config.sys file, make the changes to your copy of the Config.nt file.

15. Test your changes by running the files or shortcut.

> **Tip**   *If you want to see messages that let you know what Windows is doing when it processes your Config or Autoexec file, add the single word **echoconfig** as the last line of the file.*

The
Complete
Reference

Windows XP

Chapter 40

Automating Tasks with the Windows Script Host

If you've used computers long, you may remember DOS batch files, which are text files that contain lists of commands. Using batch files, you could store a series of DOS commands and run the whole series by issuing just one command.

When Windows supplanted DOS, many advanced users complained about the lack of a similar scripting capability in Windows. The Windows Script Host fills this lack by letting you create and run scripts. You can run scripts from Windows by using the Wscript program or from the DOS prompt by using the Cscript program. This chapter describes how to create script files, run them, and configure the Wscript program.

What Is the Windows Script Host?

Windows XP, like previous desktop versions of Windows, comes with the Windows Script Host (WSH), a program that can run scripts from either DOS or Windows. A *script* is a file containing a series of commands, like a batch file that you can use to automate tasks that you repeat often. Administrators of large Windows installations find scripts invaluable for creating and maintaining standard Windows configurations.

For example, if you administer a large Windows installation, you can write a script that logs onto your organization's LAN, connects to various servers, and runs other housekeeping programs. You can use Scheduled Tasks and WSH to run the script on a schedule (see Chapter 2, section "Running Programs on a Schedule Using Task Scheduler"). Alternatively, you can configure Windows to run WSH and the script automatically when Windows starts up (see Chapter 2, section "Starting Programs When Windows Starts").

WSH can run scripts written in a variety of languages, including VBScript (the scripting language used by Internet Explorer) and JavaScript (what Microsoft calls JScript). The makers of other scripting languages may also provide programs that will allow WSH to run scripts in their languages (Microsoft hopes that they do). Scripts are stored in text files that you can look at using Notepad or WordPad.

This chapter doesn't describe the VBScript or JavaScript languages; we suggest that you buy a book about the programming language you choose. Instead, this chapter describes how to use WSH to run scripts after you've written them.

For more information about WSH, visit its Web sites at **http://www.microsoft.com/ wsh_overview.htm** and **http://msdn. microsoft.com/scripting**.

Caution   *WSH can run scripts that are more powerful than batch files and can do a lot of damage. Viruses like the notorious ILOVEYOU virus use WSH as part of their system of infection and propagation. Checking the source and trustworthiness of the scripts you run is vitally important.*

Running Scripts from Windows

To run a script, just open the script's icon or filename in Windows Explorer or from the desktop. The Wscript program, which is part of WSH and is stored in the C:\Windows folder (or whatever folder you installed Windows in), runs the script. Alternatively, you can choose Start | Run, type the full pathname of the script you want to run, and click OK.

Wscript is registered (using Windows file associations) to run VBScript (with the extension .vbs) and JavaScript (with the extension .js) scripts. If you want to use Wscript to run scripts with other extensions, run the script's icon or filename, or type its filename into the Run dialog box. If Windows displays an Open With dialog box, you can tell Windows to run all scripts of this type using Wscript. Choose C:\Windows\System32\Wscript.exe in the Open With dialog box and select the Always Use This Program To Open This File check box. In addition to running the script you specified, Windows registers Wscript to be the program used to open all files with this extension.

Configuring the Wscript Program

To see or set properties for Wscript, run Wscript with no script by running its filename (Wscript.exe) in the C:\Windows\System32 folder. You can also choose Start | Run, type **wscript** in the Run dialog box, and then click OK. Either way, you see the Windows Script Host Settings dialog box, shown here:

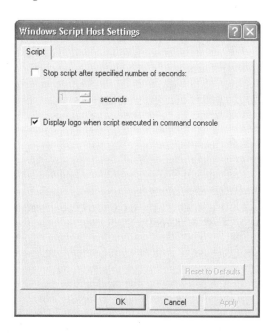

BEHIND THE SCENES:
WINDOWS XP INTERNALS

Wscript has two properties that you can set:

- **Stop Script After Specified Number of Seconds**   Specifies a maximum number of seconds that a script can run, to prevent running scripts that never terminate. This setting is the equivalent of Cscript's //T:*nn* option or the WSH file Timeout setting, which are described in the next two sections.

- **Display Logo When Script Executed In Command Console**   Displays the version number for WSH each time Wscript runs a script. This setting is the equivalent of Cscript's //logo or //nologo option or the WSH file DisplayLogo setting.

Running Scripts from the DOS Command Line

Despite the replacement of DOS with the DOS Virtual Machine (described in Chapter 39), you can still run scripts from the DOS command line by using the Cscript program. The Cscript.exe file is part of WSH and is installed in the C:\Windows\System32 folder.

To run a script using Cscript, follow these steps:

1. Open a Command Prompt window by choosing Start | All Programs | Accessories | Command Prompt. You see the DOS prompt, which is usually C:\Documents And Settings*username*>. You can also open the window by choosing Start | Run, typing **cmd** in the Open box, and pressing ENTER.

2. Type **cscript** followed by a space and the full pathname (file address) of the script you want to run. You can also type the command-line options listed in the next section in Table 40-1.

3. Press ENTER. The script runs.

Configuring the Cscript Program

You can use two kinds of command-line options with Cscript:

- **Host options**   Options that control WSH features. These options always start with two slashes (//).

- **Script options**   Information that is passed to the script itself. These options always start with one slash (/).

The command-line options you can use with Cscript are listed in Table 40-1.

Option	Description
//?	Displays information about the Cscript command.
//B	Runs the script in batch mode, so that all user prompts and script errors are suppressed. This is the opposite of the //I option.
//H:*name*	Registers the program *name* (which must be either Cscript or Wscript) as the application for running this type of script. The default program for running scripts is Wscript.
//I	Runs the script in interactive mode, displaying all user prompts and script errors. (This is the default setting.) This is the opposite of the //B option.
//logo	Displays a banner when the script starts. (This is the default setting.) This is the opposite of the //nologo option.
//nologo	Does not display the WSH banner. This is the opposite of the //logo setting.
//S	Saves the command-line options you use this time so that they become the default.
//T:*nn*	Specifies the maximum number of seconds that the script can run before Cscript cancels the script.

Table 40-1.   *Cscript Command-Line Options*

BEHIND THE SCENES:
WINDOWS XP INTERNALS

The Complete Reference

Appendix A

Installing or Upgrading to Windows XP

If you didn't buy a computer with Windows XP already installed, you face the task of installing Windows—either installing it on a blank hard disk or upgrading your existing operating system. This appendix explains your installation options and details how to install, upgrade to, and uninstall Windows. The Windows Setup Wizard runs for about a half an hour (depending mainly on the speed of your CD drive), and we tell you what questions it asks. You'll also find out Windows XP's hardware requirements, how much disk space Windows XP requires, how to check your installation, how to install optional Windows components, and other installation tips.

After installation, Microsoft's new product activation system requires you to check in with Microsoft so that your copy of Windows XP can be "locked" to your particular computer. If you are replacing an old computer with a new one, you may want to use the Files And Settings Transfer Wizard to move your files. If you want to create a dual-boot installation, this appendix has instructions, along with information about the Boot.ini file, which controls which partition your system boots from.

What Are the Windows XP Installation Requirements?

To install Windows XP, you need the following:

- A Windows XP CD-ROM and a CD-ROM drive
- A Pentium II, Celeron, or compatible CPU running at a speed of at least 300MHz
- At least 128MB of RAM memory (you can install Windows XP with only 64MB, but it's not reliable)
- A hard disk with at least 2GB total space, with at least 1.5GB free, depending on which options you choose to install (see "How Much Disk Space Does Windows Require?")
- A VGA or better monitor
- A keyboard and mouse (or other pointing device)
- CD-ROMs or floppy disks with hardware drivers for devices needing drivers that don't come with Windows

Windows itself is stored in compressed format in a group of *cabinet files* (*CAB* files) with the extension .cab on the CD-ROM. The setup program copies and decompresses the Windows programs during installation.

Note *For information on network (remote) or unattended installations, see* Windows .NET Server: The Complete Reference, *by Kathy Ivens (published by Osborne/McGraw-Hill).*

What Are Your Installation Options?

You can install Windows in one of the following ways:

- **From scratch**   Install Windows on a blank, formatted hard disk or on a blank partition of a hard disk.

- **Upgrade**   Install Windows XP over Windows Me, 98, NT 4.0 Workstation, or 2000, replacing your previously installed operating system. You can't install Windows XP Home Edition as an upgrade to Windows NT or Windows 2000; for that upgrade, you need Windows XP Professional. When you upgrade, you can decide whether to install Windows XP over your existing Windows version, leaving the program and data files intact, or delete everything and start with a clean partition or disk.

- **Dual-boot**   Create a dual-boot installation with Windows 95, 98, Me, 2000, or NT, or with Linux, Unix, or another operating system. A dual-boot installation allows you to choose to start your computer in either Windows XP or your previously installed operating system.

Each of these methods is described in detail later in this appendix.

How Much Disk Space Does Windows Require?

The Windows Setup Wizard tells you how much disk space it will need. The amount of space required depends on the following:

- What operating system, if any, is already installed.

- Whether you choose to save the previous operating system (if any) to enable you to uninstall Windows XP later. This optional uninstall file can be up to 100MB. You can delete this backup later (see "Checking Your System After Installing Windows").

- How many optional programs you install along with Windows. Windows comes with dozens of utilities and applications that aren't needed to run Windows, but may come in handy.

Depending on these factors, Windows can require anywhere from 850MB to 1.5GB during installation. It refuses to install if it doesn't find enough space.

If you don't have enough space to install Windows, try emptying your Recycle Bin, deleting your Web browser's cache (or the temporary file caches of other application programs), and deleting all .tmp and .bak files. Exit all programs and delete all the files in C:\Windows\Temp (or other temporary file folders) except those dated within the past few days. If you still don't have enough space, you can uninstall programs and reinstall them later when Windows XP is running. However, Windows XP requires a lot of elbow room; if your disk space is tight, consider buying a larger hard disk.

If your system has more than one hard disk, the free space Windows requires must be on the drive that contains your Windows program folder (usually C:\Windows).

How Does Product Activation Work?

In addition to entering a 25-character product key, Microsoft now requires you to *activate* your copy of Windows. Microsoft requires product activation for Windows XP, Office 2002, and Visio 2002. Windows XP allows you 30 days of use before requiring activation. Office 2002 allows you to run the program 50 times, and Visio lets you run it a mere 10 times before requiring product activation. When the 30 days expires, if you haven't activated Windows, it won't let you log on until you activate it. How does activation work?

Many of the components inside any computer have unique serial numbers that are routinely read by the operating system. The Windows Setup Wizard collects data about the hardware components of your computer as it installs drivers for the hardware you have installed in your system. It then creates an individually identifiable *activation ID* that it applies to your computer. When you activate Windows XP, Windows sends your activation ID to Microsoft's databank, where the information is stored, and Microsoft's activation server "unlocks" (activates) your copy of Windows. (If your computer isn't on the Internet, you need to call Microsoft on the phone to send your activation ID.) Each time you reinstall Windows XP, you must reactivate it, and Microsoft checks that the activation ID hasn't changed.

Note   *Product activation does not limit the number of times you can reinstall Windows XP on a single machine.*

You can't install the same copy of Windows XP on several different computers, because they have different hardware serial numbers. If you try, when the activation ID is checked against your original activation ID, they won't match, so Microsoft won't allow you to activate Windows XP. This is how Microsoft's product activation prevents casual piracy. For example, if you forget about activation and loan your copy of Windows XP to a friend, when he installs it on his computer it will create a different activation ID. The problems will begin when your friend tries to activate Windows on his computer and this new activation ID does not match the activation ID of the previously installed version. Even after Windows is activated, you can run into trouble, because Windows periodically checks the activation ID with the activation servers at Microsoft. (Yes, your computer will periodically report to Microsoft's activation servers, and no, you will not be asked permission beforehand.)

Note *The activation ID cannot be decoded to point directly to a particular machine, so Microsoft can't figure out (using only your activation information) who you are or what your are doing with your computer. However, future efforts could conceivably reveal a way to exploit the information about your computer that is contained in the activation ID. Even though your machine may not be able to call direct attention to you, it may draw unwanted attention to itself, which will invariably inconvenience you in some fashion.*

What happens if you reinstall Windows on what appears to be a different computer? At the time of this writing, replacing more than three hardware components in your machine causes the software to require reactivation. Once this happens, you will have from 3 to 30 days to call Microsoft to get permission to continue to use the product. If you cannot activate the product by then, you will not able to log on to Windows. You can call Microsoft to explain what has happened so that you can get your product activated.

Tip *The activation scheme appears to allow you to upgrade up to three hardware components at the same time without deciding that you have moved it to a different computer. After your new hardware has been installed for a while, the activation system automatically updates your activation ID to reflect your new hardware, and transmits that to Microsoft's activation server. You can then replace additional hardware, without fear of exceeding the three-device limit. Our conclusion: Don't plan on installing too many (more than three) new components at the same time.*

The Future of Product Activation

Microsoft is conscious of the fact that customers will intensely dislike this new procedure. By the time you read this, Microsoft may have already put in place a new activation scheme, because some folks in Germany found a way to circumvent the present system. (The Windows Automatic Update system allows Microsoft to update Windows features, even after the program is released, so the activation scheme can be updated even after you install Windows.) We expect Microsoft to retain some of the identification and data-collection methods described here, but also to give the reaction of its customers some consideration.

For the latest information on product activation or any other Windows XP-related news, check our Web site at **http://net.gurus.com/winxptcr**. If you would like to read more about this from the creator's point of view, read the "Microsoft's Piracy Basics: Product Activation" Web page at **http://www.microsoft.com/piracy/basics/xp_activation.asp**.

Preparing to Install Windows

Here are some tips, including suggestions from Microsoft, for a smoother installation:

- **Virus-checking**   Run a virus-checker on your system before installing Windows, so that no viruses interfere with the installation. You can download several good virus-checkers from the Internet, including those from McAfee (at **http://www.mcafee.com**) and Symantec (at **http://www.symantec.com**). Then disable your virus-checker before installing Windows.

Caution   *Some computers have antivirus programs stored in the computer's BIOS (Basic Input/ Output System). In this case, the Setup Wizard won't run. If you see an error message reporting an antivirus program, check your system's documentation for instructions on how to disable virus checking.*

- **Disk errors**   Run ScanDisk or ChkDsk (if you use Windows) to clean up any formatting errors on your hard disk.

- **Backups**   Make a complete backup of your system. If that's not possible, make a backup of all of your data files (see Chapter 9).

- **Program installation disks**   Make sure that you have the program disks (CDs or floppies) for all the programs you want to install. If you downloaded programs, make backups of the installation files.

- **Disk space**   Make sure that you have enough free space on the hard disk on which your Windows program folder will be stored (see "How Much Disk Space Does Windows Require?"). You need from 850MB to 1.5GB of space, and more if you plan to install many optional programs.

- **Hardware problems**   If you have problems with hardware or software on your system, fix the problems first or uninstall the hardware or software.

- **Other utilities**   Disable any non-Microsoft disk-caching programs, such as the caching programs that come with the Norton Utilities and PC Tools. Turn off other utilities that might interfere with installation, such as CleanSweep (which monitors software installations). Exit from all programs.

- **Network information**   If your computer is on a network, contact your network administrator before upgrading to Windows XP. Ask whether the computer is part of a domain, and if so, ask for the domain name and your computer's name on the domain. If your network uses static IP addresses (your network administrator will know), ask for your computer's IP address. If your computer isn't part of a domain (that is, it's on a peer-to-peer network as described in Chapter 28), ask for the name of the workgroup. Make sure that your computer is connected to the network during installation, because the Setup Wizard can detect many LAN and Internet settings and configure your computer automatically.

Starting the Installation

Before starting the installation process, you need to take a few steps, depending on whether you are installing on a blank hard disk, upgrading an existing Windows installation, or creating a dual-boot system.

Installing Windows on a Blank Hard Disk

You must be able to start up the computer to start the Windows installation. If you don't have an operating system installed on your hard disk, you need to be able to boot from the Windows XP CD-ROM.

 Formatting your hard disk (or a partition) deletes everything on it. You can't use the Recycle Bin or other unerase programs to get files back. Be sure to make and verify a backup copy of all the files you want to save (see Chapter 9).

The Windows XP CD-ROM is bootable; that is, it contains startup operating system files so that you can use it to start your computer. However, your computer must be configured to boot from the CD-ROM. Your computer may look first in the floppy drive and then on the hard drive for operating system files at startup. Try putting the Windows XP CD-ROM in the CD drive and starting your computer to see if the computer loads the Setup Wizard from the CD-ROM. If not, follow the instructions in the rest of this section.

To tell your computer to look on the CD-ROM during startup, you need to change your computer's BIOS setup. The method to do this varies from computer to computer, and you should check your computer's documentation. Generally, you press a key (usually F2, F6, F10, or DELETE) during startup, while the computer manufacturer's logo is on the screen, before you see the Windows logo. Some computers display a prompt to tell you what to press (for example, "Press <Del> key if you want to run setup").

Once you press the correct key, you see your computer's BIOS configuration screen. Follow the instructions on the screen (or in your computer's documentation) to change the boot sequence (or boot order) to start with the CD-ROM. Then follow the instructions to save your changes and reboot with the Windows XP CD-ROM in the drive. The Setup Wizard should run. Follow its instructions to install Windows XP (see "Answering the Windows Setup Wizard's Questions").

Upgrading to Windows XP

When you upgrade to Windows XP, the Windows Setup Wizard can save your old operating system's files and settings, so that you don't need to reinstall all of your programs. You can upgrade to Windows XP Professional if your computer has Windows 2000, NT 4.0 Workstation, Me, or 98. You can upgrade to Windows XP Home Edition from Windows Me or 98 (not from Windows 2000 or NT 4.0 Workstation). If you run an older version of Windows (Windows 95 or earlier) or DOS, installation replaces your old operating system entirely, and you must reinstall and restore all your programs and files.

If you want to be able to run either another operating system or Windows XP when you start the computer, you can set up a dual-boot configuration (see "Creating Dual-Boot Installations").

If your hard disk has become full of junk, or your Windows installation is unreliable, you may want to start from scratch anyway, rather than installing Windows on top of what you already have on the hard disk. Installing from scratch is called a *clean install*, and it reduces problems with older incompatible program files and with unneeded files that waste disk space. You can save the data files you want to keep, reformat the hard disk, install Windows, install the programs you want to use, and restore your data files. The Windows Setup Wizard can even do the reformatting for you. A clean install usually saves time in the long run, even though you need to reinstall your programs.

We prefer to make a separate partition for data (usually D:), move our data files there, and use the C: partition for only Windows and programs (see Chapter 32, section "What Are Partitions, File Systems, NTFS, and Drive Letters?"). This allows us to reinstall Windows any time we like without disturbing our data.

To upgrade from a previous version of Windows, follow these steps:

1. Start your current version of Windows.
2. Put the Windows XP CD-ROM in the CD-ROM drive. You see the Welcome To Microsoft Windows XP window. If you don't see this window, use Windows Explorer to look at the contents of the CD-ROM and run the Setup.exe program. Another way to run the program is to choose Start | Run, type **d:\setup**, and press ENTER (if your CD-ROM drive is drive D:).
3. Follow the instructions that the Windows Setup Wizard displays (see "Answering the Windows Setup Wizard's Questions"). The Setup Wizard creates an upgrade report that lists hardware and software issues that may arise.

The Windows Setup Wizard asks in which folder to install Windows XP (usually C:\Windows). If you choose a different folder than the one in which the previous version of Windows was installed, you must reinstall all of your application programs, and possibly all of your hardware drivers.

Creating Dual-Boot Installations

A *dual-boot* or *multiboot installation* is an installation of Windows that leaves another operating system intact on your computer. When you start your computer, you can decide which operating system to run. In order to keep the versions of Windows separate, you install each in a separate partition.

The Windows Setup Wizard can create a new partition if your hard disk has unused, unpartitioned space. It can install Windows XP into this new partition, leaving your existing operating system intact. You do not need to use a third-party partitioning program.

However, you will probably want to get a third-party partitioning program like PartitionMagic (from PowerQuest Corp., at **http://www.powerquest.com/partitionmagic**) or BootIt NG (from TeraByte Unlimited, at **http://www.terabyteunlimited.com**) to adjust the sizes of your existing partitions to make space for Windows XP. We like to create a separate partition for each operating system, plus one for our data. This arrangement enables us to switch or reinstall operating systems without disturbing our data (see Chapter 32, section "Installing Multiple Versions of Windows with PartitionMagic").

Dual-Booting with Windows 2000, Unix, or Linux

You can't use the Windows Setup Wizard to create a dual-boot system with Windows 2000 and Windows XP unless Windows 2000 is installed in a FAT32 partition. This is because the Wizard will upgrade Windows 2000's NTFS partition to Windows XP's slightly newer NTFS format, and Windows 2000 will no longer be able to read its own partition. However, PartitionMagic, BootIt NG, and similar third-party partitioning programs provide a way to create a dual-boot system with Windows 2000. Use a third-party partitioning program to create a new partition for Windows XP and to hide the Windows 2000 partition. Then install Windows XP on the new, blank partition. This method also works for creating a dual-boot system with Unix or Linux.

Dual-Booting with Windows Me or 9*x*

To create a dual-boot system with Windows XP and Windows Me or 9*x*, install the older version of Windows first, and then install Windows XP. During the installation process, Windows XP creates a file named Boot.ini in C:\, listing the bootable partitions and which partition is the default. When the Setup Wizard displays the Setup Options window, click the Advanced Options button and select the I Want To Choose The Install Drive Letter And Partition During Setup check box. This setting causes the Setup Wizard to display a list of your partitions and enables you to choose the partition in which you want to display Windows XP. You also have the option of deleting existing partitions and creating new ones. The next section steps through the installation process.

Once you have both versions of Windows installed in separate primary DOS partitions, you can switch back and forth by using the boot menu that Windows XP displays:

```
Please select the operating system to start:

Microsoft Windows XP Professional
Microsoft Windows

Use the up and down arrow keys to move the highlight to your choice.
Press ENTER to choose.
Seconds until highlighted choice will be started automatically: 30
```

Windows Me, 98, and 95 appear simply as "Microsoft Windows." You can change the text and entries in this boot menu, as described in "Setting Boot Options," later in this appendix.

On a dual-boot system with Windows NT or Windows 3.1, you can't use FAT32 for your data partition, because Windows NT and Windows 3.1 don't support FAT32 (as Windows 2000, Me, 98, and XP do) (see Chapter 32, section "What Are FAT, FAT32, and NTFS?"). On a dual-boot system with Windows Me or 9x, you can't use an NTFS partition for your data partition, since these versions of Windows can't read it.

Answering the Windows Setup Wizard's Questions

Follow the steps outlined in this section to install Windows once you have started the Windows Setup Wizard and you see the Welcome To Microsoft Windows XP window, shown in Figure A-1. (The second option, Install Optional Windows Components, appears

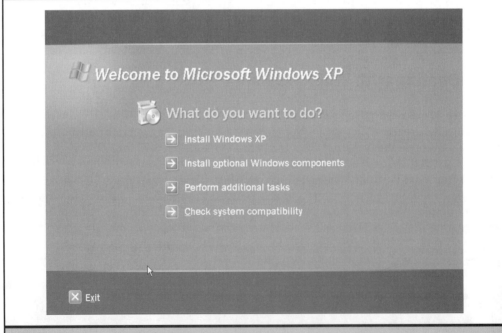

Figure A-1.   *Starting the Windows installation*

only when you run the program on a system that is already running Windows XP.) You can press ESC at any time to cancel your installation. Click Next to move from one screen of the Setup Wizard to the next.

1. Before starting the installation, click Check System Compatibility. The Microsoft Windows Upgrade Advisor checks your system for incompatibilities with Windows XP and displays a window like this:

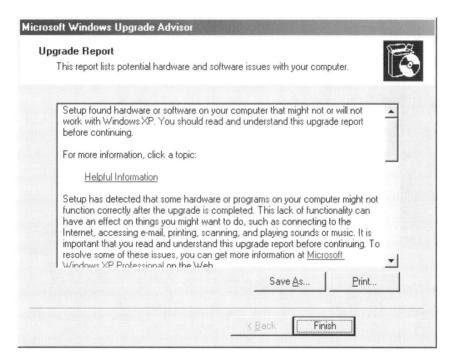

If your system includes hardware or software that Windows can't handle or that needs to be upgraded, you can click Details for a list. Microsoft's online hardware compatibility list is also on the Web at **http://www.microsoft.com/hcl**. For an installation on a blank disk, this includes information only about your hardware, since the Upgrade Advisor has no way of knowing what software you plan to install later. If the Upgrade Advisor finds Blocking Issues, you can't proceed to upgrade. If it lists only Helpful Information, you are good to go.

2. To start the installation, click Install Windows XP. The Windows Setup Wizard checks your computer for installed operating systems, and tells you whether you can upgrade or need to install Windows XP from scratch.

3. In the Windows Setup dialog box, set the Installation Type to either Upgrade or New Installation:

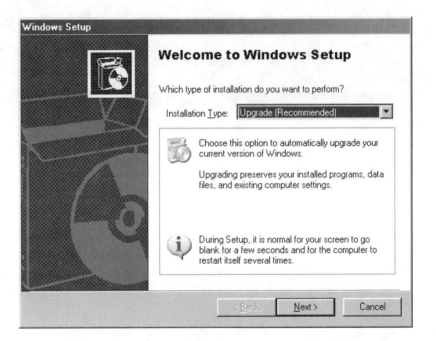

Choose New Installation to install to a new, blank partition (Setup can reformat a partition or disk for you), or Upgrade to update your Windows 98, Me, NT 4.0 Workstation, or 2000 installation. You won't see the Upgrade option if your existing version of Windows is too old (Windows 95 or earlier).

4. After you agree to the license agreement, the Setup Wizard prompts for your product key, a 25-character license number that appears on the Windows XP CD box. We suggest that you write this number right on the CD-ROM, using a fine-point permanent marker, on the same side that the printing appears on the disk. *Don't write on (or touch) the other (bottom) side of the disk.*

5. If you choose Upgrade, the Setup Wizard displays the Upgrade Report screen, which asks how much information you want on the upgrade report that it creates: hardware issues only, all issues, or no report at all. Don't choose Do Not Show Me The Report, since hardware issues may prevent Windows XP from running correctly, even if your hardware worked fine with a previous version of Windows. If you have enough disk space, the Setup Wizard stores a compressed version of your old version of Windows so that you can uninstall Windows XP later (see "Uninstalling Windows XP").

6. If you choose New Installation, you see the Setup Options screen.

- If you want to copy the installation files from the CD to hard disk, click Advanced Options and select the Copy All Installation Files From The Setup CD (this option is useful if you plan to install Windows options later and want to do so without needing to put the Windows XP CD-ROM into the drive). Click OK.

- If you are creating a dual-boot installation, click Advanced Options and select the I Want To Choose The Install Drive Letter And Partition During Setup check box. We recommend that you select this option if your system has more than one partition or hard disk. Don't change the To This Folder On My Hard Drive box to an entry other than \WINDOWS unless you have a good reason. Microsoft recommends that Windows XP be installed in the \Windows folder. Click OK.

- If you are installing from a network drive, or somewhere other than your CD, you can specify a pathname where the installation files are stored. Click Advanced Options and set the Copy Installation Files From This Folder box (click the Browse button to navigate to the folder). Click OK.

- If you have vision problems, click the Accessibility Options button. You can choose to enable the Microsoft Magnifier (if you want the contents of the screen magnified) or Microsoft Narrator (which can read the screen aloud) while the Setup Wizard runs. Click OK.

- Change the language if you want Windows to be installed with screens in another language (this option doesn't change the Setup Wizard). Click OK.

7. If you chose New Installation in step 3 and the disk partition to which you are installing Windows XP doesn't already use the NTFS file system, you see the Upgrading To The Windows XP NTFS File System screen, shown in Figure A-2. (Of course, the Setup Wizard may not yet know on which partition you plan to install Windows—it's just guessing.) If you plan to use only Windows XP on your computer, choose Yes. If you are creating a dual-boot system and you want older versions of Windows to be able to read files on the disk, choose No.

8. On the Get Updated Setup Files screen, you choose whether to connect to the Internet to check the Microsoft Web site for updated Windows XP files (this feature is called Dynamic Update). If you have a working Internet connection on the computer, choose Yes; otherwise, choose No. If you choose No, or if the Setup Wizard can't get through to the Microsoft Windows Update site, you can update your Windows XP installation later using Windows Update (see Chapter 36, section "Updating Your Computer with Windows Update").

9. The Setup Wizard analyzes your computer, figures out which files you need to install, and copies them from the CD-ROM to your hard disk. It reboots and displays a text-mode (nongraphical) screen.

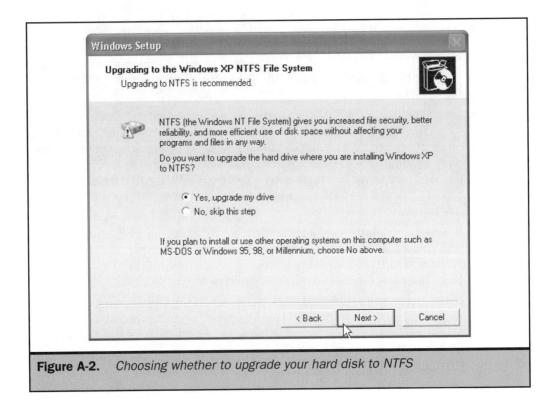

Figure A-2. *Choosing whether to upgrade your hard disk to NTFS*

10. If you selected the I Want To Choose The Install Drive Letter And Partition During Setup check box in step 6, you see several text-mode (gray on blue) menus.

■ If your system already contains an installation of Windows XP, a menu asks whether you would rather repair it or install a fresh copy of Windows. Press ESC to install a fresh copy of Windows (either on the same partition or a different one).

■ Then you see a list of your partitions, as shown in Figure A-3. You can select a partition and delete it, if it contains a version of Windows you no longer want. You can create a new partition in unpartitioned space. Don't choose a partition that already contains a version of Windows. If you are replacing your existing Windows installation, delete the partition that contains Windows and create a new partition in its place for Windows XP (just make sure that you have a backup of any files on that partition that you want to keep!).

■ If you create a partition, you can specify how much of the unpartitioned space to use (in kilobytes). Make the partition at least 2GB to leave room for Windows.

```
Windows XP Professional Setup

   The following list shows the existing partitions and
   unpartitioned space on this computer.

   Use the UP and DOWN ARROW keys to select an item in the list.

      ● To set up Windows XP on the selected item, press ENTER.

      ● To create a partition in the unpartitioned space, press C.

      ● To delete the selected partition, press D.

   ┌─────────────────────────────────────────────────────────────┐
   │ 19572 MB Disk 0 at Id 0 on bus 0 on atapi [MBR]             │
   │                                                             │
   │   C:  Partition1 (win98) [FAT32]        3012 MB ( 1470 MB free) │
   │   G:  Partition2 [NTFS]                 4991 MB ( 3801 MB free) │
   │       Unpartitioned space               5840 MB            │
   │   D:  Partition3 (DATA) [FAT32]         5729 MB ( 1603 MB free) │
   └─────────────────────────────────────────────────────────────┘

   ENTER=Install   D=Delete Partition   F3=Quit
```

Figure A-3.   *Choosing the partition in which to install Windows*

■ When you have finished, select the partition on which to install Windows XP and press ENTER. Then choose whether to use FAT32 or NTFS for the partition (use NTFS unless you have a specific reason for using FAT32). Don't choose the Quick Format options—let the Setup Wizard make sure that the hard disk has no bad sectors or other problems.

11. Windows reboots again and displays a graphical screen during the final part of the installation. (This step can take more than half an hour.)

12. If you chose New Installation rather than Upgrade in step 3, the Setup Wizard asks you a series of questions. (If you are upgrading, the Wizard can get this information from your old version of Windows.) It asks about the following:

■ **Regional and Language Options**   You can change the way dates, numbers, and money are displayed. You can also change these settings later (see Chapter 12, section "Windows' Regional Settings").

■ **Text Input Languages**   You can choose your default language and keyboard layout (see Chapter 12, section "Changing Language Properties").

■ **Name and Organization**   Applications can get your name and company name from Windows (for example, Outlook Express does this). You can change your name in most applications, but getting it right the first time is more convenient.

- **Computer name** This is the name you want to use for your computer. If your computer is connected to a local area network (LAN), the LAN administrator might want to issue your computer a name.

- **Administrator password** This is the password you'll type when you log onto Windows with the Administrator user account. Don't leave it blank. (In Windows XP Home Edition, this is the Owner password.)

- **Country, area code, and outside line number** Windows uses these numbers when configuring dial-up connections to the Internet.

- **Date and time** Set your clock, and remember to set the time zone. When you connect to the Internet, it will automatically update your clock to the correct time for your area. If Windows thinks you are in the wrong time zone, the time will be wrong!

- **Network settings** If the Setup Wizard detects a network adapter, it asks whether to create LAN connections using TCP/IP (the protocol used on the Internet and many LANs) and Client For Microsoft Networks (Microsoft's LAN client program). You can click Custom Settings to use a different protocol (like IPX/SPX) or client (like NetWare). See Chapter 27 for more information.

- **Workgroup or domain name** This is the name of the workgroup or domain your computer is part of, if your computer is on a LAN. Ask your LAN administrator for the workgroup or domain name (Windows suggests WORKGROUP or MSHOME). See Chapter 28 if your computer is part of a workgroup.

13. When Windows is installed, it prompts you to help it set up your computer. The exact order of the next couple of steps depends on whether your computer is connected to a LAN or the Internet, and whether you are upgrading or doing a new installation.

14. If the Setup Wizard detects a LAN connection, it asks whether you connect to the Internet via the LAN or connect directly.

15. When you see the Ready To Activate Windows screen, you can choose whether to activate Windows now or later. You must activate Windows (see "How Does Product Activation Work?")—you can put it off, but after a grace period, Windows won't let you log in if you haven't activated it. You don't need to register, though (registration gives Microsoft your name, address, and other information; activation gives Microsoft only the technical "signature" of your computer and your Windows XP serial number). Windows tries to connect to the Internet, and if it can't, it reminds you to activate later. If you don't have an Internet connection, you can activate Windows over the phone.

Tip *Wait a few days before activating, to make sure that the system works and that you are happy with the hardware. When you activate, the activation ID records the current state of the computer's hardware, and if you change it significantly, you'll need to call Microsoft later if you reinstall Windows.*

16. If the Setup Wizard hasn't already figured out how you connect to the Internet (if you have a LAN connection), you see the Let's Get On The Internet screen. Microsoft suggests that you sign up for their MSN Internet service. If you have another account, choose Create A New Internet Account After I Finish Setting Up Windows. If the Setup Wizard detects a modem, it may offer to call the Microsoft Referral Service to suggest one of the ISPs that has signed up with its referral program. If so, click Skip to set up your Internet account yourself after the setup is finished (choose Start | Internet and refer to Chapter 22).

17. On the Who Will Use This Computer screen, type the names of up to five people who will use this computer, so that the Setup Wizard can create user accounts for each one (see Chapter 6). If you will be the only user, type just your name (first, last, both, or whatever you would like your user account name to be). If you want to create more than five user accounts, you can add them later (see Chapter 6, section "Creating New User Accounts").

18. After you click Finish on the Setup Wizard's last screen, if you are upgrading from a previous version of Windows to Windows XP Professional, you see the Password Creation dialog box, which lists the user accounts that were created during installation, not counting the names you typed in the previous step. Windows XP Professional creates an additional user named Administrator. Windows XP Home Edition's additional user account is named Owner. Type a password to use for all the accounts listed. You can change these passwords later (see Chapter 6, section "Adding or Removing Passwords").

19. You see the Windows logon screen. Choose a user name you specified in step 17 and type the password you specified in step 18 to log on. (If Windows didn't ask you for a password in step 18, it shouldn't ask for one now, either.)

You see the Windows desktop. You are ready to test Windows and install your programs!

Tip *To see the release notes for your version of Windows XP, insert the Windows XP CD-ROM in the CD drive, start the Setup program, choose Perform Additional Tasks, choose Browse This CD, and open the Readme.htm file (click or double-click the filename to display it in Internet Explorer or your default Web browser).*

Checking Your System After Installing Windows

Here are things to do after Windows is installed:

- **Configure your hardware**   Check that all of your hardware was correctly detected by Windows, including your modem, network cards, and printer. Choose Start, right-click My Computer, and choose Properties. Then click the Hardware tab of the System Properties dialog box and click the Device Manager button (see Chapter 13, section "What Is the Device Manager?"). If any of the computer components listed in the Device Manager window have exclamation marks on their icons, something is wrong. Refer to Chapter 13 for information about how to reinstall hardware.

> **Tip**   *You can print a summary of your Windows configuration. Choose Start | All Programs | Accessories | System Tools | System Information. Then choose File | Print.*

- **Check your network connection**   If your computer is connected to a LAN, check that the network communication is functioning normally. If it's not, see "Troubleshooting Your Network" in Chapter 28, or talk to your LAN administrator.

- **Check your user account passwords**   Windows XP sets up user accounts whether you plan to use them or not, and it's important for your computer's security for your accounts to have passwords. Otherwise, if your computer connects to the Internet, some hacker may think of a way to break into your computer. Choose Start | Control Panel and click User Accounts. In the User Accounts window, choose each of the existing accounts, click Create A Password, and specify a password for the account. If "Guest account is off" doesn't appear, click it and turn it off.

- **Reinstall programs**   If you didn't reformat your hard disk to install Windows from scratch, and if you installed Windows XP in the same folder as your previous version of Windows, you shouldn't need to reinstall the application programs that were installed on your hard disk. The Setup Wizard looks for installed programs and installs them in Windows XP, too. Otherwise, get out your installation CDs and start installing programs.

- **Set up your Internet connection**   The Setup Wizard offers to help only with MSN Internet access and with ISPs who have signed up with their referral program. Choose Start | Internet to run the New Connection Wizard to set up other Internet connections (see Chapter 22, section "Running the New Connection Wizard").

- **Update your antivirus program**   If you have antivirus software (and you should if your computer connects to the Internet), check whether it is compatible with Windows XP. Go to the program's Web site and check whether you need to upgrade the antivirus program. Also make sure that you have an up-to-date virus database.

Deleting the Backup of Your Previous Version of Windows

If you upgraded to Windows XP, the Setup Wizard may have kept a backup copy of your previous operating system, which can occupy 50MB or more of disk space. If you are sure that you will never want to uninstall Windows XP, follow these steps to delete the previous operating system files:

1. Choose Start | Control Panel | Add Or Remove Programs.
2. If Windows XP Uninstall appears in the Currently Installed Programs list, there is a backup copy of your previous operating system.
3. Click Windows XP Uninstall. Additional information appears.
4. Click the Change/Remove button. You see the Uninstall Windows XP dialog box.
5. Click Remove The Backup Of My Previous Operating System, and then click Continue. Windows deletes the unneeded file.

Transferring Your Data Files and Windows Configuration Settings

If you get a new computer that runs Windows XP, you can transfer your data files and some of your configuration settings from your old computer to your new one. You can move the files over a LAN, over a direct cable connection, on floppy disks, or on other removable disks (like Zip or Jaz disks).

If you have Zip, Jaz, or other large-capacity removable disks, you can use the Files And Settings Transfer Wizard to back up your configuration and settings before you upgrade to Windows XP, and then restore them after you upgrade.

You can choose to transfer your Windows settings, your data files (specifying the folders where they are stored, or all files with specific file extensions), or both. The Files And Settings Transfer Wizard can transfer the configuration settings for Windows itself, as well as for Microsoft programs that come with Windows, like Outlook Express and Internet Explorer. The Wizard works with a small number of third-party programs as well.

If you plan to use floppies to transfer your settings, you had better have a lot of them! If you want to transfer your files, chances are that you'll have too many files to fit on floppies.

You will need to reinstall your application programs from their installation CDs or floppies. We recommend that if you installed Windows from scratch, you reinstall your programs first. Then run the Files And Settings Transfer Wizard to transfer the program settings (the settings can't be transferred if the programs aren't already installed on the new computer).

If your old and new computers are connected over a network, you can transfer your files and settings from one computer to the other over the network. Make sure that you can access the old computer's hard disk from the new computer over the network.

 When you move programs from one computer to another with the Files And Settings Transfer Wizard, you must move them to a drive with the same letter. For example, if your programs are on D: on the old computer, the Wizard moves them to drive D: on the new computer.

To transfer your files or Windows settings, you can start by running the Files And Settings Transfer Wizard from either your new computer or your old one. The Wizard runs under previous versions of Windows, as well as Windows XP. There are three ways to run the Wizard:

- Put the Windows XP CD-ROM into the CD drive on your old computer and run the Setup program. It may run automatically, or you may need to choose Start | Run, type **d:setup.exe** (replacing *d* with your CD drive letter), and press ENTER. You see the Welcome To Microsoft Windows XP window (shown earlier in Figure A-1). Click Perform Additional Tasks, and then click Transfer Files And Settings.

- In Windows XP, choose Start | All Programs | Accessories | System Tools | Files And Settings Transfer Wizard.

- Run the Wizard on another computer and create a Wizard Disk that contains the Wizard program. Run the Wizard from that floppy disk.

After you start the Wizard, you see the Files And Settings Transfer Wizard window. Click Next to move from screen to screen. Tell the Wizard whether this is the new computer or the old one, how you are going to transfer the files (cable, network, floppies, or other disks), and whether you want to transfer settings, files, or both. If you are transferring via floppies or other disks, the Wizard determines how much data is to be transferred and stores it on floppies or other removable disks, prompting for additional disks as needed.

Installing Additional Programs

The Windows XP CD-ROM contains a number of additional programs. You can install a few of them by running the Setup program on the CD and choosing Perform Additional Tasks from the Welcome To Microsoft Windows XP window. You can choose the following:

- Set Up Remote Desktop Connection (see Chapter 15, section "Accessing Other Computers with Remote Desktop").

- Set Up A Home Or Small Office Network (see Chapter 28, section "Configuring and Viewing Your LAN Connections").
- Browse This CD, to see the files on the CD in an Explorer window

The Valueadd folder on the CD contains more programs. Valueadd\Msft contains Microsoft programs, and Valueadd\3rdparty contains programs from other companies.

Setting Boot Options

Windows XP includes support for multiple partitions and multiple operating systems (it inherits this ability from Windows NT/2000). The boot program (Ntldr) is stored in the root folder of the first partition on the first disk. Ntldr reads the Boot.ini file, which is stored in the same folder, to find out which partitions you might want to boot from, which partition to use as the default, what to display in the boot menu, and how long to wait before loading the operating system from the default partition. If the boot menu contains only one option, you won't see it—Ntldr simply boots from that partition.

 Ntldr and Boot.ini are hidden, protected system files. To see them in an Explorer window, choose Tools | Folder Options, click the View tab, and deselect the Hide Protected Operating System Files check box. Also choose Show Hidden Files And Folders.

Understanding the the Boot.ini File

A typical Boot.ini file looks like this:

```
[boot loader]
timeout=30
default=multi(0)disk(0)rdisk(0)partition(2)\WINDOWS
[operating systems]
multi(0)disk(0)rdisk(0)partition(2)\WINDOWS=
"Microsoft Windows XP Professional" /fastdetect
C:\="Microsoft Windows"
```

The [boot loader] section lists the timeout (the number of seconds that it waits before loading from the default partition) and the default (which partition is the default). The [operating systems] section lists all of the partitions that contain operating systems from which you can boot.

Lines that specify partitions tell the boot program (Ntldr) exactly where to find the Windows system folder for any version of Windows, like this:

```
multi(0)disk(0)rdisk(r)partition(p)\windowsfolder
```

The "multi" in this line means that Ntldr relies on the computer's BIOS to load the system files. *R* is the number of the disk attached to the hard disk adapter (0 for the first disk, 1 for the second disk, and so forth). *P* is the number of the partition on that hard disk (1 for the first partition, 2 for the second partition, and so forth). Partitions are numbered starting with primary partitions, then logical partitions. Unused space and MS-DOS Extended partitions (which you are unlikely to have) are omitted.

If you have a SCSI disk, the line looks like the following (see Chapter 13, section "Disk Controllers: IDE, EIDE, and SCSI Devices"):

```
scsi(a)disk(s)rdisk(lun)partition(p)\windowsfolder
```

A is the number of the SCSI adapter, *s* is the SCSI ID of the disk, *lun* is the logical unit number of the disk (usually 0), and *p* is the partition number on that list. (For more information about booting from SCSI disks, see article Q102873 in the Microsoft Knowledge Base at **http://support.microsoft.com**.)

In the [operating systems] section, each partition is followed by an equal sign and the string (text) that will appear in the boot menu. Previous versions usually appear simply as "Microsoft Windows," but you can edit this to specify the version of Windows or other information about the partition. For example, you might have "Windows XP Pro Test" and "Windows XP Pro Daily Use."

You can add a few switches to the end of partition lines in the [operating systems] section. (In the example in this section, one of the lines includes the /FASTDETECT switch.) The following are some of the switches that you can use for Windows XP, 2000, and NT 4.0 partitions:

- ■ **/BASEVIDEO**   Starts up in Enable VGA Mode, which is useful for diagnosing video driver problems (see Chapter 35, section "Startup Modes").

- ■ **/MAXMEM:*n***   Allows Windows to use only a maximum of *n* kilobytes of RAM, which is useful if you suspect memory problems.

- ■ **/FASTDETECT**   Skips checking of parallel and series communications devices.

 In the [boot loader] section, set the timeout to 0 if you don't want Ntldr to display the menu. Set it to –1 if you want Ntldr to wait forever.

Editing Boot.ini

You can edit the Boot.ini file by using one of three Windows programs: the System Properties dialog box (which provides fewer choices), the System Configuration Utility (which displays the whole file for editing), or Notepad.

Editing Boot.ini from the System Properties Dialog Box

To display the System Properties dialog box, click Start, right-click My Computer, and choose Properties from the menu that appears. In the System Properties dialog box, click the Advanced tab. Click the Settings button in the Startup And Recovery section. You see the Startup And Recovery dialog box, shown in Figure A-4.

The settings in the System Startup section of the dialog box control part of the contents of the Boot.ini file. You can change the default operating system and the timeout by changing the first two settings. Don't deselect these check boxes, or you won't have time to make a selection from the boot menu. You can also click the Edit button to display and edit the Boot.ini file in Notepad—but proceed with care!

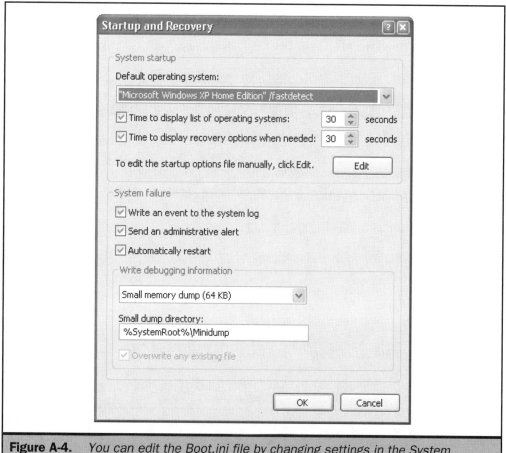

Figure A-4. *You can edit the Boot.ini file by changing settings in the System Startup section.*

The third setting in the System Startup section of the Startup And Recovery dialog box controls how long you have to choose to use the Recovery Console in the event that Windows won't start, if you have previously installed the Recovery Console. See Chapter 35 for details on the Recovery Console.

Editing Boot.ini from the System Configuration Utility

To see more of your Boot.ini options, run the System Configuration Utility by choosing Start | Run, typing **msconfig**, and pressing ENTER. Then click the BOOT.INI tab, as shown in Figure A-5 (see Chapter 37, section "Configuring Windows with the System Configuration Utility").

The BOOT.INI tab is divided into two parts. The top part shows the actual contents of the current Boot.ini file. The lower part offers options that you can use to change the file. The options that appear in the lower part of the window enable you to start up

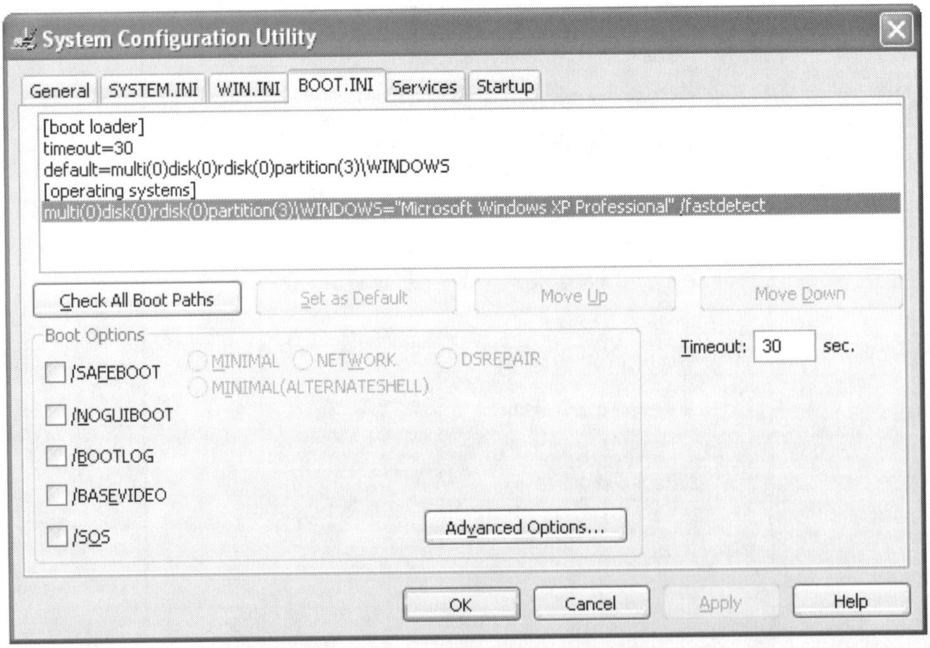

Figure A-5. *Editing your Boot.ini file*

in various startup modes (see Chapter 35, section "Startup Modes"). The options work as follows:

- **/SAFEBOOT** Boots in one of the Windows startup modes. When you select the /SAFEBOOT check box, you can choose from Minimal to start in Safe Mode, Network to start in Safe Mode With Network, DSRepair to start in Domain Server Repair mode (not used with Windows XP Professional or Home Edition), or Minimal (Alternateshell) to start in Safe Mode With Command Line.

- **/NOGUIBOOT** Boots into Windows XP without displaying the XP splash screen.

- **/BOOTLOG** Enables the verbose boot logging feature, which displays messages that can help you track down deeply embedded glitches.

- **/BASEVIDEO** Boots in the standard VGA Mode, which can operate with 99 percent of the video cards on the market.

- **/SOS** Displays all drivers and services that are loading as they load. This can be helpful if you can't finish booting.

- **Timeout** Indicates how long the menu appears before automatically selecting the default item.

You can click the Advanced Options button to display the BOOT.INI Advanced Options dialog box, with these additional settings:

- **/MAXMEM** Enables you to limit the amount of RAM that the system sees on startup.

- **/NUMPROC** Enables you to define a finite number of processors that are recognized by the system. This setting works only on multiprocessor machines.

- **/PCILOCK** Locks assigned PCI resources to already installed hardware to assist in avoiding conflicts.

- **/DEBUG** For programmers only, provides debugging features. This option offers no benefit to even the most advanced user.

Most of these options should never be used without direction from a qualified technician, if you plan to retain a stable XP installation.

Checking Your Boot.ini Entries

If you reinstall Windows or other operating systems, or copy or delete partitions, you may end up with Boot.ini entries for partitions that aren't really there. The System Configuration Utility can check the entries in your Boot.ini file and delete those that no longer refer to an installed operating system (see Chapter 37, section "Configuring Windows with the System Configuration Utility"). Follow these steps to check your Boot.ini file:

1. Choose Start | Run, type **msconfig**, and press ENTER.

2. Click the BOOT.INI tab.

3. Click Check All Boot Paths.

4. If an entry no longer refers to the location of a valid operating system, Windows displays a message asking whether to delete the line from Boot.ini.

5. Click Yes to remove the line (so the operating system won't appear on your boot menu) or No to leave it.

Uninstalling Windows XP

If you upgraded to Windows XP from a previous version of Windows, the Setup Wizard may have backed up your current operating system. (The backup files are named Backup.cab and Boot.cab, and are stored in C:\Undo, assuming that Windows is stored on C.) If so, you can uninstall Windows XP and return to that operating system. Be sure to make a backup of your data files before uninstalling Windows XP.

Note   *If you have changed your partitions or drives since installing Windows XP, you usually can't uninstall it.*

To uninstall Windows XP, follow these steps:

1. Choose Start | Control Panel | Add Or Remove Programs.

2. If Windows XP Uninstall appears in the Currently Installed Programs, you can uninstall it.

3. Click Windows XP Uninstall. Additional information appears.

4. Click the Change/Remove button. You see the Uninstall Windows XP dialog box.

5. Choose Uninstall Windows XP and click Continue.

6. Follow the directions on the screen. When the uninstall process has finished, your computer restarts and runs your previous operating system.

Uninstalling Windows doesn't delete your data files. However, any programs that you installed after you installed Windows XP probably won't work. To fix this, just install them again. If you created any documents or files, they may still be stored in C:\Documents And Settings*username*\\.

The Complete Reference

Glossary

10/100Base-T Network interface card for Ethernet or Fast Ethernet LANs.

16-bit application Program designed to run with DOS and Windows 3.1. Windows XP can run both 16-bit and 32-bit applications.

32-bit application Program designed to run with Windows 9x, Windows Me, Windows NT, Windows 2000, or Windows XP.

8-bit color Screen color setting that provides only 256 different colors (an older standard setting that provides far fewer than more recent 16-bit or 24-bit color).

access point Hub of a wireless LAN; a "base station" for the radio transmitters on the wireless LAN adapters of the other computers.

account lockout Optional security setting that tells Windows to lock a user account if someone types the wrong password more than a specified number of times.

ACPI Advanced Configuration and Power Interface, a standard for saving power by automatically turning off computer hardware when it is not in use.

action Part of the definition of a file type, specifying what Windows does with files of that type.

activation System that requires you to contact Microsoft with information about the computer system on which you are installing Windows XP (or other Microsoft programs) in order to receive an activation code that enables you to continue to use the program beyond an initial grace period.

activation ID Number that individually identifies your computer, based on its hardware characteristics and your software product serial number.

active partition Old term for the **boot partition**.

active window Window that appears "on top" of other windows, obscuring parts of other windows that overlap. The active window is the window that is currently accepting input from the keyboard and mouse.

ActiveX controls Small programs embedded in Web pages that can be automatically downloaded and run on your computer to add features to Web browsers.

adapter In LAN software, the network interface card and the driver needed to make that card work. In general, any card installed inside a computer.

adapter card   Printed circuit board that you can plug into an expansion slot inside your computer.

address   Information that tells you and Windows where to find a piece of information. *See* **e-mail address**; **file address**; **I/O address**; **memory address**; **UNC address**; **URL**.

Administrator account   Type of user account that enables the user to create, edit, and delete all user accounts; install software; and use the management tools. Administrator accounts are in the **Administrators group**.

Advanced Configuration and Power Interface   *See* ACPI.

Advanced Power Management   *See* APM.

Advanced Streaming Format   *See* ASF.

AGP   Accelerated Graphics Port, an advanced version of PCI for video cards, enabling faster screen updates.

alert   Program that sends a message or runs a program when a counter hits a preset value.

anonymous FTP   Connecting to a publicly available FTP server by using *anonymous* as the user name and your e-mail address as the password. *See* **FTP**.

antivirus software   Program that detects viruses and worms and may also delete them from your system.

APIPA   *See* **Automatic private IP addressing**.

APM   Advanced Power Management, a standard for saving power by automatically turning off computer hardware when it is not in use.

applet   Small application program, frequently downloaded as part of a Web page.

application   Program for getting real-world work done. Applications include word processing, database, and spreadsheet programs.

area code rules   Rules that describe when to dial 1 and/or the area code when dialing the phone.

argument   Additional information provided to a program on the command line.

ASCII file *See* **text file.**

ASF or **ASX** File extension for Advanced Streaming Format files, a streaming audio or video file format used by Windows Media Player.

ASR *See* **Automated System Recovery.**

ATA 2 *See* **IDE.**

attached file or File that is sent as part of an e-mail message or newsgroup
attachment article.

attribute Setting for a file or folder. The four attributes are Archive, Hidden, Read-Only, and System.

audio CD Compact disk containing audio information (rather than a Windows-compatible file system).

Audit Policy Settings that control what security events are included in audit log files.

authority Certificate authority's own certificate, used to check that other
certificate certificates it issued are valid.

Auto-hide Feature that hides the taskbar when you are not using it.

Automated System Feature of Windows XP Professional (not Home Edition) that
Recovery (ASR) backs up key system information onto a floppy disk that you can use to restart your computer in the event of a disaster.

Automatic private IP Feature of Windows that automatically assigns IP addresses
addressing (APIPA) in the format 169.254.*xxx.xxx* to computers on a TCP/IP-based LAN.

Autorun Program on a CD-ROM that tells Windows to run a program on the CD-ROM whenever the CD-ROM is inserted into the drive.

AVI file Video file with extension .avi.

background Image or color displayed on the desktop "behind" the windows that appear on the desktop. Or, program running while its window is not active.

backup Duplicate copy of information, stored separately in case something happens to the original copy.

backup job Specification of the information to be backed up by the Microsoft Backup Utility and the location to store the duplicate copy.

baseline backup *See* **full backup.**

batch file   List of DOS commands to execute, stored in a text file with the extension .bat.

BBS   *See* **bulletin board system**.

Bcc   Blind carbon copy; e-mail addresses to which to send a copy of an e-mail message without the other recipients seeing the addresses.

binding   Specification of which network protocols work with your network interface card.

BIOS setup   Or CMOS setup. Computer's low-level configuration information, including how much memory and what types of disks are installed.

bit   Binary digit, which can be either 0 or 1.

bitmap   Graphics format in which a picture or character is stored as a grid of dots. Standard Windows bitmap files have the extension .bmp. Older fonts are also stored as bitmaps.

BMP file   Graphics file in bitmap format (a Windows standard format for graphics files) with the extension .bmp.

body   Text of an e-mail message, not including the header lines at the top of the message.

boot   Start up or turn on your computer.

boot partition   Disk drive from which Windows loads on startup. *See also* **system partition**.

boot logging   Text file listing the events that occurred during computer and Windows startup. Enable Boot Logging is a startup mode.

bps   Bits per second, a measure of data transmission speed.

bridge   Connection between two networks, so that information can flow between them.

Briefcase   Folder containing files and subfolders to move between two computers.

broadband   High-speed communications, including ISDN, DSL, and cable Internet connections.

browser   Program that communicates with Web servers on the Internet and displays Web pages.

browsing   Moving from Web page to Web page, using a Web browser program like Internet Explorer.

buffer   Temporary storage area.

bulletin board system (BBS)	Text-based account that runs on a small computer (such as a PC), usually predating the widespread use of the Internet. Some bulletin board systems are also connected to the Internet, and most have been superceded by Internet sites.
bus topology	Network topology in which each computer connects to a main cable (the *bus*).
CAB or **cabinet file**	File containing a group of files for installation with the file extension .cab. The Windows XP CD-ROM contains many cabinet files.
cable	Wire that connects the computers in a LAN, or type of Internet account provided by a cable television company.
cable Internet account	Internet account provided by a cable television company.
cable modem	Device that connects your computer (through its network interface card) to a cable Internet account.
cable select (CS)	Method of determining which IDE or EIDE device is primary and which is secondary based on the position on the cable.
cache	Area on disk (usually a folder) for the temporary storage of information. Browsers store recently viewed Web pages in a cache, in case you want to see them again.
call waiting	Telephone line feature that beeps when another call is coming in on the line.
callback	Security feature of a remote access server that requires incoming connections to disconnect and for the server to call the computer back, verifying that the connecting computer is at the correct address or phone number.
calling card	Telephone credit card, which you can configure Windows to use when dialing long-distance calls.
Category-5 or **Cat-5 cable**	Unshielded twisted-pair cable used for star topology LANs.
Cc	Carbon copy; e-mail addresses to which to send a copy of an e-mail message.
CD burning	Saving files on a writable or rewritable CD-ROMs.
CD-R	Writable CD-ROM (one that can be recorded once).
CD-RW	Rewritable CD-ROM (one on which information can be recorded, erased, and re-recorded). Or, the drive that can write on writable or rewritable CD-ROMs.

central processing unit *See* **CPU**.

certificate Cryptographic data that can identify one computer or user to another. *See also* **digital ID**.

certificate authority Organization that issues certificates.

certificate file File containing a certificate (digital ID), usually with the extension .cer.

chat Online communication in real time (minimal delay between when you send a message and when the recipient receives it). Windows XP comes with Windows Messenger and NetMeeting.

check box Box onscreen that can either be blank or contain a check mark (or X), usually appearing in a dialog box.

checkpoint *See* **restore point**.

Classic logon screen Windows Me/9x-style screen that appears on systems in which multiple user accounts are set up. The alternative is the Windows XP-style Welcome screen.

ClearType Font-rendering system designed for use on LCD (flat-panel) screens.

CLI *See* **Command Line Interface** or **Command Prompt**.

client Program or computer that uses resources on a network. In Windows, a setting that identifies the type of network to which you are attaching the computer. Remote Desktop enables someone at a client computer to use a server computer.

client-server network Network on which server computers provide resources for the rest of the network, and client computers use only these resources.

clip Video, audio, or graphics file that is part of a **collection** in Windows Movie Maker.

Clipboard Temporary storage space in memory for storing cut-and-paste information.

clipboard file File saved by Clipboard Viewer, with the extension .clp.

CMOS setup *See* **BIOS setup**.

coaxial cable or **coax** Type of cable used to connect computers in a bus topology LAN.

codec System for audio or video compression and decompression.

collection   Group of video, graphic, and audio files to include in a movie in Windows Movie Maker.

color profile   System for precisely representing colors on your monitor and printer.

COM file   Executable file, with the file extension .com.

COM1, COM2, COM3, COM4, or com port   *See* **serial port**.

command button   Button you can click to perform a command.

command line   Command that you type at the DOS prompt, optionally followed by additional information.

command-line interface (CLI) or command prompt window   Program that simulates DOS, displaying a DOS prompt and running DOS programs and commands.

compatibility mode   Emulation of a previous version of Windows (2000, NT 4.0, Me, 98, or 95) so that an older program can run correctly.

compressed file   Attribute available only for files stored in NTFS partitions, causing Windows to store the file in a compressed format.

compressed folder   ZIP (compressed) file containing other files. If you have the Compressed Folders feature installed, ZIP files appear as folders in Windows Explorer.

connection   *See* dial-up connection.

contact   List of names and addresses in the Address Book.

container file   In OLE, a file that contains a link to an object in another file or that contains an embedded object from another file.

context menu   *See* **shortcut menu**.

control character   Character you type by holding down the CTRL key while pressing another key.

cookie   Small (at most 4KB) file that a Web server can store on your machine and read later.

copying   As part of cut-and-paste, copying selected information from its current location and storing it (temporarily) on the Clipboard.

counter log   Log file that reports system statistics at regular intervals.

CPU   Central processing unit, a computer chip that executes the instructions in programs. Windows XP requires a Pentium III, a compatible CPU, or a faster CPU.

crash Failure in which a program stops running.

crossover cable Category-5 cable that connects two computers' network interface cards, creating a two-computer LAN without a hub.

CSLIP Compressed Serial Line Internet Protocol, a communications protocol for computers connected to the Internet. CSLIP has been superceded by PPP.

cursor Screen element (usually a blinking vertical bar) that indicates where the text you type will be inserted. Not to be confused with the **mouse pointer**.

cut-and-paste Feature of Windows that lets you select information from one file and move or copy it to another file (or another location in the same file).

cutting Removing selected information from its current location and storing it (temporarily) on the Clipboard.

cycle Process in which the CPU completes one string of instructions.

data bits How many bits of information are included in each byte sent (usually eight).

DB-15 Standard display connector.

DB-25 Standard parallel or serial connector. *See* **parallel port** or **serial port**.

DB-9 Standard nine-pin serial connector. *See* **serial port**.

DDE Dynamic Data Exchange, a way for Windows programs to exchange information.

DDE action DDE command that defines how data moves to or from files of a specified type.

default The information or mode that a program uses unless you specify otherwise.

deferred printing Queuing print jobs on a computer without a printer to be printed when you connect a printer to your computer later.

defragmenting Moving the contents of files around on your hard disk so that each file is stored as one big chunk, speeding up access to the file.

desktop Work area on your screen on which you see your programs. The desktop can contain windows, icons, and the taskbar.

desktop theme Set of desktop background, cursor, font, and color settings to dress up your desktop.

device driver *See* **driver**.

DHCP Dynamic Host Configuration Protocol, a system that assigns IP addresses for a LAN.

DHCP server Computer running DHCP software that assigns IP addresses to other computers on a network. Internet Connection Sharing includes a DHCP server.

dialing location Location from which you place phone calls. You can tell Windows the area code and other information about the phone line at that location.

dialog box Type of window that allows you to change settings or give commands in a program. Most dialog boxes include OK and Cancel buttons.

dial-up modem Device that connects to your computer to a regular dial-up phone line.

dial-up connection Network connection that uses a dial-up telephone line to connect to the Internet or to another computer.

digital ID File containing encryption and digital identification information that you can use to digitally sign or encrypt e-mail and newsgroup messages in Outlook Express. *See also* **certificate**.

digital signature Information added to the end of an e-mail message to prove who sent it.

digitally signed message E-mail message that has been encrypted with a digital ID to prove who sent it.

direct network connection Connecting two computers with a serial cable to allow file or printing sharing. Called Direct Cable Connection (DCC) in previous versions of Windows.

direct memory access *See* **DMA**.

directory *See* **folder**.

directory server Computer that stores the addresses of people who use NetMeeting.

directory service Searchable listing of names, e-mail addresses, and other information about people.

DirectX Enhanced video system built into Windows.

disk controller Adapter card that connects a hard disk to your computer.

display properties Properties of your display and your Windows desktop.

distribution file *See* **installation file**.

DLL file Dynamic link library file, an executable file with the file extension .dll invoked from a running program.

DMA Direct memory access, a system board facility used by a few medium-speed devices to communicate with the **CPU**.

DNS or **DNS server** *See* **domain name server**.

DOC file Document file, with the file extension .doc. DOC files are usually (but not always) created by Microsoft Word or a compatible program.

docking station Hardware device into which you plug a laptop to provide connections to a monitor, keyboard, mouse, local area network, and/or additional PC Card slots.

domain On a LAN, a group of computers administered by one server. On the Internet, a two-part name used for one or more Internet hosts (for example, gurus.com).

domain-based network Server-based network, hosted on a Windows .NET Server, 2000 Server, or NT system. Domains provide network security that is controlled by the server, rather than by each computer on the network.

domain name Alphanumeric name of a computer or group of computers on the Internet; for example, **gurus.com**.

domain name server (DNS) Computer on the Internet that translates between Internet domain names and numeric IP addresses. You can specify two DNSs for an Internet connection: a primary server and a secondary server.

DOS Disk Operating System, the operating system on which Windows runs. Sometimes called **MS-DOS**.

DOS name Filename used by DOS programs and early Windows programs, limited to an eight-character name and a three-character extension.

DOS prompt Prompt that DOS displays when it is waiting for you to type a command.

DOS Virtual Machine (VM) Emulation program that allows DOS programs to run under Windows XP.

double-click speed Time period within which the two clicks of a double-click must occur, with no intervening mouse motion.

double-click style Desktop mode in which clicking an icon or filename twice runs the program or opens the file. To select the icon or filename without running or opening it, click it once.

download   Transfer a file from the Internet, other network, or mainframe to a PC.

downloaded object security   Security for information you download from the Internet.

drag-and-drop   Method of moving or copying information from one file to another, or to another location in the same file.

drive letter   Letter that identifies a disk drive, other storage device, or a partition of a drive.

driver   Or device driver. Software that allows Windows to communicate with a device, such as a display or printer.

drop-down menu   Menu that appears when you click a command on a menu bar.

DSL   Digital Subscriber Line (or Loop), an all-digital telephone line that uses the "last mile" of copper line between your computer and the central phone company offices. Actually a family of types of lines, including ADSL, HDSL, SDSL, and others.

DSL modem   Device that connects a computer (usually via a network interface card) to a DSL phone line.

DSP   Digital signal processor, a specialized computer chip for compressing video signals.

dual-boot installation   Computer that can be started in either of two operating systems; for example, Windows XP and Windows 98, or Windows XP and Linux.

DVD   Digital versatile disk or digital video disk, a digital disk that can contain video material.

DWORD   Type of Registry entry that contains a numeric value (specifically, a four-byte hexidecimal number).

dynamic addressing   System that assigns an address to a computer when the computer connects to the network. Each time the computer connects, it may get a different address. Windows supports to forms of dynamic addressing, **Automatic private IP addressing** and **DHCP**.

Dynamic Data Exchange   *See* **DDE**.

dynamic disk   Disk in which the volumes can be managed dynamically (on the fly).

Dynamic Host Configuration Protocol   *See* **DHCP**.

dynamic link library file *See* **DLL file**.

dynamic volume *See* **dynamic disk**.

ECMAScript *See* **JavaScript**.

ECP Extended Capabilities Port, a bi-directional parallel port used mainly by printers and scanners.

EIDE *See* **IDE**.

EISA Enhanced or Extended Industry Standard Architecture, an improved version of ISA, now superceded by PCI.

embedding In OLE, storing an object of one type file a file of another type, optionally maintaining linkage from the second file to the file that originally contained the object, for example, an Excel spreadsheet embedded in a Word Perfect document.

EML File extension, used for e-mail messages, that is used by the Outlook Express Inbox Assistant to reply to messages automatically.

EMS *See* **expanded memory**.

environment variable Variable used by DOS and early versions of Windows to store configuration information.

EPP (Enhanced Parallel Port) Bi-directional parallel port used mainly by devices other than printers.

Ethernet Type of local area network communication, including standards for cabling and network cards.

event Windows operation that can trigger a sound or a log entry. For example, exiting a program is an event.

executable or **EXE file** Program file, with the file extension .exe.

expanded memory (EMS) Memory management system that allowed DOS programs to use more than 640KB of memory.

expansion slot Slot inside a computer into which you can insert an adapter card.

Explorer One of two programs that come with Windows: Internet Explorer (a Web browser) or Windows Explorer (a file management utility).

Explorer window Window displayed by the Windows Explorer program.

extended memory specification (XMS) Memory management system that allowed DOS programs to use more than 640KB of memory.

extended partition Or Extended DOS partition. Section of a hard disk that stores one or more **logical drives**.

extension Last part of a filename, attached to the rest of the filename by a period (.). Extensions are usually three letters long and indicate the **file type**. For example, a file named Example.txt has the extension .txt.

external modem Modem that connects to your computer's serial port by a serial cable.

extracting Copying a file from a compressed folder or ZIP file and decompressing it as you copy it.

FAQ Frequently asked questions (and their answers).

Fast Ethernet 100Mbps Ethernet.

Fast User Switching Feature that allows Windows to switch from one user account to another, leaving the first user's programs running.

FAT *See* **file allocation table**.

FAT or FAT16 File system used in all versions of DOS since DOS 2.0, as well as Windows. FAT16 is also supported in Windows for disks up to 2GB.

FAT32 File system supported by Windows Me/9*x*, 2000, and XP, in which data is stored more efficiently than FAT16 on disks larger than 500MB. However FAT32 doesn't support file- or folder-level security.

Favorites Files, folders, Web pages, and programs to which you want easy access. Windows stores shortcuts to Favorites in your Favorites folder and displays them on the Favorites menu.

file Collection of information that has a name and is stored on a disk—for example, a document, spreadsheet, or program component.

file address Address of a file on your computer or on a network to which your computer is attached, for example, C:\My Documents\ Budgets\2003 Draft.xls. Also called a *path* or *pathname*.

file allocation table Or FAT. Table that stores information about each sector in a FAT16 or FAT32 partition.

file association Which program you use to open, edit, or print a specified type of file.

file attachment *See* **attached file**.

file icon Icon that represents a file.

filename Name given to a file. The last part of a filename, after the last period, is the **extension**.

file system Information that keeps track of which files are stored where in a partition on a disk. Windows XP supports **FAT, FAT32,** and **NTFS** partitions.

File Transfer Protocol *See* **FTP.**

file type Type of information contained in a file, indicated by the extension portion of the filename.

filter *See* **message rule.**

firewall Gateway program that provides security features when translating between a LAN and the Internet. A firewall includes or works with a **proxy server.** Windows XP comes with the Internet Connection Firewall.

FireWire Standard type of connector introduced on Macintosh computers, and also available on many PCs. Also known as *IEEE 1394* or Sony *i.Link.*

fixed spacing Typeface design in which all letters in the typeface are the same width.

floppy disk Also called a *diskette,* a removable disk that stores up to 2.8MB, depending on the capacity of the disk drive.

flow control System that controls the flow of data between your modem and your computer.

folder Special kind of file that contains a list of other files. Folders can contain other folders.

folder hierarchy *See* **folder tree.**

folder icon Icon that represents a folder; it looks like a manila folder.

folder list *See* **folder tree.**

folder template Predefined set of properties that you can choose to apply to a folder.

folder tree Diagram showing which folders are contained in which other folders. Also called a *folder hierarchy, tree view,* or *folder list.*

Folder window *See* **Explorer window.**

font All the characters in a typeface of a given size and style. Commonly but incorrectly used to mean **typeface.**

font substitution To speed up printing, using built-in printer fonts where possible for similar TrueType fonts.

formatting Writing the file system on a disk or partition of a disk.

fragmentation Storage of files in discontinuous groups of sectors on your disk. When too many files are split up into too many groups of sectors, disk performance slows down, and you should defragment the disk.

freeware Programs that are entirely free to use and frequently downloadable from the Internet.

FTP File Transfer Protocol, a method for transferring files over the Internet. The built-in Windows program that transfers files by using FTP is called Ftp.

FTP client Program that lets you upload files to, or download files from, an FTP server. Windows comes with the Ftp program. Internet Explorer and Netscape can also act as FTP clients.

FTP server Internet host computer that acts as a file archive, allowing other computers to upload or download files by using FTP.

full control Access type that allows other people to read from or write to a shared resource.

full backup Complete backup of all files and folders; also called a *baseline backup*.

game controller Device that allows you to play arcade-style games on your computer.

gateway Device or program that connects your LAN to the Internet (or one network to another network), passing messages between the computers on the LAN and computers on the Internet. A gateway usually includes a **proxy server** or a **network address translation (NAT)** program.

GIF file File in Graphics Information Format, a popular format for graphics files that is widely used in Web pages. GIF files have the extension .gif.

Gigabit Ethernet 1Gbps Ethernet.

graphical user interface (GUI) Software design that allows you to control your computer by using a mouse, windows, and icons.

group Category of which user accounts can be members. Different groups have different rights to perform tasks or open folders and files. Groups can be local (stored on your own computer) or domain (stored on a Windows XP server).

guest account User account that does not allow the user to install software; create, edit, or delete other user accounts; or the management tools. Windows comes with one guest account, called Guest.

guest computer Computer that uses shared resources from other computers over a LAN or direct network connection.

GUI *See* **graphical user interface**.

hang When a program or the Windows system stops responding to input from the keyboard or mouse.

hard disk Disk that is sealed into its disk drive.

hardware profile Description of your computer's hardware resources.

header Lines at the top of an e-mail message that contain the address, return address, date, and other information about the message, not including the **body** (text) of the message.

hibernate Method of shutting down Windows that saves the state of your desktop, so that when you start Windows again, the same windows and programs are open.

hidden file File whose Hidden attribute is selected so that the file doesn't appear in Windows Explorer.

hidden partition Partitions whose file system Windows XP can't read, and which therefore is inaccessible from Windows XP. PartitionMagic and other third-party disk utilities can mark partitions as hidden.

hierarchical file system System of storing files on disks, in which files are stored in folders and folders can contain other folders.

History List of recently displayed Web pages, maintained by a browser.

hive Group of Registry entries (similar to a folder). Each subtree of the directory-like structure of the Registry is one hive, and is stored in a separate file.

home folder Similar to the **My Documents** folder, in Windows 2000 and NT. Most programs store files in the My Documents folder rather than the home folder.

home page Main (or starting) page of a Web site. Also used to refer to a browser's **start page**.

HomeRF Standard, with **IEEE 802.11b**, for wireless LAN communications.

host address On the Internet, address of a host computer.

host computer Computer that has the resources to be shared over a LAN, direct network connection, or the Internet.

hot docking Docking or undocking a laptop without turning it off.

hot swapping   Installing or uninstalling a piece of hardware while the computer is turned on.

hover color   Color a Web page link turns when the mouse pointer is on it.

HSV   Numerical way of describing a color by its hue, saturation, and luminescence value.

HT file   HyperTerminal connection file, with extension .ht.

HTML   Hypertext Markup Language, the language in which Web pages are written. You can create files in HTML by using a Web page editor.

HTML mail or **HTML messages**   E-mail messages formatted using HTML.

HTTP   Hypertext Transfer Protocol, the language that Web browsers and Web servers use to communicate with each other.

HTTPS   Secure version of HTTP, the protocol with which Web browsers communicate with Web servers.

hub   Device to which all other computers connect in a star topology LAN.

hyperlink   *See* **link**.

hypertext   Interlinked text.

Hypertext Markup Language   *See* **HTML**.

Hypertext Transfer Protocol   *See* **HTTP**.

I/O   Input and output.

I/O address   Hexadecimal number that the CPU uses to identify a device.

icon   Little picture on your screen that responds with an action when you point to it with the mouse, single-click it, or double-click it.

ICS client   Computer on a LAN that uses an ICS server to share a connection to the Internet.

ICS server   Computer running the Internet Connection Sharing (ICS) proxy server software and serving as a gateway from a LAN to the Internet.

IDE   Integrated Drive Electronics, a standard type of disk connection, used for hard disks and CD-ROM drives. EIDE (or ATA 2) is an enhanced version of IDE.

identity In Address Book, user name that enables each user of the computer to maintain a separate list of address.

IEEE 1394 *See* **FireWire**.

IEEE 802.11b Standard for wireless LAN communications. *Wi-Fi* and *HomeRF* are both based on the IEEE 802.11b standard.

i.Link *See* **FireWire**.

IMAP Internet Message Access Protocol, used for storing and delivering Internet e-mail.

IMAP server *See* **incoming mail server**.

incoming connection Network connection that allows another computer to connect to your computer by phone (dial-up), over a cable between the two computers (direct), or over the Internet (VPN).

incoming mail server Internet host computer running a server program that stores your mail messages until you download them into your e-mail program or read them using a e-mail Web site. The two common types of incoming mail servers use the **POP** and **IMAP** protocols.

incremental backup Backup of only those files that are new or have changed since the last backup.

INI or **initialization file** File that contains configuration information used when a program loads, with the extension .ini.

installation file File that contains all the files required for a program to run, along with an installation program.

internal modem Modem on an adapter board inside your computer.

Internet account Account with an Internet service provider (**ISP**) that allows you to connect your computer to the Internet, including dial-up, DSL, ISDN, and cable Internet accounts.

Internet address *See* **URL**.

Internet Connection Firewall Firewall program built into Windows XP.

Internet Message Access Protocol *See* **IMAP**.

Internet Protocol address *See* **IP address**.

Internet service provider *See* **ISP**.

Internet shortcut   File that acts as a placeholder for a Web page, stored with the extension .url.

interrupt   Channel that a device can use to alert the CPU that the device needs attention. Also called **IRQ**.

intranet   Network installed within an organization, with a Web server that allows only people within the organization to view Web pages from that server.

IP address   Internet protocol address, the numerical address of a computer connected to the Internet.

IPX/SPX   Internetwork Packet Exchange/Sequenced Packet Exchange, a protocol used primarily in the Novell NetWare operating system.

IRQ   *See* **interrupt**.

ISA   Industry Standard Architecture, an older standard type of expansion slot or card.

ISDN   Integrated Services Digital Network, a phone line that enables your computer to connect to another computer digitally.

ISDN terminal adapter, ISDN TA, or **ISDN modem**   Device that connects your computer to an ISDN line (instead of a modem).

ISP   Internet service provider, an organization that provides dial-in Internet accounts, usually PPP, CSLIP, or SLIP accounts, but sometimes UNIX shell accounts.

Java   Language for writing applets that can be sent over the Web so that they can be executed by your computer.

JavaScript   Language often used for extending HTML by embedding scripts in Web pages. Microsoft's version is called *JScript*. The international standard version is called *ECMAscript*. JavaScript scripts are also stored in files with the extension .js.

Jaz disk   Removable disk that stores about 1GB.

joystick   Device that enables you to play arcade-style games on your computer.

JPEG or **JPG file**   File in the Joint Photographic Experts Group graphics format, a format well suited for storing scanned photographs and widely used in Web pages. JPEG files have the extension .jpg or .jpeg.

JS file   File containing a JavaScript script.

JScript   *See* **JavaScript**.

junction point *See* **mount point**.

key Component in the Registry; a key contain values and other keys. For information about encryption, *see* **private key**; **public key**.

key ring Collection of cryptography data that you need for sending secure e-mail.

LAN *See* **local area network**.

landscape Print orientation in which lines of print are parallel to the long side of the paper.

LDAP Lightweight Directory Access Protocol, a standard way for programs to search a directory service.

legacy program Program written to work with an older version of Windows or with DOS.

library Backup device (such as a tape drive) and the media that it writes on (such as tapes).

limited account Type of user account that does not enable the user to install software; create, edit, or delete other users' accounts.

link Word, phrase, or picture that you can click to display another related Web page (or another page of the same Web page). Also called *hyperlink*.

linking In OLE, storing a link in one file that links to an object in another file.

list box Box that contains a list of options, one of which is selected, usually appearing on a dialog box.

local File or device that is stored on or attached to the computer you are using (the **local computer**), rather than being stored on or attached to a computer connected to your computer by a network.

local area network (LAN) Network that connects computers that are in the same building or campus, usually with cables.

local computer Your own computer, rather than a **remote computer** connected to your computer over a network.

local disk Disk drive connected to your own computer (as opposed to a **network disk**).

local group Group stored on your own computer. User accounts can be members.

local printer Printer attached to your own computer.

lockout   *See* **account lockout**.

logical drive   Partition that is stored within an **extended partition**.

logon script   File that specifies what prompts to wait for and what to type in response when logging in to an Internet account or LAN.

Luna   Code name for the new screen design that comes with Windows. The actual name of the Luna desktop theme is *Windows XP*.

lurking   Reading the messages in a newsgroup or mailing list without posting messages of your own. Entirely respectable.

mail client   Program for sending and receiving e-mail messages, such as Outlook Express. Informally called an *e-mail program*.

mail rule   *See* **message rule**.

mail server   Computer that handles incoming or outgoing e-mail.

mailbox   Location on your mail server where your e-mail is stored until you retrieve it using your mail client (such as Outlook Express).

mailing list   E-mail-based discussion group.

manifest   File that describes how an application is to appear while using the Luna interface(Windows XP theme).

manual checkpoint   "Snapshot" of your Windows and program files created by the System Restore program at your command.

mapping   Assigning a drive letter to a network drive on another computer.

Master File Table   Table that stores information about each sector in an NTFS partition.

maximized window   Window that takes up the entire screen or is running at its maximum window size.

media pool   Category of backup tape (or other media managed by the Removable Storage service), such as Backup, Free, or Import.

memory   Temporary storage your computer uses for the programs you are running and the files you currently have open. Also called **RAM**.

memory address   Number that uniquely identifies one piece of memory storage.

menu   List of commands from which you can choose. *See* **drop-down menu; menu bar; pull-down menu; shortcut menu**.

menu bar   Row of one-word commands that appears along the top of a window, just below the title bar.

message rule Rule that specifies a kind of message and a type of action to take when such a message arrives in your e-mail program.

MIDI Musical Instrument Digital Interface, a standard for digital musical instruments and the computer hardware and software that works with them.

MIME Multipurpose Internet Mail Extensions, the most widely used method of including nontext information, such as attached files, in e-mail messages. *See also* **S/MIME**.

minimized window Window that is not displayed, so that only the window's button on the taskbar appears on the screen.

minus box Small minus sign in a box that appears to the left of an item in a list. Click the minus box to hide its subitems.

mirrored volume Volume in which the data is stored redundantly on two or more disks, so that if one disk failed, the information is available on another.

modem Device that connects to your computer to a phone line.

modifier keys Keys that you hold down while pressing another key: SHIFT, CTRL, and ALT.

motherboard *See* **system board**.

mount point Pathname to which a partition or disk drive has been assigned (mounted).

mounting Assigning a pathname to a partition or disk drive.

mouse pointer Indicator on the screen that shows where the mouse is pointing. Also called the *pointer* or (incorrectly) the **cursor**.

MPEG or MPG Moving Picture Experts Group format, a video file format based on the **JPEG** graphics file format.

MS-DOS Microsoft Disk Operating System, also called **DOS**.

multiboot Or dual-boot. Computer with two or more operating systems installed. You choose which operating to boot (run).

multilink System that allows a single dial-up connection to use multiple modems and phone lines for greater speed.

multitasking Running multiple tasks at the same time. Windows is a multitasking operating system, because it can run many tasks (programs) simultaneously.

NAT *See* **Network address translation**.

navigating   Displaying the contents of one folder after another, usually when looking for a folder or file. In your browser, moving from one Web page to another.

NetBEUI   NetBIOS Extended User Interface, the network protocol used primarily by Microsoft in its older versions of Windows.

Network address translation (NAT)   Program that translates between the IP addresses on a LAN and those on the Internet. Can be part of a **proxy server** or **firewall.** Internet Connection Sharing includes a NAT program.

network adapter   *See* **network interface card.**

network connection   Configuration information for connection to another computer via a dial-up phone line, DSL line, cable, infrared, or other device. Network connections are used mainly for LANs and Internet accounts.

network disk or **network drive**   Disk drive (or partition of a disk drive) connected to a computer that your computer can access over a network (as opposed to a **local disk**). Also called a **shared disk** or **shared drive**.

network interface card (NIC)   Adapter that connects a computer to a local area network.

network operating system (NOS)   Operating system that includes support for a client-server local area network.

network printer   Printer that is attached to a computer on a local area network and can be used by other computers on the network.

network shortcut   Entry in the My Network Places folder.

news account   Name of the news server to use when reading and posting to Usenet newsgroups.

newsgroup   Discussion group that is part of Usenet. Windows comes with Outlook Express, which lets you read and post messages to newsgroups.

newsreader or **newsreading program**   Program for reading and posting to newsgroups. Windows comes with Outlook Express, which is both a mail client and a newsreader.

NIC   *See* **network interface card**.

NNTP   Net News Transfer Protocol, the protocol used by Usenet for distributing newsgroup articles.

nonroutable protocol   Network protocol that can be used only on a simple network where routing devices are not used.

NOS *See* **network operating system**.

notification area The right end of the taskbar (what used to be called the system tray), with a digital clock and special icons for running programs.

NTFS Windows NT/2000 File System, the file system used by Windows 2000, NT, and XP; not supported by Windows Me, 9x, or older versions of Windows or DOS. NTFS enables Windows to provide file- and folder-level security.

NTFS compressed folder Folder stored in an NTFS partition with its Compress Contents To Save Disk Space attribute selected. *See also* **compressed folder**.

null-modem cable Serial cable used to connect two computers in a direct cable connection (not to connect a computer to a modem).

object In OLE, a piece of information from a file; you can link or embed an object in a different file.

Object Linking and Embedding *See* **OLE**.

offline Not connected to any network or computer.

offline files Windows feature that allows you to use network files or files stored on another computer when you are not connected to the network or the other computer.

OLE Object Linking and Embedding, a method of linking and combining information from files created by different applications.

on top Window that appears "above" other windows on the desktop, obscuring other windows where they overlap. The active window appears on top.

online help Helpful information stored on your computer that you can look at by using the Help And Support window.

online service Commercial service that allows you to connect to and access their proprietary information system (for example, America Online).

operating system (OS) Program that manages your entire computer system, including its screen, keyboard, disk drives, memory, and central processor. Windows XP is an operating system.

outgoing mail server Internet host computer running a server program that accepts e-mail messages for distributing to the Internet.

package or In OLE, a piece of information from a file that you have linked
packaged object or embedded in a different file.

packet Chunk of information transmitted on a network or other
communications line.

pane Section of a window.

parallel port Connector on your computer used for parallel
communications. You connect most printers to the parallel
port.

parity Simple method of error detection in which the value of one bit
is calculated from the values of a group of bits.

partition Logical section of a hard disk. Windows XP can read and write
NTFS, FAT32, and FAT partitions.

password hint Word or phrase used to remind you of your password if you
forget it, but that doesn't give the password away to anyone else.

Password Policy Settings that control whether user accounts need passwords,
how complex they need to be, and how often people have to
change them.

password reset disk Floppy disk that you can use if you forget your user account
password.

pasting Copying the information on the Clipboard to the location of
the cursor in the active application.

path or **pathname** *See* **file address**.

payload Infectious part of a virus or worm program.

PC Card Credit-card-sized adapter cards used mainly in laptops. They
fit in PC Card slots. Formerly called PCMCIA.

PC file transfer *See* **null-modem cable**.
cable

PCI Peripheral Connect Interface, a standard type of expansion slot
or card that fits into a PCI slot.

PCMCIA *See* **PC Card**.

PCX file Graphics file with extension .pcx.

peer-to-peer network Network on which all computers can function as both clients
and servers.

peripheral Hardware device that is attached to your computer, such as a
printer or modem.

Peripheral Connect Interface *See* **PCI**.

permission Security setting that controls what a user or group of users can do with a file, folder, printer, shared folder, or registry key. On local area networks, control users and groups throughout the network.

personal certificate Cryptographic information that identifies you when viewing Web sites or sending e-mail. Stored in files with the extension .pfx.

PGP Pretty Good Privacy, a method of sending secure e-mail.

Personalized Menus Start menu, Programs menu, and their submenus, with less frequently used commands omitted.

PIF file Program Information File with the extension .pif, containing configuration information for a DOS program.

ping Test message sent to find out whether another system will respond. Ping is also the name of a program that sends pings on the Internet; Windows comes with a Ping program.

pinned Displayed at the top of the left side of the Start menu. You can pin a program to the Start menu, so it always appears there.

pixel Single dot that can take on any color on the screen or in a graphics file.

pixelated image Graphics image in which the rectangular dots are visible.

playlist List of audio or video tracks in the order in which you want to play them.

Plug and Play Type of device that can communicate with Windows to provide its own configuration information.

plug-in Program that "plugs in" to your browser program, adding new features to the browser.

plus box Small plus sign in a box that appears to the left of an item in a list, to show that the item contains subitems.

pointer scheme Set of shapes that the mouse pointer assumes.

pointer *See* **mouse pointer**.

pointer trail Shadowy trail left behind the moving mouse pointer.

Point-to-Point Protocol *See* **PPP**.

Point-to-Point Tunneling Protocol (PPTP) Communications protocol used by Virtual Private Networking.

POP or **POP 3** Post Office Protocol 3, a program on a mail server that stores your incoming e-mail until you retrieve it by using Outlook Express or another mail client.

POP server *See* **incoming mail server.**

port Connector on your computer to which you can connect a cable. *See* **parallel port; serial port, USB port.** On the Internet, ports are numbered addresses on a computer used for specific types of communication (for example, 80 for Web pages).

port replicator Docking station that contains only additional ports.

portrait Print orientation in which lines of print are parallel to the short side of the paper.

Post Office Protocol *See* POP.

power management Settings that automatically turn off computer components to save electricity.

power scheme Group of settings that define when and if Windows should turn off the power to parts of your computer.

PPP Point-to-Point Protocol, a communications protocol for computers connected to the Internet by telephone lines.

PPP account Internet account that uses the PPP communications protocol; the most popular kind of Internet account.

PPPoE PPP over Ethernet, a communications protocol used by many DSL and cable Internet accounts between your computer and the ISP. Other ISPs use PPPoA (PPP over ATM).

PPTP *See* **Point-to-Point Tunneling Protocol.**

preference Setting or option that controls the way you want a program to work.

Pretty Good Privacy *See* PGP.

primary DNS *See* **domain name server.**

primary partition Or Primary DOS partition. Section of a hard disk that stores the main DOS or Windows file system.

print job Document sent to a printer.

print server Computer to which a shared printer is attached.

printer driver Printer control program.

printer port *See* **parallel port.**

private key One of a pair of cryptographic keys: you use your private key to decode messages you receive that were encoded with your **public key** and to encode messages you want to sign.

process *See* **task**.

profile Group of settings stored with a name. *See* **color profile**; **hardware profile**; **user account**.

program file File containing a program, usually with the extension .exe or .com.

project In Windows Movie Maker, file that contains all the graphic, video, and audio files to be used to make a movie, with filename extension .mswmm.

property Setting that affects how an object works. You can set the properties of many objects by right-clicking the object, choosing Properties from the menu that appears, and changing the settings on the resulting Properties dialog box.

proportional spacing Typeface design in which letters in the typeface are different widths.

protocol Setting that identifies the way information is passed between computers on the network.

proxy server Gateway program that provides caching, logging, and other service when translating between a LAN and the Internet.

PS/2 port Standard keyboard or mouse connector.

public key One of a pair of cryptographic keys: you use a person's public key to encode a message so that it can be decoded only with the person's **private key** and to verify signed messages.

public-key cryptography Cryptography system that uses pairs of keys, one public and one private to the key's owner. Two forms are commonly used: PGP and S/MIME.

pull-down menu Box onscreen with a downward-pointing triangle button at its right end, usually appearing in a dialog box.

QT file QuickTime video file, with the extension .qt.

queue List of tasks waiting to be done. For example, a print queue is a list of print jobs waiting to be printed.

QuickTime Video file format with file extension .qt.

RA File extension (.ra) used for RealAudio, a streaming audio file format.

radio button One of a group of round buttons that can either be blank or contain a dot, usually appearing in a dialog box.

RAID Redundant Array of Independent Disks, in which data is stored on multiple fault tolerant disks.

RAID-5 volume Volume in which the data is stored on three or more disks in alternating stripes, so that retrieval speed isn't limited to the speed of one disk (a type of **striped volume**).

RAM Random Access Memory, the memory chips used for the short-term memory of a computer. Also a file extension (.ram) used for RealAudio files.

read-only file File or folder whose Read-Only attribute is selected, so that the file cannot be accidentally deleted or modified. Shared disks and folders can be designated read-only.

real-time chat *See* **chat**.

Recycle Bin Special folder in which Windows stores files and folders you have recently deleted.

refresh Redisplay a window using updated information.

REG file *See* **registration file**.

regional settings Windows settings that control how numbers, dates, times, and currency amounts appear and what languages are installed.

registered file types *See* **file association**.

registration file File with the extension .reg, created by exporting part or all of the Registry.

Registry File in which Windows stores a database of program and system setup information.

remote access server Computer to which you can connect remotely, by dialing in from another computer or by connecting over the Internet, and which allows the remote computer to use its resources.

remote administration Facility in Windows XP Professional, 2000, and NT (but not Windows XP Home Edition) that allows someone (usually a network administrator) at one computer to change the Windows settings on another computer. For information, see *Windows .NET Server: The Complete Reference*, by Kathy Ivens, published by Osborne/McGraw-Hill.

remote computer Computer attached to the computer you are using over a local area network, Internet, or other network.

remote node Computer that is attached to a LAN via a dial-up connection.

remote storage Storage device that stores files that are used infrequently. Windows XP Home Edition and Professional do not include the Remote Storage service that comes with Windows 2002 Server.

removable disk Disk that can be removed from its disk drive (unlike a hard disk). Floppy disks and Zip disks are removable.

repartitioning Change the layout of partitions on a hard disk.

repeat delay Delay between starting to hold down a key and when the key begins repeating.

repeat rate How fast a key repeats once it starts repeating.

resolution Number of pixels (dots) your screen can display, expressed by a vertical and horizontal count. Standard screen resolutions include 640 × 480 (640 dots across and 480 dots high), 800 × 600, 1024 × 768, 1152 × 864, and 1600 × 1200.

resource Hardware, software, or data that can be shared by users of a network. *See also* **system resources**.

restore point "Snapshot" of your Windows and program files, stored by the System Restore program.

restored window Window that appears within window borders—not maximized or minimized.

return receipt request Tag attached to an e-mail message that requests a receipt so that the sender knows that the recipient has opened the message.

RGB Numerical way of describing a color by its red, green, and blue components.

Rich Text Format *See* **RTF file**.

right-clicking Clicking with the right mouse button (unless you have configured your mouse to swap the functions of the buttons).

right Security setting for groups of user accounts that allow members of that group to perform system-wide tasks (such as installing programs or shutting down Windows). *See also* **permission**.

RJ-11 jack U.S. standard telephone connector.

RJ-45 connector Connector used to connect network interface cards to Category-5 cables in a star topology LAN.

RMI File extension (.rmi) used for MIDI-format music files.

roaming profile User account profile that is stored on the server rather than on the user's computer. Roaming profiles are available only on domain-based networks.

root, root folder, or   Main or top-level folder (or directory) in a hierarchical file
root directory   system.

router   Specialized computer used to connect multiple segments of
networks; for example, to connect a local area network to the
Internet.

RTF file   Rich Text Format, a portable format for storing formatted
documents, defined by Microsoft. WordPad can read and
write RTF files, which have the extension .rtf.

RV   File extension (.rv) for RealVideo, a streaming video file
format.

S/MIME   Standard security system used by Outlook Express and other
mail programs to send e-mail securely. *See* **MIME**.

saved search   Search criteria saved in a file with extension .fnd. You use the
Start | Find | Files Or Folders command to rerun the search.

scanner   Device that digitizes pictures (or anything on paper) for use by
your computer.

scheme   Group of settings, stored with a name so that you can easily
switch from one group of settings to another (similar to a
profile). *See* **color scheme**; **pointer scheme**; **power scheme**;
sound scheme.

scrap   OLE object that has been left on the desktop or in a folder.

screen saver   Program that displays an image, frequently one that moves, on
your desktop when you are not using the computer.

screen shot   Picture of what is on the screen.

script   Program written using a scripting language such as **JavaScript**
or VBScript. *See also* **batch file**; **logon script**.

scroll bar   Vertical or horizontal bar running along the right side or
bottom of a window allowing you to scroll the information
displayed in the window.

SCSI   Small Computer System Interface, a standard for connecting
peripherals to computers. SCSI devices include hard disks,
CD-ROMs, tapes, and scanners.

SCSI controller   Adapter board for connecting SCSI devices to a computer.

SCSI device number   Unique number of the SCSI device connected to one SCSI
controller.

secondary DNS   *See* **domain name server**.

sector   Physical block of storage on a disk.

secure e-mail E-mail that has been encoded so that only the intended recipient can read it.

secure receipt Return receipt for a digitally signed e-mail message.

Secure Sockets Layer *See* **SSL**.

secure server Web server that supports SSL (Secure Sockets Layer) to encrypt data sent between the server and your computer. Pages loaded from a secure server have URLs beginning with https://.

selective startup Windows startup mode in which you choose which initialization files to process.

serial port Connector on your computer that is used for serial communication. You connect serial mice, external modems, and serial printers to a serial port.

server Program or computer that provides resources that others can use on a network. Remote Desktop enables someone at a client computer to use a server computer.

service Setting that allows you to share a computer's resources on a network. Also, a background program that is part of Windows.

Service Profile Identifier *See* **SPID**.

setup program Installation program, such as the Setup program that comes with Windows.

share name Name by which a shared drive, folder, or printer can be referred to by other users on a LAN.

shared disk or **shared drive** Disk that is shared with other users on a LAN. Also called a **network disk**. May be a hard disk, CD-ROM drive, or removable disk drive (for floppy disks or Zip disks).

shared folder Folder that has been configured to be usable by other computers on a LAN.

shared printer Printer that is shared with other users on a LAN. Also called a **network printer**.

shareware Programs that require you to register and pay for the program if you decide that you like it. They are frequently downloadable from the Internet.

shell account *See* **UNIX shell account**.

shortcut   File with a .lnk extension, used as a placeholder in your file system. *See also* **shortcut key; shortcut menu.**

shortcut icon   Icon that represents a shortcut, usually on the desktop or in Windows Explorer. Shortcut icons always include a little white curving arrow in the lower-left corner.

shortcut key   Combination of the CTRL key, the ALT key, and one other key; pressing these keys at the same time runs a specified shortcut.

shortcut menu   Menu that appears when you right-click an object. A shortcut menu contains commands that pertain to the object you right-clicked.

shutdown   Exiting Windows.

signature   Lines that an e-mail or newsreading program add to the end of each message you send, usually containing your e-mail address, name, and a witty tag line. For encrypted e-mail, *see* **digital signature; signature block.**

signature block   Encryption-related text that is automatically added to the end of your outgoing e-mail messages.

signed file   Audio or video file for which you have a digital license, usually a file you copied from an audio CD (which you presumably own).

signed mail   E-mail that has been encoded using your private key to prove that you sent it.

Simple File Sharing   New Windows mode in which user permissions are hidden (specifically, the Security tab in the Properties dialog boxes for files and folders).

simple folder view   New, uncluttered layout for the folder tree in Windows Explorer.

single-click style   Desktop mode in which clicking an icon or filename once runs the program or opens the file. To select the icon or filename without running or opening it, position the mouse pointer over it without clicking.

skin   User interface, or the arrangement of buttons, menus, and other items on the windows and dialog boxes displayed by a program. Windows Media Player comes with several skins.

SLIP   Serial Line Internet Protocol, a communications protocol for computers connected to the Internet. SLIP has been superceded by PPP.

slot   *See* **expansion slot; PC Card.**

SMTP Simple Mail Transfer Protocol, the method used by mail gateways on the Internet to send outgoing messages.

SMTP server *See* **outgoing mail server**.

snap-in Configuration program that you can add to the Microsoft Management Console. Or, a program that you can add on to the Netscape Navigator Web browser to give it additional capabilities.

snapshot *See* **volume shadow copy** or **restore point**.

sound board Adapter board that lets you connect speakers or headphones (and possibly a microphone) to your computer.

sound scheme Set of associations between Windows events and the sounds that Windows plays when that event occurs. A sound scheme also associates sounds with desktop elements.

spanned volume Volume in which many disks look like a single, large volume.

S/PDIF Digital audio port (Sony/Philips Digital Interface jack).

special characters Characters that do not appear on the standard U.S. 101-key keyboard, such as fractions and accented letters.

SPID (Service Profile Identifier) For an ISDN line, the phone number plus a few extra digits that identify the type of ISDN switch.

splash screen Screen Windows displays during startup, before you see the desktop. Many programs display splash screens while they are loading, before their windows appear.

spooling Multitasking system that allows a program to send information to a printer while performing other tasks.

SSL Secure Sockets Layer, the method that Web browsers use to provide secure encrypted communication.

star topology LAN topology in which each computer connects to a central hub.

start page Web page that the browser loads when you open the browser without asking for a specific page. Also referred to as **home page**.

startup menu Menu that appears if you press F8 while Windows is loading.

startup mode Mode in which you can run Windows if you are having trouble starting Windows in the normal manner.

static IP addressing Manually assigned IP that doesn't often change.

stationery HTML-based e-mail formats that you can use when composing e-mail to send to recipients whose e-mail programs can display HTML messages.

status bar Section of a window that displays information about the program. The status bar is usually a gray bar running along the bottom of the window.

stop bits How many extra bits of information are included after each byte sent through a serial port (usually one).

streaming audio Audio (sound) data stored in a format that allows the beginning of the file to be played, even before later parts of the file are read.

streaming video Video (movie) data stored in a format that allows the beginning of the file to be played, even before later parts of the file are read.

string Series of text characters, including letters, numbers, spaces, and punctuation.

striped volume Volume in which the data is stored on two or more disks in alternating stripes, so that retrieval speed isn't limited to the speed of one disk.

subfolder Folder contained in another folder.

submenu Menu displayed by a command from another menu.

supervisor password Password needed to make changes to Content Advisor settings.

Super VGA (SVGA) Type of display adapter with lower resolution than XGA or SXGA.

swap file File to which Windows copies data in virtual memory.

switch When typed on a command line, additional information provided to the program you are running, turning on or off features of the program. As a component of a LAN, hub with built-in circuitry to speed up transmission of packets to their destinations.

SXGA Type of display with higher resolution than an XGA monitor.

synchronize When using **offline files**, copying all the changed and new files from one computer to the other.

system board Printed circuit board that carries the CPU and memory inside your computer.

system clock Digital clock that can appear on the notification are part of the taskbar.

system file File or folder whose System attribute is selected, indicating that the file or folder stores part of the actual Windows operating system.

System menu Menu displayed by clicking the **System Menu button**, pressing ALT-SPACEBAR, or right-clicking the title bar of the window.

system partition Partition that stores the files needed to start up the computer (Ntldr, Boot.ini, and Ntdetect.com). Once the computer has loaded these files, it reads the **boot partition** to start the operating system (such as Windows XP).

system resources Memory used by Windows applications.

systemroot Windows variable that contains the pathname to the Windows system folder (the folder in which the Windows program files are stored).

system tray or **systray** *See* **notification area**.

systems program Program that performs a computer-oriented task, such as a printer driver program or a hard disk housekeeping program.

tab Page of settings on a dialog box selected by a tab shaped like a manila folder along the top of the dialog box.

task Series of instructions that your computer is executing. A program can create one or more tasks. For example, a word processing program might run one task that displays the program window and accepts your input to edit a file, and a second task that prints a file at the same time.

task buttons Buttons on the taskbar that represent each open window or running program.

Task pane Part of the Explorer window that lies between the Explorer bar and the working area. Its three sections are Folder Tasks, Other Places, and Details. Previously called the WebView pane.

taskbar Row of buttons and icons that usually appears along the bottom of the screen.

TCP/IP Transmission Control Protocol/Internet Protocol, the system that computers use to communicate with each other on the Internet or some local area networks.

telnet Program that emulates a terminal over the Internet. Windows comes with two: Telnet and HyperTerminal.

terminal-emulation program   Program that makes your computer act like a terminal, for communicating with computers that are designed to attach to terminals. You use a terminal-emulation program, such as HyperTerminal, to connect to a UNIX shell account.

terminal window   Window that allows you to see a communications session and type commands to the remote computer.

text box   Box onscreen in which you can type information, usually appearing in a dialog box.

text file   File that contains only letters, numbers, and special characters that appear on the keyboard. Text files frequently have the extension .txt.

theme   *See* **desktop theme.**

thumbnail   Tiny version of a picture.

TIF or **TIFF file**   File in Tagged-Image Format, a graphics file format. TIF files have the extension .tif.

tiling   Repeating a graphic to fill up a space (such as on the desktop).

title bar   The colored bar that runs along the top of a window.

Token Ring   Type of local area network hardware, largely superceded by Ethernet.

tool tip   Small informational box that appears when you leave the mouse pointer on something for a few seconds, usually used for buttons on toolbars.

toolbar   Row of small buttons with icons on them. Toolbars appear just below the menu bar in many windows, as well as on the **taskbar.**

toolbar handle   Raised vertical bar on the left end of a toolbar on the **taskbar,** used for dragging the toolbar to a different location.

topology   Pattern of cabling that is used to connect computers together into a LAN.

trace log   Log file that captures system state information to record what was happening at the time of particular events.

track   Concentric circle on which information is stored on a disk. Tracks are divided into sectors. In Windows Media Player, an audio or video file.

trail   *See* **pointer trail.**

transfer protocol   Method that a computer needs to use to access a file over the Internet; the first part of a URL.

tree view   *See* **folder tree**.

Troubleshooter   Part of the Windows Help system that asks a series of questions to help you solve hardware or software problems.

TrueType   Method of storing typefaces as a set of formulas for drawing the characters at almost any size.

TTL   Time To Live, how many times a packet can be passed from one computer to another while in transit on the Internet.

tunneling   Connecting to a private network over the Internet using **Virtual Private Networking**.

TWAIN   Standard for communications between scanners and computer software.

twisted pair   *See* **unshielded twisted pair cable**.

TXT file   Text file, with the file extension .txt.

typeface   Set of shapes for letters, numbers, and punctuation (for example, Times Roman). A **font** is a typeface at a specific size and weight (for example, 12-point Times Roman Bold).

UNC address   Universal Naming Convention addresses, used when referring to files on some local area networks.

undeleting   Reversing the action of deleting something.

Unicode   Character codes that allow you to use characters from practically every language on Earth.

Uniform Resource Locator   *See* **URL**.

uninstall program   Program that uninstalls another program.

Universal Plug and Play   Configuration system that allows Windows to detect new hardware and automatically install the necessary drivers.

Universal Serial Bus   *See* **USB**.

UNIX   Operating system widely used on Internet host computers.

UNIX shell account   Type of Internet account that gives you access to a computer running the UNIX operating system, which you control by typing UNIX commands.

unshielded twisted pair cable   Type of cable used to connect computers in a star topology LAN. Also called Category-5 cable.

unsigned file File for which you do not have a digital license. If you copy an audio file from an audio CD (which you presumably own), the file is **signed**.

upload Transfer a file from a PC to the Internet, other network, or mainframe.

UPS Uninterruptible power supply: a battery that can power your PC during a power outage.

URL Uniform Resource Locator, the address of a piece of information on the Internet, usually a Web page.

USB Universal Serial Bus, a standard type of connector for Windows computers.

USB hub Device that lets you connect several USB devices to one USB port on your computer.

Usenet Internet-based system of tens of thousands of newsgroups (discussion groups). Windows comes with Outlook Express, which lets you read and post to Usenet newsgroups.

user account Windows settings that are stored for use when you log into the computer. Each user's account can contain different settings.

user password Password you use when logging into your user account in Windows, or when switching from one user to another.

user profile *See* **user account.**

utility Small program that performs a housekeeping or other useful task. Windows comes with many utilities.

uuencode Method of encoding files for attachment to e-mail messages or newsgroup postings.

value Element stored in a key in the Registry. Each value consists of a name, a data type, and some data.

VBS file File containing a VBScript script, with extension .vbs.

VBScript Language resembling Microsoft's Visual Basic that can be used to add scripts to Web pages or other applications.

video capture Digitizing video information for use by your computer; for example, a digital video camera can capture video.

view settings Settings that control how folders appear in Folder and Windows Explorer windows.

virtual machine Hardware and software environment that emulates the features of one computer on another computer. The **DOS virtual machine** within Windows emulates a stand-alone DOS environment well enough to allow most DOS programs to run correctly. Sometimes called a *sandbox*.

virtual memory System that moves chunks of program and data storage between disk and memory automatically, so that individual programs don't have to do all of their own memory management.

Virtual Private Networking (VPN) Program that allows an authorized computer on the Internet to tunnel through the firewall and connect to a private network.

virus Self-replicating program, frequently with destructive side-effects.

visualization Graphical representation of a sound, displayed by Windows Media Player.

volume Hard disk partition or other form of mass storage.

volume shadow copy Type of backup that includes open files, by including the contents of each open file at the moment that the backup was made. Formerly called a *snapshot*.

VPN *See* **Virtual Private Networking**.

VPN client Computer that uses Point-to-Point Tunneling to connect over the Internet to a VPN server.

VPN connection Network connection that allows your computer to communicate with a private network over the Internet using VPN.

VPN server Computer that supports Point-to-Point Tunneling to allow computers to connect from the Internet using VPN.

wait time Length of time that your system is inactive before the screen saver starts up.

wallpaper *See* **background**.

WAN *See* **wide area network**.

WAV file Audio file with extension .wav.

Web address *See* **URL**.

Web Folder Entry in My Network Places for a Web server or FTP server, allowing you to manage files on the server using Explorer windows.

Web page HTML file stored on a Web server.

Web page editor Program for creating and editing files in HTML format for use as Web pages.

Web server Computer that stores Web pages and responds to requests from Web browsers.

Web site Collection of Web pages belonging to a particular person or organization.

Web style *See* **single-click style**.

WebView pane *See* **Task pane**.

Welcome screen Screen that appears on systems in which multiple user accounts are set up, with a button and picture for each user. The alternative is the Windows Me/98-style classic logon screen.

Whistler Microsoft's pre-release code name for Windows XP.

whiteboard Feature of Windows Messenger that allows callers to draw a shared picture that all can edit and see.

wide area network (WAN) Network that connects computers that are not all in the same building or campus.

WiFi Standard, with **IEEE 802.11b**, for wireless LAN communications.

wildcard Special character (* or ?) used when specifying a group of filenames or folder names.

window Rectangular area on the screen that displays information from a running program.

window borders Gray border running around the sides of a restored window.

WINDOWS key Key with the flying Windows logo, appearing on many keyboards to the left of the spacebar, usually between the CTRL and ALT keys.

Windows-aware DOS program Type of DOS program that handles its screen and keyboard in a way that lets it run efficiently under Windows.

Windows password *See* **user password**.

Windows program folder Folder that contains the Windows program files (along with many subfolders with Windows-related files), usually C:\Windows.

Winsock Standard way for Windows programs to work with Internet connection software. Most popular Internet programs are Winsock-compatible, including Internet Explorer, Netscape Navigator, and Outlook Express.

wireless LAN Star topology LAN that communicates by radio transmissions in the 2.4 GHz frequency band.

Wizard	Program that steps you through the process of creating or configuring something. Wizards come with Windows and other Microsoft products.
word wrap	Feature of text editors and word processors that allows the program to insert line endings automatically.
workgroup	Group of computers on a local area network.
workgroup-based network	Peer-to-peer network using Windows workgroups.
working folder	Folder in which a program reads and writes files unless another folder is specified.
workstation	Computer used by a person, rather than one used only as a server for people at other computers.
worm	Self-replicating program that can infect other computers (by e-mail or over a LAN or the Internet), frequently with destructive side-effects.
XGA	Type of display with higher resolution than a Super VGA monitor.
XMS	*See* **extended memory specification**.
XoN/XoFF	Method of flow control used by some modems.
ZIP compressed folder	ZIP (compressed) file containing other files. *See also* **NTFS compressed folders**.
Zip disk	Removable disk that stores either 100MB or 250MB.
ZIP file	File that contains compressed versions of one or more files, compressed by WinZip, PKZIP, ZipMagic, or a compatible compression program. ZIP files have the extension .zip.
zone	Categorization of the sources of downloaded information, for security purposes.

Index

INTERNATIONAL CONTACT INFORMATION

AUSTRALIA
McGraw-Hill Book Company Australia Pty. Ltd.
TEL +61-2-9417-9899
FAX +61-2-9417-5687
http://www.mcgraw-hill.com.au
books-it_sydney@mcgraw-hill.com

CANADA
McGraw-Hill Ryerson Ltd.
TEL +905-430-5000
FAX +905-430-5020
http://www.mcgrawhill.ca

**GREECE, MIDDLE EAST,
NORTHERN AFRICA**
McGraw-Hill Hellas
TEL +30-1-656-0990-3-4
FAX +30-1-654-5525

MEXICO (Also serving Latin America)
McGraw-Hill Interamericana Editores S.A. de C.V.
TEL +525-117-1583
FAX +525-117-1589
http://www.mcgraw-hill.com.mx
fernando_castellanos@mcgraw-hill.com

SINGAPORE (Serving Asia)
McGraw-Hill Book Company
TEL +65-863-1580
FAX +65-862-3354
http://www.mcgraw-hill.com.sg
mghasia@mcgraw-hill.com

SOUTH AFRICA
McGraw-Hill South Africa
TEL +27-11-622-7512
FAX +27-11-622-9045
robyn_swanepoel@mcgraw-hill.com

**UNITED KINGDOM & EUROPE
(Excluding Southern Europe)**
McGraw-Hill Education Europe
TEL +44-1-628-502500
FAX +44-1-628-770224
http://www.mcgraw-hill.co.uk
computing_neurope@mcgraw-hill.com

ALL OTHER INQUIRIES Contact:
Osborne/McGraw-Hill
TEL +1-510-549-6600
FAX +1-510-883-7600
http://www.osborne.com
omg_international@mcgraw-hill.com

WARNING: BEFORE OPENING THE DISC PACKAGE, CAREFULLY READ THE TERMS AND CONDITIONS OF THE FOLLOWING COPYRIGHT STATEMENT AND LIMITED CD-ROM WARRANTY.